D. H. Lawrence

JOHN WORTHEN

D. H. Lawrence
The Life of an Outsider

COUNTERPOINT
A MEMBER OF THE PERSEUS BOOKS GROUP
NEW YORK

Copyright © 2005 by John Worthen
Published by Counterpoint,
A Member of the Perseus Books Group
First published in the United Kingdom in 2005 by
Allen Lane, a member of the Penguin Group

Counterpoint books are available at special discounts for bulk purchases in the
United States by corporations, institutions, and other organizations. For more
information, please contact the Special Markets Department at the
Perseus Books Group, 11 Cambridge Center, Cambridge MA 02142,
or call (617) 252-5298 or (800) 255-1514,
or e-mail special.markets@perseusbooks.com.

Library of Congress Cataloging-in-Publication Data
A CIP catalog record for this book is available from the Library of Congress.

ISBN 10 1-58243-341-0
ISBN 13 978-1-58243-341-7
British ISBN 0-713-99613-7

05 06 07 / 10 9 8 7 6 5 4 3 2 1

He worked a great deal from memory, using everybody he knew. He believed firmly in his work, that it was good and valuable. In spite of fits of depression, shrinking, everything, he believed in his work. (D. H. Lawrence, Sons and Lovers)

Myself, I suffer badly from being so cut-off. But what is one to do? . . . At times one is forced to be essentially a hermit. I don't want to be. But anything else is either a personal tussle, or a money tussle: sickening: except, of course, for ordinary acquaintance, which remains acquaintance. One has no real human relations – that is so devastating.

(D. H. Lawrence, letter to Trigant Burrow, 3 August 1927)

For Conni, David, Geneviève, Joan and Mark

Contents

CONTENTS

List of Illustrations

Note: a number of photographs have been assigned dates different from those in previous publications; the new dates may be considered more accurate. Asterisks designate first-time publication of images.

1. D. H. Lawrence, Eastwood, *c.* 1886 (author's collection).
2. Lawrence Family, Nottingham, *c.* 1895: back row Emily, George, Ernest; front row Ada, Lydia, D. H. Lawrence, Arthur; photograph by Phillips & Freckleton, Market Place (Ada Lawrence and G. Stuart Gelder, *The Early Life of D. H. Lawrence*, 1932, facing page 12).
3. Beauvale School, Greasley, Boys Group III, 1894: 'Nocker' Bradley 2nd row from back, 1st on left; D. H. Lawrence 3rd row, 2nd from left; George Neville 4th row, 2nd from left (University of Nottingham, La Z 8/1/1/3).
4. Lydia Lawrence, Eastwood, *c.* 1895 (author's collection).
5. D. H. Lawrence, Nottingham High School, 1899 or 1900; Modern IVth forms (Nottingham High School).*
6. Chambers Family, the Haggs farm, 29 June 1899: May, Bernard, Mollie, Edmund, Ann, David, Jessie, Hubert, Alan (author's collection).
7. Jessie Chambers, Nottingham, *c.* 1907 (author's collection).
8. D. H. Lawrence, Nottingham, 11 September 1906 (author's collection).
9. Helen Corke, Croydon, *c.* 1903 (author's collection).
10. Louie Burrows, Leicester, *c.* 13 February 1909 (University of Nottingham, La Phot 1/38/1).

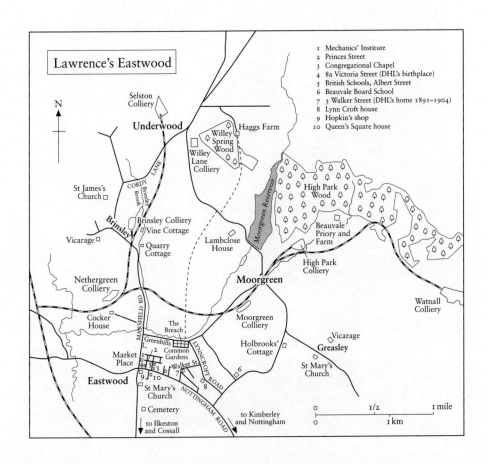

Lawrence's Eastwood

N

1 Mechanics' Institute
2 Princes Street
3 Congregational Chapel
4 8a Victoria Street (DHL's birthplace)
5 British Schools, Albert Street
6 Beauvale Board School
7 3 Walker Street (DHL's home 1891–1904)
8 Lynn Croft house
9 Hopkin's shop
10 Queen's Square house

Selston Colliery

Underwood

Willey Spring Wood

Haggs Farm

Willey Lane Colliery

St James's Church

High Park Wood

Brinsley Colliery

Vine Cottage

Lambclose House

Beauvale Priory and Farm

Vicarage

Brinsley

Quarry Cottage

Moorgreen

High Park Colliery

Nethergreen Colliery

Watnall Colliery

Cocker House

The Breach

Moorgreen Colliery

Greenhills

Holbrooks' Cottage

Vicarage

Greasley

Market Place

Common Gardens

Walker St

St Mary's Church

Eastwood

St Mary's Church

Cemetery

to Ilkeston and Cossall

to Kimberley and Nottingham

0   1/2   1 mile
0   1 km

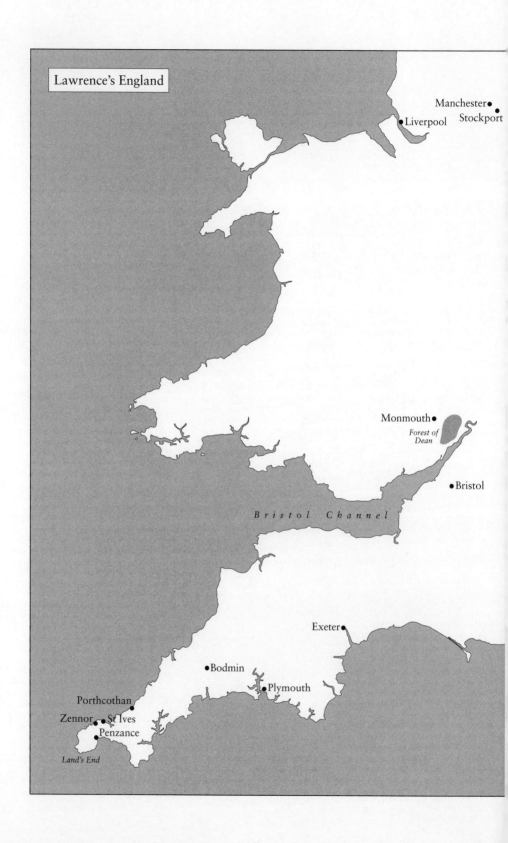

Lawrence's England

Manchester●
●Liverpool Stockport●

Monmouth●
Forest of Dean

●Bristol

B r i s t o l   C h a n n e l

Exeter●

●Bodmin
●Plymouth

Porthcothan●
Zennor● ●St Ives
Penzance●
Land's End

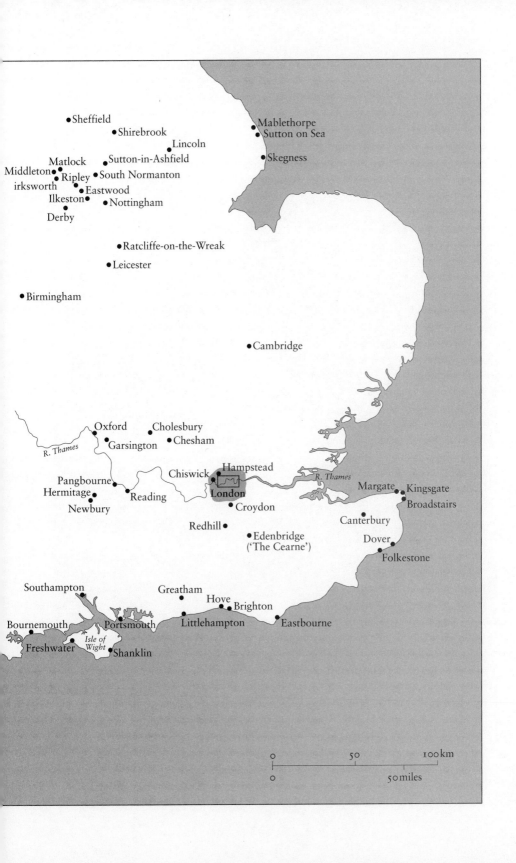

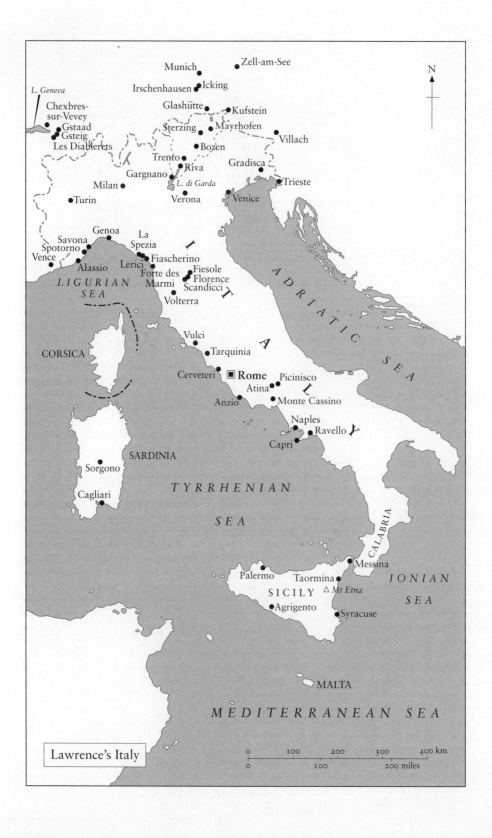

N

L. Geneva

Chexbres-
sur-Vevey
Gstaad
Gsteig
Les Diablerets

Munich   Zell-am-See

Irschenhausen   Icking

Glashütte   Kufstein
Sterzing   Mayrhofen
Bozen   Villach

Trento
Gargnano   Riva   Gradisca
            L. di Garda
Milan   Trieste
Turin   Verona   Venice

Genoa   ADRIATIC
Savona   La
Spotorno   Spezia   SEA
Vence   Alassio   Lerici   Fiascherino   I
LIGURIAN   Forte des   Fiesole   T
SEA   Marmi   Florence   A
                    Scandicci   L
                    Volterra   Y

CORSICA   Vulci

                   Tarquinia

            Cerveteri   ■ Rome   Picinisco
                         Atina
                   Anzio   Monte Cassino

                              Naples
                              Ravello
                         Capri

SARDINIA

Sorgono   TYRRHENIAN

Cagliari   SEA   CALABRIA

                                        Messina
                              Palermo   Taormina   IONIAN
                         Taormina
                              SICILY   △ Mt Etna   SEA
                         Agrigento
                                   Syracuse

            MEDITERRANEAN   SEA

                   MALTA

Lawrence's Italy

0   100   200   300   400 km
0   100   200 miles

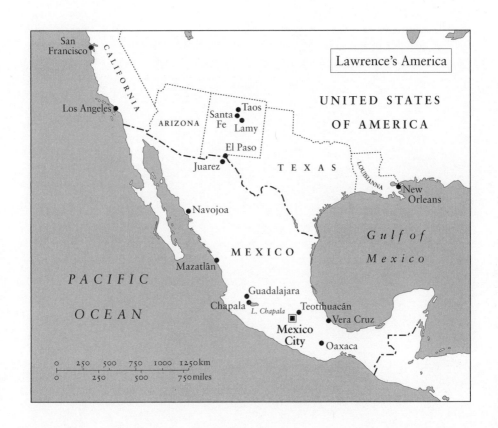

Preface

... that I have not got a thousand friends, and a place in England among the esteemed, is entirely my own fault. The door to 'success' has been held open to me. The social ladder has been put ready for me to climb ... Yet here I am, nowhere, as it were, and infinitely an outsider. And of my own choice.[1]

D. H. Lawrence wrote those words in 1927, three years before he died. He had been 'nowhere' in the middle-class literary world of early twentieth-century England; but he was equally out of place in Eastwood, the colliery village in the English Midlands where he had been born. In the most remarkable way, he had broken away from class, home and culture to grow up literary, intellectual and sophisticated: choosing to become a writer, he grew unimaginably distanced from the working class. But as a writer he also broke away again, time after time: from the literariness that had infiltrated his work and his life when he was young; from his tentative acceptance as an interesting if flawed young poet and novelist; from the literary and intellectual milieux of the First World War. He had always felt horribly uncomfortable in the world of literary insiders, and more than once jeopardized his professional career by writing things his contemporaries hated. After the banning of his novel *The Rainbow* in 1915, his sense of detachment from 'the world which controls press, publication, and all' was effectively complete. He never became the writer of acknowledged reputation which his early books had suggested he might be; he maintained a public, but a relatively small one.[2] After the war, he broke with England itself; the final eleven years of his career saw him travelling widely, writing experimentally, managing to earn his living, and at times being actively subversive in what he produced. He described his last novel, *Lady Chatterley's Lover*, as a bomb: 'let's hope it'll explode and let in a bit of fresh air.'[3] He knew very well that his writing was up against the judgement of literary insiders who, he was sure, would respond: 'Life is not like that.' And he found himself 'being told there is no such animal, by animals who are merely different. If I am a giraffe, and the ordinary Englishmen who write about me and say they know me are nice well-behaved dogs, there it is, the animals are different.'[4] Compared with his contemporaries, he *was* a giraffe: unexpected, unforgettable, and seeing a good deal further than most.

What made his writing exceptional in his time – and notorious, to the extent of bringing about his 'erotic reputation' and causing trouble with publishers and printers in book after book – was the way it centred on articulating the experiences of the body. The time is long overdue that he was given credit for this, not abuse for obscenity (in his own time) or for sexism (in ours). He had remarked in 1913 that 'it is so much more difficult to live with one's body than with one's soul. One's body is so much more exacting: what it won't have, it won't have.' Almost all his writing, particularly after he met Frieda Weekley in 1912, attempted to create a language for our experience of the body; especially of its desires. He wrote in 1929, for example, how it is 'our business to realise sex. Today, the full conscious realisation of sex is even more important than the act itself.'[5]

In his own time, however, such a preoccupation was seen as obsessive, not to say unhealthy, and was attacked by many reviewers, by the law, and by at least two other major literary figures. In 1914, John Galsworthy commented, about *Sons and Lovers*: 'The body's never worth while, and the sooner Lawrence recognizes that the better'; while in 1934, T. S. Eliot remarked that the author of *Lady Chatterley's Lover* 'seems to me to have been a very sick man indeed'. The well-known literary editor J. C. Squire would refer in an obituary in the *Observer* in 1930 to Lawrence's 'pathological traits',[6] while a note in the *Daily Telegraph* about his death in 1930 would lament how, after *Sons and Lovers*, he had written 'with one hand always in the slime'. That newspaper cutting survives in the Home Office file on Lawrence, singled out by the civil servant responsible for the file's upkeep, who noted: 'If all the critics were to write as plainly and boldly ... we should have no further cause for anxiety.'[7] The very fact that there was a Home Office file on Lawrence is another part of his history as an outsider. But disapproval had always tinged the attitude of Lawrence's contemporaries towards him, and came to dominate it. Even a friend complained that he was 'all engrossed in the body'. A vicious review of *Lady Chatterley's Lover* in 1928 had left him murmuring, 'Nobody *likes* being called a cesspool.'[8]

It was, however, as the author of *Lady Chatterley's Lover* that he would become first notorious, then famous, and finally notorious again. The book was reprinted and pirated a number of times before his death in 1930, and remained available in an expurgated edition produced by Lawrence's own English publisher in 1932; but it also appeared in innumerable unexpurgated and pirated editions.[9] The decision in 1960 of Penguin Books to bring out an unexpurgated text of the novel, in an edition costing 2s 6d (the usual price of a paperback book), resulted in enormous publicity.[10] The previous year, an unexpurgated American edition had successfully been published by the Grove Press, but the six-day trial of Penguin Books at the Old Bailey in London in November 1960 led to extensive press coverage; and the jury's decision not to ban the book (in the teeth of a judge's summing-up heavily biased in favour of the prosecution) led to a very wide dissemination of the book. Penguin's initial print run had been of 200,000 copies, and the book was frequently reprinted. What Philip Larkin called 'the end of the *Chatterley* ban'[11] marked the start of a decade of unprecedented sexual explicitness in the arts which saw Lawrence's reputation as high as it ever grew. Ironically, the decade would end with the publication of Kate Millett's *Sexual Politics* in 1970, which contained the first wholesale attack upon Lawrence as a writer whom no woman could tolerate or forgive.[12]

His writing about the body and its instincts had by no means come naturally: perhaps it never did. He had to break away from an intellectual understanding of life at which he was himself extraordinarily adept. He had to remake himself from the young man who had grown up literary, intellectual and spiritual, and his struggles to do so became the subject of some of his most extraordinary writing. 'And

Oh – That the Man I am Might Cease to Be' is a poem evocative of
the struggle. The possessor of an exceptionally keen mind wishes not
only for sleep ('which is grey with dreams') and death ('which quivers
with birth') but for the absolute end of mental experience:

> I wish it would be completely dark everywhere,
> inside me, and out, heavily dark
> utterly.[13]

Lawrence positioned himself as a writer who profoundly distrusted
the activities of the mind. This was the person he most wanted to be:
one whose instincts and passions were (so far as he could make them
so) his life. He had remarked in 1913: 'What our blood feels and
believes and says, is always true.' In 1908, he had actually listed 'sex
matters' as things for which he did not much care. But especially after
meeting Frieda in 1912, sexual desire – 'Sex is the fountain head, where
life bubbles up' – became a kind of ultimate demonstration to him of
the life of the unselfconscious body.[14] What happened when bodily
desire died is one of the stories this biography tells. But even the
seven-stone dying man, in 1929, insisted on his bodily pride. Barely
capable of walking fifty yards himself, he wrote on the final page of
his last book, *Apocalypse*: 'We ought to dance with rapture that we
should be alive and in the flesh.'[15] His acuter contemporaries recognized the extraordinarily sensuous quality of his writing: not just
its sharpness of observation, but the richness of its imagination of
experience commonly thought indescribable.

At the start of the twenty-first century, Lawrence is arguably once
again the outsider he was during his lifetime. More than seventy years
after his death, although his books continue to sell, his reputation has
fallen in the literary and academic worlds which, in the middle of the
twentieth century, treated him as a great writer. 'Something of a
national joke' was how one leading British journal recently referred to
him, and many university departments of English literature in Britain
and the USA have stopped teaching him. 'Lawrence has dropped
off the map' is a representative comment. The reasons are simple. A
contemporary American writer has declared: 'He was a sexist and a
racist, is there any argument?'[16] And to that we can add the regularly
repeated charges that he was a misogynist, a fascist and a colonialist.

Lawrence would have been savagely pleased to be condemned in all the contexts where we, as modern readers, are most sensitive. He sometimes hit his wife, which to some people proves that he was a sexist and a misogynist. Little is said about her response: 'I didn't care very much. I hit back or waited till the storm in him subsided. We fought our battles outright to the bitter end . . . I preferred it that way. Battles must be. If he had sulked or borne me a grudge, how tedious!' She hit him over the head with plates, at least twice: he also suffered sore ribs.[17] He wrote two books in the 1920s, *Kangaroo* and *The Plumed Serpent*, that explore imaginatively what happens if society is run by fascist leaders, a deeply serious subject for the period. This has been taken as evidence of his commitment to fascism, which he actually hated (he had seen it at first hand in Italy during that decade). His belief in 'the blood' has also, absurdly, been taken as evidence that he was a Nazi. How many other European writers, in the summer of 1924, when Hitler was still in prison after the Munich Putsch, could or would have written about the way in which fascism had become 'a mere worship of force', or would consequently have committed himself to 'a good form of socialism'?[18] As a young man, he wrote six lines of fantasy about leading the halt and the lame into a lethal chamber: this has been used as proof that he desired the mass murder of the unfit.[19] A working-class male character thinks that sex with a black woman would make you feel 'they're a bit like mud': this has been quoted to show that Lawrence hated women and blacks.[20] In fact his two greatest novels, *The Rainbow* and *Women in Love*, were about the independence of women; while his writings about Native Americans between the years 1922 and 1928 demonstrate the decolonization of his originally colonialist imagination. He used the words Jew and Jewess: this has been taken to show that he was anti-Semitic (though one of his closest lifelong friends was a Jew).[21] He argued that women should submit to male leadership; but he wrote fiction after fiction in which they do no such thing. In each case, the attack on Lawrence has been based on a journalistic rush to assumption and sensation. What he actually wrote is still, far too often, ignored.

He was in reality generous to women and men alike, and to all races and colours. He wrote wonderfully all his life about his experience of the natural world; he was more perceptive than almost any writer, before or since, about the effects of civilization upon instinct and desire. He has constantly been attacked because his writing constantly thought hard things through in public. But it is, uncannily, as if Lawrence knew where both his contemporaries and those after him would be most sensitive and anxious, and concentrated in his writing on those very subjects: sex, gender roles, the exercise of power. He intuitively worked his way into the concerns and anxieties of his contemporaries, though by doing so he also confirmed his alienation from his own age and (now) perhaps from ours.

This biography is the first one-volume life of Lawrence to be written since his reputation came under such assault. It tries to be honest about what he was like and to suggest as clearly as possible why he wrote as he did, rather than repeat those versions of his life and writing, hostile or favourable, which have dominated so many previous accounts.[22] His writing was richer, wittier, cleverer and a great deal more alarming and surprising than biographers and critics have commonly allowed it to be; his poems, stories and letters are at least as important as his novels; and he made his writing his life (and his life his writing) to a remarkable degree. My hope is that readers of this book will find new ways of understanding a writer whose obituary has been written many times since 1930 but who, still 'infinitely an outsider', continues to trouble and delight us.

John Worthen
Nottingham, February 2004

I

Birthplace: 1885–1895

The house where D. H. Lawrence was born in 1885 is in a row of miners' houses: redbrick, grimy, two-up two-down, just thirteen feet wide, with a shop window. It probably looks more attractive today, as a museum, than it has at any time in the last one hundred and thirty years. The street in which it stands runs away downhill to further rows and streets of similarly grimy houses: what used to be a Wesleyan Chapel stands just feet away. The place reminds us not just of Lawrence's difference from most other English writers, but pinpoints the oddity of someone born at 8a Victoria Street, Eastwood, in the English Midlands, ever becoming a writer.[1]

For very few miners – leaving school at the age of twelve as most of them did, working from six in the morning until four in the afternoon, labouring in the semi-dark through rock and coal – would spend their leisure time reading. Lawrence's father 'hated books, hated the sight of anyone reading or writing'.[2] He could pick his way through newspapers, and attempted his son's first novel, *The White Peacock*, when a copy came. But, Lawrence recalled many years later, 'it might as well have been Hottentot':

'And what dun they gi'e thee for that, lad?'
  'Fifty pounds, father.'
  'Fifty pound!' He was dumbfounded, and looked at me with shrewd eyes, as if I were a swindler. 'Fifty pound! An' tha's niver done a day's hard work in thy life.'[3]

Fifty pounds was eight months' wages for Arthur Lawrence, who had known hard work all his life. He had started at the age of ten (as was common for children before the 1870 Elementary Education Act) and continued at the colliery until his mid sixties.[4]

And how many miners' wives, beset by uncertainty, their husbands' pay variable, debts a constant threat, injury to the wage earner a nightmare, working against the odds to keep their children clean and fed, and get them educated, arguing every Friday night to ensure that enough money was handed over from their husbands' wages for food, rent, bills and insurance, and themselves cleaning, cooking, brewing, baking, ironing, sewing, darning, knitting and patching clothes all evening, when their children were in bed – how many of them would think of sitting down with a book?

One of the few men in Eastwood who would have been interested in the idea of being a writer was the socialist intellectual Willie Hopkin, who had a shoe shop and post office in Nottingham Road, and wrote a weekly column in the local newspaper. He first saw Lawrence as a baby in October 1885; from his shop, he heard Lydia Lawrence wheeling her 'three-wheeled pram; two wheels being wood and the rims iron. You could hear them coming a long way off. Mrs Lawrence was neatly dressed in black, with a little black bonnet that was always a feature of her attire.'[5] The baby was a few weeks old: 'Mrs Lawrence seemed very concerned, and she said that she sometimes wondered if she would be able to raise him.' A photograph from a little later (see Illustration 1) shows the baby's mouth open; he was 'a pasty-faced boy born to have bronchitis and a weak chest'.[6] But the white hat, lace collar and lace-edged velvet pelisse, probably supplied by Lydia's better-off sisters, offer a vivid contrast not only to her respectable black but to the prevailing grime and coal-dirt of Eastwood – the world of Arthur Lawrence.

Eastwood would not have existed had it not been for the way it was ringed by the coalmines that were responsible for the dirt. Ten pits lay within easy walking distance of the town, employing Lawrence's father and all three of his paternal uncles. One calculation suggests that '98 per cent' of the population of Eastwood (4,500 at the time Lawrence was born: wives, children, engine drivers, railwaymen, loaders, check-weighmen, miners, clerks, managers) 'depended on coal mining for their existence'.[7] The railways and the local industries such as brick making and building had all prospered because of the coal industry.

By the mid 1880s, the great coal boom was over, but Eastwood itself continued to grow. A tight-knit community of men, the safety of whose lives depended upon each other, supported wives almost none of whom had jobs, though many earned part time in various forms of sweated labour, such as stocking-knitting. Their sons could hardly wait until they were, at twelve, able to start as colliers; their daughters were likely to marry colliers. The largest local colliery company, Barber Walker & Co., owned six pits in and around Eastwood, and had built many of its houses; Lawrence's birthplace was a company house. Just down the steep little hill, Arthur's brother Walter lived in Princes Street in another company house; all six of Walter's sons would become colliers, all four daughters would marry colliers. Over at the tight-knit centre of the Lawrence family at Brinsley, just a mile away, lived Arthur's parents, John and Louisa, in Quarry Cottage; his collier brother George; and his married sisters, Emma and Sarah. John had been a tailor for the colliery company: 'a big, shambling, generous-hearted man whose waistcoat front was always powdered with snuff'. Arthur had been born in Brinsley in 1848[8] and since 1875 had been a 'butty' – the man responsible for the working of a small section of coalface (the 'stall') along with a team of workmen he organized, and paid out of the stall's earnings. In 1885, he was working at Brinsley pit (his brother Walter was in his team); his other brother, James, who had lived in Vine Cottage near the parents' home, had been killed at work underground at Brinsley five years earlier.

This was the community in which Lydia Lawrence had found herself living (she might have said 'buried') after ten years of marriage. She had been born in 1851 into a Nottingham family, the Beardsalls, in which there had once been money, even an aristocratic marriage, and 'large lands along the Trent'. The family went on thinking of themselves as gentlefolk, 'well-to-do' middle class,[9] long after their situation had utterly changed. It cannot have been an accident that Lydia's father, George, identified himself as 'Engineer' on his daughters' marriage certificates when he was only an engine fitter; nor that his daughter Lydia passed on to her son a romantic version of both her father's life and of the Beardsall family history. The Beardsalls moved around the country according to where a fitter was in demand: Lydia (the second daughter) had been born in Manchester, but had grown

3

up in Sheerness, in Kent, where the family occupied a house beyond their means. They had to take in a lodger to get by.[10] George Beardsall 'made us wait on him hand and foot': he provoked Lydia to tell him, 'I'll never have a husband like you.'[11] She was intelligent and ambitious; by the age of thirteen, she was a pupil-teacher, one who both taught and was taught, in a system introduced in the 1840s.[12] However, her family was plunged into poverty by an accident her father suffered at work in February 1870, in his mid forties, which left him crippled. George never worked again. He received the minuscule pension of £18 a year (reduced to £12 a year 1871–4, to recoup the lump sum awarded him after the accident); this at a period when an agricultural labourer would have earned something like £39 a year, a coalminer £75, a young schoolteacher in London £95, a clergyman £120. The Beardsall family returned from Sheerness to Sneinton, one of the most notorious slums of Nottingham, to live close to relatives and as cheaply as possible. Within a year, Lydia and two of her sisters had been reduced to lace-drawing. Hundreds of feet of curly cotton draw-threads separated the narrow strands of lace made on the eighteen- or twenty-foot-wide machines in the factories; outworkers 'drew' them. Every room in the Beardsall house in John Street, Sneinton, in the early 1870s must have been 'smothered in white lace',[13] and increasingly silted up with the dust that was notorious for attacking the lungs of the lace-drawer.

What way out was there for the intellectual, 'restrained'[14] and intensely moral daughter of an exacting, disappointed man? George Beardsall was sarcastic, proud, imperious – and now helpless and impoverished. Lydia was quick-witted and very attractive; and her way out of the impasse of life at home was to get married. She met Arthur Lawrence at a Christmas party in her aunt's house in 1874, and married him a year later. The ways in which he was *not* like her were especially attractive to a woman 'never effusive or demonstrative in any way'. Arthur, an exceptional dancer when young, was characterized by physical ease, warmth and vigour, 'overflowing humour and good-spirits' ('May all their rabbits die!' was a comical denunciation he passed on to his son).[15]

Her family were conventional and still optimistically genteel, and though getting her off their hands would have helped them financially, they would not have failed to tell Lydia that such a marriage was beneath her. Of the five Beardsall daughters, her marriage was by far the least respectable: she was the only one to marry directly into the working class. Arthur was 'a first-rate workman . . . invariably called upon when there was a particularly difficult job to be done in the pit', but on the borders of illiteracy (his mother could not sign her name but registered herself with a cross).[16] His promotion to butty, technically 'Mining Contractor', may have suggested a management role to Lydia, but he worked underground and came home black. Arthur's income, however, put him on a par financially with quite a lot of professional people, even though the wages were not as secure as those of a clerk and the work itself immeasurably dangerous. One conclusion is that Lydia fell spell-bindingly in love with him, with his warmth and his charm and his physique. Arthur Lawrence was strong, spare, muscular, and she went on admiring him physically into his forties, even when in other ways she 'fought her love for him, and hated him for his charm'.[17] Another conclusion, equally likely, is that she married to get away from home: he was earning more every week than George Beardsall's pension brought into a family of ten every two months.

Lydia soon felt betrayed by her marriage. She had not understood the real nature of Arthur's job, and he seems to have let her believe that he owned the house in Brinsley into which they moved, whereas he was paying his mother rent. It is impossible now to say who was the more deceived. Arthur may not have been straightforward about his job and the house, but Lydia quickly had doubts about her love for a non-intellectual man. At all events, it seems clear that many of Lawrence's problems and the sources of his unhappiness, as well as of his creativity, were acted out from the start in the troubled marriage of Lydia and Arthur. They fought the terrible conflicts of opposites: intellectual and physical, controlled and passionate, strict and care-free, genteel-minded and working-class. All these would eventually become the subject and substance of Lawrence's writing, as well as an underlying personal trouble (at times an agony) to him.

For eight years following their marriage in 1875, Lydia and Arthur were on the move. Arthur's job took them where the best-paid work was, during the boom years of the mining industry in the 1870s, and they lived in a succession of small, recently built but dirty colliery villages. George, their eldest child, was born in Brinsley in 1876, but

Ernest and Emily were both born six miles north, in New Cross, Sutton-in-Ashfield (in 1878 and 1882 respectively); the family was in South Normanton in 1880, and early on apparently in Old Radford (in Nottingham).[18] In 1883, however, they moved to Eastwood, just a mile up the hill from Brinsley. The move seems to have marked some kind of a watershed for Arthur and Lydia: they would remain there for the rest of their lives. With three small children, Lydia (now thirty-two) may well have insisted on giving her children the kind of continuity in schooling which they had not had before, and which she had never had. They settled down: Arthur (now thirty-five) worked for Barber Walker & Co. at Brinsley colliery until he retired, around 1912.

Lydia probably felt as if she were digging in for a siege. Only half a minute's walk from Walter Lawrence in Princes Street, and fifteen minutes from the rest of the Lawrences down in Brinsley, Eastwood may have been home for Arthur, but to Lydia it was just another grubby colliery village where she never felt at home or properly accepted. Her genteel version of a Kentish accent (for her English was good and her accent unusual) accentuated her difference from those around her: Eastwood people felt that she 'put it on' when she spoke. 'It was "common" to live in the Square',[19] too – something mitigated by a special feature of the house, however. The shop window, which still makes the parlour relatively light and airy, encouraged Lydia to try her hand at selling small items of clothing and lace. In part this was doubt-less to supplement Arthur's wages, but it would also have been a way of demonstrating that they were not just a miner's family, and that she was no longer a sweated labourer but a retailer. She and 'Lawrence Arthur, Haberdash.'[20] were tradespeople; and in the small mining town of Eastwood such distinctions mattered. Lawrence remembered, in the late 1920s, how his mother had looked up to Henry Saxton – the Chapel-going county councillor who ran the grocer's shop next door – as the kind of man her husband should have been.

Lawrence also recalled how his 'mother hated the thought that any of her sons should be condemned to manual labour. Her sons must have something higher than that.' But Lydia's belief in her children 'getting on' was not just snobbery or bourgeois ambition. What other way would they have of escaping the 'bloody hard life' in which she was trapped?[21] *Her* children would break the chain of an industrial class condemned to suffer, generation after generation, the same working conditions, the same awful risks, until (as happened in the mining industry in the twentieth century) they were replaced by machines, and either lost their jobs or were forced into conditions made still worse by mechanization. Lydia's children, accordingly, grew up knowing that they were different from the children of other branches of the Lawrence family. To accentuate the difference, to Lawrence his mother was 'the cultural element in the house', the rare miner's wife who 'loved to read' after her day's housework was done, borrowing books from the library of the Mechanics' Institute just two minutes' walk away from 8a Victoria Street: 'piles of books . . . to be enjoyed when we were in bed'.[22] Reading was her great escape from her community, though she loved conversation and the discussion of ideas; she also occasionally wrote poems (the only one which survives is religious).[23] Most of the time, however, the distance of her own family, her dissatisfaction with her roles as wife and mother in the mining community where the Lawrences lived, and her disillusionment with her husband, all built up in Lydia Lawrence a terrible feeling of disappointment. *Sons and Lovers*[24] confirms how Lydia and Arthur quarrelled: not just over money (in particular how much he kept for himself), but also over the children's future. Lydia wanted them at the very least to become clerks; Arthur wanted them to follow him down the pit. They also argued over what Arthur spent in the pub at night. A miner would take a bottle of cold tea with him for his eight-hour shift, but the labour was exhausting, the air always dusty and hot, and in the evening he wanted to drink. His wife would make herb-beer for him to drink at home. But it wasn't just thirst which took him to the pubs. As late as 1983, an old miner would insist on how you had 'to . . . go in the pubs: or you were out of it'.[25] After early promises, Arthur had quickly slipped back into the male life of evenings spent drinking with his mates, and (when he could afford it) coming home merry. But Lydia could never accept the working-class habit of men working together in the day and drinking together at night.

The fact that she found herself pregnant again early in 1885 would have made a difficult situation worse. The Victoria Street shop had not done well; it is hard to think of Lydia as an engaging saleswoman, and people failed to pay their debts if she sold goods 'on strap'. What is more, as Lawrence came to know, the baby was unwanted.[26] Around this time, too, Arthur turned Lydia out of the house one summer night and locked the door, perhaps while she was pregnant ('He was very bad before I was born,' Lawrence was told). This way of dealing with a recalcitrant wife was well known in Eastwood.[27] But it was the kind of thing which helped turn a rocky marriage into a disastrous one. Arthur Lawrence was never forgiven.

The baby was born on 11 September 1885. His parents called him David Herbert (the latter after Lydia's favourite younger brother): he would be 'Bert' at home and – except when young – 'Herbert' at school.[28] Lydia's need to care for him also seems to have signalled the end of her attempt to run the shop. In 1887, shortly before the birth of her last child, Ada, and with the Victoria Street house now over-crowded, the family moved down the hill into one of the long blocks of houses built by the mining company and called 'the Breach' ('It was a little less common to live in the Breach'). With a house at the end of their block, the Lawrences had neighbours only on one side and a long strip of garden of their own. The houses were well built and more spacious than those in the Squares, although the sheer concentration of families, between four and six hundred people in the eight blocks, meant that the smells of the 'ash-pits' (lavatories) in summer, along the alley where the children played and the women talked, were particularly offensive. The birth of Ada was probably another low point for Lydia; all she had to look forward to was a life of strain, penny-pinching and isolation. The successful upbringing of her sons into respectable manhood and financial independence thus became crucial to her; she seems always to have been engaged in a painful struggle back up to respectability.

In 1891, the family managed to recover (literally) a little of the ground Lydia felt had been lost when, after only four years in the Breach, they moved up to Walker Street, a quarter of a mile away, into a bay-windowed house commanding a magnificent view over Eastwood and beyond. It was not a company house but built by a local man, in a terrace of only six houses popularly known as 'piano row' from their inhabitants' relative prosperity. The Lawrences now had only a tiny garden, one of the reasons why their rent was no more than in the Breach, but it was probably around now that Arthur acquired an allotment in the 'Common Gardens' on the slopes below Walker Street. The children were very conscious of the significance of the new house. Not long after the move, Emily explained to May Chambers, a girl whose family lived along the road from the Breach, how they 'wouldn't live in the Breach for anything. We live up at Brickyard Closes in those houses with bay windows.'[29]

The same year they moved, George left school and started work as a clerk, which should have helped financially. But he remained a problem. In 1895, he ran away to join the army and his mother had to use £18 of hard-earned savings to buy him out; in 1897, he had to marry his pregnant girlfriend, Ada Wilson. Altogether, he probably seemed (to his mother and to his siblings) a great deal too much like his father; and he did not bring the money into the house that she had hoped for. It was to her second son, Ernest, however, the cleverest at school of all her children, that Lydia looked most optimistically (Lawrence was delicate in health and had missed too much school to do very well). Ernest left school in 1893 and quickly found work as a clerk; he taught himself shorthand and typewriting, and went from strength to strength.

The only extant photograph of the family (see Illustration 2) was taken around 1895, shortly before George left home. Arthur Lawrence, still flamboyant, judging by his magnificent beard, sits solidly but uncomfortably, fists clenched, in the studio chair. His clothes look unnatural on him: even his feet (shoes shining and polished) are not placed firmly on the ground. George and Ernest stand at the back, flowers in their buttonholes as in their father's: George is nineteen, dark and handsome, Ernest seventeen but already six foot tall. Below them sits Lydia Lawrence, looking at least ten years older than her age of forty-four or forty-five. She is in black, as always, but with a fine shawl around her shoulders. Her hands lie politely in her lap; she might be a matriarch but she looks worn by suffering. On her right are her two girls: Emily is thirteen but almost as tall as George; Ada is only eight, the baby of the family. And, symbolically between his parents, stands Lawrence, with the same smart breast-pocket handkerchief as his father, small and very young-looking, more like seven or eight than ten. It is a picture of a mother surrounded by her children, with the husband, sideways on to the rest, in a supporting role.

The Lawrences had the photograph enlarged, painted over and placed in a gilded frame, and hung it over the parlour mantelpiece. Lydia's cheeks were filled out and made rosy, the children's mouths closed. But the real point was to have a framed portrait. The photograph may have been accurate, but the painting was the image that reproduced what Lydia wanted them to be: well to do, professional, *getting on*.

It was the weakling, the unpromising youngest son, whom, after the death of Ernest at only twenty-one, Lydia came to love. Testimony after testimony proves it, including Lawrence's own: in a letter of 1910, he remembered what he called the 'peculiar fusion of soul' he had felt with his mother, which 'seems to distribute one's consciousness far abroad from oneself, and one "understands" '.[30] All his life, people marvelled at Lawrence's remarkable understanding of people when he first met them: how profoundly his sympathies went out to them, so that he seemed to know them through and through in ways they themselves could hardly imagine. The editor and critic John Middleton Murry, who met him in 1913, found that in 'an astonishingly short time he knew all about me'. May Chambers, daughter of a local Eastwood family, who did not particularly like Lawrence, wrote about his 'genius for making friends' when young.[31] This imaginative sympathy seems to have been something first established in his relationship with his mother: 'We knew each other by instinct,' he wrote of her just before she died. May's sister Jessie, who thoroughly disliked Lydia, could not help noticing what passed between mother and son: 'They were in close communion, swiftly responsive to one another.'[32] Lawrence knew his mother in a way that, both before and after her death, he wished to know others. Eventually he came to distrust his very capacity for intimacy, as costing too much, as well as inhibiting his need to stand back and be himself.

Home life for all the Lawrence children became polarized between loyal love for their mother as she struggled to do her best for them, saving where she could and encouraging them to take their education and careers seriously, and a rather troubled love for their father, whom

Lydia increasingly treated as a drunken ne'er do well. Arthur stayed with his friends in the pub to escape the coldness which greeted him at home (which made him all the more distant), while Lydia alienated the children from him with stories of her marriage. She 'would gather the children in a row ... while she would picture his shortcomings blacker and blacker to their childish horror'. When at home, Arthur could be an exhilarating presence: 'never more happy' than when mending the household's boots and shoes, 'seated tailor-wise on the rug, with the hobbing iron, hammering away and singing at the top of his voice'.[33] But the children never forgot the stories Lydia told, so that all of them – even George, who was particularly fond of his father – grew up with an aching, protective love for their mother.

The love and hate were, however, at their most extreme in Lawrence; his feelings for his mother and his father were different in kind from those of the other children. George's son recalled how 'Bert was very rude to [his father] as a little boy'.[34] Lawrence would later link the violent, one-dimensional separation in his feelings for his parents to an intimacy with his mother that began in the womb. 'I was born hating my father,' he insisted in 1910: 'as early as ever I can remember, I shivered with horror when he touched me.' His story 'Odour of Chrysanthemums' is rich with a mother's contempt for her spendthrift, alcoholic husband; Lawrence described it as 'full of my childhood's atmosphere'.[35] His creation of Walter Morel in *Sons and Lovers* would reproduce a parent experienced as both alien and physically repulsive. But the drunkenness and violence were drawn from uncle Walter Lawrence as much as from Arthur, and the novel would also show the father's warmth and love: a love constantly baffled by the son's nervous retreat. Late in life, Lawrence would remark: 'I was born bronchial – born in chagrin too.' He may have been using 'chagrin' in its modern sense of 'annoyance, or mortification, arising from disappointment, thwarting, or failure', but he almost certainly had the older meaning in mind too: 'care, worry, anxiety, melancholy'.[36] That was how he would characterize his mother's state of mortification and disappoint- ment when she gave birth to him, and the way in which he shared the tensions of her marriage, and inherited her legacy of anger and anxiety. Occasionally he would be explicit about the conflict of loyalties and love that had troubled him. In 1926, for example, he would write to a friend also troubled by a traumatic upbringing: 'We can't help being more or less damaged.'[37]

Arthur Lawrence, for his part, was naturally unhappy at the lack of love or respect shown him, and the way in which his male privilege as head of the household was constantly undermined. A family friend remembered him shouting at Lydia: 'Yer can mock me, an' be off hand wi' me, an' turn yer nose up . . .'[38] He reacted by insisting on his rights to a sizeable portion of his weekly wage, by spending all the time he could drinking with his friends, and by irritating and alienating his family. The tipsy return home of the miner at night was a scene Lawrence would recreate time after time in his writing; it haunted him as a kind of ritual violation of his home, potentially at least of his mother, and most of all of his own security as her child. It is plausible to link this with two other things characteristic of him as a child: a habit of crying (not knowing what he was unhappy about) and the most savage temper. He put into his novel *Mr Noon* a reminiscence of the rages which when 'he was a boy of thirteen his sister could taunt . . . up in him. And he knew he could have murdered her.'[39] The child who was normally loving and loved, quiet, shy and reserved, could lose control completely in response to humiliation, teasing, or any exceeding of the boundaries. 'And his face was transfigured. She did not know it. It was a mask of strange, impersonal, blind fury.'[40]

This needs to be kept in perspective, however. Lawrence never did murder his sister. Arthur Lawrence never left his family. If *Sons and Lovers* is to be trusted, on one occasion he did walk out: but he came back.[41] Unlike his brother Walter, Arthur never missed work because of his drinking. He was not an alcoholic. His earnings were never so channelled into drink as to leave his family hard up; and though he would go home 'merry', a contemporary believed him 'never drunk nor aggressive'.[42] Nor did the marital problems stem from one partner alone. Lydia Lawrence, disappointed with her life and her marriage, played her full part in alienating the children from their father. The sons were *not* to look forward to leaving school as soon as possible and becoming colliers, like their father, uncles, cousins and the majority of their contemporaries. All the children would stay at school; they would take the teetotal pledge, and they would go regularly to Sunday school and Chapel.

The Congregational Chapel in Eastwood had a special meaning for Lydia. Arthur Lawrence hardly ever went, but she was strict in attendance and in compelling that of her children. Although Chapel enforced a stern puritan morality, an Eastwood contemporary remarked that local women's adherence to it 'represented no sacrifice on their part as it was the only rule of life they knew and was part of the air they breathed'. Women in Lydia's situation found, in the Chapel, 'a degree of culture that was otherwise entirely lacking in their lives';[43] it was perhaps the only place where such a woman might feel at home in Eastwood. For her, Chapel insisted that the everyday world of getting and spending was not all that life amounted to; it offered a higher morality, and its values were incipiently middle class. Lydia wanted her sons not only to become clerks and teachers (and her daughters to marry such men) but also to respect morality, intelligence and spirituality. Her sons would, ideally, not grow up as men who bossed women about; they would play their part in the raising of children and they would rise into the middle class. The local newspaper's obituary of Ernest rhapsodized over his 'keen desire to get on', and as Lawrence put it, late in life: 'The reward of goodness, in my mother's far-off days . . . was that you should "get on." *Be good, and you'll get on in life.*'[44] Such a life, however, was precisely that which Lawrence came to reject.

Lydia's demands must have further angered Arthur Lawrence, who would have felt his children being taken from him. All the Lawrence children were encouraged to conform to the Beardsall family's image of itself rather than to the Lawrences'; three at least grew up to take the opportunities their mother hoped they would. But, once again, Lawrence not only experienced the parental division more violently than the others, but internalized it in a way that frightened those who knew him best. The young Paul Morel lying in bed at night, hating his father, has gone a whole journey deeper into rage than his siblings. He prays: 'Let him be killed at pit.' A late essay confirms this as a true memory of young Lawrence, awaiting his father's return and the dreaded row downstairs: 'They were not my own prayers. They were a child's prayers for his mother, who has captured him and in whom he believes implicitly.' May Chambers, invited to lunch at the Lawrences, found that the only word to sum up Lawrence's response to his father was '*vengeful*': 'Bert seemed to send out jagged waves of hate and loathing that made me shudder.'[45] He continued to work these feelings out for the rest of his life, to the extent of eventually denying his loyalty to his mother and insisting that his father had been his true parent. But quite early on, he came to realize that his love for his mother was an unfortunate influence upon him; by the time he was thirty, he knew it had distorted his life. His writing enabled him to pick apart the knots of divided love and loyalty which had entangled him since birth. But he remained torn between the intellectual and the non-intellectual, the moral and the careless, the constricted and the free, the self-sacrificing and the self-asserting, long after he left the place where he had been born.

2

Rising in the World: 1895–1902

Lawrence started at the Board school[1] in Beauvale at the age of three years and eight months, but he was by no means the youngest. Soon after his fourth birthday, however, he was withdrawn from school and did not go back until he was seven. One reason for his absence may have been serious illness; at some point in his childhood, he had his first bout of pneumonia.[2] But it is unlikely that illness caused three years' absence. In the 1911 draft of *Sons and Lovers*, the trouble of his life begins for Lawrence's alter ego, Paul Morel, because of his horror of school; in the 1912–13 version of the novel, it is a nightmare and a torture to him. Lawrence recalled: 'I shall never forget the anguish with which I wept the first day.'[3] His extreme reaction may have been why his mother withdrew him. But even after he had restarted, a neighbouring girl found him in tears, not wanting to go to school, and commented: 'I don't think there was a more unhappy child went into that Board school than Lawrence.'[4]

Part of the problem was his trouble with the other boys, who jeered at him for his 'marked difference'; he kept himself to himself and felt horribly lonely.[5] He eventually learned to spend his time with girls and (later) with books, but both of those were considered crimes in his male-dominated society. 'Dicky Dicky Denches plays with the Wenches,' the boys shouted at him; and when asked why they jeered, one answered, 'Well, he's allus wi' wenches and he never plees wi' us.' Lawrence was too frail to take part in the games and – like the neighbours' reacting against Lydia Lawrence – his contemporaries thought him 'rayther stuck up'.[6] The time he spent at home with his mother would also have ensured that his vocabulary and perhaps his accent were unusual; and like Paul Morel in *Sons and Lovers*, reacting against the 'common', he would probably have been sharply critical of people dropping their 'h's and saying 'you was'.[7] He remembered how, in Eastwood, 'most of the women said: "He's a *nice* little lad!"', although 'nice' was not an epithet many boys would have welcomed. He had always been a 'thin, pale weakly' child, but at school he was labelled 'Mardarse' or 'Mardy Lawrence' or just 'mardy' – soft, a mother's boy.[8]

It is possible that he was bullied at school, and so feared going. Yet all his life he stood up for himself and was not only courageous but also fierce in self-defence. He remained a shy and unpopular outsider, easily humiliated, who *felt* different from the others, could not cope with the feeling and ended up miserable. School confirmed how much he was his mother's son, not his father's. He claimed, later in life, to have been 'just like anybody else of the miners' children', but that was simply not true.[9]

Two surviving photographs demonstrate the extent to which he was not allowed to be 'just like anybody else'. A photograph of his Beauvale class in 1894 (see Illustration 3) shows seventy-one boys with their teacher, 'Nocker' Bradley; Lawrence is one of only two with a handkerchief in his breast-pocket, and one of the few not just with a neatly ironed collar but with a silk tie, probably the one seen in the family portrait. His clothes fit him properly; cut-down men's jackets are visible elsewhere. Lydia Lawrence was very conscious of the appearance of her children and ensured that they dressed nicely. At some point, however, someone (perhaps the multi-talented Ernest Lawrence) took a copy of that school group photograph, cut out Lawrence's head and, using ink or water-colour, drew in a kind of tasselled jerkin; the picture was then re-photographed.[10] The result is too faded to reproduce well,[11] but the effect is not only of Lawrence as a miniature Shakespeare, in a decorated doublet; by being literally extracted from the crowd of boys in which he had been anonymous, he becomes special – *apart*, unlike, distinct. Ten years later, he explained to a woman he had known since childhood, May Chambers, how his difference and cleverness had left him feeling: 'Don't you see it makes a gulf? It leaves me lonely.'[12] By the time he was eighteen, he could understand and articulate that. The child could not.

The thing that seems to have saved Lawrence from his unhappiness at school was his exceptional power of language. Those years at home, talking to his mother and listening to her, paid off: a schoolmate remembered ruefully how Lawrence started 'hittin' back wi' his tongue an' he could get at us wheer it hurt'. His brother George remembered 'that very sharp tongue' too: 'it was as our old dad used to say: "to take the skin off your back".' Vituperation was a skill Lawrence developed early, to cope with the world. On the other hand, a neighbour's girl remembered how one day 'he looked across the field and said, " 'Everywhere is blue and gold.' Now you say a line." Of course I could not.' Both kinds of language emphasized his difference.[13]

Another fact adds to our understanding of the way in which Lawrence's school years were difficult for him. Paul Morel, after the reference to his hatred of school, subsequently appears to undergo no schooling. This is odd for a novel so concerned with formative experiences; it is as if Lawrence found the subject too awkward to recreate, especially in a text stressing the *ordinariness* of Paul. The only time school momentarily gets into the novel is when Paul (who has gone to collect his father's wages on a Friday afternoon) is too overawed to add up the stoppage money. The clerk comments acidly: 'Don't they teach you to count at the Board School?' and a miner adds: 'Nowt but algibbra an' French.'[14] Paul is so angry at being humiliated that he swears never to collect the wages again, although the job provides his only pocket money. He also insists that they do *not* teach him such outlandish subjects at school: he is ordinary, not odd. Lawrence would have known such oddity all too well.

The difference between the boy at school and the boy at home was also very marked. To his sister Ada, Lawrence was a marvellous brother, intensely lively and creative. She remembered 'days of such care-free joy with Bert that I know I can never experience again. It seemed inevitable that Bert should spend his life creating things. He was never content to copy others, and perhaps found more pleasure in inventing games than in playing them.'[15] Such a boy must have been frustrated with being a despised outsider at school.

The Lawrence family dynamics would have changed when Lawrence was between nine and twelve, with George and Ernest going out to work. The eldest daughter, Emily, was not especially good at school and had always done a great deal of caring for her younger siblings (they never forgot the stories she told them); she would remain at home until her marriage in 1904 to Sam King. But by the mid 1890s, with the other boys so much out of the house, Lawrence was at last doing better at school, even if Mr Whitehead, his headmaster at Beauvale, told him that 'he would never be fit to tie his brother's [Ernest's] boot-laces'. It was just the sort of comparison which 'depressed and discouraged' an unconfident child.[16] Nevertheless, in the spring of 1898, at the age of twelve and a half, after special coaching from Whitehead, Lawrence won a scholarship to Nottingham High School. The County Council was sponsoring the access of poor children to such institutions, and Lawrence would be only the second miner's son ever to go to the High School.

There were problems with success. It would cost Lydia Lawrence (see Illustration 4) yet more struggling and saving to find the necessary money; the £14 scholarship paid only part of what was needed.[17] Ernest, for all his cleverness, had left school at fourteen, and had never been to high school. However, the family was now a little better off and, unlike Ernest, Lawrence did not seem the kind of boy who could make his way in the world at the age of fourteen. Having never been a normal Eastwood boy, he was now going to be a thoroughly abnormal one, with his high collar and dark suit, books under his arm, catching the Nottingham train in the morning when his contemporaries were employed at the local collieries, if not already working underground.

His performance at the High School, to which he went at the age of thirteen, in September 1898, was only briefly distinguished. He had a good first year (he came second out of seventeen boys at Christmas and fifth out of thirty-nine in a larger class in the summer of 1899, when he also won a mathematics prize; he had come first out of forty-three in a still larger mathematics class in his first term). But something went wrong towards the end of his second year. A school photograph of him (see Illustration 5) makes him look vulnerable, in spite of the cap angled stylishly on the back of his head and his usual breast-pocket handkerchief – he was one of the smallest in his class. He had turned out to be even more of a fish out of water, in this almost completely middle-class school, than he had been in Eastwood: 'much withdrawn into himself,' a contemporary recalled: 'the scholarship boys were a class apart.'[18]

The events of March 1900 must have made him feel even more painfully different. His uncle Walter Lawrence (now living in Ilkeston, just over the Derbyshire border) was arrested for killing his fifteen-year-old son by throwing the sharpening steel[19] at him during a row in the family kitchen at tea one Sunday afternoon. The steel penetrated the boy's ear and he died three days later: Walter was committed for trial at the Derby assizes.[20] The story was splashed over the local newspapers, and Lawrence's performance at school the following term was very poor. After gaining a term prize at the end of the Easter term,[21] he was only sixteenth out of a group of twenty-one at the end of the summer term in 1900, although he did again get a prize for mathematics. A geometry lesson is the subject of the only surviving anecdote of Lawrence at the High School. After the master, C. Trafford, 'had gone through a Geometrical rider on the blackboard . . . a small nasal voice at the back of the class said, "now you just do that again". Everyone expected the roof to fall in, but Trafford, like the gentleman he was, went through the rider once more without comment.'[22] Perhaps Lawrence only joined in when the subject excited him, though the awkwardness of a snotty-nosed[23] outsider, unable to catch the tone in which to address a master, is obvious. Trafford, however, understood the awkwardness; it was he who awarded Lawrence his term prize at Easter 1900.

Lawrence left the school shortly before his sixteenth birthday, in the summer of 1901, fifteenth out of nineteen in the Modern VIth. Two contemporaries (one from the same class) were asked in 1933 what Lawrence had been like in his last year: 'but neither remembers him at all! they infer that he could not have taken any prominent part in the life of the school; and I suppose another fair deduction would be that as a boy his personality did not impress itself on his schoolfellows!'[24] He left with rather little to show for his time at the school apart from his prizes: years that had cost him some confidence and, in spite of the scholarship, the family a lot of money (a quarterly season ticket alone cost 31 shillings). He had *not* been the outstanding academic success that some scholarship boys turn out to be, liberated by change into another sphere; he seemed (and probably felt) not cut out for higher education. In 1915, in his only fictional creation of a boy at high school, he would describe Tom Brangwen as having 'an instinct for mathematics', which immediately suggests a parallel with Lawrence, 'but if this failed him, he was helpless as an idiot. So that he felt that the ground was never sure under his feet, he was nowhere.' Tom's conclusion is that 'he knew all the time that he was in an ignominious position, in this place of learning'. That must at times have been the young Lawrence's experience: a boy from a violent and notorious family, feeling out of place and unsure, even if not, like Tom, 'aware of failure all the while'.[25] Knowing that he was not like the other children at either of his schools, or in Eastwood, his sense of separateness probably increased. In 1907, at the age of twenty-two, he described himself as having been 'naturally introspective, a somewhat keen and critical student of myself'. Two years later, he would confess that 'my youth was the most acute and painful time I shall ever see, I'll bet'.[26] Later, he would create in Ursula Brangwen a character who, after her time at high school, feels 'ashamed because she really did feel different from the people she had lived amongst. It hurt her that she could not be at her ease with them any more.' At sixteen, Lawrence was starting to find that, though he was still friendly with the girls he had got to know at Beauvale: 'I *am* a bit different – and god knows, I regret it.'[27]

But having finished school, it was imperative that he get a job. Although his high school training had equipped him to start as a pupil-teacher in a local school, it must have seemed more important to the family that he should start earning immediately than that his long-term future should be considered. At any rate, in the early autumn of 1901 his brother Ernest helped him write a letter applying for a post as a warehouse clerk at the surgical goods factory of J. H. Haywood, in the centre of Nottingham: a job in a decent old-fashioned family firm perhaps seemed the best thing for an intelligent, unconfident and rather unusual boy. 'He didn't like it, but he wanted to help mother,'[28] his sister Ada recalled. Ernest was now desperately saving for marriage to his girlfriend, but Lawrence would at last be doing something to offset the railway fares to work and the cost of the clothes he was fast growing out of. (Having always been small, he was now starting to get lanky.)

He started at Haywoods in September or October 1901. In *Sons and Lovers*, Lawrence reproduces what it was like in Paul Morel's experiences at Jordans: 'all light for the three storeys came downwards, getting dimmer, so that it was always night on the ground floor, and rather gloomy on the second floor. The factory was the top floor, the warehouse the second, the storehouse the ground floor. It was an insanitary ancient place.'[29] For the first time, Lawrence found himself getting a taste of the world outside the shelter of home and school. The work girls at Haywoods shocked him with stories of their boyfriends (a contemporary remembered him listening with 'fascinated horror'),[30] and they soon did rather more. They set on him one lunch break and attempted to remove his trousers. This may have been one of those time-honoured rites of passage for new employees, or it may have been specifically aimed at the quiet young Lawrence, easily perceived as standoffish and disapproving (so needing to be taken down a peg), or, alternatively, as an innocent abroad and so fair game. But his friend George Neville – son of a neighbour, a sportsman and athlete, and a year younger than Lawrence – says that Lawrence 'set about those girls with teeth, hoof and claw': 'Though only slim, he was tall and wiry, with very long arms and fingers, and in a rage he could be a very demon.' He drove them off; they were astonished at the fury they had aroused.[31]

It would have been just in the middle of this difficult time at the factory, in the autumn of 1901, that Lawrence's beloved brother Ernest died, very suddenly. Ernest's life perhaps demonstrates more clearly than anything else in Lawrence's childhood the pressures exerted by the parents' marriage, and their wildly different expectations. Ernest had always been a success in everything he did, whether it was bicycle racing or running or getting employment: Whitehead had proudly copied into the school log-book the letter of thanks Ernest had sent to him on getting his first job. Everyone remembered him as strong, clever, witty, gifted: 'a legendary figure' in the neighbourhood.[32] After leaving school, he was employed in a series of increasingly well-paid jobs. But the significant thing was how he got them. A family friend remembered Lydia Lawrence talking about how

He raised himself by his bootstraps, as you might say. When he said, 'Mother, I'm going to apply for that position,' I said, 'Why, my boy, you're not fitted for it – you've no business training.' But he said, 'No, but I've picked a lot up, and I've worked up pretty good in shorthand. I'm going to try for it, and if I get it I'll pick up more as I go along . . .'[33]

And that was by no means all. 'After business hours he spent his leisure in reading good books, studying shorthand and practicing type writing on a miniature toy imitation, hoping to obtain a situation eventually in that pursuit.' Those details come from the lengthy obituary the local paper gave Ernest. He taught shorthand at the local night school and gave private lessons; and although 'not bookish', he was responsible for at least two poems, both intensely religious.[34] By the age of nineteen, he was working in Coventry 'as correspondent, shorthand writer and typist' for the Griffiths Cycle Company; and before he was twenty he had a job in a solicitors' firm in London at £120 a year. He was being paid as much as some clergymen would have earned. In London, too:

there was a large scope for such ambition as his, and he settled down to work harder than ever, to apply the knowledge he had and to acquire more. His knowledge for a young man was considerable, London's gaiety could not wrest [him] from his love for work and his keen desire to get on, and after business hours his evenings were spent in the study of French and German languages, a knowledge of which he acquired sufficient to converse and write letters.[35]

Some of our knowledge of what happened to Ernest in London has to be derived from his equivalent, William, in *Sons and Lovers*, but the real-life sources confirm the novel's account. He had always been an energetic pursuer of young women and got engaged to a girl in London. Her name was Louisa Lily Western Dennis,[36] a stenographer in an office, although originally from the working class. Ernest came back for brief holidays in Eastwood where his family and friends doubtless marvelled at his style, his clothes, his girl, his camera,[37] and his success. Not everyone was impressed. Edmund Chambers, father of May and Jessie, commented: 'I never see such a young fool in my life as that lad of Lawrence's, Ernest, do they call him. There I met him walking down the street in a top hat, frock coat, and yellow kid gloves.' Ernest was dressing up to 'astonish the natives', as he put it.[38]

He had come home for a weekend early in October 1901, catching the early Monday morning train back to London, but after a day at work he collapsed at his lodgings in the south London suburb of Catford. He had developed the inflammatory disease erysipelas, which runs to blood poisoning and extremely high temperatures, and easily leads to pneumonia. As soon as his landlady sent his mother a telegram, she rushed to London to nurse him. When she arrived, 'she could scarcely recognise him, his head and face were so swollen and inflamed'.[39] Two doctors had insisted there was nothing they could do; Ernest died in her arms, not having recognized her, in the early hours of Friday, 11 October 1901. Arthur arrived in London later that day or the next, and they had Ernest brought back to Eastwood to be buried.

The Eastwood obituary lauded 'his large mind, his keen desire for hard work, his ambition to make himself thoroughly fitting to fill a high post, to get on and be useful in the world'. But *Sons and Lovers* shows William, his fictional equivalent, as an increasingly driven character: 'the carelessness went out of his eyes'.[40] He is caught between the money and glamour offered by London (and the glamorous sexuality of the girl to whom he gets engaged), and his attachment to his family, especially to his mother, whom he loves and desperately wishes to please. Lawrence later chose to sum up William's predicament in the phrase 'the split kills him, because he doesn't know where he is'.[41] It takes one to know one. Being unsure of their place in the world was an experience both Lawrence boys shared, which is why Lawrence turned them into the joint heroes of his novel. Ernest's life was brilliant, short and tragic, and yet in his death there was (to his brother) another meaning beyond that of unfulfilled promise: the tragedy of a young man who, for all his gifts – for here apparently was the perfect mixture of the charm, strength and gaiety of his father and the iron determination of his mother – did not know to what or to whom he belonged. Lawrence wrote with fascination not just about the death but also about the confusions of the life: the 'big, straight, and fearless looking' young man, who gets engaged to the sexually exciting but dressy, bored young woman who (when he brings her home to show her off) queens it over his family;[42] and whom, when he looks at her with the eyes of his mother (who else's eyes could he have, when it comes to relationship?), he despises. William has acquired bourgeois values, but also hates them; he instinctively takes as his partner someone as marginal and uncertain as himself: and she is no comfort at all.

This was what Lawrence understood and recreated eleven years later, as he followed his own troubled path and grew to understand his brother better. He saw how Ernest's vitality and enormous energy for 'getting on' had been sapped not only by his punishing work schedule and by his constant need to impress women (including his mother), but by his almost inevitable choice of the wrong partner. It became one of Lawrence's characteristic ways of understanding illness to believe that it originated in split loyalties and unanswered needs, not just in infection.

Lydia's grief seems to have made her impervious to the unhappiness of her younger son. Ernest's place in her affections can be gauged by her remark that 'she looked forward more to meeting her son Ernest in heaven than Jesus Christ Himself': a heart-breaking confession for a religious woman.[43] During the darkening autumn of 1901, Lawrence went to work at the factory (he was away from home fourteen hours a day), mourning both the beloved brother and the withdrawal of his mother's love. Just before Christmas, he too went down with pneumonia.

Even without accepting Lawrence's diagnosis of neglect turning into desperate, reciprocal demand, his illness, at such a moment, would have hit his mother especially hard. It brought her back to herself; her younger son's illness became, paradoxically, the spur she needed to attend to the living, not just to her feelings about the death of her elder boy. In *Sons and Lovers*, Mrs Morel's sister comments that Paul's equivalent illness was 'a good thing . . . I believe it saved his mother'.[44] Lydia nursed Lawrence; he came back to a new life in which he was now as intensely focused upon his mother as she was upon him. This was perhaps the period when (she would later remember) 'You used to be such a dear good boy, Bertie.' He did not return to the factory; like Mrs Morel in *Sons and Lovers*, Lydia almost certainly blamed herself for sending him to Nottingham to work.[45] After months recuperating, some of it in his aunt Nellie Beardsall's boarding house in Skegness (and after using his clerkly number-skills doing the accounts for a pork-butcher in Eastwood), Lawrence would become a pupil-teacher, eventually training to be a professional teacher. The almost uneducated father, who like Walter Morel saw his job as a miner as 'good enough for me, but . . . non good enough for 'im',[46] had acquired a son who was going to make his living by educating others, too, out of the working class.

The winter of 1901–2 thus marked a new stage in the love between Lawrence and his mother: a love that would last until her death in 1910. So long as Ernest was alive, her third son, a frail, especially cared-for child, had been only one focus of her affections. Lawrence had grown up regarding himself as no match for Ernest. The headmaster at Beauvale had told him so: his loss of confidence at the High School, and his unhappy experiences as a clerk, can be seen as the consequences of his being in Ernest's shadow. But from 1902 onwards, Lydia was devoted single-mindedly (and by no means always comfortably) to Lawrence as a young man, not as a child. It was around now that the feelings he celebrated and mourned in 1910 came about:

We have loved each other, almost with a husband and wife love, as well as filial and maternal. We knew each other by instinct. She said to my aunt – about me:

'But it has been different with him. He has seemed to be part of me.' – and that is the real case. We have been like one, so sensitive to each other that we never needed words. It has been rather terrible, and has made me, in some respects, abnormal.[47]

Such love meant that Lydia would henceforward burden Lawrence with her hopes and needs, as well as her demand for intimacy, just as she had once probably burdened Ernest. The child Paul Morel, looking at his mother, sees a woman done out of her rights: he feels helpless that he can do nothing about it.[48] Such an insight is not something even an unusually perceptive child could have worked out for himself. It is something the mother has, consciously or unconsciously, imposed upon him.

Lawrence's return to life as his mother's son and lover, in 1902, also meant that he was now more than ever polarized between his parents. His need to prove himself, to be independent, to leave home, was countered by his mother's need to possess him and by his profound responsiveness to her, his need to make up to her for what she had communicated to him as her sense of loss. In an odd way, he found that he was reproducing his father's desire to be independent of the demanding woman: knowing himself abnormal because of the relationship, but unable to break away. As late as the spring of 1902, Lydia Lawrence complained: 'He wants me to hold him on my lap like a child, but I can't.' As late as 1908, Lawrence would confess: 'I am very young – though twenty two; I have never left my mother, you see.'[49]

Becoming a writer would eventually be Lawrence's way of leaving the past and its attachments behind; of breaking out, understanding and being independent while still constantly recreating in his writing the mining village, his family, its tensions and concerns. He would, so to speak, come home repeatedly in his writing, acknowledging how intimately he belonged to his family and its quarrels and its loving mother, even as he wrote his way out of it (declaring that he rejected any idea of home, or love, and hated Eastwood and the past). In his adult life, he would regularly try to create an ideal and harmonious home of friends and partners, living and working together, as responsive to each other as his instinctive sympathy and understanding allowed *him* to be. He would first experiment with this idea in his novel *The White Peacock*, in which recognizable versions of Lydia Lawrence and his sister Ada inhabit a romantic lakeside cottage, along with a sensitive, literary son (a drunken father having been conveniently killed off). But in life Lawrence never achieved the harmonious group; he went on to live in a way that repeatedly negated the chance of any such life with others.

Being a writer, however, would offer him a way of coming to terms with the conflicts of his upbringing; and fiction in particular allowed him to create and live through the kinds of life that most fascinated him (he once wrote how his 'novels and poems are pure passionate experience'). But responding to Lydia Lawrence in 1902 meant not only adopting the role of responsible son and salary earner; it meant a commitment to a woman with 'an endless demand for love, demand of being loved'[50] without any means of dealing with the ways she inhibited his independence, carefree impulsiveness, anger and (in particular) sexuality.

In the summer of 1902, once it had been finally agreed that he should get a job in Eastwood (thus sparing him the journey to and from Nottingham), it took some time to find him a post as a pupil-teacher. The Eastwood Congregational minister, the Reverend Robert

Reid, apparently helped, but it was not until late October 1902 that Lawrence started work at the British Schools in Albert Street, just ten minutes' walk from home. He had begun to study for his teacher's certificate; he received his lessons direct from the headmaster, George Holderness, for an hour before school started, and then spent the rest of the day teaching.

If not as good as the career of a man in business, the job of a teacher would still have been close to his mother's heart. She would thoroughly approve of Lawrence becoming a professional man, doing what she characterized as 'rising in the world – on the ladder. Flights of genius were nonsense – you had to be clever & rise in the world, step by step.' But as Lawrence started out on his new career, he found himself teaching the very kinds of boy who, until recently, had mocked him and whose games and company he had refused to share. He would still be very conscious that he was 'not strong'. In the summer of 1901, May Chambers, three years older than he was, told him: 'you seem like a girl sometimes.'[51] As a young teacher, he probably suffered a version of what he created in *The Rainbow*, when he shows Ursula Brangwen trying to cope with a class of unruly children and failing horribly, though he was probably drawing on the experiences of others, too.[52] Lawrence begged May, working in the girls' section of the British Schools, to look out for him when he went from Holderness's instruction to his class; he wanted 'a smile to cheer' because he was 'frightened to death'. Lawrence was lucky, however. Holderness was a disciplinarian and 'sometimes very aggressive with the stick'.[53] His class would no more have dared start a real rebellion against Lawrence than they would against the head.

But here was proof of the distance Lawrence had travelled from the life of the colliery town. He was standing apart from it, as a teacher inevitably does, while still never having left it. Holderness wrote coolly enough in the school's log-book for 28 October 1902, as if not yet convinced of his unusual pupil's prospects: 'The third Standard has this week been mainly under the care of D H Lawrence, a young person 17 years old, who has finished a three years' course at the Nottingham High School, and who has come with a view to becoming a Pupil Teacher.'[54]

3

A Collier's Son a Poet: 1902–1905

Although working as a pupil-teacher at the British Schools in Albert Street in October 1902 was a clear indication of Lawrence's future – he would train and work as a teacher for the next nine years – another new start had been just as important. He had begun to pay regular visits to the Chambers family at the Haggs farm at Underwood, two miles north of Eastwood; usually he would walk or cycle there over the field paths from the Lawrence family home in Walker Street.

In the early 1890s, the Chambers family had occupied a house along Greenhills Lane, near the Breach, while the Lawrences were living there. The father, Edmund Chambers, a native of Eastwood (his father, 'Pawny Chambers', and mother had run a pawnbroker's shop), had a smallholding and a milk round in Eastwood. Edmund's wife Ann was, like Lydia Lawrence, a stranger in Eastwood, and a woman who never seems to have been especially happy there or anywhere; she had struck up an acquaintance with Lydia at the Chapel in Albert Street. Both of them 'hated the mining communities to which their husbands had brought them' and, according to Ann Chambers's son, they 'found in the Chapel . . . the only place in which they felt really at home in an otherwise alien world'. The children of the two families met at Chapel and Sunday school: May and Jessie, the two eldest girls, remembered Lawrence at Sunday school forgetting a poem he had learned for a recital, going white and provoking his sister Emily to hysterical giggles.[1]

In 1898, the Chambers family moved on from the smallholding and rented the Haggs farm near Underwood; an informally posed photograph (see Illustration 6) shows them the first summer after the move. Seven children cluster around a mother who is only just forty but who looks far older, and who is too busy dealing with her newest-born, David, to be concerned with the camera. The twelve-year-old Jessie kneels on the grass and seems almost the only one of the family to care much about the photograph; she smiles winsomely. May, on the extreme left, already a pupil-teacher at the British Schools in Eastwood, is sixteen. She looks thin-faced and detached. The youngest daughter, Mollie, aged three, stares open-mouthed. The three brothers are Alan (extreme right, the eldest at almost seventeen, elegantly waistcoated), eleven-year-old Hubert in front of him (a large-headed boy) and nine-year-old Bernard in front of May. The 36-year-old father, Edmund, elegantly dressed like Alan, in what looks like his best boater, is tall and thin and seems to have something in his hands which he has had no time to put down before being marshalled into the photograph.

Lydia Lawrence had a standing invitation to visit the Chambers family in their new place, but it was not until 1901 that she and Lawrence first followed the field paths out to the Haggs, on a half holiday in the early summer of his last year at the High School: he a 'tall, fair boy' with a 'swiftly changing expression', she a 'bright, vivacious little woman'. May Chambers, always an acid commentator, recognized how they came 'from the bricks and mortar of streets of houses where bay windows and front room furniture and new clothes were so very important'.[2] That was the world which the Chambers family prided themselves on having left, but which the Lawrences had risen into: the bay window, the suite of mahogany and horsehair chairs, the Brussels carpet rather than the usual rag-rugs of the miner's house, the mahogany chiffonier and the oval table. But whereas Lydia Lawrence had always fought the dominating male figures of her world, whether her father, her husband or her sons, Ann Chambers felt dominated by her menfolk; she had had her last child at the age of thirty-nine and would 'shudder when the subject of sex was mentioned'.[3] Mrs Morel, on an equivalent visit to the farm in *Sons and Lovers*, pities her friend: 'I'm sorry for her, and I'm sorry for him too.'[4]

For all its griminess, Eastwood was set in a surprisingly rural landscape. From the Walker Street house the family could look westwards to the monument at Crich Stand in the far distance of Derbyshire, nine and a half miles away,[5] and Arthur Lawrence would gather mushrooms on his early morning's walk across the fields to work. To keep his mouth moist underground, he would chew grass-stems. Although a town boy, Lawrence had grown up with a considerable knowledge of plants and the natural world. Arthur Lawrence, 'very good on wild life', according to his daughter Emily, not only knew flowers, wild herbs and plants in general, and made himself a tea mixture out of the herbs he gathered, but 'watched every bird, every stir in the trembling grass'; on one occasion, he brought home an abandoned baby rabbit.[6] He also worked the family allotment in the Common Gardens. His sons helped him; in 1900, Lawrence's acquisition of a standard flower-recognition book, *Our Country's Flowers and How to Know Them*,[7] suggests the direction in which his interests were growing, though he might have been happier learning from a book than from his father.

On his visits to the Haggs farm, Lawrence seems to have developed an altogether new awareness of the countryside and woods: its land-scapes would reappear in a great deal of his fiction, and as late as 1928 he would be recreating places and views he had first seen that day in 1901. His joy in going to the Haggs, however, was not only a reaction against the ugliness, narrowness and conventionality of his home in Eastwood. The Haggs offered something even more important: a kind of alternative family. In the spring and summer of 1902, an important part of his convalescence after pneumonia consisted of going out to the Haggs and discovering how he could participate in life there. He 'could ride up in [Edmund's] milkcart and join his lads in the hayfield'; later, the walk there and back was thought to be good for his health.[8] Lawrence first made friends with the two younger boys, and then with Alan; he once claimed that the nearest he had ever come to 'perfect love' had been at the age of 'about sixteen', which would be before September 1902, and he was probably thinking of one of the Chambers boys.[9] May was in the middle of a prolonged adolescent extraction of herself from her family, and rejected the High School boy's offer of help with her homework; but the younger daughter, Jessie, seems to have been drawn to Lawrence from the start. Although his relationship with her would develop into one of the most important of his young life, when he first started going to the Haggs regularly, in the summer of 1902, she was no more than a rather immature fifteen; he was both better read and better educated, as well as eighteen months older, and did not spend much time with her. Her reaction to being surrounded by brothers who were physically active, and rather contemptuous of her, had been to shut herself away in a world of her own in which she was the heroine of poetry and romance; her younger brothers despised this and 'took delight in bursting in on her rhapsodical moods and shattering her poetical day-dreams in a wild scrimmage of slaps and bangs'.[10] Her brother David remembered her as 'equal to anybody'; nearly as tall as her elder brothers, she was just as broad-shouldered; solidly built, disciplined, dedicated, yearning. He also recalled how she would stand up to her younger brothers: she would 'wind a scarf round each fist and challenge them both to a fight'. Her 'lighter moods', however, were rare.[11] More often, she was simply angry with men for bossing her about or ignoring her. By contrast, Lawrence was someone serious; the realization seems to have dawned around 1903, when he and she found themselves talking increasingly, and she came to regard him as the person she believed would save her from her family. Eventually he offered to teach her; and together they worked on the very subjects, 'algibbra an' French', which distinguished ordinary education from advanced.[12]

It is hard to overestimate how important the Haggs family was for Lawrence, long before he became close to Jessie. The coincidence of his return to life in the spring and summer of 1902 – and his new place in his mother's affections – with this discovery of another family to which he eagerly turned, and individuals whom he loved, suggests that he was reacting against the intimacy which made such demands on him in Eastwood. Not for the last time in his life, a passionate emotional involvement (in this case with his mother) had grown up in Lawrence simultaneously with a powerful desire to break away from the very object of his love. What many, even most people feel to some extent, in love and relationship, Lawrence lived through with an intensity that was surprising and often shocking. The way he turned to the Chambers family is perhaps the first clear instance of it.

For the angry outbursts and loud quarrels of the Chambers family would have felt very different from the moralizing, critical and emotionally stifling atmosphere of Walker Street. In Eastwood, he was up against a household dominated by women: his mother and Ada (and, until her marriage, Emily), with his father largely absent or silenced.

The Haggs offered a simpler, old-fashioned world, in which men took precedence if they could and women argued back – and did not simply feel morally superior. The Chambers boys looked down on their sisters and tried to order them about; the girls fiercely resisted. But, for adolescents in particular, other people's families are nearly always easier to deal with than one's own. The Chambers family probably felt more emotionally secure to Lawrence *because* of their constant quarrels, their overt affections, their singing and boisterous intimacy, their jokes and laughter: 'He used to say that our laughter was Homeric.' He 'made us even happy with one another while he was there, – no small achievement in a family like ours!'[13]

The Chambers family never forgot him: when he died in 1930, 'We all, as a family, mourn him, for the memories of old days were unspeakably dear to us all.' Lawrence never forgot, perhaps never got over, this new experience.[14] In a fascinating piece of passionate nostalgia, he would recreate his time at the Haggs more than twenty-five years later, in a letter to the youngest Chambers son, David:

Whatever I forget, I shall never forget the Haggs – I loved it so. I loved to come to you all, it really was a new life began in me there. The water-pippin by the door – those maiden-blush roses that Flower [the horse] would lean over and eat – and Trip [the dog] floundering round – And stewed figs for tea in winter, and in August green stewed apples. Do you still have them? Tell your mother I never forget, no matter where life carries us.

In a life so full of radical changes, it was vitally important to him that, somehow, neither he nor the Haggs should change: 'whatever else I am, I am somewhere still the same Bert who rushed with such joy to the Haggs.' Perhaps above all else, the Haggs offered both devotion and companionship: something for which he went on looking for the rest of his life. 'Then I'd sit on the sofa under the window, and we'd crowd round the little table to tea, in that tiny little kitchen I was so at home in.'[15] From 1902 to 1906, what mattered was discovering how much and how happily he could be 'at home' there; and he gave to the Chambers family as richly and lovingly as they gave to him. Ann Chambers loved him 'like one of her own', and he loved her; he was devoted to Alan; and with the family he could be the lively and cheerful son he found it so much more difficult to be at home, though his domestic training at home would have made him even more welcome. At the Haggs, he 'set about household tasks, such as cooking, and even washing, and would help to prepare the family meal and lay the table. With Bert in charge, the meal was a family party.'[16] He could be an exhilarating companion, and probably first discovered this, too, at the uninhibited Haggs. Nearly fifty years later, May recalled 'Bert with his mischievous grin':[17] his vivacity, his sense of adventure, his capacity for games and fun were what he brought to them.

It all feels a little like Arthur Lawrence escaping Lydia Lawrence, with Lawrence leaving behind the strictness of home and its moral absolutes for the farm and the 'wholesome happiness' of uncritical companionship. May Chambers's fiancé, Will Holbrook, recalled how Lawrence 'loved to come where he could do and say just what he pleased, even to using strong language to win his point'.[18] It was at the Haggs that Lawrence seemed most like Arthur. He sang with the family (his father had been in the choir of St James's Church at Brinsley as a boy), and he demonstrated how he could dance 'in our little kitchen, and once while we paused for breath he said: "Father says one ought to be able to dance on a threepenny bit." '[19] Jessie, knowing Lawrence's hatred of his father, was surprised at that little revelation; but Lawrence also demonstrated his talent (his father's too) for mimicry. One set piece was a long-drawn-out row between his father and his mother which took Arthur's side and reduced its listeners to helpless laughter.[20] Lawrence also first started painting at the Haggs, copying reproductions of paintings and encouraging everyone else to join in; two of his copies hung in the parlour of the Chambers family for years. Numerous albums – blank books for the insertion of autographs, verses, original drawings and paintings by friends – acquired inscriptions and illustrations. David Chambers, again, remembered: 'I think everyone loved him at this time; he combined with his vivacity a sweetness of disposition that was quite irresistible.' 'Ah, you Haggites see the best of me!' Lawrence remarked one day.[21]

It was hardly surprising that his mother and his sisters grew jealous of his constant visits. Very soon after he started going, he confessed to May Chambers that, though he wanted to come one Saturday, 'They won't let me'; she also heard how 'We as a family were stealing him from his mother'. Jessie, meanwhile, recalled: 'He told us rather shamefacedly that his mother said he might as well pack his things and come and live with us.'[22] The Lawrences resented his concentration on a family so unlike themselves; and they would come to be deeply suspicious of the amount of time he and Jessie spent together. Lawrence was acutely aware of their disapproval but commented, sadly: 'If it wasn't this, it would be something else.'[23] Emily once even insisted on coming out to the Haggs with him, to see what was so marvellous about it, but all she found memorable was 'that awful walk'.[24]

These visits to the Haggs remained a problem for years, but the fact that Lawrence kept going shows how necessary they were to him. There were painting parties in Eastwood, too, at the new Lawrence home in Lynn Croft; the old circles of friends – like the Limb daughters (Mabel and Emmie) from a couple of streets away, and the Cooper sisters (Frances, Mabel and Gertie) from the end of the road – joining in the fun, with Lawrence at the centre and his mother looking on admiringly.[25] In Eastwood, he felt valued at home as never before, cherished and sustained by his mother's love. However, it is never too late to have a happy childhood, and Lawrence discovered his at the Haggs.

It was probably a relief for the Lawrence family in the end to have Jessie Chambers to blame for his prolonged absences. What Lawrence and Jessie developed, around 1903 or 1904, was a common passion for reading. Both of them went to the Mechanics' Institute library in Eastwood to get books; they would meet there, and then Lawrence would walk nearly three miles back to the Haggs with Jessie, talking books. Their reading was voracious: Scott, Reade, Cooper, Stevenson to start with; then George Eliot, Charlotte Brontë and Thackeray; a great deal of poetry, mostly from Palgrave's *Golden Treasury*; and then on through Dickens and Balzac to Flaubert.[26] Jessie grew up into a brown-haired, serious young woman, 'like a lovely Italian picture', according to a contemporary. Another, more critical friend saw (as did the photographer of Illustration 7) her 'somewhat large nose and spare chin with eyes brown and steadfast – serious and rather undulating in her carriage, gay only as a duty – and then effortfully – thin lips with a very pleasant expression'.[27] Like May, she never got on very well with her family, who tended to be impatient of her 'effortful' intensity and seriousness. This was another reason why Lawrence became so important to her, why she singled him out, and why their joint reading and discussion mattered so much to her.

Books were positioned squarely on one of those fault lines that ran through the Lawrence family. Lydia insisted on their importance, though it was romances from the library that helped her escape her unhappiness. Ernest's treasured legacy of books stood in a place of honour on a shelf in the kitchen, Emily's story books were almost exclusively prizes from Sunday school, Lawrence's teaching-books proof (as Ada's would be) of how far this particular miner's child had progressed. Mr Morel's comment 'It's only fools as sits wi' their noses stuck i' books' is, however, close in spirit to what Arthur would have said.[28] Reading fiction or poetry could be a problem in Eastwood: Lawrence would sit 'ready to close the book and put it swiftly away if a step should sound outside in the entry'.[29] But with the Chambers family it was utterly different. As a girl, Jessie had heard her father reading the whole of the last part of *Tess of the D'Urbervilles* aloud to her mother, and in the Haggs parlour, passages from books were read out and the family staged readings of plays 'in their entirety'. Literature was simply part of the shared everyday life, books were everywhere, and the floods of talk about them and their authors spread happily over divisions that gaped wide in the Lawrence family.[30]

For Jessie, so often an outsider in her large and male-dominated family, a friend who shared her interests was a wonderful discovery. She saw in Lawrence that 'radiant joy in simply being alive' which was always harder to see in him in Eastwood, and which mattered so much to her.[31] She was already fascinated by poetry (she would go round the house reciting Scott and Wordsworth); and in her, Lawrence found a willing companion in reading and discussion. Lydia read a good deal, but what boy of eighteen wants to discuss romantic fiction with his mother? And although Lydia wrote poetry, she seems to have regarded it as a diversion in a busy life lived to other and more significant ends. But Jessie and Lawrence, whose reading was the natural occupation of clever, introspective but rather withdrawn children, now devoured books, lived through them, lost themselves in them: 'to say that we *read* the books gives no adequate idea of what really happened. It was the entering into possession of a new world.'[32] Lawrence also found that, in their discussions, he could express himself to Jessie as to no one else. Doubtless his mother was aware of that.

35

Between 1902 and 1906, Lawrence lived a kind of double life: hard at work in Eastwood during the week, as a model pupil, teacher and family member, but going out to the Haggs every weekend. His pupil-teacher work was taxing and very badly paid; in his first year, he earned 'a shilling a week with a yearly increase supposed to cover the cost of books'.[33] However, he impressed George Holderness with his dedication and his intelligence: his headmaster would eventually sum him up as 'hard-working and painstaking, energetic and bright in his manner, and at the same time kind and considerate for others'.[34]

From March 1904, however, a new system meant that pupil-teachers spent some time each week at the local pupil-teacher centre three miles away at Ilkeston. Holderness complained to his Director of Education that their time at Ilkeston 'would considerably interfere with School work unless more help is granted'.[35] On more than one occasion, a combination of staff illness and pupil-teacher absence meant that he was left with three or four classes – amounting to 100 or 150 children – to teach on his own. In Ilkeston, however, Lawrence met a whole group of other men and women in his situation. Jessie Chambers started to attend the centre the year after Lawrence began; his sister Ada went, so did Richard Pogmore from the British Schools, and another local girl he grew to know well, Louie Burrows, from the village of Cossall near Eastwood.[36] The centre was in every way a widening circle: it introduced Lawrence to intellectual life beyond Eastwood, very many of the pupil-teachers being, like himself, the children of working-class parents. And it was in Ilkeston that his cleverness started to show. He experienced one of those great surges forward in confidence and ability that marked his early years: it grew up alongside his newfound happiness with the Haggs family, and their encouragement of him. He thoroughly impressed the Ilkeston head, Thomas Beacroft, for example, especially with his mathematical skills. Richard Pogmore recalled how, in algebra, 'Mr Beacroft, who was always pretty hot tempered, had set us a problem. Not one of us could do it. And he suddenly stormed at us, "Oh! You – not one of you as good as Lawrence! He did it yesterday in a few minutes." And he turned the blackboard around and showed us Lawrence's working on the board.'[37]

In such ways, Lawrence triumphantly overcame the problems of the 'algibbra' he had *not* learned at the Board school. Within six months of starting at Ilkeston, he was taking the King's Scholarship examination, which would get him a place in a training college for teachers. This time he absolutely excelled: over two and a half thousand students from all over England took the exam, and only thirty-seven got into the first division of Class 1. Lawrence heard on 25 February 1905 that he was one of them. From now onwards, he recalled, he was 'considered clever'.[38] His name was printed in the local papers and highlighted in the Ilkeston log-book; he had to send accounts of himself and his working methods (plus a photograph) to the *Schoolmaster* and the *Teacher*. Holderness took the photograph of his star pupil.[39]

There was still a price to pay, however, in anxiety and nerves. Before the scholarship exam, he 'made himself look quite ill with worry and doubt', to the despair of those with real reason to worry about their performance. He was even heard tragically intoning: 'Wouldn't it be awful if I did fail!'[40] Without a real job, hardly earning (even in 1904–5 his salary was only £24 a year), he was still dependent on his family, and it was doubtless Lydia Lawrence on whose behalf he dared not fail. The brightness and liveliness of Lawrence in his late teens was overshadowed by his need to be an academic success. He would spend much of the rest of his life attempting to undo the effects of this early training, as he attempted to free himself from the control of that moralizing, authoritative mindset. Although on the one hand he was a natural intellectual, in 1904–5 he could not get away from what others expected of him and what they had invested in him financially and emotionally. Self-sacrifice, and dealing with its consequences, was something he was becoming expert in.

There remained the question of how and where he would study for his teacher's certificate. This could be done either by going full time to an institution for two years, and sitting examinations, or by fitting the study into his spare time and taking the examinations as an external student. It was decided that he would, if possible, go to Nottingham University College; this meant a matriculation examination in the summer, allowing him to enter the day-training department. He passed the exam, but not spectacularly: he only managed second class this time, 'pen-driving in the city heat'.[41] His going to college would be yet another strain on the family finances, but his recent success had made his mother hungry for more; during the next few years, she dreamed of his studying not just for a teaching certificate at Nottingham University College, but for a BA degree. It was decided that, to help with the money (a degree course would after all take three years, not two), and with George Holderness's approval, he would spend the school year 1905–6 at the British Schools as a full-time though uncertificated teacher. He would earn £50 a year: real money at last, if still less than what his father earned.

The eighteen-month interval between his learning the results of the King's Scholarship examination, and his going to college in September 1906, proved to be perhaps the most crucial period of Lawrence's life so far, for reasons that had nothing to do with education. In the spring of 1905, within weeks of his scholarship success, he started to write; the coincidence seems too strong to be *just* a coincidence. Some twenty-three years later, he sardonically recalled 'the slightly self-conscious Sunday afternoon, when . . . I "composed" my first two "poems." One was to *Guelder-roses*, and one to *Campions*, and most young ladies would have done better: at least I hope so. But I thought the effusions very nice, and so did Miriam [i.e. Jessie].'[42] The fact that he remembered it was a Sunday shows how the event stayed with him.

Why did he start? There were family reasons: he believed that he was related, on his mother's side, to the famous hymn-writer John Newton – his mother, his brother and his maternal aunt Lettie Berry all wrote devotional verse.[43] There were ambitious reasons: writing was a glamorous, middle-class profession, and as a boy he had shared with May Chambers the fantasy of his mother becoming a famous poet 'and making them rich'.[44] There were obvious reasons, too: he was steeped in the best literature of several centuries of English writing; he taught poetry, he read it aloud and he had discussed it at length. And words were his particular talent and skill; he was drawing upon the fascination with language that had been developing in him since childhood.

Nevertheless, writing poetry was not just a result of family tradition, or ambition, or linguistic skill. Secular verse of the kind with which he began was also another kind of breakout from the conventionality of home and career, from examination success and getting on. What led him to start, more than anything else perhaps, was a belief that writing would somehow be for him the way out: from Eastwood, from the working class, from confinement and restriction; from the job he was going forward into, from the division of self of which he was so very conscious. In one way, he had already declared himself as an author. He used the initials 'DHL' or 'D. H. Lawrence' as his signature on every single letter and postcard that survives from his early years (October 1903 onwards); he even signed himself 'DHL' on the single surviving postcard to his mother, from June 1905.[45] His signature was a kind of imprint: impersonal, in its way oddly professional, like a painter's. His father may have been 'Art', his brother 'Ern', but as Lawrence put it in 1928: 'I am not really "our Bert". Come to that, I never was.'[46] He was D. H. Lawrence, DHL for short.

Imaginative writing, under the banner of the new self, responded to some need to be *all* of himself, not just the exam-passing, obedient, controlled and controlling self. It became a way of uniting his sensual, emotional and intellectual selves. Lydia decried the very idea of 'Flights of genius', but Lawrence was inspired to launch out on them. Poetry and its writing represented a secret, emotional liberation from her responsible and intelligent planning for his professional life: it was more akin to a workman's skilful craftsmanship, even if Arthur would denigrate it as 'pottery'.[47]

It would have been difficult for Lawrence to have understood any of this very clearly. He 'talked about writing' long before he did any; he even announced to Jessie what was going to happen – 'It will be *poetry*' – before writing a line.[48] He began to write with an almost overpowering sense of the folly of what he was doing. 'What will the others say? That I'm a fool. A collier's son a poet!' he remarked scathingly to Jessie.[49] George Neville was there when some members of his family and his close friends heard the news. Lydia Lawrence characteristically 'sniffed', his sister Ada '"pshawed and rubbished" times without number', Emily gloomily predicted disappointment, Neville 'adopted an attitude of sheer contempt' and one of their Eastwood neighbours, Beatrice Hall, commented: 'Why David lad, tha' knows it's nobbut rubbish.'[50] Lawrence may have needed the confidence engendered by his examination success to start; but he also remained profoundly embarrassed at the pretentiousness, the absurdity, of being a writer. This was why, when he began, he kept his writing secret from everyone except Jessie. At home, often his only solution was 'writing in the kitchen where all the household affairs were going on', while pretending to do academic work.[51] His writing became public knowledge sometime around 1906. George Neville came across him and Jessie reading something; Ann Chambers knew what was going on, probably no later than the summer of 1906; and his mother cannot have found out much later. She apparently discovered his exercise book, tucked in between academic books on the kitchen bookshelf. But it is likely that when he started, in the spring of 1905, Jessie was the only person in his world to know.

He began, as predicted, with poetry: 'Isn't that the very greatest thing?' Jessie enthused when he told her. All the same, he was not very good at what he was doing. A version of 'Campions' survives from three years later, certainly much revised and improved on the original. Its first four lines run:

The unclouded seas of bluebells have ebbed and passed,
And the pale stars of forget-me-nots have climbed to the last
Rung of their life's ladders fragile height.
Now the trees with winterlocked hands and arms uplifted hold back
    the light.[52]

It is immensely careful, horribly literary writing. The images dutifully (and mechanically) follow each other, the extended metaphors are designed to be admired but also to provoke a whimsical smile. Lawrence covers his tracks and disguises his origins beautifully, but he has also produced something thoroughly self-conscious. Is this a liberation, or just another kind of entrapment? Unlike someone like the young James Joyce, who knew what he was doing from the start,[53] Lawrence had very little idea, apart from 'being a writer'. In 1905, the poem's unlikely existence was perhaps the most important thing about it, though it also gave him something to work on, to knock into shape: he was always the most tremendous reviser of his work.

For perhaps a year, he wrote poetry. It could be worked on anywhere, even in Eastwood, and in itself it did not represent a commitment to anything; it was what a literary young man would naturally produce in his spare time, and could laugh at himself for. He also kept occasional diaries; descriptions survive of the family summer holiday at Mablethorpe in 1906, for example.[54] Most significantly of all, he developed his letter writing. In some ways, Lawrence's letters are the best of all his writings – at least as important as his novels, short stories and poems. This biography will draw upon them extensively. Coincidentally, just as he was experimenting with his writing, 1905–6 brought him his worst experience yet of teaching. As a full-time teacher, he was presumably more on his own; and though Holderness continued to give him good reports (in March 1906, for example, he noted that the work of Lawrence's class was 'especially well done'), Lawrence found that he had 'to fight bitterly for my authority in school': teaching his 'collier lads' was 'savage'.[55] But his career as a teacher was what his mother had yet again sacrificed herself for.

4

Getting Weaned: 1905–1908

The seriousness with which Lawrence was starting to regard his writing in the spring of 1906 may well have contributed to his family's decision to take action against everything that the Haggs farm had, from the Lawrences' perspective, come to stand for. At best, the Haggs represented a profound distraction for a trainee teacher with a period of study just ahead; at the worst, it housed a dangerous and sexually exploitative young woman. In April that year, the literary partnership in which Jessie and Lawrence had been engaged for almost four years was brought to an abrupt end.

They had progressed from shared delight in poetry and novels to what was, by 1906, the serious work of reading and discussing Carlyle, Schopenhauer and Emerson. Lawrence would later look back rather ruefully at the intellectual strenuousness of these years.[1] He had, however, helped answer Jessie's need for intense involvement in other things than the everyday concerns of a tenant farmer's daughter, with little to look forward to except a badly paid career as a teacher, or marriage. Jessie had been not only the recipient of all of Lawrence's fledgling work but its nurse: insisting on its creation, fiercely possessive of it, loving it. Since 1905, she had played an indispensable role not only as the audience for his writing but also as an embodied, insatiable demand on him to write. She was not a critic; she was always impressed with what he did, and at times his keen analytical mind found her appreciation of his work irritating. He showed in his play *A Collier's Friday Night*, for example, the autobiographical Ernest Lambert '*slightly crestfallen*' at the predictable praise for his poems shown by the Jessie character, Maggie Pearson.[2] To a miner's son very conscious of doing something as bizarre as writing poetry, however, Jessie was crucial.

In particular to his mother and his elder sister, Lawrence's relationship with Jessie must have seemed unhealthy, and in its own way as ominous as his burgeoning literary interests. He continued to be out all hours with her, walking and talking and reading. For a possessive and anxious mother anticipating his long-awaited college career, and what she believed would depend on it, the time he spent with Jessie must have been worrying. Emily, married to local man Sam King since 1904, either imagined or pretended to imagine that her brother and Jessie were lovers, and pronounced herself shocked. At Easter 1906, Lawrence found himself confronted with an ultimatum. Even though he angrily insisted that he and Jessie only walked and talked, he was told that he was being thoughtless. By monopolizing her, he was preventing her from getting to know other men: he was wrecking her chances of marriage. If he intended to go on seeing her as he had been doing, then he should consider himself engaged; he would, after all, be twenty-one in a few months' time. In the words of a neighbour: 'She used to come to Sunday tea and sit at chapel with him. If you did things like that, you were spoken for.'[3]

Even at this stage, while he contemplated the damage Jessie, their friendship, their reading and his writing would suffer if he and she stopped seeing each other, there would have been a small part of him which agreed with, even welcomed the break. In 1908, he would write unhappily about her yearning 'to nurse me and soothe me' and continued: 'But I will not have it.' Her feelings for him had grown into love. Shortly after her nineteenth birthday on 29 January 1906, he had sent her a note: 'What am I doing to you? You used to be so vigorous, so full of interest in all sorts of things. Don't take too much notice of me. You mustn't allow yourself to be hurt.' Rather than being *normal*, he was saying, she had let her belief in him run away with her: she would later confess to being 'unbalanced by strife'.[4] The 1911 draft of *Sons and Lovers*, written with a good deal of hindsight, constantly returns to the Jessie figure's emotional needs. When Miriam looks at a bunch of flowers on a bush, she wants 'to touch, to bury her face amongst, to caress and caress as if she would eat it, as if she would absorb it'; Paul winces and shrinks when he hears her 'low, passionate, caressing laugh'.[5]

Lawrence's family would have been counting on the fact that they did not think he would get engaged. Jessie may have been the one person in the world to whom he really talked, but he was not in love with her. Jessie later offered her testimony: 'no instinct of sex was awake in either . . . it was all spiritual.' At some stage, most likely in the period 1906–8, Lawrence went out of his way to inform her: 'You have no sexual attraction at all, none whatever.'[6] This was, however, a statement which revealed him rather than her: he would confess many years later that 'when I was a very young man I was enraged when with a woman, if I was reminded of her sexual actuality. I only wanted to be aware of her personality, her mind and spirit.' But he also found Jessie's constant seriousness wearying; and her self-sacrificing love was something to which he, of all people, had no desire ever to respond. She also once remarked, about him, 'I can read him like a book',[7] and though originally it might have been flattering to be taken so seriously, he ended up unable to bear her possessiveness. What his family demanded at Easter 1906 was something to which, at some level, he would have heard a still small voice agreeing: no, he did *not* want to be engaged.

On Easter Saturday, 14 April, he was out for a walk to Dale Abbey with a party of men friends, Richard Pogmore, Leonard Watts and Fred Stevenson;[8] he had promised the Chambers family to come to them on Easter Monday. It may have been simple gaucheness, but also perhaps the relief of making some kind of emotional break, which apparently made him go straight to Jessie and tell her, 'I've looked into my heart and I cannot find that I love you as a husband should love his wife.'[9] A letter which his mother wrote about him and Jessie in 1910 shows that his language, as Jessie reported it many years later, was close to Lydia's own ('it does not seem to me like the real love he ought to have if he intends to marry her').[10]

Jessie was shocked, horribly hurt and rightly suspected his family of trying to prise them apart. She could not contemplate life without him: 'I saw the golden apple of life that had been lying at my finger tips recede irretrievably.'[11] He left her in no doubt that they must see less of each other, and if possible only when a third person was there;

younger children would soon find themselves co-opted for walks. He would go on giving her French lessons and showing her his writing, they would continue to attend Chapel together, and they 'must go on talking to one another':[12] that is, *he* would talk and she would listen. It was a savage, unexpected blow to Jessie: the ending of her implicit, unexpressed faith that she and Lawrence were destined to spend their lives together. She had never much liked his family. Now she must have hated them, and perhaps despised Lawrence for co-operating with them.

The Lawrence family, however, would have felt that they had safe-guarded Lawrence's professional future, and rescued him from a girl whose devotion they distrusted. During the summer of 1906, Lawrence continued to go to the Haggs, and Jessie even came on the Lawrences' summer holiday to Mablethorpe.[13] There was, however, an inhibition between them now, of the kind his family could observe for themselves.

Once again there was a coincidence of timing. It seems to have been at precisely this point, just after the ending of this first stage of his relationship with Jessie, that Lawrence embarked on the greatest experiment of his young life: he began to write the novel he called 'Laetitia', the earliest version of what, four and a half years later, would be published as *The White Peacock*.[14] This was more significant than poetry; it was a statement that he was not just a literary young man but that he intended to be a writer. The poetry had been written for Jessie; the novel was for a wider audience. To start a novel, too, shortly before he went to college, was its own kind of rebellion: it insisted that he had *his* life to follow too. The kind of novel it was also made it rebellious. Lydia Lawrence's only recorded comments on it were: 'To think that *my* son should have written such a story' and 'I wish you had written on another line.'[15] The heroine, Lettie, would be left pregnant by one man (Leslie) but would marry another (George) before giving birth to Leslie's child. The novel would deal overtly, that is, with sex – in a way that sounds like Hardy updated to the Midlands. Lydia Lawrence's attitude towards sexually explicit fiction was prob-ably identical to Mrs Morel's in the 1911 version of *Sons and Lovers*, where she responds to the famously bawdy opening of *Tristram Shandy* by tearing the pages out.[16]

Irony of ironies, Lawrence's novel would have the heart-seized Jessie

Chambers as its first, and at this stage only, reader. Lawrence brought her the opening at Whitsun, early in June 1906: '"We've broken the ice," he said in a tense voice. He told me to put the writing away and read it when he had gone.'[17] The writing still had to be kept secret and he still needed her; but the relationship was on his terms, not hers.

And . . . he talked to her. Seven years later, after they had parted for the last time, and she had written her own novel about their relationship, in direct competition with *Sons and Lovers*, Lawrence's response was astonishment: 'I should scarcely recognise her – she never used to *say* anything.' What Jessie did was get him to talk, and thus make him intellectually aware of what he was doing in his writing. She stimulated him into understanding the work he had produced unconsciously.[18] A version of himself as Paul in *Sons and Lovers* is seen 'discussing Michael Angelo', and the oddity of a 'discussion' in which only Paul talks is not lost on the reader. Miriam is simply aware of 'the white intensity of his search'; it gives her 'her deepest satisfaction'. The kind of monologue which Paul conducts is, however, entirely intellectual: 'so level it was, almost inhuman as if in a trance . . . He lay quite still, almost unable to move. His body was somewhere discarded.'[19] It was this kind of talking which Lawrence perfected over the years with Jessie. Paul describes how he becomes a 'sort of disseminated consciousness, that's all there is of me. I feel as if my body were lying empty, as if I were in the other things – clouds and water.'[20] Many of Lawrence's subsequent heroes have the same ability to talk, but they are matched with women who undermine their cleverness, or show them how one-sided, spiritual and disembodied their talk is. Lawrence eventually saw as the very worst kind of spiritual detachment what, in *Sons and Lovers*, is presented as really rather impressive. In his early twenties, this kind of loquacious, disembodied detachment seems to have been Lawrence's way not only of understanding what he was writing, and might produce next, but of thinking through things which concerned him. When he took up with Agnes Holt in Croydon in October 1908, she too had to listen: 'you know my kind, a girl to whom I gas. She . . . takes me seriously: which is unwisdom.'[21] That was why he needed to go on talking to Jessie in 1906.

What made the new relationship with Jessie rather easier, for Lawrence, was that in late September 1906 he was going to college in

Nottingham: another break with the old days, another readjustment to how much he could see of her, and how often he might be able to come out to the Haggs. Early that month, he brought his teaching in Eastwood to an end, apparently without many regrets. Holderness had clearly valued him, while the pupils who had given him such a hard time eventually seem to have liked him 'nearly as much as I loved them'.[22] Two photographs of him (see Illustration 8 for one of them) were taken on his twenty-first birthday, 11 September 1906, just before he started his training course. He may have been fairly frail, physically – 'because I was not strong, I thought myself of rather less account than most people: the weakling in health!' – but in his high collar and with his keen, fresh face, he continues to look very young: sympathetic, open, 'bright' (Holderness's word), 'radiant' (his own).[23] The Chambers family put both pictures on the mantelpiece at the Haggs; he was still their special extra son. He later described the photographs as those of 'an intellectual prig'.[24] Being a prig, or fearing to be one, was something he was very aware of: Professor Amos Henderson, his head of department at Nottingham University College, would sum him up as 'scholarly and refined' and 'fastidious in taste'.[25] It was a remarkable verdict on a miner's son; it suggests how much Lawrence had reshaped himself.

When Lawrence went to college Jessie must have felt more on her own than for years. Naturally enough, he moved into a new circle, of fellow students on the teaching course, and acquired a new group of friends, among them Louie Burrows from Cossall. Three years younger than Lawrence, she remembered him as 'fair with blue eyes and the nicest smile' when they first met at the Ilkeston Centre; he would later call her ' "my girl" in Coll'.[26] Back in 1905–6, his companions had been the local teachers he went walking with. He now moved into new worlds intellectually, eventually spending a good deal of his time with socialist and free-thinking companions. His sympathies with socialism seem, however, to have been less political than an instinctive reaction against poverty, combined with rebellion against the authority (of whatever kind) that maintained the status quo. In December 1907, for example, he told the Congregational minister, the Reverend Robert Reid, that religion to him was, for now, 'lessening, in some pitiful moiety, the great human discrepancies'.[27] He became a founder member of a socialist group at college, the 'Society for the Study of Social Reform',[28] and around 1908 began reading the *New Age*, a radical, socialist weekly dedicated to expounding the philosophy of Nietzsche – he would show a character in his 1909 play *A Collier's Friday Night* reading it. Back in Eastwood, he took up with Willie and Sallie Hopkin, both noted ethical socialists and readers of the *New Age*.[29] He would give a paper to a session of a newly formed debating society at the Hopkin house in the spring of 1908, to which Jessie and Alan Chambers and Eastwood socialist intellectuals, like the chemist Harry Dax and his radical-thinking wife, Alice, came. Lydia Lawrence did not approve, remarking: 'I hope he doesn't get too friendly with Willie Hopkin.'[30]

For Hopkin's lack of religious faith was notorious locally, and such a debating society was setting itself up in direct, if modest, opposition to the so-called Congregational Literary Society run by Robert Reid, which offered regular Monday evening lectures, mostly by clergymen, but not often on literary subjects. Up till then, nevertheless, it had been almost the only public manifestation of culture in Eastwood. To Jessie Chambers, who believed passionately in Reid's Society, Lawrence's developing disillusionment with organized religion, which grew steadily during his time at college, would have been hard to accept. Like Paul Morel, Lawrence had at one stage defined himself as an agnostic, but it had turned out to be 'such a religious Agnosticism'[31] that Jessie had not been too worried. Between 1906 and 1908, however, his attraction to socialism and his continued failure to experience what evangelical Christianity always valued and expected – conversion – meant that he grew increasingly critical of organized religion. In the autumn of 1907, he wrote a letter to the Reverend Robert Reid about contemporary scientific and socialist objections to Christianity.[32] Reid responded with a series of sermons in the Congregational Chapel specifically addressing the problems raised by Lawrence and his free-thinking Eastwood friends, like Alan Chambers; Lawrence wrote at least one more long letter in response to the series. Lawrence had, however, been reading Schopenhauer, Haeckel and William James since going to college, and nothing Reid could say would prevent him now moving decisively against the idea of the divinity of Christ. Eventually, under the influence of one of his teachers at college,

'Botany' Smith, he declared himself to be a Pragmatist of the William James sort: firmly agnostic, convinced there was no 'personal God'.[33] Without a personal God, there was only a 'vast, shimmering impulse which wavers onwards towards some end, I don't know what – taking no regard of the little individual, but taking regard for humanity'; on the other hand, he believed in coming to 'discover one's own creed . . . to establish one's own religion in one's heart'.[34]

'Religious without religion' might be a summary of Lawrence's state of mind. While at college, though, he had, in his sister Emily's rather bewildered words, fallen in with a set of people 'who ridiculed religion'.[35] One example would be his new correspondent Blanche Jennings, a socialist and suffragette friend of Alice Dax, from Liverpool, to whom, after Alice Dax had introduced them early in 1908, he wrote some revealing letters between April 1908 and January 1910: she was 'thoroughly out of sympathy with anything that savours of christianity', and accused 'christians' of not telling the truth.[36] Lawrence was never so cavalier, nor so brash; his reaction against formal religion was serious and carefully thought through. Although the ordinary, everyday religion of the Chapel had grown unsympathetic and irritating to him, as long as he lived in Eastwood he continued to attend Chapel with his family.

He could not always suppress his feelings, though. The Chambers family and his mother were astonished one evening in the spring of 1908 when, walking home after Chapel, he launched into a savage denunciation of Robert Reid, a man they all respected and believed Lawrence did too: 'Lawrence poured a stream of scorn and raillery upon the poor man, made fun of his ideas, and mimicked his way of expressing them.'[37] It was not just Reid whom Lawrence was attacking. A host of entangled loyalties centred on Chapel: his connection with it since childhood, his mother's belief in the basic pieties, her respect for the 'Chapel Men' who had done well in Eastwood society (the shopkeepers, the traders), her confidence in the decent ordering of society, and in the kind of authority which always must be respected. Lawrence's letters to Reid show his irritation with religion's inability to reconcile a loving, omnipotent God with human poverty, disease and deprivation. He saw himself changing – 'getting a bit weaned'[38] from his mother, for example – and at times his repressed anger came out. When it did, it could make him searchingly direct in argument; or it could render him very frightening. The 'sweetness of disposition' remembered by David Chambers was only one side of his nature. His passions could scare people: the attack on Reid was not just witty mockery but, to those who saw it, something violent and terrifying: 'a fierce, uncontrollable tirade, an outpouring of long pent-up rage that left us all silent and rather frightened. We had never seen him in such a mood before. He seemed to be beside himself. His mother was as shocked as the rest of us, and perhaps she had the most reason.'[39]

Lydia Lawrence had experienced his sudden rages and misery as a child, which had nearly always been responses to humiliation together with some kind of violent assertion of self. But this rage suggests an uncontrolled breaking down of inhibition. After an apparent lull during his teens, which may simply be because there is almost no record of his home life during that period, this tendency began to show itself again in his early twenties, as a kind of wild, almost demonic, destructive and self-destructive energy, often accompanied by verbal denunciation. At Mablethorpe in August 1906, for example, while Jessie and Lawrence were walking on the beach one evening, 'something seemed to explode inside him . . . his words were wild, and he appeared to be in great distress of mind . . . In some way I was to blame. He upbraided me bitterly.' Two years later, at Flamborough, he was even more frightening. 'Lawrence skipped from one white boulder to another in the vast amphitheatre of the bay until I could have doubted whether he was indeed a human being . . . And always, somehow or other, it was my fault, or partly my fault.'[40] David Chambers was also terrified on an occasion when Lawrence's behaviour matched the violence of his speech. He started to leap the rushing mill race at Felley Mill Farm: 'repeatedly backwards and forwards across it like an antelope, as though defying death itself, while I stood holding my breath with fear. I have seen the shute since and I still cannot see how it was done.'[41] Lawrence was very aware that he had 'a good old English habit of shutting my rages of trouble well inside my belly, so that they play havoc with my innards',[42] but these outbreaks of anger and physical rage seem for a while to have been his only way of dealing with conflicted feelings. He may well have believed in the authenticity of the rage taking him over; the violent expression of emotional need was very different from, for example, the ways in which he had tried for religious belief and conversion, and always found himself too self-conscious, too introspective. He had told Reid how 'in the moments of deepest emotion myself has watched myself and seen that all the tumult has risen like a little storm, to die away again without great result'.[43] His watching and questioning self inhibited belief of all kinds, as well as love for anyone except his mother. 'I would give a great deal to fall in love,' he remarked wistfully in June 1908.[44] The self in rage was another matter: there was no careful watching when *that* self had taken over. The split between violent rage and the self-conscious operation of control takes us straight back to his childhood, and what he had witnessed during his parents' quarrels. It also suggests some real and lasting disturbance, and continuing problems with the forms control, rage and anger might take.

The one thing which may perhaps have reconciled Jessie to Lawrence's period at college was that she remained the only person who saw his writing; and he was able to spend more time on it than either of them had probably expected. In fact, he came to feel that his two years at Nottingham were largely wasted; he strongly advised Jessie to take her certificate as an external student and not to commit her family to the expense of sending her to the college. He had gone prepared to take 'a step into a fuller life',[45] but had found the course stultifying and the teachers patronizing toward students working only for their teacher's certificate: 'I might as well be taught by gramophones as by those men, for all the interest or sincerity they felt.'[46] Ursula's experience of utter disillusion, in *The Rainbow*, offers a fictionally rounded version of Lawrence's feelings: 'the whole thing seemed sham, spurious: spurious Gothic arches, spurious peace, spurious Latinity, spurious dignity of France, spurious naïveté of Chaucer.'[47]

For a while during his first year, Lawrence had gone along with the idea of studying for a degree; he needed Latin to take a degree course and arranged with his classics professor to give him the extra coaching he needed. The arrangement fell through, however, in a way that Lawrence came to feel was typical of the college: when the moment came, the professor no longer had the time. Consequently, Lawrence seems to have done what he had to do on the day training course, and no more; and any thought of a degree was postponed. In spite of this, he came out with the best marks (B A B B in Teaching, Reading, Drawing and Music) of any man in his final year, 1908, though they were not as good as the marks of the best women students, some of whom got A A A A. His final report was very clear about the kind of teacher he was. He struck Professor Henderson as someone who with 'an upper class in a good school or in a higher school . . . could do work quite unusually good, especially if allowed a very free hand'. One reason why he needed freedom to work well was that he had grown so fiercely independent intellectually. On the other hand, with children from 'a rough district', he 'would be quite unsuitable . . . he would not have sufficient persistence & enthusiasm but would become disgusted'.[48] Lawrence may have despised his teachers, but they had noticed how he had, in effect, attained a level of education and sophistication that raised him out of the working class.

But college at least meant that he had a great deal of freedom. He boasted about working on the novel 'Laetitia' during lectures; he finished more than he expected of its first draft towards the end of his first year, and wrote the second draft the following year. 'His real interest centred on his writing and not on his studies,' as he put it in 1928.[49] He also worked hard at his poetry, and in the autumn of 1907 he started to write short stories. This may originally have been because Jessie and Alan Chambers had challenged him to enter the annual *Nottinghamshire Guardian* competition for stories with a local set-ting. Lawrence determined to enter all three available categories: he employed Jessie and Louie Burrows to submit stories for him, while he entered the story he thought had the best chance, an early version of 'A Fragment of Stained Glass'. As it turned out, the story entered by Jessie, 'A Prelude', won the category for the best story of a happy Christmas and was printed in the *Nottinghamshire Guardian*.

The story takes us into the world of 'Laetitia' as it probably was in 1907 – upper classes scornful, superior young women blushing but beautiful, young farmers handsome but disconsolate, final reconcili-ation sentimental and inevitable – but it also contains recreations of the Haggs and the Chambers family, in the very first of Lawrence's fictional versions of real life. Its prose is profoundly adjectival and charmingly sententious. The story begins: 'In the kitchen of a small farm a little woman sat cutting bread and butter. The glow of the clear, ruddy fire was on her shining cheek and white apron; but grey hair will not take the warm caress of firelight.'[50] Edmund Chambers cashed the £3 cheque for Lawrence; Jessie's headmaster recorded in the school log-book what he believed to have been her success. Lawrence eventually rewrote the other stories, Louie's being an early version of 'The White Stocking', and he wrote at least one other story ('The Vicar's Garden') around the same time. The 'Prelude', he hoped, had 'gone to glory in the absolute sense'.[51]

His final, and thoroughly symbolic, act as a student was to turn his two thick, black, nicely bound college notebooks into the working notebooks of a writer. He used them to sketch out plans of the novels he would write between 1908 and 1910; they were also a repository for fair copies of the poems he had been writing since 1905 and those he would write over the next four years. The notebooks survive to this day with his botany, French, Latin and other notes in them, but with the pages overwhelmed by poetry drafts in pencil, ink and crayon.[52]

In his college portrait, taken in the summer of 1908, he appears more solid and assured, less ethereal; the newly grown (and very red) moustache confirming his self-determination and his age of almost twenty-three. He looks his age for the very first time in a photograph, which is perhaps why he grew the moustache.[53] Although he continued to live at home during his college years, he moved further than ever before from the expectations of home. He gained another kind of confidence at college, feeling that he had seen through something which most of the world continued to be impressed by: he had 'lost forever my sincere boyish reverence for men in position'.[54] When he recreated his father as Mr Morel, he described how 'Authority was hateful to him, therefore he could only abuse the pit-managers'.[55] Lawrence enjoyed just the kind of subversive mockery Morel demonstrates: the sly stories, the sense of being the child pointing out that the emperor has no clothes. As so often with Lawrence, however, the highly intellectual person he was craved companionship and participation, and was frustrated regularly. Through education he had lost a good deal of the sense of where he came from or to what he might belong, and the role of the outsider had become natural to him.

But his immediate problem, after the exams that concluded his college career, was to find a job. Some of his friends quickly found posts: Louie Burrows, for example, began work in Leicester as soon as her exams were over; she would keep a job in the county for the rest of her teaching career. For Jessie, 'Lawrence out of work was a sardonic figure. He spent much of his time at the farm, handing his manuscript over to me, and accompanying my brother about the farm work.'[56] This must have marked the culmination of his friendship with Alan, a type of man to whom he was regularly attracted as a friend: healthy, outdoor and intellectually curious. During July and August 1908, Lawrence failed to get a post in time for the start of the school year in September, in spite of using 'pounds of paper in applications'; he could 'recite two long testimonials by heart'.[57] He was eventually interviewed at the end of September in Stockport (unsuccessfully, but he had not liked what he had seen of the place, nor Manchester). He was, however, interviewed in the south London suburb of Croydon a few days later and was offered a post as assistant master at the Davidson Road Boys' School, starting on 12 October: 'My standard – IV; my salary £95.'[58]

A full-time, qualified job was what he owed and wanted to give his mother, after her years of scrimping and saving and self-sacrificial love. But why was he leaving the Midlands? He had fixed a minimum sum of £90 a year for his salary, and that ruled out Nottinghamshire. In addition, he wanted a break from home: what became in the end a serious alienation from Eastwood started here. But there were undoubtedly other reasons, too. He may well have felt that, as a writer, he needed to expand his range of knowledge and reference. London was, and still tends to be seen as, the centre of the English literary world, and taking a job only thirty minutes away from it by train would have seemed too good a chance for a young and ambitious writer to miss. Leaving Eastwood would mean, too, that he could stop going regularly to Chapel. Any sexual inclinations he may have had at that time, except for those he insisted he did *not* have for Jessie, are mysterious. His reputation had been that of a young man who, to the relief of the women who knew him, neither spooned nor flirted. 'I never saw him make love to anybody or kiss them or anything,' remembered a neighbour. He was still fairly immature and inexperienced: at some point between the ages of nineteen and twenty-two, he had a violent quarrel with George Neville because the latter insisted that women had pubic hair.[59] His time in Croydon, however, would be marked by frequent relationships with women: another freedom contingent on leaving home.

For though, in one sense, he would never leave the place he had grown up in, he was currently committed to pursuing a professional career, and he wanted to get away. Although going to Croydon would lead to yet another break with Jessie, above all it would mean leaving his mother. However much he loved her, Lawrence would also have known that he had to leave: he knew all too well how, ever since he had been fourteen or fifteen, she had been 'guiding me into a groove'.[60]

Going away would not be inconsistent with intense nostalgia for the old place; he wrote in February 1909 how 'still I long for the country and for my own folks'. Over the years, the Haggs turned into a kind of myth of a golden time, half fictional and half real; it retained an extraordinary power over him that lasted until the end of his life. Going away 'from the valley he loved so deeply' remained a troubling decision: as usual, one half of him was in rebellion against the other half.[61]

There were various farewells to be paid, and one of the most important was at the Haggs, where he went to say goodbye to the whole family. Edmund Chambers remarked, 'Well, Bert, you're going to leave us then'; it was the 'us' that counted. Even the sardonic May confessed: 'He left a blank that no other could fill.'[62] Then it was Jessie's turn, and she recalls it in her memoir:

I walked with him to the last gate, where we stopped. He leaned towards me. 'La dernière fois,' he said, inclining his head towards the farm and the wood. I burst into tears, and he put his arms round me. He kissed me and stroked my cheek, murmuring:

'I'm so sorry, so sorry, so sorry.'

His words scalded me. I drew away and dried my tears.

'I'm so sorry for this,' he said again in a deadened voice. 'But it can't be helped, it can't be helped.'

. . . It was all utterly hopeless, there was no use beginning the old argument again.[63]

It was the end of his six-year love affair with the Chambers family and with Jessie: the words in French ('the last time') both literary and a way of hiding or diverting his feelings. If Jessie's account is to be trusted, he was – cruelly? honestly? – saying goodbye to 'the farm and the wood' as much as to her. Pity and remorse and tenderness are all he feels for her; he only rarely touches or embraces her, so this hug is very special. In 1910, he would comment that, in nine years of knowing her, 'I had hardly kissed her all that time.'[64] She draws away, so as not to be overwhelmed by her feelings, and dries her tears. But when she cries, he seems to be touched by some kind of anger (with himself, with her), perhaps because, as she knows, he has never wanted her for herself. That is what hurts her most. 'It can't be helped,' he says, twice. She has loved him for so long, and has ended up with just one more in a series of desolating partings.

Lawrence travelled down to Croydon by train on Sunday 11 October 1908, to start work the following day. All Jessie could do was accept the loss as inevitable, go on hoping against hope that somehow things might change, send him letters as often as she could, keep him in touch with their old world, and wait for his writing to arrive.

5

Croydon: 1908–1910

Lawrence started his Croydon career as an elementary teacher in the Davidson Road School, 'a great big new red-brick imposing handsome place' which had only opened the previous year: 'Inside all is up to date, solid and good . . . floors are block wood – thirty dual desks for forty five boys – all very nice.' Its headmaster, Philip Smith, was a practitioner of the 'experimental lesson', and had gathered around him a staff of young men and one older woman, Agnes Mason; Lawrence joined them as assistant master. He walked to school over 'a piece of wild waste land' on the edge of Croydon's fast-growing suburban sprawl: 'the brick-layer's hammer chinks, chinks the funeral bell of my piece of waste land.'[1] From 1908 to 1911, he lodged ten minutes' walk from school, in Colworth Road, with Marie and John Jones; she a former teacher, he a school attendance officer, both at different times confiding their marital problems to Lawrence. They had two small girls: Winifred was five, the baby, Hilda Mary, had only been born in March. Lydia Lawrence is reported to have remarked, 'austerely': 'I was glad when I knew there was a baby. It will keep him pure'[2] – innocence presumably being contagious. Lydia had reason to fear that he might need keeping pure, away from home for the first time: she could not have helped comparing him, a still-young twenty-three, with the 21-year-old Ernest, who had gone to live in London and had (disastrously) got engaged.

To start off with, Lawrence knew no one outside the Jones family and was horribly lonely; he sent Jessie Chambers a letter 'like a howl of terror', which also told her not to let his mother know how he felt: 'he had written to her that everything was all right and he was getting on well'. He found leaving home disorienting – 'I am always a bit sick as the result of my change,' he remarked in 1909 – and Croydon was not only a real break with his past but the new job turned out to be very difficult.[3] Professor Henderson had feared that Lawrence would be 'quite unsuitable for a large class of boys in a rough district'. In Croydon, that was exactly what he got. 'Think of a quivering grey hound set to mind a herd of pigs and you see me teaching,'[4] he commented ruefully on his first weeks. Too refined for the job, in other words, he should be out running races, not doing menial tasks. He found the children 'rough and insolent as the devil';[5] his Notts-Derby accent no doubt made him an easy target for mockery, and he had particular problems with children who came from institutions. The Davidson Road School included in its catchment-area boys from the Gordon Home for Waifs and Strays, and from the local Actors' Home. His pupils in Eastwood at least came from families with enough to eat, whereas poverty was a real problem in Croydon. He asked Louie Burrows, now in a country school in Leicestershire:

Louisa, do any of your youngsters limp to school; through the snow or the fine weather, limp to school because they are crippled with broken boots. Have you seen wounds on the feet of your boys, from great mens boots they wear which are split across . . . Have you seen the children gathered to free breakfasts at your school – half a pint of milk and a lump of bread – eighty boys and girls sitting down the bare boards?[6]

Not only were the children different, Philip Smith was not at all the kind of interventionist headmaster George Holderness had been. 'Discipline is consequently very slack,' Lawrence complained; Smith 'shifts every grain of responsibility off his own shoulders – he will not punish anybody'.[7] It was up to the individual teacher to sort things out, and to start with Lawrence found that he was simply 'trying to tame some fifty or sixty malicious young human animals'. What made it worse was his failure to feel much commitment towards school discipline: his instinct was to restrict as little as possible. 'How can I blame – why be angry?' But as he knew very well, that approach led to 'a hideous state of affairs': 'School is a conflict – mean and miserable – and I hate conflicts . . . I struggle with my nature and with my class, till I feel all frayed into rags.'[8] It took him back to the time when he had had to 'fight' for his authority at school in 1905. He sympathized strongly with Louie Burrows, who had also been having a rough time; as her college report had noted, 'Discipline not a strong point.'[9] Davidson Road was Lawrence's worst teaching experience yet. All he could do, after days of despair, was, like Ursula in *The Rainbow*, overcome that sophisticated, liberating nature of his by taking 'to arm me for the fight the panoply of a good stinging cane – and me voilà!' He made it sound simple, but his first months were wretched. Not until the end of December did he feel in control; only in February 1909 did he announce: 'I have tamed my wild beasts – I have conquered my turbulent subjects, and can teach in ease and comfort.'[10]

Lawrence's struggles had left his male colleagues unimpressed. He had 'failed signally to pass their tests of capacity both for sport and school discipline, so they first extended to him a contemptuous patronage'. A friend saw how 'he avoids, or is avoided by, the other men on the staff'. Later, 'when they had some experience of his intellectual fearlessness and power of passionate argument', they 'paid him a grudging respect and kept out of his way'. The fact that in his novel *The Trespasser* (published six months after he left Croydon, but written while he was still there) he satirized a couple of them, describing one as 'vulgar in the grain', would have confirmed their belief that he was objectionable.[11] He eventually got on well with the 'discerning' and 'kindly' Philip Smith, while his colleague of forty-one, Agnes Mason, tried to mother him; but the only other teacher he really liked was Arthur McLeod, a studious man of twenty-three whom Lawrence recreated in *The Trespasser* as a man of 'absolute reserve amid all his amiability'.[12] It is significant that Lawrence kept him as a friend even after leaving Croydon: the well-read young man was a natural companion for the intellectual Lawrence. McLeod lent him books, too: 'I have read much modern work since I came here,' Lawrence remarked in March 1909. 'Joseph Conrad, and Björnsterne Björnsterne, Wells, Tolstoi. I love modern work.'[13] Croydon took him in some crucial new directions. He would have known about Nietzsche since starting to read the *New Age*, but it was in Croydon that Lawrence started reading his books. Nietzsche was one of the many subterranean intellectual influences on Lawrence, who always mined such writers and thinkers for what he felt he could use; but Nietzsche – 'There is more rationality in thy body than in thy best wisdom' – was one of those who really helped educate Lawrence into new ways of thinking.[14] Yet Croydon also confirmed him in the experience – familiar from the High School and Haywoods – of being different: clever, but not someone who got on particularly well with his fellows, few of whom would have bothered about Nietzsche. He could easily be taken for arrogant and distant.

Philip Smith's enlightened approach to experiments in education, although painful in the degree of autonomy and responsibility it allotted individual teachers, at least enabled Lawrence to try out ideas; he was given the 'very free hand' Henderson had recommended. Lawrence astonished a visiting school inspector – typically a 'refined soul down from Oxford' – who walked into his class one day:

The intrusion was unexpected and resented. A curious wailing of distressed voices issued from a far corner. The sounds were muffled by a large covering black-board. The words of a familiar song arose from the depths:

> Full fathom five thy father lies;
> Of his bones are coral made.

The class was reading *The Tempest*. The presentation expressed the usual thoroughness of Lawrence's attitude to the exercise in progress. It must not be spoiled by even official comment. Lawrence rushed with outstretched hands to the astounded visitor: 'Hush! Hush! Don't you hear? The sea chorus from *The Tempest*.'[15]

He was also unorthodox in refusing to teach children moralistic poetry. Other lessons sound still more risky and exciting: when he was teaching history, for example, the boys participated 'by pretending to shoot arrows at me, drawing back the bow with vigour', while they apparently '*fought* the battle of Agincourt over schoolforms and all'.[16] His art lessons, too, were a great success: 'the whole class acquired his own free, vigorous style and painted boldly and with huge enjoyment. It was almost his one regret on leaving that his successor might cramp that freedom of handling.' Although Smith observed how he 'shirked none of the drudgery . . . of a teacher's life', Lawrence was dedicated to liberating and freeing, rather than forcing the pupils into a pattern.[17]

School was always exhausting, nevertheless. A 'wearing, nerve-wracking business', he called it: 'If ever there is a poor devil on the face of the earth it is the elementary school-teacher.'[18] The real quarrel, however, went on in his spare time as much as it did in school. It was not between his professional career and his ambitions as a writer. It was between his capacity to be detached, intellectual and incipiently middle class, and his nostalgia – 'I wish I were just like ordinary men' – for being a more ordinary kind of person altogether.[19] His attitude towards the poverty he saw in Croydon could be surprisingly superior. One of his boys has 'a strain of gipsy in him, a mongrel form common in the south of London'; a thief he accidentally traps one night in the kitchen at Colworth Road, in his fictional recreation of the incident, is 'a slum-rat'.[20] The world of real wealth was still an unimaginable distance away; the teacher's profession, as a working-class contemporary in Croydon saw it, only *just* kept the teacher out of the swamp of extreme poverty: teachers walked 'firmly along a low dyke which crosses a morass'.[21] A man like Lawrence, who had effectively moved out of one class into the classless role of the educated professional, but who had almost nothing in common with other educated professionals, was always going to be sharply aware of class distinction. He could be both callow and naïve in the distance he professed from the poor and disadvantaged. Yet he would also suggest, wistfully, in January 1909, that 'I should have been far happier and better as a farm-labourer than as anything out on the choppy seas of social life'.[22] He felt loyal to the older, non-intellectual community he also belonged to; 'social life' held very little promise for him, though he certainly wanted to be able to deal with it when he had to. But if asked who really deserved his sympathy, or who *he* was in these conflicts, or where his loyalty or his language should be in his judgements of these children, then he would have had no easy answer.

It is therefore interesting that, no sooner had he arrived in Croydon, with some ambition to 'swot', than he 'pretty well decided to give up study'.[23] He had finally turned against Lydia Lawrence's encouragement to work for a degree, which would have allowed him to move from elementary into secondary teaching, and thence perhaps into higher education. Abandoning the degree was another way of promising himself that teaching was only a temporary occupation, but it was also a way of asserting his new independence and of reaffirming that, whatever happened, and however cut off he felt, he did not want to rise in the world, socially. In that way, he was affirming something which held good for the rest of his life.

His social life, to start with, consisted of solitary visits to concerts, lectures, art galleries, the theatre and opera. London remained an enigma: enormous, brutal, fascinating. His writing about it shows us one of its major differences from a provincial city of the period: its lights.

Everywhere at night the city is filled with the magic of lamps: over the River they pour in golden patches their floating luminous oil on the restless darkness; the bright lamps float in and out of the cavern of London Bridge Station like round shining bees in and out of a black hive; in the suburbs the street-lamps glimmer with the brightness of lemons among the trees.[24]

Lawrence is self-consciously finding metaphors for his experience: he is the brilliant, observant writer, the greyhound among the pigs. His writing style in letters, in particular to Blanche Jennings, is often extremely mannered. As he put it in December 1908, though he might by nature have been passionate, he knew that he was 'too conscious, and vaguely troubled' (which is rather how he looks in a photograph of the period: see Illustration 11). He also started to write poems about the city. He cycled long distances, exploring Surrey – 'a most sweet and lovely county' – and getting as far as the south coast on one occasion. 'My hands are as red as fire-lit sands, with biking through the sunny day,' he wrote – rejoicingly descriptive even while recording sunburn.[25] He spent a lot of time at home in Colworth Road, writing; he painted, played chess, went to the pub and talked man's talk with John Jones.

'Such a pretty tart in the "Crown", Mr Lawrence – really warm and fruity.'
  'Oh,' I say, 'and didn't you cotton [strike up a relationship].'
  'No – I'd rather have a good dinner any day.'[26]

He helped with the Jones children too, in ways that their parents must have appreciated. Lawrence wrote marvellously about children; in February 1909, for example, he described the eleven-month-old Hilda Mary in a way that shows that he did not have to write metaphorically to impress. She was hanging onto my legs, laughing up at me. She has brilliant hazel eyes, so round and daring. Soon I shall take her and get her to sleep. She does not like to go to bed, but I am a good 'dustman'. I hold her tight and sing – roar away at the noisiest songs. This subdues her, she tucks her face in my neck and toddles off to 'bo', while her hair tickles my nose to a frenzy.[27]

Back in Eastwood he now had four young nephews and nieces to buy birthday and Christmas presents for; his sister Emily had had her first child (Margaret, known as Peggy) on 9 February.[28]

What really occupied his time, however, was reworking 'Laetitia'. Lawrence resolved to 'have another go at it this winter', 'to take the sentimentality out of her'.[29] He remained full of longing for the landscape of the Haggs, and for the family there; and this he poured into his rewriting of 'Laetitia', which became a kind of nostalgic recreation of a rural world which he could imaginatively inhabit while living in suburban Croydon. The novel had originally ended with reconciliation between the heroic young farmer, George, and the youthful but flighty heroine, Lettie, no longer dominated by her upper-class seducer, Leslie; it had hinted at their new life in Canada. But the whole dynamic of the piece changed, not just the ending, when Lawrence decided to write a novel about how a marriage, this time between Lettie and Leslie, goes wrong, and how George ends up alcoholic and derelict. He was trying to take the romance out of it, and to bring it into the arena of his own experience, even if it were still coloured by George Eliot, Thomas Hardy and the Brontës. At its centre, probably ever since 1906, had been the narrator Cyril Beardsall, and despite Lawrence's repeated resolution to 'stop up the mouth of Cyril – I will kick him out', he never did. His need for Cyril in the novel, given that the character talks too much – he is 'too much *me*',[30] as Lawrence knew – can mostly be accounted for by the fact that Cyril is a kind of awkward emissary to the middle-class world: intellectual, artistic, disembodied, priggish, incapable of showing or sharing feelings, even though in a position to do so. At some stage, Lawrence conceived a scene in which Cyril bathes with George, and is gently, sensuously towelled dry by him; this, however, conveys the detached character's intense need of human warmth and contact as much as any homoeroticism.[31] George was conceived as robustly non-intellectual, and Leslie as superior and middle class; but Cyril embodied all that Lawrence both feared being and thought might genuinely be his role as man and writer.

In March 1909, he was still labouring at the novel: 'I have to do it over and over again, to make it decent.' He re-christened it 'Nethermere' and showed the manuscript to Arthur McLeod 'with the anxious demand to let him know if it was good'.[32] This was the first time he had dared show it to a male friend, but he could count on McLeod's discretion. Blanche Jennings had, however, seen it in 1908, and it is probable that Lydia Lawrence was also still reading what he wrote, even if her comments continued to be disparaging.[33]

He was also embarking on a new range of poems about school, to add to those he had been writing about Hilda Mary Jones and about London. He sent everything to Jessie but still made no attempt to publish anything. He could not bear the prospect of being rejected – the collier's son getting his come-uppance – but he was also still unsure what he really wanted to achieve with his writing. This is understandable. The oddity even of the revised 'Nethermere' shows how hard it still was for him to resolve the confusion of different desires within him. However, he was starting to follow a compulsion to explore, in his writing, the body's experience (his reading of Nietzsche would have assisted here) – its sensations, its feelings, what he called 'the great impulses' that come 'through *feeling* – indescribable'[34] and to look for suitable words to express them, even if at the moment his language tended to be refined, metaphorical, poetic. That was partly because he believed he knew what would appeal to the taste of his age; he was determined to succeed, not just to crawl ignominiously into print. Jessie Chambers remembered him fantasizing: 'I'll make two thousand a year!'[35]

Writing had become the necessity of his life. In it, however clumsily, he was starting to face the divisions in his nature and of his fractured experience, even while he was aspiring to being middle class and literary, pleasing the taste of his period and hoping to be a success. The one thing he could *not* face at this stage was failure. In the spring of 1908, he had sent some writing, perhaps a version of the paper he gave to the meeting at the Hopkins', to the well-known literary figure G. K. Chesterton, whose work both he and Jessie read and admired in the *Daily News*, 'asking him if he would give his opinion as to its merit'. Some weeks or even months passed before the piece came back, readdressed by the author's wife, with a note saying that her husband was too busy to read it. Lawrence's reaction was both angry and self-defeating: ' "I've tried, and been turned down, and I shall try no more. And I don't care if I never have a line published," he concluded in a tone of finality.'[36] What he could not bear was a humiliating exposure of his absurdity. He commented in November 1908 that simply having his work *read* by others made him feel 'as if I'd stood like a naked slave in the market, under the glances of a crowd of fools safely swathed in stupidity'. When his poems were eventually taken by a magazine in 1909, he felt 'rather daft when I think of appearing, if only in so trivial a way, before the public'; and when the work was published, he described how 'one lies exposed and quiveringly vulnerable in print'.[37]

His mother's disapproval of what he was doing cannot have helped his sense of the unsheltered exposure of publication. However, the other side of his 'shyness – confusion', he knew very well, was a kind of arrogant self-belief: 'an unnecessary sort of pride' he called it in 1910. His old awareness of the strangeness of what he was doing made him desperately sensitive on both counts. But he went on writing; a few years later, he would demonstrate how well he understood why he did so: 'one sheds ones sicknesses in books – repeats and presents again ones emotions, to be master of them.'[38]

Although Lawrence offered to read and correct some short stories that Louie Burrows was writing, and to send them to a publisher for her, he made no move to try to publish any of his own work. He may have been the author of a sensitive and poetic novel, the writer of letters that were strikingly clever, mannered and elegant, and fascinated by the idea of success as a writer, but he was also Bert Lawrence from Eastwood, profoundly ill at ease with, not to say derisive about, the literary world. His mother had characterized his writing as something that simply inflated his 'soap-bubble of a soul'.[39] He would probably have agreed with her when, for example, he wrote clever nothings to another London acquaintance, Grace Crawford. His thank-you note to her for an evening party ended: 'It is a shame to break the moment from its stalk, to wither in the vase of memory, by thanking you.'[40]

That is the very accent of Cyril Beardsall in 'Nethermere' and *The White Peacock*; it was one of Lawrence's 'voices', too, at this stage of his writing life.

It was not, therefore, until Jessie Chambers proposed sending some of his poems to a literary magazine in June 1909 that any of his work was even seen by an editor. Lawrence refused to have anything to do with the proposal. 'Send whatever you like. Do what you like,' he told her.[41] He and the Chambers family had been impressed by a new literary magazine that had started publication late in 1908. The *English Review* published some of the great writers of the day; its first number had included Hardy, Henry James, Conrad, Tolstoy, Galsworthy and H. G. Wells. It was very bold to send Lawrence's work there, although its editor, the writer Ford Madox Hueffer (later Ford), had asked for contributions from new talent. What neither Jessie nor Lawrence could have known was that Hueffer was on the look-out for writing which revealed how 'what we used to call "the other half" – though we might as well have said the other ninety-nine hundredths – lives'. Hueffer wrote back to Jessie at the start of August 1909, asking to see Lawrence in London: 'perhaps something might be done.'[42] He wanted to *see* this provincial talent, not just to evaluate his work; for someone who received 'on average twenty manuscripts a day' to read, he had shown remarkable judgement in singling out Lawrence's work. Jessie gave the letter to Lawrence in triumph just as his family came back from its summer holiday on the Isle of Wight. Lawrence, murmuring '*You* are my luck' to Jessie, took the letter to show his mother, and Jessie never saw it again. Lawrence went to see Hueffer when he returned to Croydon; and Hueffer, 'fairish, fat, about forty, and the kindest man on earth', made it possible for Lawrence to become a published writer.[43]

Hueffer's account of meeting Lawrence is, like many of his memoirs, undoubtedly fictional, but accurate in terms of the exotic kind of person the young writer seemed to him to be: 'I looked up from my deep thoughts and saw Lawrence, leaning, as if panting, beside the doorpost . . . It was not so bad an impression, founded as it was on the peculiar, as if sunshot tawny hair and moustache of the fellow and his deep-set and luminous eyes . . . I had had only the impression of the fox-coloured hair and moustache and the deep, wary, sardonic glance.' Hueffer accepted five poems[44] and asked to see what else

Lawrence was writing. In one way he must have been disappointed that Lawrence was not really the working-class writer he would have liked to publish in the *English Review*. He would, however, be thoroughly convinced by the pieces of fiction set in a miner's household which Lawrence produced soon after their first meeting; it is unlikely to have been a coincidence that this was the moment when Lawrence wrote 'Odour of Chrysanthemums' and *A Collier's Friday Night* – work unlike anything he had previously written. If 'working-class' was what he had to be, then he could be that too. For his part, Hueffer was memorably impressed by the way, in 'Odour of Chrysanthemums', 'this man knows. He knows how to open a story with a sentence of the right cadence for holding the attention. He knows how to construct a paragraph. He knows the life he is writing about in a landscape just sufficiently constructed with a casual word here and there. You can trust him for the rest.'[45]

Lawrence asked two friends to help him produce a fair copy of 'Nethermere' for Hueffer: Agnes Mason played her part in writing out a number of the old pages, and so did another Croydon teacher, Agnes Holt. The 800-page manuscript, for all his objections to its lack of 'form', convinced Hueffer that he could elevate Lawrence to the category of genius. They were on a bus in London when, 'in his queer voice', Hueffer 'shouted in my ear: "It's got every fault that the English novel can have . . . But," shouted Hueffer in the 'bus, "you've got GENIUS."'[46] Hueffer's partner, the novelist Violet Hunt, also remembered the 'first blush – the blowing – of Mr Lawrence's flower of genius'; and to Lawrence's embarrassment – 'I wish Hueffer wouldn't' – it was as 'a genius' that Hueffer introduced him into literary life. The word 'genius' was not just praise, as Lawrence knew very well: it was a way of categorizing him as an untutored 'natural'. As he put it later in life, 'In the early days they were always telling me I had got genius, as if to console me for not having their own incomparable advantages.'[47] By the start of December 1909, still the published author only of those poems in the *English Review*, Lawrence had (through Hueffer) met three of the major writers of his day, H. G. Wells, Ezra Pound and W. B. Yeats, as well as the Everyman editor and writer Ernest Rhys. Hueffer had also advised him to send the 'Nethermere' manuscript to the publisher William Heinemann, and had written a letter recommending it: 'I can very fully admire your very remarkable and poetic gifts. I certainly think you have in you the makings of a very considerable novelist.' By the end of January, as a result, Heinemann had 'practically accepted' the book. A few changes were requested and, as Hueffer had criticized its 'enormous prolixity of detail', some general shortening was also recommended.[48]

Lawrence had, in a miraculously short period of time, changed from being a merely prospective writer to one with poetry, and soon stories, appearing in a prestigious magazine, who moved in literary circles and whose first novel had been accepted. Jessie Chambers saw how a 'kind of transfiguration from obscurity and uncertainty had taken place'. It would nevertheless be wrong to think of this success either as coming easily, although it came suddenly, or as changing Lawrence's life. He would get £50 for the novel, and perhaps more later; but it had taken him almost four years to write, and he had to continue depending on his teacher's salary. 'I wish I were not so handicapped for cash,' he had remarked at the end of June 1909: 'my shirts are patched, my boots are – well, not presentable.'[49] There was no way he could think of abandoning his job on the strength of what had happened.

It is much easier for biography to describe the relationships with people, and in particular the intimate relationships with women which occupied Lawrence in Eastwood and Croydon, than the writing at the centre of his life. For years he had been writing in the odd periods of time he could snatch from his college course, on holidays and in vacations, and during his working week: writing away late at night at the novel, the poetry, the plays and the short stories, with his school work still to do, laid out on the same table. 'I'm supposed to be marking Composition – such a stack of blue exercise books at my elbow,' he remarked in a letter. It took a real effort to be 'very hard at work, slogging verse into form'. A piece of advice he later gave to another writer with a full-time job suggests how he managed. He told her to take an hour every day – 'the same hour – that's very important' – simply 'to write bit by bit of the scenes you have witnessed, the people you know'.[50] He developed the ability, in Croydon, to write quite long works of fiction in just a few weeks, based on the people he knew; a skill that, fortunately, never left him.

For the moment, however, he was just an easily patronized unknown 'genius'. Ernest Rhys described an occasion when, reading his poetry to a gathering of intellectuals in Hampstead in the winter of 1909, Lawrence had no idea when to stop, and Rhys had to rescue him. The story loses nothing in the telling; Lawrence, in spite of his crass insensitivity in Rhys's account, had a self-consciously acute sense of occasion: 'I am exceedingly sensitive to other people, to their wants and their wishes.' But he was, all the same, as much of an outsider in the literary world as he had been in the school world; and people like Rhys, who stressed how 'shy and countrified' Lawrence was (reading with his back to the gathering and making 'an awkward little bow' at the end), ensured that he remained on the outside. For the literary circles of London, Lawrence was a writer who sometimes embarrassingly, sometimes thrillingly, emerged from obscurity, and then vanished again: Rhys thought him 'a young country schoolmaster somewhere in the Black Country'.[51] And Lawrence felt an ironical ambivalence towards the literary people he was being introduced to. Years later, he would still be reducing people to helpless laughter with his imitations of literary London. Ezra Pound, for example: 'there stood a young, callow, swash-buckling Ezra, with an earring in one ear.' And he was still mimicking Florence Farr reciting Yeats to the psaltery in 1927.[52]

It was Hueffer who gave Lawrence the opportunity to try to change his life, though Lawrence always acknowledged that it had been Jessie Chambers who really launched his career – 'like a princess cutting a thread, launching a ship'.[53] In the flush of confidence Hueffer's encouragement had inspired, Lawrence seems to have acquired his first Croydon girlfriend: Agnes Holt, the copyist of the first seventy-six pages of 'Nethermere'. Lawrence first told Blanche Jennings about her on 1 November 1909: 'I have got a new girl down here . . . I do *not* believe in love: mon Dieu, I don't not for me . . . I can't help it: the game begins, and I play it, and the girl plays it, and – what matter what the end is!'[54] So speaks a rather innocent young Lothario. As well as copying the novel's opening, Agnes Holt had also copied into Lawrence's poetry notebook the five poems which had appeared in the November issue of *English Review*. She was 'an erect, intelligent girl' with 'grey eyes and auburn hair', 'alert, prompt, smart with her tongue, and independent in her manner';[55] but very little about her is known, except that by the end of December 1910 her relationship with

Lawrence was in effect over. In November, Jessie had thought of it as an 'engagement',[56] probably her euphemism for some form of sexual relationship. But either it had not been sexual or, from Lawrence's point of view, it had not been sexual enough. He complained, in prose so impeccably mannered that it is hard to know exactly what *had* happened, that Agnes Holt was 'so utterly ignorant and old fashioned, really, though she has been to college and has taught in London some years. A man is . . . a more or less interesting creature, with whom one could play about with smart and silly speech – no more – not an animal – mon dieu, no! – I have enlightened her, and now she has no courage.'[57] 'I have enlightened her' sounds superior, but may mean no more than that he had made some kind of a pass at her.

He had started to move in the world of the 'advanced' (Hueffer was living with Violet Hunt), but the contrast between the Hampstead or Holland Park intellectual and the necessarily respectable schoolteacher could hardly have been more marked. Any kind of sexual contact between a female schoolteacher and a man, if it had become known, would at this date have led to her instant dismissal and the loss of her career; while a male teacher would have been hauled up before a board of governors, or the local education authority, and probably have been dismissed.[58] It was one thing to *write* about sex; quite another to risk reputation, career and income in the real world.

However, in the summer of 1909 Lawrence had written a poem in which he had fantasized about seeing a woman in the street 'who shall set me free / From the stunting bonds of my chastity'. Assuming he meant himself, sexual experience, at the age of twenty-four, was passing him by; how could he write about 'corporeality'[59] without experience? He felt disabled by this massive gap in his life: not only was he not grown up yet, but thwarted and diminished. What happened to him between 1909 and 1911 was like a long-delayed adolescence, in many ways, but happening to a man in his middle twenties, when intellectually he was far more mature than an adolescent would have been. Agnes Holt was nevertheless determined not to be the woman to set him free, however much Lawrence was attracted to her; and Lawrence was irritated by what he saw as her middle-classness. He did not, for example, forget the way she 'pursed up her mouth, and ended in a little trill of deprecatory laughter' when pretending to be amused, and included the detail in the novel he was revising.[60] It is when he tries to define the difference between them that he is most revealing: 'She still judges by mid-Victorian standards, and covers herself with a woolly fluff of romance that the years will wear sickly ... She believes men worship their mistresses; she is all sham and superficial in her outlook, and I can't change her.'[61] He implies (he is writing to Blanche Jennings) that he *had* done his best to change her; but the fact that she would get married in August 1911 suggests that he probably stood no chance in any case. But Agnes Holt did bring into the open the conflict he suffered in his attempt to believe in himself as an 'animal' – which might mean anything from 'Bohemian' or uncontrollably irritable[62] to sexually voracious – while remaining an aspiringly middle-class, intellectually detached writer of elegant prose and verse, of which Agnes copied out so much for him. Both were a kind of pose; and he had begun to realize it, without being able to do much about it.

6

Love and Death: 1910

What immediately followed Lawrence's relationship with Agnes Holt, and may well have been provoked by it, was his attempt to start a sexual relationship with Jessie Chambers, after a sexless friendship of eight years. This was extraordinary, given what Jessie felt, and everything that had happened between them since 1902. But late in November 1909, she had travelled down early on the Saturday morning to London from the Haggs, and had spent the day with Lawrence, going to galleries and then to a play. There were other sights, too: 'he took me to Waterloo Bridge and made me look at the human wreckage preparing to spend the night on the Embankment.' What shocked and fascinated Lawrence was how human beings could so lose all pride in themselves: it was the fate of George in 'Nethermere'.[1]

When they finally reached Colworth Road late that evening, Lawrence cooked some macaroni for their supper, gave her some new poems and his new play – *A Collier's Friday Night* – to read, then insisted on staying up until 2 a.m. to talk. When he asked her about her future, she cried and cried, 'because in my heart was no hope at all, but only fortitude'. Lawrence enquired whether she thought sex outside marriage was 'wrong', and she answered that, to her, it wasn't '*wrong*' but that it would be 'very difficult'. She remembered him saying: 'I think I shall ask some girl if she will give me . . . that . . . without marriage. Do you think any girl would?' Jessie astutely predicted that he'd probably not like the kind of girl who would. After finally getting to bed, she thought she heard a knock at her door, but nothing more.[2] The next day, she met Hueffer and Violet Hunt, before going back to the Midlands.

But when he came home for Christmas almost exactly a month

later, Lawrence did not so much ask Jessie if she would sleep with him as tell her that, because he loved her, it was inevitably going to happen.

When I went with him over the fields he told me he had found out – he had really loved me all along and not realised it . . . He said that all our long association was in reality a preparation for this 'une intimité d'amour'. It came as a shock to me, very disturbing, yet at the same time inevitable . . .[3]

All her life she had strenuously resisted the bullying and insistence of men like her father and her brothers, and had taken the burden of her mother's unhappiness on herself – Ann Chambers hated sex. Jessie now confronted a demand that she did not want to refuse: but even with Lawrence, 'it would be very difficult'.[4] Not only had she been fiercely independent, she was also determinedly moral. Her brother David described how her world was 'bounded by the criteria of right and wrong, of good and bad . . . she did what was right and expected to receive what was due to her for her universal rightness'.[5] Of all the women Lawrence knew, Jessie was perhaps the least likely to engage in a sexual relationship outside marriage: not because she was conventional, but because her code of behaviour was so strict and unflinching, and because sex was clearly problematic to her.

Lawrence knew that neither he nor Jessie had the income or savings that would allow them to marry, and he resisted the idea of marriage, anyway: he had told her in November that 'I shan't be able to marry for ever so long.'[6] Jessie's solution to the dilemma he thrust her into, when he announced their 'intimité d'amour', was to tell herself that the new relationship was none the less 'binding and sacred'. From her point of view, it was an 'engagement': they were going to spend their lives together.[7] Their 'engagement' thus constituted a radically new start to a relationship that, for all its rewards, had felt 'utterly hopeless' as recently as October 1908. Lawrence had found a way around his pronouncement: 'But it can't be helped, it can't be helped.'

Nevertheless, the 'engagement' did nothing to help her 'very disturbing' feelings about Lawrence's sexual demands, which not only ran clean against everything she had believed for years, but directly against what Lawrence had said to her. She would have remembered his earlier pronouncement: 'You are absolutely lacking in sexual attraction.'[8] Lawrence seems, however, to have been prepared to ignore his (and her) feelings for the sake of what he now desperately wanted. He was in a volatile, aroused state, drawn to woman after woman. The arrogant intellectual independence he had demonstrated to Blanche Jennings was only a pose; being a roué was also a pose. He desperately wanted sex. 'Une intimité d'amour' is revealing: it was an *experience of love* he wanted, not a relationship. His later writing demonstrates what a guilty and self-hating masturbator he had been: 'I know, when I was a lad of eighteen, I used to remember with shame and rage in the morning the sexual thoughts and desires I had had the night before.' And he recalled how 'the thing will keep coming on you at night . . . I've been through it all myself'. Masturbation had brought him a 'secret feeling of futility and humiliation': such chastity would have felt especially imprisoning.[9]

Lawrence wrote his story 'A Modern Lover' very soon after he made his demand on Jessie,[10] and with what reads like some genuine emotional recollection. It shows the sensitive, artistic but also insentient Cyril Mersham asking his old friend Muriel to sleep with him. Mersham says, 'if you're willing – you'll come to me, won't you? – just naturally; as you used to come and go to church with me? – and it won't be – it won't be me coaxing you – reluctant – will it?' The syntax reveals how desperately he is urging her. Muriel says to him, her face muffled in his shoulder, 'But – but you know – it's much harder for the woman – it means something so different for a woman.' What Mersham hears, however, is 'the woman defensive, playing the coward against her own inclinations': the story reveals his inability either to sympathize or to understand. He is helpless when confronted by Muriel's feelings: all he thinks she lacks is some knowledge of contraception. 'I have given you books –' he says, angrily.[11]

Even George Neville – hardly a puritan: he had fathered an illegitimate child around 1905 – thought the situation intolerable. Accidentally discovering that Lawrence was equipped with condoms, Neville commented: 'Instead of getting away and buying yourself a woman, my guess is that you're trading on somebody's regard for you.'[12] To Neville, 'buying a woman' was moral by comparison. 'A Modern Lover' shows that, at some level, Lawrence knew he was taking advantage of Jessie, but he completely forgot about 'A Modern Lover' after writing it: he would not have wanted to remember its kind of understanding.[13]

For the first weeks of his new relationship with Jessie, and before they had sex together,* their new loving warmth for each other seemed wonderful: the prose Lawrence wrote about it enacted an escape from the 'vicious circle of the self' in an experience of the other.[14] Thinking back to New Year, he would recall how Jessie

lifts up her face to me and clings to me, and the time goes like a falling star, swallowed up immediately; it is wonderful, that time, long avenues of minutes – hours – should be swept up with one sweep of the hand, and the moment for parting has arrived when the first kiss seems hardly overkissed . . . The world is for us, and we are for each other – even if only for one spring – so what does it matter![15]

The note of *carpe diem* is, however, unusual in Lawrence's writing; and Jessie, given the binding commitment she understood the new relationship to mean, would have felt betrayed by the phrase 'even if only for one spring'. Such writing so easily slips, too, into being a literary exercise: not so much a description of passion as an experiment in how passion might be written about. Lawrence's later analyses of deliberately intended and unfelt passion, in fictional characters whom he thoroughly disliked, had their origins deep within his own experience. And in some ways, nothing had changed. Jessie still felt to him like someone demanding 'to drink me up and have me';[16] her emotional needs still made him want to get away.

Running directly parallel with, and counter to, this vulnerable new relationship was Lawrence's attraction to another woman. On 28 January 1910, the very day he described kissing Jessie, he referred

---

* 'To have sexual intercourse' is long-winded and legalistic; 'to copulate' is clinical and disapproving; 'to make love' in a fully sexual sense is a relatively recent euphemism (*c.* 1950); 'to go to bed with' and 'to sleep with' are euphemisms inappropriate for many situations, including sex outdoors, and are also fairly recent (*c.* 1945). 'To fuck' is in many ways preferable to the euphemisms, and is the word Mellors uses in *Lady Chatterley's Lover*. Unfortunately, it draws self-conscious attention to itself. Lawrence is cited in *OED*2 as by far the earliest person – in 1929 – to use 'to have sex' in print ('Sex and Trust', *Poems* 466, perhaps as an abbreviation of Olive Schreiner's 'to have sex relations' from 1911). As the phrase has at least the merit of directness, I have (rather reluctantly) used it at times.

to Helen Corke as 'a new girl – a girl who "*interests*" me – nothing else'.[17] If Agnes Holt had helped provoke his desire for Jessie, so his feelings for Jessie seem to have unleashed this sudden attraction to the 27-year-old Croydon schoolteacher (see Illustration 9): small but solid rather than slight, and very fair-skinned, with light brown hair. He had got to know her through Agnes Mason, who had been at the same school as Helen before moving to Davidson Road. Helen had first seen Lawrence in the winter of 1908–9, at the Masons' house; he had been 'seated on the drawing-room floor, in the centre of a card ring, telling fortunes and chattering clever nonsense in three or four languages'. She was unfavourably struck by the company he chose to keep and by 'his chatter'.[18]

She read widely and was very interested in music, attending the opera in London and playing the violin. But by the spring of 1909, she was a deeply troubled person, preoccupied by her 39-year-old music-teacher, Herbert Baldwin Macartney. He was a married, professional violinist who lived in nearby Purley, and had been in love with her for years. He had made some kind of passionate advance to Helen in February 1909, but she had recoiled in disgust – 'it hurts me to see him lose his self control' – and, as a result, 'we were unhappy'.[19] Nevertheless, unable to stay away from each other, they continued to meet for Helen's weekly lesson, and remained in love with each other in quite different ways. In spite of his wife's suspicions, Macartney managed to get Helen to spend five days with him secretly on the Isle of Wight in August 1909. By chance, it was the same brilliantly hot and sunny week when Lawrence and his family were also on the Isle of Wight, but the two parties were at opposite ends of the island (the Lawrences in Shanklin, Macartney and Helen in Freshwater) and they never met. During the five days, however, Macartney at last had sex with Helen, and also felt profoundly rejected by her; after extracting herself from 'the passionate grip of his arms', she would think of him as 'beaten at last'.[20] They returned to London on Thursday 5 August: on the morning of Saturday 7th, with Helen down in Cornwall on a 'respectable' holiday with two women friends (one of them Agnes Mason), Macartney hanged himself from the back of his bedroom door. Helen, desperate at hearing nothing from him, returned to London to find the news in the local paper: '"It was like a brick" . . .

that brutal simile was the only one she could find, months afterwards, to describe her condition.' She was nursed through her shock and loss by her parents and Agnes Mason, but remained distressed for months, not to say years. It was crucial for her career as a schoolteacher that no word of her role should leak out. She thought she might be pregnant, but there was no child.[21]

In the autumn of 1909, Lawrence learned something of what had happened from Agnes Mason, and played his part in keeping Helen's depression at bay during the winter of 1909–10. They went to concerts together, exchanged books – Nietzsche, for example – and he taught her some German. He showed her his writing and also encouraged her to write. At some stage, she confided her story in him; this may have been what he was hearing from the 'girl who "*interests*" me' in January 1910. In turn, she helped him with the later stages of getting 'Nethermere', shortly to be re-christened *The White Peacock*, ready for Heinemann; she corrected its grammar and checked its spelling. Eventually, late in February or early in March 1910, as a sign of her special trust in him, she lent him the writing she had done about the Isle of Wight: either the 'Freshwater Diary' she had written during the autumn, or the long 'Letter' to Macartney which she had started after his suicide and which she was still writing in 1910. In both these she called Macartney 'Siegmund': to him she had been 'Sieglinde' (siblings and lovers in Wagner's *Die Walküre*, which they knew intimately and for which Macartney had played professionally).

It was at just the same time that Lawrence's new relationship with Jessie Chambers was taking its course. Jessie and he had managed a secret weekend in London together at the end of March, but Jessie now thought it 'not honourable' to accept the Jones family's hospitality: they probably went to a hotel. Lawrence wrote to her the following week: 'You have done me great good, my dear. Only I want you here with me. It is as if I cannot rest without you near me, you goodly thing, good to be near, to touch and to hold . . .'[22] It seems probable, however, that they were still not having sex. An indication of the problems underlying their relationship had been revealed when Lawrence's old Eastwood friend Alice Dax had come to stay in London earlier in the month, and Lawrence had found himself on the very verge of being seduced by her. Alice was married to an Eastwood chemist and already

77

had one child; she was a socialist and suffragist, had read 'Nethermere' back in 1908, and she and Lawrence had had a sparring, flirtatious kind of relationship for a couple of years. He now told Jessie how 'I was very nearly unfaithful to you. I can never promise you to be faithful. In the morning she came into my room, you know my morning sadness.'[23] A great deal more would happen with Alice Dax the following year, but Jessie must have been left uneasy. During the Easter holidays at the start of April 1910, at home in Eastwood, he spent a lot of time on the final revision of *The White Peacock*, and only 'walked out' with Jessie and talked; both were being carefully watched by their respective families. She recalled how happy they were during this holiday, probably because they felt warm and tender to each other, but were still not sleeping together. Lawrence returned to Croydon in mid April but 'Almost immediately' wrote to Jessie, 'apparently very much disturbed, saying that he found he had to write the story of Siegmund . . . It was in front of him and he had got to do it.'[24] It was just a week after he had submitted *The White Peacock* manuscript to Heinemann. In one sense, he was simply eager to start on a new novel, for a fascinating subject had forced itself on his attention. However, he had already written the name 'Siegmund' in error for 'Leslie' three times during his final revision of *The White Peacock*.[25] He had not only been deeply impressed by Helen's experiences but for weeks had been imagining writing about them.

The new novel's first draft ('The Saga of Siegmund') would be a way of helping Helen come to terms with her tragedy and of addressing her grief that Siegmund's musical art had died with him: she wanted 'voice for his silence'.[26] But it would also mean Lawrence getting very much closer to her. She was that exceptional thing in the respectable professional classes, a single woman with a sexual history; and Lawrence was recreating her relationship with a man with whom (it turned out) he identified profoundly. Macartney had been a sensitive, artistic and passionate man who had made an unfortunate marriage, was beset by money problems, and had fallen in love with a young woman only to find that she hated the 'sex impulse' in him – she called it 'the beast' – although she had submitted to his sexual demands during those five days together.[27]

It was at Whitsun (14–21 May), just when Lawrence was writing the new novel exploring the contradictions of Helen's affair, that he and Jessie engaged in their own brief sexual relationship. He had gone back to the Midlands for the holiday in excited anticipation and in dread, telling Helen: 'Muriel will take me. She will do me great, infinite good – for a time. But what is awake in me shivers with terror at the issue.' In fact, it worked out badly from the start. 'The times of our actual coming together,' in the heart-rending words of Jessie's private memoir, 'under conditions both difficult and irksome . . . would not exhaust the fingers of one hand.'[28] They borrowed May Holbrook's house in Moorgreen on one occasion, but otherwise adopted the age-old strategy of sex outdoors among the marsh marigolds, cowslips and dead leaves. It was an awful experience for them both. Lawrence imagined, with horror, how it felt 'like death' to Jessie, and felt ashamed at forcing himself on someone so repelled: for her, he sensed, the male body was only 'a clogged, numb burden of flesh'. For her part, Jessie never forgot how 'Lawrence implored me not to attempt to hold him': a terrible limitation on love. The fact that, five weeks after Whitsun, his love affairs going 'criss-crossy', Lawrence feared that he would 'have to return in September to home', may well indicate that Jessie thought she was pregnant and that they would have to marry.[29] Fortunately, she wasn't. For Jessie, too, any publicity about the affair would have meant the end of her career as a teacher.

It seems at least possible that that they never had sex together again; but Lawrence's writing of 'The Saga of Siegmund' between April and August 1910 must have done their chances a lot of damage. The novel was a real achievement for a man in an exhausting full-time job – the first of those outpourings of writing in which Lawrence regularly wrote the first drafts of his subsequent novels. He had promised Helen not to publish it without her permission, but his understanding of its central characters (Helena and Siegmund) criss-crossed his relationship with Jessie in a way that probably made 'The Saga' as much about himself and Jessie as about Helen and Macartney. Siegmund's feelings of rejection by Helena certainly relate to Lawrence's sense of Jessie's sexual horror; and the ending of the novel coincided with the end of Lawrence's affair with Jessie. In the novel, after all, Lawrence had been creating a man who knows that his partner 'rejects me as if I were a baboon, under my clothing' after allowing him to have sex with her.[30] The novelist found Siegmund profoundly sympathetic. He wrote to Helen, 'You don't know how inimical I feel against you'; 'I feel often inclined, when I think of you, to put my thumbs on your throat.' He may have felt similarly about Jessie, telling her: 'I have always believed it was the woman who paid the price in life. But I've made a discovery. It's the man who pays, not the woman.'[31] On 1 August, having arranged to go over and spend some days with the Chambers family at their new farm at Arno Vale, he met Jessie and, having given her no inkling of what was in his mind, 'broke off our engagement completely'.[32]

He may have been waiting to make sure she was *not* pregnant before breaking off. But the novel seems to have helped bring him into a state in which being honest about his feelings mattered more than the devastation of Jessie's hopes. The day before he saw her, he had written to Helen Corke, feeling 'as miserable as the devil'. When Jessie kissed him, it 'makes my heart feel like ashes. But then she kisses me more and moves my sex fire. Mein Gott, it is hideous . . . we ought finally and definitely to part: if I have the heart to tell her.'[33] What was 'hideous' was the discrepancy between Jessie's devoted love ('she demands the soul of me'), his awareness of his own lack of any such devotion to her, and the fact that in spite of everything she went on arousing him sexually. He knew that he was being desperately cruel to her – 'can I hurt her so much' – but her demand for intimacy was something he could no longer cope with. He described it as feeling her 'plunge her hands through my blood and feel for my soul': an astonishing image of physical and psychical encroachment. He preferred to 'set my teeth and shiver and fight away'.[34]

However attracted he was to Helen in the summer of 1910, he was not leaving Jessie for her. Helen simply did not want him as a partner; and he had, after all, worked through the horrors of her relationship with a man who had killed himself after spending five days with her. Helen disliked sexuality profoundly; she believed the husband of her cousin Evelyn was 'guilty of a kind of manslaughter' because Evelyn had died in childbirth,[35] and her revulsion had been reinforced by what had happened with Macartney. Lawrence was none the less staggered – 'you take the wind out of my sails' – a fortnight after his break with Jessie, to find that Helen had invited Jessie down to Croydon and to

Newhaven, to share her summer holiday.[36] They had first met in July; Helen recalled how gentle Jessie was with Lawrence, how irritable Lawrence was with Jessie, and how uncertain he was about marrying her.[37] The two women had a lot in common, they found. Both of them feared and disliked sex with the men they loved, and had recently lost them, partly in consequence. Both were attracted to Lawrence and believed in his exceptional abilities; but they were also repelled by his sexual demands. Both had become barely disguised heroines in his fiction, both would come to feel exploited by the way he had used them in his work, and both eventually wrote alternative versions of the fictional accounts he produced.[38] They saw a good deal of each other over the next few years. When Jessie went to see Lawrence in Croydon at the end of 1911, it was with Helen that she stayed, and after Lawrence had gone to Germany with Frieda Weekley in May 1912, Jessie and Helen went on a boat journey up the Rhine together that summer. And because they preserved their letters from Lawrence, or at least the memory of what the letters contained, and in the 1930s both wrote books about him, to some extent they were responsible for writing his public epitaph. To them, he was someone remarkable but emotionally dominated by his mother – and a ruthless exploiter.

Did he exploit them? Jessie, certainly. Yet although Alice Dax threw herself at him in March 1910, he did not have sex with her; and even after Jessie had agreed to their affair, they did not have sex for months. Her dislike of it was not something he ignored: it made him want to end their relationship. He made no sexual advances to Helen Corke throughout the writing of 'The Saga' in 1910; on one occasion, he 'clasps me longer than is necessary, and when we move, holds my hand fast, protectively and possessively' – but no more.[39]

What Lawrence was doing, however, can never really be separated from what he was writing. Having decided to make the revised 'Nethermere' of 1909–10 a more realistic text, he found himself committed to describing how Lettie's marriage to Leslie fails, and how George surrenders to despair after failing to marry Lettie; he felt impelled to write about sexual relationships that came to such ends. His compulsion to have sex with women in the autumn of 1909 and the spring of 1910 was not just because he was going through a kind of delayed adolescence, but because his writing was forcing upon him the major subject of his entire writing career: the way in which relationship, in particular sexual need, redresses the lonely, detached individuality of the participant, while also endangering that individuality. The individual is threatened by the very thing that he or she craves, and is likely to veer between a desire to lose him or herself in passion and a desperate longing for detachment. Lawrence had suspected it in the relationship of his parents; he had found it terribly true of himself. What he did was feel, which in his case meant write, his way into the problem. The writing enacted the problem, and offered some understanding of it. He would in some ways have preferred to have shown how the experience of being *in the body* is the most significant of all, and to have been an untroubled propagandist for such a state. In that way, he would happily have been subverting what he felt were the middle-class proprieties of the novel, just as the gamekeeper Annable in *The White Peacock* subverts the politer discourses of the text. But to do so would also have denied a great deal of what he knew to be true of himself and of his family.

This realization seems to have struck him while he was working on 'Nethermere', and perhaps explains why he needed to go straight from the revision of that novel into the creation, at breakneck speed, of 'The Saga'. He had suddenly found his subject as a writer: a taboo subject, in so far as it meant constant writing about sexual desire. But he saw, in the story which Helen had told him, the opportunity for a quite different exploration of catastrophe from the one she had offered, and one which clarified the confusions of the novel he had just so painfully finished. The new novel would not show physical desire to be pitifully unimportant compared with the meeting of minds, which was how Helen Corke's own account had presented her relationship with Macartney. Lawrence's book would insist on our experience of the body as the most important fact about us, and on intellectual detachment as our greatest danger. Siegmund would no longer be Helena's clumsy, earth-bound, self-divided seducer, but would become a tragic hero of the body's fulfilment; and where Lettie in *The White Peacock* had been a spirited but well-meaning woman who makes the wrong choice of husband, Helena would become a frightening, detached, bodiless, dreaming woman – an anti-heroine, knowing nothing outside her immediate needs. On the other hand, Siegmund's bodily heroism would also be his undoing. Where George commits a kind of slow suicide, as he drinks himself to death, Siegmund would end up deliberately destroying the very body which had brought him passionate fulfilment but which Helena rejected. Helena would survive, meanwhile, wistful but unchanged, unable to learn from her experience, condemned to go on playing 'the same old delicate game',[40] as Lawrence put it in a poem about Helen Corke.

The writer and the man wanted to discover new, post-religious ways of describing fulfilment: a state of self (or being) in which detached consciousness and body were not fatally divided but somehow brought together. From 1912 onwards, Lawrence appears consciously and unconsciously to have explored how he might be able to make *fulfilment*, rather than tragic failure, his subject as a writer. In 1910, he would have realized in the process of writing that the horribly exploitative relationship he had developed with Jessie Chambers simply had to end. He would have known that from the poems he was starting to write about it, even if not from the experience itself.

> I am ashamed, you wanted me not tonight –
> Nay, it is always so, you sigh with me.
> Your radiance dims when I draw too near, and my free
> Fire enters your petals like death, you wilt dead white.[41]

Lawrence made mistake after mistake in these years and was, in particular, desperately unfair to Jessie Chambers; but it is equally clear that his writing, while liberating him from the tensions of his origins, was also a way of imagining (or dreaming) through his most disturbing experiences and so beginning to resolve them. He remarked in January 1912 how 'my dreams make conclusions for me. They decide things finally. I dream a decision. Sleep seems to hammer out for me the logical conclusions of my vague days, and offer me them as dreams.'[42] That was what his writing did, too. In the summer of 1910, he was still unable to resolve the real problems of his 'vague days': all he could do was imagine them clearer, in his writing.

At all events, he had little enough time to regret what he had done to Jessie, though it was certainly right that such a relationship should have been brought to an end. We may hope that Jessie was as savage at its ending as Miriam is with Paul in *Sons and Lovers*: 'I have said you were only fourteen – you are only *four*! . . . Always, it has always been so! . . . It has been one long battle between us – you fighting away from me . . . It has always been you fighting me off . . . Always – from the very beginning – always the same.' Paul is deeply hurt that Miriam should say such things, and should nullify what to him have been their 'eight years of friendship and love, *the* eight years of his life'.[43] Lawrence and Jessie agreed not to see each other, not to correspond. For Jessie, it was by far the worst of all their partings. Four months later, she was writing to Helen: 'I think I must not talk about him at all . . . If an artery were cut, you would tie up the end of it, wouldn't you!'[44]

Within a fortnight of her son's break with Jessie, Lydia Lawrence fell seriously ill with cancer. It was characteristic of Lawrence that, a couple of years later, he would interpret her illness as her recognition that her love for him had been malign,[45] but it was all the same an amazing coincidence. She had been visiting her sister Ada in Leicester, there being no Lawrence family holiday this year; Arthur Lawrence was moving towards retirement, was no longer a butty, and money was probably tight. Lawrence had gone to Blackpool – 'a crowded, vulgar Lancashire seaside resort . . . I shall enjoy it' – for a week with his 'Don Juanish' friend George Neville, and had been flirting happily with a Yorkshire girl, as well as keeping the hotel 'uproarious with laughter'[46] – once again the exhilarating, high-spirited companion the Chambers family had so often seen. His break from Jessie must have been one immediate cause of his relief. However, when he got back to Leicester around 14 August, to accompany his mother home, he found that she was confined to bed. A tumour had been discovered in her abdomen; for the moment she could not be moved. Lawrence's school term in Croydon started on 29 August and he had to go back, but he travelled up to the Midlands at weekends as often as he could.

The mainstay of his contact with Leicester became his college friend Louie Burrows, 'who has always been warm for me – like a sunny happy day',[47] and who (at Ratcliffe-on-the-Wreake) lived near enough to get over to Leicester regularly to visit Lydia and to pass on news of her condition. In 1910, Lawrence described Louie as 'an old girl friend of mine, with whom I've always kept up a connection'. Willie Hopkin remembered her as 'a big strapping girl'; to Lawrence she was 'big and dark and handsome'.[48] Illustration 10 shows her as she looked around 1909. She now became very valuable to Lawrence. What his mother wrote couldn't be trusted; Lawrence knew that she 'would never let me know how bad she was'. He was correcting the proofs of The White Peacock – Helen Corke remembered his face 'set with pain' as he did so – and he sent his spare set up to the Midlands for his mother to see, so that she could share in his achievement. It was, however, Louie who actually read them; and it was Louie who turned out to be able, for moments at least, to save him from being 'as miserable as the devil'.[49]

Somehow he managed to keep up his writing. It offered him a world to escape into; as he would put it in 1912, the artist 'lets go and loses himself'. 'The Saga' had proved a disappointment; Hueffer had dismissed it as a 'rotten work'; the fact that he added 'of genius' hardly helped.[50] Lawrence had accordingly started planning his next novel; and his mother's illness, combined with his acute sense of what kind of a life she had had, probably inspired him first to plan and then to start writing a novel which would include both her girlhood and her marriage, moving on to his own upbringing.[51] It was also a sign of his determination to come to terms with the world of his upbringing that, in this book, however far he moved away from the facts of his life, he would write an account not only of a child growing up in the industrial working class but of a family riddled with conflict. In mid October, he was able to inform Heinemann that the new book ('Paul Morel') was 'plotted out very interestingly' and that about one-eighth was written.[52] It would have been natural for his mother, spending hours with him, to talk about her life; a letter he wrote to a Scottish poet, Rachel Annand Taylor, early in December even provides a glimpse of the kind of thing Lydia may have been saying, and the kind of novel he might as a result have been writing: 'My mother was a clever, ironical delicately moulded woman, of good, old burgher descent. She married below her. My father was dark, ruddy, with a fine laugh. He is a coal miner. He was one of the sanguine temperament, warm and hearty, but unstable: he lacked principle, as my mother would have said. He deceived her and lied to her. She despised him – he drank.'[53] This is obviously told from Lydia's point of view. Telling and retelling the story of the marriage, and showing how he was its product, was something which Lydia's final illness compelled Lawrence to do: 'Paul Morel,' he knew, 'belongs to this.'[54]

Lydia was moved back home to Eastwood, probably late in September, 'horribly ill'. Louie continued to come over to visit, and early in October, when she and Lawrence 'walked home by the canal & then to his train at Ilkeston', she felt sure that the 'first knowledge of our love came on that evening – but it was unexpressed though both knew.' She was falling in love with him: much later she would write how 'Love took away all selfishness & I had no life apart from him.'[55] Lawrence's feelings for her at this point are unknown; but he continued to come home at weekends to see his mother, and to see Louie too. In the last week of November, he got permission from the Croydon authorities to return home for what he believed would be a very brief time with his mother, to share the nursing and the all-night vigils with his sister Ada. Any time to himself he now had, back in the Midlands, he seems to have used in seeing Louie; otherwise he would simply 'sit upstairs hours and hours, till I wonder if ever it were true that I was at London'.[56] The Eastwood miners went back to work on 25 November after a five-month strike; in *Sons and Lovers* the dying Mrs Morel astonishes the servant Minnie by suddenly asking: 'Have the men been saying their hands are sore . . . But at any rate there'll be something to buy in with this week.' That kind of active awareness of what was happening around her was characteristic of Lydia Lawrence; she was still capable of delighting in the flowers that Louie sent her at the end of November.[57] Lawrence wrote, painted, talked with his mother and helped care for her; by early in December, she was too weak to move herself and had to be lifted and turned over in bed.

On 2 December, an advance copy of *The White Peacock* came; Lawrence inscribed it 'To my Mother, with love, D. H. Lawrence.' She, however, took no particular notice of the book when it was given to her, simply asking about the inscription: 'What does it say?' Lawrence believed 'I've nothing to offer her' and insisted that she didn't approve of the book: 'She didn't like it. Even disliked it.'[58] She certainly paid little attention to it; but she loved him so much that she did not want him to waste his time believing in himself as a writer.

On the evening of the following day, Saturday 3 December, while once again seeing Louie home, Lawrence suddenly asked her to marry him: and after a moment's hesitation she agreed. Lawrence told Arthur McLeod about it: 'What made me do it, I cannot tell. Twas an inspiration. But I can't tell mother.' The vivid contrast between Louie – 'swarthy and ruddy as a pomegranate, and bright and vital as a pitcher of wine' – and his mother ('her face has fallen like a mask of bitter cruel suffering') tells its own story.[59] Louie suddenly seemed to promise relationship without suffering and angst, to save Lawrence from all the desperation and bitterness of his childhood and adult cares, from the complexities and conflicted loyalties which living at home had reawakened in him. It was not a substitute mother he wanted, but 'Somebody to rest with – you perhaps don't know what a deep longing that may be.' Louie offered affection that was warm, vital, outgoing and, above all, straightforward and untroubled; she was a girl Lydia Lawrence approved of, 'good, awfully good, churchy', a good deal more conventional than Jessie, and far less demanding.[60] Yet although she liked Louie, Lydia Lawrence could not be told about the engagement. As Lawrence explained to Louie the following week, 'my mother has been passionately fond of me, and fiercely jealous'; he could not now allow her to feel that Louie was replacing her in his affections. May Chambers, when told that his mother had not approved of his book, asked him: '"What *did* she want?" "Me," he said softly. "Just me." '[61]

The days dragged past, through the first week of December; Lydia's cancer tormented her and those watching over her. On the night of Saturday 3 December, on returning home after proposing to Louie, Lawrence recorded what his mother was saying: ' "Not pain now – Oh the weariness" she moaned, so that I could hardly hear her. I wish she could die tonight.' He felt sure that she was 'very near the end'.[62] On the Monday, however, 'still she is here, and it is the old slow horror'. On the Tuesday, 'she is still here . . . so grievous, pitiful this morning, still and grey and deathly'. He may even, as he later made Paul Morel in *Sons and Lovers* do, have added water to the milk he gives his dying mother 'so that it should not nourish her. Yet he loved her more than his own life.'[63] Lydia Lawrence's dreadful dying made Lawrence articulate about his feelings for her as he had never been before. He wrote to Louie: 'She is my first, great love. She was a wonderful, rare woman . . . as strong, and steadfast, and generous as the sun. She could be as swift as a white whip-lash, and as kind and gentle as warm rain, and as steadfast as the irreducible earth beneath us.'[64] But now all he wanted was for her to die. Finally, on the Thursday night, he and his sister Ada conspired to give her an overdose, in her nightly milk, of the morphia that the doctor had left.[65] Even then she lived on until the Friday morning.

'I think this is finally the bitter river crossed,' Lawrence wrote to Louie, entirely exhausted. 'It certainly feels like one of the kingdoms of death, where I am. It is true, I have died, a bit of me.'[66] He registered her death that Friday afternoon and made the funeral arrangements; they buried her in the Eastwood cemetery on the following Monday, down beside her son Ernest, in pouring rain and a storm of wind: 'and there is gone my love of loves'. On Tuesday 13th, he went back to school in Croydon, after taking to the Eastwood cemetery a wreath from Louie. 'I wore one or two of the violets, and I kept catching their scent all the way down to London, in the warm carriage,' he told her.[67]

The night his mother died, he had started to sketch a painting of which he eventually made four copies: the *Idyll* (1891) by Maurice Greiffenhagen.[68] He had known it for a couple of years, but copying it when he did shows its connection with his feelings about his mother. An Arcadian shepherd embraces a shy woman; the ground is strewn with white, blue and red flowers, the sun sets redly. The contours of the woman's body and the heap of her breasts crushed together by the pressure of the man's body made it a little shocking, in its period. Lawrence had never copied or painted anything like it before (he had copied only landscapes and still-lifes), nor had he made multiple copies of any of his paintings. He gave a copy of the *Idyll* to Agnes Holt as a wedding present, another copy to his sister Ada, a third to Louie Burrows and a fourth to McLeod.

In one way, it is a portrait of the uninhibited 'animal' man he was now, after his mother's death, promising himself he could be, even if, in Agnes and Louie, he felt confronted by just the kind of woman he wanted not to experience again: 'passive . . . a wee bit frit [alarmed]'.[69] It was, however, an intensely artificial, romantic, even literary painting: and the sensual and uninhibited were conscious experiments for Lawrence. On the other hand, given that his 'father was dark, ruddy, with a fine laugh ... one of the sanguine temperament, warm and hearty', it is natural to identify him, too, with the man in the painting, whom Lawrence depicted as even more of a contrast with the woman than the figure in the reproduction from which he was working. In October, Lawrence had insisted that he had 'never had but one parent': the copying suggests differently. It would follow that Lydia Lawrence – 'clever, ironical delicately moulded'[70] – might be seen in the carefully moulded, over-civilized woman of the painting. Whereas Greiffen-hagen's woman modestly lowers her eyes, in Lawrence's copies she stares out at the onlooker, discomforted. For all Lawrence's grief at his mother's death, and anger with his father, Lydia was also a woman repelled by the sexuality which now fascinated Lawrence: the great red splashes of flowers on the grass suggest the crushed carnations on the ground where Clara Dawes and Paul Morel first make love in *Sons and Lovers*.[71] As that novel would show, loss can also be a stark kind of liberation.

7

The Sick Year: 1911–1912

It seems unlikely that Lawrence would have got engaged had it not been for his mother's illness and death; indeed, none of the letters he wrote subsequently to Louie Burrows have the simple happiness of those written immediately after their engagement. It is possible that he quite quickly came to regret his proposal; more likely that he simply made the best of it. Working hard to earn enough to get married on, as any young man might, as a continuation of his old, dutiful, caring self, was one of the things he set himself to do during the first half of 1911; burying himself in work would have helped him try to get past the awful feeling of loss and to forget the dreadful events of the winter. Early in 1911, however, he found himself taking the same stand against Arthur Lawrence that his mother had taken, when it became clear that Ada could not cope with their father and was suffering both due to his coming home tipsy and to the fact that he was keeping for himself nearly a quarter of his earnings. Lawrence wrote to the Reverend Robert Reid to enlist his support, and (just like his mother) denounced his father as 'disgusting, irritating, and selfish as a maggot'[1] – an extraordinary image, the maggot having no existence except parasitically to feed. The publication of *The White Peacock* on 20 January 1911 might have been a moment for simple rejoicing – Lawrence had hoped that it 'would break me an entrance into the jungle of literature' – but he had a new perspective on that, too. He told Louie: 'I shall be very sorry if I get no success . . . because it will leave me miles further off from marrying you.' His engagement reveals how powerfully he wanted to be committed, in love and life, to a woman he characterized as 'fine, warm, healthy, natural';[2] in utter contrast to the ultra-intellectual and exploitative being he had been with Jessie, or the person suffering from the complex mixture of conflicting impulses he had set out to explore in 'Paul Morel', or the writer committed to self-exploration, no matter what the cost.

He was earning £95 a year, Louie (a headmistress at Gaddesby in Leicestershire from January 1911) £90. The financial facts for young professional and incipiently middle-class people were, however, inexorable. They had agreed that they could not marry without a lump sum of at least £100, in addition to £120 a year income. They knew that Louie would give up her job either on marriage or very soon afterwards; Lawrence would have to become a headmaster in a country school. Hence the potential importance of his novels, poems and short stories; a group of poems might earn £5, a story £10, and *The White Peacock* had earned £50, a lot of it spent on doctors' bills and train fares during the autumn of 1910. In July, Lawrence would define 'success' as meaning 'an assured income of £150' a year.[3] Louie happily saw Lawrence's writing as a way of earning the money they needed: especially the lump sum. It was not long before Lawrence was ironically reporting to her the number of pages of 'Paul Morel' he had written that week. 'Am I a newspaper printing machine to turn out a hundred sheets in half an hour?' he grumbled.[4] He ground out the novel painfully over the spring and summer; against all his expectations, it reverted to a kind of romance. Mrs Morel becomes a saintly woman trapped by an unredeemable, drunken husband; Morel kills his son Arthur, is sent to prison and dies; Paul is left at home with his mother; Miriam is a kind of middle-class foundling. It seems to have stalled finally around the start of July, just as Paul is meeting a married woman who attracts him (Clara in *Sons and Lovers*). But this in its turn may have been something Lawrence did not want to embark on. An affair with a married woman would not have been an encounter Louie could easily have borne in her fiancé's autobiographical hero. Reading about Paul and Miriam in the novel would have been bad enough; Louie had been upset by Jessie sending Lawrence a letter at the end of January 1911.[5]

Such feelings nevertheless meant that Louie could not be the kind of partner or reader Jessie Chambers had been. Lawrence had hidden nothing from Jessie: with Louie he always had to be circumspect. He had hardly seen Jessie since August 1910; in December, he had simply

shown her some of the poems he had written about his mother's illness
and death. Louie had copied those poems into his poetry notebook,
but Lawrence dared not show her the other poems he had been writing,
although she asked to see them. His writing contorts itself as he tries
to refuse deferentially: 'If you will allow me, I will not give them to
you. They are all very well dancing up and down the pages of my little
note book, shut safely in the cupboard – but wandering, even as speech
from me to you, as yet, "no", permit me to say.'[6] There were poems
about his attraction to Helen, about making love to Jessie, about a
woman who may have been the married Alice Dax, and about Louie.
'The Saga', too, which Hueffer had hated when he read its first half –
'it would damage your reputation, perhaps permanently'[7] – was not
something that Lawrence would have wanted Louie to see; she would
have been deeply suspicious of his relationship with Helen. He did not
often show Louie his short stories, as she thought they distracted him
from 'Paul Morel'; but 'Paul Morel' had come to a halt, for reasons he
probably understood better than she did.

His real trouble with Louie, however, was that his attraction to her
neither held him nor brought them close. He told Helen Corke in July
that 'I love Louie in a certain way that doesn't encroach on my liberty',[8]
and this was not just a libertine's excuse. He loved her as one of the
sorts of person he certainly was. But trying to be normal, decent,
conventional, professional and middle class was an attempt to ignore
his difference, his rebelliousness, his pride, his profound desire to 'Be
a good animal',[9] his rage and depression, his intensity and intelligence,
and his terrifying (if intermittent) capacity for insight. The engagement
meant that his genuine fondness for her turned into a series of nagging
complaints about her refusal to respond sexually: Louie, in a tart
comment made some eighteen years later, would mock his complaints
as 'the miseries of continence'.[10]

Lawrence appears to have seen rather less of Helen Corke in 1911,
but things came to a head with her following a weekend which Louie
spent with him in London in March. After the weekend was over,
he had written Louie a fiercely honest letter about his desires and
frustrations: this was as near to having a row with her as he could
manage. He did not want to wait for the money they needed for
marriage; he wanted her now.

I cannot, cannot slowly enjoy watching the rose open: I can't help it, Louie, I can't. I am really dangerous in my fixed mad aim. I love my rose, and no other: and when I can have her I shall want no other. But when I have her not, I have nothing. Your pleasure, which you enjoy, in the thought of me, is nothing to me. What I want I want . . .[11]

Shortly before this, he had asked Helen if she would sleep with him; she was very tangibly the 'other' he wanted if he could not have Louie. Helen had admitted that she desired his 'intimate company', but she was only prepared to allow their intimacy to extend to kisses and embraces.[12] After the appalling outcome of her relationship with Macartney, there was every reason for her to have conflicted feelings about men and sex. It is a measure of Lawrence's dreadful loneliness and craving for relationship during this year that he should have gone on in such frustrated confusion; 'more or less in love' with Helen, knowing that she was 'a woman whom one knows one can't love altogether, nor really',[13] while still engaged to Louie. Nor was he just caught between them, either. At some stage, he developed a considerable *tendresse* for his landlady, Marie Jones, although this may not have been until the autumn of 1911, after she had made various confessions to him, 'marital and faintly horrifying'. There was also a mysterious woman in London known as 'Jane'.[14]

Things flared up again between Lawrence and Helen in July, and once again his anger with Louie, this time specifically over money, was the spur. The *English Review* had just paid him £10 for his story 'Odour of Chrysanthemums', which was at last published in June. Lawrence had found ways of spending all of it, almost at once. Louie had accused him of not even trying to save any of it, which was a way of accusing him of not wanting to marry her, and so partly true. One thing she objected to was a trip he had made to Dover by himself for half a day. He had done this, in fact, on the rebound from Helen Corke, who had yet again rejected his sexual advances. As a result, he had ritually thrown away 'the two little articles . . . of temptation' (condoms) with which his landlord had provided him. In Dover he had tried to reach a decision about the future. He explained to Helen: 'I think I can manage to live alone body and soul as long as must be . . . never never will I ask a woman for anything again: I will pay her market price.' This was the theory. A fortnight later, he would be on holiday with Louie, George Neville and Ada in North Wales; Jessie Chambers heard 'that he absolutely refused to be left alone with Louie and insisted on Ada accompanying them wherever they went'.[15] That might have been because he was so attracted to Louie, rather than because he did not want her. But either way, he knew that their relationship was going nowhere.

As he went from woman to woman, a number of them were badly hurt, while he experienced a good deal of guilt and misery. But it is too easy to adopt a comfortable attitude of moral disapproval towards the half-truths he was now telling women, the promises he was failing to keep, his loveless pursuits. Lawrence's situation must have felt maddening in the late summer of 1911. *The White Peacock* had been published in January, and the reviews were very mixed: often patronizing, at times enthusiastic, but – from the very start of Lawrence's career – stressing the physicality of his descriptions of people: 'We are never allowed to forget their most goodly bodies.'[16] Worse still, no publisher had offered him a contract for a second novel. As the months went by, the little reputation he had earned simply leaked away. He had written two more plays, *The Widowing of Mrs. Holroyd* and *The Merry-go-Round*, both set in the Midlands, one a tragedy and one a comedy, and had sent them to Hueffer; but nothing had come of them. The publication of 'Odour of Chrysanthemums' had led to a young publisher (Martin Secker) asking whether he could publish a book of Lawrence's stories: but he had only three or four and no time to write more. He remained an oddity in the London literary world; as much of a fish out of water as he had been at Nottingham High School, or at the literary social events through which Hueffer had paraded him in the winter of 1909–10. His taste was clearly for 'fine-writing', but his life experience, both as a child in Eastwood and now at the Davidson Road School, could not be further from the literary. His nature was caught between the refined and the outspoken, the cultivated and the natural, the awkwardly unconfident and the arrogantly confident, between depression and anger. After his mother's death, he might have felt liberated, his own person, at last able to make his own choices. As a man engaged to be married, he could do none of those things. He was thoroughly unsure of 'The Saga' after

Hueffer's criticisms of its 'execrably bad art',[17] and the new Heinemann novel, 'Paul Morel', was getting nowhere. Yet it was on these books that his future as a writer, if he had a future, depended. And Hueffer, having damned 'The Saga' and temporarily lost the two plays, had left the *English Review* and gone abroad; while his successor at the magazine, Austin Harrison, before he would even publish 'Odour of Chrysanthemums' (the story Hueffer had so joyfully welcomed), had demanded that Lawrence cut five pages. Lawrence's literary career, unassisted by Jessie, Helen or Hueffer, was at a standstill. All he could do was submit the occasional story to the *English Review*, try to write some more, and at some point try to rewrite 'Paul Morel'.

At the back of everything was the death of his mother, which continued to leave him feeling lonely and miserable. The best it seemed that he could look forward to would be another few years of school-teaching, trying to save, or, if he abandoned Louie and teaching, a continuing series of frustrating relationships with women, without any income to speak of. Abandoning teaching would mean an ignominious return home to his Eastwood family, where it would be deeply unfair to try to live off his schoolteacher sister Ada, herself trying to save for her forthcoming marriage to a local draper, Eddie Clarke. Lawrence's turning to woman after woman was, in one way, a search by a de-manding, complex and contradictory man for a partner. In another way, it was just part of a much larger pattern of estrangement, dissatis-faction and frustration. He simply did not know what he wanted, nor how he could reconcile the differing demands of his nature. Late in life, he would refer to 1911 as his 'sick year', meaning the year between his mother's death and his collapse with pneumonia. It was also the year when he was probably more depressed and unhappy than at any time in his entire life (he used the words 'ghastly' and 'dreadful' in July); and while never being in danger of alcoholism – 'Think of the paternal example' – he did begin to drink. As he put it to Louie: 'The Good God made whiskey, as I have rather lately discovered': 'Sometimes when I have horrors – the ashy sort – I drink a little – to mend the fire of my faith and hope, you see . . . too much whiskey is better than too much melancholies: and a drinking bout better than a bout of ferocious blues.'[18] He could not deal with Helen Corke without alcohol, for example; it kept him 'just sufficiently dimmed', and reduced his tendency to become either ironical or over-demanding. He had escaped to Dover in July precisely so that he would find 'nothing to push back, nothing to get ironic over'.[19] Twelve years later, he exactly identified his situation. In *Aaron's Rod*, Aaron confesses to himself 'a secret malady he suffered from: this strained, unacknowledged opposition to his surroundings, a hard core of irrational, exhausting withholding of himself. Irritating, because he still *wanted* to give himself. A woman and whiskey, these were usually a remedy . . .'[20] In 1911, those were Lawrence's solutions too. But to whom or what could he give himself?

The start of the autumn term in August 1911 found Lawrence as depressed with school, and himself, as he ever chose to reveal to Louie; he makes casual something that was very troubling:

Two days of school over – and I must say they have been pretty rotten. My new kids – well, they are not my old ones: and I have 50 – and, at the bottom, I don't like teaching – it wearies me to death . . . I feel very unsettled. I should like to lift up my feet and depart again from here – to Hades or elsewhere, I don't mind. Really, I think I shall have to turn that proverbial tramp.[21]

He was still doing his best to write stories, and it may have been Austin Harrison who suggested that he contact the publisher's reader Edward Garnett, currently gathering stories for the American magazine *Century*. American publication would add to Lawrence's reputation and his income.

This was a crucial contact, as it turned out, though it began badly enough with Lawrence sending off two new stories (early versions of 'The Witch à la Mode' and 'Daughters of the Vicar'), neither of which Garnett was able to place. Garnett, however, suggested that they meet, and Lawrence managed to get a couple of hours off in the middle of one Wednesday to go into London. He was so impressive that Garnett invited him down to the Cearne, his house in Kent, for a weekend. This was a chink of light to a man who had been feeling 'as if I'd got a bandage over my eyes and mouth ugh!'[22] Garnett, seventeen years older than Lawrence, was famous for having discovered Conrad back in the 1890s; he knew the literary world through and through, and now took Lawrence on. He was determined to introduce Lawrence to literary people: 'I am not keen on it, but he says my business is to get known.' Garnett was impressed with Lawrence's work – 'He praises me for my sensuous feeling in my writing'[23] – and hoped to acquire it for his employer, Gerald Duckworth; but it is clear that Garnett was also excited by a new talent, as yet undeveloped, which he would be able to nurture. He wanted Lawrence to recover his two plays from Hueffer so that they could be published with *A Collier's Friday Night*; and he wanted Lawrence to put together a volume of his poems. He read Lawrence's stories too and criticized them ferociously, while remaining friendly and supportive. Lawrence wrote with utter happiness about that first weekend at the Cearne with Garnett, how they had 'discussed books most furiously, sitting drinking wine in the ingle nook'.[24] Personally, Garnett was extremely sympathetic; neither over-impressed by Lawrence's working-class origins, nor desirous of showing him off as a curiosity. Garnett went his own way and had an unconventional marriage (he and his wife, the translator Constance Garnett, did not often live together).

The conflict in Lawrence between teaching and writing grew worse. He found himself busier and busier as October 1911 went on: 'I have only time to think about work and the things I've got to do tomorrow ... Things I've got to do, things I've got to do – there seems nothing else in the world but that.'[25] Garnett's encouragement had succeeded in making Heinemann re-evaluate Lawrence's prospects; they decided they wanted the book of poems, and 'Paul Morel' by March. For this, Lawrence went back to Jessie Chambers. He sent her the manuscript, asking her if she would tell him what she thought of it.[26] She would take it seriously, not just see it as a money-spinning venture. Sending it to her was also a way of asking, 'is this how I came to be as I am?' – a kind of apology.

He was, however, still rightly sceptical about whether he could survive financially as a writer; and so long as he remained engaged to Louie, he felt obliged to keep on teaching. All the while, he remained attracted to her in what he once called 'inflamed necessity'.[27] They spent the weekend of 27–9 October together, for example, in Leicester and Eastwood, and Lawrence wrote to her on the Monday:

the long slow drag of hours is very trying. I've now got to digest a great lot of dissatisfied love in my veins. It is very damnable, to have slowly to drink back again into oneself all the lava and fire of a passionate eruption . . . The most of the things, that just heave red hot to be said, I shove back. And that leaves nothing to be said. All this, you see, is very indelicate and immodest and all that . . . and I always want to subscribe to your code of manners, towards you – I know I fail sadly.[28]

The language is astonishingly sexual. But the apologies invited her to ask: 'shouldn't we bring our engagement to an end, if this is how you feel?' As they said goodbye on the Sunday, he had said to her, 'you must not be surprised if I give you up' and she had been baffled: surely they were happy? She had told herself, naïvely, that 'in marrying him I must not expect happiness but only love'.[29] They struggled on until November but, to make matters worse, this seems to have been the moment when his affair with Alice Dax started.

Alice was a married woman of thirty-four; her daughter, Phyllis Maude, would be born on 6 October 1912 and Alice was convinced that the child would 'never have been conceived but for an unendurable passion which only *he* [Lawrence] had roused and my husband [Harry] had slaked'; she kept the link with Lawrence by giving her daughter the names that he had suggested for a daughter back in 1908.[30] (Mother and daughter can be seen in Illustration 12.) Alice was notorious for being 'advanced' in almost every way; she took an uncompromising stand on women's rights, and a friend commented that 'most of the men of her generation' were frightened of her. She absolutely refused the role of the conventionally unobtrusive woman; local people hated her 'loud laugh' and 'sudden explosion into laughter'.[31] She could inflame Lawrence's feelings whenever she wished, whether during his crisis with Jessie in the spring of 1910 or, as now, in 1911. At the end of the Whitsun holiday in June, Louie had been suspicious of a woman who may have been Alice, and Lawrence and Alice were lovers no later than November. She may have come down to London; they may have met in Nottingham or in Shirebrook: on one occasion, they made love while Harry was asleep upstairs.[32] Lawrence was desperate for a relationship that was neither exploitative nor commercial. Tom Brangwen's experiences with a prostitute in *The Rainbow* are 'so nothing, so dribbling and functional', and Lawrence may well have been writing from experience; although in December 1908 he had no idea how to spot 'a "femme perdue" by the look of her', in 1918 he would comment that he had 'an aesthetical or physical aversion from prostitutes'.[33] By the autumn of 1911, he was getting into the habit of pursuing sexual relationships with women he did not love. Five years later, he would recreate the condition of a man very like himself, who hates his 'profligate intercourse' with women; and Alice Dax wanted him badly, to judge by her later account.[34]

It was in the middle of all this, on 3 November, that with trepidation he restarted 'Paul Morel'. 'I really dread setting the pen to paper,' he told Louie.[35] He had doubtless talked to Garnett about it, while Jessie had advised him to stick much closer to the facts about his early life; she offered to write down some memories of their relationship. Despite Lawrence's determination to write the story of his parents' marriage as it really had been (the essential problems of Paul's life, and his own, thus being brought into focus), early on in the new work he would write: 'No man can live unless his life is rooted in some woman: unless some woman believes in him, and so fixes his belief in himself.'[36] He was as yet incapable of the analysis of male dependence which *Sons and Lovers* would become.

At this stage, anyway, he had no more time than to compose its first seventy pages; and his struggle to write it probably contributed to what happened next. For months, he had been distressed, tense and unwell. His brother George had remarked, after staying at Colworth Road early in October, that he 'isn't at all well . . . He calls out in his sleep, thinks somebody's trying to kill him.' He had constructed a frantically busy social life, visiting acquaintances or going to concerts three or four times a week, and had an acute sense that things were going wrong. He not only felt 'really rotten – it is the dry heat of the pipes in school, and the strain', but his 'mouth seems to be lifted blindly for something, and waiting, puzzled. It is shocking how I curse within myself.' In modern parlance, he was on the verge of some kind of breakdown; he hazarded, 'I am on the brink of a complaint.'[37] His affair with Alice Dax was part of the same pattern of desperation seeking relief, and would have brought as much guilt as satisfaction. A week after they probably had sex together, Lawrence travelled down to Garnett's again, to meet the editor of a London newspaper; he got wet, but stayed in his wet clothes. Back in his Croydon lodgings on the night of Sunday 19 November, he developed double pneumonia. Ada Lawrence had to hurry down to Croydon to nurse him; he 'wanders a great deal' (she told Louie) and needed morphia to sleep; the real question was whether his heart could stand the ragingly high temperatures he was running. It was even worse than his childhood illness of 1901 had been. The 'crisis' came around 29 November. 'We are all fighting hard for him,' Ada wrote to Louie: by then, a nurse had been brought in, too.[38]

Lawrence survived. Not until 9 December, however, could he even sit up, and he was not allowed out of bed until the 15th. What is more, he told Garnett, who was now almost a kind of elder brother to him, 'The doctor says I mustn't go to school again, or I shall be consumptive' – that is, develop tuberculosis. He would never return to teaching.[39] What made it possible to give up school was the fact that, while he was ill, Garnett had seen the old manuscript of 'The Saga' and told Lawrence what he would need to do to improve it; Duckworth would then accept it. Lawrence was already expecting another £50 from Heinemann in February for *The White Peacock*. 'Paul Morel' was promised to them too, but with the money for a novel from Duckworth as well, a career as a writer looked to be a real prospect, at least for a year or so. He had not planned it, but it had forced itself upon him.

First he had to get well. On 11 December, propped up with pillows, he shaved off his (first) red beard, a demonstration that his hand no longer shook. In spite of her protests, Louie was not allowed down to Croydon until Christmas Eve, though Jessie Chambers had been to see him ten days earlier; but Lawrence and Louie then spent Christmas and New Year with Ada and Eddie Clarke, in Croydon, and went on to friends in Redhill. At the start of January, Louie returned to the Midlands while Lawrence went to Bournemouth to spend a month convalescing; he took the manuscript of 'The Saga' with him and, on the rare fine days within view of the Isle of Wight, did a thorough and transforming revision of the manuscript into his novel *The Trespasser*. He could not change it completely. Though he removed handfuls of adjectives, it was still 'too florid, too "chargé". But it can't be anything else – it is itself.'[40] He also started to walk long distances again, he ate properly and he seems thoroughly to have enjoyed himself in the boarding house, as he so often did in a group. Just as at the Haggs, the other guests became a kind of family for him.

There remained his engagement, however. At the start of January, he had unwisely but decently offered to marry Louie anyway, in spite of abandoning his job; and she had lovingly accepted. So he was still not free. But he also wanted to go abroad; he had an 'old desire' to travel, and a number of the heroes of his early autobiographical works have links with France.[41] His letters to Louie during January 1912 show that nothing had been finally decided. Writing *The Trespasser*, however, may well have had the same effect upon Lawrence's engagement to Louie as writing 'The Saga' had had upon his affair with Jessie. He was once again thinking through the effects upon a couple of a woman's inability to respond to her partner, and the man's growing isolation from her, in spite of his attraction to her. Although he knew the decision about Louie could no longer be put off – so that for all the pleasure of coming back to life, 'at the bottom I am rather miserable . . . I don't know what ails me'[42] – he also knew that he was not going to be self-sacrificing Siegmund.

It was not until he had left Bournemouth that he finally wrote to Louie. He had gone down to stay with Garnett for five days, incidentally seeing Helen Corke on the way, and then writing to her proposing that she should come down to the Cearne as well, Garnett being 'most beautifully free of the world's conventions'.[43] Siegmund, for the last time, claimed Helena; luckily she did not go. For months now Lawrence had been taking Garnett into his confidence about his relationships with women, and Garnett would certainly have insisted on the writer's need for his freedom. Lawrence wrote as gently as possible, but the letter he sent Louie was that of a man quite determined to be free:

I ask you to dismiss me. I am afraid we are not well suited.

My illness has changed me a good deal, has broken a good many of the old bonds that held me. I can't help it. It is no good to go on. I asked Ada, and she thought it would be better if the engagement were broken off; because it is not fair to you.

It's a miserable business, and the fault is all mine.[44]

Louie was thus given no chance of saying 'no' but, to her credit, insisted on seeing him: she would not accept the ending of her engagement by post. Lawrence agreed to meet her when he got back to the Midlands.[45]

It was at this point that he encountered the mysterious 'Jane'. Who was she? On Friday, 9 February 1912, Lawrence returned to Eastwood from the Cearne. He travelled up from Limpsfield to Victoria by train, crossed London by bus or underground and went to see Ford Madox Hueffer and Violet Hunt in Holland Park Avenue. In the early afternoon, Violet Hunt went to a meeting and Hueffer took Lawrence to a theatre matinée at the Royal Court: a Yeats play and two others. Afterwards, Lawrence went to Marylebone station to catch his evening train to the Midlands. No more is known about Jane than is contained in a sentence he wrote to Garnett the following day: 'I met Jane and kissed her farewell at Marylebone – my heart was awfully heavy.'[46] That last phrase demonstrates that it was another romantic attachment which Lawrence was ending; but he *was* ending it, presumably because he was leaving London. His arrangement to meet her on 9 February must either have been made in person – by knocking on her door – or by post; but his address book for the period provides no clue. Either he kept her address in his head (he made no entries for people he knew well, like Jessie or Helen) or 'Jane' was not her real name. It is tempting to identify her with Marie Jones,[47] to whom he *did* send one of his precious copies of Sons and Lovers in 1913, suggesting a special relationship: the novel, of course, shows Paul Morel having an affair with a married woman. Yet it would have been easier to see Marie Jones in the morning, at Victoria station; there seems no obvious reason why she should have trailed right across London to Marylebone at night to say goodbye. 'Jane' was a special friend: someone whom Lawrence never saw again, but who mattered none the less.[48]

Lawrence was returning to Eastwood in time to celebrate his niece Peggy's third birthday on 9 February. Emily, Sam and the little girl were now living with Ada, and Arthur Lawrence, in a rented house in Queen's Square, Eastwood.[49] It was a remarkable place in which to write 'Paul Morel': the novel had been promised to Heinemann for March, though it would be delivered late. His father would have occupied his old chair in the kitchen, just as he used to; a young child was at play and a young woman in charge of the house; and Lawrence was writing away in the corner, imagining the world of his childhood even as a version of it played itself out in front of him.

Things now had to be finally brought to an end with Louie. Lawrence had written to her again, saying as honestly as he could, 'I dont think now I have the proper love to marry on.'[50] They met at the Castle Art Gallery in Nottingham on 13 February (Louie's birthday, unfortunately, her twenty-fourth), and Lawrence sent Garnett a marvellous, if devastating, account:

She had decided beforehand that she had made herself too cheap to me, therefore she thought she would become all at once expensive and desirable. Consequently she offended me at every verse end – thank God. If she'd been wistful, tender and passionate, I should have been a goner . . . She stared at the naked men till I had to go into another room – she gave me a disquisition on texture in modelling: why clay lives or does not live; – sarked me for saying a certain old fellow I met was a bore: could not remember, oh no, had not the ghost of a notion when we had last visited the Castle together, though she knew perfectly . . . I took her to a café, and over tea and toast, told her for the fourth time. When she began to giggle, I asked her coolly for the joke: when she began to cry, I wanted a cup of tea. It's awfully funny. I had a sort of cloud over my mind . . .[51]

The letter is both wonderfully written and a heartless exercise in literary control, but Lawrence was writing to entertain Garnett as well as attempting to show how untouched he was by the experience. Louie read the letter when it was published fifty years later, and annotated it. In reality she had been 'simply dumb with misery'. She remembered that Lawrence had been in evening dress; he was going to the theatre with someone that evening (probably Alice Dax). Louie wrote in the margin of the published letter: 'I said Is there another girl He said Yes, if you'd *call* her a girl.'[52] She never saw Lawrence again.

It is, however, hard to see any kind of future which Lawrence and Louie might have shared. If they had got married back in December 1910 and had settled down together in that north Cornish school of which Lawrence had almost immediately written for particulars, with Lawrence's writing a hobby that brought in a welcome bit of extra money, then it is possible that they could have lived together happily. They might have had children, Lawrence could have studied for an external degree and might in time have become a distinguished teacher and writer. Yet no sooner is that future imagined than it sounds unlikely. Lawrence wanted so much more than that; he always hated the 'eternal cultivation of the habit of going without what one wants – needs'.[53] A relationship with Louie would have offered no more than a decently happy marriage; and the happiness would have been bought at the price of Lawrence not having to face up to the consequences of his love for his mother. Eight years later, in his unfinished novel *Mr Noon*, he would question the fate of an autobiographical self who married 'some *really* nice woman'. The answer sounds horribly likely: 'he would never have broken out of the dry integument that enclosed him. He would have withered with the really nice woman inside the enclosure.'[54] Lawrence would draw heavily on Louie's life and family for Ursula and her family in *The Rainbow*, which was a kind of tribute. In 1919, he remarked in a letter: 'I was fond of her, and have always a good feeling for her in me.'[55] She never forgot him; she did not marry until she was fifty-three and never had children, despite wanting to.

Having thus made himself, at last, a writer with no responsibility except to himself, Lawrence had two urgent needs: to finish 'Paul Morel' for Heinemann, making it the novel which might build him a reputation, and to do whatever he could, with Garnett's help, to develop his career. He had returned to the Midlands on the eve of the National Miners' Strike, which would last until April. Almost immediately, he wrote 'The Miner at Home', about the situation in a miner's household when the husband brings home his strike-ballot paper. Garnett had it printed in the *Nation* in March. Lawrence also wrote three other pieces about the strike in the course of February and March, and although none were published, all four show, for the first time, that he could now write about Arthur Lawrence's world without subjecting it to Lydia Lawrence's disapproval.[56] He was learning to write straight realism of a most impressive kind; the pieces were in effect exercises in non-metaphorical writing. Garnett's guidance may well have lain behind what he was doing; and Garnett also introduced him to the poet Walter de la Mare, who recommended Lawrence's poetry to the *Saturday Westminster Gazette*.

Yet 'Paul Morel' was even more important. Lawrence collected from Jessie Chambers the notes she had made for him, and then (as in the old days) began giving her the finished pages of manuscript to read, either at the Arno Vale farm or at her lodgings in Nottingham. As a result, he saw more of her than for the past eighteen months. After her visit to Croydon during his illness in December, he had written another wistful, fictionalized piece which would become the story 'The Shades of Spring', about the Haggs farm and the family. Here the Jessie figure confronts the passionless, artistic, detached man (Syson) who used to be so close to them all but who has gone away: his linguistic and intellectual superiority fatally distance him. Lawrence becomes savagely dismissive of Syson; an analysis of the bodiless, sublimated self, dependent on the woman for drawing him out, was a breakthrough in Lawrence's understanding of the person he used to be with Jessie. Writing 'Paul Morel' in its new form, and revisiting the territory of the Haggs yet again, Lawrence would do so without nostalgia, and without using the old, self-mocking figure of the refined and detached onlooker. He would recreate, fictionalize and develop his young life and his relationship with Jessie as that of Paul and Miriam; but this would be the Paul who had to leave Miriam.

At moments, this spring, both he and Jessie were tempted back into their old relationship. On one occasion, seeing what she perceived as 'his intense loneliness, his separation', she took his hand: 'His arms closed round me in a moment, he drew me to him, begging me to "come to him".' But that was only for 'a moment', too.[57] Not surprisingly, Jessie was finding what he was writing in the novel harder and harder to accept. Paul Morel is a painter, not a writer, who leaves school at fourteen and works as a clerk; he has no such literary apprenticeship as Lawrence had had with Jessie. Paul and Miriam read few books, there are few discussions of literature, and Miriam is not an intellectual woman. Jessie's years of struggle for self-fulfilment are reduced to Miriam's rather foolish failure to learn algebra, and Jessie inevitably felt that such a depiction was a denial of the realities of their early life. Even worse, Lawrence also began to draw upon their sexual experience of 1910, putting it chronologically far earlier, presenting Miriam as someone whose emotional needs make any relationship with her almost impossible, and who drives Paul to give her up for another woman. Lawrence may well have thought it impossible to give any realistic account of his years with Jessie, but she felt hopelessly betrayed. He left off going to see her, but still sent her his manuscript through the post.

For the first time in his life, too, he could decide where to live. He could have stayed in Eastwood, in that crowded household which reminded him so much of his past; but the experience of going back probably convinced him that he needed to make a break. There had been that despairing day back in July 1911 when, on the rebound from Helen Corke, he had gone down to Dover and had stared out across the Channel to another kind of life that might be lived, abroad. In January 1912, his mother's sister Ada, married to Fritz Krenkow, a bookish and scholarly German merchant who became an academic, had suggested that Lawrence might like to go to the Krenkow cousins in Waldbröl, in the Rhineland. He could acquire a real fluency in German there, as well as travel and try to get work, and he could write. That prospect must have seemed immensely attractive: if he found he could not live by his writing, he could always return to England. He was a qualified teacher, and the knowledge of languages he could acquire abroad might help him get into secondary teaching. He told Jessie, 'rather dismally', that if, when he came back, 'neither of us had found anyone we preferred, then we would marry'.[58] He believed he owed her that from 1910; he still felt guilty about taking advantage of her, and was determined to be honourable.

However, he must have hoped to live by his writing. Above all, he believed in it; which was why he had been so reluctant to risk its publication in the first place and had spoken and written so deprecatingly of his work to almost everybody, while simultaneously agonizing over it and continually revising it. When Lawrence writes about Paul's painting in *Sons and Lovers*, he mirrors his own experience: 'He worked a great deal from memory, using everybody he knew. He believed firmly in his work, that it was good and valuable. In spite of fits of depression, shrinking, everything, he believed in his work.'[59] He would go abroad in May, after finishing 'Paul Morel', and when his health had settled. This would at last offer the kind of break from the past which so attracted him.

He needed, naturally, whatever advice he could get about making his way in Germany. Lawrence knew one person who might be able to help. He had admired the teaching of the professor of modern languages at Nottingham University College, Ernest Weekley, who was not only a fluent Germanist but had married a German woman.

Weekley seems to have remembered the student-poet who had attended his lectures; his wife remembered him once commenting: 'I am sure he is a poet I could see it in his face, when I referred to the "blessed Damozel".'[60] When Lawrence got in touch with Weekley, at the end of February 1912, he was immediately invited to lunch. On the morning of Sunday 3 March, Lawrence took the train into Nottingham; he would have walked up from the Carrington Road station to the Mansfield Road, into the airy, middle-class, northern suburbs. The day was sunny and warm; the walk would have taken him perhaps thirty minutes. He may have been early: for some reason, Weekley was not there, or not available. (In his study would have been the proofs of *The Romance of Words*, the book that launched him as a writer.) Lawrence was shown into the sitting room, with its French windows open on to the garden where the three Weekley children were playing; he was introduced to Weekley's wife, Frieda. And the next half an hour changed his life.

8

Frieda Weekley: 1912

When Lawrence first met Frieda Weekley, she was thirty-three, but had already lived a remarkable life. She had been born Frieda von Richthofen in Metz, the second of the three daughters of Friedrich and Anna von Richthofen. Friedrich was a career army officer and baron of a branch of the famous family, but a struggling branch since they had suffered 'a succession of disasters' in farming.[1] Friedrich's own disaster had come when his forefinger was shattered during the Franco-Prussian War of 1870–71; his active military career had been reduced to a job in the administration of the garrison town of Metz, in the occupied territory of Alsace-Lorraine. The three daughters had grown up very aware of their parents' 'fierce hatred'[2] of each other, their quarrels and incompatibilities. Their father was, in one way, rigidly disciplined, but with an awful capacity for anger and self-hate; an unlucky gambler with a mistress who had to be paid off, and an illegitimate child. Their mother was constantly angry with the mess her husband's life generated, and struggled to prevent him from ruining them all.

The children grew up in the heart of German militarism, 'with its bands and brass and spurs'; Frieda always remembered the singing of the young soldiers, and ended up with a great repertoire of songs and a total ease in male company.[3] But, of all her family, she was also the one to whom the titles *Freiherr* (Baron) and *Freiin* (Baroness) mattered most; daughters, under the old system, inherited the title too. All her life she remained cheerfully superior: Lawrence remarked, ruefully, 'she makes the *de haut en bas* of class distinction felt . . . It is as she was bred and fed, and can't be otherwise.'[4] All three daughters had been presented at court in the 1890s, but lived the usual teenage life in Metz of balls, clothes and boyfriends. Frieda's first beau had been a young officer cadet, Karl von Marbahr; her younger sister, Johanna, at the age of eighteen, would marry the career officer Max von Schreibershofen. The girls were raised in a society in which the woman's role was that of mistress or wife, neither working nor earning, but caring for her family without the support of the regularly absent husband, who lived for the army and its comradeship.

Anna and Johanna were just the kind of resourceful women who could deal with the absences, the upsets, the debts, the conflicts between aristocratic aspiration and the grim reality of military marriages; but neither Frieda nor her elder sister, Else, married into the military. Both chose men with respectable professional careers, academics in both cases, who offered middle-class security. Else's husband (Edgar Jaffe) was a professor of economics, and Frieda's (Ernest Weekley) of modern languages. The girls' education had been minimal, but Else showed what could be done, against all the hopes and wishes of her father, by going to university and obtaining a PhD. Frieda was neither as well educated nor as bookish as her sister, but at the age of eighteen fell for the first man who would take her away from the tumultuous life of home. Weekley was sixteen years older than her, in his own way remarkable, a man born in the lower middle class who had left school at fifteen but had educated himself to the rank of professor. He had recently been appointed to a Chair at Nottingham University College, was away from England for the first time, and was overwhelmed by the astonishingly beautiful girl whom he met while on holiday in Freiburg in 1898. Illustration 13 shows them at the place where they originally met, probably a couple of summers after they married (in 1899): Frieda's bonnet making her look nun-like; Weekley close and protective. He kept the photograph all his life.[5]

By marrying Weekley, Frieda committed herself to a middle-class life in a country where she did not speak the language. However, she embraced the advantages that her home life had lacked: respect for women, male devotion, financial security. She had three children in quick succession, Monty in 1900, Elsa in 1902 and Barby in 1904. In Illustration 14, Frieda looks magnificent as she grasps Monty and baby Barby. But she was still only twenty-five when Barby was born, and her life was in fact lonely, dull and predictable. She had quickly learned in Nottingham, for example, that she had to shop in the morning: the afternoon was for rest, social calls and afternoon tea. 'To shop in the afternoon would have been unthinkable.'[6] Like both her sisters, she began to have love affairs, the first in 1905 with Barby's godfather, William Enfield Dowson, a neighbour and local industrialist;[7] then, on a visit to Germany in 1907, with the psychoanalyst Otto Gross (a pupil of Freud and Jung, and her sister Else's lover). In 1910, another German lover, Ernst Frick, came and lived in England for some months and saw Frieda when he could. These last two men were the very antithesis of the respectable: Gross a married drug-addict who slept with his patients, Frick a painter and anarchist.

Frieda never contemplated abandoning her husband for them; in Gross and Frick she had chosen men quite unsuitable as long-term partners. All three von Richthofen sisters ended up married to men they no longer loved; all three had affairs with men whom they admired. Else even had a child by Otto Gross, and Edgar accepted it into the family. Frieda's affairs appear to have satisfied her need for sex and for self-determination. While being drawn to men with life-styles and purposes very different from the bourgeois, and whose ideas impressed her, she none the less loved her children dearly, feeling 'so much nearer to them than the grown-up people'.[8]

When Lawrence walked into her life that March morning in 1912, her reaction was probably simple pleasure that this clever and unusual young man was attracted to her, coupled with a fascination about his class and his refusal to adopt conventional manners. When he first spoke to her about women, for example, 'I was amazed at the way he fiercely denounced them.' The second time they met, he told her: 'You are quite unaware of your husband, you take no notice of him.' This was not at all how Frieda was used to being addressed: 'I disliked the directness of this criticism.' Yet the fact that 'we talked about Oedipus, and I agreed eagerly to all he said' is a clue to the intellectual stimulus they could share.[9] He seems to have been just on the point of writing a new version of the scene in 'Paul Morel' in which Gertrude Morel and Paul kiss each other, but this time he would show them interrupted by Mr Morel: after which Paul pleads with his mother not to sleep with her husband. Lawrence knew *Hamlet*, and the son's demand there for his mother (another Gertrude) not to sleep with her husband. What was new was this version of the Freudian Oedipus complex, the son caught between hate for his father and incestuous love for his mother, to which Frieda may well have been able to give a Freudian gloss: Gross, she recalled, had 'revolutionised my life with Freud'.[10]

Frieda once told her daughter that all she expected from this striking young man was 'an affair and no more'; and though she would have embarked on this as soon as possible, the story that they were in bed within twenty minutes of first meeting, or even the same day, is a myth.[11] Lawrence left the Weekleys that afternoon to go to the Chambers family at their farm, and he went up to Shirebrook the following day to see Harry and Alice Dax. But over the next three weeks there was opportunity enough for Frieda to see a good deal of her new admirer; his intensity, eagerness and intelligence strongly attracted her. At the divorce hearing, Weekley said that he 'had to remonstrate with his wife for going about too much with Mr Lawrence'.[12] They went to the theatre in Nottingham, for example, to see Shaw's *Man and Superman*; on another occasion, with the children out of the way and the maid enjoying her afternoon off, Frieda invited Lawrence back to the house in Private Road, where he found that she had no idea how to turn on the gas to make them a cup of tea (kitchens had played no role in *her* kind of untroubled life: the household had three servants).[13] More than once she met Lawrence in the country; on one occasion, May Holbrook loaned Lawrence and Frieda the cottage in Moorgreen, and Lawrence recalled a month later how 'Moorgreen seems sweet to me'.[14] He none the less refused to have sex with Frieda in the Weekleys' house. That would have been too gross a betrayal of Weekley, who had shown him nothing but kindness.

For Lawrence, Frieda really was 'the woman of a lifetime'; within a few days, he told her she was 'the most wonderful woman in all England'.[15] How did he recognize so quickly that she was not just another Jessie, or Agnes, or Helen, or Louie? First, because she was sexually uninhibited. For the first time in his life, a woman who attracted him was prepared to have sex with him, though at this stage the sex was brief and occasional. Not for another two months would they celebrate their first night together. But for a man who only a year earlier had been writing about the way his own sexual feelings 'escaped from prison', her lack of inhibition was exhilarating. Secondly, he was desperately attracted to her carefree manner, her directness, sensuality and living-for-the-moment: she was wonderfully 'indifferent to the small things'.[16] This was something he envied profoundly. He also discovered that she responded strongly to him, and had little feeling for her husband. What most distinguished her from Jessie was that she not only said what she thought, but was fearless in opposing and contradicting him. It was knowing Frieda that made Lawrence reply, when asked why he had not married Jessie, 'It would have been a fatal step. I should have had too easy a life, nearly everything my own way, and my genius would have been destroyed.'[17] Genius not only thrived on opposition; it needed it, to exist at all. A new life as an independent writer had recently opened out in front of him, and he must have felt that he had found the ideal partner for it.[18]

But although Frieda was attracted to him, and eventually found herself in love with him, she had not the least intention of leaving her husband or children. The adaptability which had allowed her to walk out of her life as a teenager in Metz into life as a wife and mother in England had also allowed her to adapt to her marriage, and then to affairs within marriage. In old age, she was happy to repeat the story of how Lawrence entered her life and she left Weekley. But that simply did not happen. She liked Lawrence, but it was his creativity and his attraction to her that seem to have mattered most. Her twelve-year-old son, Monty, watched her lying in bed reading pages of manuscript; she must have acquired 'Paul Morel'. Jessie Chambers, catching sight of Lawrence on Easter Monday 1912, was struck by how miserable he looked ('beyond anything I had ever imagined').[19] Jessie put this down to the fact that, writing 'Paul Morel', he had found himself torn between *her* and his love for his mother. His misery was far more likely to have been due to the fact that, having discovered the 'woman of a lifetime', Lawrence had then found that she wanted just an affair, and was going her sunny, cheerful way regardless. As Frieda put in later: 'He forced the responsibility of himself on to her; she did not want to take it.'[20]

Lawrence, meanwhile, immediately broke off from Alice Dax and devoted himself to Frieda. When she watched him absorbed in floating paper boats and daisies for her little girls on one of their trips into the country, she found that he 'touched a new tenderness in me'.[21] She was attracted to a man who responded to her children as well as to her. Lawrence had to go to London in April and she was able to visit him there; Edward Garnett – 'free of the world's conventions' – invited the couple down to the Cearne for the day, and Frieda gratefully recalled 'your friendly cottage and the appleblossoms and your own wonderfully hospitable self'. In addition, they could look forward to going to Germany for 'at least one week together',[22] which must have sounded a romantic ideal to Lawrence. He was due at his cousins the Krenkows in May, and by wonderful luck Frieda was also going to Germany at the start of that month, for the celebration of her father's fifty years in the army.

Lawrence also believed that, before leaving for Germany, Frieda was going to inform Weekley that she was having an affair. But she did not do so. What she did was tell Weekley about her affairs with Otto Gross and Ernst Frick. Barby may have witnessed the end of the confession: 'I sat on the stairs one day and saw Frieda coming out of Ernest's study in tears.'[23] Frieda told her confidante Frieda Gross (Gross's wife) what she had done, and the latter informed Else how her sister 'has told her husband about Otto and Ernst. He has been very good . . . I've understood the thing so as very much to admire her, and say to myself, that recent events have revealed something wonderfully lively and renewing in her.'[24] It is possible that she had been unable to complete the confession she had been working up to; a good deal more likely that she had begun to feel that the code of free love exemplified by Gross's wife, Frieda, and by her sister Else and brother-in-law Edgar, was something which felt right for her too, and that Weekley ought to accept it. The fact that she wrote to Frieda Gross immediately afterwards backs up that interpretation; Lawrence's demands, and her own feelings, were encouraging her to try and start a new kind of marriage with Weekley. Otto Gross had told her that she was the woman of the future;[25] she stowed his letters in her luggage for Germany, suggesting the extent to which she still counted on his support. It is, however, impossible to sustain Frieda Gross's self-congratulatory conclusion that Weekley had been 'very good' in response to Frieda's announcement; on 11 May, Weekley said he had been 'insane for ten days'.[26]

Frieda left her two little girls with her parents-in-law in Hampstead, her usual practice when she went away (Monty stayed with his father in Nottingham). At 2 o'clock on Friday 3 May 1912, she met Lawrence outside the first-class ladies' room at Charing Cross, to catch the boat train; he had just £11 in his pocket. They crossed the Channel in the bows of the steamer; Lawrence liked the feeling of being at the forefront of their enterprise – 'at the tip of their projection', as he later put it – as he escaped at last from England.[27] They reached Metz just after 6 o'clock on the Saturday morning.

What happened there would have been comic had it not been so painful. Lawrence had, of course, to be kept out of the way as a 'distant friend';[28] he was lodged in a respectable family hotel (smuggling a woman up to his room was almost impossible) and Frieda lived with her family. She at once told her mother and Else about what she had said to Weekley, and about Lawrence. On Saturday afternoon, Lawrence was introduced to her mother, who naturally cast him in the role of Frieda's 'latest gallant'. His, however, was not yet a starring part in this particular drama. On one occasion, Frieda apparently managed to get up to his room;[29] but, most of the time, all he could do was hang around the garrison town, which he hated, draft two essays in the series he eventually called 'In Fortified Germany' for a newspaper he had contact with, the *Westminster Gazette*, and find that he had now far less chance of seeing Frieda than in Nottingham. On Monday, the day of celebration, they saw each other only for a few seconds across a crowded fairground.

By Tuesday, Lawrence was desperate and angry. He was acutely conscious of the brevity of Frieda's 'days in Germany' compared with 'the days that are to follow in Nottingham';[30] neither of them doubted that she was going back. All her mother and sisters would talk about were strategies for deceiving Weekley and allowing Frieda to take the occasional lover, keep her children, and remain financially secure: this, after all, was what Frieda had started off by wanting. 'I can't stand it any longer,' Lawrence wrote to her: 'no more subterfuge, lying, dirt, fear . . . no, I won't utter or act or willingly let you utter or act, another single lie in the business.' He had to write; she was living three miles away, and he did not even know when he would next see her. He was having to tell a 'thousand baffling lies'[31] to explain his presence in Metz; and there was now a new reason for lying.

A letter had come from the distraught Weekley, insisting that Frieda tell him whether she was still having affairs. If so, she must send him a telegram reading 'Ganz recent' (i. e. 'very recent': the mixture of languages hopefully ensuring the bafflement of the postal staff in both countries). The shrewd Else, who had stayed in Nottingham and disliked Weekley, feared that he would react violently to such an answer; Lawrence, too, saw Weekley as a man 'in whom the brute can leap up'.[32] An ambiguous reply must be sent, the next step carefully negotiated.

Lawrence hated this. Frieda recalled how 'he would hammer away at her, trying to make her commit herself finally'; he drafted his ultimatum in the form of a letter to Weekley which stated: 'I love your wife and she loves me.' But he did not post it. He sent it to Frieda, telling her that she must send it, or must write herself. She promised to do so, but felt utterly confused; she loved Lawrence 'with a 1000 different loves'[33] and believed in him as an extraordinary person, but she was subjected to the terribly sensible advice that her family were giving her. And however much she loved Lawrence, he was in his way as unsuitable as Gross or Frick as a partner. How could she entrust her future or her children's future to him, a barely published author with no money, only an utter certainty that they were right for each other? To her, 'it seemed just madness – and it was'.[34]

On Tuesday morning, black comedy turned to farce. While out briefly with Frieda, Lawrence was arrested for trespassing, thus possibly spying, in one of the military areas that ringed the city. They had to give their names and addresses to the soldier who had spotted them. In self-defence, they disclosed the name of Friedrich von Richthofen, and so Lawrence, in all his ambiguous status, had quickly to be presented to Frieda's father. The meeting, that afternoon, was a catastrophe. Friedrich von Richthofen realized that his daughter was having an affair; he liked Weekley and the last thing he wanted was Frieda mixed up with an 'ill-bred, common, penniless lout', which was how, apparently, he referred to Lawrence.[35] When Lawrence returned to his hotel, he was told by the military authorities to leave; he was still suspected of being a spy. On Wednesday, he caught the train to Trier, eighty miles away; Frieda probably helped him out with some money, borrowed from one of her sisters.

It is clear, however, that he and Frieda had reached some kind of a decision before he went; and she had agreed to write to Weekley. Lawrence's letters from Trier were calm and optimistic, full of certainty that Weekley knew (or very soon would know) what was happening and that Frieda would be coming to join him at the weekend. His letter to Weekley, posted from Metz or from Trier, remarked confidently that 'Mrs Weekley will have told you everything'. Frieda would have liked his letter – it was almost entirely about her needs (she was 'afraid of being stunted and not allowed to grow')[36] – although she was frightened of what it might precipitate. She still did not write to Weekley herself. But Lawrence's letter was on its way.

In Trier, all Lawrence could do was go for walks around the town and wait; he drafted another essay, 'How a Spy is Arrested', for his series 'In Fortified Germany'. Frieda arrived on Friday 10th, but she had had to promise her father that she would return that night, and she brought her mother and sister Johanna as chaperones. Lawrence discovered that she had still not written to Weekley. He acted decisively: 'we were sitting under the lilacs in the garden at Trier. Oh Lord – tragedy! I took F. straight to the post-office, and she wired "ganz recent".' Her telegram and Lawrence's letter would thus both have arrived in Nottingham that Friday and Weekley may well have assumed they were meant to arrive together, with the letter supplying the name missing in the telegram. It was the climax of his 'insane' ten days. He dashed off letters to Frieda and her father for which he later apologized – 'I was really not responsible' – and he dispatched a telegram to Metz to say that the marriage was over.[37]

In Trier, Frieda and Lawrence went for a walk together and apparently had sex in a dry ditch outside the town; but that was their only consolation.[38] There then followed a farce-like sequence of losing each other and not seeing each other again before Frieda had to return to Metz. The next day, Lawrence had to go to Waldbröl for his visit to the Krenkow family, but he hoped that at last the way was clear for him and Frieda. On the journey, which took eleven hours, he drafted his first love poem to her, 'Bei Hennef', and wrote his first real love letter, on a postcard of Trier: 'Now, for the first time during today, my detachment leaves me, and I know I only love you. The rest is nothing at all. And the promise of life with you is all richness. Now I know.'[39] It had taken the events of the past eight days to make him realize that not only did he want her unbearably but, as the poem put it, 'At last I know my love for you is here.' In a letter to Garnett, he would later write: 'I *do* love her. If she left me, I do not think I should be alive six months hence. And she won't leave me, I think. God, how I love her – and the agony of it.' It wasn't until after his death that Frieda saw these letters: 'I have just wept bitterly over L's letters to Garnett & I felt I didn't deserve his love, but then how dull if I had deserved it!'[40] Realizing that he *could* love Frieda was another kind of breakthrough for Lawrence. Up until then, he had only ever been certain that he loved his mother; she had been the only person he had ever responded to without any kind of saving detachment. Ten days after her death, he had written: 'I think I loved my mother more than I ever shall love anyone else.' Now he told Frieda: 'You make me sure of myself, whole.'[41]

Frieda's family were, however, furious that she had allowed the situation to get out of hand. Her father informed her that he would never see her again if she went off with Lawrence: 'I know the world,' he told her. Weekley veered between laconic acceptance – 'I . . . hope you will be happy with him' – and hysterical threats that, if he ever saw her again, 'I would kill myself and the children too.' He also asserted that, for his parents, 'it is ten thousand times worse than death', and warned Frieda that if she did not help sort things out quickly, 'it might cost me my post here, and our children could starve'. He wrote to her mother, more coherently: 'She must understand that she has no more rights but she knows I am honourable.'[42] He probably meant that she no longer had any rights to an income, nor of access to her children – but he was not going to ruin her reputation.

All Frieda now had from Lawrence in Waldbröl were letters saying how much he loved her, but how they must wait until they could come together and begin their marriage. She would much have preferred him to rescue her, and criticized him at least once for having forced the issue, to which he responded: 'I did not do wrong in writing to Ernst.'[43] She could not bear staying with her parents, and escaped to

Munich with Else. Lawrence worked away at 'Paul Morel' in Waldbröl, an utterly remote village up in the Rhineland, which 'will always be to me a land of exile – and slow, slow cattle drawing the wagons'.[44] He wrote to Frieda regularly; five letters from Waldbröl survive, and there were probably more. The Krenkows were friendly to him, and he got on especially well with the recently married, 31-year-old Hannah, though his report that she was growing 'fonder and fonder of me' was just for Frieda's benefit, to counteract her more lurid accounts of her encounters in Metz with her old admirer Udo von Henning. The Krenkows took him on little trips, Lawrence practised his German and wrote yet another sketch for 'In Fortified Germany'.[45] But for him nothing now really mattered except rejoining Frieda. He spent just under two weeks in Waldbröl, 11–24 May, probably as brief a visit as he could manage without appearing horribly rude; and then went down to Munich.

Else was convinced that her sister was behaving foolishly. She had nothing against Lawrence, yet she found it hard to accept Frieda's failure to negotiate successfully with Weekley over money and her children. But in the village of Icking she was able to find Lawrence and Frieda a flat; usually rented by her lover Alfred Weber (brother of the famous sociologist Max Weber), this would be free for a couple of months from the start of June. While they waited to move in, Lawrence and Frieda went further up the Isar valley to another tiny village, Beuerberg, to the local inn; and here their joint life started.

It began both joyously and badly: not surprising, perhaps, after the turmoil of the last three weeks. Lawrence felt 'here's my marriage',[46] but although Frieda loved him, how could she feel the same? His poem 'First Morning' (written later) starts, boldly, 'The night was a failure / but why not – ?' and describes how 'I could not be free, / not free myself from the past, those others –'; Jessie Chambers, Alice Dax, 'Jane'? Lydia Lawrence? Weekley, too? Outdoors in Beuerberg, their daytime selves loved the place, the sheer beauty of everything; it was a dream of spring, and they took an exhilarated, childlike pleasure in it. 'All the exuberance of my childhood came back to me,'[47] Frieda recalled. But they were tormented by their links with the past, and utterly uncertain about the future. When they moved to Icking after the week's 'honeymoon' (beautiful, but even more problematic than most honeymoons), Lawrence could never be certain that Frieda would not walk out and leave him. He was deeply in love with her – 'I love her more every morning, and every night' – but 'Where it'll end, I don't know.'[48]

Meanwhile, he had to earn their living. During their first week in Icking, he finally finished revising 'Paul Morel' and sent it off to William Heinemann; throughout the rest of the month, he worked on four short stories. 'Paul Morel' had been started during his mother's final illness, and before he had even been engaged to Louie Burrows; its previous revision had marked the ending of his relationship with Jessie Chambers. Now it was the novel which he hoped would support him and Frieda, and into which she would eventually put her energies too, as mother and lover. It had originally been written by someone who felt very like Paul, derelict after his mother's death. It was now revised by a man who felt that he was at last freeing himself from the love of his mother, and who was partnered by a married and honey-skinned Clara, who was not (he hoped) going back to her husband. Paul was a tragic figure but Lawrence was becoming liberated.

Life in Icking veered constantly between the wonderful and the dreadful; dreadful because of the 'storms of letters' from England and from Frieda's relations, and because of their violent quarrels: 'the great war is waged in this little flat on the Isarthal' – 'I didn't know life was so hard,' Lawrence confessed in July. He felt guilty in particular about the pain they had caused. 'It has been rather ghastly, that part of the affair. If only one didn't hurt so many people.'[49] At one point, Frieda moved out for some days, to stay with her sister; and Weekley constantly changed his mind. He offered to divorce her, so that she could marry Lawrence; he then refused a divorce but offered a separation. At one point, he seems to have offered her a separation, a flat, her children and financial support, if she would leave Lawrence and live with her parents.[50] He told her: 'You know I would have died for you.' He also insulted her with remarks like: 'Isn't the commonest prostitute better than you?'[51]

Yet in spite of everything, Icking seemed wonderful because their joint life was so rich. In a letter to Garnett, Lawrence described Frieda 'in a scarlet pinafore, leaning out on the balcony, against a background of blue and snowy mountains' saying: 'I'm so happy I don't even want to kiss you.' For the first time, Frieda experienced Lawrence as entertainer and mimic, acting out revival meetings in the Eastwood Chapels, and being both minister and terrified congregation: he was wickedly funny. They both felt they had escaped the restraints of their old lives; they lived cheaply and simply, on less than £10 for two months. 'The lovely brooks we have paddled in, the lovely things we've done!'[52] It was a kind of long-lasting holiday, but with Lawrence also seriously employed at his writing.

Then, in July, disaster hit them. Heinemann turned 'Paul Morel' down flat. He declared it too sexual, he hated what he called the 'degradation' of Paul's mother, a sensitive woman condemned to the working class, and he thought the whole book badly structured.[53] Lawrence sent a letter of comic rage to Garnett, but undoubtedly felt hurt and worried beneath it all: 'Curse the blasted, jelly-boned swines, the slimy, the belly-wriggling invertebrates, the miserable sodding rotters, the flaming sods, the snivelling, dribbling, dithering palsied pulse-less lot that make up England today.'[54] He knew it was his best book; and it was his first to be rejected. But he was lucky. Garnett had seen the novel before and liked it; now he made many suggestions for one final revision and recommended its acceptance to Duckworth. After his initial anger, Lawrence does not seem to have been too upset, though the delay in publication was financially worrying. He may have recognized that he now wanted to include in the book something of his new experience with Frieda; not just in Paul's love for Clara, but in the ways in which mothers love their children.

The loss of her children was becoming Frieda's real agony. She refused even to consider abandoning them; and Weekley realized that they were his strongest suit. Accordingly, he ensured that she heard how the children were 'miserable, missing her so much'. At one point, he even sent a photograph of Elsa and Barby, 'with a letter saying "You will never see your children again."' Lawrence described how Frieda

lies on the floor in misery – and then is fearfully angry with me because I won't say 'stay for my sake'. I say 'decide what you want most, to live with me and share my rotten chances, or go back to security, and your children –

decide for *yourself* – Choose for yourself.' And then she almost hates me, because I won't say 'I love you – stay with me whatever happens.'[55]

Frieda never accepted that she should have to give the children up; she pursued them for the next eleven years. Lawrence's view was that, by not going back to Weekley, she had elected to stay with him, and must accept the consequences. But for the people involved, logic was impossible; they experienced the most fearful pain and anger. The quarrels over the children went on and on: 'we nearly murder each other.'[56] One reason would be that Lawrence was simply jealous; but that is only partially true. The more Frieda was compelled to make an exclusive choice between him and her children, the more her regrets seemed to Lawrence regrets about the choice she had made. He also felt he knew so much about mother love that he could not stand back and watch his partner desperately clinging to her children. But at bottom, he resented the children because he believed his partnership with Frieda had led them to break away from their old selves. Frieda also acknowledged this: 'He seemed to have lifted me body and soul out of all my past life . . . I only wanted to revel in this new world Lawrence had given me.' Every time Frieda returned to the subject of her children, she seemed to Lawrence to be betraying his idealism for their life together. It attacked the core of his belief, and he raged against her.[57]

At the beginning of August, they had to give up the Icking flat; Lawrence had managed to complete seventy pages of the new version of the novel, and put the manuscript in his knapsack. He and Frieda had reached another turning point in their relationship. It was Else who had suggested that they might go to Italy, where living was cheap. Lawrence asserted that 'I have at last nailed F.'s nose to my wagon', but immediately qualified his own confidence: 'At last, I think, she can't leave me.'[58] They sent their belongings ahead to the Austrian border at Kufstein and before dawn on Monday 5 August, carrying knapsacks and a little cooking stove, and with '£23 between us' (some more of his poems had been published),[59] they set off on what turned out to be the great adventure of their early life together.

A combination of walking and trains took them through the rain and past the wayside crucifixes of southern Bavaria to Bad Tölz: the crucifixes offered Lawrence a subject for his essay 'Crucifixes Among the Mountains'. On the second day, they climbed high up into the border country between Bavaria and Austria. But as evening came on, a short cut went both disastrously wrong and marvellously right: they ended up at nightfall with a choice between a hay-hut and a tiny wooden chapel (the size of a small shed) to sleep in. Lawrence preferred the chapel, with its candles and dry wooden floor; but Frieda had always wanted to sleep in a hay-hut. So they did, with anything precious wrapped up in Lawrence's waistcoat for safety. They tossed and turned all night, and in the morning found that snow had almost come down to their level. Another five miles walking and scrambling in the rain brought them down to a house in Glashütte, where they took a room, dried their clothes and slept until mid afternoon. Lawrence probably also began to write about the journey.[60] The rain was now pouring down again, which persuaded them to take a horse-drawn post-omnibus across the Austrian border and on to the Achensee, under dark mountains shrouded in mist, where their bedraggled appearance would have barred them from the hotel; they went to a cheaper farmhouse. On Thursday, they recovered their suitcases from the customs at Kufstein, fifteen miles up the Inn valley, and slept there; having sent the luggage on to Mayrhofen, a further day's walking and a train journey got them safely there by Friday night. Here, in 'a farmhouse at the foot of the mountains, just by a lovely stream, that tears along, and is as bright as glass', they took a room for a couple of weeks. Lawrence wrote, they recovered, and spent their days walking and exploring: 'we *can* be happy, nobody knows how happy.'[61]

After a week, they were joined by English acquaintances: Garnett's twenty-year-old science student son, David, known as Bunny (who had enjoyed their company briefly in Icking), and a friend of his, the 21-year-old Harold Hobson. Life continued to be exhilarating: 'we are fearfully happy together,' wrote Lawrence, and Bunny confirmed that 'I never saw him so well or so happy, so consistently gay and light-hearted as he was then'.[62] Suitcases were again dispatched, to Bozen (Bolzano now, but at that time in the Austrian Tyrol), and the four of them set out to walk over the Pfitscherjoch pass. They spent one night in a hay-hut near Ginzling, this time under the tutelage of Bunny, the outdoor expert, and a second night at the 'Dominicus-

Hütte', then on the third day walked over the pass and down the far side into the Pfitscher valley, to the Gasthof Elefant. These days of hard walking with the two young men were exhausting, and on the fourth day (a Thursday) Lawrence and Frieda stayed in bed and only later ambled down to Sterzing, after Bunny and Hobson had walked on before dawn to catch a train back north.

They never recovered quite the same joy in things after this. Sterzing was dull; and when they set off again, on Sunday morning, Lawrence badly miscalculated how long it would take them to walk up to the mountain hut on the Jaufen pass. They ended up exhausted, after eight hours of walking uphill, with night falling, a bitter wind, and great steep slopes ahead. It was apparently at this point that Frieda told Lawrence that she had had sex with Hobson some days earlier, while Lawrence had been off with Bunny looking for alpine plants. 'He had me in the hay-hut – he told me he wanted me so badly – '63 She was asserting to Lawrence (and to herself) that she was not giving up her independence, despite making a new life with him, though it would also have been her 'free love' way of helping a troubled young man. But as Lawrence had written to Weekley, only three months earlier, 'Mrs Weekley must live largely and abundantly. It is her nature.'64 If Lawrence wanted her, then he had to accept that she would not always stay faithful; and she did not.

Frieda's announcement would at least have stopped Lawrence in his tracks, and let her pause for breath. Lawrence bottled up his misery over it, which was characteristic of him too (he would later comment: 'Harold is no gentleman').65 They arrived at their destination after dark, imagining, as they had come over a ridge and then walked down to the Jaufen-Haus, that they had crossed the pass. The following morning, seeing the road winding away down into the valley, they assumed that this was their route to Meran and Italy, and happily followed it all day; only to end up, at four in the afternoon, walking back into Sterzing. Lawrence, map-reader and organizer, would have been extremely angry with himself; Gilbert Noon, in an identical situation, feels 'shame and ignominy'.66 They were, literally, getting nowhere, and Lawrence could not resist Frieda's demand that they spend some of their dwindling supply of money on a train. They went straight to Bozen, but an unpleasant night's lodging there propelled them still further south, again by train, to Trento. They bought an Italian dictionary and tried with its aid to find lodgings; but in stained, torn and creased clothes, Lawrence's trouser ends frayed, Frieda's panama hat streaked with dye from its ribbon, they were offered nothing except filthy rooms and had doors slammed in their faces.[67] Frieda ended up in floods of tears in the Piazza di Dante, by the station. On an impulse, they took the train to Riva; a poster showed a picture of the Lago di Garda, which from the start they had considered a possible destination.

This was the warm south they had been looking for. They rented a room in a house belonging to two old ladies, and waited for their luggage to arrive, so as to dress presentably again. They were desperately short of money, having exactly one English pound unspent, but then £50 in cash for *The Trespasser* arrived: Garnett had organized an advance. The novel had had fewer reviews than *The White Peacock*, and at least two had been addressed to its sexual explicitness, one reviewer referring to a 'nakedness of physical detail that is almost morbid in its ugliness'.[68] But all that mattered now was the cash it brought in. Lawrence started work on 'Paul Morel', a sign that he had become what he once called 'sufficiently inrooted'. They stayed in Riva for only a fortnight: their lovely room cost too much. But further down the lake they found Gargnano, over the Italian border, and a flat in the Villa Igea looking over the lake, 'dark blue, purple, and clear as a jewel'. Life improved in other ways: Frieda's sister Johanna sent some fashionable hats and a dress; her mother dispatched sheets and towels.[69] At the Hotel Cervo in Gargnano, the hotelkeeper's wife was German and could offer Frieda some company. All Lawrence had was Frieda and his writing, but he wanted nothing more.

9

Sons and Lovers and Marriage:
1912–1914

In the course of the next two months in Gargnano, with Frieda listening to him read the book aloud – 'we fight like blazes over it' – Lawrence transformed 'Paul Morel' into *Sons and Lovers* in one of his great bursts of creative energy. Such creativity made Frieda feel in October that 'though I am never *quite* sure whether I love or hate L, I only know I would rather die then do without him and his life along of mine'.[1] For the first time, he presented both the Morel sons as damaged by their relationship with their mother: interesting, this, for a writer living with a woman increasingly desperate to be with her children. For the first time, too, he explored the catastrophe of Paul's sexual relationship with Miriam, and described the death of Mrs Morel in all its slow horror. This was a necessary step: the poems he had written after his own mother's death had been rigidly locked into love and suffering. Frieda had scribbled on one, in his poetry notebook, 'I hate it/I hate it/Good God!!!!'[2] *Sons and Lovers* sets the death in the context of what happens to the son, and thus attempts to lay to rest one of Lawrence's alternative lives. There, but for Frieda, he might have gone, in subjection to his old love; a love which he continued to worry about all his life, because he had repudiated it. The new understanding had its limits, however. A letter describes drinking at Bogliaco, the next village down the lake, in 'the living room of the house'. The father there, 'his shirt sleeves rolled up and his shirt collar open', 'nods and "click-clicks" to the small baby, that the mother, young and proud, is feeding with soup from a big spoon. The grand-father, white moustached, sits a bit effaced by the father. A little girl eats soup. The grandmother by the big, open fire sits and quietly scolds another little girl.' This working-class family reminded Lawrence 'so of home when I was a boy. They are all so warm with life.'[3] But only at times did he allow this kind of feeling into a novel that had always centred on Mrs Morel and her ambitions. The moral condemnation of Mr Morel and his world was, nevertheless, one of the things that started to grow problematic in this version. Above all, in writing the novel – it felt 'slow like growth'[4] – Lawrence was attempting to write a new self into existence, as he would always do in his major fiction.

He took only one break from rewriting the novel and, in three days, managed to write *The Fight for Barbara*, a play about an unmarried couple in Italy who are confronted by the woman's parents and her abandoned husband. At the end, Barbara agrees to stay with Jimmy Wesson, but it has been a very close thing. By the time Lawrence and Frieda had reached Gargnano, they were exhilarated at sharing the same adventure; but Frieda, with more time to reflect, pined for her children, now further off than ever. She and Lawrence had only each other to turn to; after some friendly feelings towards Weekley in mid September – describing the beauty of the Lago di Garda, she felt sad that he 'cannot see all this, because he has so much feeling for nature'[5] – they both felt horribly pressurized. 'Letters would come. The harm we had done, my grief for my children would return red hot'; 'Weekley threatens us alternately with murder and with suicide (the latter his own). I always expect a streak of greased lightning to fly out when we open an envelope from him.'[6] Lawrence was, as ever, a brilliant mimic and comedian: his tone in that letter suggests one of his ways of resisting the pressure, and *The Fight for Barbara*, which he dispatched full of optimism to Garnett, was another. But the horrible unhappiness of all parties continued. Barby later summed up the effect on Weekley of Frieda's departure: 'It was a mortal blow to my father; he never recovered. He was a remarkable, kindly man, a man of the world, but where Frieda was concerned he was like a mediæval Italian, very unforgiving. He was the cuckold, he felt it very much.'[7] And Lawrence and Frieda, with their constant arguing, put each other under dreadful stress. They had done their best to escape from the past: so why did they still torment each other so much? Frieda recalled how, during the last winter of his life, eighteen years later, Lawrence was still worrying 'that we had quarrelled so, and I had to console him and tell him, as we were with our characters it couldn't be helped'.[8]

It was not just character. One reason was that their relationship was, as Frieda confessed, 'Not a sort of love affair', in which individuals lovingly sacrifice their rights and independence; nor was it a 'grand passion' of mutual dependence. It began as 'just an affair', thought Frieda, which grew into a desire to share 'all that life had to offer':[9] both remaining independent, both determined to live their own lives. Lawrence described Frieda reading Tolstoy's *Anna Karenina* in October 1912 'in a sort of "How to be happy though livanted" spirit'; she sent the book to Weekley when she had finished it, to show him why Anna abandons her husband for a lover. She forgot, however, that she had slipped into it the note which William Dowson, her first lover, had sent her on hearing that she had left Weekley: 'If you wanted to run away with someone, why didn't you run away with me?' Weekley forwarded the note to Lawrence.[10]

The battle in Gargnano was about the children, but it was also about self-sacrifice and independence. Weekley had offered Frieda what her mother and sisters had been angling for from the start – a flat of her own, in London, and access to her children – but she had to give up Lawrence. Frieda's sister Else told Lawrence he was a hero, but one who should now stand aside: Frieda must accept Weekley's offer. Lawrence's counter-argument was that Frieda's self-sacrifice, in giving him up, would be thoroughly bad for her children: 'They would not be free to live of themselves – they would first have to live *for her*, to pay back.'[11] And if Lawrence stepped gracefully aside, he would be sacrificing himself. But if Frieda did not take up Weekley's offer, would she not then be sacrificing her own independence? She ended up believing that she could stay with Lawrence but would all the same manage to see her children in England in the spring, and somehow thereafter.

Living with Frieda, Lawrence had grown to hate being self-sacrificial in love: he wanted love (or was it independence?) in which he did not feel given up or sacrificed but, on the contrary, revivified and reaffirmed. Frieda had regularly complained that he couldn't love, that he was too self-contained. She wrote in his poetry notebook: 'I have nearly killed myself in the battle to get you into connection with myself and other people, sadly I proved to my self that *I* can love, but *never* you.'[12] That got under his skin; he knew how near the truth it was.

Nevertheless, he was doing his best to change. Italy and Frieda were not just breaking down some of his old intellectual reserve, but freeing him in more profound ways. He noted, of the Italians: 'They haven't learnt not to be themselves yet.'[13] He had learned such self-control all too thoroughly, and now wanted to unlearn it. He was starting to write about what his upbringing had most deprived him of: any realization of his sensuality and its needs; any possibility of loving anyone except his mother. And he started to recognize how 'so damnably violent, really, and self destructive' he was; he had always bottled up what he called his 'rages of trouble'. He had, for example, only just realized how much he had loathed 'the Jones ménage' in Croydon: 'I am just learning – thanks to Frieda – to let go a bit.'[14] At the same time, Gargnano, an immeasurably alien place, offered neither of them any escape: 'always just us two and we live so hard on each other'. And this demanded of them a kind of practical exposure to the problem of being together, yet remaining independent, with, all the time, what Lawrence called 'this drawn sword of the children between us . . . We have both of us got some pretty bad – half healed – cuts from it.'[15]

Though it set the pattern for the rest of their life together, partnership in a foreign land was exhausting and often intensely lonely. Lawrence told Garnett in December how 'I'm dead tired inside – fit to drop. It's just the strain of resisting, of seven months resistance.' Christmas-time was the nadir for Frieda: no presents, nothing from or for her children, while 'I was ignored by all my friends, the outcast'.[16] At some stage during these months in Gargnano, she had a fantasy of drowning herself in the lake; she may even have attempted it. They had a visitor or two; surprisingly, Harold Hobson turned up in December. His self-confidence had always been thick-skinned. Lawrence did not much like it, but felt he could just about 'trust H. as my friend now'.[17] And in the spring came Antonia Almgren, a friend of Bunny Garnett, on the run from her husband.

And so their six months in this far-flung outpost went by, the novels sent on by friends for Frieda – 'a cormorant of novels' – being 'Almost our only connection with outer life!'[18] For Lawrence as a writer, however, those months were incredibly important. He had finished *Sons and Lovers* in mid November and sent it off to Garnett; another part of his and Frieda's joint future was thus financed. Garnett's rather angry criticism that the book was still far too long, and that he would shorten it, made Lawrence 'wither up',[19] but Garnett was the one person he would have trusted to do the job. What mattered was that the novel would be published and might make Lawrence's name. It received the dedication: 'To Edward Garnett'. Without him, neither the novel nor Lawrence's career would have had any chance.

Lawrence had also, for the first time, begun to work out, in letters and in experimental prose such as his 'Foreword' to *Sons and Lovers*, the things in which he believed. 'My great religion is a belief in the blood, the flesh, as being wiser than the intellect,' he wrote to the English writer and artist Ernest Collings, in January 1913.[20] That was perhaps implicit in the recently finished *Sons and Lovers*, but it is important that, at such a moment, he should have arrived at a formulation which encapsulated his major realization of these years: an understanding of himself and his world, not just a reaction to it. It was part of his project to change himself. He went on: 'We can go wrong in our minds. But what our blood feels and believes and says, is always true. The intellect is only a bit and a bridle. What do I care about knowledge. All I want is to answer to my blood, direct, without fribbling intervention of mind, or moral, or what not.' And he concluded: 'The real way of living is to answer to one's wants.'[21] This was what he felt he could learn from Frieda; it was something he very much *wanted* to learn, which was why he wrote at such length about it. It was inimical to his habitual carefulness and detached intelligence; both by nature and by upbringing he was, as he complained the English always were, 'ridiculously mindful'.[22] But he very much wanted to be a new kind of self. He would write about this for the rest of his life, and would regularly insist on its importance; he would endeavour to transform himself through his writing and (ideally) transform his reader too. But though he had broken away from his past, he remained an outsider to the middle-class world. For a securely middle-class person like Bunny Garnett, Lawrence remained 'the type who provokes the most violent class-hatred in this country: the impotent hatred of the upper classes for the lower'.[23] As a permanent stranger, Lawrence would find himself bringing his new gospel of the body, the blood and the feelings into polite drawing rooms, for politer readers: and being hated and resented for it. Three years later, he would claim that this 'religion' was what he had believed when he 'was about twenty',[24] but he had only dared make it an article of faith after meeting Frieda.

The money from *The Trespasser* would have confirmed that writing novels still offered the best chance of financing his career, and during the winter of 1912–13 Lawrence started no fewer than three which he then abandoned. In February 1913, he wrote to Garnett: 'I hope to God I shall be able to make a living – but there, one must.' His best prospect was a new novel called 'The Sisters', begun in despair as a 'pot-boiler' because the novel of which he had written over two hundred pages ('The Insurrection of Miss Houghton') turned out too sexual in content to be publishable.[25] Over the next four years, the pot-boiler proved to be a kind of ur-text which, repeatedly reconceived, became *The Rainbow* and *Women in Love*. Lawrence had also written some sketches of Italian life which would become his first travel book, *Twilight in Italy*; and in January 1913 he wrote his best play, *The Daughter-in-Law*, wholly in the Notts-Derby dialect of his youth, and a kind of savage commentary on the mother and son in *Sons and Lovers*. As such, he believed it was 'neither a comedy nor a tragedy – just ordinary'. Duckworth had published his first book of poetry, too, *Love Poems*: the poet, critic and travel-writer Edward Thomas gave it a good review but remarked that 'Mr. Lawrence sacrifices everything to intensity, particularly in amorousness'. Frieda had not much liked it – it contained 'too many heroines other than herself'[26] – but it represented another kind of farewell to the past. And he had made contact with the editors of the magazine *Rhythm* who, though they could not afford to pay, accepted a review and a short story.

After months in Gargnano, Lawrence and Frieda had no desire to live anywhere quite so remote again. He had always had his writing, which, although she admired it, could also get on Frieda's nerves: 'he goes on working and it's simply ghastly; he becomes a writing machine, that works itself out, it made me quite frantic.' She would think of him as a 'a big fountain pen which was always sucking at her blood for ink'.[27] What mattered even more to her, however, was that Weekley had suddenly gone back on all his previous offers. His new position was: 'I have done with you, I want to forget you and you must be dead to the children. You know the law is on my side.' Frieda was desperate. One of Weekley's sisters came out to Italy in January to gather evidence for the divorce Weekley had decided to obtain; it is possible that Lawrence and Frieda did not know she was there but more likely that they collaborated with her need to see them together.[28]

In late March, to get away from the Villa Igea, Frieda and Lawrence went for ten days to a farm up above the lake, at San Gaudenzio. They loved the company, the dancing and the household, although even here Lawrence went on writing, perched in the high and sunny lemon-house, looking out over the lake; it was one of those places that he loved. From there they went to Verona to meet Else, then back to Germany, south of Munich, to stay in yet another of the Jaffe houses, a little wooden one this time, in a corner of a pine forest at Irschenhausen, and again with a marvellous view down to the river Isar. Here, where they hardly meant to stay more than a few days, Lawrence was strikingly productive. He finished the first draft of his 'Sisters' novel – 'it is *the* problem of today, the establishment of a new relation, or the re-adjustment of the old one, between men and women'[29] – and wrote three stories, including 'New Eve and Old Adam', which gives a sense of what this stage of his relationship with Frieda was like. There is constant tension and argument: the woman wants a 'simple, warm man who would love me without all these reservations and difficulties', the man feels that he 'loved her' but that 'it would never be peace between them'.[30] He also wrote the extraordinary story published as 'The Prussian Officer', in which the instinctive self-possession of an army officer's young orderly is breached by the bullying and jealousy of his superior. The boy kills his assailant, only to find himself not liberated but psychically destroyed. Lawrence was exploring the fearful consequences for the instinctive self when forced into self-consciousness: precisely the opposite of the process he himself was engaged in, but very near the bone in the way it explored the central subjects of his life and writing.

Their quarrels about the children continued. Frieda was determined to return to England in the summer, to make contact with her children 'by hook or crook – chiefly by crook', as Lawrence put it, but she felt she had no choice. Lawrence confessed that he had to let Frieda choose 'her own way', and 'that includes my being there'. Yet 'the trouble about the children has knocked us both a bit loose at the joints'. Frieda smashed a plate over his head during one row; she also went to stay with Else at her house in Wolfratshausen.[31] What would contact with the children mean for their relationship, for the kinds of new start that they had given each other? And how would the children react, after a year of being told by their aunt and grandparents that their mother did not love them? 'She-who-was-Frieda' was probably the phrase used about her in the Weekley household of grandparents, aunts, uncles and children now brought together in Chiswick, just outside London. The children would have heard it, either now or later.[32] Lawrence was thoroughly apprehensive about returning to England, but he would not let Frieda go alone.

Other things were also going awry at Irschenhausen. Jessie Chambers had been one of the few people who knew that Lawrence had gone abroad with Frieda; he had told her 'to leave her a chance of ridding herself of my influence'.[33] He had recently sent her a set of proofs for *Sons and Lovers*; it would not be fair to publish a fictional account of their sexual relationship without telling her. She reacted violently and sent his letter back. This made him unhappy, but he could cope with it: 'God bless her, she always looked down on me – spiritually . . . And look, she is bitterly ashamed of having had me – as if I had dragged her spiritual plumage in the mud. Call that love! Ah well.' But then she sent, via Garnett, a fictional account of her time with Lawrence; she called it *The Rathe Primrose*, from Milton: 'the rathe [early] primrose that forsaken dies'. Lawrence grew 'so miserable I had hardly the energy to walk out of the house for two days'.[34] Even Frieda was now aware of what she called 'the amazing brutality of *Sons and Lovers*'. Lawrence would remark, fifteen years later: 'You have to have something vicious in you to be a creative writer.' To a friend in 1916 he would describe how – 'to be a real writer or artist or recorder' – the artist needed to be 'so intrinsically detached, so essentially isolated and separated, as . . . to remain intact, *essentially*, whatever your experiences may be'.[35] The fact that he could not feel detached from Jessie Chambers indicates one of the points at which convenient theory collided with awkward fact.

While not keen on going to England, Lawrence did want to attend his sister Ada's wedding in Eastwood at the start of August, although he and the socially unacceptable Frieda could not go together: 'We shan't be able to see folks much in England. I *do* feel cut off from my past life – like re-incarnation.' But it would make sense to sort out his literary affairs, in particular the publication of his essays and short stories; the fact that he had not been in London to look after his career, and still had no literary agent, had a good deal to do with the continuing limitation of his appeal. The thought, too, of being at the Cearne again 'fills my heart with relief'.[36] On 17 June 1913, he and Frieda set off: Lawrence coming back to England as the author of Sons and Lovers, which had been published on 29 May; Frieda coming back as a mother, to reclaim her children.

Garnett was mostly in London, but the Cearne was the only house in England where they could be welcomed as a couple; even the Hopkin family in Eastwood were asked only to put *him* up. On arrival, Lawrence helped Constance Garnett with netting the raspberries; she found him 'full of bonhomie & genuine friendliness & kindness'.[37] But now they had arrived in England, he and Frieda quarrelled worse than ever. Their ferocity left Constance feeling it was pointless for them even to try to continue their relationship: she advised Lawrence to leave Frieda 'before he makes things too hard for her'. It would be this kind of comment which made Lawrence eventually certain that 'I don't like Mrs G.'. But it must have been hard for her suddenly to receive this violently warring couple into a house dedicated to her quiet translating and Bunny's exam revision; Lawrence reassured Garnett that 'we are trying to be good for David and his exam'.[38]

The quarrelling, though now habitual, was in part their response to a cruel situation. Frieda insisted, even in a forgiving old age, that Lawrence had 'a very nasty temper'; she meant that, like his father, he fired up quickly, sometimes for very little reason. In 1913, there were reasons enough. But Frieda increasingly found him unwilling to sympathize with her suffering: this in spite of the fact that her separation from her children was (Bunny felt) 'as painful to watch as an animal in a trap'.[39] From Lawrence's point of view, with Frieda now waiting for her divorce, the decision about the custody of her children could only go still more decisively against her if she were to upset things. He would perhaps not have come back to England at all, to witness her painful pursuit of the children, had he not been, as Frieda rejoiced, unable to 'bear to be away from me, hardly for hours'. But his very dependence on Frieda would also have troubled him. An entry in Constance's diary reveals what he told her: 'his love is of the permanent sort – and that it's all that F. only *half* loves him – but he'll make her love him altogether.'[40] This suggests that Lawrence's quarrel with Frieda was not really about the children but another development of his insistence that their love must be open, honest, total. It would have been much easier for him simply to capitulate and support her in her silliness, as he probably saw it, over the children. Instead, he argued with her, and at times helped, and at other times refused to help her, all because he loved her.

They went to London together on Thursday 26 June, met Bunny in South Kensington around 3 p.m. and then, while Lawrence went to have his photograph taken in High Holborn, Bunny did what he could to help Frieda – 'hanging round St Paul's School in the hope that she could intercept her son and see him for a moment or two' (Monty was actually at Colet Court School in West Kensington, the preparatory school for St Paul's).[41] This reconnoitre was preliminary to Frieda going back four days later – Lawrence with her this time, staying in the background – and managing to talk to Monty; she asked him to try and bring his sisters to meet her the following day. She also gave him money and a letter. The consequences were dreadful. The money was discovered and sent back; Monty was made to confess what he had been doing, and Frieda's letter was found. Weekley's sister Maude, in charge of the Chiswick household, told Weekley, who applied for and by the end of July obtained a court order against Frieda which restrained her 'from interfering or attempting to interfere with the said children'.[42] He also sent Frieda a 'hideous' letter via her mother, telling her that she was no longer just 'dead to the children' but, so far as they were concerned, a 'verfaulte Leiche' (a decomposed corpse).[43] As a direct result of what Frieda had done, he was awarded legal custody of the children, months before the divorce proceedings. Frieda had, in effect, lost her children because of her attempts to see them, though she did not yet know this.

Back at the Cearne, Lawrence went on making himself useful, in spite of the fact that he and Frieda 'quarrelled just as arduously as ever'.[44] It would have been in yet another attempt to assert her independence from him, as well as to show Bunny her gratitude, that, one hot and sleepy afternoon in the woods above the Cearne, Frieda (according to Bunny in old age) 'suggested that we should make love'. He did not respond, although he would have liked to have done so; he believed, probably rightly, that 'Frieda was far too outspoken to keep her mouth shut'.[45] Illustration 15 shows the Lawrence whom Bunny might have betrayed, in one of the photographs taken on 26 June by W. G. Parker so that Lawrence could supply a picture to newspapers.[46] Lawrence appears vividly alert – and Bunny responded to that: 'once you looked into his eyes you were completely charmed, they were so beautiful and alive, dancing with gaiety. His smile lit up all his face as he looked at you, asking you silently: "Come on . . . let's have some fun," and the invitation of this look was irresistible, at least to me.' People saw a 'broad, jutting brow, and clear, sensitive, extremely blue eyes – very wide apart': his moustache was red, his hair rich brown, his complexion very pale.[47]

Frieda, ignorant of the impending court order, must have felt that she had proved to Lawrence that she *could* establish contact, of a kind at least, with her children. The time had been useful in other ways too. Their most significant new encounter, on the London visits, had been with the editors of the magazine *Rhythm*, who turned out to be another unmarried couple: the 24-year-old journalist and critic John Middleton Murry and the New Zealand writer Katherine Mansfield, a year older than Murry, who had a growing reputation for her short stories. The two couples got on well from the start: 'We rode in a bus to have lunch together in Soho, and Frieda was surprised and delighted to catch Katherine and me making faces at one another. For Lawrence and she had formed the curious idea that we were wealthy and important people.'[48] Katherine sympathized with Frieda; she met Monty once, and went fruitlessly to Colet Court by herself on at least two other occasions. Murry was lower middle class, a scholarship boy and Oxford educated, but had given up his degree for the sake of writing and publishing. Lawrence had lived an extremely lonely existence over the last fifteen months; only Edward Garnett had really been a trusted friend, and Lawrence immediately turned to Murry as a man who seemed responsive, was attractive and charming, and whom in his own way he could help: his first surviving letter to Murry is full of good advice. Murry, intellectual and inhibited, was deeply impressed by Lawrence's intuition and understanding: 'I was quite unprepared for such an immediacy of contact.'[49]

Lawrence had originally promised that they would not stop at the Cearne longer than a fortnight, and they had been there three weeks, while making these visits to London. On 9 July, they went to the seaside, to rooms in Kingsgate, in Kent, where they made Katherine and Murry promise to come and visit them. Kingsgate was just along the coast from Margate, which Frieda remembered from her time with Weekley; she would write to Frieda Gross in September: 'Think, I was in *Margate*, could not help dwelling on the time when I was there with Ernst and the children – I miss the latter so much, it takes so much strength and it is also so hard for L.'[50] Lawrence wanted to stay put and do some work. He was revising and getting typed some of the short stories he had been writing over the past two years, and Garnett was still advising him what to try to publish and where, though one story was forwarded to the agent J. B. Pinker to place – 'If you succeed with this, there will be others to follow.'[51] Garnett was trying to put Lawrence's career on a securer footing; a literary agent might therefore be advisable.

Lawrence was depressed when they got to Kingsgate: 'I do not belong to it at all, at all.'[52] There is no way of establishing exactly why he felt like this, or why now, or why in Kingsgate, though his feelings may be reflected in 'The Shadow in the Rose Garden', one of the short stories he was rewriting. A newly married couple go on holiday to the seaside, to a place where the woman is acutely conscious of a sexual relationship that she had once had there. The new husband finds out about it; as Lawrence revised the story's ending, 'he had nothing to do with her'.[53] Lawrence may well have found galling Frieda's joyous memories of Margate five years earlier: 'so beautiful here, so really beautiful, the days by the sea, in the sea, on the sea, near the sea'.[54] What did he have to do with *her*?

Lawrence must have been acutely aware of being cut off from his past. His family, with the exception of Ada, must have wondered why, having been away for so long, he was not going to see them; he did not visit George Neville; and there were quite a lot of his old acquaintance he positively did not want to see (Jessie, Louie, Alice, Helen: he asked the Hopkins not to tell Alice that he would be coming to Ada's wedding).[55] He had still seen almost no one from 'the old days' in Croydon and London: not the Joneses, nor Arthur McLeod nor Agnes Mason nor Philip Smith, not Hueffer nor Violet Hunt nor Walter de la Mare. And what was for him in elegant Kingsgate, with its 'babies and papas'?[56] He had neither money, children nor middle-class ambitions.

New friends were therefore important, with Frieda 'dwelling' on the past and needing to leave it behind, and Lawrence badly wanting 'people'. He had been sent money for a poem included in Edward Marsh's second *Georgian Poetry* anthology; Marsh, who worked as Winston Churchill's private secretary at the Admiralty, was a dapper figure who combined the life of a man-about-town with sympathy and practical help for the work of young poets and artists like Katherine and Murry. Lawrence found, astonishingly, that Marsh was coming down to see friends in Kingsgate that weekend. Marsh was promptly invited to tea but, when he arrived, insisted that Lawrence and Frieda come and meet his friends Beb and Cynthia Asquith; he thought they might like each other. This contact delighted Frieda. Beb was the second son of the Prime Minister and Cynthia the daughter of Lord Elcho (she would become Lady Cynthia shortly); and they were living at the end of the Lawrences' road! Lawrence and Frieda went to tea, their marital status concealed. Frieda was gratified at meeting a genuine English aristocrat – 'I too am a "success"' – and she also quickly learned the difference between Kingsgate, in superior Broadstairs, and the 'really too dreadful' Margate. But they were both 'a tremendous success',[57] and they subsequently spent quite a lot of time with Cynthia, with whom they got on extremely well. That was some compensation at least.

They had been sad that Katherine and Murry had not come down the same Sunday as Marsh; but Marsh explained that they were desperately hard up, overturning Lawrence and Frieda's assumption that people running a magazine must have money. Lawrence sent advice to Murry and (ingeniously) a sovereign to Katherine, for her to give half the money to Monty if she could catch him at school, while the rest would subsidize a visit to Kingsgate.[58] They came the next weekend, along with Murry's barrister friend Gordon Campbell, and once again they all got on wonderfully with each other: 'We bathed together in the dusky evening, and feasted sumptuously on beefsteak and tomatoes.' Murry said he and Katherine first experienced the Lawrences' 'desperate quarrels' the following year, in October 1914, which suggests that an 'armistice' Lawrence mentioned on 13 July was still holding.[59]

Frieda summed up their time in Kent: 'It has been good for L. that we came to England, money and people etc.'[60] The fact that *Sons and Lovers* had been getting some excellent reviews would have helped; the only problem was that reviewers were starting to categorize Lawrence as a sexual specialist. Ethel Colburn Mayne in the *Nation*, for example, had criticized the 'incessant scenes of sexual passion' and 'this morbid brooding on the flesh', while Lawrence recognized that the refusal of the libraries to take the book (they had been put off by what one reviewer referred to as its 'offences against reticence') had serious implications for him. 'The damned prigs in the libraries and bookshops daren't handle me . . .'[61]

It was during their time in Kent that Frieda began to find out what a hornet's nest she had stirred up in the Weekley family. She received Weekley's 'hideous' letter; and Monty refused to respond to Katherine when the latter went to see him with Lawrence's money: 'he sent word by another boy "that he was not to talk to people who came to the school to see him".' Frieda was agonized: 'it is as if living pieces of flesh were being torn out of one.'[62] They returned to London for a couple of days to stay with Gordon Campbell, who had a house in Selwood Terrace, Kensington, not far from Monty's school. It is possible that by now Frieda had heard of the restraining order, which would probably have been served on her while she was at the Cearne. Campbell, a lawyer, would have left her in no doubt about its meaning; she later told him how 'I used to think you beastly unsympathetic, you said such commonsense hard things'.[63] But she had to accept that nothing would be gained by her staying longer. On Thursday 31 July, she set off for Bavaria to visit her parents, who were staying with Else; she had not seen her father since leaving Metz fifteen months earlier. It was probably a good idea for her to see him while accompanied by other members of the family. Lawrence remained in England to be at his sister Ada's wedding in Eastwood at the start of August.

After an often painful but reasonably productive and financially rewarding summer (one newly revised and typed story published in August, three Italian sketches and two more stories in September, and another couple of stories accepted but not yet published), Lawrence and Frieda met up in Irschenhausen on 9 August. Here Lawrence wrote the first hundred pages of a revised second version of 'The Sisters' before, in mid September, they set off again, Lawrence hoping that Frieda was 'getting better of her trouble about the children, for the time being, at least'.[64] Again they separated for a week; Frieda went to her parents, now in Baden-Baden (she went alone, just as Lawrence had gone alone to *his* family), while Lawrence embarked on another of those mountain walks that could be written up as travel sketches, this time over the Swiss Alps. They met in Basel and went by train to meet Else's husband, Edgar Jaffe, who was holidaying with his mistress in Lerici on the northwest Italian coast, on the gulf of Spezia. They loved the place, and found a cottage almost on the beach in the nearby fishing hamlet of Fiascherino; here they settled for their second period in Italy.

But Frieda was worried about Lawrence. She told Else, late in September or early in October, that 'he is simply helpless without me, when I am not there you must take care of him, really you must, he simply becomes thoroughly melancholy'. This was the kind of admission that Lawrence himself very rarely made. In general, he would simply say from time to time – as, for example, in March 1913 – that 'I feel about as cheerful as Watts' *Hope*' (a notoriously gloomy picture), whereas Frieda spelled it out: 'He *has* got the humpiest hump, O Gawd! I am a heroic person, to stand him day for day.' She had been relieved to hear from Ada that he had always suffered such moods: 'I thought it was my fault!'[65] Early in July, he had admitted to a new acquaintance, Henry Savage, that he was 'a sad dog myself, pretty often. But then again, I'm not'; though when he got to Kingsgate a few days later, he was '*thoroughly* miserable'.[66]

There seems no particular reason for him to have become depressed in September 1913, though his walk through Switzerland had been very driven: Frieda thought he 'had walked himself thin, like a pencil-stub'.[67] The narrator of 'The Return Journey' in *Twilight in Italy*, encountering a Londoner, is shocked that the man, 'sick with fatigue', has 'done over a hundred miles in the last four days'.[68] Lawrence himself had walked rather further. He didn't like Switzerland, he said; on his own, he would have found the language especially hard to cope with. Frieda happily saw herself as indispensable, because Lawrence had been depressed but on her return stopped being so. But the problem was profounder than that. Lawrence unburdened himself to Murry on 30 September. Not only did he confess to having been 'acutely unhappy', but continued, 'I seem to have a bent that way – I am a fool',[69] though the rest of the letter is cheerful enough. A comment he had made to Savage, in July, is apposite. Hearing that Savage was temporarily engaged in the hotel business, Lawrence commented: 'I envy you . . . So many types with whom one is always in contact. I'd like to have a pub myself.'[70] Being *out* of contact, just ferociously dedicated to fighting his own battles, was something to which he had always been prone. Frieda saw it the same way; she felt she was struggling to get him 'into connection with myself and other people',[71] and this was a problem which did not go away. His writing both established contact and separated him: that was its paradox.

Yet it is also true that his admission of unhappiness – and of his 'bent' for it – was a sign that he was increasingly prepared to acknowledge feelings which previously he would have concealed or refused to admit. In *Mr Noon*, written eight years later, Gilbert feels that one result of living with Johanna is that his 'old, closed, more-or-less self-sufficient heart had been broken open'.[72] The same was true of Lawrence during these first years with Frieda. He was not just broken open, but exposed as needy, too. The very project of change on which Lawrence was embarked would leave him feeling vulnerable, unsure, lonely, even if increasingly he preferred to be angry rather than depressed. His writing, which for eight years now had been his great resource and recourse, was naturally changing too, becoming more risky and less controlled. A sign of that had come in August, when he described his work as that of 'a somnambulist'; 'it's like working in a dream, rather uncomfortable – as if you can't get solid hold of yourself.'[73]

But at least he and Frieda began their time in Fiascherino knowing that Frieda would shortly be divorced and that, the following summer, they could get married and no longer be regarded as social outcasts. And Frieda would have hoped that that in turn would lead to access to her children. Lawrence's priority in the autumn of 1913 was to finish 'The Sisters' (he had not completed a novel for a year), but first he had to prepare for publication his old play *The Widowing of Mrs. Holroyd*. Garnett, who had always admired the play, had got it accepted by the American publisher Mitchell Kennerley; Lawrence revised it heavily, in accordance with his new thinking about marriage. 'It seems to me that the chief thing about a woman – who is much of a woman – is that in the long run she is not to be had,' he remarked in a letter he wrote in October. 'She is not to be caught by any of the catch-words, love, beauty, honor, duty, worth, work, salvation – none of them – not in the long run.' What she wanted, instead, was satisfaction: 'physical at least as much as psychic, sex as much as soul'.[74] That remarkable new formulation of female independence also suggests the direction 'The Sisters' was taking; in the autumn of 1913, it grew enormously long as it charted the emotional and sexual lives of Ella and Gudrun Brangwen. Not until January 1914 did Lawrence finish its first half and send it to Garnett, by which time he was calling it 'The Wedding Ring', confirming how the theme of marriage had become central: Ella probably marrying Rupert Birkin, Gudrun on the point of marriage with Gerald Crich. It had been just a year since Lawrence had promised Sallie Hopkin to 'do my work for women, better than the suffrage'.[75] This was the work he meant.

Fiascherino had in every way turned out better than Gargnano. Lawrence and Frieda loved their house, a 'little, pink, four-roomed cottage in a big vine-garden, on the edge of a rocky bay'; they employed a young woman, Elide Fiori, and her mother, Felice, 'about sixty, and wizened, and barefoot', though only after Lawrence had got to work with a scrubbing brush on the floors could they see 'the dawn of deep red bricks arise from out this night of filth'. Frieda was even less occupied than before, but wrote happily to Garnett about 'my reputation for laziness'.[76] Lawrence hoped to earn some £150 during the winter; they could afford to lay down wine and also to hire a piano, which was brought round the coast to them in a boat. It was Frieda's joy to play and to sing whenever she could; she had asked Else the previous year: 'Be an angel and send me Beethoven's songs – no higher than G.' She sang well but, like Paula in 'New Eve and Old Adam', made a composer's music 'sound so different by altering all his time'.[77]

On 18 October, Weekley's decree nisi was granted. Frieda and Lawrence would have been glad to escape the publicity: the case figured on the front page of the Sunday *News of the World* – 'TO LIVE HER OWN LIFE / LADY LEAVES HER HUSBAND AND JOINS AUTHOR'[78] – and a crucial piece of evidence was the letter Lawrence had sent to Weekley from Metz. It would take six months for the divorce to be made absolute. In November, Lawrence – honoured foreigner in Fiascherino – served as a witness at the marriage of Felice's son Raffaele Azzarini; he appears in the marriage register as 'Loris, David', the local priest's attempt to spell his name.[79] The festivities and food (nine chickens as well as freshly caught octopus) were oddly tempered by the arrival of three acquaintances from London: the *Georgian* poets R. C. Trevelyan, Lascelles Abercrombie and Wilfred Gibson, together with Abercrombie's wife and Aubrey Waterfield, the English owner of a nearby castle. Waterfield in turn would introduce the Lawrences to the English expatriate community; they ended up with an extensive social life. But Lawrence registered the poets' *distance* as much as their companionship. 'They make me feel ashamed of myself, as if my human manners were very bad' is how he summed it up to Savage; they seemed 'shadowy and funny'[80] after the passionate, ordinary people at the wedding with whom Lawrence found himself in sympathy. In the spring, more visitors came: a young woman who had written Lawrence a fan letter about *Sons and Lovers*, Ivy Low (daughter of one of the first British Freudian analysts, Barbara Low) rather outstayed her welcome by remaining for six weeks. Constance Garnett came to Lerici and lived in the hotel for a while. And all winter and spring, Lawrence felt able to spend the time he wanted to on the novel, which was growing and growing.

On being sent the first half of 'The Wedding Ring', however, Edward Garnett responded thoroughly negatively, and his second letter was even more critical. For the first time, Lawrence felt, Garnett was attacking 'the thing I *wanted* to say: not me, not what I had said, but that which I was trying to say, and had failed in'.[81] Lawrence tended to agree with the comments, though not with what he felt was a patronizing attitude. In the spring of 1914 – and this was probably a final tribute to Garnett's perspicacity – Lawrence abandoned the unfinished draft and embarked on yet another rewriting, which went far faster and this time more satisfactorily. But he was now wondering whether Garnett's taste for realism could be reconciled with the way in which he wanted to write about experience, feeling and physical awareness. No sooner had he established himself with one kind of fiction in *Sons and Lovers*, than he was breaking away into a new kind of writing. He tried out the superseded draft of 'The Sisters' on Constance Garnett in Lerici, and she criticized the characters as 'simply invented to hang the pages of description of sexual experiences and emotions on to ... there's no light & shade – it all seems cheap intensity and violence at the same hysterical pitch all through'. These were criticisms that Lawrence's writing would often receive subsequently, though the surviving eight-page fragment of this draft of the novel, sensitive and careful, bears out none of them.[82]

The novel's future was also beginning to be affected by the way in which, in the aftermath of *Sons and Lovers*, Lawrence was being treated by publishers and agents. J. B. Pinker, for example, made an approach to Lawrence with a lucrative three-novel contract with the publisher Methuen (£300 per book), and Lawrence was strongly attracted by it. It seemed as if he might be on the point of breaking through successfully into the commercial market. Joseph Conrad, whose 1913 novel *Chance* had changed his career, so that in future he earned spectacularly well, had an identical three-volume contract with Methuen, arranged by Pinker.[83] Lawrence had his new, spring 1914 draft of 'The Wedding Ring' typed in two copies while he was still writing it: a sign of his confidence, but also an indication that he was thinking of putting it into the hands of publishers other than Duckworth.

Crucially, Edward Garnett turned out to object almost as strongly to the new version as to the old; he wrote that it was 'shaky' and that the psychology was wrong.[84] Lawrence must have felt he had now reached the end of the road of Garnett's helpfulness. With such an opinion, Garnett could not be expected to recommend the book to Duckworth; what he seemed to be demanding would need a further massive rewriting, which Lawrence no longer wanted to do. There were two consequences. Lawrence decided to try and interest another publisher, and he concluded that his friendship with Garnett was, in practical ways, at an end, though they never quarrelled.

Lawrence and Frieda had planned, as the previous year, to spend time in London in the summer, though Frieda wanted three months and Lawrence only a few weeks. They travelled separately; Frieda via Baden-Baden, where she saw her father – 'ill and broken' – for the last time, Lawrence walking some of the way across Switzerland with A. P. Lewis, a young engineer employed in La Spezia, near Lerici, who was returning to England.[85] When Lawrence and Frieda arrived back, on 24 June 1914, they stayed in London with Gordon Campbell; Katherine and Murry were also sharing the house. Lawrence went to ask Duckworth, a smaller and less commercial publisher than Methuen, if he could match Methuen's offer of an advance of £300; and of course he could not. So, having unsuccessfully tried to see Garnett, on 30 June Lawrence 'went to Pinker, and signed his agreement, and took his cheque, and opened an acc. with the London County and Westminster Bank – et me voilà'. He received £135 (£150 less Pinker's 10 per cent) just for signing the contract and submitting the novel's typescript: more than the total of £100 he had received from Duckworth for *Sons and Lovers*.[86] All Lawrence could now give Duckworth, to make up for Garnett's investment of time and patience in the 'Sisters' project, was a collection of short stories: it became *The Prussian Officer and Other Stories* when published in November. But he now seemed set up as a successful author, and was commissioned to write a short book on Thomas Hardy in the series 'Writers of the Day' by the young publisher Bertram Christian (Middleton Murry was almost certainly the contact).

Frieda's divorce had been made absolute at the end of April, and Lawrence – 'with neuralgia in my left eye and my heart in my boots'[87] – married her in a south London registry office on 13 July 1914. He would not be the only person to feel depressed about taking this step, but he also believed in the idea of marriage as Frieda never had, and perhaps never did. None of his own family came; his increasingly pious brother George, for one, would profess himself disgusted by this liaison with a married woman. It was from Campbell's house in Selwood Terrace that they got married, and photographs were taken in the back garden before and after the ceremony. In Illustration 16, Frieda's old jacket can no longer be brought to meet around her waist; a sash holds it together. Katherine is neat and demure-looking, her darkish straw hat at a stylish angle; Murry is conventionally smart. The book under his arm and the sheet on the washing line suggest how informal the photograph was. Lawrence's boater looks new but his suit is distinctly shabby. Edward Marsh, knowing of the Hardy commission, in a gesture that was both brilliant and practical sent them a set of Hardy's works as a wedding present – novels for Frieda, work for Lawrence. Their two-year exile was at an end and the respectable couple, supported by the money from an excellent novel contract, could at last live as they wanted to.

Within days of getting married, Frieda (ignoring the previous year's court order) made a new attempt to see her children. She intercepted the girls on their way to school with Maude Weekley, 'a fattish white unwholesome maiden aunt who, when she saw their mother, shrieked to the children – "Run, children, run" – and the poor little things were terrified and ran'.[88] Frieda then took the law into her own hands. Without Lawrence knowing, she tracked down the house in Chiswick where the family now lived: she had spotted her Nottingham curtains in one of the windows. One evening, she got into the house, 'creeping by the back way'.[89] Presumably she thought that if she could actually confront her children, they would rush into her arms. What happened, Barby remembered, was that 'she entered the nursery and found us at supper with Granny and Aunt Maude . . . And while she stood at bay before our relations, we children gazed in horror at the strange woman she had then become.'[90] To have her children not only run from her but look at her in horror was worse than Frieda could have imagined, and still harder to deal with because Lawrence had so often insisted that the children no longer wanted her.

All that could sustain her in this new loneliness was the fact that she and Lawrence were starting to acquire a large group of friends. Through Ivy Low, Lawrence had made the acquaintance of the writer and reviewer Catherine Jackson, later Carswell, and a whole group of intellectuals (including Freudians like Ivy Low's aunt Barbara) in Hampstead. For the first time in his career, he was being accepted into artistic and literary London, not just being steered through it or patronized by it. Because of his continuing friendship with Marsh, he met the painter Mark Gertler and lunched with the poet Rupert Brooke at the end of June; and at the end of July he was invited to dinner with the American poet Amy Lowell. At that dinner, he also met the young English poet Richard Aldington and his wife, the American poet H. D.

His career at this point looked wonderfully promising. Not only did he have his contracts with Methuen and Duckworth, and the Hardy book to write, but the *English Review* was taking three stories, including 'The Prussian Officer' which he had been so proud of writing in 1913. He had also made contact with the American magazine *Poetry*, which had accepted a selection of his work for its December number. But at the same dinner where he met Amy Lowell, he brought news from Marsh that England would shortly be involved in the European war currently dominating newspaper headlines and placards. On 31 July, leaving Frieda in London, Lawrence went off to the Lake District for a week's walking tour with a group of men; one was Lewis, and another the Russian translator S. S. Koteliansky ('Kot'), who was to become a friend for life.

Months later, he recalled when and how he heard of the outbreak of the war: the moment which people of his generation never forgot. His prose takes us into the experience of a sensitive, troubled observer:

I had been walking in Westmoreland, rather happy, with water-lilies twisted round my hat ... and we shouted songs, and I imitated music hall turns, whilst the other men crouched under the wall and I pranked in the rain on the turf in the gorse, and Kotilianski groaned Hebrew music ... It seems like another life – we *were* happy – four men. Then we came down to Barrow in Furness, and saw that war was declared. And we all went mad.[91]

They probably reached Barrow on 4 August. Some would have been mad with anger that war had been allowed to happen; others mad with desire to seize the moment.

I can remember soldiers kissing on Barrow station, and a woman shouting defiantly to her sweetheart 'When you get at 'em Clem, let 'em have it', as the train drew off – and in all the tram-cars 'War'. – Messrs Vickers Maxim call in their workmen – and the great notices on Vickers' gateways – and the thousands of men streaming over the bridge. Then I went down the coast a few miles. And I think of the amazing sunsets over flat sands and the smoky sea – then of sailing in a fisherman's boat, running in the wind against a heavy sea – and a French onion boat coming in with her sails set splendidly, in the morning sunshine – and the electric suspense everywhere – and the amazing, vivid, visionary beauty of everything, heightened up by immense pain everywhere.[92]

This was his last vision of the world at peace. His life and his work would never be the same again. He would never recover any similar sense of delighted ease with success, or companionship, or even social acceptance. His work would not again be in such demand for the next decade and a half; nor would he ever be in such a happy relationship with his own country. The war put paid to all that.[93]

10

In England at War: 1914–1915

Lawrence would have taken some time returning home to London. On Monday 3 August, the decision to mobilize was taken; on the Tuesday, the government announced that the bank holiday was being extended to Friday morning, and the state took over the railway system for troop transports. Vast numbers of army reservists were being called up, as Lawrence had seen in Barrow. When he did get back, probably by the Saturday, he found everything changing with astonishing speed; and, to prove it, on Monday 10 August, he received back the typescript of 'The Wedding Ring' from his publishers. Methuen had returned the novel, like most of their recently submitted fiction, to be resubmitted in six months' time, when they hoped the economic and business situation would have stabilized, though they also made some criticisms of the book's sexual outspokenness. This meant that it would be months before Lawrence would get the money due on its publication, on which he had been relying. He and Frieda had been spending a great deal since June; they had run through the advance.[1] There must have been debts to pay off: Frieda had received money from her family at various times, and Lawrence would have been very keen to repay it. A trip planned to Ireland in August to see the Campbells was abandoned, while the cheap living abroad they had planned to return to in Fiascherino became impossible: 'what is going to become of us?' Lawrence wrote to Pinker.[2]

All they could do was find somewhere cheap to live outside London, where Lawrence could write his Hardy book and they could wait for the war to end. Most people expected it to be over by Christmas; the Kaiser had told his troops, 'You will be home before the leaves have fallen from the trees.'[3] After a few days at Gordon Campbell's home in Selwood Terrace, they heard through Murry and Katherine that the young novelist and playwright Gilbert Cannan and his wife, Mary,[4] had a friend with a cottage to rent near Chesham in Buckinghamshire. So that was where they went: a cheap ride out of London on the Metropolitan railway line. It was 'tiny, but jolly' Lawrence said, making the best of it; a visitor described it as 'a dreary little structure of crimson brick and blue slates standing in a decayed orchard overgrown with nettles'.[5] Lawrence employed his formidable skills of painting and cleaning: he whitewashed upstairs and scrubbed the floors downstairs. Frieda and he quite liked it, but it was not a patch on Italy: 'the apples blown down lie almost like green lights in the grass. Kennst du das Land, wo die Citronen blühen? Yes, so do I. But now I hear the rain-water trickling animatedly into the green and rotten water-butt.'[6]

That was by no means the worst of it, either. There was the problem of nationality: 'we are so miserable about the war. My wife is German, so you may imagine.' The Lawrences were *very* aware of how Frieda ('the Hunwife')[7] and her family were now 'the enemy'; and Lawrence refused to accept the hysteria implicit in the perception of 'enemy', the 'obsolete' version of societies and civilizations which the war implied, or the anti-German propaganda which quickly began to circulate. He and Frieda suffered something of this in Buckinghamshire when, presumably at blackberry time, 'the local inhabitants concocted some preposterous, strange story that they were poisoning the berries in the hedges'.[8]

Lawrence, too, knew more than most civilians about the mechanized nature of modern warfare, having observed the Bavarian army on manoeuvres in 1913; he used his first-hand knowledge to write an article ('With the Guns') for the *Manchester Guardian* in mid August 1914. The coming war, he suggested, would be 'an affair entirely of machines, with men attached to the machines as the subordinate part thereof, as the butt is the part of a rifle'. It is not the accuracy of his prediction that is so surprising, but the way in which he foresaw such a development so keenly, so early. 'My God, why am I a man at all, when this is all, this machinery piercing and tearing?' His conclusion was: 'It is so unnatural as to be unthinkable. Yet we must think of it.'[9] Few would now disagree with him. The reports in the papers of preparations and troop movements might have allowed any sensitive man to recognize the 'ghastliness and mechanical, obsolete, hideous stupidity of war',[10] but the majority had no such feelings. Bunny Garnett nearly joined up ('I felt that the war was a great human experience which I ought not to miss'); Murry actually did so, though he extricated himself again on medical grounds.[11] There was widespread popular enthusiasm. London had been 'packed with cheering masses' on the afternoon and evening of the day war was declared; the departing soldiers found crowds 'shouting, singing, waving their handkerchiefs, and showering us with sweets and packets of cigarettes'. But Lawrence felt nothing but 'immense pain everywhere'. Soon after the declaration of war, he wrote: 'The war is just hell for me. I don't see why I should be so disturbed – but I am. I can't get away from it for a minute: live in a sort of coma, like one of those nightmares when you can't move.'[12]

Why should the first two weeks of the war have had such a profound impact on him? He would declare in January 1915 that the 'War finished me: it was the spear through the side of all sorrows and hopes'.[13] Not only did it dash all hopes of returning to Italy, living happily with Frieda, or having his novel published; the war damaged his very belief in his country and his age. In this, again, he might seem farsighted: how could one believe in a civilization responsible for such wickedness and carnage as the war would generate? Yet Lawrence formulated his opinions long before trench warfare started, before there had been much fighting, and before the first stories of atrocity began to circulate around 18 August.[14] He was reacting to the very idea of the war, rather than to anything that had occurred. When the real 'war and its horrors'[15] came, they did no more than confirm what he had felt from the start.

It took him years to understand quite what had happened to him in 1914. But he was one of the first to grasp what an extraordinary moment it was, in culture, consciousness and modern memory. He would write a good deal about war in *Aaron's Rod* and eventually, in the summer of 1922, would compose a version of his experience, in the account he added to his novel *Kangaroo*. It would be wrong to imagine him realizing anything very definitely in August 1914: he simply knew that he was desperate. But what was at stake seems to have been his very belief in English civilization. While growing up, he had nursed (like many other people) a Whitmanesque surety that 'the great procession is marching, on the whole, in the right direction' and that 'I can help the march if I like. It is a valuable assurance.'[16] Up until 1914, he had written with the largely unspoken and in many ways nineteenth-century self-assurance that what he wrote addressed the deepest needs of his society; and he had felt that he was, with his subversive perspective, in a unique position. He had remarked, early in 1913, 'I think, do you know, I have inside me a sort of answer to the *want* of today: to the real, deep want of the English people.' Every so often, he would articulate this kind of confidence, as in 1912, when he remarked of his countrymen that 'I should like to bludgeon them into realising their own selves', or in 1913 when he commented, more blithely, 'I do write because I want folk – English folk – to alter, and have more sense.' What the war destroyed, in the end, was his certainty that any such alteration was possible, as well as his belief that he could do anything about it. From perhaps the end of 1915, Lawrence's 'old great belief in the oneness and wholeness of humanity' was 'torn clean across, for ever'.[17]

The consequences for someone with the conviction that 'Belief is . . . the only healer of the soul's wounds' can be imagined.[18] Lawrence would end up doubting whether he could help heal the 'soul's wounds', or recover for his society a recognition of the body's central place in experience; or even *be* a writer for his society. He always linked the creative and the religious, once referring to 'the essentially religious or creative motive'; his only real means of being purposive was his writing. Now he watched his country's energies redirected into hatred, the mechanisms of war and communal, not individual, barbarism. ' "When you see 'em *let* 'em have it." "Ay, no fear",'[19] was what he had heard shouted at Barrow. The writer who had up to now believed in the development and utterance of 'the great racial or human conscious-ness, a little of which is in me', who wanted people to read his fiction and be made 'alert and active',[20] to alter their relationships, to realize their desires, found his whole *raison d'être* as a writer being called in question. He also started to comprehend, more sharply, the extent to which he *was* an outsider, not only in the literary world but in the smoothly functioning middle- and upper-class worlds of politics and government. 'England, my England,' he would later quote, to ask immediately: 'But which is *my* England?'[21] Without a belief in 'the world', or in something beyond the merely personal, there remained just the individual concerns of individual men and women to believe in.

His unhappiness showed itself immediately, in 'With the Guns', and then in the Hardy book. He should have been working on this in Buckinghamshire. 'Writers of the Day' was a new series with a conventional format of 'Life' and 'Works', each volume running to 15,000 words.[22] It would earn him £15 as an advance, maybe more in the end – a similar sum to what he would get from a magazine for a 'long' short story like 'The Prussian Officer'. He had probably thought he could do it in a month: 'the work won't be very much'.[23] Marsh's present of the works of Hardy may have meant that he did more reading than planned. But he worked on the book from September to late November, and was still typing it up in mid December. In the course of it, he went far beyond the idea of the literary-critical and biographical book he was supposed to be writing. It turned into a 50,000-word exploration of his thinking; although 'supposed to be on Thomas Hardy', it 'seems to be about anything else in the world but that'.[24] It would have been pointless even to submit it to 'Writers of the Day'. But while the piece gave him a new understanding of abiding human dualities that he would employ directly in the revision of his novel for Methuen, it also stood out as a new and rebellious refusal to conform. Although 'very badly off' and not knowing 'what money will come, if any, during the winter',[25] Lawrence felt compelled more than ever to use his writing to find out what *he* and the people of his society truly wanted and needed. How should he simply co-operate with a society from which he was starting to feel so alienated? He was consciously standing apart from it for the first time, though also doing imaginatively what he thought was best for it.

He returned to 'The Wedding Ring' late in November 1914; he was probably thinking of Methuen's suggestion that it should go back to them after six months. But the novel went in its own new direction. Its final rewriting changed it, and Lawrence's career, irrevocably: he feared that, when Methuen saw it, 'he'll wonder what changeling is foisted on him'.[26] For one thing, Lawrence had split the novel into two: the material that had been accumulating around the original

'Sisters' of the title had become too long for one volume. The first book, to be called *The Rainbow*, would tell the story of the sisters' grandparents, Tom and Lydia Brangwen, their parents, Will and Anna Brangwen, and the early life of one sister (now called Ursula), including her first, unhappy, love affair with a young soldier, Anton Skrebensky. The second book would show the subsequent relationships of Ursula and Gudrun Brangwen: Ursula successful with Rupert Birkin, Gudrun unhappy with Gerald Crich. But *The Rainbow* also became the story of the need of all three generations for fulfilment. Its idea of 'the beyond' as the conceptual goal of the characters was probably new in this version, and related directly to what Lawrence thought he should be stressing in wartime. As it concentrated increasingly on what it was like to be a woman in the modern world, standing back from it in horror, the book also dwelt even more explicitly upon the body and its experience as well as becoming sexually overt – exactly what had already troubled Methuen in the summer.

For the moment, Lawrence was simply happy to have a novel to be involved with, to take his mind off the war and to give him a role in the society he now distrusted so much. And in spite of the retreat to Buckinghamshire, he was still encountering people who impressed him and whom he impressed. On a visit to London, the old friendship with Bunny Garnett, now working in zoology at Imperial College on the unicellular creatures *Paramecia*, led Lawrence into a new way of imagining what Ursula might see through her laboratory microscope when examining a unicellular creature and thinking about self-fulfilment.[27] It was Bunny who brought him into contact with Lady Ottoline Morrell, a great hostess for artists, writers and other intellectuals, whose house was increasingly a centre for those opposed to the war. In her turn, Ottoline introduced him to the novelist E. M. Forster and the philosopher and mathematician Bertrand Russell. His meeting with Cynthia Asquith in 1913 had also developed into a steady friendship, in spite of the pressures of the war on a woman in her position: she was the Prime Minister's daughter-in-law, and her husband was already on active service. These friendships gave him some continuing context for his ideas and what he wanted to write, though he would end up alienated from a number of the individuals concerned.

The cottage, as winter set in, turned out to be damp as well as cramped, and even the companionship of Murry and Katherine, who in October moved out to Buckinghamshire to be near them, could not reconcile the Lawrences to living there. Frieda remembered how 'we walked over to you for dinner over those wet fields with smelly decaying cabbage stalks in them in the gloomy twilight and it was the only fun we had!'[28] It was Lawrence's first winter in England since his bout of pneumonia in 1911, and he took to his bed repeatedly. Perhaps for the first time, Frieda acquired a sense of his physical frailty; his Alpine walking for three summers running would have given her a very different impression. It was during one such illness that he stopped shaving: 'I've grown a red beard, behind which I shall take as much cover henceforth as I can, like a creature under a bush. My dear God, I've been miserable this autumn.'[29] At a time when the male population was shaving as never before – the army allowed its soldiers only moustaches – the beard implied difference and separateness.

The memoirs and diaries of Murry and Katherine give us a series of insights into the Lawrence household and its stresses. The 'armistice' had clearly came to an end: according to Murry, one evening, probably early in November 1914,

we were talking gaily enough, when there was a mention of Frieda's children, and Frieda burst into tears. Lawrence went pale. In a moment, there was a fearful outburst. Ominously, there was no physical violence. Lawrence, though passionately angry, had kept control; and it was the more frightening. He had had enough, he said; she must go, she was draining the life out of him. She must go, she must go now. She knew what money he had; he would give her her share – more than her share. He went upstairs, and came down again, and counted out on the table to me sixteen sovereigns. Frieda was standing by the door, crying, with her hat and coat on, ready to go – but where?[30]

Lawrence's sympathies for Frieda's quest seem to have ended with her expulsion from the Chiswick nursery in the summer of 1914. But, compelled to stay in England, she found the near proximity of her children too much to bear. One of their new Hampstead friends, Catherine Carswell, had noticed how 'the links between Frieda and her children had reasserted themselves'; during a weekend in London in September, by hiding and waiting she had managed to see 'Ernst and children (not to speak to)'.[31] It may have been on that occasion that Campbell's wife, Beatrice, found her at the door,

her face blotched and red with weeping. She had a wide straw hat on[,] which hung down all round her face, shapeless with water, and her hair was wet and straggling; she looked quite mad ... she had been standing behind a hedge ... waiting to see her children return from school. The rain had poured down on her; she had no umbrella. When at last the children appeared and went into the house she was so blind with weeping that she could hardly see them.[32]

Her campaign for her children in 1914 came to a head when, getting herself shown in under an assumed name, she managed to see Weekley in Nottingham in December. Lawrence dramatized her account:

'You –' said the quondam husband, backing away – 'I hoped never to see you again.'

Frieda: 'Yes – I know.'

Quondam Husband: 'And what are you doing in *this* town.'

Frieda: I came to see you about the children.

Quondam Husband: Aren't you ashamed to show your face where you are known? Isn't the commonest prostitute better than you?

Frieda: Oh no ... You see I must speak to you about the children.

Quon. Husb.: You shall *not* have them – they don't want to see you.[33]

In that last assertion, Weekley was unfortunately right: she remained the 'strange woman' Barby remembered from 1914. And Frieda would only see her children in a lawyer's office for thirty minutes in August 1915, again in April 1917, and in April and August 1918.[34]

Nevertheless, her quarrels with Lawrence about them went on. His empathy with her – she knew his 'oversensitive, oversympathetic nature'[35] – and, ultimately, his responsibility for her situation were such that he could not just ignore her. It was because he responded to her that she had either to drop the subject or leave. Right into the 1920s, her children were a taboo subject for them. Their friend Knud Merrild, in the winter of 1922, remembered Frieda saying: 'He won't let me talk about them, or even mention their names.'[36] But although mentioning the children was taboo, it was a topic to which Lawrence and Frieda constantly returned. It is especially interesting that it came up when the Murrys were with them. Frieda may have wanted

sympathy, or been trying to embarrass Lawrence, or to show him up
as heartless, or all three. She recalled, late in life, how they would
quarrel 'mostly when other people were around'.[37] Both of them played
to their audience; Lawrence's division of the money was nothing if not
theatrical. In the play *The Fight for Barbara*, which he had written in
October 1912, almost exactly the same division of money occurs
before 'Barbara', dressed up with her hat on, is supposed to leave, but
doesn't.[38] The division of the money and preparations for leaving were
a scenario Lawrence and Frieda probably enacted more than once;
and in 1914, Frieda again did not leave, in spite of donning hat and
coat. She *could* not just walk out: where was she to go? Murry
responded to the episode by launching 'into a kind of theatrical har-
angue' to reconcile the Lawrences, so that, in his words, they 'were
smiling together before we left'.[39] It may not have needed Murry to
bring them together again; they had achieved that before. The quarrels
were always exhausting, but perhaps necessary for a passionate
relationship bottled up in a damp cottage in the English winter. Frieda
knew how to 'unbottle' the conflicts and tensions, for sure, and did so.
But she was testing to the limit Lawrence's capacity for imaginative
sympathy. He found himself responding to her unhappiness and her
anger, and in turn seems to have switched between an intellectual
response – that she could not have her children *and* stay with him –
and violent anger.

Murry's diary entries, one-sided as they are, are ruthless about
Frieda. After it had been explained how, when Lawrence wanted
Frieda, often Frieda did not want sex 'at all', Murry concluded: 'Sin-
cerely I do not believe that she loves *him* at all.'[40] He and Katherine
were, by contrast, 'deeply in love', despite the fact that Katherine was
planning an affair with an old friend, whom she went to for a few
days in the spring of 1915, although she came back.[41] In July 1914,
Lawrence had offered his friend the La Spezia consul Thomas Dunlop,
who seems to have been in marital difficulty, some very precise advice
about love and marriage. Loving his wife 'completely', Lawrence had
said, would bring 'peace and inner security'.[42] He had believed that
since 1912. But the very assertion to Dunlop seems to have marked
the end of that belief; by the autumn of 1914, Lawrence had moved
away from the very idea of mutual, peaceful love, to a belief in growth

through opposition and conflict. Frieda remained sure that 'L. and I really love each other at the bottom', though she also said that 'he is so furious with me because of this very fact sometimes', and there is some truth in that. Lawrence found dependence hard. As Frieda put it, after his death, 'He cared only too much.'[43] At times, they were very happy, but the violent quarrelling had become a way of life, which had its pleasures too, not usually shared by those who were present. By the early summer of 1915, they would be spending time apart from each other because of their differences about the children;[44] and yet these separations were still only breathing spaces in the relationship, not indications that it was likely to end. A friend noticed how Frieda, after being shouted at by Lawrence, responded proudly that Lawrence 'is so violent, so fierce', while she wrote admiringly how he was 'so tender, generous and fierce'.[45] Frieda – in theory the vulnerable one, with her children irrecoverably lost, cut off from her German relatives as well as from her English ex-family, with nowhere to go – seems to have remained more blithe through it all, more easily herself, so long as she was not pushed into a subordinate role. She walked out on Lawrence more than once, only to come back without apologies or pleas for forgiveness. It was Lawrence, with his whole sense of himself as a writer called into question, who in the late autumn of 1914 felt more insecure. Catherine Carswell noted how he 'seemed to be holding on to himself against depression'.[46]

One thing that kept Lawrence going through the darkest and deepest part of the winter was a kind of fantasy he originally worked out with Murry, the Cannans, Mark Gertler and Koteliansky, who had visited for various New Year parties in Bucks. Following Kot's singing of 'Rannani Zadikim Zadikim l'Adonoi' ('Rejoice in the Lord, O ye righteous'),[47] they invented Rananim, or 'The Island'; they worked out the objectives, aims and laws for communal life in some place far from England, at times literally on an island. So much has been written about Rananim as Lawrence's long-term goal – the 'ideal community ... which Lawrence hoped to establish', for example – that it comes as a shock to realize that it was, rather, a pleasing festive fantasy concocted by four or five people over a few days when the various households visited each other. Frieda remembered the occasion as 'the last time for years to come that we were really gay'.[48] Not all those present for the New Year parties even participated. Katherine, for example, 'felt *very* antagonistic to the whole affair'. The fact that a similar later scheme left Frieda 'so amused by it all' suggests that she did not take it very seriously herself. For Lawrence, however, the idea and the word became a kind of unwritten, but strenuously imagined, fiction about living with a few friends in a better way than conventional society permitted; he wanted a community 'established on the assumption of goodness in the members, instead of the assumption of badness'.[49] Planning it as a liberating communal fiction with his friends, and at times involving others who also became friends, mattered a great deal more than actually setting off, which no one ever did. It involved not just Lawrence's own powerful imagination but his fantasy of living and working with others; such planning and fantasy extended his affective circle well beyond that of his marriage.

At the end of January, the Lawrences managed to leave the damp little house for a cottage at Greatham in Sussex offered them rent-free by Viola Meynell, a friend of Catherine Carswell; here they had space to invite friends to stay. Frieda seems to have relished the fact that she was now able to move among the higher echelons of English society, with visitors like Ottoline Morrell, Cynthia Asquith and Bertrand Russell, while Lawrence felt taken seriously by them, which at such a time was especially important to him.

Russell was courageously embarked on a pacifist campaign against the war that would end his academic career at Trinity College, Cambridge, and put him in prison in 1917. He was enormously impressed with Lawrence when they discussed society and its ills together. Lawrence's passion and emotional commitment were overwhelming: Russell found him 'infallible. He is like Ezekiel or some other Old Testament prophet ... he sees everything and is always right.'[50] That initial response was followed by a more considered reaction; but for months, Russell saw Lawrence as a man gifted with startling insight. He invited Lawrence to visit Trinity, to exhibit this amazing talent to those he felt needed the challenge Lawrence represented. The visit to Cambridge in March went badly, however. Lawrence got on well with only one or two of the fellows, and when he met J. Maynard Keynes, the economist, he experienced a violent reaction (discussed below). Through the late spring and summer,

Russell and Lawrence planned to work together; they would give a joint lecture course, 'he on Ethics, I on Immortality'. The difference of topic is suggestive. Lawrence wanted to talk about people's deepest needs and beliefs: by 'immortality' he meant the fulfilment of desire.[51] Russell wanted to discuss what was to be done in England at a time of war. They finally disagreed over the outline for Russell's lecture course on the 'Philosophy of Social Reconstruction', which Lawrence thought insufficiently radical, while at the same time he saw with startling clarity into Russell's deeply contradictory nature.[52] The plans came to nothing.

Lawrence's letters of the spring of 1915 are among the most remarkable he ever wrote. Like *The Rainbow*, they chart his new understanding of how to symbolize the historical development of human consciousness, society and self-responsibility: how, for example, it came to be that 'one is not only a little individual living a little individual life, but that one is in oneself the whole of mankind, and ones fate is the fate of the whole of mankind'.[53] Such a philosophy had come to be at the heart of *The Rainbow*, which had begun as a novel about how two sisters got married but was now developing into an analysis of how Ursula (the most 'modern' member of the Brangwen family) becomes a highly developed individual ending up on the very fringes of her society, though gifted with a final vision of its renewal. Whatever Lawrence wrote in this first year of the war was going to have the individual's relationship with society at its core. He finished the novel, triumphantly, on 2 March 1915: 'bended it and set it firm. Now off and away to find the pots of gold at its feet.'[54] Having done his best to ensure that it earned his living (there was a final instalment of the advance to come), he immediately turned back to rewriting the philosophy that had taken over his Hardy book. He felt he could afford to write that, now that the novel was done; and over the next six months it crystallized into a series of six essays, 'The Crown', which he would publish as a kind of *cri de coeur* about what was wrong with England at war, and how it might be brought back to purpose and belief.

He had, all the same, not finally finished with *The Rainbow*. When he received the typescript, he decided that it needed extensive revision; and the proofs, later in the summer, would be revised still further, taking the end of the novel into the vision of a changed and renewed society which the philosophy was also exploring. In between work on the novel, he wrote at his philosophy, with occasional breaks. During one such break, early in June, he completed the first version of his story 'England, My England', which summed up his new insight into why men are so eager to fight. Its central character, Evelyn Daughtry, a failure in his marriage, abandons 'love and the creative side of life' when he joins up. Daughtry – typical of the helpless, self-conscious artistic intellectual so common in Lawrence's early writing – turns out in wartime to be the perfect 'destructive spirit entering into destruction'.[55] Lawrence was thinking of a neighbour in Sussex, Percy Lucas, but Beb Asquith (full of loyalty and patriotism) would have been in his mind too, as would, oddly, Bertrand Russell. In such imaginative ways, Lawrence expressed his fundamental opposition to the war and to the spirit of war. He could see how a man like Russell, although passionately against the war, was also, as Lawrence wrote to him, 'too full of devilish repressions to be anything but lustful and cruel': 'The enemy of all mankind, you are, full of the lust of enmity.' Lawrence had no time for anyone who compromised with what he was now calling the 'envelope of nullity within which mankind is enclosed, the envelope of the achieved self, the womb of the past era'.[56] His letter finally alienated Russell: what might have been impressive insights Russell found too terrible to contemplate. In his turn, Russell was finding Lawrence increasingly absurd, incapable of real thinking and madly unrealistic in his hopes for change: 'undisciplined in thought, & mistakes wishes for facts'.[57]

But Lawrence's opposition to the war was growing into an extraordinary reconceptualization of the nature of his society. For humankind in its 'envelope', 'nothing but reduction, disintegration can take place ... And war is usually, or very often, part of this great flux of reduction.'[58] There is a nightmare quality to these images of the 'achieved past' which are both enclosing and also in 'flux'. Lawrence was trying desperately to find a language for his intuition of how English society was both horribly compelling and yet disintegrative. In 1915, he struggled to be honest to his insights and his need to detach himself from a society which felt so utterly imprisoned within the past and which stopped at nothing to destroy those societies or individuals in opposition to it. In 'The Crown' he would be very clear about this: he referred to the poison gas attacks which had first been launched on the Western Front in April 1915 and had continued throughout the summer. In a death-focused society, he concluded, one is very aware 'of the gas clouds that may lacerate and reduce the lungs to a heavy mass'. Escaping from the 'corrupt enclosure' of such a society was all he now felt he could attempt to do: 'Some few, very, very few, have an inkling of this.'[59] His feverish engagement during 1915 with concepts of society, and how it might be changed, shows how desperately he clung to the idea of the social role of the writer, in spite of all his feelings of difference and the role of the outsider to which he felt condemned. Works like 'The Crown' show us very vividly Lawrence's capacity for intense thought, his super-subtle and ingenious mind constructing analogy after analogy. His kind of thinking can also, however, be private, enraptured, reminiscent of the ecstatic outpouring which Jessie Chambers so admired, and which the later Lawrence thought analogous to 'going up in smoke'.[60] His fiction compelled him, as Frieda did, to recognize opposition, which was why it was so important to him.

But the kind of intensity of choice between right and wrong, which he was now forcing upon himself, led to problems with several friends. He and Frieda had been very fond of Bunny Garnett since their time at Icking in 1912; but during April 1915 they became convinced that their friend was in trouble. They noticed how shaky his handwriting was when he wrote to them; they believed him miserable. Lawrence was convinced that this was because Bunny had become entangled in homosexual relationships. While he had been in Cambridge visiting Russell, Lawrence had experienced some kind of a trauma about what he perceived as self-enclosed, predatory homosexuality: he had seen Keynes standing in his pyjamas, at midday, and 'a knowledge passed into me, which has been like a little madness to me ever since'. As he thought back to it, three times Lawrence called himself 'mad' or 'insane'. His feelings were immensely disturbed, presumably because they were so compelled; he was aware of 'the most dreadful sense of repulsiveness – something like carrion – a vulture gives me the same feeling'.[61] He insisted that this had nothing to do with any moral objection to homosexuality. It was, instead, a physical repulsion from the idea of the solitary, encased self preying off vulnerable or innocent selves like a vulture off dead meat, and from the smell of the tightly closed room he associated with Keynes: 'a horrible sense of frowstiness, so repulsive'. Lawrence *knew* this feeling, which was why he found it so disturbing. It was a revelation to him of the way in which he himself might be homosexual, and did not want to be.[62]

He linked this version of the predatory homosexual with what he saw of Bunny's intellectual, immensely talkative male friend Frankie Birrell, later in the spring of 1915:

To hear these young people talking really fills me with black fury: they talk endlessly, but endlessly – and never, never a good or a real thing said . . . They are cased each in a hard little shell of his own and out of this they talk words . . . They made me dream in the night of a beetle that bites like a scorpion . . . It is this horror of little swarming selves I can't stand: Birrells, D. Grants, and Keynses.[63]

Birrell was in love with Bunny, and the painter Duncan Grant was sleeping with him. Lawrence and Frieda both wrote Bunny letters of loving care, trying to turn him against the men they believed were exploiting him. Lawrence's, in particular, was extremely tender. But it was also profoundly interfering: it told Bunny which of his male and female friends he should give up. It was the kind of letter that either makes you love the writer for caring so much, or hate him for such unconscionable meddling. Bunny hated Lawrence for it. He ignored the insights and the proffered love; and Lawrence lost a good friend.

It was with the feeling of having stayed too much on the fringes of life that, in August 1915, Frieda and Lawrence moved back to London, to Hampstead, where they had a circle of friends; the poet and playwright Dollie Radford, whom they had first met in Sussex, turned out to be especially loyal. Certainly, Frieda needed all the friends she could get at such a time. In May, they had nearly rented a London flat for her, just to give her some company and put some distance between her and Lawrence – 'L is very wearing and also I will see the children on their way to school.' Despite his new acquaintances, Lawrence too had been fairly isolated; he had made just one or two visits, such as when he had dropped in on Aldington's wife, H. D., in London, and seemed to her the only person who understood how she felt after losing her baby: they had a special tenderness for each other thereafter.[64] But now he felt he should be back in London. The autumn publication of *The Rainbow* meant that he would be receiving rather more publicity than before, as well as being paid his final advance.

But he still wanted, rather desperately, to *do* something about his society. He revised his old Italian essays for publication, and wrote new ones that embodied some of the thinking of 'The Crown'. Russell's criticism of him as not practical had perhaps put him on his mettle not just to think and feel but also to find ways of acting directly. He and Murry planned a small magazine that would publish their writing and Katherine's; it would say the kinds of thing he thought needed saying to the public at large, at a time of war. Like William Blake, whose painting he admired, he was too much of a believer in conflict ever to be a pacifist; in 1916, for instance, he would call some pacifist pamphlets 'too squashy altogether'.[65] But he wanted people to understand the real nature of their society. He planned a series of small public meetings, to be advertised in the magazine, which might draw together a body of sympathetic people. It was characteristic of Lawrence at this stage of his career that he should be doing so much to make contact with people and to change their ideas: through his writing, the magazine and the meetings. He wanted to play an active part in his society, and he believed in his capacity to make people 'alert and active', as he put it in March.[66]

However, the autumn of 1915 turned out to spell one disaster after another. First, the magazine (called *The Signature*) failed to pay its way, in spite of Murry and Lawrence sending subscription forms to all their friends, old and new. They raised only enough to produce three issues, rather than the six they had planned, so that only three parts of 'The Crown', rewritten for it, got into print. The public meetings, too, were a fiasco: only two were apparently ever held and 'about a dozen people' came.[67] By far the worst blow, however, was the attack on *The Rainbow*. Methuen had tried to impose some censorship on it at the proof stage, though Lawrence, in spite of having to accept some small changes, had managed to evade many of his publisher's efforts. Now, after its very first review, it was viciously dealt with by almost everyone. One reviewer (Catherine Carswell) who found things to praise in it lost her job as a result, and another favourable review was pulled by the newspaper about to print it.[68] Crucially, two reviews called for the book to be suppressed. Reviewers found they could easily inflame public morality at a time of national crisis. 'A thing like *The Rainbow* has no right to exist in the wind of war,' wrote one. 'It is a greater menace to our public health than any of the epidemic diseases.' He went on to insist that the 'young men who are dying for liberty are moral beings. They are the living repudiation of such impious denials of life as *The Rainbow*.'[69]

Although by late October there was some public celebration of the successes of the battle of Loos, there were also distressing reports of casualties, together with a general sense that the war was going to continue for a long time and that people at home must stand firm. Because of its sexual content, the book was not bought by the public libraries or taken by the bookstalls. Methuen withdrew it from their advertisements; and early in November, on the orders of the Director of Public Prosecutions (encouraged presumably by the reviews, and certainly by the National Council for Public Morals), the police collected all undistributed copies from Methuen. On 13 November, the Bow Street Magistrates heard a prosecution under the Obscene Publications Act of 1857. Methuen, though they had a lawyer present in court, refused to defend the book. Their only significant statement was that 'they regretted having published it';[70] they hoped to avoid a fine. The magistrate ordered the book's destruction: Methuen were not fined but had to pay £10 costs. Lawrence could do nothing to prevent the book he was so proud of, and had worked on for two and a half years, being destroyed in a few minutes, along with his reputation and his capacity to earn his living as a professional writer. He knew that they were 'robbing me of my freedom':[71] not just the freedom to publish what he liked, but the freedom to live the independent life that his writing had earned him. Ottoline Morrell's husband Philip, an MP, raised the matter in the House of Commons on 14 December but achieved nothing, and none of Lawrence's literary friends, it turned out, was prepared to argue for *The Rainbow*, only against censorship: even Murry and Katherine thoroughly disliked the book. Lawrence felt 'you don't know how much, sick and done'. He was asked ten years later whether the suppression made him bitter. He denied it, but the way he responded in 1915 shows how passionately he felt about the attack on his book, though his saving sense of absurdity was not lost: 'I am not very much moved: am beyond that by now. I only curse them all, body and soul, root, branch and leaf, to eternal damnation.'[72]

During October, following the failure of *The Signature*, but before the fate of *The Rainbow* became known, Lawrence had been thinking of going abroad. The USA seemed the obvious place: still out of the war but a country where an English writer could be published and where Lawrence believed his work might be appreciated – all of his books except *The Prussian Officer and Other Stories* had had US editions. From mid October to mid December, the Lawrences tried to get passports, to go to Florida. The move seemed even more urgent after the novel's suppression; they borrowed money and people made them gifts, so that in the end they had around £100. Lawrence had made new acquaintances and friends; the young composer Philip Heseltine and the undergraduate writer Aldous Huxley were sufficiently impressed by him to agree to come to Florida. Lawrence intensely enjoyed the shared planning, the hopefulness, the idea once again of a colony;[73] but he was shrewd enough not to set off unless he was sure he could make a success of it. As with Rananim in Buckinghamshire, the feeling of a body of friends looking forward, and planning together, mattered more than the actual move.

In November and December, he and Frieda made two visits to Garsington Manor, the sixteenth-century house in Oxfordshire to which Ottoline and Philip Morrell had recently moved. He wrote lyrically about the house in a prose poem he gave to Ottoline:

Shafted, looped windows between the without and within, the old house, the perfect old intervention of fitted stone, fitted perfectly about a silent soul, the soul that in drowning under this last wave of time looks out clear through the shafted windows to see the dawn of all dawns taking place, the England of all recollection rousing into being . . . It is me, generations and generations me, every complex, gleaming fibre of me, every lucid pang of my coming into being. And oh, my God, I cannot bear it. For it is not this me who am drowning swiftly under this last wave of time, this bursten flood.[74]

Lawrence's sense of England, as he saw it embodied in Garsington, reveals him not just preparing to leave his country, but ceremonially bidding it farewell, as it drowns in the new and apocalyptic flood that, for him, marked the end of a civilization. His writing has a Swinburnian quality (Lawrence would recite Swinburne to the guests at Garsington) quite different from anything in 'The Crown' or *The Rainbow*. Did Lawrence really feel, like any aristocrat, that for 'generations and generations' he had *been* England? The answer is clearly 'yes'. Back in March, he had attempted to express his feeling that 'ones charge is the charge of the whole of mankind'.[75] It was this feeling of responsibility that in December 1915 he felt to be profoundly endangered; for England belonged to the past, and he did not intend to drown along with it. He was the one who knew what was happening, while others either simply followed their countrymen into battle, or campaigned for peace while remaining 'achieved' selves within 'the womb of the past era'.[76]

All this is so very strange that it must bring us up short. The war made a huge difference to the way Lawrence was now feeling about the past. It pointed up sharply his powerfully nostalgic sense of the 'beautiful, the wonderful past', which preyed on his heart[77] and which gave him some feeling of a community to which he belonged and found sustaining, and a present in which he felt merely an isolated individual. It was for this reason, among others, that in October 1915 he had wanted to go to America: it was not just somewhere his work could be published, but seemed to offer a public in which he might believe, and a place where he might belong. Matters came to a head on 12 December when, in order to get a passport to travel abroad, he had to queue up to attest: that is, swear the oath of allegiance as a military recruit and thus enrol as ready for military service when called up. Between 25 October and the middle of December 1915, some two million men attested under the so-called 'Derby Scheme'.[78] Swearing an oath of alliegance was, of course, something in which Lawrence simply did not believe. None the less, for the sake of obtaining the passports, he went down to Battersea Town Hall, over the river from Westminster and the Houses of Parliament, and joined the queue.

But I hated it so much, after waiting nearly two hours, that I came away. And yet, waiting there in the queue, I felt the *men* were very decent, and that the slumbering lion was going to wake up in them: not against the Germans either, but against the great lie of this life . . . In the long run, I have the victory: for all those men in the queue, for those spectral, hazy, sunny towers hovering beyond the river, for the world that is to be.[79]

Because he had left the queue, he would probably not get a passport. Florida would remain a dream. Yet his report is also optimistic; and while such optimism came only at times, it is interesting that it should have been provoked by Lawrence's feelings about the men in the queue. This reminds us of his potential loyalty to the working class, at such a time of isolation. As he could not go to Florida, might the Midlands now be a home to which he could return? He and Frieda went there at Christmas 1915, but while he was there he wrote disturbing letters about how he now felt about it:

These men are passionate enough, sensuous, dark – God, how all my boyhood comes back – so violent, so dark, the mind always dark and without understanding, the senses violently active. It makes me sad beyond words. These men, whom I love so much – and the life has such a power over me – they *understand* mentally so horribly: only industrialism, only wages and money and machinery. They can't *think* anything else . . . The strange, dark, sensual life, so violent, and hopeless at the bottom, combined with this horrible paucity and materialism of mental consciousness, makes me so sad, I could scream. They are still so living, so vulnerable, so darkly passionate. I love them like brothers – but my God, I hate them too . . .[80]

It was not just the materialism of the miners that made them so alien, though that was a kind of intellectual explanation for his feelings. Their reality was violently attractive; they were the male sensual body and self that he had been promoting in his work, yet they also seemed utterly alien, narrow, hopeless and incomplete. So what, now, did he believe in? Where were his loyalties, and where was *his* home? Not here, at any rate.

The question of where to go next was fortunately answered. The novelist and writer J. D. Beresford had a holiday house on the north Cornish coast which he had lent Katherine and Murry in 1914, and was now prepared to lend the Lawrences for a couple of months. Cornwall at least looked out over the Atlantic towards America, as far from warmongering London as they could get. They would have to live as cheaply as they could, with the prospect of no income at all – just that £100. On the penultimate day of the old year, 1915, Lawrence and Frieda travelled down to Porthcothan, not knowing what they would live on or what in the long run they could do. But, as Lawrence optimistically declared in one of his characteristic images of looking out and breaking free, it was 'like being at the window and looking out of England to the beyond. This is my first move outwards, to a new life.' He said he felt 'Vogelfrei',[81] which he probably hoped meant 'free as a bird'. It actually means 'outlawed', which was even more appropriate. The liberation of life in Cornwall, writing and looking outward 'to the beyond', was symbolically what he wished for himself: to be outlawed and free. 'Apart he would remain' would be the conclusion of the central character in *Kangaroo*, Richard Lovatt Somers, after thinking through his war experiences to see where he is now.[82] In December 1915, Lawrence had not yet reached such a conclusion, but Cornwall shows that that was the direction in which he was moving: towards the edge, the margin of his world.

11

Zennor: 1916–1917

Cornwall represented an extraordinary change for Lawrence and Frieda. Going to Porthcothan was like going to the Lago di Garda: a retreat into isolation and poverty. They were, Lawrence realized, going to be 'very very poor': the Florida money was all they had.[1] Lawrence had just one book on its way towards publication, his collection of essays about Italy; he would revise the book into its final state at the proof stage in January 1916 and it would be published in June as *Twilight in Italy*. But there was little prospect of anything more, beyond a second volume of poems (*Amores*) that Duckworth was prepared to publish. The two books together cannot have brought him more than about £50, and probably less.

Illustration 17, a photograph taken in the late summer of 1915, demonstrates the culmination – and conclusion – of Lawrence's reputation as a writer. There is no other Lawrence photograph like it. Some people in studio portraits have birds in cages at their feet; others have potted palms. Lawrence has been given a book: he is posed as 'the author'.[2] From the date of the photograph, we may be meant to assume that the book is the brand-new *Rainbow*; one hand and arm lie along the table as Lawrence pretends to read it, the other hand makes to turn its pages. He is not, however, reading *The Rainbow*. For one thing, he is not wearing the spectacles he needed when reading and writing; he had worn them since 1908, but was never photographed in them.[3] For another, the book is loose-hinged and slightly dog-eared: a studio prop. Only weeks later, the banning of *The Rainbow* had destroyed everything that this pose of the authorial self had been designed to convey. The man in Cornwall was no longer able to earn his living; could no longer *be* the author posed by the photograph.

In the early months of 1916, Lawrence worked his way through his old college notebooks, digging out and rewriting poems, to construct 'a sort of inner history of my life, from 20 to 26';[4] the book came out in July. In spite of the apparent pointlessness of writing fiction, he wrote 'a mid-winter story of oblivion' – perhaps 'The Miracle', the early version of 'The Horse-Dealer's Daughter'.[5] But what other prospects did he have? His notoriety was bad enough, but the war was also causing a steep decline in the publishing industry. Firms had cut wages on the outbreak of war and by 1916 were finding it hard to keep employees, as more and more men joined up or, from June, were conscripted. Paper was increasingly expensive, fewer books were published, and publishers were choosing to bring out no-risk material. Lawrence's image of himself at the time was that of 'a man pushing an empty barrow up an endless slope'.[6] He and Frieda would survive on money that Pinker advanced, on the occasional magazine publication, on charity from institutions like the Royal Literary Fund and on friends and family (which Lawrence hated having to do). And in the winter of 1915–16 he was ill again, this second winter in England no better than the first.

Yet he and Frieda liked Cornwall. The Porthcothan house overlooked rocks and a small cove, and gave them a sense of being almost out of England; it felt like 'the first move to Florida'. Lawrence enjoyed the feeling of having left everything behind, the rest of the world going on like 'a sordid brawl in last night's café-restaurant', and on 6 January 1916 he made one of his periodic declarations that he was 'willing to give up people altogether'.[7]

However, Lawrence's letters, remarkable though they so often are, are only a partial guide to what he was thinking. Letters were creative work, never simply confessions. They were occasions for trying out a language to express feelings as those feelings were immediately present to him; and very often he experimented with a language that he reckoned appropriate for the person to whom the letter was being written. The man who declared that he was willing to give up people altogether was, at the time, living happily with his wife, a friend was staying and two others shortly expected, and he was engaged in an extensive correspondence with a great many others. Giving people up meant that he was very conscious of having tried (and failed) to change them with writing like *The Rainbow*. As he went on to say in another letter, 'why should they be as I want them to be'. He insisted that he did not want 'to urge and constrain any more';[8] a resolution, however, immediately countermanded by his development of a plan for the private re-publication of *The Rainbow* by subscription. He was provoked into this by Philip Heseltine, who had come down to live with him and Frieda at the start of January; Heseltine's girlfriend, Minnie Channing (always known as the 'Puma'), and his friend the Armenian-born writer Dikran Kouyoumdjian also came to stay, though they had returned to London by the end of February. Kouyoumdjian, who had grown increasingly unwelcome, took back material for a malicious satire he published in March in the *New Age* on 'a Brilliant Author with a Red Beard and Spiritual Eyes' whose 'Great Philosophy . . . was too Good to be Published'.[9] Heseltine, however, developed a scheme for the 'Rainbow Books and Music', and appealed for subscribers.

Yet Lawrence was not simply a creature of whim. His letters, like everything he wrote, were the direct consequence of what was happening to him at the time. A woman who met him in 1915 commented: 'Nobody . . . cared so little for the embarrassments he caused.'[10] Letters were written to the person and for the moment, not for posterity; and the resulting contradictions were far less important to him than his attempts to keep in touch with what was happening to him – to know it, to express it, to share it. He argued himself (and his fictional characters) into full, imaginative realization of all kinds of contradictory positions: for example, that men were (and needed to be) 'master' in their relationships with women,[11] but – also – that they wanted equal partnership with them; that men must go their way regardless of women, but that men could only act when they had women behind them; that women needed to find sexual freedom, but that men must always lead the way in matters of sex. He believed it his job as a writer to find out what he and others thought and felt; and that meant a continual effort of imagination. He constantly outflanked himself as a thinker; but that was the point. He never imagined that he should be establishing some kind of final conclusion. He was not a teacher or a philosopher. He was as wedded to contradictions as Blake or Whitman had been, in their own ways; as happy to think of people as 'not homogeneous or even coherent. They are dual and opposite.'[12]

And for all his talk of 'giving up' people, the idea of living together with others, especially with Murry and Katherine, remained very appealing. He wrote to them: 'I've waited for you for two years now, and am far more constant to you than ever you are to me – or ever will be.'[13] Those last four words were perhaps a joke: but they were also a deadly prediction. Lawrence often very much wanted to live with other people, in spite of his repeatedly expressed desire for isolation. For all his determined self-reliance, or perhaps because of it, he became very lonely; and one of the differences between life on the Lago di Garda, or in Fiascherino, and life in Cornwall, was that in 1916 he was no longer content with just Frieda. When he had been first passionately attracted to her, she had been enough for him, but now, with a strong sense of her as his necessary opposite as well as his complement and partner, he wanted people with whom he could have a different kind of relationship.

In particular, he wanted a man with whom he could be close. It is clear that by 1916 he was consciously acknowledging the side of his nature that had always found men as important as women. Living with Frieda for almost four years had satisfied him emotionally and sexually, but he was still left with a sense of a gap – a need for 'another kind of love', as Birkin would put it in *Women in Love*.[14] This meant love for a man with whom he would actively *do* things, walk and work and talk, and to whom he would pour out his heart; who was not a sexual partner but a kind of brother. He had perhaps first experienced love for such a man in his relationship with Jessie's brother Alan, back at the Haggs. Since then, there had been his Eastwood friend George Neville; in Croydon, Arthur McLeod; from 1912, Bunny Garnett; since 1913, Murry. Lawrence's writing about a person such as 'Il Duro' in *Twilight in Italy* in the autumn of 1915 had shown his specific attraction to a man's body: Il Duro 'was very handsome, beautiful rather, a man of thirty-two or -three, with a clear golden skin, and perfectly turned face, something godlike'; 'his beauty, so perfect and defined, fascinated me'.[15] And *Women in Love* would explore the idea still further, in Birkin's attraction to Gerald Crich.

Of these men, real and fictional, all except Bunny were exclusively heterosexual, so Lawrence was not portraying, nor looking for, a homosexual relationship. As shown, he had developed a considerable aversion to some kinds of homosexuality, for what he thought was its self-enclosed and sexually predatory nature (he recognized this in himself). It had taken him a long time before he was prepared to admit that his need of men *did* have a component of physical attraction. But attraction was not the same as desire. He never seems to have wanted to have sex with a man. If anything, the opposite: he actively wanted *not* to. He offered himself the intellectual justification that sexuality should always entail conflict, opposition to the necessary other; his feelings for men could not, therefore, be concerned with sexual gratification. They were, however, 'attempts to assuage early disturbances and divisions in the self';[16] what he wanted was a beloved male companion, with whom he could talk and to whom he would not be opposed, unlike the self involved and oppositional in his relationship with Frieda. Early in the twentieth century, he was thus articulating and feeling what other Englishmen by the end of the century had begun to feel: that in heterosexual relationship, *other* kinds of love, especially same-sex loving friendship, are necessary. Back in 1912 he had written to McLeod about this: 'Do you know, I don't think you were fond enough of me. I was very fond of you. But . . . You won't let yourself be really fond, even of a man friend, for fear he find out your weaknesses.'[17]

Luring Murry to Cornwall was a real ambition for Lawrence, though he also welcomed the idea of living with people he liked. He was a constantly frustrated social being, as every account of his exhilarating presence in company shows. He played and worked *with* people extremely happily, even if he wanted to take the lead. Groups, over and over again, brought out the best in him; whether at the Haggs as an adolescent, or having a wonderful time in Blackpool with George Neville in 1910, or with Bunny and Frieda in Icking and Mayrhofen in 1912, or participating in the peasant wedding in Fiascherino in 1913, or playing charades in Mecklenburgh Square in 1917. One example must stand for all. In August 1912, Lawrence had acted out 'ridiculous versions of a shy and gawky Lawrence being patronised by literary lions, of a winsome Lawrence charming his landlady, a sentimental Lawrence being put in his place by his landlady's daughter, of a bad-tempered whining Lawrence picking a quarrel with Frieda over nothing'. Frieda and Bunny had 'laughed at him until laughing was an agony'; they acted 'complicated nonsense charades', and were 'fearfully happy together'.[18] In Cornwall in January 1916, before Lawrence became ill, group life took the form of writing a play, 'all of us together, a comedy for stage, about Heseltine and his Puma and so on'.[19] It sounds like a comic version of Rananim in Buckinghamshire: the making of a consoling group fiction against the ravages of the moment. Lawrence could lose himself in such activity and find it fulfilling, but his sense of failure and disappointment militated against this outgoing social self and, as the years went by, he tended to grow warier, more guarded, more self-contained. Rather ominously, he would comment in 1918, while living again with his family, that 'I have almost a passion for being alone'.[20]

In spite of his marriage and the company of friends, the disaster (for him) of the start of the war, together with the suppression of *The Rainbow*, meant that he was again subject to real melancholy and to a violent hatred for institutional England, while knowing that he must remain a part of it. What else could he be a writer for? His father had always instinctively reacted against authority; one of Lawrence's patterns was also to rebel, whether against Christianity, or parenting, or philosophy or literature. He resisted *influence* very strongly ('We have to hate our immediate predecessors, to get free from their authority,' he once remarked).[21] Although he liked Cornwall and the sense it brought that he had left everything behind and that nothing mattered, this also made him feel terrible. By the middle of January he had not only been 'ill for weeks', on and off, but he had 'got the sense of dissolution, that horrible feeling one has when one is really ill'. What he called 'the slightest upset' could plunge him into depression. He told Murry that he felt 'always on the brink of another collapse'; and when he saw Lawrence in April 1916, Murry thought that 'his present carelessness seems to me due to a despair'.[22] Things had, after all, turned out badly with Heseltine. Lawrence had not only tried to partner him with a woman he thought right (a regular, well-meaning concern for Lawrence and Frieda) but, by telling Ottoline about Heseltine's Puma, he had wrecked Heseltine's chances with a young woman Ottoline was taking care of at Garsington.[23] After returning to London, Heseltine had denounced Lawrence for his interference.

The publishing scheme had also come to nothing: thirty responses to six hundred proposal leaflets. And the war ground on remorselessly. At the start of March, Frieda would tell Katherine that 'Lawrence has had a bad time . . . Some of the *wonder* of the world has gone for him.' He needed people, he needed belief, above all he needed work in which he could escape. Four years later, sympathizing with Catherine Carswell about her depressed husband, Donald, he would remark: 'It is absolutely killing, I know, to keep wrestling with the void. I can feel that he gets depressed.'[24] Wrestling with the void and getting depressed were things he knew very well. Frieda, who, without regular employment, might have been expected to suffer more in the remote places in which they lived, again seems to have coped with the isolation better, and actually to have preferred the company of Lawrence alone. She wrote, later, how richly and happily they had spent time together in isolated places – 'months of quiet, peaceful living'[25] – but she was, all the same, prepared to put up with the presence of the people Lawrence needed.

At the start of March 1916, with his health rather better, Lawrence and Frieda went to Zennor, even further west, and found two cottages side by side, 'just under the moors, on the edge of the few rough stony fields that go to the sea'. Higher Tregerthen Farm lay just below, and the Hocking family there were friendly and helpful. Lawrence decided immediately that the second cottage would be for Murry and Katherine, and sent out an appeal for them to come.[26] The rent was only £5 a year (so reasonable it was positively Italian); the Lawrences lived in the local inn while they painted and decorated one cottage, and bought second-hand furniture for it. Then they moved in and waited for the arrival of their friends. Murry and Katherine had been happily living in Bandol, in the south of France; returning to England seemed, for them, a step in the wrong direction. But they did not want to ignore Lawrence's appeal. Frieda wrote to them that 'we are *friends* and we wont bother anymore about the *deep* things, they are all right, just let's live like the lilies in the field'. They arrived early in April and also painted and decorated, 'working furiously' – not like lilies at all.[27]

Lawrence responded strongly to emotional and personal support, and was wonderfully creative while Murry and Katherine were with them. He had, apart from the one story, written no new fiction for almost eighteen months; but he was waiting to see if he could recover from Germany those two hundred pages of manuscript, abandoned in 1913 when he had started 'The Sisters'. Getting the manuscript out of wartime Germany proved an insuperable problem; but in the last ten days of April, before the decorating was finished, he had gone back to the second half of the *Rainbow* material.

For the first time in months, he was engaged in something that really occupied him. The tensions of life at Tregerthen found their way into the novel, as did a vision of small, brightly coloured figures moving against an alien landscape, and an attitude towards the past (and places like Garsington) which defined them as 'accomplished' – finished, rigidly in place – and therefore oppressive.[28] Lawrence's conflicted desire to retreat into social isolation with a single partner, ideally abroad (as Birkin wishes to go with Ursula), and the contradictory idea of love between two men (Birkin and the coal-owner Gerald Crich) became central to the novel. Work on it went rapidly from the very start, and Lawrence was both proud and relieved; the making of such a book, after all, *was* his life. 'When one is shaken to the very depths, one finds reality in the unreal world.' He could not afford to think of how pointless it was to write what could not be published: 'one goes on writing, to the unseen witnesses.'[29] He had finished the first writing by the end of June. The novel took Birkin, Ursula, her sister Gudrun and Gerald to the Alps: unable to establish a relationship with Gudrun, and furiously jealous of her, Gerald finally dies frozen in the snow: Gudrun goes off with an artist (a memory of a sculptor Lawrence and Frieda had met in 1913)[30] and Birkin mourns the man he loved, while Ursula criticizes his refusal to admit that his love was hopeless.

The dream of a settled, creative life for the four in Cornwall worked out badly in reality, and in ways that echo the novel. Frieda was jealous of Murry and Katherine for monopolizing her precious Lawrence, while Katherine wanted a life with Murry, not a communal life with friends (Frieda wrote, years later: 'I think K. didn't want it to work!'). Murry and Katherine reported to Ottoline Morrell that Lawrence was worryingly unstable, though both were trying to ingratiate themselves with her and to tell her what she wanted to hear. Katherine thought 'he has gone a little bit out of his mind', Murry asserted that, in everything Lawrence did or said, 'I detect a taint of illness or hysteria'.

In fact, Lawrence's letters read very sanely; what was happening was the break-up of the relationship between the two couples. Lawrence came to feel that Murry disliked him intensely, and that Murry had only ever wanted simply 'the warmth and security of personal affection'.[31] Lawrence always wanted more than that from his friends, however: loyalty, for a start, but also responsiveness to ideas and purposes; this is what he had had with Alan Chambers. And this, Murry had never been good at giving; in general, all he could do was mimic what he thought Lawrence wanted to hear from him. In Cornwall, Murry and Katherine grew to hate Frieda; and, above all, Murry and Katherine found unbearable the Lawrences' vicious language to each other, the occasional physical assaults, the subsequent making-up, the renewal of conflict. The Lawrences' marriage in this state was too much for most people, as they themselves knew. Lawrence had acknowledged in January: 'Perhaps the way we behave to one another she and I makes everybody believe that there is real incompatibility between us'; while Frieda wrote around the same time how – if people thought she was bad for Lawrence and that Lawrence did not care for her – 'both his behaviour and mine stupidly give this impression to other people'. Someone sensitive and middle-class, like the writer Eleanor Farjeon, who admired Lawrence enormously, hated him when he launched into 'some atrocious outburst against Frieda'.[32]

People as fragile in their own relationship as Murry and Katherine found the Lawrences especially hard. Frieda's lost children remained one source of anger, but almost anything could be. An apparently innocuous remark by Frieda about Shelley during tea one day, for example, was actually an attack on something Lawrence had been arguing for, as both would have known, and it led to a row. It should be noted that Katherine is the only witness, and any account by her of violent behaviour is going to be biased.[33] The Lawrences started shouting (Katherine called it 'roaring') with Frieda exclaiming: 'Out of my house – you little God almighty you. Ive had enough of you. Are you going to keep your mouth shut or aren't you.' Lawrence's Notts-Derby voice is audible: 'I'll give you a dab on the cheek to quiet you, you dirty hussy.' Katherine got out fast, but the row followed her into her own cottage a couple of hours later: the Lawrences apparently *demonstrating* their quarrel. Frieda had gone to see Murry and Katherine in the evening, telling them: 'I have finally done with him. It is all over for ever.' Lawrence, however, did not follow her, as she had perhaps expected. So she went outside, in the dark, and began to walk around the house, met Lawrence (as presumably she meant to), and 'they began to scream and scuffle'.[34] Katherine adds: 'He beat her – he beat her to death – her head and face and breast and pulled out her hair.' But as this happened outdoors, in the dark, Katherine couldn't have seen much; and Frieda was far from dead. 'All the while she [Frieda] screamed for Murry to help her. Finally they dashed into the kitchen and round and round the table. I shall never forget how L. looked. He was so white – almost green and he just hit – thumped the big soft woman. Then he fell into one chair and she into another.'[35] Gradually they struck up a conversation with Murry, then with each other, and finally left.

Lawrence was in a state of mind in which almost any kind of criticism made him angry, but in particular 'I . . . can't stand showing off'. He found it 'nauseating and humiliating'. Yet there seems no doubt that both the Lawrences were increasingly violent in acting out their feelings. Frieda had recently cracked Lawrence over the head again with a plate, stoneware this time.[36] He was very aware of his old tendency to stifle feelings, so now made it a point of principle (as he stated it in 1920) to 'prefer my strife, infinitely, to other people's peace, havens, and heavens'. Again, they were aware of this: Frieda told Ottoline 'how he has grown and so have I and our fights have been the lesser unreal thing'. But each was bossy, and their determination to keep the other in her or his place, using any 'unreal' means possible, left their friends alienated and themselves exhausted. Nearly ten years later, Lawrence told their friend Dorothy Brett: 'You have no idea, Brett, how humiliating it is to beat a woman; afterwards one feels simply humiliated.'[37] Neither public embarrassment nor private shame worried him; what mattered was the loss of self-containment and control, however much he attempted to be 'unbottled' and uninhibited.

Murry and Mansfield were shocked by the assaults, but the aftermath seemed worse. The next day they saw Lawrence trimming a hat for Frieda and the couple in perfect amity. Katherine found this 'so degraded'. To her it was worse than the physical violence; what she saw as Lawrence's 'humiliating dependence' made her 'too furious'.[38]

It took her a couple more years before she admitted that she was extremely like Lawrence emotionally: '*unthinkably* alike, in fact'. They both knew the capacity for rage of the self-conscious, controlled, fastidious person; they were both intensely aware of consequent humiliation. Indeed, Lawrence often felt closer to Katherine than to Murry: 'I like her better than him.'[39]

In the middle of June, Murry and Katherine moved out, abandoning the carefully chosen furniture, the painting and floor staining and distempering, along with Lawrence's hopes of a shared life. Lawrence was left with an angry self-accusation that he had misunderstood Murry; he now thought the two of them were 'not really associates. How I deceive myself.'[40] Their departure was nevertheless a blow: another kind of support suddenly gone. Murry and Katherine were also now telling themselves (and anyone else who could hear) that the Lawrences were impossible, in particular Frieda. They were not the only people to say this about her. Ottoline Morrell had received acrimonious letters from her and had grown to hate her; Russell had come to dislike her, Koteliansky could not bear her. Such antagonism usually came from people jealous of her special access to Lawrence, which Murry and Katherine were not alone in seeing as her domination of him; such people found her loud, aggressive and fat (Katherine called her an 'immense german christmas pudding').[41] She had an aristocratic contempt for the bourgeois world; she did very little house-work, she sat with her legs apart, she smoked, she said what she thought, she expected to be waited on. She also refused to be charming or 'female' in any conventional sense. She never simpered or flirted; she told people what she wanted. Her liberation from Weekley and bourgeois Nottingham exaggerated such traits; her natural careless-ness became a point of principle, her clamour for individual freedom almost deafening (as early as 1912 her ex-lover Ernst Frick, writing from police detention, had cautioned her for her 'over-evaluation of freedom').[42] If you were attracted to her, you found her miraculously direct, uninhibited, sensual, unafraid and, like Bunny Garnett, would forgive her anything. If you were not attracted, you found her coarse, rude, vulgar and exhibitionist. Murry in 1916 was appalled by her 'ultimate vulgarity' and called her (in Latin) 'monstrous, horrible, shapeless, huge'; but in 1923 and 1930, he desperately wanted to sleep with her.[43] Everyone agrees that she was 'voluble'; she repeated, and sometimes trivialized, Lawrence's ideas, some of which were, in fact, development of insights that had come from her. This gave some people the idea that she had him under her thumb.[44]

Lawrence, however, knew that however irritating he found her, he needed to hear what she was saying. What made things especially difficult for Frieda in 1916, of course, was the war; and it is striking how most of the real antagonism to her arose after its outbreak in August 1914. In 1913, Constance Garnett had hated Frieda and Lawrence quarrelling, but had been sorry for them (and had gone to Lerici to stay near them in 1914); a casual acquaintance in Kingsgate thought her 'a first-rate poet's wife'.[45] Frieda had had to remake her life completely at the start of the war. She feared internment, and she was suffering the loss of her German family shortly after losing her English family and her children. At the start of May 1912, her affective existence had been made up of three children, a beloved nanny, a husband, two parents-in-law, a father to whom she was devoted, a mother and two dear sisters, along with nephews and nieces. She lost the first seven overnight in May 1912 and the rest effectively in August 1914 (mail from Germany arrived only very rarely and had to come via Switzerland). When her father died in 1915, and the news finally got through to her, she could neither go to Germany nor see her mother or sisters; she could not even write to her mother with any certainty that the letter would arrive. She was an astonishingly adaptable woman, but the emotional deprivation and pain she suffered during these years was remarkable, and Lawrence the only person she could take it out on. In her own remaking of herself as a natural, uninhibited, sensual and independent woman, she became, at times, a parody of herself. She asserted her nationality; she was proud of the successes of her distant cousin the air-ace Manfred von Richthofen. With wonderful tactlessness, in 1917 she told a member of the Household Cavalry to whom she was introduced 'how very much smarter she thought the Prussian Guards than the Household Brigade'; and in the spring of 1915, when Brave Little Belgium had long been a national piety, she may have commented: 'Dirty Belgians! Who cares for them?'[46] But however much all of this might have been offensive to the inhabitants of Porthcothan or Zennor, such sentiments would not have troubled

Lady Ottoline or Russell, Murry, Katherine or Kot. What mattered to them was the combination of competitiveness, assertiveness and *vulgarity* she demonstrated. Frieda easily found herself dismissed as a 'quantité négligable',[47] and became still more insistent.

All this was happening, too, exactly when Lawrence was at his most depressed since the summer of 1913. For one thing, the failure with Murry and Katherine weighed on him. And then, at the end of June, came his first brush with the military; he had to attend a medical examination at Bodmin. He received a total exemption, but responded violently to the 'degradation' of the experience; the very pillow on his army bed had been like 'an old withered vegetable marrow tied up in a bag'.[48] The war was entering a new phase: the Somme campaign of the summer of 1916, hailed as a push deep into German territory, turned out to be the greatest disaster of the war; there were 60,000 British casualties on the first day alone. Lawrence commented, on 16 July: 'This is a winter.'[49] He worked harder than ever at his novel (another cause of both irritation and pride for Frieda: she saw herself as Ursula), and grew still more run down. To save money, he was typing the first half out, revising it as he went along; he was not a skilled typist (it took him months) and the work was 'like a malady or a madness while it lasts'.[50] In the early autumn, he abandoned the typing and wrote the rest out by hand, for someone else to type. By October 1916, he was complaining that 'I seem half my time, and more, to be laid up in bed. I think the terrible moisture of England does it: it has rained every day now for nine weeks.'[51] The weather, his preoccupation and his illness would not have improved Frieda's temper, either. She was rarely ill and felt that she was the one who should be waited on. The loneliness of Cornwall, however well she managed to cope with it, did get to her at times. In mid September 1916, using money the Lawrences could not afford (the fare was £2 5s), she went away to London for a week.

Lawrence finally finished *Women in Love* late in October. It was something that *he* believed in, as a piece of creative work, though he feared that 'everybody will hate it'. But it offered an extraordinarily courageous final word about wartime England, its violence and insanity: 'the bitterness of the war,' he wrote later, 'may be taken for granted in the characters.'[52] The novel suggests that one should go away from such a society, to create one's own world. As Birkin insists: 'One wants to wander away from the world's somewheres, into our own nowhere'; Gudrun Brangwen parodies him by saying that 'the happiest voyage is the quest of Rupert's Blessed Isles'. Six years later, Lawrence would sum up Birkin's state of mind (and perhaps his own), while writing about Herman Melville: 'Choosingly, he was looking for paradise. Unchoosingly, he was mad with hatred of the world.' Yet for all his own attempts at single-minded hatred – 'I hate humanity so much, I can only think with friendliness of the dead' – Lawrence, like Melville, was also 'at the core, a mystic and an idealist'.[53]

In 1916, he continued to write about and to look for a way of life which would be closer to what he thought he and his society needed, and his acute hatred of the world at war ('I am the enemy of mankind') sat uneasily with that; it could lead to a sense of strangeness, even madness at times. He wrote some disturbed and disturbing letters at the start of September, for example: 'When I see people in the distance, walking along the path through the fields to Zennor, I want to crouch in the bushes and shoot them silently with invisible arrows of death.' In the novel, Birkin – 'wondering if he were mad' – nevertheless decides that he prefers 'his own madness, to the regular sanity'.[54] For Lawrence, *Women in Love* was a book in which he worked through feelings of savage antagonism ('the only righteousness is the destruction of mankind'), while it was also a fictional world 'in which I can live apart from this foul world which I will not accept or acknowledge or even enter'. On 31 October, he sent its last pages to Pinker: 'It is a terrible and horrible and wonderful novel. You will hate it and nobody will publish it. But there, these things are beyond us.' Frieda wanted it called *Dies Irae*, 'Day of Wrath'; she thought it apocalyptic.[55]

Some part of Lawrence must have hoped that it *would* be published; he had dropped a Prologue chapter (about Birkin's attraction to men) which publishers would have found impossible,[56] and had had the book typed in two copies, for English and American publication. He also felt sure that it was his best novel. He was obliged to offer it first to Methuen, and they refused it, but then so did the 'decent' Duckworth[57] and all the other publishers Pinker tried. It was a profound rejection, and yet another indication of his foreseeable future as a writer. The circulation of one of the two typescript copies among his friends also put paid to his already damaged friendship with Ottoline Morrell, who detected in the character of Hermione a portrait of herself (I shall discuss Lawrence's fictional kinds of portraiture in Chapter 13). Lawrence vehemently rejected the connection; but he lost another supportive friend. He put as brave a face as he could on the various kinds of rejection he suffered: 'what does it matter? All that side of the old show is dead for me.'[58] But such bravado was terribly hollow. Like many sensitive people, his reaction to being hurt was to hit back and to insist that he did not care.

The rejection of *Women in Love* was, in its own way, as bad for Lawrence as the suppression of *The Rainbow* had been the previous year. He was a creative person who needed to feel that his writing was in some way affecting people; he believed passionately in 'the great articulate extremity of art'.[59] He had been a writer for more than ten years; he had been publishing for seven. And now he had been rendered inarticulate. Two short stories were his only fiction to be published between the banning of *The Rainbow* and the end of the war: and they only appeared in the USA. The frustration of an imaginative writer in such a situation is hard to conceive. After finishing the first version of *Women in Love*, Lawrence continued to work over the unpublishable typescript, to such an extent that during the next three years he would rewrite about a tenth of it. Revision at least allowed him to remain enclosed in his novel; as he had put it in October 1916: 'The world of my novel is big and fearless – yes, I love it, and love it passionately.'[60]

The rewriting, however, meant his importation into the text of some extraordinarily esoteric interests; a kind of deep texture of contemporary alternative thinking, to which he now felt free to devote himself. For who would publish his fiction now, or read it? He could do with it what he liked. Ideas drawn from theosophy, about cosmic energy – kundalini, the 'central serpent ... at the core of life' – entered the novel; so did a bizarre description of Birkin driving his car seated like a Pharaoh, with arms, breast and head 'like those of a Greek'.[61] Something similar happened to his next project, first contemplated in the winter of 1916–17: a series of essays about American literature, which became extraordinarily esoteric before (six years later) being rewritten to become the book *Studies in Classic American Literature*. They had nevertheless started as a very practical, money-earning project. Publishing in the USA was a better idea than trying to earn in England, and Lawrence's thoughts were increasingly turning again to the possibility of going there: 'that far-off retreat, which is the future to me'.[62] The dream was encouraged by a new friendship with two young Americans, Robert Mountsier and Esther Andrews. Mountsier, in England to write for US magazines about the effects of the war, had met Lawrence in 1915; he got himself invited to Cornwall with Esther, who was starting as a journalist. They came down for Christmas and New Year in 1916 and had an extremely cheerful time; Stanley Hocking, from the farm, remembered 'taking my accordion and playing them songs, and they were singing. They all enjoyed themselves very much.' What may have contributed to the cheerfulness was the 'junk' (either heroin or some other narcotic) that Mountsier enjoyed but Lawrence disliked.[63] But Mountsier helped Lawrence develop his plans for his essays on American literature, and they also talked about travel to the USA. The American essays, on writers such as Poe, Hawthorne, Melville and Whitman, were obviously a practical way of addressing himself to that potential US audience. Lawrence was determined to 'go soon' and applied for passports; he told his agent how 'One's psychic health is more important than the physical.' He told Catherine Carswell how 'my heart never felt so down in the dirt, as it does now'.[64] At the start of 1917, he was ill again and spending a lot of time in bed.

In 1911, one of his reasons for giving up school had been the fear that he might grow 'consumptive', and long before 1924 people linked his pallor (that of the fair-skinned and red-bearded man), his thinness and his frequent chest illnesses with tuberculosis.[65] However, although he had developed tuberculosis by 1925, he didn't have it in 1916.[66] Like 80 per cent of the population of Europe, he would have had tubercles – areas of infection which had been hardened over and were no longer infectious – in his lungs, but the vast majority of that 80 per cent never developed the disease. Lawrence had what was called a 'weak chest': he was particularly subject to colds, coughs, inflammation and bronchitis. 'I have had bronchitis since I was a fortnight old,' he lamented.[67] His liking for living in places that were set above a view, or by the sea or lake, may have had some physiological component (he welcomed fresh air and ozone); but he also developed metaphors of oppression and suffocation that were as much psychological as physiological. On 16 January 1917, for example, while waiting to hear about his passport application, he wrote: 'All the oxygen seems gone out of the vital atmosphere here, and one gutters like a suffocated candle'; three days later: 'I can't live in England any more. It oppresses one's lungs, one cannot breathe.' His application was refused; the next day, Lawrence wrote how the 'vital atmosphere of the country is poisonous to an incredible degree: to me at least. I shall die in the fumes of their stench.'[68] All he and Frieda could do was sit tight in Cornwall, Lawrence in 'a state of tension against everything', 'thwarted, cribbed, stunted'. Back in December, Asquith's Liberal government, which for Lawrence had represented the last of the 'old, stable, measured, *decent* England', had been ousted by a war coalition headed by David Lloyd George ('The man means nothing: he has no more inside to him than an empty tin').[69]

For relief and escape, Lawrence immersed himself in his American essays. He had a quick, capacious, sceptical mind, adept at taking what he wanted from books that others would dismiss as absurd. What he liked was a 'learned' book, 'not too big, because I like to fill it in myself'.[70] He had always read widely, and during these years of the war had lots of time to do so. The essays for *Studies*, in their long and immensely complex gestation, would, like *Women in Love*, take their readers through ideas drawn from psychoanalysis, religion, anthropology, theosophy and magic. He had always found fascinating the subjects of religion and belief, and of the esoteric, and described one of the famous theosophical books (Madame Blavatsky's *Secret Doctrine*) as in 'many ways a bore, and not quite real. Yet one can glean a marvellous lot from it, enlarge the understanding immensely.'[71] He took nearly two years, in the first instance, to write the twelve *Studies* essays. But for all the abstraction of this work, which had a profound appeal for him, as usual there was a strongly practical streak in Lawrence that never let him completely abandon himself to the esoteric. Early in May 1917, for example, working on another version of his old philosophy, 'suddenly I felt as if I was going dotty'. He 'left off' at once. The 'wonderful things' which he discovered in his reading of the esoteric, however 'marvellously illuminating', were also, he felt, 'all part of the past, and part of a past self in us: and it is no good going back'. He summed up the paradox the following year in his conclusion that the occult 'is very interesting, and important – though antipathetic to me'.[72] It offered useful metaphors, but not truths. There remained in Lawrence a stubborn determination to be himself, and of his age, and to write for his age. And of course he had a constant, stultifying (not to say suffocating) awareness that, during the war at least, there was hardly any point in even *trying* to publish. The American essays, when stripped of some of the strangeness, would one day also be publishable as a book: but not yet. The fact that the USA had declared war on Germany on 6 April 1917 had done a good deal to blunt his keenness to go there.

Another form of distraction, late in April 1917, came in the person of Esther Andrews who, after Mountsier had left England for the continent to pursue his journalistic work, had returned to Cornwall, to lodge in the house vacated by Murry and Katherine and now regularly used as extra space by the Lawrences. The American patron of the arts Mabel Sterne Luhan later claimed that Esther had had an affair with Lawrence. Mabel was wrong;[73] nevertheless, Frieda was, unusually for her, ill in bed much of the time, and Lawrence must have spent lengthy periods with a young woman who, to judge by her star-struck account of her time in Cornwall, was strongly attracted to him.[74] The fact that, in her account, Lawrence emerges as rather depressed ('there seems to be always a weight on him') suggests that he may not have enjoyed her company as much as she enjoyed his.[75] Her relationship with Mountsier, whatever it was, seems to have come unstuck, and she was profoundly unsure of herself. Back on her feet, Frieda 'showed the young lady the door' and she went back to London. A long and extremely cheerful letter that Lawrence wrote to her in August indicates that he felt no awkwardness with her, though he did ask: 'Why didn't you answer Frieda's letter?'[76] There is another way, however, of confirming that nothing happened between Lawrence and Esther. Nothing really significant that Lawrence experienced ever failed to make its way, in some form, into his writing, often recreated in his fiction. And of Esther there is no trace.

Lawrence dug around for things he might publish in 1917. There were two more rewritings of his philosophy; in the spring he called it (in direct opposition to the war) 'The Reality of Peace', and by the end of the summer it had turned into a short book, 'At the Gates', which no longer survives. The *English Review* continued to offer some support, especially when he told Austin Harrison in April that he was anxious to have 'The Reality of Peace' published 'and quite realised that it was hardly a commercial proposition'. He accepted 20 guineas for the four essays they printed;[77] before the war the magazine had paid him £10 or £15 for a single story. 'At the Gates' was considered by a number of publishers, but all turned it down. All Lawrence could do was grow vegetables – in their own way 'a triumph of life in itself'[78] – work at Higher Tregerthen farm, read, and occasionally add revisions to his American essays and to the typescript of *Women in Love*. The ending of the latter changed, to one of those characteristically mid-air Lawrentian endings, where one insistence (Ursula saying that Birkin's love for both men and women is 'false, impossible') is met by another (Birkin's 'I don't believe that') with the novel remaining suspended between the two points of view.[79]

Lawrence's only book publication in 1917 would be a small volume of poems, *Look! We Have Come Through!* (which earned him just £20), revised from poems written in 1912–13 and centred on his love for Frieda. He had always held these back from publication, feeling 'most passionately and bitterly tender' about them, and desperately nostalgic: 'I feel more inclined to burst into tears than any thing.' They were 'my last and best. Perhaps I shall never have another book of poems to publish'; the book was 'a sort of final conclusion of the old life in me'.[80] He had told Murry in October 1916 (during the last fortnight of the draft of *Women in Love*) that 'Frieda and I have finished the long and bloody fight at last, and are at one. It is a fight one has to fight – the old Adam to be killed in me, the old Eve in her – then a new Adam and a new Eve. Till the fight is finished, it is only honorable to fight.'[81] He now felt that he had been wrong about love. His previous collections had been entitled *Love Poems* and *Amores*, but Birkin had denounced the 'horrible merging, mingling, self-abnegation of love', and Lawrence was struggling through to a new philosophy of relation-ship in which individuals, single and separate, are 'constellated together like two stars' in 'a pure balance of two single beings'. This was a way of responding both to Frieda's insistence on love *and* to his own long-term hankering for detachment. He wanted the new kind of partnership not to be dependent on love: the poems of *Look!* revisited 1912 but were revised to acquire the very different voice of 1917.[82]

The year 1917 passed in much the same way as 1916; Lawrence made just one brief journey away from Cornwall, to see his family in the Midlands and doctors in London. Military conscription was, however, coming closer. The number of casualties continued to be appalling, and new conscripts were vital. Lawrence was examined again at Bodmin in June 1917 and put in category C3 (the lowest possible grade apart from rejection). But some of the local Cornish people were not at all happy about having this uninhibitedly anti-war individual (with a German wife) in their midst. Rumours abounded. Frieda running along the coastal path with her scarf flapping must be signalling to submarines: was there a stock of petrol for these German craft at the bottom of the cliffs near the Lawrences' cottage? The main Atlantic convoy route lay along the north Cornish coast, and during 1917 there was a massive increase in the numbers of attacks on shipping. Only fourteen ships had been sunk in the area by submarine activity during the whole period between August 1914 and December 1916. However, after a change of strategy by the German navy, no fewer than forty-nine ships were sunk during 1917. At the start of February, Frieda recorded: '*Three ships* have been torpedoed *just here*, gone, the men seen struggling in the water (Stanley saw them) for a few minutes, I tell you it's *very* bad.'[83] Even tarred repair work on the Lawrences' cottage chimney could be interpreted as a coded signal. They were spied on, and German songs would have been heard. They were stopped on one occasion by a military patrol and their bags searched (a square loaf of bread was seized on as a camera until unwrapped).[84] The situation was made worse by the presence in the neighbourhood of other non-conscripted, artistic individuals. Heseltine returned at intervals to a house nearby, and his friend the musician Cecil Gray had come to live at Bosigran, three miles down the coast road. The Lawrences helped Gray move in, as they had helped Murry and Katherine; Gray and Lawrence discussed how the war might be brought to an end (Lawrence apparently favoured a disruptive and pacifist campaign in industrial areas); and all three of them, doubtless overheard, sang German lieder and the Hebridean songs (some of them in Gaelic) that were a recent musical discovery.[85]

For his part, Lawrence got on better and better with the Hockings at Higher Tregerthen. In 1917, 'whether it was hay-making or harvesting', he worked in the fields along with the family, 'the same as if one of us', and this accounted for his subsequent feeling of being 'mostly happy at Tregerthen'. It sounds like the Haggs again. The Hockings observed that he 'could work very hard indeed, but not for a whole day like we would'; during one meal break, the handsome eldest son, William Henry Hocking (see Illustration 18), then around thirty-five years old – Lawrence was thirty-two – said to him: ' "You are getting more like one of us every day, Mr Lawrence." He made a smile at that.'[86]

He was spending a lot of time with Hocking, who had 'thought deeply and bitterly'; Lawrence brought his reading of mysticism to the conversation, the Cornishman his instinctive comprehension. Lawrence had singled him out as 'most marvellously understanding' back in October 1916. As the summer of 1917 went on, Frieda felt increasingly neglected because of the time Lawrence was spending with the young farmer. She probably saw it as one of her husband's 'uncritical intimacies with people',[87] in which he was the intellectual superior. Hocking, as usual in these relationships of Lawrence's, was heterosexual (he married the following year and had had two children by 1920), and the idea of sex with another man would probably have been anathema to him. It was an intimate relationship, in which Hocking relieved Lawrence of the lonely burden of himself; emotional yet not sexual; capable of making Frieda jealous, certainly, but all Lawrence's friendships did that.[88] It seems more like Lawrence's friendship with Alan Chambers than anything else: Lawrence the contained, demanding, intellectual partner, needing companionship and warm response, Hocking the instinctive man, with his own needs. Lawrence never forgot Hocking's habit of putting his hand to his chest 'with a queer, grasping movement' while saying 'there's something one wants . . . I can feel the want of it here – but shall I ever get it?'[89] Lawrence got on well with the young farmer's friends, too: Hocking recalled how he 'had some of my friends coming in the evenings, and we made a kind of merry group at times. He was never short of a story or an answer for us, and, well, I think we amused him and he also amused us.'[90] It would be hard to imagine such a group of men having anything to do with Lawrence if they had doubted his sexual inclinations.

Three years later, however, on Malta, Lawrence's homosexual friend Maurice Magnus wrote that Lawrence 'opened his "heart" (!) to me here accidentally', in another of those 'uncritical intimacies' which Frieda so distrusted:

He is looking for bisexual types for *himself*. Spoke of his innocence when he wrote 'Twilight' and 'Il Duro'. Evidently innocent no longer. Didn't like Malta because he thought that the religion or something prevented their sexual expression! I didn't elucidate [enlighten] him as I could have done even after a few days stay! He revels in all that is not just within his reach. He wants it to be within his reach. Arrived too late – regrets it. Never speaks of it unless bored to tears by women as here by Mrs Cannan and his wife.[91]

This is three years later, it should be emphasized, and Magnus is an unreliable reporter: always with an ear cocked for scandal, he is writing to his gossipy, boy-loving friend Norman Douglas, who would have enjoyed hearing such things about Lawrence. There is no other evidence that Lawrence was on the lookout for 'bisexual types', though such people intrigued him (both Douglas and Magnus were married homosexuals, and he certainly enjoyed their company). But by 1920 Lawrence seems to have regretted that he had spent so long refusing to acknowledge his attraction to men. His friendship with Hocking in 1917 shows him starting to do this.

Magnus's letter reveals, too, that in 1920 Lawrence believed that 'sexual expression' was just as much the right of the homosexual as of the heterosexual. He was perfectly fearless in doing what he wanted, and would have acted on his own feelings if he had really desired to. If Lawrence never did make sexual advances to a man, that would have been because the feelings he had for men were not strong enough: undeniable attraction not carried through into actual desire.

What is most illuminating about Magnus's comment, however, is the way it shows how profoundly Lawrence was fascinated by experiences and feelings outside the grasp of his own intuitive understanding. He was an extremely detached person, in spite of his friendships and his marriage; and in his attraction to men had at least three times been disappointed or let down. Bunny Garnett had flatly rejected his loving friendship in 1915; Murry and he were estranged; Hocking would stop answering his letters. In *Kangaroo*, Somers feels taken advantage of by John Thomas Buryan, rather as Lawrence came to feel he had been by Hocking; and Lawrence may well have come to feel the same about Magnus, who took advantage of him financially because of Lawrence's interest in him. A successful, loving relationship with a man was probably one of the things that seemed to Lawrence to be, although desirable, beyond him. The only occurrence in the biographical record suggestive of his even touching another man is his 'bundling' Murry into bed in February 1915, when the latter was ill with influenza and miserable; but all he was doing was (Murry recalled) 'looking after me as though I were a child'.[92] What Magnus ignores is the way in which, as a writer, Lawrence experimented with the lives and feelings of people lying just beyond his reach, by recreating them. In fiction, he would imagine a scene in *Aaron's Rod* in which Rawdon Lilly not only cares for an influenza-sick Aaron Sisson but also massages him with oil; in the first writing of *Women in Love*, he had shown Birkin loving men rather than women, wrestling naked with the man he is close to, and desiring 'to have and to possess the bodies'[93] of the men to whom he is physically attracted. Lawrence used his writing as an imaginative space in which to act out his feelings. Fiction brought those feelings and such people within his reach.

The war reached a new pitch of awfulness in the autumn of 1917, with the long-drawn-out horror of Passchendaele; there were nearly 90,000 Allied casualties in the first two months. According to Stanley Hocking, the Reverend David Rechab Vaughan, vicar of Zennor, hated the Lawrences and was 'largely responsible' for them being investigated by the authorities (who even questioned whether Lawrence was English). Non-conscripted friends were also natural targets for attack; Cecil Gray was fined punitively in September 1917 for letting a light show in his house after dark in a window facing the sea, during an evening spent with the Lawrences.[94] Lawrence's friendship with Mountsier, too, would have been regarded as compromising: Mountsier had been arrested and strip-searched as a possible German agent on his return from Cornwall in January 1917.[95] In the end, it was probably easier for the authorities to act rather than spend time finding out the truth about the spying and collusion with the enemy: and the writer with the German wife was the obvious target. Although Lawrence protested

– 'We are as innocent even of pacifist activities, let alone spying in any sort, as the rabbits of the field outside' – formal steps were taken. On Thursday 11 October, their cottage was searched while they were out and some papers taken away, including the text of a Hebridean song (a coded message?), Lawrence's address book and 'a few old letters in German'.[96] The following day, they were searched again: one of Lawrence's old poetry notebooks from college, with its drawings of sections of plant stems (gun emplacements? shell designs?), was examined. And they were served with a military exclusion order under the Defence of the Realm Act (DORA), forbidding them to reside in Cornwall or in any coastal place. They had to be out within three days. On Monday, 15 October 1917, Hocking drove them to the station in St Ives, to catch the train to London: 'and there the police were again'.[97]

Up in London, Cynthia Asquith, viewing the matter with the eye of responsible authority, confided to her diary that 'after all, the woman *is* a German and . . . Their exclusion seems so very reasonable.'[98] But Lawrence, already extraordinarily sensitive to the rejection of *The Rainbow* and *Women in Love* and the wrecking of his life as a serious writer, and horribly aware of wartime lies and propaganda ('all the world, as represented by the newspapers, is just prancing about in a meaningless sort of nightmare'), felt that his ejection was a proof of the rule of the mob, personified by the press. There had been vicious anti-German attacks in the papers: Germans were Germ-Huns in *John Bull*, and the *Daily News*, like other papers, had adopted a nasty moral superiority. Lawrence felt that there was no longer any such thing as a free citizen of England; his expulsion from Cornwall changed him for ever.[99]

12

Isolated and Independent:
1917–1919

Nothing would have prepared the Lawrences for their eviction from Cornwall, where they felt 'rooted', but it was also a disaster financially. The cottage was cheap and its rent had been paid until March 1918;[1] because they lived next to a farm and grew their own vegetables, they also had cheap food. In London, they had no money to pay for accommodation; for the first time in their life together, they were homeless. They had to rely on friends such as H. D. and Dollie Radford, and Cecil Gray's mother.

They were also still being tracked by the police. The authorities (having told them to register at the nearest police station) sent constables around to check up on them anyway, but they were also now under more worrying surveillance. In November, Richard Aldington met a detective from Scotland Yard whose job it was to follow them, and Lawrence encountered two plain-clothes police officers listening at the door of H. D.'s flat. Gray, visiting his mother's flat in December, found himself 'subjected to a mild form of third-degree examination concerning the Lawrences and my relations with them' by a CID officer; even Ernest Weekley was questioned.[2] During 1918, the Lawrences' neighbours would experience 'many visits from the police making enquiries', and as late as April 1919, the Censor was still opening Lawrence's mail. All this, Lawrence found 'hateful and humiliating and degrading'.[3]

Yet the expulsion did have a certain enlivening effect. Life at Zennor had increasingly become a killing experiment in isolation; being 'wound up in a dreadful state of resistant tension' there was exhausting.[4] Lawrence had been growing strange, describing in May 1917 that odd moment when suddenly he felt he was going 'straight out of my mind', while in September he had exclaimed: 'God, I *don't want* to be sane, as men are counted sane.'[5] The relationship with William Henry Hocking had been another sign of how far beyond his old self he was now prepared to go, and how much he was prepared to ignore Frieda and her claim on him: not because his relationship with Hocking was sexual, but because it consciously did what previous relationships with men had not done. It abandoned intellectualism; it was deliberately careless and took emotional risks. In London in October 1917, Lawrence missed Zennor and the freedom dreadfully, and he and Frieda quickly caught colds ('It is London'); but to be forced back into everyday relationships was in some ways a relief. At the end of October, he told Gray that 'somehow I don't want to be in Cornwall for the present'. Over the next twelve months, he lost touch with Hocking, who by January 1919 was not even answering letters to do with the disposal of the contents of the Lawrences' cottage.[6]

The people they now began to see a lot of became very important to them, as well as a relief to Frieda. H. D. was undergoing a time of dreadful stress. Richard Aldington was not only in the army, and unsure how long he would survive, but he had also found a new woman, Arabella Yorke, 'elegant but poor . . . usually lives in Paris'. Nevertheless, H. D., 'like an angel',[7] put up both Lawrence and Frieda for six weeks in her tiny flat in Mecklenburgh Square, which already contained Arabella and at times John Cournos, the translator; while Aldington also came to stay on occasion (though the Lawrences then made themselves as scarce as they could). There is no doubt that H. D. was drawn to Lawrence. In 1934, undergoing analysis with Freud, it was the meaning of her relationship with Lawrence she found she needed to deal with, and she wrote a novel centred on it.[8] Lawrence admitted to Gray, in November, that H. D. was, like Esther Andrews, one of his 'women': *not* sexual partners, but those who took him seriously, 'deeper than love, anyhow'. He felt that 'though there is a certain messiness, there is a further reality'.[9] Frieda would probably have reacted violently to this: soul-mush, she would have declared. She would have been happier with other friends, such as the Jungian analyst Dr David Eder and his wife, or when Gray came up from Cornwall, as he did at least once that autumn.

Lawrence and Frieda both, however, enjoyed themselves at times in ways that had rarely happened in Cornwall; they could be 'really jolly, notwithstanding everything'.[10] One evening of play-acting and charades in Mecklenburgh Square was especially memorable: Aldington and Arabella playing Adam and Eve (Aldington with a chrysanthemum for a fig-leaf), Frieda cast as the serpent (Otto Gross would have been pleased with that) obliged to writhe on her stomach on the carpet. H. D. was a dancing tree of life, Gray the angel at the gate (with an umbrella for a sword) and Lawrence typecast himself as God Almighty, organizer and narrator; thus dramatizing many of the problematic relationships of real life. And the local police to whom the Lawrences reported (as persons expelled under DORA) turned out to be nice enough, even sympathetic.[11]

But, as homeless people have to, they moved from room to room: Gray's mother's flat for a fortnight (they hated its bleached middle-classness) then back with H. D. for a few days. Lawrence found it 'a more wintry winter of discontent than I had ever conceived'.[12] It was perhaps not surprising that at precisely this point, he developed another of his unwritten, desperate 'Island' fantasies; it allowed him to bring together the people who were now important to him and, like a novelist, pitch them into a new location. This time, 'we shall sail away to our Island – at present in the Andes'. The location was chosen because Eder 'knows the country *well*'; the islanders would be an ill-assorted bunch of the people Lawrence was seeing every day, and therefore the ideal enactors of the fiction. Others did not know the extent to which they were participating: Gray was put down for £1,000, which he did not have. William Henry Hocking was also named as an islander; his farming skills would have been useful, but he may well not even have been told of the plan (and he would certainly not have come: he never even travelled to London, in spite of many invitations). But the idea occupied Lawrence for days. Unlike a novel, it was not a solitary preoccupation; it involved working with and talking the ideas through with the people whom he needed so desperately: 'it seems to occupy my heart.'[13]

In the real world, two people rescued the Lawrences. Dollie Radford from now onwards regularly lent them her country cottage in Hermitage, in Berkshire, when she or her daughter Margaret did not need it, and Lawrence's sister Ada rented a house for them in the Midlands from May 1918. Those became their main addresses for the next two years. In London, even Lawrence, good as he was at writing in a room occupied by other people, could not work: 'I get irritated here,' he explained.[14]

Look! We Have Come Through! had come out at the end of November 1917, while they were still shuffling between flats: an ironical reminder of those pre-war days in Icking and beside the Lago di Garda, when Lawrence's love for Frieda had been the most important thing in his life. He now felt that his job as a writer was to be concerned with the struggles of opposites and, in particular, with how the male struggles to escape what a year later he would memorably call 'the devouring mother'. That was where a new direction was taking him: to the position where he would say, 'I do think a woman must yield some sort of precedence to a man, and he must take this precedence.' Frieda thought that attitude ridiculous; she called him 'antediluvian'.[15] In 1917, Lawrence had only an instinct about this new formulation of the partnership between man and woman; but he was starting to gauge how much he had suffered (and been damaged) by his love for women, and by theirs for him. This sounds like the beginning of prejudice, not to say misogyny, but it was a genuine reaction: it encompassed his worry about the way he had developed. He was wondering if he had been too loving, too self-sacrificing, too ready to give way to Frieda's demand to be loved, exactly as he had to his mother's. It was in that sense that Frieda was the devouring mother; he was repeating with her what he had done before. (A great deal of his theoretical writing over the next four years would centre on the relationships between parents and children; one potential title for his 1921 book *Fantasia of the Unconscious* would be 'The Child and the Unconscious'.)

It was probably because of the development of this kind of idea about relationship, one that emphasized the lonely male, that, in London in the autumn of 1917, Lawrence started another novel:[16] always a sign in him that new thinking had to meet the tests of relationship and opposition within his fiction. It would be about a man who walks out on a conventional marriage to find a new life; and for whom love is not the answer to his problems. *Aaron's Rod*, all the same, did not get very far. Shifting from one friend's flat to another was not good for Lawrence's writing of large-scale fiction; and with one lengthy, unpublishable novel on his hands, writing another might have seemed even more absurd, however natural. His American essays were the only prose to which Lawrence could sensibly apply himself (he was at work on them from January 1918), and he made another small collection of poems. But *Bay* would earn him only £10. 'I go on working, because it is the one activity allowed to one, not because I care,' he insisted.[17] He knew the link between writing and caring, even as he dismissed it.

By February 1918, living out at Chapel Farm Cottage in Hermitage – 'cold, a little comfortless' – he and Frieda were getting desperate. They collected fuel by trawling the woods after the professional woods-men had finished, gathering in sacks the yellow wood chips left behind. Lawrence told his agent how 'in another fortnight I shall not have a penny to buy bread and margarine', and Pinker helped with a loan, as did other friends (so did the Royal Literary Fund). All Lawrence could do was struggle away at the American essays, and though at times they could 'of course rejoice my soul', even they were also 'a weariness to me'.[18] In some ways, the *Studies in Classic American Literature* at this stage became symbolic of Lawrence's state of mind: acutely analytical, profoundly abstract and detached. So much in them was in danger of becoming purely theoretical, as they worked out the patterns of 'self' and 'other.' They were hermetic, esoteric, internalized, a way for Lawrence (as he put it) to get it 'all off my chest'. He felt that he was in a deep rage most of the time, describing himself as 'a walking phenomenon of suspended fury'.[19] And yet the essays still paid acute attention to the authors and writing with which they dealt; he went on working on them until August. It was the everyday which haunted him, made him paranoid and angry: 'Nowadays one can do nothing but glance behind to see who now is creeping up to do something horrible to the back of one's neck'; 'At present there is some intang-ible counteraction between us all – so I find it – between me and everybody.'[20]

Settling down was, therefore, a problem. In the spring of 1918, Lawrence was likely to feel a kind of panic about being pinned down, or being with anyone, or living near anyone; his desire for lonely individuality was intense. 'The one thing I don't seem to be able to stand is the presence of anybody else – barring Frieda, sometimes.'[21]

(Ironically, he was just trying to get published another short book of poems he had provisionally called 'All of Us'.) 'I *hate* and *abhor* being stuck on to any form of society,' he insisted: 'it would be wrong to assume that one is quite sane just now.' The writer who could not get his books published continued to write with his usual brilliance, however: 'yesterday there was deep snow, though the trees are in bloom. Plum trees and cherry trees full of blossom look so queer in a snow landscape. Their lovely foamy fullness goes a sort of pinky drab, and the snow looks fiendish in its cold incandescence.'[22] Lodging in Hermitage, seeing few people apart from the family next door, was what he wanted; he gardened, and helped ten-year-old Hilda Brown, the neighbours' daughter, with her mathematics homework. But he could not afford to refuse Ada's charity; a visit to the Midlands in early April discovered Mountain Cottage at Middleton, near Wirksworth, 'a bungalow, on the brow of the steep valley'. He and Frieda moved up there at the start of May, Lawrence 'queer and desolate in my soul – like Ovid in Thrace': that is, in exile. It was 'exactly the navel of England, and feels exactly that', to which he had 'come home, in these last wretched days'. Although the place was beautiful, 'and the house quite nice',[23] returning 'home' to the Midlands must have felt like defeat to them both; they had gone away together in 1912 precisely to escape such a home.

For although Mountain Cottage was another house with a view out over the land falling away in front of it, it was hardly an outpost of freedom for either of them. Lawrence inevitably saw more of his family and of old Eastwood friends ('people of my pre-London days') than he had for years, and he found it 'queer – and a bit irritating, to be en famille again',[24] while for Frieda such an immersion in his family was quite new. Both his sisters came regularly, with their children, and his father came, too (and met Frieda for the first time); they saw the Lawrences' old neighbours the Coopers in Eastwood, and also the Hopkins.

But although Lawrence hated his dependence – 'We live practically on my sister – and that is very painful, too' – he also recognized that 'it is good for me for some time to be with people, and en famille. It is a kind of drug, or soporific, a sort of fatness; it saves one.' There were compensations. In particular, he enjoyed the children (Emily's nine-year-old Peggy, Ada's three-year-old Jack – 'a very delightful boy'), whom he was 'all the time rescuing' from their mothers, 'who have jaguars of wrath in their souls'.[25] Peggy and Jack actually came to live with the Lawrences for a few weeks during June and July, and Lawrence was 'very glad of their presence'. He also published 'War Baby' to coincide with the birth of Catherine Carswell's son, John: 'Blessings on the infant – and may it be blest.'[26] Children were perhaps the only beings he excepted from responsibility for the madness of his country; every account of his spending time with them suggests that he liked them, understood them, made friends with them, taught them things, played with them but, to follow his striking dictum of 1920 about children, left them alone ('First rule, leave him alone. Second rule, leave him alone. Third rule, leave him alone').[27] But 'leaving alone' was not neglecting: he saw it as a responsibility to educate them, whether by giving lessons in 1915 to ten-year-old Mary Saleeby, effectively parentless and running wild ('I'm not taking on Mary because I *like* it! *But somebody has got to,*' he had exclaimed), in 1918 teaching Hilda Brown short-cuts at mathematics, and in 1919 treating the five-year-old Bridget Baynes just as she treated him (she hit him with a thistle: he hit her back, just as hard, which 'astounded her who had never before been treated in such a downright manner') or showing reproductions of Goya pictures (no bull-fights or violence allowed) to the eight-year-old Myfanwy Thomas, talking to her about them, and then doing so all over again the following morning.[28] He respected children for what they were and treated them *as* they were, with delicate, amused perception; and they responded. Frieda had seen him like this with her own daughters in the spring of 1912, and it must have reminded her yet again of her loss.

By the end of the summer of 1918, he had finished his American essays, at least in draft form, and he put together that little book of old poems – misleadingly called *New Poems* – this time for a new publisher, Martin Secker, who would one day become very important to his career. But there was no change to his prospects, as man or writer. He confessed that 'I am very tired of it, and *irritated* by it – terribly irritated. And it is not the slightest use my trying to write selling stuff, in this state of affairs.' Lawrence was a fluent, able and energetic writer: these months and years, dragging on since 1915, were the most awful waste of his talents. Frieda would state the obvious at the start of 1919: 'I feel so bitter, so bitter against the world, if they had only given him *some* response, he would be happy!'[29] The war went on, in spite of rumours of its ending; visitors came and went; Lawrence grew more desperate. 'I look at the months and *know* there must be a change.' Even the view out from the heights of Mountain Cottage became an image of his desperation: 'I feel as if I were on a sort of ledge half way down a precipice.' And all he could see was the way down, not the way back up. What he wanted was 'to get out, to get across into something freer and more active'.[30] All they could afford was a week in August 1918 in the Forest of Dean, with Catherine and Donald Carswell and the new baby, because the house there was rent-free and Catherine had sent them the train fare, which Lawrence reluctantly accepted. (As he remarked to another friend who found him some money: 'I would give you money, if I'd got any.') They walked in the day, and played and sang in the evenings, which left the Lawrences with 'good memories – worth a lot, really. And it pleases me that we carried the child about. One has the future in one's arms, so to speak.'[31] He also carried away with him an idea for a short story: 'The Blind Man'.

Less than a fortnight later, on 11 September (his thirty-third birth-day), a friend about to give lectures in America on contemporary English writers asked him for some biographical details, and he wrote a sardonic miniature biography, which ended 'always lived with no money – always shall – very sick of the world, like to die with the nausea of it'. The same day, however, he received his third notice to report for military call-up; by this stage of the war, practically no one was being rejected. Illustration 20, taken by the Hopkins' daughter Enid, shows how he looked in the summer of 1918. One of the young men summoned to the barracks down in Bodmin had commented, about the beard, 'all that'll come off tomorrow – Qck, Qck!' as he 'gave two long swipes with his finger round his chin'.[32] Not just the beard: the unkempt hair would have gone too. Somers in *Kangaroo* is well aware of his oddity, just as Lawrence would have been: 'a queer figure, a young man with a beard'. It was not only the military who would have objected, either. Lawrence had linked being followed by detectives in 1917 to the fact that 'one has a beard and looks not quite the usual thing'; while Richard Aldington would observe how a theatre crowd in London, in November 1919, seemed immediately hostile to Lawrence: 'there were gibes and sneers at Lawrence's red beard . . . it was simply the ugly instinctive hatred of the crowd for the person who is different.'[33] But not only different: he was publicly proclaiming that he was a non-combatant.

Lawrence was medically examined by the military at Derby on 26 September. He found the experience utterly objectionable, done by people whom he despised and whom he believed despised him. His testimony to having had pneumonia was greeted (he thought) with disbelief; and this time he was classed 'Fit for non-military service'.[34] Rationally, he was very aware that many men in the war, even most, went through far worse experiences; he knew he had to be examined. 'Of course it was all necessary, the conscription, the medical examination, the putting of the beastly puppy's hand between a man's legs, the looking into a man's anus. Of course, of course.' But reason had nothing to do with it. His society had evicted him and treated him like a criminal; now it laid its hands on him and humiliated him. He gave Somers in *Kangaroo* a version of what he felt to be his own biblical curse: 'because they had handled his private parts, and looked into them, their eyes should burst and their hands should wither and their hearts should rot'.[35] As it turned out, he was never called up. But Derby was a defining moment. His was no longer a theoretical rejection of society and England but a very actual one: and focused by *touch*. He had been physically invaded. 'They shall *not* touch me again – such filth': 'from this day I take a new line. I've done with society and humanity – Labour and Military can alike go to hell. Henceforth it is for myself, my own life, I live.'[36] It was the culmination of his hatred, and rejection, of English society.

His aversion extended to what he wanted to do as a writer. 'I'm not going to squat in a cottage feeling their fine feelings for them, and flying for them a flag that only makes a fool of *me*.'[37] It was not often that he expressed so clearly his sense of his role as a writer. But if anything had been calculated to drive him still further into a kind of ultimate nonconformity, it was this period in his life. He and Frieda ran away from the Midlands for practically the whole of October and November, in spite of having Mountain Cottage. They went to stay with various friends in London from 7 October; it was probably not a coincidence that Lawrence thus made himself unavailable at the address the military authorities had. He had, after all, told Kot that he would rather be 'put in prison than endure any more'. Gray was determined that if ever *he* were conscripted, he would just disappear. Lawrence and Frieda shifted between London and the Radford cottage out in Berkshire: 'big, yellow woods. I never saw them more lovely'.[38] But during this period in the south, the Armistice was declared. On the afternoon of that momentous day, the Lawrences were in London at a party with friends and acquaintances, Lawrence irritating everyone by insisting that the war was not really over: that the violence it had set loose would recur, that Germany would rise again. He was maintaining his outrage; he had remarked as early as April 1916 that 'I feel the war must end this year. But in one form or another, war will never end now.'[39] By the evening, he and Frieda were back in Hermitage, sitting by the fire and singing German songs, with Frieda in tears.

The pieces of writing with which Lawrence was engaged during the autumn and winter of 1918 provide a perfect cross-section of the problems of his life as a writer at that moment. They might be thought of as Notes from the Underground. He had written a play, very quickly, in October 1918: *Touch and Go* drew in part upon still unpublished *Women in Love* material, but concentrated upon the industrial unrest in the Midlands. He was very excited about it, feeling that he had written it 'out of my deep and earnest self . . . I believe the world yet might get a turn for the better, if it but had a little shove that way':[40] thus characteristically going back on all his professed detachment after the medical examination in Derby. Yet the play is a curiously unsatisfactory piece of work; and in spite of one wonderful moment of confrontation towards the end, when the miners spreadeagle the coal-owner Gerald Barlow, it is oddly undramatic. However could Lawrence have thought it might change anything? Compared with his journalistic pieces of the spring of 1912, and his accomplished, problematic play *The Daughter-in-Law* of January 1913, the last time he had written anything directly about 'the industrial situation', *Touch and Go* looks doctrinaire and (in its use of the 'Birkin' character, Oliver Turton, to offer a solution to the industrial problem) wooden and well meaning. There was a price to pay for Lawrence's detachment, as well as for his lack of practice as a writer of drama.

The next project marked the only time in his career when he wrote something entirely for money. He had accepted a commission from Oxford University Press to write a brief history for schools, entitled *Movements in European History*; it would pay him £50. In one way, it fitted rather well into the reading he had been doing earlier in 1918, when he had found great satisfaction in Gibbon's *Decline and Fall of the Roman Empire*: 'the emperors are all so indiscriminately bad'. He took the school-history job seriously, and did quite a lot of research for it; but apart from a few moments of pleasure, as he grasped 'the thread of the developing significance', mostly he hated it 'like poison'. Again, it now seems simply a waste of him as a writer that he should have been bothering with what he called 'the broken pots of historical facts'.[41]

He also wrote some essays on education for *The Times Educational Supplement*, referring to them as 'nicely curried'. All we know of them is the revised version he made in 1920, when he gathered them into a book, 'Education of the People'; it was not published in his lifetime. Judging by that rewriting, the essays would have been deeply argumentative ('the old idea of Equality won't do'), thoroughly practical ('Begin at the age of seven – five is too soon') and squarely aimed at 'advanced' thinking about education.[42] They probably drew on the same analysis of society and its idealisms which can be seen in the essays on 'Democracy' he wrote in September 1919; to that extent, they would have been what Lawrence called them in 1918: 'most revolutionary'. He could not, however, make them attractive to the newspaper: 'I *can't* do the *Times* work – I gnash my teeth.' And the essays were not accepted. The editor was 'deeply interested, but feel myself rather out of my depth . . . we feel that this is rather matter for a book than a supplement'.[43] It would not be until the late 1920s that Lawrence would successfully develop a style (or styles) appropriate to journalism.

But at almost precisely the moment the Armistice was announced, on 11 November, he wrote his first new short fiction for two and a half years. He finished one excellent piece after another: 'The Blind Man' and 'Tickets, Please' and the first version of 'The Fox'. This re-immersion in the imaginative worlds of his fiction was a sign of what he had lacked: his philosophical work had been fiction with both hands tied behind its back. 'I hope we shall sell them, for I can't live,' he remarked to Pinker, but for the moment, Pinker was only able to place 'Tickets, Please'. A couple of years later, Lawrence would again explain the importance to him of writing fiction: 'these damned books . . . somewhere they are the crumpled wings of my soul. They get me free before I get myself free.'[44] This new start coincided with his seeing, once again, Katherine Mansfield and Murry in London. She had been diagnosed with consumption; Murry, on the other hand, 'is quite flourishing – rather to my disgust, seeing she is so ill'. It sounds like Frieda and himself, reversed. Lawrence, however, developed (or rediscovered) an immediate responsiveness to Katherine. A sign that he knew what ailed him was his comment to her, in December 1918, that 'I begin to despair altogether about human relationships'. His situation as 'a sort of lone wolf' had been enforced and self-enforced: 'Really, I need a little reassuring of some sort.'[45] The letters to Katherine show him giving and finding such reassurance. He loved writing, and she loved receiving, letters about the every day, as from Mountain Cottage at the start of February 1919:

Yesterday I went out for a real walk – I've had a cold and been in bed. I climbed with my niece to the bare top of the hills. Wonderful is to see the footmarks on the snow – beautiful ropes of rabbit prints, trailing away over the brows; heavy hare marks; a fox so sharp and dainty, going over the wall; birds with two feet that hop; very splendid straight advance of a pheasant; wood-pigeons that are clumsy and move in flocks; splendid little leaping marks of weasels, coming along like a necklace chain of berries; odd little filigree of the field-mice; the trail of a mole – it is astounding what a world of wild creatures one feels round one, on the hills in the snow.

This is a writer showing us how to see the world. The letter ends: 'Well – life itself is life – even the magnificent frost-foliage on the window. While we live, let us live –'[46]

But it was not surprising that someone as unhappy and physically run down as Lawrence should, within a couple of days of that letter, nearly have died 'with that damned Flu.' which killed millions in Europe the first winter and spring after the war. He was, luckily, at his sister Ada's house in Ripley when he fell ill in February 1919, and that may have saved him. Out at Mountain Cottage, with only Frieda to nurse him, and a local doctor's visits limited by the winter's snow, he might not have survived. As it was, Ada's doctor 'said he feared I should not pull through'.[47] And this time it took him months, not weeks, to get well again: 'I have never felt so down in the mud in all my life.' Friends rallied round with presents of wine, spirits and food, but he remained depressed and weak, and the spring never seemed to come. He wanted to escape Ripley ('it is so shut in here') and was back in Mountain Cottage by 17 March, but snow was still deep around the cottage late in the month: 'I stare stupidly out of the window like a sick and dazed monkey.'[48] He was still convalescing in April. His illness left him raw, depressed, feeble and bitter, and he wrote to Kot with less reserve than usual about Frieda just before they left Ada's:

My sister goes with us to Middleton. I am not going to be left to Frieda's tender mercies until I am well again. She really is a devil – and I feel as if I would part from her for ever – let her go alone to Germany, while I take another road. For it is true, I have been bullied by her long enough. I really could leave her now, without a pang, I believe. The time comes, to make an end, one way or another.[49]

We could ascribe such feelings to the after-effects of the illness; elsewhere in the biographical record for the period, there are, if anything, fewer reports of quarrels between them, and Lawrence's comment only three days earlier to Beatrice Campbell – 'I suppose I'll get strong enough again one day to slap Frieda in the eye, in the proper marital fashion. At present I am reduced to vituperation' – suggests his usual attitude. Frieda's point of view may be represented by her comment to Katherine Mansfield that she was feeling 'a little stronger & more able to cope with him':[50] by no means all the wilful behaviour was on Frieda's part. In 1922, Lawrence told Mabel Sterne that Frieda had the soul of a German soldier, 'strong because it does *not* understand – indelicate and robust!'[51] She could, in the end, live blithely through most things, with a certain insentience; years struggling with the loss of her children had taken their toll. In the end, it became part of their common myth that, although he went to bed frequently, his being 'seedy' was not, after all, being ill, and that she saved him from real illness. This was, as it turned out, a dangerous myth to develop, but one can see how it would have helped them get past less important crises than this. Usually, Frieda did not need to be a nurse; by being robust, she healed him. When she had to nurse him, however, they were both miserable.

But leaving her and being wholly independent of her was at the same time a fantasy which Lawrence enjoyed sharing with Kot in that letter: Kot had been angry with Frieda for years. Now the war had finally ended, it *would* have been possible for Frieda to return to Germany and be supported by her family; so the fantasy could be voiced. But what we are probably seeing, provoked by illness and short temper, is the next stage of Lawrence's lifelong working out, through his writing, of the relationship of men and women. He would no longer emphasize the ideally polarized relationship of man and woman (with the concomitant man–man friendship as 'another kind of love'), but the wholly unapologetic struggle of the man to be himself: going his *own* road, experiencing sexual desire but neither love nor dependence, and not asking for 'permission or approval' of any kind. The woman as 'devouring mother' about whom he had written to Katherine in December 1918 was the provocation for this change.[52] Having escaped the loving mother in Lydia, he had since 1912 been focused upon and polarized by the female. Now he wanted to be himself: partnered, but not dependent. It was neither a swing to the 'antediluvian' (as Frieda had called it) nor a regression to the nineteenth-century male – Arthur Lawrence writ large. It was an attempt by a man who had once been extraordinarily progressive in his ideas of male–female relationships to deal with the results of having been progressive. He felt he had been insufficiently himself; he had made himself too much a cypher to the powerful female.

The year in Derbyshire, which on so many counts had been a depressing failure ('I am weary beyond thought of this winter,' he wrote at the end of March 1919), was ending, doubtless to Lawrence and Frieda's relief. Intensely irritating to Frieda would have been Ada's loving hero-worship of her brother, likewise his sister's recent role as 'the responsible nurse'.[53] Ada could not have helped showing, either, that she could not only care for Lawrence, but also run a Ripley drapery business *and* bring up a child. (What did Frieda spend her time doing?) At the start of April, Lawrence was at last able to take up his writing again. The first task was to revise *Movements in European History*, which he had finished just before going down with flu. By the end of the month – rejoicing 'I am a free man'[54] – he had at last got it ready for the publisher. He and Frieda were then able to travel back down to Dollie Radford's cottage.

Publishing would soon be getting back on to a proper footing, and Lawrence had to do something to try and re-establish himself as a writer; his only book publication in 1919 would be the tiny volume of poems, *Bay*. Murry had asked Lawrence for contributions to the *Athenaeum* (of which he had taken over the editorship), while Pinker suggested that short stories might be sold to American magazines. Lawrence promised to write nothing but short stories for six weeks, 'if the short stories will come'.[55] Three of them did: 'Fannie and Annie', 'Monkey Nuts' and 'Hadrian' (published as 'You Touched Me'). But the best news, in July 1919, was that 'The Fox' had been accepted for publication and paid for handsomely, while another publisher had decided to take *Touch and Go*. Lawrence's career was, little by little, being rebuilt. It was no thanks to Murry, however, who, in spite of Lawrence doing his best to be 'pleasant and a bit old-fashioned', and deliberately writing a couple of short pieces about his childhood, 'Adolf' and 'Rex', only took one of the pieces written specially for him. This angered Lawrence violently: 'Good-bye Jacky, I knew thee beforehand.' Murry in his new role as establishment figure simply confirmed Lawrence in his feeling of being the outsider.[56]

It seems probable that Lawrence was now starting to go behind his agent's back from time to time, and not to pay Pinker the required 10 per cent on work whose publication he had himself arranged: the piece that Murry took, for example, was published under a pseudonym. Lawrence had also made the contact that led to the publication of *Touch and Go*, and was increasingly wondering whether he needed to continue with an agent. He had certainly never made Pinker much money; but nor, he thought, had his agent really exerted himself on his behalf. He had broached the idea of leaving Pinker in November 1918; but now, in the middle of 1919, he became increasingly disillusioned with what Pinker was doing for him, especially in the American market. Things came to a head over *Women in Love*. It turned out that Pinker had never even sent the novel's typescript to Benjamin Huebsch, who had published all Lawrence's works in America since 1914.[57] Lawrence only discovered this failure after he had arranged (without Pinker's assistance) for the American publisher Thomas Seltzer to take the novel, and Seltzer had sent him a £50 advance. Huebsch was extremely annoyed (*Women in Love* was potentially a book which might have made him some money, after the lean years of the war), but all Lawrence could do was blame Pinker. Anyway, 'I would like the book to come first in America. I shall never forgive England *The Rainbow*.'[58] He revised the novel slightly in September for Seltzer and wrote a foreword, while in England Martin Secker expressed interest.

Most of Lawrence's energies were now concentrated on the matter of winding up things in England so that he and Frieda could go abroad. Frieda badly wanted to see her German family; she had originally hoped to go as early as March 1919, only there was a continuing problem with passports (none would be issued until the peace treaty had been formally ratified by all the governments concerned). This took months. Lawrence would mainly have been concerned to be out of England before the winter came. The initial plan was for Frieda to go to Germany and Lawrence to America, where she would join him; Lawrence investigated the possibilities of organizing a lecture tour to support him when he first arrived. In the meantime, they had to shift houses more than once: first to London, then Hermitage and then Pangbourne, in Berkshire, into yet another borrowed house. Lawrence had known the poet and writer Eleanor Farjeon since 1915; her brother Herbert was married to Joan Thornycroft, whose sister Rosalind had recently separated from her husband (the doctor Godwin Baynes). Rosalind was planning an escape to Italy with her children. More than once, while living in Hermitage, the Lawrences had gone out into the woods to picnic with the extended family and when, in August, Rosalind house-sat for her sister Joan, she invited the Lawrences to occupy her own Pangbourne house. The month turned out 'Monstrous hot' but the chance of a holiday home in the south, near the river, was not lost on Lawrence's sisters and children, who all came to stay at different times. Though 'Myrtle Cottage' was 'a pleasant house', Lawrence also declared that he could only 'hate Pangbourne itself': as with Mrs Gray's flat in Earl's Court, 'the whitewashed devil of middle class-dom sends me mad'. After that, the Lawrences made two further moves, to different addresses near Hermitage; it was astonishing how Lawrence got any writing done at all. 'How many times have I packed our miserable boxes,' he grumbled, but he still professed liking 'not to have a home'. This was in direct opposition to Frieda, who 'craved for a home and solidity'.[59] He finished revising Kot's translation of the Russian author Leo Shestov's *Apotheosis of Groundlessness* (which Lawrence wanted to call *All Things are Possible*); he was irritated at having to deal with what seemed the everlasting production of *Bay*; there was still another version of the unpublished *Studies* essays to be got ready to be sent to Huebsch in America; and there were essays on 'Democracy' to be done for a peculiar multilingual magazine based in The Hague.

But by now both the Lawrences were itching to leave England. 'The thing to do is to get on the move,' Lawrence remarked (his old friend Mark Gertler had sympathized with his 'depressed' state in August),[60] but he had given up the idea of America for the moment and now intended returning to Italy. They developed the plan that he and Frieda should go to investigate the house in the Abruzzi that Rosalind Baynes was considering for herself and her children (she wanted to get out of England while Godwin's uncontested divorce action went through). But the Lawrences had to wait until October for passports to arrive. Frieda's came by the 8th (see Illustration 19), though she still needed a visa for Holland, but she was at last able to leave to see her mother in Baden-Baden on the 15th.

Lawrence stayed a month longer, doing business with magazines and publishers, not only not wishing to go to Germany so soon after the war, but also because he seemed to want to be apart from Frieda for a while. Aldington, whom he saw in London, thought that Lawrence 'seemed not to care if he never saw her again'.[61] It was a year after the Armistice but only eleven years since, at the age of twenty-four, he had been nursing his mother in Eastwood, coming up every weekend from Croydon, and growing intimate with Louie Burrows. Since then, he had met the 'woman of a lifetime' and his life had changed out of all recognition. But his writing career, initially so promising, had also been wrecked and he was in a most peculiar position of detachment from and animosity and resistance towards his country: feelings that now to some extent also marked his relationship with Frieda.

At last, on 14 November 1919, after being seen off in London by the Carswells and Kot (two Scots and a Russian thus bidding him farewell from England), he sailed for the continent from Dover. He would return only three more times (in 1923, 1925 and 1926), spending no more than twelve weeks in England, in all, during the final ten and a half years of his life. At least twice he recreated in fictional form his feelings on leaving. The version he wrote just six months later, for *The Lost Girl*, contains a vision haunting in its power: 'there behind, behind all the sunshine, was England. England, beyond the water, rising with ash-grey, corpse-grey cliffs, and streaks of snow on the downs above. England, like a long, ash-grey coffin slowly submerging. She [Alvina Houghton] watched it, fascinated and terrified.'[62] This is more than alienation. Lawrence felt that England was literally dead to him: a submerging coffin. There were of course sensible reasons for living abroad. Winter in England was always bad for his health. He could not, either, 'forgive England *The Rainbow*': but even that was only part of it. His need to leave England, like his reaction at Derby, went well beyond any rational explanation. The hurt and rage of someone who had 'always *believed* so in everything', and now did not, went terribly deep.[63] He was consciously, symbolically attempting to reject his country, to drown any connection he might have with it.

When he had last sailed from Dover, in August 1913, it had also been on his own, on his way to rejoin Frieda, who had left earlier on a visit to her family in Metz. But he had then been full of plans to go on with the most thrilling piece of writing of his life, as well as feeling buoyed up with vivid memories of his recent visit to Eastwood and his old friends there; he had been excited about the idea of writing a series of sketches about Eastwood. In 1913, too, he had admitted that he was glad to leave England, but also acknowledged that 'I rather love my countrymen'. Six years later, like his character Somers in *Kangaroo*, Lawrence must have felt 'loose like a single timber of some wrecked ship, drifting the face of the sea. Without a people, without a land. So be it. He was broken apart, apart he would remain.' It is tempting to discount the passion of Lawrence's utterance: to see it as an exaggeration. His passion to leave England was not: 'I don't care where I go, so long as I can turn my back on it for good.'[64]

His fiction expresses such a feeling dramatically and one-sidedly; it allows him to develop what was in reality a constantly shifting point of view into a determined, unambiguous standpoint. But, none the less, it pointed to the primary direction that his life, career and beliefs had now taken. For five years he had felt (as his character Aaron Sisson would feel in *Aaron's Rod*) a 'strained, unacknowledged opposition to his surroundings', and had been aware of his 'hard core of irrational, exhausting withholding of himself'. His old capacity for detachment and distance had, during the years of the war, hardened into a kind of solitary 'withholding' that at times came close to solipsism. In *Kangaroo*, Somers discovers 'the great secret: to stand alone as his own judge of himself, absolutely'.[65] Somers's hard-edged decisiveness about his situation is, once again, a kind of perfected version of Lawrence's anguished and more ambiguous feelings ('One has been so much insulted and let down'). The real-life Lawrence was never capable of adopting such an absolute position, though he liked the feel and sound of it. As a writer and as a man, he needed people too badly, was too sympathetic with others. Like Aaron, 'he still *wanted* to give himself',[66] and as a writer Lawrence had a particular need to go on doing so. But this old, continuing need was up against the stubborn, solitary opposition which he had developed over the past five and a half years to almost everything and everyone. His previously optimistic belief in society was now replaced by cold anger towards it and a kind of holding back, contained and judgemental.

That would turn out to be rather bad for his writing of novels, which, from the early 1920s, would at times be strained, univocal and liable to preach: and sometimes all three. He did not, however, become a writer for the countries he would now make his home. He went on feeling English and loving his country, even if 'so bitterly, bitterly'. As he had confessed in 1915: 'I am English, and my Englishness is my very vision'; he continued to see things on behalf of his country, and to write in his own language. He remained passionate, intensely concerned with human relations and how they might change (and be changed) for the better. But he was now contemptuous of his country's inhabitants and of its institutions, to a degree that at times left him (like Somers) 'expressionless'. He believed that he had to live away from it, so as not to be depressed by it; he would say in June 1921, 'I simply don't want to come to England. I know it would only make me feel dreary: and I can't work in England.'[67] As he looked back at his country from the Channel steamer, that November afternoon in 1919, it 'seemed to repudiate the sunshine, to remain unilluminated, long and ash-grey and dead, with streaks of snow like cerements. That was England!'[68] But whatever he felt and wanted to feel, there was no final escape from the England he left for dead in November 1919. He went on writing for it.

13

Italy and Sicily: 1919–1920

Lawrence was leaving for a continent where once again he would be a stranger, and a poor one. In 1912 he had had £11 with him, in 1919 only £9, though money was on its way from London. The railways were *'slow slow – slow'*;[1] Paris to Turin took twenty-one hours and had no restaurant car. Lawrence stopped in Turin for a couple of nights on the way; his old acquaintance Thomas Dunlop, who had been British Consul in La Spezia, had arranged for him to stay at the house of the ship-owner and philanthropist Sir Walter Becker. Becker later remembered the arrival, while the rest of the household was at dinner, of 'a homespun-clad figure, carrying some sort of travelling bag'. Both points are deliberately made: gentlemen do not carry their own bags, and Lawrence was doubtless wearing either the tweed jacket visible on his passport photographs or his old brown suit (see Illustrations 22 and 27).[2] When Lawrence finally reached the dinner table, Becker recalled having 'a good deal of conversation' with him, and rather unwisely assumed that they were 'on terms of friendship and sympathy'. But Lawrence never found those he called *'les riches'*, the English abroad, very sympathetic (they 'dried me up'), and he recalled a few days later a 'sincere half-mocking argument' with Sir Walter: 'he for security and bank-balance and power, I for naked liberty'.[3] Sir Walter would later find a lengthy recreation of his house, his guests, himself and these conversations in Lawrence's novel *Aaron's Rod*, and was outraged, as much for what he thought was a breach of hospitality as for anything insulting in the recreation.[4]

It was, however, characteristic of Lawrence to have no scruple in using such material. He would do the same in one of his greatest but least celebrated pieces of writing, his introductory 'Memoir' to the reminiscences 'Dregs', about life in the Foreign Legion, by the American writer and journalist Maurice Magnus (see Illustration 21). Lawrence started the 'Memoir' with a recreation of his arrival in Florence on 19 November 1919, when he saw again his raffish old acquaintance the novelist and essayist Norman Douglas, who had been obliged to live abroad since 1917,[5] and first met Magnus: the latter always hard up, living by his wits, knowing 'all the short cuts in all the big towns of Europe'.[6] Douglas would profoundly object to what he felt were the liberties Lawrence took in this 'Memoir' in recreating his friends and acquaintances although, from the point of view Douglas chose to adopt, Lawrence's real crime was a breach of manners. Douglas had, moreover, specifically given Lawrence *carte blanche* to do what he liked in the 'Memoir': 'Put me into your introduction – drunk and stark naked, if you like. I am long past caring about such things.' He appeared there as 'Douglas, who has never left me in the lurch': he had found Lawrence a room in a pension and left him a note with the travel agency Thomas Cook. But Douglas would also appear as James Argyle in *Aaron's Rod*, which he had *not* sanctioned, and Lawrence wondered if he would be offended.[7] Magnus, too, would not only appear in the 'Memoir' but as Mr May in *The Lost Girl*.

It had long been Lawrence's practice to take what he chose of real-life people and recreate them in the forms he wanted. As most of Lawrence's acquaintance knew, including Douglas, he was 'a damned observant fellow'. The passage of years means that today characters are taken as fictional who are in fact composite and sometimes close portraits or re-inventions. Lawrence would certainly be ruthless in fictionalizing, to take another example, the 'secrets of my heart' to which Faith, the wife of the novelist Compton Mackenzie, unwisely allowed him access.[8] He was possessed of enormous charm if he wanted to use it; his early correspondence is a constant essay in how to please different people successfully. Being so observant and attentive, as well as capable of immediate sympathy and understanding, he quickly grew intimate with people, so that they gave themselves away to him to 'an extraordinary degree'. This habit was something he characterized as essentially female: for him, women 'can set up the sympathetic flow and make a fellow give himself away without realising what he is doing'.[9] Lawrence remembered a great deal of what he was told but, even more significantly, was able to re-imagine it afterwards, in his writing. All his life, people he knew suffered, or just occasionally enjoyed, this fate. In his first novel, *The White Peacock*, the character Alice Gall recreated his old Eastwood friend Beatrice Hall; examples from the middle of his career would be Julius Halliday and 'Pussum' in *Women in Love* (recreations of Philip Heseltine and Minnie Channing – 'Puma'); in 1927, Michael Arlen (formerly Dikran Kouyoumdjian) professed himself 'greatly elated' to have starred as the popular playwright Michaelis in *Lady Chatterley's Lover*.[10] If Lawrence were confronted by complaints and threats of legal action, as he was by White Holditch (the man Beatrice Hall subsequently married) and by Heseltine, he would either offer to have the names changed (as he suggested to Holditch) or deny that he had created a portrait ('I think it all perfect nonsense – as if there weren't dozens of little Pussums about Chelsea, and dozens of Hallidays anywhere'). Holditch did not sue: Heseltine threatened to, and – much to Lawrence's annoyance – was paid off by Lawrence's publisher. In private, Lawrence was dismissive: 'away with anyone's feelings – they won't recognise themselves when they read it, so why worry?' So he would admit to 'the representation of Alice', and confess that 'Halliday is Heseltine, The Pussum is a model called the Puma, and they are taken from life'.[11]

For obvious reasons, equal offence could be caused by recreations that combined recognizable aspects of a figure with other material. People (including Ottoline Morrell) naturally took Hermione Roddice in *Women in Love* to be some kind of a portrait of Ottoline, even though many details were different. The offensiveness was not thereby diminished; it might well be increased. In *Aaron's Rod*, which Lawrence wrote at intervals between 1917 and 1922, he went further than ever before, perhaps in consequence of severing his ties with England: the originals of almost its entire cast can be located in the circles of his acquaintance between 1917 and 1922.[12] A very few people (almost always those who were very close to him) never seem to have been involved in such portraiture: Kot, for example, as well as his sister Emily and perhaps Catherine Carswell.[13] These were people who he knew would be lastingly hurt by such recreation.

But what might, for some of Lawrence's original readers, have been the material of a *roman à clef* has, over the years, inevitably had to stand on its own feet. Now that the ethical issue of the propriety of drawing on life in this way has mostly been taken care of by the passage of time, any element of malice (or, more accurately, wicked pleasure) inherent in, say, the figure of Halliday, is no longer very important. There is a vast amount of original creation in the 'portrait from life', and the common ways of thinking about it are inadequate. Lawrence has been called 'one of literature's scavengers',[14] but simply picking up bits and scraps is far less interesting, or disturbing, than the kind of creation in which he actually engaged.

It is in their language and dialogue that his characters come alive. The truly effective mimic (like Lawrence) not only reproduces the sound of the voice but the kinds of thing the voice might express. The 'transparent disguise' of himself to which Douglas, as predicted, strongly objected in *Aaron's Rod*, James Argyle, has been mocking Algy Constable (a version of the journalist and novelist Reggie Turner) in a café at night. Algy has gone home, and Argyle comments:

'But you know, they get on my nerves. Little old maids, you know, little old maids. I'm sure I'm surprised at their patience with me. – But when people are patient with you, you want to spit gall at them. Don't you? Ha-ha-ha! Poor old Algy. – Did I lay it on him, tonight, or did I miss him?'

'I think you got him,' said Aaron.

'He'll never forgive me. Depend on it, he'll never forgive me. Ha-ha! I like to be unforgiven. It adds *zest* to one's intercourse with people, to know that they'll never forgive one.'[15]

Nobody ever conveyed the flavour of Douglas's wicked talk – 'I think he is so funny,' Lawrence confessed – better than the man whom Douglas would accuse of having no trace of humour.[16] A man and a voice are there, with their savoured repetitions, the old-fashioned manner ('I'm sure I'm surprised', 'Depend on it'), the hiss of '*zest*', the epigrammatic conclusion, the malicious phrases ('lay it on him' is from hunting, laying a trail to lead to the quarry, coupled with the old-fashioned sense of 'hit him').[17] Lawrence may not have remembered a word from his encounters with Douglas in 1920 and 1921; but he *made* Argyle out of such language.

Lawrence did not baulk at using Frieda in precisely the same way, while portraits of himself, in one guise or another, were his most constant recreations of all: and very often unflattering. He advised Mabel Sterne in 1922 on the making of an autobiographical novel: 'You've got to remember also things you don't want to remember.'[18] *The Rainbow* and *Women in Love* both drew on the Lawrence marriage in different ways; the novel he started in the middle of 1920 and abandoned in 1921, *Mr Noon*, turned into the most extraordinary recreation of their experience of each other between May and September 1912. *Aaron's Rod* offered an update on the progress of a marriage after that; *Kangaroo* took the process still further.

For the life of the emotions was what he had always wanted to explore through his writing, his fiction in particular; and this was why the writing was so important to him, and the blank periods when he was writing little fiction so destructive. Such times left him with the purely intellectual apprehensions of a very intelligent man, and often almost uncontrollable rage at being shut in, enclosed. This he regularly transformed into anger with the place he was in, with other people, with the very climate or weather: it closed him in, and he needed to break out of it. Writing fiction seems to have been his best way of freeing up the logjam of his feelings, of realizing in language what he was experiencing. It may well be true that it was not until he had *written* it that Lawrence felt he had had an experience; and this would go some way to explaining why he used this recreative method so very often. People he apprehended intellectually, or as a mimic might remember them, came alive all over again as (in a deep, even tranquil sense)[19] he recollected them, and remade them. The habit of remaking did not make him especially liked or likeable. But in remaking people in a new language, he seems to have *experienced* them and their needs and feelings more fully than he had previously been able to do. And if that was true of others, it was even more true of himself.

In some ways, returning to the continent, and to Italy in particular, would have been a journey of great symbolic importance for Lawrence. It had been mostly in Italy, originally on the Lago di Garda and then in Fiascherino, that he had first learned (through Frieda) not only to love and to feel and to be himself, but to start to know what it was like to escape the prison of his shut-in self. In November 1919, he did something rather unusual (for him) and went back to La Spezia and Fiascherino on his way from Turin to Florence; by the sound of it, he did his very best to revisit the past, being there for two nights and seeing almost 'all the people'.[20] Their servant Elide, of whom he and Frieda had been so fond, had died in 1914 (Frieda had marked her name in their address book with a large cross, in the German way), but he would have seen her mother, Felice Fiori, who lived on until 1930, as well as other acquaintances in Fiascherino.

This time he was going to live somewhere new in Italy, simply pausing in Florence on the way so as to meet Frieda; they had friends there, which was why they had chosen it. Douglas and Magnus turned out to be a great deal more sympathetic than the inhabitants of the house in Turin had been, even though conversation with Douglas would naturally have sparked disagreements. (Frieda loved the 'fireworks of wit' she heard them generate.) Magnus also fascinated Lawrence – 'just the kind of man I had never met: little smart man of the shabby world' – and Lawrence immediately recreated the sound of his voice: 'very much on the spot, don't you know'.[21] For the moment, Lawrence hugely enjoyed being out of England in the company of congenial people. Italy remained a magical place to him, even though it rained a lot, so that the Arno was often 'noisy and swollen'; but Florence, with English friends, was 'so nice: its genuine culture still creating a certain perfection in the town'. When Frieda arrived, a good bit thinner (her diet in a post-war Germany of acute shortages having consisted mostly of carrots), he met her train at 4 o'clock in the morning and immediately took her for a drive in an open carriage to show her the town he had been exploring. She recalled how 'I saw the pale crouching Duomo and in the thick moonmist the Giotto tower disappeared at the top into the sky'.[22]

But they were there together for only a week. The next move was to Picinisco, in the wilds of the Abruzzi mountains, where Rosalind Baynes had thought of living, in the house of one of her sculptor father's old models. There, Lawrence hoped to sit still and do some work.[23] Not only did he have to finance their travels, but Italy had always been fruitful for his writing, and he had a new project underway. Because of Sons and Lovers, he had long been linked in the minds of reviewers with Freud, and Frieda's 1907 relationship with the psychoanalyst Otto Gross had strengthened his own insights. But he had also had far closer contact with contemporary psychoanalytical ideas than most people could have had at the time. From 1914, he had known the English Freudian analysts Barbara Low and Ernest Jones, and his friendship with Dr David Eder (who had been a Freudian but whose interest in Jung's work was well developed by 1917) had carried these interests still further. He now decided to write about the subject himself. In 1919, it was a highly contested field, only just on the edge of intellectual respectability, commanded by specialists and practitioners. It took Lawrence, however, directly into the subjects of self and sexuality that had always been his main concerns; and he first mentioned the project in a letter at the start of December 1919. It would be a development of what he had been doing in the *Studies*, but this time, he conceived the essays as popular material for magazines. He wanted to get round behind psychoanalysis, with its stress on the unconscious mind, and stress instead the unconscious body: the essays he wrote obstinately refuse everyone else's ideas, and combine esoteric terminology with a lucid account of actual bodily experience. Few writers have ever come as near as Lawrence did here, for example, to describing the experience of the very young child.

The trip to Picinisco began with the train from Rome to Monte Cassino, then a bus journey along winding mountain roads to Atina, a horse and trap for the first part of the way to Picinisco and the last part on foot, climbing 'unfootable paths, while the ass struggles behind with your luggage'. They arrived well after dark, to find a house with

a rather cave-like kitchen downstairs – the other rooms are a wine-press and a wine-storing place and corn bin: upstairs are three bedrooms, and a semi-barn for maize cobs: beds and bare floor. There is one tea-spoon – one saucer – two cups – one plate – two glasses – the whole supply of crockery. Everything must be cooked gipsy-fashion in the chimney over a wood fire: The chickens wander in, the ass is tied to the doorpost and makes his droppings on the doorstep, and brays his head off.[24]

The Lawrences could rough it when required, but Picinisco was 'a bit staggeringly primitive', and the gathering winter made everything worse. The only food was at the market in Atina, five miles off: 'no wine hardly – and no woman in the house, we must cook over the gipsy fire and eat our food on our knees'. The post came to 'the God-lost village' up on a rocky outcrop, a 'goats climb' taking over an hour. They organized the construction of a fireplace in one of the bedrooms (there was no heat of any kind upstairs), but it was '*so* primitive, and *so* cold' that it was impossible to settle there, or for Lawrence to write.[25] And although it was marvellously beautiful – 'all round circled the most brilliant snowy mountain-peaks, glittering like hell' – it would have been out of the question for Rosalind, three children and a nurse. The Lawrences spent a memorable week there, on the verge of being snowed in, with bagpipes played under the window every morning, accompanying a wild howling 'Christmas serenade'; Lawrence must have realized that Picinisco was just the kind of location he could write about. But he had to send a letter telling Rosalind not to come. There wasn't even anything approaching a bath; she would have to wash her children in 'a big copper boiling-pan, in which they cook the pigs' food'.[26] He and Frieda had to stagger back to Atina, carrying their luggage, to escape over the mountains before the snow came for good and all.

They travelled down to the island of Capri, where the successful writer Compton Mackenzie (whom they had known since 1914 in Buckinghamshire) had promised to find them a room if ever they needed it: 'Capri will be warm.'[27] By Christmas Day, they were settled in a little apartment in an old palazzo 'on the neck of Capri', over-looking the tiny square, the cathedral dome just in front of them ('the apple of our eye – gall-apple'), with views out towards Vesuvius and Naples on one side, and the open Mediterranean on the other. They shared their kitchen with a voluble Romanian, and their servant, who was 'handsome, and eats the jam', with the whole floor.[28]

Yet another Italy thus suddenly burst on them: life at the very heart of an expatriate colony, 'the uttermost uttermost limit for spiteful scandal'. As well as Mackenzie and his friends, their old friend Mary Cannan was there (last seen in Buckinghamshire in the winter of 1914–15 but now separated from Gilbert: 'she's very nice and brought us some butter'), as were the English doctor-turned-novelist Francis Brett Young and his wife. Lawrence observed them with the relish with which he enjoyed, for a while, all absurdity: Mackenzie, for example, 'walking in a pale blue suit to match his eyes, and a large woman's brown velour hat to match his hair'. When he got fed up with the bitchiness, he called Capri 'a stewpot of semi-literary cats': 'Cat Cranford'.[29]

Although the social life was so engaging that Lawrence claimed several times that he wasn't writing, he was actually hard at work. He took his old essays on education, done in the autumn of 1918, and turned them into a short book. More important were the six essays on psychoanalysis. These would be published as *Psychoanalysis and the Unconscious*, and would take his philosophy a stage further; they were primarily dedicated to setting out a new idea of the unconscious, locating it in 'the great ganglia and nodes of the nervous system', Lawrence thus differentiating his unconscious from what he regarded as the psychoanalytic cul-de-sac of 'mental-consciousness'. The essays also mounted his first attack in print on Freud. By late March, they were ready to send out.[30] He may possibly have sent an early version of one or two to Murry for the *Athenaeum*, in December 1919; he had read and discussed Jung with Katherine Mansfield the previous year.[31]

At the end of 1919, as another sign of his new determination to take a proper grasp on his future as a writer, he had written to J. B. Pinker to end their relationship, and confirmed this in January 1920: 'What bit of work I have to place, I like to place myself. I am sure it isn't worth much to you . . . I feel I have been an unpleasant handful for you, and am sorry.'[32] He thus brought to an end the agreement signed on 30 June 1914: a world away. He intended to act as his own agent in England, while Robert Mountsier, although not a professional agent, agreed to act for him in America, which was where Pinker had failed him most. The trouble over *Women in Love* was continuing; Huebsch still very much wanted the book (and felt he had a right to it). Lawrence wrote to Seltzer asking to have the original typescript back, and volunteering to return his £50 advance. But Seltzer clung to the novel, and the chance it gave him to become Lawrence's American publisher; while the promise of the set of six psychoanalysis essays did nothing to mollify Huebsch.

Lawrence also promised Huebsch a new novel, but doing business from Italy had complications. A postal strike was followed by a railway strike and these not only delayed until Good Friday morning the only one of his Christmas parcels to arrive[33] but prevented his getting hold of the 200-page novel fragment 'The Insurrection of Miss Houghton', dating from 1913, which he had tried to recover in 1916 and which he still felt he could either finish or rewrite into a new, commercial novel. Eventually it came and he was able to start work on it. It looks as if he were attempting a two-pronged attack on publishing: he would produce stories and novels (popular if possible) for his publishers, but also essays on the subjects close to his heart, which could be published in magazines and might become books in their own right. Negotiations with Secker for the publication of *Women in Love* in England were constantly delayed, but in making such agreements, Lawrence had at least the advantage of advice and help from Mackenzie, who had made a lot of money for and with Secker and was his unofficial business partner. But the negotiations would also have reminded them both of the extent to which Mackenzie was the successful writer (even after the war, his novels sold over 30,000 copies) and Lawrence the unsuccessful. Indeed, Secker thought Lawrence's books 'not worth competing for from a money making point of view'. He offered to republish *The Rainbow* if he could purchase its copyright outright, but Lawrence baulked at this: 'I believe in my books and in their future.'[34] He wanted royalties. A publisher might still be pleased to have Lawrence in his list, however, and Secker stuck with Lawrence, even though he never made much money.

The postal strikes and delays also contributed to another break with the past: an intensely painful and angry episode with Murry and Katherine. Lawrence was already feeling thoroughly irritated by those who were publishing (or failing to publish) him. Cyril Beaumont had made a real mess of *Bay*: he had taken two years over it, left out the inscription, omitted two poems and printed one illustration upside down. Then on 29 January, Lawrence found out that Pinker had let him down over *Women in Love*, having never even sent the typescript to America. The following day, the articles that Lawrence had sent to Murry for the *Athenaeum* were returned. Lawrence can only have sent them because he'd been invited to and had, perhaps foolishly, gone back on his decision not to offer Murry anything again. Lawrence sent Murry a coldly vicious response: 'as a matter of fact, what it amounts to is that you are a dirty little worm, and you take the ways of a dirty little worm.'[35] But what made it much worse was that the articles had been returned from Katherine's address in Italy (where Murry had, unknown to Lawrence, been at the end of December and early in January); their arrival in Capri had coincided with a letter (held up by the postal strike) from Katherine, not mentioning the articles but desperate about herself: her 'appalling isolation' and her feeling 'that I had consumption and was tainted – dying here', in a house where 'I could get no maid because of my DISEASE'.[36] She was moving to France. Lawrence jumped to the conclusion that she had colluded with Murry in turning down his articles, but was still pleading for his sympathy. He sent her the nastiest response he could: 'I loathe you, you revolt me stewing in your consumption. The Italians were quite right to have nothing to do with you.' 'Katharine – on ne meurt pas,' he had written to her in December 1918: 'I almost want it to let it be reflexive – on ne se meurt pas [one does not die . . . one does not *let* oneself die].'[37] Where was her courage now? But Lawrence's letter, as presumably he wanted it to, attacked her exactly where she was most vulnerable. It was a desperate and horrible farewell to a relationship. The ruthlessness with which Lawrence now overcame all his feelings of fondness for Katherine is very striking; the episode gives us a momentary revelation, for once preserved, of what he could be like when really vengeful. He not only believed in saying what he felt; he could be calculatedly vicious, too. In November 1921, he would refer contemptuously to her as a 'long-dying blossom'.[38]

What perhaps made the letter worse for Katherine was the fact that in the winter of 1920–21 she was suffering a traumatic breakdown of relationship with Murry. On his most recent visit to Italy, they had not shared a room, as they usually did, and her journals and letters of January and February 1920 are anguished. She only quoted Lawrence's letter in passing in her first mention of it to Murry; in her journal for 6 February, she had simply noted: 'Received Lawrence's last letter and reply from J.'[39] She was in a desperate state; but not because Lawrence had hurt her.

On 6 February, before he knew anything of Lawrence's letter to her, Murry had forwarded to Katherine his own letter from Lawrence, commenting that 'I feel he is something of a reptile, and that he has slavered over me'. On 10 February, Katherine answered Murry: 'Note this coincidence. I wrote to Lawrence "I detest you for having dragged this disgusting reptile across all that has been." When I got his letter I saw a reptile, felt a reptile.'[40] This was extraordinary. How could they both independently have used the word 'reptile' for Lawrence? It was probably a word they had used about him before, however. Twelve years later, Murry quoted in his journal, as another phrase he remembered from Lawrence's letter to Katherine, 'You are a loathsome reptile – I hope you will die.'[41] That would certainly account for Katherine's 'I saw a reptile, felt a reptile', but would add yet another to a weird series of coincidences. (The phrase was probably not a quotation, but Murry's half-remembered conflation of what Katherine had felt and he had written.)

Equally, Lawrence, using the word 'worm' to insult Murry ('you take the ways of a dirty little worm'), had also chosen a word with a special significance. It belonged to the 'little language' Murry and Katherine had shared for years. 'Worm, worm,' Murry wrote desperately to Katherine on 10 February, in an attempt to make her feel his love: it was a profoundly intimate term of endearment between them.[42] Was it only a coincidence that Lawrence should have used it?

Again, though both Murry and Katherine were sure that Lawrence had done something unforgivable, they both forgave him. In December 1921, Katherine wrote how 'one must always *love* Lawrence for his "being"'; in August 1922, she confessed that 'I feel nearer L. than anyone else'.[43] In 1923, Murry started the *Adelphi* primarily so that he could print Lawrence's work in it. Lawrence, however, who looks so much more like the offender than the victim, never forgave either of them.

Rational explanations of the episode may account for what he did, and in the end it is not even Lawrence's words that seem so very significant. But what was it about self-pity that he hated so violently (in Katherine, in himself)? He later called it 'pitying yourself and caving in', 'sloppy self-indulgent melancholics, absolutely despicable'. Katherine's ability to be wrapped up in herself was something that he knew and shared to an extent that made him react against her so very, very angrily. She brought him to experience a violent encounter with what has been called the 'unconscious desire which is personal history':[44] this was something he too had to get over.

In mid February 1920, while still waiting for the novel manuscript from Germany, Lawrence left Capri and went to Monte Cassino for a couple of days to see Magnus in the monastery where the latter was staying, and where he had begged Lawrence to visit him. Lawrence was both intrigued and fascinated by Magnus, and may also have been relieved to get away for a few days after his violent eruption of feelings about Murry and Katherine. In January, Lawrence had been kind but also unwise enough to send Magnus £5 because the other man appeared to be in financial difficulties (Lawrence had just received an unexpected windfall of $100, so could afford to be generous). Magnus had been hugely grateful. He was at the monastery because he was on the run; his cheque for a hotel bill in Anzio (for several weeks' stay) had bounced.[45] Lawrence's account of his visit appears at length in his 'Memoir', and contains an astonishing recreation of his feeling at Monte Cassino of being caught between the past and the present. He became very aware of the 'past, the poignancy of the not-quite-dead past', in the old rituals and habits of the monastery; but down below, in the valley, he could see the railway lines, the roads, modern life, all the bitter, barren world of the present: 'Both worlds were agony to me . . . I feeling as if my heart had once more broken: I don't know why.'[46] The war lay like a crevasse across Lawrence's life; he felt caught between an irrecoverable, beloved past, in which he had believed, and a present in which he was in danger of believing in nothing. Experiences like the one at Monte Cassino triggered once again a realization of the gap which for him never lay far below the surface of the everyday.

The fact that he was with Magnus may well have contributed to this feeling. Magnus was homosexual: Lawrence had even been subjected to an appreciative chat-up line when they had first met in Florence – 'How lovely your hair is – such a lovely colour! What do you dye it with?'[47] But Magnus was not the kind of predatory homosexual that Lawrence, back in 1915, had felt Keynes to be and with whom he had feared Bunny Garnett had become entangled. The 'Memoir' constantly stresses Magnus's yearning, tenderness and vulnerability; Magnus was a man to whom Lawrence could 'open his "heart"', and he did so on at least one occasion. He may have gone to Monte Cassino in hope of a warm response, even love, from his new friend. But at Monte Cassino, in the company of Magnus – a deeply troubled, sensitive man – Lawrence was struck once more by feelings of his own irretrievable loneliness, and realized once again that homosexual love was, for him, a road not to be taken, in spite of his sympathy with Magnus. Lawrence usually felt that 'most people one can hardly bear to come near', but here he found no problem with the fact that Magnus 'seemed to walk close to me, very close'.[48] Yet this in turn made Lawrence realize that his own 'heart', his whole emotional life, belonged to his original love for his mother and then to his love for Frieda. And those past loves now seemed lost to him; that heart broken for ever. A couple of years later, thinking specifically of his mother, he would confirm this by writing how love 'belongs to the old life'; and in October 1921, feeling that Europe 'was dying under my eyes', he wrote, revealingly: 'It's almost precisely as if somebody were dying: one's mother, for example.'[49] All he could now do, stoic and courageous, was assert: 'One can't go back.' And it was at Monte Cassino in February 1920 that he said to Magnus something like: 'I think one's got to go through with the life down there – get somewhere beyond it.' There was no going back to the comforting past. Rather, he felt that 'one must strike camp, and pack up the things, and go on'; he imagined his own life would now be a matter of 'some sort of action and strenuousness and pain and frustration and struggling through'.[50]

His journey to Monte Cassino is not mentioned in any surviving letter; something about it made him want to keep it 'veiled'.[51] When he returned to Capri on 21 February, it was to find that the old novel manuscript ('The Insurrection of Miss Houghton') had at last arrived, and he set to work. Although he may originally have hoped to go on from where he had stopped, using the original starting date (1913) and the central character's situation, he ended up rewriting the book completely: not surprisingly, given his thoughts about 'going back'.

Within a week of returning to Capri, however, he was on the move again. Magnus had convinced him that he should try Sicily, telling him that it 'had been waiting for him since the days of Theocritus'; and Capri, however pleasant, remained 'a nice cats cradle of semi-literary and pleni-literary pussies', most of them English: 'Oh my dear English countrymen, how I detest you wherever I find you!' Both the Lawrences preferred the idea of living more independently (they were still sharing their Capri kitchen) as well as being in a place where they had only Italian neighbours.[52] They also wanted somewhere less in the public eye than it was ever possible to be in Capri. Because it was so tiny, Capri offered a very special example of the temptation and threat of English expatriate society, which Lawrence would first be drawn into, then find himself bored by; he would end up longing for solitude.

Around 26 February 1920, Lawrence took the boat from Naples to Sicily (a twelve-hour crossing), with the Brett Youngs for company.[53] He travelled extensively, getting as far as Agrigento in the southwest of the island (Magnus had recommended it), but it was in Taormina, which Mary Cannan knew, that he discovered the Fontana Vecchia, a house standing by itself outside the town, among fields and gardens, with its upper half to let and its Italian owner's family downstairs. It looked out eastwards, from high up, over the straits of Messina and the Ionian sea. It was almost as far south in Europe as he and Frieda could go; living there, he felt, would in effect be 'with one's back on Europe forever'. They moved in on 8 March 1920: 'High on the top floor we live, and it feels rather like a fortress . . . Here one feels as if one had lived for a hundred thousand years.' He and Frieda came to love the Fontana Vecchia deeply: Lawrence felt marvellously at home 'in the garden and up the hills among the goats',[54] and he would write some of his best poems about the natural world there, including 'Snake', 'She-Goat' and 'Bare Almond Trees'. This first spring, he would write lyrically about the dawn and sunrise:

I open my eye at 5.0, and say Coming; at 5.30, and say yellow; at 6.0, and say pink and smoke blue; at 6.15 and see a lovely orange flare and then the liquid sunlight winking straight in my eye. Then I know its time to get up. So I dodge the sunlight with a corner of the blanket, and consider the problem of the universe . . . so warm, so first-kiss warm.[55]

But they also had to remain until Lawrence had earned enough for them to travel on.

That was not his only difficulty. He confessed a very considerable problem in a letter to Mackenzie that he wrote shortly after moving in. 'Hope your book goes – perhaps I shall write here – if only I could care again.'[56] Just because he had got safely out of England, he was not thereby released into easy productivity. On one level, he professed himself happy not to care; he insisted that he went his own way regardless, remarking in January 1921, quite seriously, 'If you knew how I don't care about it all.' He would often write about his hopes to go to the South Seas and somehow run a small ship, doing a little trading, so as to 'break from the last deep land-connections: with society, essentially'. Like Rananim, 'The Island', the ship was another fruitful fictional fantasy, just on the edge of the practical. The fact that, later on, Frieda grew 'terrified' of it suggests that the fantasy had grown too serious; at which point Lawrence, too, grew worried about being 'tied' to the ship. He remarked to Catherine Carswell how, in Sicily, 'I sort of get indifferent to the world . . . The South cures one of caring.'[57] That spring, his essays on psychoanalysis and his little book on education were specifically designed to change people's ways of thinking; yet they were extremely idiosyncratic, and took a particular pleasure in outraging both conventional *and* progressive attitudes. Such writing both adopts and denies a persuasive role, which gives it a peculiar quality. It was all very well Lawrence declaring, 'I want to live my life, and say my say': the very *saying* involved an audience. He remarked in March 1920: 'I am not interested in the public'; eighteen months later, he would write that he felt 'hopeless about the public'. But such comments imply the possibility of hope. He had quickly to add: 'Not that I care about them.'[58] Detachment from his human connections, which the Fontana Vecchia appeared to encourage and endorse, was never enough for him, however much he craved detachment. At some level he knew that too.

14

Ending with Love: 1920–1921

Lawrence's work in hand, all the same, occupied him; and it continued to be centred on England. Between 9 March and 5 May, he worked with great energy at *The Lost Girl*, which was what the 1913 manuscript had turned into: a wryly comic account of the breaking away from small-town morals and expectations of Alvina Houghton, a young woman from 'Woodhouse'. He scrapped what he had done in Capri and started again; but he finished the book with astonishing speed, given that he, Frieda and friends from Capri also made a five-day trip to Syracuse and to Etna. In *The Lost Girl*, he wrote a novel far less demanding on its readers than *The Rainbow* or *Women in Love*, and one which he thought 'amusing, and might be quite popular'[1] – his words to the publisher he hoped would take it, Martin Secker. Its conclusion (Alvina goes to Italy with her new husband, Ciccio) was a wonderful recreation of Picinisco, with an account of the coming of spring, imagined in place of the midwinter landscape the Lawrences had actually experienced.

On their return from Syracuse, Lawrence found himself unexpectedly saddled with the problem of Magnus, who, having escaped from Monte Cassino, had turned up in Taormina, relying on Lawrence for money and accommodation. He had meanwhile taken a room in the most expensive hotel in the town. Magnus told Douglas that Lawrence was at first 'most sympathetic & ready to help me', but he blamed Frieda ('the bitch') for the fact that he was not made welcome at the Fontana Vecchia. Lawrence recalled:

'But what am I to *do*?' he snapped ... 'I came here ... thinking you would help me' ... He put his hand on my arm, and looked up at me with tears swimming in his eyes. Then he turned aside his face, overcome with tears. I looked away at the Ionian sea, feeling my blood turn to ice and the sea go black. I loathed scenes such as this.[2]

Lawrence persuaded Magnus to move into cheaper accommodation and agreed to pay his hotel bill, also to advance him some money. But Lawrence was impatient and angry, too; he himself was marvellously economical when it came to accommodation and food, yet had ended up paying the bills of someone with no such cares.[3] Magnus also tried to persuade him to go up to Monte Cassino to rescue his belongings, but Lawrence refused. Eventually Magnus left, planning to go to Malta.

In the middle of May, Mary Cannan offered to pay for the Lawrences to keep her company on a trip to Malta; postal difficulties were making it almost impossible for Lawrence to stay in contact with publishers and typists, so a few days' break seemed a good idea. They were held up in Syracuse by a steamer strike, and while they were waiting Magnus turned up again, desperate; he begged another loan from Lawrence to pay his hotel bill and get away on the same boat. Once aboard, the Lawrences watched with anger and amusement as Magnus, though only with a second-class ticket, mingled with the passengers on the first-class deck.[4] On Malta, where Magnus intended to settle, Mary Cannan and the Lawrences were delayed by a renewal of the steamer strike. As a result, Lawrence saw more of Magnus than he had planned; they discussed Magnus's literary affairs, and Lawrence met two new Maltese friends of his. Lawrence was led into two uncharacteristic pieces of behaviour. He had a suit made of Indian silk (tussore) costing £6: there was a price to pay for travelling with someone of Mary Cannan's elegance and going about with Magnus in his 'smart white duck suit, with a white piqué cravat'. He was also confidential with Magnus about his sexuality; Magnus 'seemed to understand so much, round about the questions that trouble one deepest . . . he was so intelligent and sensitive'.[5]

Magnus now owed Lawrence some £23, and would end up owing a further £60 to the Maltese. When the travellers finally managed to return to Sicily, Lawrence must have felt relieved at the thought that he was leaving Magnus behind. None the less, Magnus was able to make Lawrence feel a kind of responsibility for him, as well as admiration for his resourcefulness in face of a hostile world. The responsibility and admiration would last long after November 1920, when the authorities caught up with Magnus over his unpaid bills and he committed suicide rather than be arrested and taken back to Italy.

Both Secker and Seltzer were pleased with *The Lost Girl* when they saw it. Secker responded: 'I am quite sure of your future', eliciting Lawrence's sardonic 'What Jehovah is this squeaking.'[6] The novel was never the popular success both Lawrence and Secker hoped it would be (the latter confidently printed 4,000 copies); but, almost as soon as Lawrence had finished it, he started sketching out another novel, *Mr Noon*. The first part would also be set in a recreated English Midlands, but it would then draw heavily on what had happened to Frieda and him in 1912.

But not only did he have *Mr Noon* as a project from the summer of 1920, he also went back to *Aaron's Rod*. Together with *The Lost Girl*, the three novels comprise a kind of comic, fragmentary trilogy of disillusionment with English society, with marriage, and with love: *Aaron's Rod* would eventually come closest to the modern times of Lawrence's relationship with Frieda. The uncomfortable processes of human relationships would also be sharply defined in writing he started in September.

He and Frieda had moved north in the summer, to get away from the heat. By the end of May, Sicily was 'yellow witheredness and sundried earth, and Etna dim in the glare'; by mid July, 'already the leaves are falling' and it was 'too hot to do anything, save at morning and evening'. 'I live in pyjamas, barefoot, all day . . . or when I must put my suit of pyjamas in the tub, behold me *in puris naturabilis*, performing the menial labours of the day.' They escaped: Frieda to Baden-Baden to see her mother, and Lawrence by way of Milan, Lago di Como and Venice – 'Love Venice to look at, but not to smell, and not to live in – melancholic with its dreary bygone lagoons'[7] – to Florence, where Rosalind Baynes (see Illustration 23), her children and their nurse had come to stay.

Since November 1919, Lawrence had been writing to Rosalind with a great deal of practical advice about travel, prices and life in Italy; like him, she stayed at the Pension Balestri in Florence when she arrived. Shortly after her arrival, he had written asking a friend to look in on her: 'I'm afraid she feels a bit forlorn.'[8] She and her family had moved to the Villa La Canovaia, just outside Florence, in a narrow lane leading up to Fiesole, but in August their windows had been shattered by an explosion in the powder factory just below ('Powder factories always explode in Italy,' remarked Lawrence). They took another house, the Villino Belvedere, in Fiesole; but La Canovaia, 'a great rambling old place'[9] with its front windows blown in, remained empty, apart from the gardener's family. Lawrence, unhappy with his accommodation in Florence, was very pleased to camp there. He moved in about 3 September 1920.

It was at this time that he had a very brief affair with Rosalind. David Garnett had known her in England before the war: 'a lovely creature – a russeted apple in face, cool, delicate and critical in spirit'; her laughter was 'thin and a little fastidious', 'like a spoon ringing against a china cup'.[10] All that is known about what happened comes from Rosalind's account of how, around Friday 10 September (the day before Lawrence's thirty-fifth birthday), she and he, out walking, talked about sex and how 'damned fastidious' they both were; until to her surprise he wondered aloud if they might 'have a sex time together'. 'Let us think of love as a force outside and getting us. It is a force; a god.' She felt astounded and extremely happy, answering: 'indeed I want it'. But she also asked him: 'how do you account for the fastidious-ness we have been talking about if there is no personalism in love?' A good question to an enemy of the personal ('Personal means mental consciousness of self').[11] Lawrence dealt with the objection ingeniously, if just a little hastily: ' "Oh yes," says he "there must be understand-ing of the god *together*".' On getting home, she recalled, 'we embrace and kiss our promise'. For a day nothing happened; but on Sunday 12 September, he walked up from La Canovaia (it would have taken him an hour or so), and they spent a happy lunch, afternoon and evening together, walking out and seeing 'the black grapes . . . the grand turkey cock . . . Sorb apples we buy', and so home to make supper. Lawrence said: ' "How good it is here. It is something quite special and lovely, the time, the place, the beloved".' They sat on into the dark, 'our hands held together in union. And so to bed.'[12] It sounds, in her account, extra-ordinarily tender and non-exploitative. They would, however, have had to be discreet; Rosalind had three children and a nurse in the house.

As usual, Lawrence's experience turned itself directly into writing. He had never, before September 1920, written poetry as now he did: wittily and vividly, and also very fast (some poems needed almost no revision),[13] about fruits, trees and animals, and always in ways that evoked and involved the human being participating in or narrating the poem. Some of the poems he drafted in September are luminous and descriptive, like 'Cypresses' and 'Turkey-Cock'; others are thoroughly flirtatious, like 'Pomegranate', 'Peach' and 'Grapes'; while 'Figs' is sexually outrageous, stressing (like 'Grapes') the brave, adventurous 'rosaceae' (for Rosalind) while toasting the *'thorn in flower'* (Rosalind's maiden name was Thornycroft). The oddest fruit poem, however, 'Medlars and Sorb-Apples',[14] is touchingly, at times tenderly, valedictory; the fruits not only suggest autumn and farewell, but their sweetness comes *only* in decay and ending. Although many of the poems survive only in the form in which Lawrence revised them, 'Medlars and Sorb-Apples' can be read exactly as it was written in September 1920. It was finished by the 16th; and the way partners move away from each other is its central subject: 'Each soul departing in its own essence / Never having known its own essence before.' The poem speaks about sexual relationship in ways that are quite different from anything Lawrence had previously written. It evokes a post-coital loneliness: 'The exquisite fragrance of farewell'. Relationship ends as inevitably as the fruit decays and the year ends.

> A kiss, and a vivid spasm of farewell, a moment's orgasm of rupture,
> Then along the damp road alone, till the next turning.
> And there, another parting, a new partner, a new unfusing into twain,
> A new gasp, of isolation, intense,
> A new pungency of loneliness, among the decaying, frost-cold leaves;
> Going down the road, more alone after each meeting,
> The fibres of the heart parting one after the other,
> And yet the soul continuing, naked-footed, ever more vividly embodied,
> Ever more exquisite, distilled in separation.[15]

The 'exquisite' quality exists not in the sweetness of experience, but in the inevitability of the ending; and this only four days or so after Rosalind and he had first slept together.

The six 'Tortoise' poems, about the tortoises in the garden of La Canovaia, for all their brilliant descriptiveness are not so much studies of the natural world as comic revelations of human beings. Whereas the first three depict the lonely individuality of the male tortoise, the last three are about the way in which sex breaks that down, and about the farcical male, 'Doomed to make an intolerable fool of himself'.[16] The female is bored by his persistence; sex is as inevitably a crucifixion of the individual as the cross is inscribed in the shell of the tortoise. It was a remarkable thing to write about the horrible intractability of the sex urge – 'Want, / Self-exposure, hard humiliation, need to add himself on to her' – during an affair. Whatever tenderness Rosalind seems to have found, and to have retained a memory of, Lawrence's experience appears to have been very different.[17]

The poems also offer a running commentary on his marriage: the littleness of the male tortoise pursuing a larger female a comment on Lawrence and Frieda. According to Lawrence, Frieda hated the first draft of the book of verse made up of the 'Fruit Studies', the 'Tortoise' poems and a few others.[18] She must quickly have found out about Rosalind, and that would have been a reason for anger: there was really no way in which the actual subject of the 'Fruit Studies' or the 'Tortoise' poems could have been disguised. She told Mabel Sterne in 1922 that Lawrence had only once been ' "unfaithful" to her' with another woman, at a time 'when she was absent for a visit to her mother'; when she saw him again, there was 'a feeling in the air that she had not left there'. According to Mabel, Frieda 'forced Lawrence to tell her about it'. Mabel, however, who knew of Esther Andrews's huge admiration for Lawrence but knew nothing about Rosalind Baynes, confused the woman Frieda had 'showed . . . the door' to in Cornwall in 1917 with the woman Lawrence slept with in 1920.[19]

Only five days or so after the affair with Rosalind had started, Lawrence wrote to a friend in Capri suggesting that he might soon travel down there, rather than wait for Frieda to come back from Germany: 'I dont want to wait for her here in Florence.'[20] He actually left Florence for Venice ten days before he needed to. That might add substance to the only other detail in Mabel's account: that Lawrence had confessed that the affair had 'been a miserable failure, anyway'.[21]

When Lawrence left, Rosalind gave him some panforte for his

journey to Venice, but the postcard in which he thanked her for it says not a word about any past or (indeed) future relationship, and he never saw her again. Though he continued to write to Rosalind, his correspondence with her reveals not the least trace of what had happened.[22] He would of course, in gossipy Florence, have been extremely careful to safeguard her shaky (in-divorce) reputation. But he could also step back from a relationship into detachment, and back into his marriage; in October, Frieda would remark: 'We are glad to be together again.'[23] In March 1921, Lawrence asked Rosalind how her divorce was proceeding, but learned only in August that it had gone through in April, which suggests the distance that had grown between them. Again, with Frieda suddenly returning to Baden-Baden in March 1921, there would have been an opportunity for Lawrence to see Rosalind during his own journey through Italy. He seems not even to have told her he was coming, however, and spent more time in Capri than in Florence.[24] But when, in the early summer of 1921, he created the relationship between Aaron Sisson and the Marchesa in *Aaron's Rod*, he would incorporate an extended reflection on what had happened.

Because he had left Florence early, on 28 September 1920, Lawrence found himself hanging around in Venice waiting for Frieda. An explosion of anger would have followed her extraction of the facts from him: in *Aaron's Rod*, Lawrence's next fictional account of a marriage, the wife ('with her flushed, tear-stained, wilful distress, she was beautiful') accuses her unfaithful husband of being a coward: 'Tell me ... Tell me! Tell me what I've done. Tell me what you have against me.'[25] Lawrence and Frieda went back to Sicily, arriving by mid October, Lawrence eager 'to get back, and work'. All he had done over the summer was create that first draft of his 'little book of vers libre', which by mid October had acquired the name *Birds, Beasts and Flowers*. It felt marvellous to be back in Sicily: 'peace and stillness and *cleanness*, flowers, rain, streams, birds singing, sea dim and hoarse: valley full of cyclamens: poem to these'.[26] Shortly afterwards, copies of Secker's *The Lost Girl* arrived, along with proofs (at last) of the English edition of *Women in Love*.

But then, in ways to which Lawrence was sadly accustomed, things went wrong. The lending libraries refused to take *The Lost Girl* as it stood, and Secker implored Lawrence to make changes. Lawrence made one big alteration to a sexual encounter (for which the offending page had to be sliced out of copies already bound, and a new page 'tipped in'), and Secker subsequently made three cuts of his own.[27] Before the end of November, Lawrence also had Secker asking him to make changes in *Women in Love*, while warning him that he would be getting an advance of only £75 on the book, because it was obvious that the libraries would refuse it (he had originally threatened Lawrence with an advance of only £50). And this for 'the book I have most at heart'. Lawrence wondered whether it would be best 'not to send out review copies *at all*, but just to publish and leave it at that'. After all this time, nothing seemed to have changed in the conditions of English publishing, and how it treated him, or how critics reacted either; 'they are such poisonous worms,' Lawrence wrote, still perhaps thinking of 'murry-worms'.[28]

It was against this background that he began *Mr Noon* at the start of December 1920. His dislike of the English reading public had been sharpened by the reception of *The Lost Girl*; Virginia Woolf's review, for example, had described him as one for whom 'the problems of the body' were 'insistent and important': sex for Lawrence, she wrote, 'had a meaning which it was disquieting to think that we, too, might have to explore'. Lawrence was contemptuous ('snap my fingers at them: the drivel of the impotent') and, returning to his attack on English stuffiness, he started on a scandalous text constantly attacking both its readers and its critics:

So, darling, don't *look* at the nasty book any more: don't you then: there, there, don't cry, my pretty.

No one really takes more trouble soothing and patting his critics on the back than I do. But alas, all my critics are troubled with wind.

The polite address to the 'gentle reader' is constantly undermined, as on the last page: 'oh gentle but rather cowardly and imbecile reader: for such, really, I find you'.[29] The book was also proof of how much Lawrence had changed since 1912 – as a novelist, a partner and a thinker. The delighted partnership and love of eight years earlier is recreated with loving tenderness, and also subjected to wicked sarcasm and irony. Just as he used the experience of others, so he would use his own experience as a way of thinking through his problems and, in this case, getting past them. As he would put it most positively, in his Magnus 'Memoir': 'We have got to *realise*. And then we can surpass.' What he would have been attempting to 'surpass' in *Mr Noon* was the very idealism about love that had mattered so much to him in 1912. It was probably the first of his texts that aimed to show, without reservation, how love needs to be surpassed.[30] But to do this the novel had to remake the past; there is a paradox in the way it lovingly re-creates the actual events of 1912, only to discount them, to make comic figures of the participants, and to take their essential story in quite another direction from the ideal of love as an identification with the other towards which, in 1912, Frieda and Lawrence had mutually been heading.[31]

At the same time, the novel also allowed Lawrence to investigate aspects of himself which he had barely admitted to, but which can be observed in the biographical record. As Gilbert Noon watches the farm hands scything the meadow, he wishes that he 'were one of them': 'To be at one with men in a physical activity. Why could he not? He had only his life with Johanna [Frieda], and the bit of work he was doing.'

The life with Johanna was his all-in-all: the work was secondary. Work was always a solitary, private business with him. It did not unite him with mankind.

Why could he not really mix and mingle with men? For he could not. He could be free and easy and familiar – but from any sort of actual intimacy or commingling, or even unison, something in his heart held back, tugged him back as by a string round his heart. He had no comrade, no actual friend. Casual friends he had in plenty – and he was quite popular. He had even friends who wrote and said they loved him. But the moment he read the words his heart shut like a trap and would not open.[32]

When working on Tregerthen farm in 1917, Lawrence had appeared 'free and easy and familiar' with other men. That role he could very easily adopt; but the problems of intimate friendship remained. With William Henry Hocking, he *had* tried 'actual intimacy', though not sexually, but by 1920 he had become convinced that 'commingling' was wrong, as much in friendship as in love.

Mr Noon allowed Lawrence to go back and examine his younger self, to see how his life had led him to his situation in 1920. One of his insights was that although he had always been 'cut off – and more or less he knew it', so that naturally he 'almost envied' the mowers, yet he had always previously stood self-consciously back from any desire to identify with them: 'Not quite. Not altogether.' In 1912, he would not have been able to state that paradox so starkly. In 1920, it was as clear as daylight to him.[33]

The novel abandons the lovers in mid-sentence in Riva, with the arrival of clothes for Johanna [Frieda]. An experience for Gilbert of sensual realization of his sexual partner, and which the novel has just located in Riva, parallels something Lawrence himself apparently only experienced around 1915, as one of the stages of his escape from the idealism of love.[34] Gilbert (at this stage of his life with Johanna) naturally cannot understand what is happening: he 'would not have conceived, as you cannot conceive, gentle reader, that a man should possibly have a sensual *soul*'. Lawrence would have found it impossibly difficult to recreate the following winter with Frieda in Gargnano, and its loving tenderness, given that he had just thrust Gilbert into a much later stage of experience; especially in the knowing, superior, overtly comic style of *Mr Noon*. The past could, after all, not so completely be remade. Not surprisingly, writing the novel was getting 'a bit of a strain'.[35] He abandoned it in February 1921: it had been a kind of experiment that he now saw no way of carrying through, and its sexual explicitness would, anyway, have made it impossible to publish.

In America, however, *Women in Love* was finally published, without the extensive cuts and alterations Secker was asking for (though with two small cuts Seltzer had made without telling Lawrence, to passages which seemed overtly sexual), and Lawrence told Seltzer that he hoped 'we can go on all the way together, you as publisher and me as writer'. But Seltzer was running only a small business, and so was less able to weather the storms of the market. Although Mountsier would have preferred to work from the start with 'big publishers like Doran and Co', Lawrence liked the idea of the dedicated, small-scale, 'art' publisher, both in England and in America. His one experience of a large commercial publisher had been a disaster: 'they are excellent sellers of old hat, but fatal for new: witness Methuen and *The Rainbow*.' He wanted simply to earn his living, not to be rich or famous.

He had a simple faith that 'One must be, first and foremost, clear of the money complex: even if one earns one's living', and by living close to the edge of poverty he managed to keep faith with that ambition, down to the end of his life. But all the same he very much wanted to establish an American market for his work; and he would be loyal to Seltzer, who between 1920 and 1923 would publish no fewer than twelve of his books. 'England,' Lawrence told Secker in September 1922, 'makes me about £120 a year ... Well, if that is all England cares about my books, I don't care if England never sees them.'[36] For the first time in his career, Lawrence deliberately arranged for the American publication of his work to take priority over the English: nine of Seltzer's books either came out before the English first publication, or had no English equivalent. Lawrence now told Mountsier that he was not sending the *Birds, Beasts and Flowers* poems to England. When he heard from Secker asking for yet further cuts to *Women in Love*, his attitude hardened still further. Seltzer had issued a fairly minor book like *Psychoanalysis and the Unconscious* in 1921 in an edition of 2,000 copies; Secker produced the English edition of *Women in Love* in an edition of only 1,500 copies. Lawrence also preferred Seltzer's larger, more elegant books to Secker's 'shoddy' volumes; he 'fairly spat' when he saw Secker's *Women in Love* ('dirty paper').[37]

It was thus natural that his thoughts should return to the idea of going to the USA. He had stated to Kot at the start of December 1920 that 'I will go to that "far country" ... as soon as I can afford', and early in February 1921 he told Mountsier: 'I really feel I must come to America.'[38] At one stage, he was set on leasing a derelict farm in Connecticut owned by Carlota Davis Thrasher (whom he had met in Florence in September 1920); and he went on fantasizing about running a ship. As was his habit, he worked out detailed and extensive plans about how to finance, staff and run both ventures: 'You imagine ... the rage with which we make plans.'[39] Such schemes seem, once again, to have been a kind of imaginative fiction that he *needed* to work through.

Yet why was he apparently so keen on moving when he and Frieda were happier than for a long time, securely at home in the Fontana Vecchia during nine months of the year and happily travelling to Italy and Germany in the summer? Lawrence could react very unhappily to new places; and he loved life at the Fontana Vecchia. After rain, Calabria was 'such a blue morning-jewel I could weep', while 'the sun rose with a splendour like trumpets every morning, and me rejoicing like a madness in this dawn, day-dawn, life-dawn, the dawn which is Greece, which is me'.[40]

Restlessness, even the 'devil of restlessness' which possessed Lawrence, is not a sufficient answer, however much 'a seat burns my posterior if I sit too long. What ails me I don't know – but it's on and on.'[41] Getting to know (and being known by) publishers and literary editors in America would probably have helped his career, and it would be wrong to underestimate the annoyance caused all round by the dreadful postal delays in Italy during 1920 and 1921, which made long-distance correspondence frustrating and misunderstandings almost inevitable. Being in the country that was apparently going to be his main market was an attractive proposition. A desire to find an ideal place to live is still closer to the truth, even though Lawrence knew very well that he would find America in many ways quite horrible.[42] But he was fundamentally an idealist, though he also regularly attacked idealism: 'I loathe the ideal with an increasing volume of detestation – *all* ideal.' To start a life better than he thought was now possible in Europe meant finding somewhere freer, less constricted, less industrial, less civilized even than Sicily ('I am feeling absolutely at an end with the civilised world'); somewhere where the dead weight of the past and society's 'barrenness and its barren laws' were not so oppressive.[43] Coming from the working class made him especially sensitive to the structures of English middle-class society. In the aftermath of the war, he was very aware of the way England 'makes everything feel barren', 'the impudence and disorder' of the struggles of the fascists and communists in Italy, the end of 'the old order' in Germany: 'Hohenzollern and Nietzsche and all. And the era of love and peace and democracy with it.'[44]

Yet he also knew that his wish for 'freedom' was suspect. As he would put it in *Studies in Classic American Literature*, 'The most unfree souls go west, and shout of freedom. Men are freest when they are most unconscious of freedom. The shout is a rattling of chains, always was.'[45] Lawrence had fewer pre-existing sensitivities than most middle-class people about where English people should live and how they should behave. He was strongly attracted to communism, as a way of changing the world and remaking it *out* from the image of the past which so annoyed him. 'If I knew how to, I'd really join myself to the revolutionary socialists now,'[46] he remarked in January 1921, the year when the communists showed their strength in Italy.

But, fundamentally, he did not believe that any political movement would change the world. He thus felt, at times reluctantly, forced back on his capacity as an independent writer to change his *own* world, by making it for himself, and living and writing where best he could. However sympathetic Sicily was, he believed that he should 'come unstuck from the old life' and the Europe he had so richly experienced 'this unsatisfactory year'.[47] Being a writer demanded this of him.

An idea of finding a house in Sardinia – which they had imagined to be simpler, not so full of foreigners, 'uncaptured'[48] – was ended by a lightning visit there in January 1921; the trip was (anyway) made partly so that Lawrence could get a book out of it. He did; the book was finished by the start of March, and, with illustrations by the artist Jan Juta, was published in 1923 as *Sea and Sardinia*. It is perhaps the most immediately accessible and attractive of his prose books; not only a miraculous feat of recreation but alive with the comedy of everyday experience, and written with that 'artful' spontaneity which so often marks his writing at its best. Take, for instance, the depiction of Lawrence's fury at being forced to stay at an awful inn at Sorgono (there is no other, and no bus leaves before the morning). What annoys him more than anything, he finds, is the wine-stained shirt front of the landlord; but he also is driven into a rage by finding himself in the lane used by the locals as a lavatory. Back at the inn, he furiously asks, 'Could I have milk?' of 'the dirty-breasted host who *dared* to keep such an inn':

No. Perhaps in an hour there would be milk. Perhaps not.

Was there anything to eat?

No – at half-past seven there would be something to eat.

Was there a fire?

No – the man hadn't made the fire.

241

And so on: the ferocious questioner, the lethargic landlord. The q-b (Queen Bee, i.e. Frieda), observing her furiously buzzing husband, very sensibly asks, 'Why are you so indignant? . . . Why take it morally? You petrify that man at the inn by the very way you speak to him, *such* condemnation! Why don't you take it as it comes? It's all life.'[49] That was true too. In such ways, Lawrence creates a book both comic and beautiful, filled both with his frenzied impatience and with his patient understanding.

Having abandoned *Mr Noon*,[50] he instead turned back to the recalcitrant but continually fascinating *Aaron's Rod*, the book which, more than any other up to this point in his career, had become a kind of journal for his changing ideas and experiences. He had decided to ask the agent Curtis Brown to act for him in England ('I'll stick to him if he does me square and *energetic*');[51] the relationship would continue until his death. Much as he liked the idea of working independently, there were practical drawbacks; and with his new productivity (and the new interest being taken in his work), the effort of placing it himself had become too much.

In March, Frieda's mother fell ill with heart trouble and Frieda hurriedly went to Germany: all ideas of the American farm were abandoned. As Lawrence wrote: 'I made all preparations to go – and then suddenly feel I cant.' A month later, he went north. But before going, he arranged to keep the Fontana Vecchia for another year and to postpone any move to America. He explained to friends: 'With one thing and another, I can't manage my plan.'[52] What he probably meant is that his idealistic desire to go was in head-on conflict with the practical good sense of not going. He was still not sure of his earning power, and *The Lost Girl* had not been a popular success or earned him very much capital, which he wanted to have had before embarking on a new life in America. As he confessed to Robert Mountsier: 'I am so *afraid* of expenses', 'I am so terrified of borrowed money.' Committing all his resources to America, where for the moment all he and Frieda could get were visitors' visas, was too much of a risk; quite apart from the fact that the Thrasher farm would have pinned him down. He wrote how 'the farm scares me, with too much responsibility'.[53] There was, too, the realization (just forced upon them) that Frieda's mother's health was not what it had been, and to leave when she was ill was impossible. None the less, Mountsier felt let down at the cancellation of the plans. It was his first experience of Lawrence engaged in this particular kind of absorbing fantasy.

In Capri, on his way north, Lawrence met an American couple, Earl and Achsah Brewster – painters, Buddhists and intellectuals in their forties – with their daughter Harwood, aged nine; it turned out that they had spent their honeymoon in the Fontana Vecchia. They would be good friends for the rest of Lawrence's life, and tempted him with talk of the East and of Ceylon; they engaged him in discussion of their beliefs, and he sent them a cheerful postcard a few days later, telling them how they were wrong: '*your* Nirvana is too much a one-man show: leads inevitably to navel-contemplation. True Nirvana is a flowering tree whose roots are passion and desire and hate and love. Your Nirvana is a cut blossom. – Pardon this on a p.c.'[54] Although naturally short, it is a lovely example of Lawrence's liveliness as a companion and talker. He spent a couple of days in Florence and on 26 April reached Germany, where for the first time since the war he was going to stay with Frieda on a visit to her mother, who was now living in a *Stift*, a kind of old people's home for aristocrats.

Living in Ebersteinburg in a 'peasant inn', 'black and white village – old castle above – Rhine plain, and Vosges, far beyond', in a climate much cooler than Sicily, and writing during the day in the woods ('very big and lovely – a sense of a big wide land and strong deep trees'), Lawrence finished *Aaron's Rod*: the 'flowering' ending he had been looking for had suddenly come to him.[55] The novel is especially important for offering the overview, abandoned in *Mr Noon*, of what Lawrence felt had happened to him and Frieda since 1912. Towards the end of *Aaron's Rod*, the narrator suggests: 'When a man writes a letter to himself, it is a pity to post it to somebody else', and adds: 'Perhaps the same is true of a book.'[56]

The start of the novel shows Aaron Sisson walking out on his marriage to Lottie; a marriage in almost every way unlike the Lawrences'. Aaron and Lottie have lived together for twelve years and have two children; Aaron has never left the Midlands before the action of the novel, and remains working class. Yet, as the story is told, it draws more and more on the Lawrences' marriage. Aaron's 'detached and logical soul' is a revealing insight:

Of two people at a deadlock, he always reminded himself, there is not one only wholly at fault. Both must be at fault. Having a detached and logical soul, he never let himself forget this truth. Take Lottie! He had loved her . . . And the love had developed almost at once into a kind of combat . . . both he and Lottie had been brought up to consider themselves the first in whatsoever company they found themselves. During the early months of the marriage he had, of course, continued the spoiling of the young wife. But this never altered the fact that, by his very nature, he considered himself as first and almost as single in any relationship. First and single he felt, and as such he bore himself.[57]

He possesses 'the arrogance of self-unyielding male'. He also loves his wife; which for a long time deceives her. She thinks she can love him and he can love her, and then everything will be fine. But Lottie gradually realizes that her husband's withholding of himself is what she is up against; and that this is what makes her so angry with him. 'He never yielded himself: never. All his mad loving was only an effort. Afterwards, he was as devilishly unyielded as ever.' While *she* believes in passion, ecstasy and loss of self, 'All the time, some central part of him stood apart from her, aside, looking on.'[58] If this were only half true, it would be a courageous self-analysis, as Lawrence was recalling things he did not want to remember, but it seems a great deal more than that. It summarizes what Frieda had been saying for years; in 1912, she had concluded that *she* was capable of love, 'but *never* you', while in the 1913 story 'New Eve and Old Adam', Paula Moest's parallel charge against her husband had been: 'You – you don't love. I pour myself out to you, and then – there's nothing there – you simply aren't there.' As early as 1907, Lawrence had written about his capacity for self-conscious looking on: 'myself has watched myself'; in 1913, he had identified Whitman's writing as the 'self revelation of a man who could not live, and so had to write himself', an insight vivid with self-doubt.[59] By the early 1920s, his creation of Aaron's marriage was radical in its grasp of his own predicament.

What the novel does is place this individual up against another central figure, Rawdon Lilly, who seems equally like Lawrence, but in a very different way. The divided hero was an old device for Lawrence, though rarely as starkly presented as in *Aaron's Rod*. Lilly is a kind of alter ego to Aaron; he is married but his relationship looks like a perfected version of Lawrence's idea of what he should have with Frieda: the couple are together or apart just as it suits them. Lilly in general seems to have his life, as well as his marriage, sorted out – interestingly, people think he has recently been psychoanalysed[60] – but for him, isolation is the only justifiable position. (His wife, Tanny, is not present when he justifies it.) Lilly's contradictions abound, however. He finally enunciates his theory that individuals, men and women, must admit their subordination to beings they know to be superior. He tells Aaron that his heart will tell him to whom he must submit, and it looks as if he had only one person in mind: himself. But Aaron remains sceptical about 'deep, unfathomable free submission': ' "You'll never get it," said Aaron.'[61] Lilly, on first acquaintance, 'paid such attention, almost deference to any chance friend. So they all thought: Here is a wise person who finds me the wonder which I really am.' He then forgets them; and it is only then that 'they realised his basic indifference to them, and his silent arrogance'.[62] Another Lawrentian self-insight there, for sure. Frieda had always been critical of his being 'too sweet and smarmy with other people', but it wasn't that he made 'casual acquaintances' too easily. Just the opposite: he took people very seriously. Frieda commented that he always approached people, 'women specially', 'as if they were Gothic cathedrals, then he finds that they are little houses and hates them for it!'[63]

The relationship which Lawrence develops towards the end of the novel between Aaron and the Marchesa, in Florence, offers a kind of commentary on what had happened between him and Rosalind the previous September. As the relationship starts, Aaron looks at his flute, 'Aaron's Rod', and smiles: 'So you blossom, do you? – and thorn as well.'[64] The Thornycroft leitmotif is thus touched on, as in the poems 'Figs' and 'Grapes'. For a long time, Aaron has 'wanted nobody, and nothing'. But now his desire comes back: 'The phoenix had risen in fire again, out of the ashes.' Emotions are not involved: 'I want none of that,' the Marchesa says, recalling how Rosalind had very much liked the 'off-hand' way in which Lawrence suggested they have sex. In the ecstasy of his orgasm, Aaron has the feeling that the Marchesa 'was not his woman' and feels 'somewhere beyond himself – as it were shipwrecked'. Yet when he leaves, he feels 'blasted', 'blazed', 'withered': the same experience Gerald Crich has after sex with Gudrun in *Women in Love* – as if struck by lightning.[65] The experience seems, however, to have little to do with the woman: it is the self-inflicted damage to a man's integrity that results when he has given himself up to sexual desire.

The next day, Aaron feels that 'the need to be alone still was his greatest need' and his instinct is to be angry with the Marchesa. But, he realizes, 'she too was struggling with her fate. He had a genuine sympathy with her. Nay, he was not going to hate her.' He spends a day on his own, out in the country, and although his instinct is 'never to see her again', he ignores the feeling. 'Nay, that would not be fair. For how had she treated him, otherwise than generously.' He tells her that he still feels married to his wife: 'when one has been married for ten years – and I did love her – then – some sort of bond or something grows.'[66] The Marchesa generously accepts that she and he will just be friends.

They stay apart until chance throws them together again a week later, and she asks him: 'Won't you stay?' Aaron does; and this experience is terrible. The sex is 'an excruciating, but also an intensely gratifying sensation'. He stays the night, and makes love to her repeatedly, but 'it simply blasted his own central life. It simply blighted him.' 'He didn't want it, not at all.' (Lawrence later described this stage of Aaron's life as 'the lowest depths'.) She lies curled on his breast, 'with her wild hair tangled about him', but sex feels like the attacking violence of birds of prey, and his feeling is once again that of being dead meat (carrion) to her, as she in her way is to him. In the morning, he has to let himself out and has difficulties with the locks, so that he 'began, in irritation and anger, to feel he was a prisoner, that he was locked in'. But he gets out finally and spends the day alone, knowing that 'he would never see her again. A great gulf had opened, leaving him alone on the far side.'[67]

There is no evidence that these episodes reproduce the details of Lawrence's relationship with Rosalind Baynes. His fiction would usually develop the tendencies of an experience into something a good deal more absolute, so that it no longer simply reproduced, as a diary might, what had occurred. But the other depictions of male sexual activity in Lawrence's fiction have autobiographical origins, and his affair with Rosalind is very likely to have been incorporated into his fiction, especially as he was looking for a way to finish *Aaron's Rod*. The place, what is known of the circumstances, the fact that it ends with the man so absolutely determined to get away, even the fact that Lawrence had been with Frieda more than nine years, all relate the fiction to reality.[68] Having, too, so recently written (in *Mr Noon*) about Frieda's unfaithfulness to him with Harold Hobson in 1912, Lawrence may have thought it only right to use similar material about himself.[69] When Lawrence created Constance Chatterley in *Lady Chatterley's Lover* six years later, he would draw on Rosalind's background, and would repeat the Marchesa's characteristic clinging and feeling small.[70]

The experience with Rosalind seems, however, finally to have confirmed to Lawrence that he did not want sexual relationships. He wanted to get away and recover his sense of himself. Sexual desire, tearing the self out of its integrity (Gilbert Noon is so compulsively drawn to Johanna as to ejaculate 'three times in a quarter of an hour'),[71] was likely to leave him also feeling 'blasted and withered'; and, above all, wanting not to be touched. It was probably this insight which unblocked *Aaron's Rod* in the early summer of 1921. While in its very final stages, Lawrence had commented to Earl Brewster about '*not grasping*: first because of the thorns, then because it's so horrid (not sorrowful but enraging) to be grasped'. It is the very idea of touch which Aaron most hates: the way the Marchesa clings to him makes him want to get away from her. (A couple of months earlier, Lawrence had commented, about the resurrection of Jesus: 'There's a lot lies behind that *noli me tangere*.')[72]

If anything, the affair with Rosalind had strengthened his commitment to his marriage, just as Aaron's relationship with the Marchesa confirms his sense of being married: 'I am a husband, if I am anything. And I shall never be a lover again, not while I live.'[73] At this stage of their lives, Lawrence and Frieda seem to have related to each other not with the accustomedness of a long-married couple, but in a stranger and less intimate way. They were no longer the children in a new world they had been when first together, but people who, although knowing each other very well, maintained their distance from each other. They naturally did things together, as a couple, but they might just as easily do them apart. Yet they were, in their own way, intensely dependent on each other. When Frieda went to Germany in the spring of 1921, for example, Lawrence would find 'the house very empty without F.'. The writing Lawrence did in the summer of 1920 envisages the culmination of this idea of marriage: 'two beings, who recognise each other across the chasm, who occasionally cross and meet in a fiery contact, but who find themselves invariably withdrawn afterwards'.[74] That may have been what Lawrence thought he wanted, as a kind of self-liberation, but it seems unlikely that Frieda would have agreed with him; she would probably have insisted that he was still dependent on her.

Whether they still regularly had sex is unknowable. Lawrence had discovered in Cornwall that he was physically attracted to men rather more than to women, in ways that he had always previously denied, though he also wanted a woman as his partner. He had also thought harder about sexual desire being blasting and withering, a feeling which he gave to both Gerald and Aaron. The woman is 'so beautiful, so perfect, you find her *so good*, it tears you like a silk, and every stroke and bit cuts hot – ha, that perfection, when you blast yourself, you blast yourself! . . . it is a great experience, something final – and then – you're shrivelled as if struck by electricity'.[75] In January 1920, Lawrence apparently discussed with Compton Mackenzie the rarity of simultaneous male and female orgasms, which sounds as if achieving it may have been a problem for him. This suggests a continuing sex life, but it may also relate to the 'blasting' experience of the helplessly orgasmic male, out on his own.[76] As early as August 1919, Frieda at least ('she did not wish to be too much married') preferred to occupy a separate bedroom; this was middle-class practice, certainly, but Frieda was far from conventionally middle class. Living as they had done, 'so much alone, and in isolated places', meant that 'we suffer badly at being cooped up with other folk'; but they did not enjoy being cooped up with each other either. Lawrence explained: 'We both like to keep sufficiently clear of one another.'[77] It is most likely that sex sometimes just happened between them, but that it was not now the centre of their relationship. This is what appears to be the case with Harriett and Somers in Lawrence's next novel, *Kangaroo*, in which Somers remarks: 'Now I don't like love, and I don't like sex . . . I don't want to cast out sex, or cut it out. But to set it subordinate to the living male power in my soul.' That was, however, why Harriett and Frieda had to be suspicious of their husbands' desires for 'Something beyond sex'.[78]

In its final manifestation, *Aaron's Rod* became not simply a demonstration of how Lawrence had changed but, like all his novels, a statement of how he saw relationship and marriage at that time. Following his encounters with the Marchesa, Aaron wants relationships into which love and sex do not enter: the novel 'spits on ecstasy'.[79] Just a fortnight before he finished the book, Lawrence told Achsah Brewster that 'the word *love* has for me gone pop: there isn't anything any more'. Without the 'torment of the spell of this desire', a man could 'preserve himself intact'.[80]

Lawrence would tell Seltzer in October 1921: 'It is the last of my serious English novels – the end of *The Rainbow*, *Women in Love* line. It had to be written – and had to come to such an end.'[81] Not one of the novel's conclusions about relationships was something in which Lawrence would continue to believe, but as he said after finishing it, the book 'is what I mean, for the moment': 'It is my last word in one certain direction.' Many readers objected to the novel, though Lawrence exaggerated when he said: 'Everybody hated *Aaron's Rod* – even Frieda.' Seltzer cabled that he thought the book 'wonderful, overwhelming', a 'publisher's pat', which Lawrence greeted sardonically: 'Glad to hear it, I'm sure.'[82] Frieda would have objected to the novel's rejection of love and sex; but the whole book was aimed at her, and at the relationship she and Lawrence had had since 1912. Even though it incorporated the results of his experience with Rosalind Baynes, the book could have drawn only on Lawrence's relationship with Frieda and reached the same conclusion.

Lawrence would develop these ideas further in the second of his psychoanalysis books, *Fantasia of the Unconscious*, which he drafted in Germany immediately after *Aaron's Rod*: 'We have a vice of love, of softness and sweetness and smarminess and intimacy ... We think it's so awfully nice of us to be like that, in ourselves.'[83] The theory thus grew (as he liked to think it did) out of the passional experience of writing and engaging in fiction, so that the theory was both a confirmation of the fiction and a development away from it. But both the fiction and the theory expressed the conviction that this was the end of the road for the 'vice of love'. When he revised *Fantasia* eight months later, Lawrence would go still further: love becomes 'a piece of indecent trickery of the spiritual will. A man should smack his wife's face the moment he hears her say it. The great emotions like love are unspoken. Speaking them is a sign of an indecent bullying will.'[84] And this from the man who in 1912 had proclaimed himself 'a priest of love', and who had imagined that his life's work would be 'sticking up for the love between man and woman'. He now makes himself the priest of freedom: 'one fights one's way through it, till one is cleaned: the self-consciousness and sex-idea burned out of one, cauterised out bit by bit, and the self whole again, and at last free'.[85] If only.

15

Forwards, not Back: 1921–1922

Although Frieda would have preferred to stay in Baden-Baden 'all summer long', after eight weeks Lawrence wanted to move on. He had finished *Aaron's Rod* and the first draft of *Fantasia of the Unconscious*, but in spite of getting on well with his mother-in-law felt: 'One can have enough of relations at close quarters.'[1] He had also seen Robert Mountsier, who was in Europe; but this time Lawrence got on badly with him. Ideas of sailing away with Mountsier or moving to a farm – 'We'll make a life somehow,' Lawrence had written to him, back in February – came to an abrupt end. It is easy to forget that Lawrence had seen very little of Mountsier, in spite of their extensive correspondence; briefly in London and then for a few days in Cornwall in the winter of 1916–17. Now Lawrence discovered that he 'is one of those irritating people who have generalised detestations: his particular ones being Jews, Germans, and Bolshevists. So unoriginal.'[2] Even more to the point, Mountsier disliked Lawrence's recent work; he had read the first half of *Aaron's Rod* and lectured Lawrence about it, nor did he care for Lawrence's writing about the unconscious. The problems of having chosen an individual rather than a firm to represent him became clear to Lawrence in the course of the year, as Mountsier was away from New York a good deal and Lawrence did not even know where to write to him. At the start of July 1921, Lawrence and Frieda went to visit her sister Johanna at Zell-am-See in Austria, where she was holidaying with her two children (Anita now twenty and Hadu sixteen) and her husband, Max von Schreibershofen, whom she would shortly leave for the banker Emil von Krug. The Lawrences saw Mountsier again in Austria, and this time, too, he 'got on my nerves badly'.[3]

It would, though, continue to be a creative time for Lawrence. The visit to Austria provided the setting for several poems as well as for the second part of his short novel 'The Captain's Doll', written in the autumn. But just as in Baden-Baden, he was keen to move on. In spite of the friendliness of the von Schreibershofens, who were 'really *very* nice with us', Lawrence had his old feeling: 'Everything is free and perfectly easy. And still I feel I can't breathe.' Frieda was 'quite bitter that I say I want to go away. But there it is – I do.'[4] After an expedition to the nearby Karlinger glacier, Lawrence and Frieda went back to Florence; and there, in September, he wrote some of the best poems for *Birds, Beasts and Flowers*, including 'Bat' and 'Man and Bat', before he and Frieda returned to Sicily. Finally at home, Lawrence experienced a renewed onrush of love for the place: 'But how lovely it is here! . . . the great window of the eastern sky, seaward. I like it *much* the best of any place in Italy.'[5]

He had, nevertheless, come back only to leave again. 'What ails me I don't know – but it's on and on'; it was like a sickness, and not to be gainsaid. He would at last fulfil his promise to Katherine Mansfield, made at the end of December 1918, that he would '*get out* – out of England – really, out of Europe'.[6] While still in Austria he had been arranging for new passports, and by the start of winter had had his old brown suit 'turned ready to set off'.[7] For a long time Sicily had seemed like the last of Europe: 'it all seems so far off, here in Sicily – like another world. The windows look east over the Ionian sea: somehow I don't care what happens behind me, in the north west.' But now he not only felt that he could not '*belong* any more' to Europe, but that 'my heart – and my soul are broken, in Europe. It's no use, the threads are broken.'[8] This was a way of talking about loneliness as much as a way of describing Europe; but it was a loneliness that he now did his best to embrace. He linked it with the completion of *Aaron's Rod*: 'I am tired of Europe – it is somehow finished for me – finished with *Aaron's Rod*. Done.' He had written a series of challenging novels and stories; he had argued himself into a position of almost total self-reliance, just as the novel had argued Aaron and Lilly into such a position. Moving on was now 'the next step'.[9]

But there was a lot that still made him feel angry about England, so that at the end of October he would note in his diary: 'Have had a month of loathing everybody, particularly the canaglia of England.

Canaille!'[10] In August he had seen the reviews of *Women in Love* in England, including a vengeful one by Murry, which asserted that the novel was 'deliberately, incessantly and passionately obscene in the exact sense of the word': such a review might have been designed to invite the book's prosecution. A month later, Murry would remark in another review that Lawrence was one of those novelists who 'appear to have passed their prime long before reaching it'.[11] Lawrence also discovered, when he got back to Taormina, that Secker had capitulated to Philip Heseltine's threats of a libel action over *Women in Love*, and needed the descriptions of Halliday and the Pussum in the novel altered. With a very bad grace ('I think it all perfect nonsense'), Lawrence made the changes he was asked for, noting in his diary: 'I give Halliday black hair & Pussum yellow, & send pages back.'[12] Secker also paid Heseltine £50 and reimbursed his legal costs, which made Lawrence 'sick with rage': '*Really*, one should never give in to such filth.' Heseltine was, however, trying to do the novel even more damage. He wrote to his lawyers that 'if ever a book afforded grounds for prosecution on a charge of . . . the glorification of homosexuality in particular, this one does'. Such talk was exactly what Secker was most scared of; but Heseltine could not afford to continue his legal action. Lawrence was also sent the review which had appeared in *John Bull*, calling for the novel to be suppressed because of its presentation of men in love: 'in the hands of a boy in his teens', the book 'might pave the way to unspeakable moral disaster'. Lawrence commented: 'Don't give a fig for the canaille.'[13]

Such things confirmed his belief that neither he nor his novels would ever do well in England; and he was increasingly aware, with Seltzer bringing out book after book of his in the USA, in spite of the slump in the book trade, that 'Nowadays I depend almost entirely on America for my living'. As a writer, he was starting to think of himself as 'more than half American. I always write really towards America: my listener is there.' Once again, he was prepared to be convinced that North America was his land of the future, and that helped make him 'tired of Europe.'[14] He began to gather together his unpublished work, in particular his short stories, revising and rewriting them (for example, the 1916 story 'The Miracle' became 'The Horse-Dealer's Daughter'): Lawrence was setting his house in order. Out of this burst of work between October 1922 and February 1923 came the final version of *Fantasia of the Unconscious*, his book of ten short stories *England, My England* and the short-novel collection *The Ladybird* (also comprising 'The Fox' and 'The Captain's Doll'), the novel of the title being brand new, only finished in December. 'The Captain's Doll' was another work that tested out the consequences of a marriage abandoned and a new relationship, without romantic love, attempted. Alexander Hepburn ends up claiming that all he desires in marriage is the fulfilment of the promises in the Anglican prayer book: he wants to be honoured and obeyed, and he will love and cherish his wife. Hannele, whom he loves and who loves him, calls him a 'solemn ass' and insists that at any rate she will not promise anything *before* the marriage service. The story ends with Hepburn vanishing 'quickly into the darkness'[15] after making his claim. But it *is* only a claim; and the fiction brilliantly dramatizes both Hepburn's longing for a new kind of relationship and what he is up against, in himself and in Hannele.

Lawrence also wrote his lengthy 'Memoir' of Maurice Magnus: his first work to make a homosexual its central figure and so position itself outside the marriage debate. After Magnus had killed himself in Malta on 4 November 1920, Michael Borg, whom Magnus owed £60, had sent Lawrence the typescript of 'Dregs', about Magnus's life in the Foreign Legion. Borg did not trust Norman Douglas, Magnus's literary executor, to do anything towards settling outstanding debts, and Lawrence came to think that he might pay them off (as well as the debt to himself) by getting the book into print, with the introductory 'Memoir' he would write. He acquired Douglas's permission to try to publish it. That, at least, was his excuse for investing a lot of time in writing and then trying to publish the 'Memoir', which he thought was the 'best piece of writing, *as writing*' that he had ever done.[16] The 'Memoir' seems above all to have been a piece designed to discover what Magnus had taught him about himself. During the period 1916–20, he had constantly told himself that friendship with another man was what he wanted: when he got to Monte Cassino, he had found that he didn't want it, after all. And when the friendship deposited itself on his doorstep in Taormina and Syracuse, demanding money and accommodation, he had been dismayed. But he had, thereafter, spent time with Magnus on Malta, and had stayed in touch with him by letter. He would write of Somers in *Kangaroo*: 'he wanted *some* living fellowship with other men; as it was he was just isolated.' That was the risk that Lawrence himself ran. When he heard of Magnus's suicide, it came fully home to him what it would have meant to be 'the hunted, desperate man'; he wrote, admiringly, of Magnus having 'the courage of his own terrors'.[17]

The conclusion of the 'Memoir' was that, although Magnus was a 'scamp', who took advantage of people like Borg, and let down those who felt warm-hearted towards him, like Lawrence, because he had gone into human experience so deeply and profoundly, and refused to give in during his time in the Foreign Legion, he claimed Lawrence's loyalty 'through eternity'. It was one of the oddest of all Lawrence's expressions of friendship.[18] The fact that the Foreign Legion experiences are not particularly gripping, in Magnus's account, suggests that Lawrence's interest in the writer made him over-value the writing. Magnus's position as outsider certainly fascinated Lawrence; he once discussed Magnus with Douglas, sharing the 'grave and brotherly pitifulness that men who have found it difficult to accommodate themselves to their fellow men feel for those who have found it impossible'.[19]

What complicated his American plans was that he now had a powerful inclination to travel east rather than west. His friendship with the Brewsters had developed, and they had invited him and Frieda to follow them to Ceylon, where Earl was taking Buddhism seriously enough to be studying at a temple. Lawrence was tempted: 'I'm rather inclined to think, myself, that people matter more than place.'[20] But Ceylon could only be for a while; and he still wanted to go to the USA, though where and how was more problematic than ever. What finally settled the matter was a letter from Mabel Sterne that arrived unexpectedly at the start of November, inviting him to Taos in New Mexico. Mabel was a wealthy woman, interested in the arts, who had read part of *Sea and Sardinia* and believed that Lawrence could write about New Mexico with new insight. She offered him a small adobe house near the Native American Pueblo in Taos, and sent things to tempt him. 'I . . . smelt the Indian scent and nibbled the medicine: the last being like licorice root, the scent being a wistful dried herb.'[21] Lawrence was strongly attracted and replied at once, with a list of questions. It was by far his best opportunity yet to experience North America: better than a farm, or a lecture tour, or a visit to a publisher.

For all his harsh words about Europe, he was still developing new interests; for example, he was considering translating the novels or stories of the Sicilian author Giovanni Verga. 'He would be most awfully difficult to translate. That is what tempts me.'[22] His 'Memoir' of Magnus was also causing him to revisit his feelings about Italy and the past, while he had an irrepressible sense that he would hate North America. Even Taos had 'a colony of New York artists' and he felt 'I never want to see an artist again while I live': 'Evil everywhere.' All the same, 'I want to go – to try.'[23]

Late in November, however, he found himself reacting badly for the first time to Seltzer, who wanted revisions in *Aaron's Rod* for 'the general public'. Seltzer was, after all, a publisher with a business to run; and Curtis Brown, in England, was also clear about the 'necessity of eliminating the portions of "AARON'S ROD" that deal in such anatomical detail with sex'. There were, of course, no 'anatomical' details, but there *was* a lot about sexual experience; and to begin with, Lawrence had been helpful and thoughtful, suggesting that Seltzer might cut a sentence or two. But when the publisher asked for more substantial rewriting, Lawrence dug his heels in. 'It's your dilemma,' Seltzer was told: 'say no more to me. I am tired of this miserable, paltry, haffling and caffling world – dead sick of it.'[24] Were North American publishers just as pusillanimous as their European equivalents? After his hopefulness of an American readership, too, the reviews of *Psychoanalysis and the Unconscious* had been thoroughly depressing. In this spirit, Lawrence addressed himself to American readers in the foreword he was writing to *Fantasia*: 'I warn the generality of readers, that this present book will seem to them only a rather more revolting mass of wordy nonsense than the last. I would warn the generality of critics to throw it in the waste paper basket without more ado'; and he answered his critics point by point. Seltzer, fearful of the effect of this, cut the passage, thus protecting Lawrence (and the critics).[25]

By January 1922, Lawrence's mind seemed finally made up: he was coming to Taos. (It was the period of a number of 'final' things; in November, he had even considered making a will, 'to give myself a nice sense of finality'.)[26] But during the winter, he felt run down. He had been working very hard, completing three books in seven weeks, and kept getting colds and flu; he may also have had a touch of malaria, endemic in parts of Sicily. This made him put off a date for leaving; and there came the occasional day when, he confessed, 'I love Taormina still'. This went clean against all his determination to go, so that he felt as if he were 'messing about on the edge of everything'. By now, he was also recreating his first huge enjoyment of Sicily in the 'Memoir': 'dawn-lovely Sicily, and the Ionian sea'.[27] Memories of old times in England also haunted him – the Christmas in Buckingham-shire, for example, when the original ideas of Rananim had been discussed: 'If only there were some of the dark old spirit of that left in the world!' He was recalling a time when a small group of friends, in the darkness of the winter and the war, had planned and fantasized optimistically together. 'Meanwhile one is eight years older, and a thousand times more disconnected with everything, and more frus-trated.'[28] He was even so irritated with his sisters (both of whom had been 'loftily disapproving' towards Seltzer's little book of the 'Tortoise' poems) as to feel 'I really am through with them: shall send them no more of my books'. Early in 1922, he would send a copy of the 'Canovaia Tortoise poems' to Rosalind Baynes; she may have seen some of them at an earlier stage, but the whole set represented another kind of ending.[29] He was in the process of severing still more of his links with people, with the past and with anything to which he might belong.

Between March 1920 and February 1922, Lawrence and Frieda had spent longer based in Taormina than anywhere since 1912. He had been astonishingly productive; he had written eight books (two about psychoanalysis, two novels, a book of stories, a book of three short novels, a travel book, and a tiny book of poems). All that remained incomplete, of work he had started and intended to finish, were his Studies in Classic American Literature (but he would send off yet another set of them to his publishers shortly before leaving Sicily, and believed the book was now done), his translation of Verga's Mastro-don Gesualdo, which he would finish on the boat to Ceylon, and the full-length Birds, Beasts and Flowers, of which about two-thirds was ready. And he had written about 100,000 words of the unfinishable *Mr Noon*. He may at times have been very unhappy, but he had loved the Fontana Vecchia and had worked there as a responsible and dedicated professional writer. His writing had constantly generated new ways of understanding how he and Frieda should live; their marriage had remained the basis from which he would time and again take imaginative flight, and Frieda had continued to be the person with whom he argued through his ideas of the new.[30] One of the happiest images of Lawrence in Sicily comes in his landlord's recollection of how his short journey with 'a big terra cotta jug' to the well would sometimes take Lawrence 'several hours', 'for he would loiter along the way and then relax on the little wall surrounding the reservoir, watching the other people come and go'. Not just people, either. His famous poem 'Snake' belongs to the Fontana Vecchia: the narrator 'in pyjamas for the heat', as Lawrence would be in high summer, the poem itself probably written in the middle of winter.

> He reached down from a fissure in the earth-wall in the gloom
> And trailed his yellow-brown slackness soft-bellied down, over the edge
>   of the stone trough
> And rested his throat upon the stone bottom,
> And where the water had dripped from the tap, in a small clearness,
> He sipped with his straight mouth . . .[31]

Taormina had brought them 'months of quiet, peaceful living', like the months in Berkshire in 1919 which Frieda once wrote about as the staple of their lives. Yet in November 1921 she had described how dull Taormina had grown, too: 'it *is* time for Lawrence to get out of this, this is no life for a man and a man who wants something genuine.'[32] Towards the end of January, Lawrence went through some kind of a crisis, feeling 'so ridiculous, wavering between east and west. I believe I shall not go to America.' The thought of Mabel's friends in Taos – 'the analytic therapeutic lot' and 'that "arty" and "literary" crew' – depressed him. He may once have called going to America 'my destiny', but it was a very desperate destiny. He was also filled once again with the pain of leaving Europe, 'the wrench of breaking off'; and his remark the previous March that 'I've got to come unstuck from the old life and Europe' shows that, although he had decided to *come* unstuck, it had not yet happened. America only 'half-cajoled' him.[33]

He finally resolved the dilemma by deciding to go east first, 'intend-ing ultimately to go west'. Ceylon might conceivably give him 'rest, peace, inside', and staying with the Brewsters would be an opportunity for 'solitude and labour'. From there, if he still wanted to, he could travel to the USA's west coast, and thus miss something he dreaded: the dynamic capitalist culture he had come to associate with 'that awful New York'.[34] He would also not need to maintain his current steely *opposition* to things, which seemed to him crucial for arrival in North America. 'I am tired of the world, and want the peace like a river,' he told Catherine Carswell. What currently he most desired, he would tell Rosalind Baynes while on the boat leaving Europe, was not to 'feel any more that tension and pressure one suffers from in England'. The tension was what he had always lived with; the pressure was that of the individual who felt *enclosed* ('England-stifled') and who wanted to break 'out of it all!'[35] This had become an extraordinary need in him, and it is hard to say whether it was more psychological or physiological (he would have seen no difference).

To leave Europe – the Roman fountain in the garden of the Fontana Vecchia, the Greek archaeology of Sicily, the complex mixture of past and present implicit in such a place – was finally necessary to Lawrence, in order to demonstrate his abandonment of his *belief* in Europe. This was the culmination of what he had been thinking about society since 1914. He had been addressing European society since the start of his career. 'But I want to go.' He was thirty-six, 'poor as ever', a not very successful writer with a very small public ('the appreciation of the few'), whose work was 'not of the character that makes a popular appeal'. In fact it was just the opposite, much of the time; he summed up his recent reception as 'mostly abuse'.[36] He certainly had an unsavoury reputation. But he hardly cared about that. He was defiantly disillu-sioned with the literary world, and eager to experience what lay outside Europe. Writing for him was inevitably linked with his capacity to feel, and he was going away not just to travel but to write: to acquire, if he could, 'a sense of the future'. This he had been conscious of lacking since 1919, when he wrote about how uncertain life felt, 'with no past to stay one, and no future to wonder over'. He wanted to get past 'this crisis of the world's soul depression, into a new epoch'. He hoped he would find an idea of the future generated by 'some kind of emotional impetus from the aboriginal Indian and the aboriginal air and land'.[37] But he was also going to try to find a way of life that would satisfy his complex nature and needs; where he would not be so subject to depression and anger as he had been, and where he would not want to oppose everything in his path. Ideally, too, he would find a few people with whom to share his life, though by now that must have seemed rather a forlorn hope.

The *RMS Osterley* left Naples on 26 February 1922, with the Lawrences, 'one household trunk, one book trunk, F's and mine – and then two valises, hat-box, and the two quite small pieces'. They also had with them the painted side of a Sicilian cart, a joust painted on one panel and St Geneviève on the other: a memorial of the world they were leaving. As they sailed through the straits of Messina, they could look back to Etna and Taormina. Lawrence 'wept inside with pain – pain of separation'; leaving symbolized the kind of separation that he was increasingly aware of as the problem of his life. His leaving nevertheless satisfied his desire to make a symbolic break with the past; it was a conscious willing of himself 'to come unstuck'. 'I look forwards, mustn't look back.'[38]

16

On and On: 1922

Leaving Europe, Lawrence not only wanted to experience more of the world, but to 'get a new *start*'. Ever the realist, however, he also knew how much easier it was, as he told Rosalind Baynes, 'to make more ends'.[1] How he prepared for his new start is demonstrated by his passport photograph of 19 September 1921 (Illustration 22), which shows him in his 'same-as-ever old grey jacket' and his old tie;[2] his handkerchief bulges out a breast pocket marked by his habitual pen clip. The shirt is not of the old, English kind, however: his beard is trimmed close to his face, presumably by the kind of 'foreign barber' whom in 1919 he had not wanted to visit, preferring to leave his beard 'bushy and raggy'.[3] After nearly two years abroad, he looks for the first time a non-English Lawrence; the studio backdrop shows a couple of fake columns.

He must have wondered whether his voyage to Ceylon wasn't just a way of demonstrating his anger with Europe. He would have been very conscious of how much that anger was costing him, if so: the steamer tickets had been the most expensive purchases of his life. Fortunately, shortly before they sailed, the otherwise unlucky *Lost Girl* was awarded the James Tait Black prize for fiction, which brought in £100: that made the purchase of two £70 tickets easier to bear. And Ceylon was only two weeks away. He and Frieda could stay if they liked it, and if he could write; or they could travel on to America, or even 'go to Australia if we can manage it': a new plan, developed on the *Osterley*, because there were some 'Australians on board – rather nice people' whom he very much liked.[4] Anna Jenkins, a wealthy Australian widow, had actually brought *Sons and Lovers* with her to read on the journey. Lawrence seems to have taken to boat life with relish, not just for the wonderful views of the desert and the mountains as they came through the Suez Canal – 'Mount Sinai like a vengeful dagger that was dipped in blood many ages ago, so sharp and defined' – but for the companionship. It was a richly filled space between more anxious concerns, and he enjoyed it to the full while, in turn, people saw him at his best, and he did not have time to develop the kinds of feelings that made him critical of them. As a result, he found that he didn't feel angry while travelling: 'no more of my tirades – the sea seems so big'.[5] But it was also characteristic that he should have spent the fortnight's voyage earning his living. He was doing his translation of Verga's *Mastro-don Gesualdo*, which he finished before the ship docked at Colombo: 'The *Osterley* shall always wear my black mark' (he had dropped his inkbottle on the deck).[6] After the weeks and months of indecision, too, travelling was satisfying: 'I feel so glad I have come out, but don't know how the money is going to behave: Can't help it.'[7]

Almost as soon as they arrived in Ceylon, they watched the spectacle of the Pera-Hera, when the 28-year-old Edward, Prince of Wales, 'so thin and nervy', visited Kandy for the annual celebration of the 'tooth' of the Buddha: the night-time procession involved dancers, chiefs and elephants. Lawrence described it in a number of letters, as well as in his poem 'Elephant':

> Enormous shadow-processions filing on in the flare of fire
> In the fume of cocoa-nut oil, in the sweating tropical night,
> In the noise of the tom-toms and singers;
> Elephants after elephants curl their trunks, vast shadows, and some
>   cry out
> As they approach and salaam, under the dripping fire of the torches,
> That pale fragment of a Prince up there, whose motto is *Ich Dien*.[8]

Yet Ceylon was to play almost no part in his subsequent writing, which was extraordinary, given his hopes for 'a new *start*' on this journey. He knew almost from the moment they landed that 'I don't believe I shall write a line in Ceylon – at least not here in the hot part'. That was the initial problem: the heat. The Brewsters' bungalow, well outside Kandy, was right on the edge of the forest:

1. D. H. Lawrence,
Eastwood, *c.* 1886

2. Lawrence Family,
Nottingham, *c.* 1895. BACK
ROW: EMILY, GEORGE,
ERNEST; FRONT ROW: ADA,
LYDIA,
D. H. LAWRENCE, ARTHUR

3. Beauvale School, Greasley, Boys Group III, 1894: 'Nocker' Bradley 2nd row from back, 1st on left; D. H. Lawrence 3rd row, 2nd from left; George Neville 4th row, 2nd from left

4. Lydia Lawrence, Eastwood, *c.* 1895

5. D. H. Lawrence,
Nottingham High School,
1899 or 1900

6. Chambers Family,
the Haggs farm,
29 June 1899: May,
Bernard, Mollie,
Edmund, Ann, David,
Jessie, Hubert, Alan

7. Jessie Chambers, Nottingham, *c.* 1907

8. D. H. Lawrence, Nottingham,
11 September 1906

9. Helen Corke, Croydon, *c.* 1903

10. Louie Burrows, Leicester,
c. 13 February 1909

11. D. H. Lawrence, Croydon,
c. 12 December 1908

12. Alice and Phyllis Dax, Shirebrook, *c.* 1915

13. Frieda and Ernest Weekley, Freiburg, *c.* 1901, PHOTOGRAPH CUT DOWN BY Ernest Weekley to fit a watch or locket

14. Monty, Frieda and Barbara Weekley, Nottingham, *c.* 1905

15. D. H. Lawrence, London, 26 June 1913

16. D. H. Lawrence, Katherine Mansfield, Frieda and John Middleton Murry, South Kensington, 13 July 1914 (the Lawrences' wedding day)

17. D. H. Lawrence, London, late summer 1915

18. William Henry Hocking, Cornwall,
c. 1917

19. Frieda Lawrence, London, October
1919

20. D. H. Lawrence, Derbyshire, *c.* June 1918

21. Maurice Magnus, *c.* 1920

22. D. H. Lawrence, Florence,
19 September 1921

23. Rosalind Baynes with her daughter Bridget, 1914

24. Mabel and Tony Luhan, New Mexico, *c.* 1925

25. D. H. Lawrence, Bibbles and Frieda, Del Monte ranch, Taos, February–March 1923

26. Frieda Lawrence,
Guadalajara, Mexico,
May–June 1923

27. D. H. Lawrence, Santa
Fe, 19 or 20 March 1923

28. D. H. Lawrence and Frieda, *SS Resolute*, New York, 21 September 1925

29. BACK ROW: Harwood Brewster, Earl Brewster; front row: Dorothy Brett, Achsah Brewster and D. H. Lawrence, Capri, late February or early March 1926

30. Angelo Ravagli in Bersaglieri uniform, *c.* 1926

31. Ada Lawrence and D. H. Lawrence, Mablethorpe, week of 21–26 August 1926

32. BACK ROW: D. H. Lawrence, Emily King, Maude Beardsall, Ada Clarke, Gertrude Cooper; front row: Joan King, Jack Clarke, Bert Clarke, St Peter's Church, Markby, Lincolnshire, week of 21–26 August 1926

33. D. H. Lawrence, Villa Mirenda, San Polo
Mosciano, *c.* 1926–7

34. 'Pino' Orioli, Frieda and D. H. Lawrence, Ponte Santa Trinita, Florence,
c. May 1928

35. and 36. D. H. Lawrence in the bookshop of Davis and Orioli Ltd, Lungarno, Florence, May 1928

37. *Family on a Verandah*, painted late April 1928

38. D. H. Lawrence,
Ad Astra Sanatorium,
Vence, 26 February
1930: CLAY HEAD BY
JO DAVIDSON

We sit on the verandahs and watch the chipmunks and chameleons and lizards and tropical birds among the trees and bamboos – there's only a clear space of about three yards round the house. We've got four servants – two men, one ayah, one boy of fifteen – but nothing is ever done: except meals got ready. It is very hot in the sun – we have sun helmets and white suits – but quite pleasant sitting still. If one moves one sweats. There's a good deal of room in the bungalow, and practically no furniture except chairs and a table or two. It is rather fascinating, but I don't know how long we shall stay.[9]

His sister Emily heard how 'one doesn't do much here, I tell you.' His account simmers with the impatience of a man used to working: the fact that no one *does* anything and *he* can't do much either. Although the place was 'lovely to look at', he was simply overwhelmed by 'the terrific sun that makes like a bell-jar of heat, like a prison over you'.[10] Because the bungalow was so close to the forest, they all experienced 'the metallic sense of palms and the horrid noises of the birds and creatures, who hammer and clang and rattle and cackle and explode all the livelong day, and run little machines all the livelong night'. They slept badly, with the noise and the heat: 'even at night you sweat if you walk a few yards.' The Brewsters were, as always, kind and helpful, if otherworldly, and Harwood a child whom both Lawrence and Frieda liked very much, but Lawrence continued not to be 'quite sure where I am'. The Brewsters visited the old rock temples, where they would take off their shoes and hats before going in, but Lawrence refused to accompany them: 'coming out, there would be Lawrence standing in his shoes, hat tight on his head, declaring that there was no use, he did not belong there and could not join in.' 'I feel I don't belong and never should.'[11] He did, however, acquire a couple of extraordinary performances for his repertoire of mimicry. Four years later, his friend Rolf Gardiner watched Lawrence imitating the 'Singhalese dervishes or devil-dancers' he had seen. He did not just demonstrate the dancers' steps. Not a particularly well man, he suddenly gave, to Gardiner's astonishment, 'an imitation of their frenzy, quite terrifyingly, his piercing blue eyes popping right and left out of his pale face as he twisted like a cobra, shuffling in his carpet slippers like one possessed by demons'. And Richard Aldington, in the late 1920s, experienced Lawrence's recreation of life on the edge of the forest: 'he once asked me if I had heard the night noises of a tropical jungle, and then instantly emitted a frightening series of yells, squawks, trills, howls and animal "help-murder" shrieks.' Lawrence obviously responded to every feature of his surroundings in Ceylon, and a recollection by Achsah Brewster shows that, in spite of everything, he was still doing some work; at night 'he would read what he had written during the day' – his new translation of Verga's *Novelle rusticane*, presumably, though he was also drafting his 'Elephant' poem.[12]

Apart from the poem, he did no original work at all, in spite of having told his publisher that he hoped to write a 'Ceylon novel'. One reason is that early on he picked up a stomach bug which led to constant stomach trouble and diarrhoea: 'my inside has never hurt me so much in all my 36 years as in these three weeks.'[13] This certainly conditioned his responses to what he saw. He told Brewster that, because of his illness, 'he did not trust his impressions', and he was thoroughly bad-tempered much of the time. It was literally a physical distaste that he experienced:

the scents that make me feel sick, the perpetual nauseous overtone of cocoanut and cocoanut fibre and oil, the sort of tropical sweetness which to me suggests an undertang of blood, hot blood, and thin sweat: the undertaste of blood and sweat in the nauseous tropical fruits; the nasty faces and yellow robes of the Buddhist monks, the little vulgar dens of the temples: all this makes up Ceylon to me, and all this I cannot bear.[14]

And the old feeling of suffocation started to creep into his letters. He wrote of 'the thick, choky feel of tropical forest' and of how the 'place, Ceylon, is a real prison to me, oppressive, and I want to get out'; a week later, it felt as if there was 'a lid down over everything', so that even when, for the sake of coolness, they went up to a hill station at 6,000 feet and 'I thought we should get through the lid', he found that 'no, it presses tighter there'.[15]

His comments on Buddhism cannot have endeared him to his hosts either, especially not to Earl, who would publish a *Life of the Buddha* four years later. 'Oh I wish he would *stand up!*' was his comment on Buddha, and by implication on Buddhism's lack of engagement with the world. In one of his politer remarks, he called it 'a barren, dead affair'; it 'affects me like a mud pool that has no bottom to it'. Even the Brewsters, forgiving as ever, must have wished at times that this vituperative snake had not come to their tropical paradise. But, at all events, in spite of his original intention to stay a year, later modified to 'six months at the least', he and Frieda would not be staying on after the Brewsters themselves left at the end of April.[16]

Lawrence's first experience of life outside Europe, however – 'I . . . sort of look round for myself among all this different world' – produced one unexpected effect. It made him deeply regret leaving England and Europe: 'I break my heart over England when I am out here.' Frieda remembered how 'terribly English' he became: 'English in the teeth of all the world, even in the teeth of England' is how he put it. He wrote: 'I do think, still more now I am out here, that we make a mistake forsaking England and moving out into the periphery of life.' Such a 'periphery' included, astonishingly, not only Taormina but 'Ceylon, Africa, America';[17] the bitter disgust with Ceylon evinced in his letters reminds us how disappointed Lawrence was, and how easily at this stage he ran to colonial and racist explanations. (Such a reaction would be challenged and eventually utterly changed by his experiences in America.) In correspondence with another English expatriate, he had a sudden insight into what it would be 'to care', to be responsible, to write for his country. In Ceylon, it had seemed that 'nothing ever *could* matter, not really, not in our sense of the word'; and like his character Somers in *Kangaroo*, Lawrence 'felt himself to be one of the *responsible* members of society, as contrasted with the innumerable *irresponsible* members'. In Ceylon, he felt he was 'running away from the place where we belong'; he announced that he was trying to make up his mind 'to return to England during the course of the summer'.[18] He did not act on this fantastic reversal of almost everything he had been saying and thinking for the last seven years, but it is a useful reminder not only of his contradictoriness, but of how divided he was, even when sounding most certain. He frequently enacted alternative needs and feelings in his letters and, at times, in his travels. Another stance he took while in Ceylon is a good example. He told Mabel Sterne, in a letter, that he believed not in democracy but in 'actual, sacred, inspired authority: divine right of natural kings. I believe in the divine right of natural aristocracy.' When, however, it came to riding uphill in a rickshaw in the heat, he refused to do it. Ill as he was, 'he simply could not allow a rickshaw boy to pull him, but got out and walked'.[19] Lawrence was also far too intelligent not to be aware of the oddity and in some ways the absurdity of his flight from Europe, nor of the likelihood of his encountering disappointment after disappointment on his travels.

After only six weeks, he and Frieda left. The Australians they had met on the journey out to Colombo had invited them to stay, and Western Australia, now in the late autumn of the southern hemisphere, sounded far more like the England for which he was nostalgic. He and Frieda headed there, though not with any particular expectation: 'one may as well move on, once one has started. I feel I dont care what becomes of me.' That was Lawrence acting irresponsible. Having cut loose, loose he would remain: 'I like the feeling of rolling on.' On the other hand, just travelling was futile, and he confessed in May 1922 how the 'sense of futility grows'. He now intended to 'go on and on till I am more or less sure': sure, that is, that there was nowhere he preferred to England and Europe. He commented ruefully, in May, that 'I love trying things and discovering how I hate them'.[20] But he would have to settle and write somewhere, come what may; to remind him of how expensive 'discovery' was, the tickets to Australia cost another £66 each. Back in 1920, while planning an escape by boat to the South Seas, he had felt as if he were 'victualling my ship, with these damned books'.[21] That was almost literally what he now had to do.

The Lawrences would spend, altogether, only just over three months in Australia. After a journey over 'a very big blue choppy sea with flying fishes sprinting out of the waves like winged drops', they landed in Perth, in Western Australia, on 4 May 1922, but stayed there for only a fortnight. They were a little overwhelmed by the hospitality of the Jenkins family and friends, though the climate was exactly what Lawrence wanted after Ceylon: the sky felt 'high and blue and new, as if no one had ever taken a breath from it'. He was not the least oppressed. The most significant thing in Western Australia, for Lawrence, was the bush he saw near Darlington, which both fascinated and scared him: 'hoary and unending, no noise, still, and the white trunks of the gum trees all a bit burnt . . . somewhat like a dream, a twilight-forest that has not yet seen a day'.[22] The silent contrast with Ceylon's suffocating forest could not have been starker. Lawrence's most significant contact in Western Australia, made via Mrs Jenkins, was with the nurse and novelist Mollie Skinner, who lived not far away. She reckoned him frail, with scarlet lips and a 'hectic flush' on the cheekbones of his otherwise white face.[23] But she was impressed by his advice to write about what she knew: this led her to write the book that, the following year, Lawrence would transform into their joint novel, *The Boy in the Bush*. In this, he would create what it was like for Jack Grant to be lost in the bush, and almost to die in it.

Neither Perth nor Darlington offered the Lawrences the opportunity to settle down that they were looking for, however, and their tickets took them on to Sydney. On 18 May, they left to try New South Wales. Sydney itself turned out too expensive; so, in spite of the excellent advice he would give himself shortly – 'to get to know anything at all about a country', one should 'live for a time in the principal city'[24] – he and Frieda retreated down the coast forty miles to the small and declining holiday resort of Thirroul, and took a house there: 'a very nice bungalow with the Pacific in the garden'; 'the surf seeming to rush in right under our feet as we sit at table'. They knew no one – 'within 1000 miles there isn't a soul that knows us' – and their neighbours, much to Lawrence's relief, did not cross-examine them. 'I suppose there have been too many questionable people here in the past.'[25] There, despite all his forebodings about writing in a place he didn't know at all, and his anxieties about his recent novels – *Aaron's Rod* had 'stuck for two years' and *Mr Noon* was still unfinished[26] – Lawrence started a novel. He found himself able to write over 3,000 words a day for six weeks, with only one serious break in his progress. Ceylon should have been marvellous, but he had written almost nothing. They had expected little of Australia: but here was Lawrence, writing furiously.

He had originally considered something popular: 'a romance – or begin one – while I'm here and we are alone'.[27] But *Kangaroo* was in no way a romance. It was a progress report from a European in the middle of his travels, and not just travels across oceans, but in a political sense, too, as he considered the ways in which an individual might best belong to his society. Australia both impressed Lawrence and made him intensely wary. He liked the uncaring quality; but he also found it the most democratic place he had ever been to. Lawrence was already a self-convinced opponent of the levelling-off effects of democracy, though he had hated the fascism he had seen in Italy. Above all, Australia made him ask how society might change. The novel took the European problems that had concerned him – who is to rule, who is to submit; what the exercise of power should be like; how society might alter; how individuals can both remain themselves and be social beings – and explored them in this new/old world, where every issue seemed clearer. Here in Australia, not only could socialism realistically be polarized against authoritarianism or fascism, but the old civilized ideas of love and trust and belief could be stacked up against a genuine, realizable idea of individual separateness; and, as in any novel, these ideas could be sustained and subverted fictively. Lawrence used the socialists and fascists he had seen in Italy, and the ideas about socialism which stemmed from his youth in Eastwood, as well as the attitudes of the discontented ex-servicemen he was seeing in Australia itself. On the boat he may have made the acquaintance of some people who were at least toying with the idea of a revolutionary group made up of such servicemen; and it was characteristic of him that he should have developed what he guessed and imagined into a complex, fictional organization, the Diggers. The central, invented figure of 'Kangaroo' – the lawyer Ben Cooley, the representative of the idea of love who is both fascist and Whitman-like – is far more than a cardboard figure. His emotionalism, his rhetorical power, his appeals to Somers, are the kinds of thing which only a man and a writer who had been deeply committed to such feelings at some stage of his life could now have created or attempted to reject. The same is true of the socialist Willie Struthers. Lawrence was revisiting his own and his culture's past, but using his insight into a new country and society to make them real and compelling. Somers, however, ends up feeling that the whole of the past, with its fixation on politics, 'authority', 'love' and 'democracy', is a mere 'decomposed body . . . whirling and choking us, language, love and meaning'.[28] This was a depressing enough conclusion. For all its newness and agelessness, Australia was not offering *this* novel (or novel-writer) any way out, except into the beauty and isolation of the bush, or into Somers's solitary meanderings along the shore, peering at sea creatures and shells.

Somers's marriage is even less of a partnership than that of Tanny and Lilly in *Aaron's Rod*. He and Harriett exist in continual flux, between the possibilities of masculine lordship, female love, and mere companionship. *Kangaroo* offers another updating of Lawrence's thinking, and shows the husband more than ever determined to be obeyed, as lord and master, and the wife more than ever contemptuous of such a role. 'Him, a lord and master! Why he was not really lord of his own bread and butter, next year they might both be starving.'[29] The marriage seems almost a side issue to Somers, who, pulled in all directions by society's claims, its old ideas of rootedness in love, in marriage and in responsibility, finally comes down even more firmly than previous Lawrentian heroes in the role of the lonely individualist. In *Aaron's Rod*, Aaron had asked the question 'to whom should I submit?' In *Kangaroo*, Somers's answer is, in effect, 'to no one'.

For the first time in a Lawrence novel, too, a belief is asserted in the non-human world rather than in relationship as *the* crucial context for a human being's sense of self. While offering ideas about how twentieth-century people might work out ways of changing their society, a novel that might have been completely political chooses instead compelling visions of a world free of the constraints of society. Australia offered a superb context for this way of thinking and writing: 'The soft, blue, humanless sky of Australia, the pale, white unwritten atmosphere of Australia. Tabula rasa. The world a new leaf . . . without a mark, without a record.' Lawrence commented that he'd not want to stay there 'unless I'd had enough of the world altogether, and wanted to lose myself. It would be a good place for that.'[30]

He found 'a great fascination in Australia' and remarked that 'But for the remains of a fighting conscience, I would stay'. That is, he felt he could not *be* responsible in Australia and, like Birkin in *Women in Love*, he felt still 'damned and doomed' to the old effort of working out (and fighting for) what he believed, as man and writer.[31] And this in spite of the chapter 'The Nightmare' which had poured out of him in *Kangaroo*, setting out what was to him the real history of the war. The chapter had recounted his experiences in Cornwall and Derby, and in it he now finally worked out how he had lost his belief in his country. That would have proved to him, if he had been in any doubt, that Australia offered insufficient challenge to the European he still was; it provided simply a larger landscape in which the old concerns could be positioned. But what a landscape: 'when the sky turns frail and blue again, and the trees against the far-off sky stand out, the glamour, the unget-at-able glamour!'[32]

After the initial rather pressured intimacy with the people he met in Western Australia, Lawrence seems to have done very little in New South Wales apart from look, think and write: 'still' was the word he used to characterize the time they spent there. The novel was, however, a real, odd achievement, and remains one of the most significant twentieth-century perceptions of Australia. After becoming 'slightly stuck' around 21 June,[33] it was quickly on course again; but as soon as Lawrence was sure that he could finish it, he and Frieda booked their tickets for the USA. He posted his manuscript ahead to Mountsier, for it to be typed and waiting when he arrived; he knew he would want to revise it. But America could no longer be put off. It remained 'the only country in the world that I shrink from and feel shy of: Lord knows why'.[34] At different times, he asked Seltzer, Mabel Sterne and Mountsier whether they would like to meet the *Tahiti* when it landed in San Francisco, though in the event none of them did. On 11 August 1922, Frieda's forty-third birthday, they sailed for San Francisco, via Wellington, Raratonga and Tahiti.

The last words in Lawrence's manuscript of *Kangaroo* had been: 'Goodbye to you, goodbye to everybody. I've finished on this side.' When he arrived on the *other* side, in America, Lawrence tried out three more endings. One depicts the threads of streamers between ship and shore at Sydney Harbour snapping: the last words – 'like broken attachments, broken' – suggest Somers's state of mind. A slightly longer ending, but no less bleak, shows Somers and Harriett on the boat, sailing away: 'It was only four days to New Zealand, over a cold dark, inhospitable sea.' In the longest of the endings, the boat has got as far as Tahiti, but is now leaving for America, 'towards sunset, and the evening all intensely gold'. Somers has a long and intimate conversation with a young American which ends with them separating to dress for dinner: 'they jerked apart again as if they had never spoken.' All three endings demonstrate different kinds of isolation. 'He was broken apart, apart he would remain' summarizes all of them.[35]

As usual, this was the kind of condensed truth that Lawrence's writing encouraged him to develop. Travel was bringing out in him the chance of not just believing in his solitary self but enacting it. And yet, travel was going to bring him some very new and varied experiences. He had been hoping to see the Pacific islands ever since reading Melville and discussing *Typee* in *Studies in Classic American Literature*; he had fantasized voyaging there with Mackenzie and subsequently with Mountsier. He also wanted to see where another of his heroes, the writer Robert Louis Stevenson – wirily energetic and consumptive novelist, poet and essayist, whose initials are acquired by R. L. Somers – had gone, to find the earthly paradise and to write. Lawrence, however, had lost his faith in 'earthly paradises': 'You can have 'em.' Papeete, the capital of Tahiti, turned out 'a poor, dull, modernish place'. And although Raratonga was 'really almost as lovely as one expects these South Sea Islands to be', he found the same metaphor for his experience he had used in Ceylon: 'One's soul seems under a vacuum, in the South Seas.'[36] He felt cut off, apart, unspeaking, uncaring. He seems to have got as much pleasure out of a crowd of film people who came aboard in Tahiti, en route to San Francisco, as out of the islands. Although his letters are contemptuous of the cinema crowd, a letter from Frieda remarked that he 'doesn't work, people amuse him' – 'a new kind of people these' – and he went on talking about them:

Their unrestraint and their wild, care-free love-making amazed and at the same time infuriated him. He became acquainted with some of them. They were like a new species of creature he had never seen before. He watched and registered every move . . . [he] made us *see* that ship; the long, slow passage through the blue sea, the reckless, sensational crowd on board . . . [37]

The uninhibited ease of beings who had so far escaped their isolation as to make unrestrained love may have angered him, but it compelled him too. When the boat finally reached San Francisco, not only did he and Frieda go on seeing their 'shipboard friends' – they were 'still a friendly company' a couple of days after landing[38] – but he also went to the cinema and saw the developments in cinema technique which the west coast of America fostered. Could this have been with some of the film crowd?

But the cinema, like the rest of the 'iron-noisy', expensive city, 'a sort of never-stop Hades', failed to impress him. His prose mimicked his disturbance: 'I went to a cinema and with jazz orchestra and a huge and voluminous organ. Either it is all crazy or I am going.' On the evening of Friday 8 September, after just five days of city life, he and Frieda left by train for New Mexico: the journey was still 'two days by train and 100 km. by motorcar'.[39] Mabel Sterne and her Native American lover, Tony Luhan, met them at Lamy station on the Sunday, and took them to Santa Fe to spend the night. They stayed with friends of hers, the poet Witter Bynner and his lover, Willard 'Spud' Johnson; and the next day Mabel and Tony drove them up the long, rocky, canyon-lined road to Taos, fifty-five miles away. It was 11 September 1922, Lawrence's thirty-seventh birthday.

17

New Mexico: 1922–1923

New Mexico turned out to be the place Lawrence had been looking for all his life. But if it represented a kind of breakthrough, that was not because the people he found there were the people he wanted to be with. New Mexico gave him an experience of a surviving religious culture such as he had never expected to find; and on the Kiowa ranch, some eighteen miles from Taos, he managed to establish a life lived more independently and richly, up against the natural world, than he had thought possible. As a contemporary wrote: 'On his small ranch near Taos his life nearly came true.'[1]

But Taos didn't at first strike him as a breakthrough. His essay 'New Mexico', written in December 1928 in response to a suggestion from Mabel Luhan, gives a fascinatingly one-sided account of what he had encountered in 1922. He wrote there how 'New Mexico was the greatest experience from the outside world that I have ever had . . . the moment I saw the brilliant, proud morning shine high up over the deserts of Santa Fé, something stood still in my soul, and I started to attend.'[2] That may have been an undercurrent in his response; but what impressed him when he first arrived was the artificiality, indeed the superficiality of life. Three days after he and Frieda arrived, Mabel sent him off with Tony Luhan to see Apache ceremonies in Arizona, another long car journey; and in the essay he wrote in response, 'Indians and an Englishman', Lawrence made the Southwest in turn a stage, a circus, a farce, and a comic opera: 'here am I, a lone lorn Englishman, tumbled out of the known world of the British Empire onto this stage: for it persists in seeming like a stage to me, and not like the proper world.' Following his return to Taos, he would tell Robert Mountsier, in a broad hint at the problems of life in

'Mabeltown', 'If it doesn't *suit* me here, I shan't stay more than a month.'[3] And three days later, he wrote to Earl Brewster dismissively about the 'Land of the Free': 'It's free enough out here, if freedom means that there isn't anything in life except moving *ad lib* on foot, horse, or motor-car, across deserts and through canyons. It is just the life outside, and the outside of life. Not *really* life, in my opinion.' He had experienced nothing except the 'outside'; his heart was 'never touched at all – neither by landscape, Indians, or Americans'. The Pueblo tribe of Taos he found 'much more remote than negroes', and as late as December 1922 he would dismiss them as 'very american – no inside life'.[4] At the end of September, he had written in the same terms to Catherine Carswell, whom he imagined envying him and Frieda their new experiences. 'It only excites the outside of me. The inside it leaves more isolated and stoic than ever. That's how it is. It is all a form of running away from oneself and the great problems: all this wild west and the strange Australia.' And he felt like leaving: 'I don't know how long I shall stick it: probably, as a sort of lesson to myself, until the spring. Then I shall come away. But if I dislike it *too* much, I shall leave as soon as I decide that it is too much.'[5]

What he was up against was Mabel Ganson Evans Dodge Sterne Luhan; Tony would become her fourth husband in April 1923 (see Illustration 24). The letter Lawrence wrote to Brewster makes plain how she was the problem:

What you dislike in America seems to me really dislikeable: everybody seems to be trying to enforce his, or her, *will*, and trying to see how much the other person or persons will let themselves be overcome ... I dislike that: and I despise it. People must be very insufficient and weak, wanting, inside themselves, if they find it necessary to stress themselves on every occasion.[6]

He had come to America for a new experience and a non-European world. What he discovered were utterly alien Apache and Pueblo tribes, and a white world at its most wilful and domineering. He and Frieda could have had no idea in advance quite what they were getting into. The house with four rooms and a kitchen in which they lived during those first weeks, in theory Tony's house because built on Pueblo land, was a mere satellite of the big house 200 yards away. Having invited him to New Mexico, Mabel wanted Lawrence to talk to her for hours, to fit in with her plans and imaginings, to be the grateful recipient of her kindness, to be shown off to her guests and, above all, to write for her, as he had written about Sardinia. 'I wanted Lawrence to understand things for me. To take *my* experience, *my* material, *my* Taos, and to formulate it all into a magnificent creation. That was what I wanted him for.'[7] Mabel's writing about Lawrence, from ten years later, conveys her character irresistibly: energetic, determined, almost comically self-regarding, acknowledging nothing except her own desires. It offers a kind of crazed parody of Lawrence's insistence on responding to one's own needs.

Though the Lawrences went on hoping that Mabel would 'leave us alone', and *not* be 'a padrona', and though she regularly maddened them, arranging them 'too much as if one were a retainer or protégé of hers', they continued to be grateful for her invitation, for the meals and the rent-free house. And as the months passed, and Lawrence started to become aware of the power which the Native Americans of the Pueblo, so close to the centre of Taos, held over his imagination, he began to appreciate the place far more. Everyday life in Taos, too, because of Mabel as well as in spite of her, had its compensations. A stream of interesting people flowed through her house; and Lawrence and Frieda also very much enjoyed learning to ride. Lawrence rode clumsily but fast, and utterly fearlessly. The man who had so contemptuously described 'moving *ad lib*' on horseback ended up loving 'to ride alone – in the sun in the forever unpossessed country – away from man. That is a great temptation.'[8] He was also able to do some sustained work; *Kangaroo* was almost the only original thing he had written since February. He now revised it and gave it a new last chapter, as well as writing two poems – 'my first in America' – and some essays and journalism about New Mexico. He also wrote a review for the student magazine *Laughing Horse* which Spud Johnson worked for; he had been sent Ben Hecht's avant-garde novel *Fantazius Mallare*, which for its time was extremely explicit, its hero 'fondling a warm thigh and steering his phallus towards its absurd destiny'. Lawrence set out to show that there was more than one way of being outspoken. 'The word penis or testicle or vagina doesn't shock me. Why should it? Surely I am enough a man to be able to think of my own organs with calm, even with indifference.'[9] The magazine editors, however, replaced the underlined words with bracketed dashes to give an added comic frisson to the piece (and so wrecking Lawrence's point), but the uncut review stands as one more of those declarations of faith with the language of the body which would culminate in the writing of *Lady Chatterley's Lover*.

Under pressure from Mabel, he also started 'a M. Sterne novel of *here*: with her Indian: she makes me notes'. However, after writing only a few pages, he abandoned Mabel's hoped-for 'magnificent creation', potentially his long-planned novel of the American continent. It survives as the fragment known as 'The Wilful Woman'; its version of Mabel brief but wonderful, the energy, the candour and the allure all combined:

She was a sturdy woman with a round face, like an obstinate girl of fourteen ... Her thick, dark brows like curved horns over the naïve-looking face; and her bright, hazel-grey eyes, clear at the first glance as candour and unquenchable youth, at the second glance made up all of devilish grey and yellow bits, as opals are, and the bright candour of youth resolving into something dangerous as the headlights of a great machine coming full at you in the night.[10]

Lawrence's work on 'The Wilful Woman', however, reminded Frieda of how 'I had always regarded Lawrence's genius as given to me'. Although she admired the writing – 'It's *very* clever the beginning, it will be rather sardonic!' – she simply did not want Lawrence collaborating with Mabel. Lawrence had his reservations too: 'I think ... it would be just *too* impossible. Might make me also *too* sick.' In that characteristic mode of feeling which was both response and assertion, Lawrence first remarked that he felt he needed 'breathing space' – 'we gasp on the breath of hurry' – and subsequently commented: 'I don't breathe free.'[11] Rather than going on with 'The Wilful Woman', in mid October he returned to the *Studies in Classic American Literature* and in two months rewrote them completely, in a new, punchy, hard-hitting style which he developed as peculiarly appropriate to North America. The essays were his first real work for America, a sign of his new relationship with it, and they still stand as 'the most interesting book ever written about American culture'.[12] But they were extremely abrasive:

White Americans do try hard to intellectualise themselves. Especially white women Americans. And the latest stunt is this 'savage' stunt again.

White savages, with motor-cars, telephones, incomes and ideals! Savages fast inside the machine; yet savage enough, ye gods![13]

Mabel was the obvious target of such an attack.

The Europe where he had first created the essays must have seemed very far away, though he would be poignantly reminded of it early in the New Year when he heard that Katherine Mansfield had died of her tuberculosis, aged only thirty-two. He would write to Murry at the start of February 1923 that, in spite of their differences, 'I always knew a bond in my heart'. Even his rage with her had acknowledged the bond. Her death also made him comment to Murry, in one of his very few recorded moments of nostalgia and regret, how 'I wish it needn't all have been as it has been: I do wish it'.[14] But he responded even more strongly and strangely to the death of his Eastwood friend Sallie Hopkin, at the age of fifty-five. When he first heard the news, six weeks after arriving in Taos, he wrote a loving letter to Hopkin, which ended:

Sallie had a fine adventurous life of the spirit, a fine adventurous life. And it's the adventure counts, not the success . . . the rest of the journey she goes with us like a passenger now, instead of a straining traveller.

. . . There will be another grave in that cemetery now, down Church Street. It makes me feel I am growing old.

Never mind, one must strike camp, and pack up the things, and go on.

With love, that belongs to the old life.

D. H. Lawrence

England seems full of graves to me.[15]

The Church Street cemetery was where his mother and elder brother were buried. But he also wrote a poem, 'Spirits Summoned West', starting from the letter's postscript, which explicitly linked his mother's death with that of Sallie Hopkin. The two women – mothers, loved ones – are in the poem's terms now 'virgins' once again. Released from their marriages, 'disburdened of Man', they gravitate to Lawrence as he summons them: he undividedly loves them.

Come back to me now,
Now the divided yearning is over . . .

Come back then, you who were wives and mothers
And always virgins
Overlooked.

. . . Come home to me, my love, my loves, my many loves,
Come west to me.[16]

This appeal was nothing new in Lawrence's life: he had written his poem 'The Virgin Mother' after the death of Lydia Lawrence in 1910.[17] And despite the final, cathartic writing of *Sons and Lovers*, he had not worked past all such feelings in the novel either. To sharpen our sense of the strangeness of this 1922 fantasy of the sexless woman *'loved for gentleness'*, we have only to consider what Frieda would have made of the new poem. Herself a mother, and far from feeling virginal, Frieda knew how her sexuality defined her sense of herself. It is as if the poem were contrasting such a conception of woman with one in which sexuality played no part. But the poem also shows how much Lawrence needed Frieda to counterbalance such a depiction of the sexless and the yet desired:

Come to me and be still . . .
The overlooked virgin,
My love.[18]

Back in 1912, Frieda had scribbled angrily and contemptuously over one of his poems to his mother.[19] But he believed in indulging the demands of his imagination; Frieda was there to refuse him its consequences.

Something else underlying the poem would have been his new awareness of sexual jealousy. As well as being interfering, Mabel had also done her best to pit herself against Frieda, to attract Lawrence. Not that she was in love with him, but he was a challenge she could not resist. She told him that Frieda had 'mothered his books long enough. You need a new mother!' More mothering was exactly what Lawrence did not want; such a remark reveals how little Mabel understood him. Frieda, however, very quickly came to feel jealous of Mabel: more jealous than she had been of any other woman. Eight years later she accused herself: 'Why was I such a fool and couldn't manage the situation, why did I doubt that he loved me?'[20] That question is easily answered. He was now sure he did not love her in the old way. For him, 'the old life' of selfless, devoted maternal and romantic love lay dead, 'down Church Street' along with the women who loved as he had once loved his mother, and had at first loved Frieda. He would write in February 1923, when thinking about the subject matter of contemporary novels, about how 'I simply don't care whether I love the girl or not . . . or what my mother feels about me . . . though I used to'. He now insisted that 'the purely emotional and self-analytical stunts are played out in me. I'm finished.'[21] The point of fiction was to find out what was important, instead of concerning itself with such things; he wanted the same in his life too.

And, as 'The Wilful Woman' shows, Lawrence was attracted to as well as repelled by Mabel, though not as a sexual partner. He would have recognized her as one who attempted to deal with the problems of life by being stronger-willed than those around her. He insisted that she had to give up attempting to impose her will on everything – 'Unless you do, you will be destroyed' – but she recalled his admission of parallels between them: 'you have gone far, but I have gone further.'[22] Where he had his writing, however, and the worlds he created and inhabited imaginatively, she had an income of $14,000 a year, abundant energy and charm, a wide circle of friends and acquaintance, property and land, along with a considerable desire to make the real world, not the imaginary one, conform to her desires.

By November a crisis had been reached. Mabel had apparently sent him a letter with numbered points, and he responded in kind. These are three of his responses:

1. I don't believe in the 'Knowing' woman you are.
2. I don't believe in the 'good' woman you are: that 'good' woman is bullying and Sadish. i.e. I utterly disbelieve in your 'heart'.

. . .

7. It strikes me that I have paid you pretty fully for all the 'emotion' you have expended, and more than paid for all the 'goodness'. I have still to pay for some of the bullying and mischief.[23]

His absolute plainness, without either malice or rudeness, is admirable in such a situation; he was able to write such letters to her, of clear-sighted criticism, as well as letters of understanding and sympathy. He would eventually advise her, for instance, to 'learn to abstain from that vice of "knowing" . . . because there's no end to it, like a bottomless pit: which swallows every human relation'. He was also determined not to be 'bullied, even by kindness'.[24] Those were things he certainly knew about, and would write about in the *Studies*.

One solution would have been for him and Frieda to leave Taos. But they had spent a lot of money getting there, Lawrence wanted to write in America, and the place was remarkable: he called it 'unpossessed'. With the mountains full in view, 'standing heavy on the plain', one escape route was clear.[25] At the end of October, in the company of Mabel, they had visited a rather ruinous ranch owned by her son John Evans, eighteen miles away, up Lobo mountain. Lawrence and Frieda had fallen in love with it; it would be 'really free, far more than here'. It would be difficult to cope there in winter as the cabins were not in a good state but, accompanied by a young Mexican, Lawrence and Frieda went to try it out for four days.[26] Mabel scuppered the plan by declaring that the cabin would have to be kept for her son John, in case he wanted it, but the Lawrences were not so easily thwarted. Just two miles away was the sprawling Del Monte ranch, owned by the Hawk family; here the Lawrences could rent a couple of cabins, only about five minutes' walk from the Hawks' house, so they would not be entirely cut off.

After nearly three months in Taos, Lawrence was feeling 'sore with all Americans'.[27] He and Frieda had met two young Danish painters (Kai Gótzsche and Knud Merrild) who also needed somewhere to live; Lawrence had the cash to buy what was wanted and to pay the rent, and Gótzsche and Merrild were easily persuaded to come up and spend the winter in the mountains. They had a car and also the necessary physical strength – Merrild had qualified for the Danish Olympic swimming team in 1920. Trees would have to be felled for wood, and great quantities of wood cut and transported; the ranch would get snowed in at times. They borrowed horses from Tony; Lawrence bought his first pair of cowboy boots to go with his cowboy hat, his sheepskin coat and corduroy riding breeches. Early in December 1922, they went to live up at Del Monte, borrowing just a water carrier and a couple of blankets from Mabel. The Lawrences thus neither compromised with her, nor finally quarrelled with her – 'We are still "friends" with Mabel' – nor were so ungrateful as to reject her out of hand. But they got away: 'Mabel was too near a neighbour.' She felt the slight very badly, and her relations with the Lawrences were bitter for a while; John Evans spread the story that 'Mother had to ask the Lawrences to get out' because they had been spongeing on her, which infuriated Lawrence.[28]

With the Danes, whom they hardly knew, the Lawrences almost by accident managed that first real escape with a few others which Lawrence had so often fantasized about. They worked and lived together in harmony for three and a half months; they rode together, sometimes ate as a group, played and sang together in the evenings; and the fact that the relationship worked out so well seems to have had a considerable effect upon how Lawrence and Frieda lived for the next couple of years. It was how Lawrence had hoped to live with Katherine and Murry, back in 1916. From the start, a lot of physical work was involved: 'roofing, carpentering, plastering, glazing, paper-hanging, painting, whitewashing, etc'. There was also a lot of going out together into the wilds; and apparently no sexual attraction between the two couples. The Danes were aged twenty-eight and thirty-six, and Frieda's feelings for them appear to have been entirely maternal: while Merrild solemnly reported that when he, Lawrence and Gótzsche went to the hot springs at Manby together, he watched Lawrence 'very carefully' but concluded that 'he was as sound as I and not the pervert he was accused of being'. Someone must have told him that Lawrence was homosexual: Taos gossip may have seized on the friendship he had struck up with Bynner and Johnson in Santa Fe.[29] For their next journey, Lawrence and Frieda would again choose two companions – Bynner and Johnson – and the following winter, Lawrence would do his best to acquire other friends to come and live with them. In the past, the presence of others seems to have triggered rows between the Lawrences. Now, the opposite seems to have been true: they actively wanted company. In a state of harmony, Lawrence finished his work on the *Studies* at Del Monte, both the major revision and then an extensive correction of the typescripts. He was, after all, at last confronting his American public, and ended the essays with the proud declaration 'LOBO, NEW MEXICO', to announce them as an American work.[30] He also revised some of his Verga translations, and wrote a number of poems for *Birds, Beasts and Flowers*.

Seltzer and his wife, and Mountsier, all came to visit, and stayed on the Hawks' ranch; the Seltzers for New Year 1923, Mountsier just afterwards. Mountsier then stayed on in Taos, but his relations with Lawrence were very strained. He had not liked *Aaron's Rod* and objected to *Kangaroo*, and Lawrence was finding him increasingly awkward to work with; Mountsier seemed determined to be abrasive in his relations with Seltzer, upon whom Lawrence was depending more and more for his income. (Seltzer had failed to sell many copies of Mountsier's 1922 book, *Our Eleven Billion Dollars*, and Mountsier did not forgive him.) Lawrence finally broke with Mountsier in February 1923, and put his American business, like his English, in the hands of the Curtis Brown agency.

The Danes, like the Brewsters in Ceylon, had been given a first-hand opportunity to report on life with the Lawrences, and in 1938 Merrild published a book about it. Lawrence emerges as a charming and energetic centre of activity; an excellent companion and friend, direct, kind, fair and helpful, always playing his part in what they were doing, constantly making those around him see the world differently, and with no affectations of any kind. 'One was never bored in his society. On the contrary, no matter how often one saw him, it was always a revelation.' However, he *was* bossy. Merrild once had 'to engage in a bodily struggle to get my brush back'[31] when Lawrence attempted to take over a painting Merrild was doing, and he easily came to the boil, though not very often with Götzsche and Merrild. There were some tremendous quarrels between him and Frieda, however, and violent anger towards his dog.

Lawrence had always loved animals. He and Frieda, travelling as they did, never kept pets, but were sometimes adopted by them: in Bandol, in 1929, a marmalade cat would insist on living with them. Up at the ranch, dogs and cats were part of everyday life; in 1925, a cat ('Miss Timsy Wemyss') would be a particular favourite.[32] In 1922, Lawrence had acquired a black female puppy from one of Mabel's bull-terriers: 'First live thing I've "owned" since the lop-eared rabbits when I was a lad.' Illustration 25 shows them on the porch of the Del Monte cabin; Frieda commented: 'I love that one of Lawrence and Pips and me.' Lawrence was so fond of the dog – whose name seemed to change as often as the days: Bibbles, Bimsey, Bambino, Bibsey, Bubsey, Bubastis, Bubbles, Pebbles, Pips, Pipsey, the Omnipip – that in the spring of 1923 he planned to take her to Mexico, and only left her because 'I can't trail her round hotels. If we had a house to go to I would take her at once.' In July, he was still dreaming of her.[33]

But he insisted on being the dog's master. After he had prevented her from eating the remains of a dead bullock, she did so, got sick, was 'well spanked – and so has gone to live with the Danes'.[34] The dog had to be loyal, but she also had to be stopped from doing stupid things. Merrild recounts an extraordinary episode when, in rage with Bibbles (on heat) for going off with an Airedale, and then staying with the Danes, Lawrence walked into their cabin without even taking off his wet boots, chased the dog out of the door, kicked her through the snowdrift into which she had blundered, then finally picked her up and threw her as far as he could, which cannot have been very far: and luckily it was into another snowdrift, so that she was not hurt. He had to be physically confronted by the athletic Merrild to prevent him attacking her again. As Merrild remembered it, although Lawrence was 'panting for air' – struggling through the snow was exhausting for man and dog alike – he was quite unafraid: 'still his eyes dared me to strike.'[35]

He was, according to Frieda, 'never sorry',[36] and never apologized, but he knew how to restore friendly relations. The next day, he brought the Danes some of his freshly baked bread and cake. They were reconciled; and he went on loving the dog profoundly, and continued to get on well with his friends.

How could a person so sane, sensible, caring and loving, and wise in many respects, one who insisted, 'I do believe in self-discipline', and who hated bullying, kick a dog so brutally? It was the dog's in-discriminate 'loving' of Gótzsche and Merrild, of the Airedale, of anyone or anything which he blamed. But it was his loving of the dog which got him into the mess in the first place: 'love always exposes one's incompetence.'[37] Like an 'animal poem' in which human beings are shown up for their failures, his relationship with the dog showed up painful needs which went right back to the puppy, 'Rex', his family had taken care of when he was a child, and which was repossessed by his uncle, 'ruined' (said the uncle) by being too much loved. 'Nothing is more fatal than the disaster of too much love. My uncle was right, we had ruined the dog,' Lawrence commented. Nevertheless: 'My uncle was a fool, for all that.'[38] Lawrence had worked out his emotional life with humans so that failures in loving did not, in the end, affect him too badly; he had recently been insisting that love belonged to 'the old life' and that he, at least, was living in a kind of post-emotional state. But he loved the dog too much – the fact that it was female surely mattered – and lost himself in need and rage.

The situation in which the violence occurred is significant. Lawrence remarked at the start of January 1923 that although Del Monte was marvellously beautiful – 'Very fine indeed, the great space to live in' – and his friendships there were firm, it was all the same 'humanly nothing'. He had cut himself off, was out on a limb, so that just three people were his world. He would tell Murry in February: 'It has been a savage enough pilgrimage these last four years.'[39] If a cynic is a disappointed idealist, a misanthrope is one whose social desires have been savagely disappointed. The new world of America still meant very little to him. But, just for once, another being apart from Frieda was directly on the receiving end of his frustrated rage. Merrild recalled Lawrence's face when he was pursuing Bibbles through the snow: 'a pair of burning piercing eyes of such strength that I saw nothing else, only sensed the bloodless, pale blue-pink lips in a wilderness of beard'. Lawrence was utterly possessed by his anger, as he had been all his life; his childhood rages as 'a boy of thirteen' had been just the same. He was on the verge of attacking Merrild as savagely as he had attacked the dog.[40]

In her book, Mabel Luhan says that she saw bruises on Frieda when they went to the Manby hot springs in the autumn of 1922: 'great black and blue bruises on her blond flesh'. She encourages her reader to assume that Lawrence was responsible, and ignores the fact that Frieda would, for example, have got badly bruised while the Lawrences were learning to ride (on at least one occasion she came off her horse, 'hanging ludicrously, head down, from her saddle'). Mabel also asserts that whenever Lawrence 'capitulated to Frieda and sank into the flesh'

– presumably meaning had sex with her – 'he beat her up for it afterwards'. But how could Mabel have known? Lawrence did hit Frieda, as least as often as she hit him. And yet Frieda still wanted to be 'off alone somewhere, with him writing his books in the next room while she did her housework in peace'.[41] The violence between them was something they had managed to incorporate into their marriage. She was never frightened of him for more than a few seconds at a time; nor he of her.

With the coming of the spring, Lawrence decided that he and Frieda should go to Mexico. The winter had been stressful and long, at the altitude of Taos, and Lawrence also wanted to write. They had to leave, anyway, as they had only six-month visitors' visas; but Lawrence had come to think 'the U.S.A. so terribly sterile, even *negative*. I tell you what, there is no life of the blood here. The blood can't flow properly.' Though he had finished the *Studies* and written seven American poems (one about Bibbles, another of them 'Spirits Summoned West', to complete *Birds, Beasts and Flowers*), from the start he had been hoping to write fiction: 'I think I'll do a novel out here.'[42] But nothing, apart from the abortive novel about Mabel, had come: neither blood nor ink was flowing properly. Fiction occupied a very special place in his life, where he dealt with his most intimate concerns, and where he confronted his imagination with the reality he had experienced. But what would 'post-emotional' fiction be like?

18

Loyalty and Betrayal: 1923

Lawrence and Frieda went first to Santa Fe in March 1923, where they stayed with Witter Bynner and Spud Johnson, before going on to Mexico. They would have liked to travel with Götzsche and Merrild, but the latter couldn't afford it; however, 'the Bynners' (as Lawrence wickedly called them) agreed to come, and they all met up again in Mexico City. It is obvious that Lawrence and Frieda were not spending so much time on their own as they had, for example, in Australia, or indeed at any time since 1912. Other people seem to have provided a kind of buffer between them. They spent a month with Bynner and Johnson in Mexico City, and visited outlying places: Lawrence was particularly impressed by the pyramids at Teotihuacán and the House of Quetzalcoatl, where 'huge gnashing heads jut out jagged from the wall-face of the low pyramid . . . The great stone heads snarl at you from the wall, trying to bite you.' For perhaps the first time, he became vividly aware of the pantheon of the old Mexican gods and goddesses; and though for the moment he thought of Quetzalcoatl as 'just a sort of feathered snake', he was also starting to feel that he would like to settle down in Mexico and write a novel there.[1]

Throughout the month, too, he had been noticeably tetchy and restless, as often while in the early stages of planning a novel. A lunch appointment with the Minister for Education, José Vasconcelos, had been arranged by mutual friends, following Lawrence's expression of interest in the 'Indian revival' which the state was encouraging; but at the last minute the minister was too busy to see them. Lawrence was enraged by what he took to be an insult, and refused to return for the rearranged appointment. Those with him were shocked at the violence of his rage;[2] but, like his father, he had absolutely no respect for people

286

in authority. Bynner wrote an account of another flare-up, after a meal at their hotel. Frieda had just lit a cigarette:

I saw his attention light on it, saw him watch grimly fascinated till she gave a pull on the dangling stub and then tilted her head up to ease her eye from watering. Though the dining room was full, he stiffened suddenly, jerked himself to his feet and blared, 'Take that thing out of your mouth!' She gazed at him, wide eyed, without answering. 'Take it out, I say, you sniffing bitch!' And then, though she was seated behind a corner table, half hidden from everyone by the cloth, 'There you sit with that thing in your mouth and your legs open to every man in the room! And you wonder why no decent woman in England would have anything to do with you!'[3]

As Bynner published this some forty years after the event, there is reason to doubt the actual words, though not the tone. Lawrence always despised the dangling cigarette. The abuse, too, was habitual, which was why Frieda hardly reacted; she would write to Murry, in 1955, 'Do you remember the sweet names he called me?' 'Pull in your belly, you big bitch,' an acquaintance was shocked to hear him say, the following year. Her comment to Bynner after the Mexican episode was: 'I have to put up with him but I do not answer him.' That was not true; she regularly answered him. 'Oh! You are such an ass!' was one retort; 'You shut up, or I will tell about *your* things,' was her below-the-belt response to being told to pull her stomach in. Her answers may not have been as eloquent as Lawrence's attacks, but they were just as abusive.[4] However, as Frieda explained to Bynner and Johnson, Lawrence was still not writing. Bynner had noticed that when Lawrence was 'genial' it was linked with the fact that 'he wrote a little then'. All that he seems to have produced during the month in Mexico City was an essay for Johnson's *Laughing Horse* about the carvings at Teotihuacán.[5]

But just a week after despairing of the place and of ever creating fiction in America – 'I should never be able to write on this continent' – and having even set in motion plans to return to Europe, Lawrence thought he would try one final place: Chapala, situated on the only large lake in Mexico. And just when Frieda must have been expecting to see her family again, he telegraphed her: 'CHAPALA PARADISE. TAKE EVENING TRAIN.' 'He will be writing again there,' Bynner reports her as saying: 'He will be happier.'⁶ Bynner and Johnson came too, and stayed in a hotel overlooking the lake. The Lawrences moved into a house in Calle Zaragoza and Lawrence started on a novel, as he had written *Sons and Lovers* beside the Lago di Garda, 'The Sisters' beside the sea in Fiascherino, *Women in Love* high above the sea in Cornwall, *The Lost Girl* and *Mr Noon* overlooking the Straits of Messina, and *Kangaroo* beside the Pacific in Australia. 'Quetzalcoatl' was the first version of *The Plumed Serpent*: 'It interests me, means more to me than any other novel of mine. This is my real novel of America.' New Mexico had impressed him only with the soul of violent white America. What he felt he had uncovered in Mexico was 'the sort of solar plexus of North America': the bundle of nerves at the pit of the stomach.⁷

Writing a novel is in itself an act of hope: 'It allows us to imagine that things may be other than they are.'⁸ 'Quetzalcoatl', the first draft, and its successor were founded on a compelling fantasy: a European woman visiting Mexico experiences, at first hand, a religious revolution, in which a military though generally bloodless coup replaces Christianity with elements of the old Mexican religion. Society, in the control of the charismatic leader Don Ramón, undergoes radical change; it becomes wholly religious again. The central female character of 'Quetzalcoatl', Kate Leslie, is without a partner (her dead husband sounds rather like Lawrence); she is attracted to a new kind of partner in the military leader Don Cipriano. Change in the novel, however, is violent and can be arbitrary. Whereas Bynner believed in progressive socialism, Lawrence's version of change involved violent conflict and summary punishment, as when those who have tried to assassinate Ramón are executed. (The fact that they are given a chance to save themselves by choosing from a handful of dried grasses, one of which is green at the tip and offers life, suggests how powerful the arbitrary is in human affairs.) But the book was attempting to answer the despair about the individual, politics and society into which novels like *Aaron's Rod* and *Kangaroo* had led Lawrence; it was characteristic of his writing that a new novel should take on the problems which the previous novels had thrown up. It was hugely ambitious in setting out to answer the most fundamental problems of society, and was almost certainly going to fail in one way or another; but Lawrence would rather grandiosely remark in August that he was only interested in people who 'make the destinies of the world'.[9] Even this first draft had something of the same portentousness.

Lawrence wrote his book beside the lake: 'generally down towards a little peninsula where tall trees grew near the water. He sat there, back against a tree, eyes often looking over the scene that was to be the background for his novel.'[10] An ex-student of Bynner's, Idella Purnell, who lived in Guadalajara (where the Lawrences visited her and her family more than once, and Bynner photographed Frieda: see Illustration 26), wrote her impressions of him in Chapala in April 1923:

so thin, so fragile and nervous-quick, and with such a flaming red beard, and such intense, sparkling, large mischievous blue eyes, which he sometimes narrowed in a catlike manner. His rusty hair was always in disorder, as though it never knew a comb. But otherwise the man seemed neat almost to obsession and frail, as though all his energy went into producing the unruly mop on top and the energetic, stiff beard.

'Energetic' is apt because Lawrence's face was mobile and because he talked a great deal; but it is useful to set such an impression against the sternness of many of the photographs of him:[11] for example, Illustration 27, showing Lawrence leaning against the adobe wall of Bynner's house back in March, with one hand in his pocket and the other against the wall behind him; an odd mixture of the formal and the casual. He is not actually as thin as before; his waistcoat is even a little tight. The suit is his 'old brown suit' which he had had 'turned' in preparation for setting off a year earlier. That explains why the trouser flies are the wrong way round, and the breast pocket on the wrong side for a man's jacket. His shoes have their laces threaded in different ways; but Frieda had taught him 'not to do things *too* well'. His forehead shows just how deep the frown lines now are, as he screws up his eyes against the sun.[12]

Lawrence decided fairly early on that the novel he was writing in Chapala was only a 'first draft'.[13] For the first time since 1914, he planned radically to revise his novel before publishing it. He could now afford to do this; Seltzer was still publishing book after book of his in America and for the first time since 1914 Lawrence felt assured of an income. A novel needed time and effort when it was doing something so new in his creative life as recreating a whole, thoroughly alien society, and then showing it changing absolutely, under the pressure of religion. Not since *Women in Love* had a work of fiction meant so much to him.

He reached a suitable stopping point at the end of June. The time with Bynner and Johnson had been fruitful but never peaceable; Bynner's account shows something of Lawrence's extraordinary capacity to immerse himself in the new. Bynner had lived in Santa Fe for a long time without learning Spanish; Lawrence had learned it in Taos, in preparation for the journey. On all their trips, he was the one who had read up and made notes on history and archaeology before they went, and he educated himself into Mexican life: though he also simply sat and watched it. 'Quetzalcoatl', written in less than seven weeks, is a tribute to his sympathetic immersion in a country that, like Australia the previous year, he had inhabited for just three and a half months.

Lawrence and Frieda left Bynner and Johnson in Chapala on 9 July, re-entered the USA and travelled slowly up to New York, where Seltzer had offered them somewhere to live and where Lawrence could work, mostly on the proofs of the books which Seltzer was bringing out, until he and Frieda went back to Europe. Although they both wanted to return to the ranch in Taos eventually, they were not keen on spending another long winter at altitude. Even more crucial for Frieda was the fact that her son Monty was now twenty-one and her daughter Elsa soon would be, on 12 September; both could thus now make up their own minds about seeing her. She had also been away from her German family for nearly two years, and especially wanted to see her mother. Murry had just started his new magazine (the *Adelphi*) in England, too, and wanted Lawrence's commitment to it as 'the only writer of modern England who has something profoundly new to say'; and in spite of his previous determination to have nothing more to do with Murry, Lawrence had expressed interest in the venture.[14] He was still attracted by the idea of 'doing something' with another man. It remained an article of faith with him that he *ought* to try; and Murry had written very pointedly in the first issue that, as editor, he was 'only a *locum tenens* for a better man'. Lawrence's essays and poems would appear in all but one of the *Adelphi*'s first seven issues. But when Lawrence saw the *Adelphi* for the first time, in June, he was horrified, probably by Murry's effusive editorial tone ('The magazine is run . . . by a belief in life'): 'How feeble it is! Oh God, am I going back to Europe to that?'[15] But he was in no real doubt that he *was* going; and Frieda was equally sure.

However, a fortnight before the boat was due to sail from New York, and after they had bought their tickets, following several days of saying that he really didn't want to go, Lawrence decided not to accompany Frieda back to England. He told Murry that, now it came to it, he could not bear the thought of 'England and home and my people', nor even of the Fontana Vecchia, which he had loved so much. Back in April he had worried that England might 'try to drag me down to the old thing', as if it were emotional attachment that he feared: love 'that belongs to the old life' repelled him.[16] He had not been close to his family since leaving England in 1912, in spite of his time in Mountain Cottage, but his sister Ada had always been devoted to him, and he had loved Emily's daughter Peggy and Ada's son Jack. Emily now had a second little girl, Joan, just past her third birthday, whom he had never seen, while Ada was expecting her second child (to be called Bert) just when he and Frieda were due to sail. But he could no more bear the claims of his own 'people' than he could stand Frieda's continuing demand for her children. 'Such melancholy comes over my senses, when I only think of it, that I believe it would be better to stay here.' He recognized that he was in some kind of trouble, however, commenting, 'I suppose I'm the saddest, at *not* coming.' It certainly wasn't that he wanted to stay in America. 'America means nothing to me,' he confirmed. 'I wish that things were real to me.'[17]

At some point, he and Frieda had a dreadful quarrel: Catherine Carswell believed it took place on the quay in New York on 18 August. It was not just about his refusal to sail. On the boat, Frieda wrote to Adele Seltzer:

I feel so cross with Lawrence, when I hear *him* talk about loyalty – Pah, he only thinks of himself – I am glad to be alone and I will *not* go back to him and his eternal hounding me, it's too ignominious! I will *not* stand his bad temper any more if I never see him again – I wrote him so – He can go to blazes, I have had enough – The worm that turns – [18]

The quarrel was still going on in Frieda's mind, and for once she enjoyed the feeling that she had the upper hand. She makes two main points: that Lawrence had not been loyal, and that she felt hounded. Certainly, he never let her rest in opinion or attitude or feeling: he always expected her to respond. She always remembered how 'he would hammer away at her, trying to make her commit herself finally'.[19] He was a driven person. But he was perhaps now accusing her of disloyalty in trying to restart a relationship with her children; the very day he made up his mind not to travel, he had remarked to Murry that he couldn't 'stomach the chasing of those Weekley children'. As far as he was concerned, they were not her children any more, and wanted nothing to do with her; he preferred to believe that, if Frieda were honest with herself, she would realize that. This was perhaps at the bottom of his refusal to sail, and then of the quarrel. The children had been a 'drawn sword' between them since 1912.[20] Even at Del Monte, on at least one occasion Merrild had been charged with giving the mailman a letter that Frieda had written to her children; she had not dared let Lawrence catch sight of the envelope. And Mabel Luhan had helped her in the same way.[21] But now she was on the verge of starting to reclaim her children, and Lawrence found her desire to do so unbearable. He feared it would change the whole nature of their relationship: one that had been dedicated to the two of them going their own way together. That was probably what he claimed her loyalty to, as he had been claiming it since 1912. She, however, would have seen at issue only her loyalty to her children.

After the quarrel, Lawrence did not see Frieda off. He gave an interview to a reporter for the *New York Evening Post*, Seltzer probably making the arrangement, in the course of which he 'drew out his watch' and remarked that his wife would be 'going back to England in half an hour'. Murry, however, came to believe that Frieda 'had left him. She felt – rightly enough – no more loyalty to him.'[22] She struck out on her own, making a break for her old life with her children, attempting to recover what she had been deprived of for so long. She believed 'I shall like England', and indeed she did. Frieda saw all three of them, even though Barby was still only nineteen, and started the process of re-establishing her relationship with them; she also got on much better with Kot and with Murry than she did when Lawrence was there. She felt proud, for example, to be able to introduce Monty to Murry, and see the young man making a 'big impression' on her old friend.[23] Lawrence continued to make financial arrangements for her: on 27 August, he wrote her a cheque for £25, sent another on 10 September, and arranged in November for £100 to be transferred to her.[24]

He then returned to travelling through America, across to Chicago and the west coast, and finally down to Mexico: there followed three miserable months for him, some of the time again with Götzsche and Merrild. It was in California that he had a second brush with the film industry. At a party in Hollywood, an actor dressed in white jodhpurs, and carrying a riding crop, thrust 'an appalling pint of whiskey and soda' into Lawrence's hand. If life in Taos had seemed to him to be lived 'from the outside', what he saw on the west coast felt much worse. 'Drunk with trivial externalities: that is California.' Eventually he went down to Mexico with Götzsche, Lawrence feeling 'as if I should wander over the brink of existence'.[25] To begin with, he probably expected Frieda to see her children and come back. Some postcards to her written in September scrupulously avoid inviting her to return, but nevertheless assume that she will. 'Don't stay any longer in Europe if you don't want to': 'Come west when you feel like it.' At the end of September, he told her that he had returned his own steamer ticket, 'to get the money back'; she was thus the one who would have to travel.[26] But Frieda, enjoying herself in Europe, had very little inclination to go back to a demanding life with Lawrence in North America.

What Lawrence turned to was writing a revised version of Mollie Skinner's new novel that she had sent him from Australia: his second novel to be written on the American continent. It seems to have come terribly fast and easily, and he used it to develop the next stage of his thinking about relationships. His habit of almost ceaseless literary activity meant that other people's ideas were often extremely useful; he made her novel, 'The House of Ellis', into *The Boy in the Bush*, and developed the idea of an independent-minded hero into one who

293

refuses all emotional ties and obligations in favour of doing what he wants. Jack Grant marries, for example, but feels that, if he wants two wives, he should have them: he also believes that his wife 'knows she can't get past me. Therefore, in one corner of her, she hates me, like a scorpion lurking.'[27] And Jack wonders about turning into a kind of patriarch, with several wives, cattle and land. Mollie Skinner would be bewildered and hurt to see what Lawrence had made of her book, especially of its ending; but it was what he wanted to write. It would be wrong simply to identify Lawrence with Jack: but the novelist was taking the chance of allowing his hero to explore feelings and reactions very close to his own. Jack feels persecuted – 'Because I'm not one of them . . . they would like me destroyed'[28] – and absolutely different from the majority of people; Lawrence took such attitudes seriously, as he always did in his fiction, and saw where they led. The Mexican landscapes he was travelling through helped make his creation of the Australian outback more vivid; a cattle ranch he visited in October between Navojoa and Mazatlán, for example, struck him as 'wild, weird, brutal, with a devastating brutality'. He had written in a book review, at the start of September, that there was no point in a writer wasting time, 'playing word-games around the camp fire. Somebody has to jump like a desperate clown through the vast blue hoop of the upper air.' His new novel became wild and desperate. In it, however, Jack and his ideas come in for no criticism or opposition. It ended up as a book in which the hero is finally indulged, unquestioned; only Jack is allowed to criticize Jack. As a result, the portentousness of 'Quetzalcoatl' is never too far away: Jack fantasizes at the end of the novel about being 'a lord in death' and being able to 'sway the destinies of the life to come'.[29] It is a novel lacking Frieda's response.

Götzsche, at just the time Lawrence was writing *The Boy in the Bush*, was struck not by how liberated Lawrence was, without Frieda, but by how tortured he was by his months of independence. The Dane wrote to Merrild about Lawrence *in extremis*, in the Mexican town of Guadalajara towards the end of October 1923:

I am avoiding L. as much as possible at present, because, considering all things, he is really insane when he is as now . . . You know his ways, and how he bends his head far down, till his beard is resting on his chest and he says (not laughing) 'Hee, hee, hee' every time one talks to him. A cold stream always runs down my spine when he does that. I feel it is something insane about him . . . I realize it would be too difficult to live with a man like L. in the long run. Frieda is at least an absolute necessity as a quencher. I have sometimes the feeling that he is afraid she will run away from him now, and he cannot bear to be alone.[30]

Lawrence gave himself as hard a time as he gave to those who were with him. But Gótzsche's insight into the effect of Lawrence's separation from Frieda was acute. Lawrence may well have started to believe that his marriage had come to an end; hence the extravagancies of *The Boy in the Bush*. His indulgence in his imaginative worlds had become too complete, and destructive.

Lawrence still refused to go to England, however; he complained to his mother-in-law that Frieda would only 'think and write and say and ponder *how* she loves me. It's stupidity. I am after all no Christ lying on his mother's lap.' He thus equated her love for him with misplaced maternal love. On 10 November, he wrote cordially but quite unemotionally to Frieda, telling her not to bother about money: it looks as if he were arranging for her to have about £400 a year: 'a regular arrangement for you to have an income, if you wish'. He also hoped she was having 'a good time with your flat and your children'.[31]

But Frieda kept insisting that she loved him – 'my religion is that I want people to *love* . . . And I know I can love' – and she kept asking him to come to England. So did Murry, who insisted that he needed Lawrence for the *Adelphi*: and it was not as if Lawrence's experience since August had been very satisfying, in spite of the book he had written. On the contrary, he had spent some of the most arid months of his life. The west of Mexico had been 'much wilder, emptier, more hopeless than Chapala', he had written to Bynner at the start of October: 'It makes one feel the door is shut on one.' What finally made up his mind for him was the realization that he had, literally, nowhere he now wanted to go. On 20 November, he put it like this: 'I don't want much to go to England – but suppose it is the next move in the battle which never ends and in which I never win.'[32] He was committed to struggle, in writing and in marriage and in living: he made all of them a point of principle. But in this case he did not even know whether

Frieda was prepared to continue the struggle; or, indeed, whether he wanted to go on struggling with *her*.

Yet he could not simply give up all ties to the old life, much as he wanted to. After almost exactly three months on his own, he went back to Frieda and England; Götzsche and he sailed from Vera Cruz on 21 November. In his later, unfinished story 'The Flying Fish', Lawrence recreates the voyage and his experience of watching flying fish and porpoises from the bows, and it is again the mesmerizing power of the non-human world he watches (and mourns) in the speeding, playful fish:

This is sheer joy – and men have lost it, or never accomplished it. The cleverest sportsmen in the world are owls beside these fish. And the togetherness of love is nothing to the spinning unison of dolphins playing under-sea. It would be wonderful to know joy as these fish know it. The life of the deep waters is ahead of us, it contains sheer togetherness and sheer joy. We have never got there – [33]

But the boat on which Lawrence experienced that, or something like it, was irrevocably returning to the human, all too human world, and to his family and his marriage. There wasn't much sheer joy in *those* things. His letters to England were correspondingly gloomy, and annoyed Frieda: '*Why* can't he say he will be glad to see me? Always a misery and pain! It makes me *sick*!'[34]

England, too, could hardly have been more of a contrast with the life he had been leading. His first reaction, after four years away, was characteristically about his feelings of enclosure and suffocation. Even on the train to London, 'The place feels tight: one would like to smash something. Outside, a tight little landscape goes by, just unbelievable, with sunshine like thin water, a horizon half a mile away, and everything crowded forward into one's face till one gasps for space and breath.'[35] And London was worse: 'loathe London – hate England – feel like an animal in a trap. It all seems so dead and dark and buried.' He went down with a cold in no time and retreated to bed: 'I don't belong over here any more. It's like being among the dead of ones previous existence.' The images of death, burial and enclosure are constant. He felt 'buried alive, under the yellow air and the vast inertia': 'one seems to creep under a paving-stone of a sky': 'it's like being in

Lawrence, breaking a glass at every sentence end, after which Lawrence 'just put his head down in his arms on the table and cried'.[46] Love was always a puzzler for him. At some stage, too, Murry kissed Lawrence and declared: 'I love you Lorenzo, but I won't promise not to betray you.' This may have been a drunken warning that he might still sleep with Frieda: interesting from someone who had said he would travel to America with them. The fact that Lawrence put his arm round Murry's neck – 'for the first and last time', according to Murry – saying, 'Do not betray me!' reveals Lawrence's awareness that betrayal was very possible.[47]

It was becoming an evening of drunken emotionalism, Lawrence's included: drink always affected him badly. In Taormina, he had once become 'terribly jovial and friendly' with some guests after drinking too much; insisting on getting some mimosa for them, he had fallen out of the tree he had been trying to climb.[48] At this point in the Café Royal – and we might link the alcohol with all the emotional appeals being made – the port which he had been drinking made him violently sick over the table, and he passed out. The evening dissolved into a kind of messy disaster. Gertler and Mary Cannan left; Donald Carswell had to take over the business of paying the bill, as Lawrence was in no state to do so; the waiters had to be tipped to clean up; and Lawrence was taken home in a taxi to the Carswells' house in Heath Street, where he was still sufficiently ill to have to be half carried upstairs by Kot and Murry. He was revolted when he later thought back to 'that fatal evening' at the Café Royal: 'That is what coming home means to me. Never again, pray the Lord.'[49] He wrote to Murry six weeks later to denounce his friend's loving tendencies: 'I don't care a single straw what you think of me ... Leave off being emotional.' (This had absolutely no effect on Murry, who began his 1931 book on Lawrence by saying that Lawrence was one of those 'who cannot be judged, but only loved'.)[50]

The only certain outcome of the evening, Dorothy Brett coming to the ranch with them, the Lawrences had known from the start. Brett, who 'paints, is deaf, forty, very nice, and daughter of Viscount Esher', had spent her adult years devoting herself to one person after another. She was, however, extremely independent too. She did not mind getting her hands dirty; she could (she was, after all, an aristocrat) ride, fish and shoot, as well as paint and play the banjo; and she could adapt to the unfamiliar. Lawrence was 'intrigued' by her; he thought her 'a real odd man out'[51] who would be a companion for both him and Frieda. She could also type: very useful for a writer in the wilds. She used a tin ear trumpet they called 'Toby', but even her deafness might have seemed an advantage to Lawrence and Frieda; it would allow them some continuing privacy, even in close company with her. Lawrence welcomed the thought of her living with them: he believed she would stand between them and other people.

To any outsider, however, knowing Brett's habits of devotion, and aware of what happened when a woman competed with Frieda for the attention, let alone the sexual attraction, of Lawrence, Brett's presence would have looked like trouble being stored up. Koteliansky, who knew Brett and Murry well, actually accused Brett of going to America in pursuit of Lawrence.[52] That Lawrence's motives were also mixed in welcoming her to America is suggested by an addition he would make, during January 1924, to the ending of *The Boy in the Bush*, when he developed a previously minor figure, Hilda Blessington, into a character with a great desire to 'get away' into the Northwest of Australia. The physical description of the character, and her combination of determination and timidity, point to Dorothy Brett. Jack Grant invites Hilda to join him and his wife; she says that although she hates men and the idea of marriage, she would not mind being a man's second or third wife 'if the other two were living'. And though Jack feels no sexual attraction to her, he is very aware of her physically: 'She was slim and light, with an odd, remote reserve.' But what most impresses him is the way she is 'one of the odd, border-line people who don't, and *can't*, really belong. She kept an odd, bright, amusing spark of revenge twinkling in her all the time.' If Lawrence saw Brett like that, then he was seeing something of himself too.[53]

After Christmas, without Frieda, Lawrence visited his family for a few days; he had put the visit off as long as possible. 'It's all the dead hand of the past,' he commented, gloomily. He also went to Shropshire to meet the author Frederick Carter, who had been writing about astrology, the occult, and symbolism in the book of Revelation; he and Lawrence had been in correspondence for a year. Carter took him walking through border landscapes that would help Lawrence create the English background to *St. Mawr* later in the year. Having climbed up to the Stiperstones, a rocky outcrop looking towards Wales, they could see a tiny wisp of smoke in the distance. Carter remembered Lawrence sniffing the wind, and crying: ' "There is never any clean air in this country. It smells smoky to me even here. Don't you think so?" That pale, faint drift of smoke as far off as we could see, miles away, and all wild Wales before us. He challenged it as he challenged everything.'[54] Back in London, Lawrence worked on his essays for the *Adelphi*: 'On Being Religious' appeared in the February issue. He also began the first version of his story 'The Last Laugh', which used versions of Brett and Murry as its central characters. One passage – 'They had been friends like that for almost two years. Never lovers. Never that at all' – reveals that he still did not know about their affair. During January and the first days of February, both Brett and Lawrence continued to assume that Murry would be coming to America: if not with them, then shortly afterwards – 'we can wait for you in New York.'[55]

At the end of January 1924, Lawrence and Frieda went to Paris before going on to Germany to see Frieda's mother. Frieda had been in Paris back in September, at the start of her trip on the continent, and had loved it. But while in Germany, Lawrence embarked on his story 'The Border-Line', in which a widowed woman named Cynthia is fascinated and compelled by a dead, long-lost husband whose loving power overwhelms her new partner, named Jack. Lawrence had by now clearly learned about Frieda's German excursion with Murry;[56] she must have told him about it in Baden-Baden, or on the way. Strasburg in winter is brilliantly evoked in the story, and is where the woman becomes aware of her dead husband. Aldous Huxley would later say that Lawrence was normally aware of Frieda's 'erotic excursions' and 'got angry about them sometimes',[57] though the excursion with Murry hadn't come to anything; but it would have been characteristic of Lawrence to have blamed Murry rather than Frieda, and also to have made a point of appearing not to care. He had refused to mind about Frieda having sex with Harold Hobson, back in 1912. But around 9 February he stopped encouraging Murry to come to Taos, simultaneously with starting the story. The very day he and Frieda arrived in Baden-Baden, Lawrence wrote to Murry: 'Let us clear away all nonsense. I don't *need* you. That is not true. I need nobody. Neither do you need me. If you pretend to need me, you will hate me for it.' He wouldn't have dreamed, however, of telling Murry not to come, though he did confess to Kot: 'I don't want him, flatly.'[58] But if, like Cynthia in 'The Border-Line', Frieda had been considering two male partners, Lawrence had also (via Brett) been imagining what 'two wives' would be like. So Murry was left to do as he wanted; and by February that seemed increasingly to be *not* to travel with them. Well and good.

On the way back from Baden-Baden, Lawrence would write his remarkably prescient 'Letter from Germany' about the breakdown of the country's old values and the rise of the 'queer gangs of *Young Socialists* . . . Whirling to the ghost of the old Middle Ages of Germany.'[59] His recent writing about politics may not have been especially profound, but he reacted instinctively against National Socialism in Germany: he found it terrifying. All that he wanted to do now, however, was get back to America. Frieda and he returned to London for a week, to settle matters with publishers, and to collect Brett and her painting things, and during this week Lawrence helped rescue Murry from yet another emotional entanglement with a woman, the one he later commemorated in his story 'Jimmy and the Desperate Woman'. Then he, Frieda and Brett sailed for America on the *Aquitania* on 5 March 1924.

Lawrence had felt, throughout his visit, that Europe was 'weary and wearying': 'Sometimes I really get discouraged: quite discouraged altogether.'[60] But he was going back to a place that fascinated and intrigued him, with the wife whom he might have lost, accompanied by a new and very loyal companion; and at some point, perhaps in Mexico, he would be rewriting what he thought was his most important novel. Not a bad outcome, considering Frieda's flirtation with Murry, or his own arid wanderings during the autumn, or the humiliations of the evening at the Café Royal.

19

America Again: 1924

After months of silence that had thoroughly worried Lawrence, Thomas Seltzer met him, Frieda and Brett in New York and was as friendly as ever; but he could not disguise the fact that his business was in trouble. All Lawrence could do was hope that his publisher would stay afloat long enough to pass on what Lawrence had earned (over $4,100 in 1923). Lawrence had also put some of his earnings into Seltzer's business, on condition that Seltzer maintained a constant $2,000 credit in his bank account: that money, too, was at risk. So that after all Lawrence's optimism about the future, financially everything was in doubt again. In fact, Seltzer was never able to repay Lawrence. In the slow collapse of his business, the bulk of Lawrence's American unpaid earnings (over $8,000) would vanish. All that Seltzer seems to have paid Lawrence after September 1923 were small sums adding up to another $1,200. For the moment, that was that; further small sums of money would come in over the next two years, as his agent managed to extract them.[1] Lawrence was back to having to live hand to mouth.

After a fortnight of sun and snow in New York, Frieda, Lawrence and Brett took the train to Taos, to make a second attempt at living in Mabel Luhan's orbit: the balance of relationships was changed, anyway, by the presence of Brett. But this time the Lawrences had prepared their arrival. Frieda had written to Mabel back in February, in what sounds like Lawrence's voice: 'I dont see why with some good will on all sides we shouldnt live near each other . . . we have all reached the same point as far as the world is concerned and we *must* go *on* further together; nobody else will.' She and Lawrence lived again in one of Mabel's houses, Brett in another, and 'we eat in the big house'. To start with they got on better than in 1922; 'Seems to me quite all right now,' Lawrence commented.[2] There was a lot of shared pleasure in the evenings: charades, readings, dances, Lawrence's comic play 'Altitude'. Mabel, however, found Brett and her ear trumpet a problem. 'Do you think I liked it when I saw that brass dipper swallowing up Lorenzo's talk to me? Good heavens! It was worse than Frieda's restraining presence!' She came to despise Brett as one who 'sat in the doorway of life with her mouth slightly open, like a paralyzed rabbit'.[3]

Lawrence was already at work, this time on his essays 'Indians and Entertainment' and 'The Dance of the Sprouting Corn': each of them an attempt to say what it was about Native American culture that had become so important to him. His time in Mexico had made him think and see differently. Now he believed that the work of even the experts on the Southwest, such as Adolph Bandelier, was misleading, because it did not take account of the fact that the 'Indian way of consciousness is different from and fatal to our way of consciousness'.[4] Lawrence chose to write about that difference. He was now confronting not an *idea* of what instinctive action might be, but its enactment. He used every bit of his intuitive skill to feel as the Native American feels; to find the words, for example, for saying what a religion was like that was not god-centred. Older, animistic religions seemed to him to have a huge advantage over Christianity, or Greek culture, in not being at bottom idealistic:

There is strictly no god. The Indian does not consider himself as created, and therefore external to God, or the creature of God. To the Indian there is no conception of a defined God. Creation is a great flood, forever flowing, in lovely and terrible waves. In everything, the shimmer of creation, and never the finality of the created . . . Everything, everything is the wonderful shimmer of creation, it may be a deadly shimmer like lightning or the anger in the little eyes of the bears, it may be the beautiful shimmer of the moving deer, or the pine-boughs softly swaying under snow . . . There is, in our sense of the word, no God. But all is godly.[5]

This was a way of thinking through what he would want to say in 'Quetzalcoatl' about religion; but it was also a response to the first society he had experienced, and the first place he had been, which made the Christian world of his upbringing seem no longer relevant.

Breaking free of that old world was something that he profoundly wanted.

After a couple of weeks of relative harmony, Mabel 'legally made over'[6] to Frieda the near-derelict ranch on Lobo mountain they had made plans for in October 1922, before settling at Del Monte. This was intelligent and generous of her: she still wanted Lawrence to write about New Mexico. Both the Lawrences, however, worried about the obligation that such a gift put them under. By coincidence, Frieda's sister Else had just rediscovered and sent Lawrence the original manuscript of *Sons and Lovers*, and Frieda presented it to Mabel. It was a spectacular gift but one that left Mabel perfectly unimpressed.

On 5 May, after having some preliminary work done on the buildings, Lawrence, Frieda and Brett moved up to the ranch they had christened 'Lobo', the Lawrences sharing the three-room cabin and Brett taking a far smaller one nearby. The work of repairing and rebuilding took five weeks, into June; the larger cabin had to have its chimney rebuilt with adobe bricks, and they re-roofed both cabins. Lawrence worked with a number of Native American labourers and a Mexican carpenter; and characteristically made no distinction between the heavy or difficult work he expected them to do and what he did himself. When someone, with a wet handkerchief over mouth and nose, had to crawl along under the large cabin's corrugated iron roof on a hot day, to clear out the old rats' nests, then he was the one to do it. Brett, too, 'was amazing for the hard work she would do'.[7] Mabel and Tony came up to see them on a couple of occasions, sleeping in a big tepee up on the hillside, as the Native Americans did; at night, they all ate together, sang together, and planned the next day's work. A letter to Mabel when she was back in Taos gives a flavour of what needed doing even when the building work was finished: they requested adobe tools, whitewash, white and turquoise paint, brushes, a packet of tin-tacks and another pound of putty, hinges for cupboards, screws, and the loan of a little grindstone. Lawrence did almost no writing, though he does seem to have finished his essay 'Pan in America'; but 'naturally I don't write when I slave building the house'.[8] The five of them went on a couple of trips together, however: during a journey to Taos on horseback, for example, Mabel and Tony took them to the 'ancient ceremonial' cave at Arroyo Seco which Lawrence would use as the setting for his story 'The Woman Who Rode Away' the following month. In summer, there would probably have been a steady drip of water over the cave mouth that, in winter, would become the long fang of ice that plays such a crucial role in the story. Mabel conveyed to Lawrence her fears of the place, and told him that the local Native Americans would not camp there; but it would be Lawrence who imagined its fearful past as a place of human sacrifice.[9]

For weeks there had been no word of Murry. In mid May, Lawrence heard from him again, 'still putting up little catty defences – leaves me cold'. It was Brett who, a couple of days later, received the letter announcing that, at the end of April, Murry had married Violet le Maistre, just seven weeks after saying goodbye to them all at Waterloo station and promising to come soon. Lawrence wrote to congratulate him, but his letter was both sharp and sour. 'I am sure it is the best for you,' was all he said about the marriage: 'Better, as you say, than wild-goose-chasing in other continents' – presumably Murry's phrase for what the Lawrences and Brett were currently doing. It was probably at this point that Brett felt released from her promise and told Lawrence about her affair with Murry. Living so close to Lawrence, she could not 'bear feeling I have deceived him', though she certainly gave Lawrence the impression that it had been she, not Murry, who had insisted on their sleeping together. Lawrence would later refer to her having 'dragged sex in' to her relationship with Murry; but even that may have been true, in her desire to serve dead Katherine.[10]

It is striking that Lawrence should have spent five weeks rebuilding a couple of cabins on a run-down ranch where he could never live more than six months at a time; it suggests his extreme attachment to the place. Although he was a professional writer, his books never sold in very large numbers, so that he depended upon publishing a great deal, and so writing a great deal. The ranch was punishingly remote and life there always taxing; as he told Witter Bynner when the latter was about to visit, 'you'll have more or less to *camp*, help with the chores and all that. You won't be particularly comfortable.'[11]

Lawrence and Frieda were, however, enormously pleased to have their own place at last. Frieda had been pining for a house since 1918, while at the back of Lawrence's mind would have been the memory of his days at the Haggs farm between 1902 and 1908, and at San Gaudenzio in 1913. The ranch – they changed its name to 'Kiowa' as soon as they found that that was what the Pueblo tribe called it – was the first place they had ever occupied which they did not have to pay rent for, or look after for someone else. Lawrence had always resisted the constraints of ownership; all his life he had paid rent, as his family had done, which was perhaps another reason why Mabel had given the ranch to Frieda. Now he threw himself into the work and the working of it. It offered him a wholly new sphere to explore and master, and he became expert in new skills. He had always cooked, baked bread and cleaned; now he learned to mend fences, make adobe bricks, a chair, shelves, cupboards, a meat-safe to hang from a tree branch; to look after horses and to milk a cow (he had milked goats in Berkshire, back in 1919). He loved 'doing for myself all I need',[12] and at the ranch, he had to.

It was also the most beautiful and the most difficult place they had ever lived. 'One doesn't talk any more about being happy – that is child's talk. But I do like having the big, unbroken spaces round me,' Lawrence wrote to Catherine Carswell. He told Murry how 'one has to bear up hard against it'. The animal life could nearly defeat human occupation: pack-rats bounced on the ceilings at night 'like hippopotamuses' and gnawed through almost anything left unattended; furniture had to be slung up to the ceiling on ropes when the human occupants went away. Black ants swarmed into the kitchen, animals would fall ill; there was an 'underlying rat-dirt, the everlasting bristling tussle of the wild life'.[13] Water had to be carried from the spring: the water which they finally made flow through pipes the following year was only for irrigation. Wood had to be chopped; and every evening there was milk and mail, and sometimes butter and eggs, to collect on horseback, two miles down to the Del Monte ranch, and then back before dark. The horses needed to be fed and cared for, and there was unremitting hard physical work, even when the main rebuilding was done. Lawrence and Brett added a wooden porch to the main cabin; Frieda knitted, cooked, made butter and (in 1925) looked after chickens, so they could regularly have eggs. Fish could be caught in the Hondo river; Brett was skilled at that, and she could also take out a rifle and pot a rabbit for supper.[14] The nearest store was ten miles away in Arroyo Hondo, half a day's journey on horseback.

It was turning out, however, to be a wonderfully creative and fulfilling summer: first in the work on the ranch, and then for Lawrence's writing. He recreated the place for the conclusion of his short novel *St. Mawr*: 'The landscape lived, and lived as the world of the gods, unsullied and unconcerned. The great circling landscape lived its own life, sumptuous and uncaring.' They could see down to the desert a thousand feet below, the houses of a Pueblo looking like crystals, and away for twenty miles to where the Rio Grande canyon wound its way; and then beyond that to the far distant mountains, 'like icebergs showing up from an outer sea'. Lawrence wrote to his German mother-in-law: 'Here, where one is alone with trees and mountains and chipmunks and desert, one gets something out of the air: something wild and untamed, cruel and proud, beautiful and sometimes evil, that really is America. But not the America of the whites.'[15] Unlike Mexico, which had offered him a human world that was dangerous and ripe for change, Kiowa gave him life with nature almost untrammelled: 'something savage unbreakable in the spirit of place out here'. It gave him a strong sense of what he really wanted in his life: 'I myself find a good deal of satisfaction living like this alone in this unbroken country, which still retains its aboriginal quality.'[16] *St. Mawr* opens in England, but it becomes Lawrence's first novel of North America. When the fictional Lou of the story first sees the ranch,

In an instant, her heart sprang to it. The instant the car stopped, and she saw the two cabins inside the rickety fence, the rather broken corral beyond, and behind all, tall, blue balsam pines, the round hills, the solid uprise of the mountain flank: and getting down, she looked across the purple and gold of the clearing . . . '*This is the place*,' she said to herself.[17]

Kiowa offered them the chance to 'live, circumstantially, from day to day, with the hills and the trees'. Human beings could struggle, work, get tired, do what they wanted: but above all, they experienced life, as Lawrence put it, '*out of the world*', away from conventional civilization. 'It was very beautiful up here. We worked hard, and spent very little money. And we had the place all to ourselves, and our horses the same. It was good to be alone and responsible. But also it is very *hard* living up against these savage Rockies.'[18]

Being 'alone and responsible' did not preclude quarrel and anger, however. As might have been predicted, Brett attached herself increasingly to Lawrence; Frieda developed a marked dislike for Brett; and Lawrence did his best to cope with the different demands and temperaments of the two women. Two incidents during the composition of *St. Mawr* (which Brett would type) take us a little closer to the realities of life with a writer. Brett remembered Frieda calling out, while riding her horse Azul, 'Oh, it's wonderful; wonderful to feel his great thighs moving, to feel his powerful legs!' Lawrence was not going to have his ideas parroted like that. '"Rubbish, Frieda!" you call back. "Don't talk like that. You have been reading my books."' So much for her experience of the 'vividly embodied'.[19] Brett also remembered a day soon after Lawrence began *St. Mawr*. Her record of what she saw and heard was so fixated on Lawrence that, throughout, she addressed him in the second person, as though talking to him:

I am blowing and blowing my whistle. Not a sign of you . . . lunch is ready and piping hot. Frieda and I decide to start without you, so down we sit on the porch – which is finished and where we now have all our meals.

At last you come. You had not heard the whistle – you never do hear it, as a matter of fact. You are full of your new story . . . You sit down in your place, and between bites you read out to us the pages you have just written. You are still twinkling with amusement, and you are still living more with them than with us . . . With each character your voice and manner change: you act the story rather than read it, and we sit entranced, horrified, amused – all by turns, while your lunch gets colder and colder on your plate.

How rare it is that you read out anything . . . [20]

That last sentence changes everything. The bravura performance is an exception: a momentary overwhelming of the writer who normally keeps his writing to himself by the writer who needs an audience. Usually only the squirrels and chipmunks would have enjoyed the performance.

Lawrence had prefaced writing *St. Mawr* with another North American story which he had probably been thinking about during the weeks since Arroyo Seco, 'The Woman Who Rode Away'. He wrote this very fast (again, Brett typed it for him), and showed it to Mabel Luhan down in Taos at the end of June. These were his first two North

American fictions: both, strikingly, about the danger, for twentieth-century white consciousness, of America; both attempting to suggest how modern men and women are confronted by the challenge not just of *place* but of another kind of consciousness. 'The Woman Who Rode Away' describes a white woman who unthinkingly decides to go and see an isolated tribe of Native Americans; to her they are no more than a kind of tourist attraction, and she blindly gives herself up to them. They are indifferent to her sexuality; they see her as a way of getting back at the American white man, and regaining their own lost power. Lawrence may have been impressed by animism, as a religion; when he came to imagine its operation, he found it as threatening as anything he knew of from Christianity. In the story the woman is drugged and eventually taken to the cave at the winter solstice to be sacrificed to the sun: the story ends at the moment before the sacrifice, with the setting sun about to strike through the great fang of frozen ice at the cave's mouth.[21] Such a fiction was a way of showing what Lawrence knew, in himself, that the white races lacked: a sense of religion growing out of an immediate relationship with the natural world and the universe. But the story also reveals just how opposed to white civilization he felt Native Americans were, how much they hated it. 'The Woman who Rode Away' is a story (like *St. Mawr*) utterly ambivalent about the opposition of the cultures it reveals.

A copy of *A Passage to India* sent by E. M. Forster in July must have added to his sense of the efforts which other writers, too, were making to confront their European characters with alien worlds: 'The day of our white dominance is over, and no new day can come till this of ours has passed into night.'[22] But he was also very critical of Forster's work. In his view, the book only served to enforce a kind of ironical separation of the Western and the Indian, whereas what Lawrence wanted to do was to get inside non-European ways of thinking and feeling. After all the hard work at Kiowa, it was now possible to live relatively quietly from day to day, and the writing of *St. Mawr* flowed through the summer, though 'this isn't a good place to write in – one does too many other things'. He finally finished it around the middle of August: 'It took it out of me.' But it was, he thought, 'a corker. It's much better if I'm not *popular*.' To Seltzer's anguish, it became Lawrence's first work for his new American publisher, Alfred Knopf.[23]

There had been a disturbing moment, however, shortly before he finished it. His health had been good for months; but around 2 August, when going down with a cold, he began to spit blood. He was suffering a bronchial haemorrhage. Frieda arranged for a doctor to come up to the ranch to see him, which drove him into a 'wild fury'; he threw at her the iron ring he normally used as an egg-cup.[24] But the doctor, probably realizing that the patient would settle for no other diagnosis, declared that all Lawrence was suffering from was a bit of bronchial trouble, to be dealt with by mustard plasters. This treatment, because it was combined with rest, seems to have worked, in the short run, though the haemorrhage marked the development of the third (active) stage of the tuberculosis that would dominate the last five years of Lawrence's life. But it is notable that this very first indication of the disease was accompanied by Lawrence's determination to have nothing to do with a doctor. His pride and self-belief extended to his health. He had, eight years before, created in Birkin a character who 'liked sometimes to be ill enough to take to his bed. For then he got better very quickly, and things came to him clear and sure.'[25] Illness for Lawrence had, since 1912, been something that he and Frieda dealt with together. Others didn't come into it.

In August 1924, anyway, he was well enough to be up and about in a few days, to finish *St. Mawr* and prepare for a visit to Hotevilla to see the Hopi tribe's snake dance, in which the priests carry rattlesnakes in their mouths. They would go with Mabel and Tony but without Brett: there would not be room for five in the car. Lawrence's ambivalent reactions to the dance are beautifully set out in the two quite different pieces he wrote. One, which thoroughly annoyed Mabel – 'I had not taken him to the Snake Dance to have him describe it in this fashion,' she grumbled – he called 'Just Back from the Snake Dance – Tired Out'. It sees the whole event as a show put on for the white man: 'The south-west is the great playground of the white American.' The second essay, 'The Hopi Snake Dance', written a few days later, is one of the profoundest of all Lawrence's writings about America: 'it defines somewhat my position,' he told Murry.[26]

We dam the Nile and take the railway across America. The Hopi smooths the rattlesnake and carries him in his mouth, to send him back into the dark places of the earth, an emissary to the inner powers . . . The American aborigines are radically, innately religious. The fabric of their life is religious. But their religion is animistic, their sources are dark and impersonal, their conflict with their 'gods' is slow, and unceasing.[27]

The honest outsider's point of view of the first essay, detached and ironic, and Lawrence's serious enquiry into another culture and religion in the second, could hardly be better demonstrated than by these two pieces of work.

The trip with Mabel had, however, been spoiled by her own growing problems. She was heading for a nervous breakdown, and would soon afterwards put herself into the hands of the famous American Freudian analyst A. J. Brill. She would eventually settle his bill by handing over the manuscript of *Sons and Lovers*: a witty gesture, if ungrateful to Lawrence and Frieda. Lawrence was at first sympathetic and helpful, in spite of his distrust of psychoanalysis, and wrote her a couple of letters of stern encouragement. She, however, seems at this point to have given up any idea of making him her lover. She was angry about what she had heard he had been saying: that she was 'hopeless', 'destructive' and 'dangerous'. That finished things: 'I gave up expectation, so far as he was concerned.'[28] He had actually been saying such things to her face almost from the time they had first met. But they never met again, although the Lawrences would not leave the American continent until September 1925.

The Lawrences and Brett had only a month left at the ranch before leaving for the winter. Lawrence had long planned to go back to Mexico to write the final version of his 'Quetzalcoatl' novel; he needed to be there to finish it. And then came unexpected news from England. His father had died in September, very suddenly, at the age of seventy-eight. 'It is better to be gone than lingering on half helpless and half alive,' Lawrence wrote to his sister Emily, thinking back to their mother's illness in 1910. 'But it upsets one, nevertheless: makes a strange break.'[29] He had never been close to his father, though he had grown out of the hate he had felt as a child and adolescent. But Arthur's death was another kind of ending; Lawrence was left feeling oddly isolated. He wrote elegiacally in a letter to Murry three weeks later, linking the death with the coming of autumn.

The country here is very lovely at the moment, aspens high on the mountains like a fleece of gold. Ubi ist ille Jason? The scrub oak is dark red, and the wild birds are coming down to the desert. It is time to go south. – Did I tell you my father died on Sept. 10th., the day before my birthday. – The autumn always gets me badly, as it breaks into colours. I want to go south, where there is no autumn, where the cold doesn't crouch over one like a snow-leopard waiting to pounce.[30]

The autumn breaking into colours doubtless also recalled the autumn of his mother dying.[31] That was something else, far off but unforgettable, belonging to the old world he had tried so hard to escape, and never quite managed to get away from.

Lawrence had responded all his life to his father's independence, his love for animals and nature, his dancing, and his practical outdoor knowledge (gathering herbs to make tea, for example),[32] not to speak of his determined refusal to listen to nagging women. Almost nothing is known of their relationship after Lawrence left England in 1912; there is just the occasional flash of insight, as when in 1922 he told Achsah Brewster that a workman in Ceylon 'resembled his father – the same clean-cut and exuberant spirit, a true pagan. He added that he had not done justice to his father in *Sons and Lovers* and felt like rewriting it.'[33] Emily sent him a photograph of their father in January 1925. 'It's very nice: I see a good deal of myself in it,' Lawrence commented. In his last years, he would increasingly mythologize Arthur Lawrence as a man of warmth and unspeaking intimacy, belonging to 'the old wild England'; and in that guise he came to haunt Lawrence's later work, influencing, for example, the gipsy in *The Virgin and the Gipsy* and the gamekeeper in *Lady Chatterley's Lover*. His father became one of Lawrence's life-alternatives: not just a progenitor but a road not taken.

In 1924, Lawrence wrote just one more major piece, to complete the summer's writing: the short novel 'The Princess', in which once again a white woman goes out to explore the Southwest. But Dolly Urquart, 'the Princess', is a victim of her father's protective love, which has left her alone in the world and utterly detached from it. On a trip into the mountains, she is bitterly cold at night, and invites her Mexican guide, Romero (who is tenderly attracted to her), into her bed; but in

the morning, she hates him and lets him know it. This is the last straw
for a man who in the past has lost everything to the white, colonizing
power; he takes away her clothes, rapes her, shoots a man who comes
to rescue her; is eventually shot himself.[34] 'The Princess' is a story
about the inability of the white, colonial consciousness to realize its
self-enclosure. Lawrence would not have written it, perhaps, without
knowing Brett. But the essential experience described in it is his own.
He knew, all too well, what it was like to be self-contained and, like
Dolly Urquart, to refuse the actualities that lay outside his contained,
controlling white self.

Lawrence could look back at the summer as one of substantial
achievement: three major works of fiction about North America, and
a foothold established at the ranch. He had also successfully answered
the question he had been asking since 1912: he knew where and how
he wanted to live. But now it was time to go. In some ways, the essays
and other fiction writing had been preparations for the novel: he
needed to be back in Mexico. On 11 October, Brett, Frieda and he
went down to Taos; by the 23rd they were in Mexico City.

20

The Lost Depths of Mexico:
1924–1925

In October 1924, Lawrence was only thirty-nine, though looking rather older in the face.[1] Youthful in figure, however, he had defeated the expectations of the passport official at El Paso, when he arrived with Brett and Frieda to cross into Mexico. 'Your wife?' asked the official, pointing to Brett, and when Lawrence answered 'no', tried again: 'Your sister?' Informed that Brett was only a friend, the official then pointed at Frieda and 'with an engaging smile' asked Lawrence: 'Your mother?' Brett would have enjoyed that.[2]

It is significant that Lawrence wanted to be in Mexico in order to rewrite 'Quetzalcoatl'. He had not needed to be in Australia to write a new last chapter for *Kangaroo* or to write *The Boy in the Bush*; in Italy, he had written *Sons and Lovers, The Lost Girl, Aaron's Rod* and *Mr Noon*, and there he would write his thoroughly English novel *Lady Chatterley's Lover*. But *The Plumed Serpent*, as it would now become, meant the recreation of a society that, although fascinating, remained essentially alien to him. He wanted day-to-day and first-hand experience of Mexico to do it, especially to expand it. It was, too, a significant time to be going back to Mexico. In December, the new president, Plutarcho Calles, supported by the labour movement and fiercely anti-clerical, was going to be inaugurated; and a man writing about a change of government in Mexico (and the abandonment of Catholicism) would certainly have liked to be there at such a moment.

But they did not go to Chapala. Lawrence must have felt he had sufficiently vivid a memory of it to continue using it as a location, but he wanted to settle somewhere with a greater indigenous population and fewer tourists. The southern town of Oaxaca was recommended to him as having a 'perfect climate' by the British Consul in Mexico

City, whose brother (Edward Rickards, a priest) worked there.[3] After a fortnight in Mexico City, the Lawrences and Brett travelled south 350 miles to Oaxaca, which took two days by train, with 'endless unexplainable stops'; and after a short time in the Hotel Francia, the Lawrences moved into two wings of Rickards's slightly dilapidated adobe house, built around two sides of a garden patio. Brett stayed on in the hotel, however. As Lawrence told his sister Emily: 'One gets tired of being always with other people.' Frieda was more direct, informing Brett that there wasn't room enough there 'for all of us'.[4]

The town felt politically even more unsure than Chapala in 1923, as well as a good deal more remote. Earlier in 1924, the Governor of Oaxaca province, the ex-general García Vigil, had taken on the forces of the federal government, and had been shot after surrendering. The 'thread of a narrow-gauge railway' between Oaxaca and the outside world could easily be broken: it had only recently been repaired, after a four-year gap. The minister Lawrence had been so angered by in April 1923, José Vasconcelos, had been a candidate for the post of Governor, but had lost an election which he claimed to have been full of vote rigging and intimidation; his rival, Onofre Jiménez – 'an Indian from the hills' Lawrence tetchily called him – took up the post the same day as Calles became President, just after the Lawrence party arrived. Oaxaca, deep in 'dark, dangerous Mexico', was thus wonderfully appropriate for a book about political and religious revolution and change.[5] Although Lawrence remained unsure about Mexico as a place to live, he had already realized the opportunities it gave him in creating in his writing a society that might be utterly transformed.

On 19 November 1924, he started work on his novel again: 'on the deep, shady verandah facing inwards to the trees, where there are an onyx table and three rocking chairs and one little wooden chair, a pot of carnations, and a person with a pen'.[6] He worked almost unremittingly for six weeks, from mid November to the end of January, with just a break in mid December to write four pieces about life in Oaxaca which later formed the central part of *Mornings in Mexico*, and which demonstrated yet again his extraordinary gift for recreating the everyday. Unlike, however, his six-week novel *Kangaroo*, or later *Lady Chatterley's Lover*, also written in six weeks, the new book proved exhausting to write, although it built on its predecessor,

'Quetzalcoatl'. Frieda was constantly angry with Brett, and it seems likely that Lawrence's tuberculosis was now active, bringing a high temperature and exhaustion; while much of the work he found himself doing went against the grain. Just before starting, he had felt 'a bit sick of' America, 'put out by the vibration of this rather malevolent continent'. Early in January 1925, as he grew angry and tense as well as more ill, he remarked ominously: 'It's so queer here . . . always a feel of being hemmed in, and shut down. I get sick of it myself: feel I shall bust.' Oaxaca had turned out tropical in climate and vegetation, and in some ways reminiscent of what he had found so oppressive about Ceylon: 'at this moment the patio is reeking with the scent of some sweet tropical flower. Damn tropical flowers, anyhow.'[7] The Lawrences and Brett had been warned not to take long walks into the countryside, and to keep their windows closed night and day, with their doors secured; there were rumours of attacks on houses and on isolated whites. As a result, feeling 'never free, never quite safe', Lawrence often wrote at home rather than under the shade of some tree in the countryside. The novel was growing enormously, ending up almost twice as long as 'Quetzalcoatl'; as Lawrence noted, 'It is good, but scares me a bit, also.' He must have been writing between 2,000 and 3,000 words a day, which was nothing unusual for him, but, Frieda remembered, he 'got run down'.[8] And he was composing from scratch nearly all the hymns and other poetry that the Quetzalcoatl religion required; he always slaved at writing and revising poetry.

For the duration of the writing, Lawrence was putting to one side his objective, detached critical spirit; he was writing in an almost trancelike way about his imaginary Mexico. The main problem for most readers of *The Plumed Serpent* is not that it is too violent (many good novels are more violent), or too concerned to preach a gospel of power, but that it has too little connection with the awkward, mundane, ordinary world that Lawrence was normally so good at creating. The very language the characters speak frequently reads like translation: Ramón says, for instance, 'I must keep myself together, keep myself within the middle place, where I am still'; and when Cipriano asks Kate, stiltedly, 'Shall we not make a civil marriage,' she replies, bewilderingly, 'And if the star has risen between us, we will watch it.'[9] Almost everything that happens or is uttered in *The Plumed Serpent* is made heavily symbolic, hieratic and significant. For many readers, the most memorable episodes are those almost incidental to both plot and theme: the bullfight at the start, Kate's journey down the lake, the child who tortures the duckling.

Keeping up such a pressure of intensity and significance in the novel must have made it compelling to write, however, as well as a strain. It does not fall to many people to invent the rituals of a new religion, and Lawrence took his chance. He was also following through the ambivalent logic of his feelings about this violent, Aztec-influenced world. In a letter, he quoted *Macbeth* at a friend: '*I dare do all that may become a man*, said somebody. It's the becoming.'[10] But his difficulty was not that of staying human. His problem was to push his characters to extremes, and simultaneously keep them sympathetic and realistic. The central male characters, Don Ramón and Don Cipriano, are intensely unreal: idealists, with few weaknesses, inhabiting roles rather than living them out. The central female character, Kate, had, in 'Quetzalcoatl', shown wonderfully Frieda-like qualities of resistance to male idealism: if Lawrence had not had Frieda's opposition to contend with, he would have had to invent it. In *The Plumed Serpent*, Kate has neither the sharp particularity of Ursula Brangwen nor the autobiographical richness found in a character like Somers, although she is being used to work through many of Lawrence's ideas about Mexico. It is not Kate's objections which now chiefly interest Lawrence but the effort of imagining, in precise detail, the mechanisms and rituals of the new religion of Ramón and Cipriano. Crucially, at the end of the book Kate not only marries Cipriano but also brings herself to stay with him. In 'Quetzalcoatl', she felt she had to leave; she had experienced a world in which she could not believe, run by 'mystical' men 'with their hateful abstraction and imagery'.[11] But she now submits to that very mysticism and imagery.

To add to Lawrence's problems, and in a way that could not get into the novel, as such things often did, Frieda's anger with Brett was proving irrepressible. Brett came over from the hotel every day, 'and I thought she was becoming too much part of our lives and I resented it', Frieda told Lawrence, and they quarrelled about it: Lawrence 'said I was a jealous fool'.[12] His concentration on his writing, the state he was getting into because of it, and the way they felt themselves closed in, would have made things worse. Frieda probably felt she only had him to herself after the day's writing was over and Brett was gone; and Brett was slow to recognize when she was not wanted. Things got more and more tense after the turn of the year. In a rather uncharacteristic way, which suggests what stress she too was under, Frieda seems finally to have forced Lawrence to choose: 'She goes or I . . .'[13]

Lawrence wrote to Brett in distress: his letter started 'one can't shout everything', suggesting how difficult communication was with Brett at the best of times. Brett professed to be astonished: ' "Do you mean to say that all this time while I have been thinking Frieda likes me, that she has been hating me?" "Of course she hates you".'[14] But she obediently offered to leave, and undertook alone the journeys from Oaxaca up to Mexico City, to El Paso, back up to Taos, and finally up to the Hawks' Del Monte ranch, where she would stay until the Lawrences returned. It was an almost inhuman journey to send her on alone. But Lawrence was still grappling with his novel, and Frieda, as well as feeling jealous, must have grown increasingly worried about him: he needed all the peace he could get, and his health was getting worse. During the last week of January, he was 'seedy' – 'well you must be exhausted after such work like the novel,' commented Frieda – but he would insist that it was Brett's dependence on him ('Your "friendship" for me') which had made him ill.[15]

Around 29 January 1925, he finished the book. Almost simultaneously, he suffered a physical collapse. It was as if the onset of disease had been kept at bay by the excitement of the writing and his total involvement with it. Lawrence always linked his illnesses to his state of mind, but in this case refused to look at the evidence of his inhabiting too exclusively the world of his imagination, as opposed to the world of the everyday. He blamed others, not himself, for what had happened: 'that's why I too am ill. The hurts, and the bitternesses sink in, however much one may reject them with one's spirit.'[16] A few days later, he was almost dead. His temperature soared, he had inflammation of the bowels and a 'tortured inside'; he also had influenza, and his tubercular lungs were active. And then there was an earthquake. For the first time, he seemed to give up hope; Frieda thought he would die. 'It was as if he couldn't or wouldn't live on.' 'You'll bury me in this cemetery here,' he told her. Hardly able to stand, he was moved back into the Hotel Francia, with Frieda regretting that they had ever come to Oaxaca: 'I really never wanted to come here, but he was as if bewitched by his Mexico.'[17] Oaxaca, like *The Plumed Serpent*, had raised him to a weird pitch of estrangement, of going as far as he could into the unknown of his imagination. The tortuous, hot, uncomfortable train back to Mexico City at the end of February was 'a *dreadful* journey from that hell of a country'.[18] They had planned to sail back to Europe from Vera Cruz, but when they reached Mexico City, they moved into a hotel for Lawrence to recover. He then suffered a relapse, and was unable to travel on for almost another month.

It had been during the journey to Mexico City that Frieda too gave up: she remembered how 'something broke in me. "He will never be quite well again, he is ill, he is doomed. All my love, all my strength will never make him whole again." I cried like a maniac the whole night.' Characteristically, Lawrence 'disliked me for it'. Just as he had rejected Katherine Mansfield's self-pity in 1920, so he rejected Frieda's despair as well as his own. It was during Lawrence's illness in Mexico City that a doctor had him X-rayed, and said straight out to Frieda, 'rather brutally . . . "Mr Lawrence has tuberculosis." And Lawrence looked at me with such unforgettable eyes.' The doctor told Frieda that it was 'tuberculosis . . . in the 3rd stage' – active, in other words – and urged her: 'Take him to the ranch; it's his only chance . . . A year or two at most.'[19]

It was just at this point that Lawrence dictated to Frieda the first few pages of a new story, 'The Flying Fish': something he had never done before.[20] The doctors had said that he must not work and must 'become a vegetable' (the only non-surgical treatment for tuberculosis at that date); but his need to write it impelled him to start work, in spite of the fact that *The Plumed Serpent* had almost cost him his life. The 'Flying Fish' fragment begins with its central figure, Gethin Day, desperately ill in Mexico. Using material from Lawrence's 1923 return voyage with Götzsche, it creates, most beautifully, the sense of a 'Greater Day' surrounding the little concerns of everyday existence. Its account (quoted in Chapter 18) of the dolphins running ahead of the ship, in sheer playful joyfulness, is mesmerizing. But the part dictated to Frieda was haunted by a vivid distaste for the 'lost depths

322

of Mexico'[21] and an intense nostalgia for the English Midlands. Day wants 'to go home. He didn't care now whether England was tight and little and overcrowded and far too full of furniture. He no longer minded the curious quiet atmosphere of Daybrook in which he had felt he would stifle as a young man.' It is probably not a coincidence that the remaking of England as a heavily mythologized, rural world, to which Lawrence clearly had a profound attachment, came just when the sentence of his own mortality had been pronounced: 'he felt that home was the place.'[22]

But the plans he and Frieda had been making to return to Europe from Vera Cruz were countermanded by the advice of the doctor to go to a higher altitude. So in spite of that 'lurking hankering for Europe', they put off their journey. Lawrence recovered a semblance of health during March, and at the end of the month he and Frieda travelled north again; they acquired their usual six-month visas at the American Consulate in Juarez, on the Mexican side of the border. But at the border, they had serious trouble. Lawrence was still unwell; in Mexico City he had started using rouge to stop people staring at him in the streets, and used it 'all the time until I reached New Mexico – until I got past that terrible doctor at El Paso'. The US doctor, presumably observing in Lawrence the symptoms of tuberculosis, and not fooled by the rouge, refused him permission to enter; he was forced to strip 'and kept stripped', and examined: 'Sheer degrading insult!'[23] It was the army medical examination at Derby all over again. Only after an appeal to Juarez, and a two-day wait, were they finally allowed in. They struggled up to Santa Fe, where the actress Ida Rauh and her partner, Andrew Dasburg, whom they had got to know in 1924, took care of them. Lawrence seems to have been possessed with the belief that if he could get back up to Kiowa he would recover; and early in April, they got as far as Del Monte, where Brett was waiting for them.

Lawrence was desperately weak; but as soon as possible, they went up the final two miles to the ranch, and Lawrence, sleeping much of the time, began to improve. Kiowa, even in spring, was hardly a place for a convalescent. But for a while they had a young Native American couple, Trinidad and Rufina Archuleta, to look after them, and Frieda did more household work than usual, announcing that she was 'developping into a "chef"'. Later in the summer, things returned to normal: 'I cook when he'll let me, but he does it much better himself.' This time they insisted on Brett living down at Del Monte, even though she could have been of some practical help. Frieda had told her, before they even got back, that she could not bear feeling Brett 'waiting and watching': but it was now more than that. 'You will hate me for this, but I also have my life to live and the responsibility.'[24] She felt committed to caring for Lawrence; that had become her new priority.

And, amazingly, Lawrence got better. Frieda wrote: 'We are very still and peaceful, it is incredible, I felt there would *never* be any more peace.' And Lawrence described 'Lying on the porch this warm afternoon, with the pine-trees round, and the desert away below, and the Sangre de Cristo mountains with their snow pale and bluish blocking the way beyond'.[25] Typically, he not only celebrated his recovery by starting to write, but as usual found that writing *was* his life. Back in March, the desperate creation of an alternative fictional world in 'The Flying Fish' had obviously been necessary for him. It was if creativity and imagination were themselves sustaining: 'Being able to express one's soul keeps one alive.' As he would write later that summer: 'And that again is what I think about writing a novel: one can live so intensely with one's characters and the experience, one creates or records, it is a life in itself, far better than the vulgar thing people *call* life.'[26] After a false start in Mexico City on a play he called 'Noah's Flood' (which only survives as a fragment), he now created the play he had been promising Ida Rauh for months. In *David*, modern man develops out of the remnants of what consciousness and the old religious self had been like, before the flood; Lawrence is both David, articulate, self-conscious, modern and intelligent, and Saul, the representative of the older, and in this case Native American, world that Lawrence was now trying, in work after work, to recreate. In the play, he offers a kind of alternative myth to the version of human progress and development that had so dominated his early thinking. *David* dramatizes the end of the old world, of animist religion and the revelation of God in nature: at the end, Saul dies, and the old order with him. The Bible text is thus profoundly subverted.

By early May, the play was done; and life at the ranch re-established its old pattern, though with Lawrence much less active than before. They managed to get the spring water irrigating the field, and bought a buggy to be pulled behind one of the horses. Early in June, they also acquired chickens, which Frieda cared for, and a cow they called Susan, Lawrence's responsibility. Though he had to spend an inordinate amount of time looking for her, to milk her, this still saved them the daily journeys down to Del Monte, where Brett continued to type for Lawrence and to irritate Frieda, who would snarl: 'You did things for Lawrence but *never* for me – You just thought me an inferior fool.'[27] They had relatively few visitors. Frieda's German nephew Friedel Jaffe came to stay for a couple of months, and helped with the everyday work. A young American journalist, Kyle Crichton, came with his wife, and spent a very cheerful afternoon with the Lawrences and Brett; as Brett recalled: 'You give yourself freely, laughing and talking unreservedly.' Crichton observed that Lawrence 'was thin, about five eight in height, and had a dark reddish beard and the same wart on the right side of his face that appears in all his photographs . . . His lips were full and quite red; his eyes were small but astonishingly bright and blue, and he looked steadily at you when he talked.' But Brett saw how, after the guests were gone, 'you are tired: it has taken a lot out of you'.[28] Ida Rauh came to hear Lawrence read *David* out loud; Lawrence compiled the book which became *Reflections on the Death of a Porcupine and Other Essays*. He included a revised version of 'The Crown' from 1915, but mostly wrote completely new essays during July and August. The new work was consistent with positions he had been arguing himself into during the last couple of years. On the one hand, he insisted that the 'great relationship, for humanity, will always be the relation between man and woman. The relationship between . . . parent and child, will always be subsidiary.'[29] That was a conclusion which the author of *Sons and Lovers* would have approved of, and the Lawrence of the summer of 1925 would reassert it. But in another essay he would write about the ways in which 'art is always ahead of the "times," which themselves are always far in the rear of the living moment'. His honesty to the 'living moment' would be borne out by the way he wrote over the next four years about his belief that relationships 'with all things' are as necessary as human relationships: 'stone, earth, trees, flowers, water, insects, fishes, birds, creatures, sun, rainbow, children, woman, other men'. More important still was man's relationship 'with the sun, the sun of suns: and with the night, which is moon and dark and stars'. The circumambient universe was the *real* context of human life: 'The Greeks, being sane, were pantheists and pluralists, and so am I.'[30]

Brett typed for him and came up occasionally; Frieda continued to send her regular brickbats – 'I wish you no ill, but dont want you in my life': 'It's all very simple we *want* to be *alone*' – with which Brett seems to have coped rather well. And Lawrence was sent the typescript of *The Plumed Serpent*, but could hardly bear to look at it. 'I think of Mexico with a sort of nausea,' he commented. When he finally went through it and corrected it, he found he felt the same about it as he had about *The Trespasser* and *Women in Love*: 'I hate giving it out to be published. It is different from my other books: and to me, the one that means most to me.'[31] He still clung to his belief in the intensity of the state of mind in which he had created it. The book said what he most wanted to say: it was an extreme example of his decision to write so as to change hearts and minds, to *do* something.[32] At one point during his visit, Kyle Crichton had asked what made a writer write. Frieda had answered, provocatively, 'Egotism'; she saw it as her role to discourage Lawrence from being too solemn. Lawrence had protested: 'No, no . . . It isn't that. You don't write for anybody; you rather write from a deep moral sense – for the race, as it were.'[33] He had written *The Plumed Serpent* for – and against – his contemporaries.

The weeks meandered past. 'We've just sat tight and considered the lily all summer,'[34] Lawrence proclaimed, though for a convalescent he had been extremely active; there was the play, the book of essays and other essays too, as well as the regular hunting for Susan, and rides in the buggy down to San Cristobal or Arroyo Seco. It was on one of these rides, just before his fortieth birthday, that Lawrence remembered a letter sent by Austin Harrison in 1910 to Lydia Lawrence about her son:

'By the time he is forty, he will be riding in his carriage' . . . And sitting in my corduroy trousers and blue shirt, calling: 'Get up Aaron! *Ambrose!*' then I thought of Austin Harrison's prophecy . . . 'Get up, Ambrose!' Bump! went the buggy over a rock, and the pine-needles slashed my face! See him driving in his carriage, at forty! – driving it pretty badly too! Put the brake on![35]

He points the irony beautifully between the outsider and maverick he actually was and the prosperous professional he had fantasized about being when he told Jessie Chambers, 'I'll make two thousand a year!'[36] A good model would have been Compton Mackenzie, who had published his first novel in 1913, and who by the mid 1920s had a regular income of more than £1,000 a year, a secretary, a Bond Street tailor and membership of the Savile Club. Lawrence was perfectly aware that the fact 'that I have not got a thousand friends, and a place in England among the esteemed, is entirely my own fault'.[37] He was writing what he wanted to, and was free to travel where he wished: but was only barely able to make his living. Frieda would not have let him forget this: she once commented, 'Ach, Lorenzo, for a genius you are a poor ting.' He would turn forty on 11 September 1925, just after they left the Kiowa ranch: 'lovely autumn, pity to go'.[38] But the six months were up. They travelled via Denver by train to New York, and by the 21st were on the *SS Resolute*, bound for Europe; Brett stayed on.

Leaving the USA in 1925 was as symbolic a journey for Lawrence and Frieda as when they had left Europe for Ceylon three years earlier. Lawrence had always dreamed of America; he had written extensively about it and had explored through his writing what it meant to be there, as well as finding a place to live which surpassed anywhere he had previously lived, and had more of the qualities he really wanted. Living at Kiowa, as he had written compellingly in *St. Mawr*, may have meant being up against 'the insidious malevolence of the country', but he never felt oppressed there, and had no sense of the prison that seemed to enclose him almost everywhere else. It was the ultimate place *out of the world*, with its amazing view looking 'out' and over: the ideal place to be 'a bit of a hermit'.[39]

But the ranch was not only a difficult place to be: it was also in the USA. Unless his tuberculosis went into extended remission, he would not get a visa to return. This was a very sensitive matter to Lawrence and Frieda. Accepting the likelihood that he could not come back would have involved an admission that he was genuinely ill: an admission of a kind that he and Frieda did not make. It was also impractical to live up at the ranch without being fitter than Lawrence was now going to be. They would need people like Trinidad and Rufina around, and that was not what they wanted; while the winter's snow and cold would be an even greater problem. However marvellous it was, Kiowa after 1925 was too much of a strain for Lawrence. Its wildness and teeming wildlife undermined all human purposes; it was exhilarating but it was also 'everlastingly tough'.[40] After the discovery of Kiowa as the place where, above all, he wanted to live and work, and after all the time and money and energy they had put into it during the summer of 1924, he now had to give it up.

At the age of forty, he was coming back to Europe. New Mexico reverted to being the country of his dreams and fantasies; it grew un-American to him, being 'so different, and Mexican really'. The ranch became the great good place to which, to the very end of his life, he imagined returning: one of his finest late pieces of writing would be an essay about New Mexico, composed in the middle of the winter of 1928, which remembered the summer of 1925 in particular: 'for a *greatness* of beauty I have never experienced anything like New Mexico'. As he recreated it then, with the unimaginable splendour of its view 'far over the desert to the blue mountains away in Arizona', he wrote how only 'the tawny eagle could really sail out into the splendour of it all' – only the eagle, that is, besides the imagination of the man creating it.[41]

21

Return to Europe: 1925–1926

The Lawrences were returning to Europe for rather different reasons than those which had brought them back in 1923. Frieda would have especially wanted to see more of her younger daughter, Barby, twenty-one at last; but Lawrence now wanted to come as much as she did, and it was England he wanted to see. He had told the Hawks, with grim irony, 'one's native land has a sort of hopeless attraction, when one is away'.[1] But where did he belong, now? He had always insisted that coming back was not 'coming home': 'I won't say home, it isn't home.' In June 1925, hearing of cherry-blossom back in England, he had compared New Mexico unfavourably with Europe: 'here the country is too savage, somehow, for such softness. I get a bit of a heimweh [homesickness] for Europe.' He felt that 'a little relief from the American Continent will be good for me' and was very drawn to the Mediterranean again. 'I don't suppose we – or I – shall stay long in my native land. I expect to go south – Italy, or Sicily, or Egypt – for the winter.'[2]

A news photographer on board the SS Resolute took a picture of them before the boat sailed, suggesting the extent to which Lawrence was now a public figure.[3] At first glance he appears unchanged by illness, in spite of what had happened in Mexico; but the shoulders are narrower than ever, with the chest more tightly contracted (see Illustration 28). His 'slim fragility' is obvious besides Frieda's handsome solidity; in the summer of 1925 she would have been about twenty pounds heavier than he was. Her dress looks home-made: 'She had her own way of cutting out the garment and the form was always the same – a straight from the shoulder affair caught in at the waist with a belt or girdle.' She was, however, perfectly happy with her appearance: 'My waistline is a great comfort to me and I wouldn't be cardboardy elegant, not I!'[4] Lawrence's hand is self-consciously pushed into his pocket as he looks straight ahead; he is clearly not touching Frieda with the other hand, although they stand so close. Lawrence's visit to New York had confirmed that Seltzer's business 'is hardly held together by a safety pin'; Lawrence was very conscious of his affairs being financially as uncertain as in 1912.[5]

He had not been in England since March 1924. Since then, his father had died, but there were Ada and Emily and their families to see, and the Hopkins in Eastwood. Lawrence commented, after being back for a week, on how he missed 'the peaceful ranch, and the horses, and the sun': not, however, the people. He may still have been hoping to find 'in my native land' the people who mattered to him.[6]

But in London, Frieda and he had for the first time taken rooms in a hotel, rather than living with friends, which suggests that rest and quiet were even more important than money; and although writing only a few book reviews, Lawrence deliberately saw nothing of his old friend Koteliansky: 'felt I couldn't stand any more'. Perhaps this was because Kot and Murry had quarrelled; but he did not want to see Murry either. Gertler was in a sanatorium in Norfolk, recovering from tuberculosis; Lawrence saw the Eders, but the Carswells were living out in Buckinghamshire and, without Frieda, he only stayed with them a single night. Catherine noticed that 'he seemed very solitary in London', but realized that it was because 'he had hardly told anyone of his arrival. He could not bring himself to do so.'[7]

What made it all much worse was the weather. There were only 'feeble attempts at sun'; it was 'rather foggy, and gives me a cough'.[8] His old feelings of oppression and constriction returned. But it was not just the rain which made him write to Murry about looking on 'with wonder instead of exasperation, this time. It's like being inside an aquarium, the people all fishes swimming on end. No doubt about it, England is the most fantastic *Alice-in-Wonderland* country.' It was his way of saying that it was all *so* unreal that there was still 'nothing to be "done"' in the way of changing England. He couldn't change it, and his writing couldn't; he was alien to it. He felt 'queer and foreign'.[9]

After a week in the London hotel, Lawrence and Frieda spent nearly a fortnight in the Midlands, first with Emily and then with Ada. But he was in bed with a cold as soon as he reached Nottingham, and was soon complaining how the 'weather's awful, and we simply hate it up here'. He was correcting the proofs of *The Plumed Serpent* on the journey and was particularly aware of the contrast between his created Mexico and the 'rain and dark and dismalness' of England; though his continuing claim that it was 'the most important of all my novels' came with an insistence which now might suggest uncertainty. Ada and Eddie Clarke had been prospering; in Ripley, Lawrence noticed the 'Comparative opulence here – *comparative*, of course'.[10] When the weather improved a little, they toured around in Eddie's new car, and Lawrence also went walking near Eastwood. But even that was painful. Although the country around Eastwood was 'the landscape I knew best on earth', he would write about this visit: 'Nothing depresses me more than to come home to the place where I was born.' Images of death possessed him: 'I can't look at the body of my past, the spirit seems to have flown', 'England just depresses me, like a long funeral.'[11]

Why was he so unhappy, after what had been such a powerful impulse to return? It wasn't just the awful weather. He wrote angrily about the 'general effect of paltriness, smallness, meanness, fathomless ugliness' that he had discovered all over again, in the Midlands.[12] But he had also discovered his almost total lack of contact with the place or the people. First in London, then in the Midlands, he found that he had been away too long. Whom did he know any more in Eastwood? The last surviving Cooper sister, Gertie, his old Eastwood friend and exact contemporary, now stricken with tuberculosis, was living with Ada; his only remaining old Eastwood friend was Willie Hopkin.[13] And there were his sister Emily and family in Sneinton, and Ada's family in Ripley. But that was the extent of his acquaintance; the rest was the past, buried in his recollection. He insisted aggressively, while actually staying with Ada, 'I'm weary of past things – like one's home regions – and dont want to look at them.' In 'The Flying Fish' he had speculated about the way in which the ordinary day starts to 'lose its reality' for someone who has had a revelation of the 'Greater Day', the genuinely real behind the apparently real.

But Gethin Day also starts to feel 'as if at the very middle of him, beneath his navel, some membrane were torn, some membrane which had connected him with the world and its day'.[14] This sounds like the experience of losing both a mother *and* a place (the sister whose death brings Gethin home to England is called Lydia). The real anguish of Lawrence's return in 1925 was, Catherine Carswell remembered, how 'especially on that visit, the horrors of his childhood had come up over him like a smothering flood'. This had been why 'my home place is more depressing to me than death'.[15] Recollection of the horrors of childhood, at this stage of his life, went well beyond the violence offered to his mother by his father, or his father's alienation. Lawrence was now especially conscious of his mother's constant moral pressure on her children, and their devoted love for her. He had ended up with a profound dislike of love, and without any sense of a place that he wanted to call home; he wanted to cut loose but also felt scarred and constrained.

An evening at Ada's house at Ripley offered him further confirmation of how he no longer belonged. Frieda's daughter Barby recalled how she had visited Ripley, and planned to stay overnight, but the friends of her father with whom she was staying in Nottingham implored her, over the telephone, to return: they were horrified at the 'idea of my spending a night under the same roof as Lawrence'.

Lawrence sprang to his feet, white with rage.

'These mean, dirty little insults your mother has had to put up with all these years!' he spat out, gasping for breath . . . Feeling something like a criminal, I crept dejectedly back to my Nottingham friends in the dark.[16]

It is one of the few occasions which shows us Lawrence's sympathetic rage on Frieda's behalf, in her loss of family, friends and respectability: but what triggered it seems not to have been feeling for Frieda so much as a revelation of what he called the 'sort of chapel-going respectability' of the Midlands, the 'self-rightness' which had oppressed his childhood: something he had been rebelling against for nearly twenty years. His gasping shortness of breath shows not only that England was taking its toll, but that he was experiencing, all over again, how tightly enclosed he felt there. 'I coughed like the devil, with the filthy air.'[17]

Barby was very astute in her observation of the other tensions at Ripley. She noted what she called Ada's 'rather unhappy adoration' of Lawrence, judged Frieda 'a little out of place' in Ada's company, and concluded: 'I do not think Ada ever liked her, or forgave her for going off with her favourite brother.' His naming Gethin Day's sister 'Lydia' in 'The Flying Fish' suggested that he saw Ada, as she grew older, in the role of the controlling, repressive but also desperately loving mother whom he knew so well, and from whom he still needed to escape. He thought this through in relation to Ada: 'What sort of daughters came from these morally responsible mothers? As we should expect, daughters morally confident . . . there it was, the inevitable sense that I-am-right.'[18] Ada was very like him: but she had not got away.

Such things, combined with Frieda's attachment to her children – in November he would comment that they 'have a sort of suburban bounce and *suffisance* which puts me off'[19] – and the dreadful weather, quickly turned his original plan of staying in the Midlands for a month, and perhaps taking a house by the sea, into a determination to leave. They toyed with the thought of Paris, and of Ragusa in Dalmatia, but finally settled on Germany and then Italy: Lawrence would give 'Anything for space, and sun'. Back in London, it was 'pouring with rain here now, and dark as death'. This time, they did see a few more people from the old days: Murry, for example, Cynthia and Beb Asquith ('rather sad – and a feeling of failure')[20] as well as some of the younger people of literary London. Almost without becoming aware of it, Lawrence had grown to be a senior figure in the literary world, and no longer belonged to the rebellious young. One of those he met, William Gerhardi, told him: 'You're the only one we younger men can now look up to', and later sourly wrote how Lawrence 'lapped it up'. But Lawrence was completely unimpressed by Gerhardi: 'nothing that makes any difference – nothing to matter at all. Not much point in being here.' He was left with the strong impression, which he voiced the following June, that it 'seems I don't know anybody in London any more'.[21]

They had, however, discovered that the family of Martin Secker's wife, Rina, lived in Spotorno, on the Italian Riviera, an area they did not know at all; and that was where they determined to head, after first visiting Frieda's mother. Lawrence's failure to say goodbye to Murry was characteristic of this unhappy visit. Murry, now married, with a child, had come to London to stay overnight; Lawrence had gone out to buy him a bag of fruit to take home to Dorset, had been delayed, and the taxi taking Murry to the station failed to collect him and the fruit. Although Murry had been 'very quiet, and quite nice', Lawrence had already decided that there was 'nothing between us'.[22] He resisted Murry's subsequent invitation to edit the *Adelphi* with him – 'My dear chap, people don't want . . . the punch and Judy show of you and me' – and on reflection thought that Murry's response to that refusal had been filled 'with more spite and impudence than I have yet had from him'. His advice to Murry had been to throw over the magazine and not be so self-important: 'Earn a bit of money journalistically, and kick your heels. You've perhaps got J.M.M. on the brain even more seriously than JC' (Murry – John Middleton Murry – was writing a book about Jesus Christ). Eventually Murry asked him, 'man to man', to supply essays for the *Adelphi* without payment. Lawrence replied that, 'man to man, if ever we were man to man, you and I, I would give them to you willingly. But as writer to writer, I feel it is a sort of self-betrayal.'[23] Between October 1925 and the following February, all that was left of the old relationship unravelled completely. Another link gone.

The Lawrences stayed a fortnight in Baden-Baden, Lawrence 'playing whist with old Baronesses, Countesses and Excellencies, and behaving like the sweetest house-spaniel'. The occupants of the *Stift*, needing an appropriate title for a literary man married to a Baronin, called him *Herr Doktor*, while Lawrence could 'hardly believe my own ears when I hear myself saying (in German, of course) – But, Excellence, those are trumps!' He wrote a couple of essays on books; Frieda had her hair fashionably 'bobbed, permanently waved, fluffed'. But Baden-Baden was as unreal to him, though not as painful, as England – 'like something one remembers in a dream, not quite actual or present' – and he was very happy to move on to Spotorno.[24]

Within three days, they had taken the Villa Bernarda for four months. As usual, it had a wonderful view: 'just above the village and the sea. The sun shines, the eternal Mediterranean is blue and young, the last leaves are falling from the vines in the garden.' It was also cheap: necessary for someone determined to economize. He would have made a distinction, however, between not allowing money to rule one's life, and being careful and provident. Hearing that Brett, back in Taos, had given a shopkeeper a cheque which she knew would bounce, he was shocked. 'I do think you ought to keep track of your spending and incoming . . . I would loathe to draw a cheque if I thought it wouldn't be covered: it's sort of false.'[25]

But as usual when he had found a new place where he felt liberated, he could write: and in Spotorno he wrote his first piece of fiction since *The Plumed Serpent* in Oaxaca and 'The Flying Fish' in Mexico City. The tiny short story 'Smile' was a tailpiece to his three anti-Murry stories of 1923–4; 'Glad Ghosts' was a ghost story commissioned by Cynthia Asquith which, of all things for a ghost story to do, celebrated the body, stressing 'how *very* extraordinary it is to be a man of flesh and blood, alive'.[26] The third piece, however, 'Sun', grew straight out of the situation in Spotorno, where Juliet, suffering from 'nerves' and with a small child, goes to live and to take sun baths, until her grey-suited business-man husband, Maurice, comes out to her. Secker's wife, Rina, nervous and with a twenty-month-old son, was waiting for her husband to arrive from England. For the setting, Lawrence recreated the Fontana Vecchia in Sicily, in what was to be another of those stories exploring the relationship between the human being and the circumambient universe: but this time it was a story in which the new relationship fails, and the woman is driven back into her old frustration. Juliet fantasizes about an affair with a peasant on the estate, but knows that 'Nevertheless, her next child would be Maurice's. The fatal chain of continuity would cause it.'[27]

In one way it seems impossible that Lawrence should have written so directly and so closely about what he could see in front of him: Rina 'a living block of discontent', Secker 'a nice gentle soul, without a thrill'.[28] The latter arrived early in December, Lawrence sent the story off for typing on the 12th, and Secker would eventually publish it. But that was what Lawrence had always done. Part of knowing him was being aware that this might happen to you; his analyses and judgements were frighteningly acute, and could never simply be dismissed as the result of envy, resentment or malice. His creation of Juliet's experience of the sun, however, is the first example of his writing, in these last years of his creativity, on the theme of the relationship between a person and 'the elemental life of the cosmos'. The sun heals, regenerates, makes new in *The Escaped Cock, Sketches of Etruscan Places, Lady Chatterley's Lover* and *Apocalypse*. It was something Lawrence was very aware of, both when he didn't find it (as in England) and when he did, especially after New Mexico. One of his aims as a writer, now, was to get people to see how their lives could be in 'direct contact with the elemental life of the cosmos, mountain-life, cloud-life, thunder-life, air-life, earth-life, sun-life'. His poem 'November by the Sea', written in the winter of 1926–7, would suggest how 'they race in decline / my sun, and the great gold sun', while a poem he wrote in January 1925, 'Mediterranean in January', preferring Europe to America, stated: 'I like better this sea, I must say, / Which is blue with the blueness of one more day.'[29] *Kangaroo* had made the non-human world something to which the human being could escape. It now became a final kind of 'home' for Lawrence.

Another, even more significant result of living in Spotorno was that Lawrence and Frieda met Angelo, husband of their landlady Serafina Ravagli and an officer in the Italian Bersaglieri (see Illustration 30). Frieda described him as 'a nice little Bersaglieri officer . . . I am thrilled by his cockfeathers he is almost as nice as the feathers!'[30] The Lawrences saw him most weekends; Ravagli took English lessons from Lawrence, and did jobs around the house. He helped fix a smoking chimney, for example, which made Lawrence comment to Frieda, in a way that clearly envisaged her life after his demise: 'That is a man who would be useful to have at the Kiowa ranch.' Ravagli was non-intellectual, with no literary interests; he remarked in old age how he had once 'tried *Sons and Lovers* but it was too heavy – *much* too heavy. We don't need literature to know what to do.' At some stage, and it would have been unlike her to have any doubt about her feelings, the 46-year-old Frieda found herself strongly attracted to the 35-year-old Ravagli; and attraction in her case was always likely to be sexual. Ravagli 'resisted Frieda's blandishments for a time but eventually they came to some arrangement'.[31] It sounds as if she fell for him, while initially his feelings were rather less strong. How much she saw of him depended on where he was stationed in northern Italy; but it seems certain that they eventually became lovers at intervals over the last three or four years of Lawrence's life.

At some point, Lawrence must have learned about it: his remark about Ravagli's usefulness at the ranch suggests, indeed, that he saw it coming. It is even possible that, in the end, Frieda confessed it to him, as she had told him about von Henning and then Hobson in 1912 and had discussed Gray with him in 1917. One reason David Garnett would give for not having sex with Frieda that hot afternoon at the Cearne in 1913 was his certainty that, if they did, Frieda would tell Lawrence about it. But Lawrence guessed about Ravagli; after his death, Frieda told Mabel Luhan: 'He just got it out of the air!' A remark which Barby Weekley remembers him making at some point during these years – 'Every heart has a right to its own secrets' – was, for her, as near an acknowledgement of the relationship as he would have wished to make.[32] Frieda's affairs up to this point in their marriage seem to have made rather little difference to her relationship with Lawrence, or to her sometimes grudging belief in him as *the* extraordinary man in her life, whose understanding of her and of the world surpassed that of anyone else she knew. Being with him was by no means always a happy or pleasant experience, but she had always felt inescapably involved with him. She and Lawrence both lived, deliberately if at times painfully, by the conviction that 'honour did not consist in a pledged word kept according to pledge, but in a genuine feeling faithfully followed'.[33] The real quarrels of their lives do not seem to have occurred over her affairs, or his, but over her jealousy of the people he insisted on bringing into their lives (like Ottoline, or Mabel, or Brett, or his sister Ada), and over the people she insisted on as being part of her life (her children and her family). It was people who threatened to disrupt their partnership and living space who mattered, not those who temporarily occupied their beds. Lawrence's friends and family were the people Frieda was most likely to hate, because when they were present, and being given his very special and intense kind of attention, she always felt most ignored.

Frieda seems to have been more jealous of her husband's independence and non-sexual relationships than he was of her sexual ones; but, then, she had more reason to be alarmed. She had complained to Witter Bynner about her financial dependence: 'how could I earn a living? I was never taught anything which might earn me a living ... I am helpless. I am caught.' Lawrence would, however, certainly have tried to support her if they had separated. In 1914, he had divided their funds, and in the autumn of 1923, thinking they might have separated for good, he had offered her an income. But she did not *want* to leave him: 'I wish to be caught. We love each other.'[34] Lawrence may well have regarded her affairs as the price he had to pay for going his own way regardless, in his pursuit of ideas, and choice of places and relationships, if not of sexual partnerships, as well as for her opposition to him. This she had known for a long time. She told Bynner that 'he quotes me and often what he quotes from me is attacking what he himself says and in the book he lets me have the best of it . . . He knows that I'm useful. He likes to have me oppose him in ideas, even while he scolds me for it.'[35]

It has been suggested that Frieda began her relationship with Ravagli because Lawrence was impotent. Richard Aldington would inform the biographer Harry T. Moore, years later, that Frieda had told 'her intimates . . . "Lawrence has been impotent since 1926"',[36] and in spite of the fact that Frieda denied it, biographers and critics have constantly taken it for granted.[37] The matter might have been settled by Frieda's testimony: she remarked, in a private letter, 'Fancy, Murry says he was impotent, the lie, the lie, I ought to know, far from it.' In fact, it was Aldington who spread the story: he certainly had reasons for his vindictiveness. A man under severe attack by tuberculosis has rather little, or only occasional, desire for sex, and Lawrence certainly wrote, very movingly, about his lack of desire; but not wanting sex does not mean a 'loss of sexual potency'.[38] Frieda had never needed any excuse to have affairs, either; and the reality of the Lawrences' sexual relationship seems to have been more complex still, as the writing of *Lady Chatterley's Lover* would show.

Frieda's relationship with Ravagli seems at any rate not to have come between her and Lawrence. Frieda's children, whom Lawrence had so often resented, were another matter and far more likely to precipitate a row. Barby was staying in Alassio, quite near Spotorno, during the winter of 1925–6 and they all saw a good deal of each other. At first this led to the usual quarrels, with Frieda telling Lawrence, according to Barby: 'now I was with her at last, he was to keep out of our relationship and not interfere. This had infuriated Lawrence.' In turn, Barby lectured Frieda about her relationship with Lawrence, being concerned to see, after one of their quarrels, that Lawrence 'had tears in his eyes . . . a rare thing for him'.[39] But anyone coming between Lawrence and Frieda and their complex need of each other, and their need for space between them, too, was going to become a focus for quarrels; though Lawrence gradually grew affectionate towards Barby and ended up very fond of her.

Things grew calmer for a while when Frieda's daughter Elsa arrived at the start of February 1926; Barby remembered that 'Unlike me, she hated "rows"'. Back in November, Lawrence had been dismissive of both girls.[40] But now he started to warm to them, especially after hearing about their lives following Frieda's departure in May 1912. Now they told him all about their father, and life with their aunt and uncle and dominating grandmother in Chiswick, and later with their father's clergyman brother in Essex; and these conversations became the source of the short novel he almost immediately began to write, *The Virgin and the Gipsy*, in which the character Yvette is a good deal like Barby, the Reverend Mr Saywell very like Weekley, and other characters entirely recognizable recreations or conflations.[41] This gave him the chance to bring together the real-life situation of the Weekley sisters with his fascinated hatred of the dominant matriarch, such as he knew in his mother, had seen differently in Mabel Luhan, and was hearing in the girls' stories of their grandmother. He could also incorporate his observations of the landscapes he had seen when touring around Derbyshire in October, as well as his sense of the kind of shut-in, stuffy and respectable Midlands lives that had made him so eager to break away. He created the flavours of middle-class life horribly well, even in food: 'Roast beef and wet cabbage, cold mutton and mashed potatoes, sour pickles, inexcusable puddings'.[42] A good adjective, 'inexcusable'. The flood at the end of the story is a perfect device, as it quite literally cleanses the cabbage-stinking rectory with rushing water, which also washes away the dominant grandmother. Lawrence, as usual when writing, was entirely caught up in his imaginary world, while Barby's painting was also going well; she recalled how the 'creative atmosphere of the Lawrence household was like a draught of life to me'. When he had finished the novel, however, it became something rather rare: a work he decided not to publish. He thought that it would be unfair to the girls and their continuing relationship with Weekley: 'after all, he *is* their father'.[43] After he died, Frieda showed no such concern and published it at once.

Early in February, Frieda translated Lawrence's play *David* into

German. She 'loves it, and has become the authoress, I the cook and the captain bold, and housemaid of the Villa B. –' But, a few days later, Lawrence suffered another bronchial haemorrhage: 'like at the ranch, only worse'.[44] This was an ominous prelude to a period of intense disturbance. On 10 February, Lawrence's sister Ada was coming to visit them for the first time in their marriage, while Frieda would have her daughters staying in a nearby hotel. The weather turned out to be dreadful, and everyone got on everyone else's nerves; Lawrence was still convalescent, and 'everything feels in a great muddle, with daughters that are by no means mine, and sister who doesn't see eye to eye with F. What a trial families are!'[45] Frieda also chose this moment to make yet another of her declarations of final opposition to Brett, now back in Europe and staying in Capri with the Brewsters: the latter had returned to Europe but were on the point of returning to the East. Although Frieda was determined never to see Brett again, Lawrence remained in correspondence with her, and it is possible that this initially provoked what Lawrence casually called 'another rumpus'. This was a savage 'bust-up' between Frieda and Ada.[46] Ada had been shocked, as other observers would be, by Frieda's view of her nursing responsibilities; Frieda and Lawrence had argued and been reconciled, but Frieda had subsequently quarrelled horribly with Ada, who told her: 'I hate you from the bottom of my heart.' And then, when Frieda went up to Lawrence's room, she had found it 'locked and Ada had the key'.[47] Expelled thus from her marriage, Frieda walked out, to stay in the hotel with Barby and Elsa. Lawrence declared that he felt 'absolutely swamped out, must go away by myself for a bit, or I shall give up the ghost'. To escape the conflicts of Spotorno – to 'get away a bit by myself, I may get a clearer mind' – he accompanied Ada to Nice and Monte Carlo on her way home. And when Ada returned to England, he didn't go back to Spotorno but to Capri to see Brett and the Brewsters just before they left (Illustration 29 shows them all together). In the dismantled library of the Brewsters' house, stripped of its books, they played charades one evening. Lawrence sounds perfectly manic, 'with his hair plastered down into bangs, a red bow tie under his chin, he was a clerk in a shoe-shop – the empty library shelves stocked with all the stray shoes the house had. The skill with which he argued his customers into buying what they did not want would have been the envy of any salesman.' Brett heard how he might 'stay alone in S. France for a while'. Four weeks after the 'bust-up', when Frieda had started to write 'much more mildly', Lawrence was still resentful of the way she was trying to 'lay the law down. That sort of thing is no good.'[48] Again it seemed possible that this would be the end of their marriage.

It was at this juncture that Lawrence and Brett had some kind of miserable sexual encounter. After the Brewsters had left, he and Brett went to Ravello to see the painter Millicent Beveridge; he had got to know her in Sicily in 1921 when she painted his portrait.[49] Frieda would have dismissed her as 'One of Lorenzo's old maids', knowing his 'weakness for these English spinsters'. By 11 March, he and Brett had ended up in the annexe of the Hotel Palumbo in adjacent rooms. Brett had been devoted to Lawrence for more than two years; and, according to her, Frieda had said in Oaxaca that, rather than behaving 'like a curate and a spinster', they *should* sleep together; Brett told herself that Frieda 'resents the fact that we do not make love to each other'.[50] And Lawrence was still extremely angry with Frieda.

Brett's account was only published, and perhaps only written, in the 1970s, when she was over eighty, and after she had started working with her business partner and friend John Manchester, who included it in the reprint of her book he brought out in 1974; another version was typed at around the same time. Twice, on consecutive nights, runs Brett's account, Lawrence came to her room; she felt 'desperately inexperienced' (very odd, considering her affair with Murry); on the second occasion, Lawrence was struggling 'to be successfully male'. She presumably meant that he had trouble getting or maintaining an erection. On both occasions, her story says, nothing happened; Lawrence stalked out of her room, saying in one version 'your pubes are wrong' and in the other 'your boobs are all wrong'.[51]

That peculiar difference between both versions suggests, however, a mishearing of an anecdote by a third party. Deaf as she was, Brett would surely have remembered, or have decided, what the phrase had been. Lawrence, who had used 'boobs' to mean 'fools' in one of the hymns of Quetzalcoatl in *The Plumed Serpent*, is very unlikely to have used it for 'breasts' in 1926. There is reason for linking him with some particularity about the presence or absence of pubic hair, but 'pubes' would have been a weird word to use: he never used it elsewhere.[52] The fact, however, that 'boobs' was printed in the reissue of Brett's book is a little worrying. By 1974, too, Brett's memory was not good; other things in her account vary from their equivalent in 1933. Equally unreliable is her account, given by Manchester, of Lawrence telling her that if they 'could develop a successful physical relationship as well as the spiritual, he would leave Frieda'.[53]

Frieda did not believe that any such thing could have happened. In 1932, she wrote to Koteliansky about his belief that Brett had been Lawrence's lover: 'Lawrence was too much of an *artist* to want her, he had a real affection for her & she adored him, though *her* Lawrence is a kind of Buddha – He couldn't bear to touch her, don't you know that?' Frieda told Brett in Oaxaca that 'Lawrence says he could not possibly be in love with a woman like you – an asparagus stick!'; while Lawrence himself had told Brett in January 1925 that 'between you and me there is no sensual correspondence'.[54]

A letter Brett wrote in 1931, however, shows that something awful had indeed happened in Ravello: she claimed grandiosely that that 'one week of intense living, two nights of tragedy, have given him the only widow he is likely to have'. And evidence for the encounter exists from just after the event. On 18 March, Lawrence wrote to Brett:

One has just to forget, and to accept what is good. We can't help being more or less damaged. What we have to do is to stick to the good part of ourselves, and of each other, and continue an understanding on that. I don't see why we shouldn't be *better* friends, instead of worse. But one must not try to force anything.[55]

That is certainly an attempt at bridge-building after something un-happy. One of Brett's reactions was, characteristically, 'caving in', as Lawrence put it, meaning that she felt sorry for herself.[56] If, rather than Lawrence imposing himself on Brett, Brett had selflessly imposed herself on Lawrence, as she had on Murry in 1923, he would probably have written in just the same way. But there is now no way of knowing exactly what occurred in Ravello, except that it was sexual and miser-able, and happened twice, as well as leaving Lawrence determined to free himself from a woman he had once been close to (Brett left Ravello immediately). In that way, though perhaps in no other, there are similarities with Lawrence's affair with Rosalind.[57] Brett wanted to see him again, but he wrote: 'I don't think it would be any use our meeting again just now, we should only be upset.' He himself was upset, just like the central figure in 'The Man Who Loved Islands', a story he wrote just three months later; Cathcart is attracted to his housekeeper's daughter – 'it was almost a kind of pity for her' – but is eventually caught by the 'automatism of sex'. At Ravello, there would have been a ledge near the sea, where Lawrence might well, like Cathcart, have sat for hours, 'motionless, gazing miserably at the sea, and saying unconsciously to himself: Not that! Not that! Not that!'[58] That would have been Lawrence's conclusion if he had responded to advances Brett had made; while if he had initiated things, and hoped to rekindle desire by going to bed with her, he would have cursed himself afterwards for a fool and worse. He had had a lifetime's history of detaching himself from attachment; he told the Brewsters in April about Brett that 'I can't stand it when she clings too tight'.[59] He never saw her again, though they corresponded regularly. She said that she wanted to make a life at the ranch, and Lawrence advised her to get on to the quota of immigrants allowed into the US; within weeks, she had gone back and continued as a kind of custodian of Kiowa. She always remained devoted to him; her 1933 book *Lawrence and Brett* offered its own kind of claim on him, even without mention of the Ravello encounter.

By 18 March, Frieda had written to Lawrence 'much more quietly and humanly', saying 'we must live more with other people . . . not cut ourselves off'. He reported that sentiment to Brett. But Frieda's daughters had been giving her advice. They 'are very fierce with her, and fall on her tooth and nail' reported Lawrence maliciously: 'Being her own family, they can go for her exactly in her own way, and pretty well silence her.'[60] The Lawrences' most serious rows were provoked by other people intruding into their relationship; if they could find a way of living 'more with other people', so that those 'other people' did not divide their loyalties, that would have been all to the good.

They tried a new start. Lawrence went back to Spotorno after an absence of seven weeks, to find 'the three females very glad to see me', though he had a 'bit of anger still working in my inside'.[61] After a brief time there – the term of the rent of the Villa Bernarda was almost up

– the four of them went to Florence for a while; and then Frieda's daughters went back to London, leaving the Lawrences to find somewhere to live. Lawrence had plans to write about northern Italy, and believed that Umbria and the Etruscans were possible subjects, but for the moment he opted for Tuscany. Very quickly, he and Frieda found an old villa at San Polo Mosciano, about eight miles southwest of Florence, where they could rent the top floor cheaply.

It was a way of saying that he was not going to return to America. Brett had returned to her cabin at Kiowa, doubtless hoping that Lawrence too would be back; but he decided not to try. After his haemorrhage in February, he would have known that he was *not* getting better; and the danger of being refused a visa, or entrance, would have been uppermost in his mind. There was, too, the enormous journey, which he could not easily face; he was more than ever conscious that 'even the ranch is a sort of effort, a strain – and for the moment I don't want to make any efforts'. He concluded that 'I really don't want to go to America: and am getting weary, and wearier, of the outside world. I want the world from the inside, not from the outside . . . I don't want to go west.' Fortunately, for the moment 'Italy is still very nice, and I feel more at home here than in America'.[62] But although he was apparently setting himself to do a different kind of writing – 'the world from the inside, not from the outside' – he would never be so concerned with the contemporary world as in his last four years of writing. He may have been considering a wise retreat; he actually entered the public arena as never before.

The 'big old heavy villa, square', 'crowning a little hilltop' like so many of the Lawrences' houses, was called 'Mirenda' after its owner; it looked 'far out over the Val d'Arno' and was surrounded by 'lovely slopes of vines and olives', 'all poderi and pine-woods, and no *walls* at all'.[63] An English family, the Wilkinsons, lived just two minutes' walk away; but the Mirenda was the centre of a peasant community too, and the Lawrences got to know their neighbours, especially the Pini family, very well. And, unlike the ranch, the six rooms at the Villa Mirenda not only entailed no responsibilities, they were rented 'with service': Giulia Pini was their housekeeper. It was fairly easy to get to Florence, too: 'One can stay out and be quite remote. Or go into Florence in an hour, and see a few people who aren't exciting, but all

344

the better.'[64] The Mirenda would be the Lawrences' base for just over two years.

But always 'base' or '*pied à terre*', rather than home. The top floor was sparsely furnished and there was no running water. It was very cheap, however, they didn't spend much money on it, and they were away a good deal. They lived there for just a couple of months now, during which time they also visited the English aristocrats Sir George and Lady Ida Sitwell at their nearby castle; they had probably all met in Florence. A Florentine connection they did not, however, renew was with Norman Douglas, who had viciously attacked Lawrence's introduction to Magnus's book, and then reprinted the attack in a book in 1925.[65] Douglas had suggested that Lawrence had written irresponsibly about Magnus, and that he had profited from a manuscript that belonged to him, Douglas, as the literary executor. Lawrence, on the insistence of Secker, published a brilliant rebuttal of the charges in a letter. In Florence in June 1926, Lawrence confessed: 'I saw Douglas in a cafe and didn't speak to him: felt I couldn't stand him.'[66]

But Lawrence was now properly back at work, typing out Frieda's translation of *David*, though he hated doing it ('I loathe the typewriter'), writing essays about Florence and producing two pieces of work provoked by conversations, in Capri in March, with Compton Mackenzie's wife, Faith: 'another who loves her husband but can't live with him'.[67] That wasn't exactly true of him and Frieda, but the subject obviously appealed. 'Two Blue Birds' was a skit and no more, but 'The Man Who Loved Islands' became one of Lawrence's great works: a profound criticism of the temperament that seeks out separation from the world. The first island that the central figure, Cathcart, occupies is a development of Lawrence's various old Island schemes, though it also uses elements derived from Mackenzie's life on the islands of Herm and Jethou. Cathcart, 'the Master', builds a perfect community, and everything goes wrong: people betray and cheat him, the animals die, and he is almost bankrupted. He abandons the community and moves to a second, smaller island, where he lives with just a few people about him, and a widow and her daughter working as housekeepers. He writes, with no sense of urgency; it seems as if an earthly paradise has come into being. And again it goes wrong: this time because he gets the daughter pregnant and feels obliged to marry her. The idyll ends: he sells up again and heads straight for his third island, where he will be completely alone. And there, cut off from the world, Cathcart goes mad. He 'ceased to register his own feelings'. He destroys, for example, every trace of writing around him, even the brass label on his paraffin stove. The story ends with his crazed loneliness, as he looks over his island and does not know if it is summer or winter. It seems deep in snow, but he knows that it 'is summer . . . and the time of leaves'. That single trace of the natural world exists only in his mind, however; he is irretrievably solipsistic. And the conclusion shows him confronting death. It is a story which draws on so many of the tendencies and potentialities in Lawrence's life and temperament that it goes far beyond the elements of Mackenzie's life which had been its starting point: recreation had become creation. Lawrence was testing out what happened, under the stress of experience, to his old philosophy of individualism. As he would remark: 'The Man who loved islands has a philosophy behind him.' The next book he planned offered an absolute contrast. The fact that there 'really is next to nothing to be said, *scientifically*, about the Etruscans' meant that he felt free to take an 'imaginative line'; his book *Sketches of Etruscan Places* would create a richly detailed account of what a happy and contented communal life might after all be like.[68]

By the end of June 1926, it was getting hot. On 12 July, the Lawrences left for Baden-Baden: Frieda's mother was about to celebrate her seventy-fifth birthday. They spent a fortnight there, Lawrence maliciously picturing the *Stift* as 'a sort of Holbein *Totentanz* [dance of death]: old, old people tottering their cautious dance of triumph: "wir sind noch hier: hupf! hupf! hupf!" [we are still here: hop! hop! hop!]'; but by the end of the month they were in London, in a rented flat. It may seem surprising that Lawrence should have gone back to England so soon, especially as 'the thought of England . . . depresses me with infinite depression'. But he badly wanted to see the early rehearsals of his play *David*, which the Stage Society were putting on – 'I should like to have a finger in that particular pie' – and he planned this visit very differently.[69] While he was in the Midlands or the north, Frieda stayed in London with her children. They also made an effort to see old friends: Koteliansky, Richard Aldington, and Arabella Yorke, whom they had known as Aldington's partner since their stay at H. D.'s flat in Mecklenburgh Square in 1917: 'very nice'. Lawrence also met Frieda's son Monty for the first time, Monty being struck with Lawrence's Notts-Derby accent: 'Sargent,' he remembered Lawrence saying, 'sooch a bad peynter.'[70] Lawrence made a ten-day visit to Scotland, too, to see Millicent Beveridge. He had never been further north than the Lake District, but although Scotland was beautiful, 'the air so fresh, and the harebells just like the Black Forest', the tourists irritated him and it rained a good deal. In spite of his finding the Isle of Skye 'so remote and uninhabited, so northern, and like the far-off old world, out there', Scotland was '*too* northern for me'. 'But we had one perfect day, blue and iridescent, with the bare northern hills sloping green and sad and velvety to the silky blue sea.'[71]

On the way back from Scotland, Lawrence visited his sisters and their families, including Gertie Cooper, on the Lincolnshire coast (see Illustration 32),[72] and this stay beside the sea turned out an unexpected pleasure: 'England seems to suit my health.' He recalled 1901 on the east coast: it was 'very bracing and tonicky – picks me up like a shot', and he felt that he had got 'into touch with my native land again, here – and feel at home'.[73] That was very unusual for him, and he took advantage of it to extend his stay. It linked directly with his health; he was 'at home' where he felt well. He had great resources of humour and fun, which came out at such a time; 'delicious laughter' was as much his style as serious talk. Illustration 31 shows him and Ada fooling about on the beach at Mablethorpe, Lawrence with a child's parasol. An Eastwood neighbour remembered them as children: 'He was a comic. Their Ada was too, they had us in stitches.'[74] Frieda joined the party briefly before the sisters went home; but Frieda and Lawrence then stayed in Sutton-on-Sea for another fortnight, in theory waiting for the Stage Society to sort out their plans for *David*, but really so that Lawrence could go on feeling 'at home'. Frieda swam; Lawrence did not risk it, being still 'scared of my bronchials'. Frieda then went back to London and Lawrence briefly went over to see Ada in Ripley. Here, however, the effects of the miners' industrial action depressed him; the national strike of nine days in May had ended, but the miners were still out. As a consequence, 'there is a lot of misery – families living on bread and margarine and potatoes – nothing more'.

Lawrence felt both 'devouring nostalgia' and 'infinite repulsion'.[75] It may have been 'home to me'; but it was becoming only bearable in his writing about it.

Back in London, they saw some more of the 'old people' (Kot, Enid Hopkin, Margaret Radford, Aldington) as well as Frieda's children; and for the first time since 1915 Lawrence met the successful writer Aldous Huxley and his wife, Maria. This had far-reaching consequences; they developed a lasting friendship and saw a great deal of each other over the next four years. But *David* had been postponed, so after lunching with the director, Lawrence and Frieda left on 28 September, eager to be back at the Mirenda for the celebrations surrounding the grape harvest. Although they had enjoyed the trip, it had been tiring and rather expensive: 'one wastes every sou in this moving around.'[76] Lawrence was becoming sharply aware of how little he was currently earning. His new American publisher, Knopf, had not yet published much of his work, for (by his standards) Lawrence had not written much recently; he had not started a new novel since 1923. What had happened during the writing of – and after – *The Plumed Serpent*, as well its reception, certainly inhibited him from beginning another. T. S. Eliot would write the following year of how in 'his series of splendid, but extremely ill-written novels – each one vomited from the press before we have had time to finish its predecessor – there is nothing to relieve the monotony of the "dark passions" which cause his Males and Females to tear themselves and each other to pieces'. Lawrence told his sister-in-law Else on 18 October that he felt 'I'll never write another novel.'[77] In spite of this, but perhaps because of his new sense of England as a place where he might feel at home, around 22 October he started a story set in the Midlands. And this had altogether unexpected consequences: for it was to become *Lady Chatterley's Lover*.

22

Other Forces: 1926–1927

Lady Chatterley's Lover occupied Lawrence from October 1926 to the publication of its third version in the summer of 1928 and well beyond, as in the spring of 1929 he would go to Paris to arrange for publication of a cheap edition. The book forever altered his reputation. From being a not especially well-known author of a number of books in different genres, he became the author of *Lady Chatterley's Lover*. The book made him what he feared to be: 'a lurid sexuality specialist'. But it was also the one best-selling book of his life and earned him more money than he had made in his entire career, which came just when it was most wanted: when his strength did not allow him to write much, when he was ill and needed doctors, and eventually a sanatorium, and when Frieda would have to live on without him, supported by his literary earnings. At some level, he must have suspected that this is what *Lady Chatterley's Lover* might turn out to be: he wrote it when what he called 'my poverty' was especially worrying him.[1]

He began it around 22 October 1926, as what Frieda called 'a short long story' of the kind he had written several times during the previous five years, and he wrote it whenever possible outdoors: 'he would sit, almost motionless except for his swift writing. He would be so still that the lizards would run over him and the birds hop close around him. An occasional hunter would start at this silent figure.' The Wilkinsons' dog went with him; he noted, on page 41 of his manuscript: 'Smudges made by John, the dog, near the stream behind San Polo Mosciano! 26 Oct 1926.'[2] (Illustration 33 shows him near the Mirenda, one sunny afternoon: the ground drops away behind him, down to the valley and the stream.) Everyday details appear in the new work: Constance Chatterley's room has 'Italian rush matting, that smelled sweet of rushes', the same thick pale rush matting which the Lawrences were using at the Mirenda. And it can hardly have been an accident that a story containing a recognizable portrait of Rosalind Baynes should have been started at the Mirenda, with its superb view across the Arno valley to Fiesole, where he had had his affair with her in 1920.[3]

On 28 October, Frieda referred in a letter to the new work as 'breaking new ground, the curious class feeling this time'. Her meaning becomes clearer from a row she and Lawrence had had on the 24th. They were at tea with the Wilkinsons, and Arthur noted in his journal: 'The talk soon got on to Revolution & stayed there & was really impassioned. We all generalised a bit – but he did so tremendously & swears by his class & death & damnation to the other class. He's done with them. "They're hard – cruel cruel (crescendo)".'[4] From a man who had made good friends with Lady Ottoline Morrell and Lady Cynthia Asquith, and who was married to the daughter of one of the oldest German aristocratic houses, this may seem odd. Lawrence was, however, starting to regret his exaltation of the idea of aristocracy; Duncan Forbes in *Lady Chatterley's Lover* would confess that 'I've hated democracy since the war. But now I see I was wrong, calling for an aristocracy.' Creating the Chatterleys, Lawrence discovered anew how the 'well-bred, polite, considerate treatment' of class inferiors concealed 'the cold inhumanity, the lack of heart-throb, the mere curiosity, and the inward arrogance of the class-superior'.[5] He attacked Frieda for being superior, too:

He was so rude & cross to her & she retaliated with spirit – 'Why didn't you marry one of your own class then' she said 'You'd have been bored stiff.' Says he very sad & vinegary 'I may have my regrets' & she retorted 'Well you can be off you can go now if you like.' It was rather tense – but we got them off that tack & though the talk on their part was so savage we daresay it did them good to let off steam.[6]

Her phrase about the novel – 'the curious class feeling' – shows that she found merely quaint and odd what was for Lawrence a fundamental division in English life. The novel was borrowing an idea which lay behind the as yet unpublished *Virgin and the Gipsy* but which in his early years had been at the centre of Lawrence's writing: the experience of the middle- or upper-class woman who embarks on a transgressive relationship with a man from the working class. *The White Peacock* had been the tragedy of George's failure to marry Lettie, and contained the story of Annable, the cattle-dealer's son who marries an aristocrat. *Sons and Lovers* had been the tragedy of a family in which the mother felt she had married beneath her; 'Daughters of the Vicar', finished in 1914, had shown a clergyman's daughter preparing to marry a miner. But *The Virgin and the Gipsy* and the first version of *Lady Chatterley's Lover* are so 'savagely' concerned with the barriers of class that the latter could not show how Constance and the gamekeeper Parkin might make a life together. By the time Lawrence came to write the third version of the *Lady Chatterley* novel, more than a year later, he was determined to make such a relationship possible, which meant considerable adjustments to the character and class of the gamekeeper. Working-class Parkin had to become *déclassé* Mellors.

More was at stake than realism about class. The first *Lady Chatterley* novel, on just ten occasions, had used the words 'cunt', 'fuck', 'fucker' and 'fucking': and this at a time when even words like 'phallus' or 'phallic' were considered risqué in print. Anyone publishing the 'indefinable sexual words of the dialect'[7] in England, however accurate they might be as denotations of speech, would have been prosecuted. Lawrence had been up against censorship ever since publication of *The White Peacock*, but now, although the first version of *Lady Chatterley* was not sexually explicit, it would do some extremely unusual things, such as describe a woman's 'short, almost whimpering cries of passion', and suggest what an orgasm feels like. Lawrence was on the edge of writing a novel in which there would be *no* restrictions at all on what could be included.[8]

He started writing the second version of the novel almost immediately after he finished the first; it looks as if he only finished the first (it had taken a little over a month) in order to find out where this tale of transgressive love would go. He must have known he would be rewriting it, and would be developing things so far only experimented with. The second version became the first sexually explicit book he had written, and may even have been the first sexually explicit book he had ever seen.[9] Not only would it describe sexual encounters; it would allow Parkin to use a sexual vocabulary. It took Lawrence far longer to write than the first version, and grew to almost twice the length, though it told an almost identical story. He finished it late in February 1927, and found it 'good, I think, but a little too deep in bits – sort of bottomless pools'.[10] What had been, at the start, a novel primarily about class division coming up against sexual desire, turned in the second version into a novel in which class division was just one element in a sexually explicit love story.

What is striking is that Lawrence should have embarked on such a project when Frieda had taken a lover (Ravagli), and when his own illness probably ensured that he was less sexually involved with her than in their entire life together. But Frieda recalled reading every day what he had written, and the following year a visitor heard 'at intervals' Lawrence calling Frieda to his room, where he was writing in bed, to read to her: 'Sometimes they laughed together and at other times she would sound a little shocked and in her deep, throaty voice, said: "Lorenzo, you cannot say that." '[11] She was thus the first audience for the novel. Their own relationship had been unusual, in something of the way the novel was depicting, Lawrence working class and Frieda aristocracy, yet in many ways, in 1912, Lawrence had been closer to the position of Constance (detached and inexperienced onlooker) and Frieda to that of Parkin/Mellors (instinctive, sympathetic, experienced married partner). The dismissive judgements of Jessie Chambers and Helen Corke put into the mouth of Mellors in version three would be a great deal closer to the way Frieda would have preferred to sum up Jessie and Helen than to how Lawrence originally felt about them.[12] And if there is one character in the novel with whom Lawrence might have been expected to sympathize, it would be Clifford Chatterley, demoralized by illness, whose wife wants more of her marriage than he can give her, and who is prepared to turn a blind eye to her taking a lover. Instead, the novel takes the woman's point of view, and the sexually active woman abandons the sexually non-active but literary and intellectual husband for the non-intellectual gamekeeper. The novel shows less sympathy for the husband than would seem possible for a writer who must have been concerned by Clifford's predicament, and whose own lack of desire troubled him so much. The idea that

Frieda might leave him for Ravagli would have occurred to Lawrence. How could he make himself more like Parkin/Mellors and less like Clifford?

His answer was, paradoxically, by writing the novel. If on the one hand its sexuality was an astonishing tribute to Frieda, and to how Lawrence felt about her feelings and her experience, it was above all a final tribute to the life of the body, male and female, which now occupied him more in imagination and recreation than it could in actuality or in desire. It is not too much to say that the second and third versions of *Lady Chatterley's Lover* were verbal acts of love to Frieda, written in the words she would have read or heard each time he came back from writing, towards the end of a partnership which had started out as violent sexual attraction. These versions of the novel did what Lawrence could always do best, which was imaginatively develop the crucial experiences of his own life: and his sexual life had been overwhelmingly what he had shared with Frieda. *Lady Chatterley* was, then, a way of insisting that he was not too withdrawn, ill or fragile to imagine making intense love to Frieda, as he always had done; and to experience (and make his reader feel) what she felt. By unwisely calling Lawrence 'a sexual weakling' in 1951, Edward Gilbert provoked Frieda into saying something unguarded. She responded: 'It is just absurd to call L. a sexual weakling, anything but: with his intensity. You don't know how a man like he was, could give himself, body and soul. I experienced this miracle.'[13] It was the 'intensity' that she insisted on: the experience she had of his giving himself absolutely. She may even have envied him; she gave herself quickly and temporarily, to men like Hobson and Gray, often with regret. Lawrence's final act of sexual giving was to write the second and third versions of *Lady Chatterley's Lover.*

Almost exactly two years after starting the first version of the novel, Lawrence made a hesitant remark to the writer Brigit Patmore that suggests another reason behind the book's development from a short fiction about class into a novel primarily concerned with sex and the experiences of the body. He told her about his loneliness, and went on: 'you think you have something in your life which makes up for everything, and then find you haven't got it . . . Two years ago I found this out.'[14] He cannot have meant Frieda's sexual loyalty to him, which he had never had. He might have meant Frieda as a sexual partner, but he is much more likely to have meant his capacity to experience desire: including (but not exclusively) sexual desire.

The novel was, thus, written by a man reaffirming the life of the body that, for him, had always found its culmination in sexual desire. After finishing *Lady Chatterley*, he began to use the phrase 'phallic consciousness' to describe its central experience. He was attempting to channel an exclusively male word into a special term for awareness of the body; and he used it to imply something conventionally associated with women rather than men. He would, for example, call his book a nice, tender phallic novel: a warm phallic novel. He even thought of calling it 'Tenderness',[15] which would have been a way of explicitly asserting its 'female' quality of responsiveness and denying its traditionally 'male' characteristics of demand and rapacity. The novel was also a final, perfectly deliberate attack on the conventions of decorum and taste that had dogged him as a writer all his life. The project occupied him profoundly: it offered a chance to win the arguments with censorship and prudery which he had up to now always lost, as well as to take his writing in a new direction.

His other new occupation this first winter at the Mirenda was painting. He had always painted; had made innumerable copies as a boy, in those sessions in Walker Street and at the Haggs, 'with almost dry water-colour, stroke by stroke, covering half a square-inch at a time, each square-inch perfect and completed, proceeding in a kind of mosaic advance'.[16] A few of his copies had achieved a kind of luminous intensity, and one or two of them he had carried with him on his travels; Knud Merrild saw his copy of the *Death of Procris* in 1922, and his version of Masaccio's *Adoration of the Magi* had hung over the cabin fireplace at Del Monte. In his essay 'Making Pictures', written in April 1929, he described how art lessons had convinced him that 'I couldn't really paint. Perhaps I can't. But I verily believe I can make pictures, which is to me all that matters in this respect.'[17] He had continued making copies of paintings, and doing occasional originals. In October 1926, when the Huxleys came to visit, Maria presented him with four or five stretched canvases, one of which had been started but left unfinished by her brother. The Lawrences were just decorating their south-facing *salotto* for winter use, and the newly whitewashed walls were bare. Lawrence used what remained of the decorating paint, and produced a batch of large original paintings. Nearly all are on taboo subjects, all are about the experience of the body, and many of them are depictions of desire. Coincidentally, with the start of the second version of his *Lady Chatterley* novel at the beginning of December 1926, for example, he designed and then painted his *Boccaccio Story*, with its half-naked gardener lying on his back and its bevy of startled nuns, acutely set on seeing his '*glorietta*' but also shocked at the idea.[18] His paintings are never very skilfully handled but often powerful. They were for him ways of losing himself in work which took less out of him than writing did; but they were also ways of making actual the feelings of the body, in particular the sexual body; and above all of imaging what is desirous about the body, and about being in the body. He remarked: 'I like a picture to be a picture to the whole sensual self.'[19]

This was, however, by no means easy to paint, and one of Lawrence's problems was that he took on difficult subjects. He had sufficient technical skill to do roughly what he wanted; but it was hard for him to depict a man and a woman wrestling with wolves howling around them (*Fight with an Amazon*), or a woman escaping into Paradise from the industrial world (*Flight back into Paradise*), or a couple embracing (*Under the Mango Tree*), or men wrestling (*Spring*), or brutalized men under soaring swans (*Singing of Swans*), or indeed any of the paintings in which bodies are in close conjunction with each other, while simultaneously moving. One or two of his paintings stand as pictures in their own right, but most are interesting only because a great writer painted them. The static figures in *Family on a Verandah* (see Illustration 37), *Contadini*, *Red Willow Trees*, *The Lizard* and *Renascence of Men* show him at his most accomplished, but those – apart from their qualities of 'luminosity' and '*glow*'[20] – are not what he most wanted to paint. He had another ambition for his paintings. 'I paint no picture that wont shock people's castrated social spirituality,' he told his painter friend Earl Brewster; the Brewsters were back in Europe, and Lawrence saw them again in March 1927.[21] During the years spent writing *Lady Chatterley's Lover*, he was redeveloping a powerful sense of his role as a writer and painter for his society, especially English society. He again saw himself as someone who would change people for the better, both in painting and in writing: in the summer of 1927, he had a compelling dream about being made 'head of a school somewhere': 'I half wonder if it is *my* destiny!' The difference from teaching was that, in painting and writing, he was using shock tactics, so that, recovering from their shock, people would realize that the sexuality of the novel or painting was no more than 'part of every man's life, and every woman's'.[22]

Christmas 1926 was marked by a break in his writing and by a celebration with the local community of peasants. Years later, Frieda would write how the 'handful of peasants round us in that remote part of Tuscany gave Lawrence more unvoiced recognition than he had had anywhere we had been. He was not even very friendly, but rather aloof with them. But instinctively they felt: here is something special. They did not jeer at him and they jeer easily. They would have done anything for him.'[23] None of the local children had ever seen a Christmas tree: they were full of talk about some English people who had had one. Pietro Pini, Giulia's half-brother, whom Lawrence had asked to buy a tree, instead stole one from the wood belonging to the priest. The Lawrences decorated it with ornaments and candles and presents; they gave every man who came to the celebration a glass of sweet wine and a cigar and every woman a glass of wine and some sweet biscuits; while there were dates and sweets for the children – 'washed beyond recognition' – and heaps of wooden toys. There was singing and dancing, too; with all twenty-seven visitors there, it was 'like Ripley fair in this salotta'. The Lawrences were worn out when their guests left. The occasion was nevertheless a kind of demonstration of Lawrence's loyalty to the working class; something he became very conscious of during these last few years, as his contempt for the middle classes grew more pronounced. It was solidarity he felt with the local peasants, not identification with them. 'I don't want to live with them in their cottages; that would be a sort of prison.' But it was they 'who form my *ambiente* . . . I want them to be there, about the place, their lives going on along with mine, and in relation to mine'. That was as close as he now preferred to get to his chosen society: 'a certain silent contact'.[24]

The fiction he went on with after Christmas was far more experimental and accomplished than the painting he enjoyed so much. After three months' work, around the start of March 1927 he finished the second version of *Lady Chatterley's Lover* – 'verbally terribly improper' – and did not know what to do with it. It was quite unpublishable as it stood. This is significant. He was publishing less, and the exchange rate in Italy had become distinctly unfavourable. As he would remark in June: 'it's God help us, when it comes to earning money by sincere work. I manage still to scramble through, but no more.' He survived only by 'living like a road-sweeper'.[25] He certainly could not afford to waste months writing the unpublishable. And yet he had done just that: his need to write the book over-rode his good sense as a professional writer who needed to make best use of his resources. All he could do with the novel for the moment was let it wait. He did not even have it typed, as he would normally have done with a work he wished to revise or offer to a publisher. He probably felt that, one day, he would be able to let both novel and paintings (now decorating the Mirenda) have an impact on people. In the meanwhile, they simply stayed with him.

He needed to publish, however. The cheapness of the Mirenda did not make up for a lack of earnings, and besides the novel he had written only book reviews and some poems. With the novel out of the way, he wrote the short story 'The Lovely Lady' and went back to his idea of a book about the Etruscans, an older civilization he could perhaps recreate without plunging into the morasses of *The Plumed Serpent*. Lawrence concentrated on what he saw in the paintings that decorated Etruscan tombs; he would include many illustrations of those. The Etruscans' attitude towards death was something he found immensely attractive; and he took his clue from what he saw as the 'peculiar physical or *bodily*, lively quality of all the art' and the 'spontaneity of the flesh itself' which he presented as the *feeling* of the Etruscan world. There are no armies, no chants, no ceremonies; individuals sit, drink, dance, caress, touch: are located in 'phallic consciousness'. 'Here, in this faded etruscan painting, there is a quiet flow of touch that unites the man and the woman on the couch, the timid boy behind, the dog that lifts his nose, even the very garlands that hang from the wall.'[26]

The Etruscan project involved a lot of preliminary reading, which he had already started to do, and then visits to Etruscan sites. He

357

rejected scholarly suggestions of 'the barbarously cruel sports of the Etruscans'; he carefully recreated an old world, but found no need to assert its power and cruelty. He speculated that Etruscan religion was more like Native American animism, and god-less: in that way, too, the book was a kind of criticism of *The Plumed Serpent*. In many ways, *Sketches of Etruscan Places* would come nearest to showing what he had said 'The Flying Fish' would reveal – 'regenerate man' – than anything else he wrote.[27] He had not been particularly well during the winter of 1926–7, but in mid March while Frieda went to visit her mother, and probably Ravagli too, Lawrence first went to see the Brewsters in Capri, and then set out on a fortnight's tour of Etruscan places, accompanied by Earl Brewster: from Rome they went to Cerveteri, Tarquinia, Vulci and Volterra. During the next three months, he would use the experience to write his essays about the Etruscans, a number of which were taken by magazines. He never finished the book he planned; its essays were only published together posthumously. It nevertheless gave him the chance that for several years he had been looking for, to recreate a primitive society which would model the things which he felt the modern world had lost. He had attempted this in *The Plumed Serpent* and then in the fragment 'Noah's Flood' written shortly afterwards, and then at length in *David*. But this was his best chance yet; and he wanted to reach a wide audience with it, telling Secker that 'I want this book – which will be a bit expensive to you, owing to illustrations – to be as popular as I can make it'.[28]

'The Lovely Lady' had begun as a commission from Cynthia Asquith for a book of murder stories she was now compiling. If Lawrence were writing a murder story, whom would he choose to murder? The answer was, a marvellously well-preserved woman of seventy-two who continues to control her middle-aged son and his affections, and who years ago effectively killed her other son: 'Handsome . . . Tall, good at games; rather freckled, with mother's soft brown hair with a gleam of red in it . . . Open, rather boisterous. Women all loved him.'[29] Lawrence is unquestionably recreating his elder brother Ernest; the woman to be murdered, Pauline Attenborough, is another reworking of Lydia Lawrence. When Pauline dies, her surviving son sees in her 'the pathos of a maid who has died virgin and unlived': Lawrence's 1910 poem about Lydia, 'The Virgin Mother', and his 1922 poem about her as one of the 'Spirits Summoned West' – 'The overlooked virgin / My love' – had been countered, clearly and forcibly. The tenderly loved mother, assisted out of life in reality, dispatched again in the fiction of *Sons and Lovers* with some anxiety about the way she 'holds' her sons, is at last given the *coup de grâce*: her 'look of wilfulness and imperviousness . . . now fixed and gone cold'. The surviving son in 'The Lovely Lady' confesses: 'One can go so awfully wrong, without knowing.'[30]

An equally significant story that Lawrence started a couple of months later was a short work called 'The Escaped Cock'. Just as the second version of *Lady Chatterley's Lover* had broken sexual taboos, and 'The Lovely Lady' had transgressed his old emotional loyalties (he would write in April how 'one has lost for good one's old self – some of it'),[31] this new work would infringe religious pieties. It described Jesus, after the crucifixion, coming back neither as the Son of God, nor to his mission as a teacher or healer, nor to ascension in the biblical sense, but to the life of the body and resurrection in the flesh. Lawrence celebrated the same idea in his painting *Resurrection*, finished after his return from the Etruscan tour, which shows the newly resurrected Christ leaning towards Mary Magdalene and the latter 'easing him up towards her bosom'; she is bare-breasted.[32] In that way, the story was like the *Lady Chatterley* novels: a work exploring the extraordinary phenomenon of being alive in the body in the physical world. Lawrence was able to publish 'The Escaped Cock', even though it caused a storm for the magazine involved, the *Forum*.

During the early summer of 1927, he was busy with short essays and some new short stories, 'None of That!' and 'Things', drawing on acquaintances as diverse as Mabel Luhan, the Wilkinsons and the Brewsters. He was still working outdoors when possible; in May he would be 'out in the woods by eight oclock'. His health was not good, however. In the winter he had suffered what he called 'a bit of malaria', but which may well have been a renewed onset of tuberculosis, with its sweating, exhaustion and sudden rises in temperature. He was confined to bed at the end of February and again in mid April, and he was still not very well at the end of the month. At the start of May, he

was too ill with 'malaria' to go to London to attend the first performances of his play *David*.[33] He had been following tuberculosis-sufferer
Gertie Cooper's progress through the winter and spring, advising and
cheering her; though the decision taken in January 1927 that she
should have a lung removed had made him absolutely certain that *he*
would not have such an operation: 'it leaves a little thorn stuck in
one's mind, which makes one jump when it is touched.' Things got
still worse for Gertie. By the end of April, she had not only had the
lung removed, but also six ribs and glands in her neck: 'too horrible –
better die,' exclaimed Lawrence. 'What is left, after all those oper-
ations? Why not chloroform and the long sleep! How monstrous our
humanity is! Why save life in this ghastly way?' In spite of the horror,
he offered his sister Ada £50 a year for Gertie if it was needed: and
this at a time when he was getting increasingly anxious about his own
capacity to earn. He made Ada swear not to reveal his offer: 'I hate
these money things talked about.'[34] He had, however, been confirmed
in his determination never to put himself in the hands of doctors by
his knowledge of what Gertie had gone through; he told Ada, 'There's
nothing to do but not think of it.' He continued to refer to his own
problems simply as 'bronchial trouble'.[35]

The performances of *David* at the end of May were slated by the
critics; Lawrence's response was to call the critics 'eunuchs' with 'no
balls'. 'The worst of the youngish Englishman is, he's such a . . . prig,
one imagines he must either be a lady in disguise, or a hermaphrodite.'
But it was not as if *David* had been daring in its treatment of sex. The
acting left much to be desired and the play also proved extremely long.
The violence of Lawrence's response simply shows how annoyed he
was; the Wilkinsons saw how both the Lawrences were 'bitterly disappointed about the play'.[36] A stage success would not only have been
very cheering, but also financially welcome; Lawrence's reputation by
the late 1920s was that of a writer who had peaked around the time
of the war, but was now distinctly in decline, after a succession of odd
and not especially distinguished novels.

Lawrence felt well enough to go swimming in mid June when the
Huxleys were on the coast at Forte dei Marmi, but then, at the Mirenda
early in July 1927, he suffered the first of a frightening series of
haemorrhages. Frieda recalled:

One hot afternoon Lawrence had gathered peaches in the garden and came in with a basket full of wonderful fruit – he showed them to me – a very little while after he called from his room in a strange, gurgling voice; I ran and found him lying on his bed; he looked at me with shocked eyes while a slow stream of blood came from his mouth. 'Be quiet, be still,' I said. I held his head, but slowly and terribly the blood flowed from his mouth. I could do nothing but hold him and try to make him still and calm and send for Doctor Giglioli. He came, and anxious days and nights followed.[37]

The Pini family helped in every possible way: Giulia went down to Scandicci at four in the morning and brought ice in sawdust in a big handkerchief. The doctor came every day; a Florentine bookseller, Guiseppe ('Pino') Orioli, with whom they had made friends, also visited. The Wilkinsons did what they could when they came back; as Lawrence convalesced, Lily did some typing for him, and they shopped and cooked for Frieda. The Huxleys also came, and spent time with the patient. On the 18th, he haemorrhaged again, while out walking, and this time the doctor impressed on him how he had to 'stay in bed & rest, & this time he really seems to have made up his mind to do so'. The heat of July made everything more difficult; he badly wanted to get into another climate, but was too delicate to travel. It was on Frieda that the bulk of the nursing fell, and she wrote in her book on Lawrence how she 'nursed him alone night and day for six weeks'. That was doubtless how it felt, but she told a horrified friend in 1930 that when 'the crisis had passed . . . she allowed him to get up and make her coffee in the early morning' – 'Oh Frieda, how could you?' – which sounds very like her: but very like Lawrence, too.[38] The Wilkinsons were wonderfully helpful during the whole period, but relieved when, just four weeks after Lawrence's first attack, he and Frieda caught the night train from Florence to go and stay with Frieda's sister Johanna at Villach in Austria. Their departure was 'a load off our minds', commented Arthur. Lawrence found Austria a marvellous relief: 'I feel a different creature here in the cool.' 'It is such a mercy to be able to breathe and move.'[39]

In the immediate aftermath of the attack, as the Wilkinsons observed, he had been 'so good & patient that one hardly knows him'; both they and the Huxleys made a point of how 'touchingly gentle' he had been: 'so gentle & that's so unlike him'.[40] His usual rage and fierceness were things he actively encouraged in himself, however, to escape from his 'complaining melancholy', and he went on doing that: at the end of July, Huxley summed him up as 'passionate, queer, violent' and thought he 'preferred to be angry'.[41] His anger was a way of living with inadmissible knowledge; Huxley would judge that the 'secret consciousness of his dissolution filled the last years of his life with an overpowering sadness . . . It was, however, in terms of anger that he chose to express this sadness.' On 29 July, his first day 'up for tea and looking better' after his relapse, Lawrence 'had a great talk about where he would like to live . . . in England', which culminated in his 'finally turning round & bursting out into a frenzy against England & the English'.[42] He was starting to ascribe his illness to what he called 'chagrin': 'My illnesses I know come from chagrin – chagrin that goes deep in and comes out afterwards *in hemorrhage* or what not.'[43] He had always preferred psychological explanations of illness to physical; he now made his illness inherent and therefore untreatable. Anger was a good way of coping with that, too.

He was again doing almost no writing, just some translations of Verga, which seem to have been his stand-by when he did not feel up to his own work; as late as 25 August he told Mabel he still felt 'only about a third' of him had come back.[44] After Austria, he and Frieda went on to their long-planned return to Bavaria, to stay in Else's (once Edgar Jaffe's) little wooden house in Irschenhausen, where Lawrence had written 'The Prussian Officer' in 1913, and where Anna, the servant he had recreated in 'The Thorn in the Flesh' with her distinctive flower-sprigged dress, still worked. This was a real journey back into the past, 'with forest behind, looking across a wide valley at the blue mountains'. 'I like it very much – there is no time, and no event – only the sun shines with that pleasant hotness of autumn, and in the shadow it is chill.' He sent the Wilkinsons a letter full of vivid detail, of just the kind they would love: 'The jays are so cheeky they almost steal the tears out of your eyes.' Again, he did very little writing apart from his translations and letters: 'I am glad when I don't work – I have worked too much.'[45] They had a good, quiet, social life, being visited by old friends, including their 1912 Icking landlady. Lawrence felt better too, 'swallowing malt and beer and milk and chalk, for my fatal tubes', and even allowing himself to be examined by the poet-doctor Hans Carossa – 'a nice man, mild as mashed potatoes' – who specialized in tuberculosis. Lawrence told Frieda's sister Else that Carossa 'could hear nothing in the lungs, says that must be healed – only the bronchials'. Lawrence was reassuring Else as well as maintaining his own fiction, but a friend asked Carossa what he really believed: 'He hesitated a moment before he said, "An average man with those lungs would have died long ago. But with a real artist no normal prognosis is ever sure. There are other forces involved. Maybe Lawrence can live two or even three years more. But no medical treatment can really save him." '[46]

23

Lady Chatterley's Lover: 1927–1928

Because he felt so well, Lawrence would have liked to stay in Bavaria in September 1927, but Frieda very much wanted to get back to Italy. And so, via Baden-Baden, they went, with Lawrence acknowledging illness to the extent of doing an inhalation cure in passing: 'sit in a white mantle and hood in a cloud of vapour, with other ghostly figures, for an hour every morning!' But he refused to take the advice of his doctor to go into a sanatorium. The reason was simple. 'Look at poor G[ertie] and sanatoriums. I'm sure the thought of her simply breaks my heart: a year now.' He offered a self-diagnosis: 'since, with me, it's nearly all a question of spirits; and since doctors and sanatoriums only depress me; and I'm just beginning to get back a bit of my *real* self, and my appetite, why should I stick myself in a German sanatorium?'[1] He was suffering from a fatal disease for which absolute rest was the only known treatment. If he could keep up his spirits, then he might indeed delay the illness; but spontaneous remission was his only real chance. He was not, however, living the kind of quiet life likely to induce it.

He felt very differently about the Mirenda when he got back: 'I've sort of lost my attachment to the place.' The Wilkinsons saw how ill he still was, and how 'he refused to be pleased or glad – said it was all like a dream & Italy had no life in it'. The bareness and loneliness were now things he reacted against: 'how can I sit in this empty place and see nobody and do nothing!' But he was also feeling poor – 'have not much money to go anywhere with'[2] – and fragile; it would be a month before he even ventured into Florence. Accordingly, rather unwillingly he set to work on various projects: a new volume of short stories, and a new collection of all his poems, which Secker had asked for, which meant typing them out and arranging them; and he also started painting again.[3] It was at this low point, however, that he wrote something quite new, in response to his friend Koteliansky's attempt to launch a series of little books containing the 'intimate' revelations of various well-known authors. What might have been an essay in the caustic 'Return to Bestwood' vein became a complex fantasy of what a new society might be like: not this time located in Mexico or Etruria, but in Eastwood. While working on it, Lawrence remarked in a letter that he felt like living 'somewhere nearer home. Time to go home, I feel.' The narrator of the piece falls asleep for a thousand years, and comes back to find Eastwood/Newthorpe reborn as Nethrupp, the mining community replaced by an agricultural community similar to the Etruscan communities Lawrence had been re-imagining, and ex-periencing something like the life of the harvest around the Mirenda: the climate is warm and people can go naked. The time-travelling narrator finds himself suffering 'a curious, sad sort of envy' of those he meets: 'It made me feel like a green apple, as if they had had all the real sun.'[4] For a moment, it is vividly clear how such a descrip-tion of unselfconscious behaviour was not an account (like a diary) of Lawrence's own experience, but a fictional creation of what he desperately wanted.

He never finished the piece, partly because Kot's scheme never got off the ground, but partly because, like 'The Flying Fish', this 'intimate' revelation was turning into a kind of fiction in which he could not quite believe: 'a real life in this Garden of Eden'.[5] However, in Florence he was about to embark on a publishing scheme that would flourish. He had recently been reconciled with Norman Douglas; Orioli had ensured a meeting and, after a 'moment of embarrassed silence', Douglas had offered Lawrence his snuff box:

'Have a pinch of snuff, dearie.'

Lawrence took it.

'Isn't it curious' – sniff – 'only Norman and my father' – sniff – 'ever gave me snuff?'[6]

With Orioli's help, Douglas had begun to publish his books privately, and Lawrence realized that he too could publish *Lady Chatterley's Lover*, by having it printed in Florence and distributing it himself.

It was financially rather risky, but the idea appealed to him enormously. It would be the perfect enterprise for an outsider like himself and it would cut out the middlemen. After a chance meeting, around the same time, with the successful popular novelist Michael Arlen (the transformed Dikran Kouyoumdjian), he noted: 'Definitely I hate the whole money-making world, Tom & Dick as well as en gros. But I won't be done by them either.' He set himself to make '£600 or £700'. 'It is not cheap, being ill and doing cures.'[7]

But Lawrence then did something strange. He rewrote the novel. This was a remarkable feat in itself, for someone who had been as ill and depressed as he had been; only a week earlier he had told Huxley how he was 'in a state of despair about the Word either written or spoken seriously'.[8] Why did he not simply publish the extant second version, well over 140,000 words long?

Lawrence drew on it when writing the new version, but he needed to reconceive the novel all the way through because he wished it to end differently: he wanted a book in which Constance could plan a future with a working-class gamekeeper husband. Parkin is remade as Mellors: no longer a man with Parkin's awful family, no longer someone about whom people exclaim 'what a man to be mixed up with'.[9] Mellors is also frailer than his predecessor and suffers from a persistent cough. He is born into the working class, becomes an officer during the war, but chooses to go back to the working class; he can, when he wishes, 'talk proper'; he reads widely and discusses the world intelligently; and when he stops working as a gamekeeper, does not (like Parkin) get a job as a labourer in a steelworks but is employed on a farm. One of the major problems of the novel – how could such a cross-class relationship be more than an affair? – was thus removed; but the book's realism was also undermined. It was now becoming a genuine romance.

Lawrence worked with an astonishing burst of energy, the equivalent of anything he had done previously. He wrote between 2,000 and 4,000 words a day between late November 1927 and early January 1928, and transformed a novel which had been about sexual desire and class barriers into one in which a gamekeeper can become Lady Constance Chatterley's future partner, as they plan a world of their own, cut off from the awfulness of the rest of England. The sexual explicitness remained, was indeed slightly expanded, but the novel also acquired a new, simpler, hard-hitting quality that went with its new, slimmed-down shape. It was some 20,000 words shorter than its predecessor (unique in Lawrence's revisions) and had a new task: asserting its defiance of the conventions. Having discovered a way of getting it into his readers' hands, Lawrence could insist: 'It's a bit of a revolution in itself – a bit of a bomb.' Like his paintings, the novel aimed to wage a kind of artistic terrorism.[10] Clifford becomes an even less sympathetic character: he is treated with the kind of savage irony and malice which Lawrence had previously reserved for characters like Rico in *St. Mawr* and the Reverend Mr Saywell in *The Virgin and the Gipsy*. And the novel acquired an exemplary tone: this is how to live and to love, it says; it becomes a kind of testament. Frieda observed this with her usual shrewdness: '*The First Lady Chatterley* he wrote as she came out of . . . his own immediate self. In the third version he was also aware of his contemporaries' minds.'[11] It ends not with one of Lawrence's debating and debatable endings, but with an angry voice, solitary yet confident: Mellors speaking out about what is wrong with the world. Lawrence's only comment (in May 1928) on how he might revise the novel for a possible second edition was that he might rewrite or lengthen that final monologue.[12]

In versions one and two, Lawrence had made a direct attack on the idea of the isolated individual which he had first begun to critique in 'The Man Who Loved Islands'. In the first version of the *Lady Chatterley* novel, Constance reflects on the problem of whether it wouldn't be better to be 'free', because marriage must be some kind of prison: 'No, not a prison! . . . If one wanted to be so tremendously free, one must evaporate into nothingness. That hard little freedom of a separate, completely separated individual, that was worse than a prison. It was just a nail through one's heart.'[13] Such a development ran in parallel with a correspondence Lawrence had in the summer of 1927, between writing the second and the third versions of the novel, with the American psychoanalyst Trigant Burrow, who made Lawrence reconsider his relationships with other people and with society. Lawrence concluded that

What ails me is the absolute frustration of my primeval societal instinct. The hero illusion starts with the individualist illusion, and all resistances ensue. I think societal instinct much deeper than sex instinct – and societal repression much more devastating. There is no repression of the sexual individual comparable to the repression of the societal man in me, by the individual ego, my own and everybody elses.[14]

The third version of the novel is, however, in a state of acute anxiety over this idea. Like Birkin in *Women in Love*, both Mellors and Constance hate and fear society; and the novel's version of society makes it indeed something to be feared. Their future looks as if it will consist of them together, on a farm, with no connection of any kind to the rest of the world. Societal man (and woman) will be almost completely repressed. Mellors's final letter in the novel is mostly about society, but only to say that it is all wrong, needs to change, won't change, and so must be avoided. Lonely individuality *à deux* is, once again, the future. But there is no figure in the novel like Ursula in *Women in Love* to say, 'You see, my love ... while we are only people, we've got to take the world that's given – because there isn't any other'; there is no ominous sense, as in 'The Man Who Loved Islands', of what happens to the perfect worlds which people construct for themselves, so as to escape society. Instead, the other voice of Ursula dominates: 'You've got me ... Why should you *need* others?'[15] This is what makes *Lady Chatterley's Lover* a romance: it becomes the story of a couple whose love survives and surmounts every obstacle, and who can be happy ever after because separate and alone.

This is especially odd because Lawrence had reviewed Burrow's book *The Social Basis of Consciousness* in August 1927 and had declared: 'it is most in sympathy with me of any book I've read for a long time.' In these years, Lawrence became aware as never before of the split in him between a belief in lonely individuality, modified only by partnership, and a profound nostalgia for the communal. He would never be very happy with other people; he knew that. 'I don't see how one can even begin to be honest with other people. And as I hate lying, I keep to myself as much as possible.'[16] That was a handy intellectual justification. But the alienation he had felt in the Midlands in 1925 was caused in part by his failure to find any link with the place or with his family or the past; his pleasure there in 1926 had been because he had found a seaside resort where he felt well, and which offered him the milieu that he wanted: 'I really rather like being back in my native Midlands ... the people are common, but alive.'[17] The fact that in 1927 he responded so powerfully to Burrow confirms that he knew the detachment at the centre of his experience was wrong. It was perhaps not a coincidence that, in the late summer of 1927, he began for the first time to engage with the general reading public, by accepting an invitation to write articles for a popular London newspaper, the *Evening News*. The Lawrence of the war years would not have done any such thing as write chattily for the newspapers (if indeed anyone had asked him), not even for an income of which he was desperately in need. On the other hand, *Lady Chatterley's Lover* shows his fiction returning to the familiar proclamation of loneliness and a thorough-going, polemical rejection of society.

Throughout the winter of 1927 and the early spring of 1928, Lawrence would continue to be as busy and energetic as he could; as ever, it was one of his ways of dealing with feeling miserable. In spite of his initial insistence that he wanted no repetition of the previous year's festivities with the local peasants – 'there's such a host of them now, it wears one out' – they had a tree after all, once again stolen by Pietro, and the peasants came in on Christmas Eve, though this time only seventeen of them. The children had toys, the men had 'toscani – cheroots' and the women had sweet wine. They also 'sang to us, and were happy'.[18] In spite of Lawrence's own impatience about living there, the Mirenda offered both Lawrences a better solution than most of their recent homes to the old problem of how and where to live. It was isolated; but it had neighbours they were fond of, a community around it, and was within an hour of a major city. Frieda's old desire to cherish and keep her extraordinary husband to herself, often in places far removed from the world, was now in conflict with her desire to have a less boring and more varied life than was offered by days alone with a sick man. A letter she wrote to her mother just after Christmas 1927 gives an insight into her impatience with his illness, as she recounts in desperate detail an ordinary day. Dr Giglioli in Florence, like the doctor in Baden-Baden, had been consulted about the idea of Lawrence going into a sanatorium, but had responded, according to Frieda,

that Lawrence cannot do better than stay here, nowhere is perfect; he lives here better than in a sanatorium. Normally his day goes like this: I make a cup of tea on the spirit stove beside the bed at about half past seven, then Giulia comes and makes breakfast. If L feels well and if it's a nice day he gets up, otherwise he has his breakfast in bed – then he writes or reads, is given milk with extract of malt, and then at 12 the post comes, then we eat at quarter past twelve or half-past – then we go for a walk, and have tea; we light a fire only at tea-time, we have only had 3 cold days but now it's raining, very necessary! Then I sometimes go to Florence, sometimes with Giulia, and eat with Orioli or somebody else – At times Lawr seems to me to be so weak. Yesterday the Huxleys were there for lunch, when they left he just fell asleep, absolutely tired out!! He cannot stand making the slightest effort, but eats well and sleeps and works . . . I go on hoping that, if Lawr gets a little better, he'll go briefly to Capri, and I'll come to you . . .[19]

That account of the life of an invalid must be set against the fact that Lawrence was simultaneously rewriting *Lady Chatterley's Lover* at the rate of around 3,000 words a day. Huxley made a diary entry about the very visit Frieda describes: 'D. H. L. in admirable form, talking wonderfully.'[20] To the healthy Frieda, Lawrence in these years *was* an invalid, no matter what he did; even though – the same day she wrote her letter – he wrote at least three letters and two postcards, as well as doubtless doing his stint on the novel. But it was also true that he had not recovered from the state in which he had returned to the Mirenda in mid October. He had told Koteliansky on 23 December that 'I do think this is the low-water mark of existence. I never felt so near the brink of the abyss.'[21] The narrow routine of the sick man, and Lawrence's unhappiness and exhaustion, to which the punishing schedule of writing the novel would have contributed, inevitably combined to make Frieda feel trapped.

And as soon as he finished the novel, early in January, he turned back to his poems: work was very necessary to him. Secker wanted to produce a *Collected Poems*, but Lawrence wanted to make extensive revisions, especially to the early ones. Re-reading them was a strange experience: 'My word, what ghosts come rising up! But I just tidy their clothes for them and refuse to be drawn.' He rewrote some on the grounds that, when young, he had been muffling the voice of his 'demon';[22] but he was re-inventing his younger self so that it appeared as outspoken, detached and determined as he was now. A very successful dialect poem he had written in 1911, for example, 'Whether or Not', had as its central character a young woman coping with the fact that her young policeman fiancé has had an affair with a much older, local woman; at the end of the poem, she forgives him. In 1928, Lawrence rewrote the poem so that the young man rejects both the older woman *and* the fiancée: 'As for marryin', I shanna marry / Neither on yer.' The young man is unrepentant about the affair, and blames his fiancée for it. She has refused to sleep with him: 'Yer too much i' th' right for me.' But he dismisses the older woman too: 'What bit o' cunt I had wi' 'er / 's all I got out of it.'[23] Secker failed to notice the word 'cunt', deep into a lengthy poem; but in such ways, the author of *Lady Chatterley's Lover* imposed himself upon his old text. It represented what Lawrence felt he *should* have written as a young man, but it is not what he ever *could* have written.

His main concern, however, was to look after the publication of *Lady Chatterley's Lover*. Typing began in January, though one typist cried off because of the book's explicitness: part of the manuscript had to be sent to London, and Lawrence did not have a complete typescript until the end of February. Maria Huxley lent a hand with the typing while the Huxleys were spending time at Les Diablerets in Switzerland, between January and March 1928; the Lawrences had gone to join them. Lawrence commemorated Maria's work on the novel in his poem 'To Clarinda'. She was a terrible typist, and the poem conveys something of the sheer fun they all had in Les Diablerets.

> And you cried: 'Ooray! Play up John Thomas!
> Let's have no full stops, let's just manage with commas! –
>
> And the white snow glistened, the white world was gay
> up there at that height in the Diablerets.
> And we slid, and you ski'd, and we came in to tea
> and we talked and we roared and you typed Lady C.[24]

He had been fantasizing about going back to the ranch in New Mexico – 'sometimes I pine for it' – and perhaps for that reason enjoyed being at a high altitude. The place was 'very high, very sparkling and bright and sort of marvellous ... it sort of puts life into one'.[25] Lawrence learned from Huxley's range of reading and knowledge, even if he also defied Huxley's scientific rationalism; he would describe 'outlandish events in Mexico, trying to frighten Aldous off his four-square rationalist perch'. For Huxley, Lawrence was, as he had been in 1915, a revelation of a mind and personality utterly different from his own. Maria – exquisite, fine, sensitive – had grown extremely fond of Lawrence, as he was of her. As he put it, 'We don't fit very well outside – but the inside corresponds, which is most important.'[26] The Huxleys gave Lawrence a good deal of what he needed at this point: love and admiration, support and advice, especially as they were not just a couple, but a family which included a sister, a brother, and several children. Julian Huxley and his wife, Juliette, were also at Les Diablerets; Juliette noticed Lawrence's 'very special way of laughing, tilting his head and pointing his small red beard at one, his bright blue eyes twinkling'. She remembered both the 'radiating creativeness' of his presence and the 'delicious lemon-curd on crisp little pasties' which he baked there, but – angered by *Lady Chatterley's Lover* – she told him he ought to call it *John Thomas and Lady Jane*. 'Many a true word spoken in spite,' commented Lawrence, and promptly did so.[27] Once again, it was Frieda who, feeling that the group was overmuch in awe of her husband, and his attention too much directed away from her, tended to quarrel with the others. Aldous in particular would get irritated: 'being with her makes me believe that Buddha was right when he numbered stupidity among the deadly sins.' Only after Lawrence's death did he and Maria really come to appreciate her. The time at Les Diablerets ended with Frieda going to visit her mother, but Juliette suspected that she was really seeing Ravagli, on one of her 'periodical prowls'.[28]

Back in Florence after Les Diablerets, at the start of March, with the complete typescript of the novel at last ready, Lawrence now had to find a printer, and a binder: and there were publicity leaflets to print and distribute. 'D. H. Lawrence / Will publish in unexpurgated form his new novel / LADY CHATTERLEY'S LOVER / OR / JOHN

THOMAS and LADY JANE / limited edition of 1000 copies, numbered and signed / at £2.0.0. net (of which 500 copies for America / at $10 net). / Ready May 15th 1928.' Orioli recommended a printer; and Lawrence thought he had better tell the man, who had no English, exactly what it was he was handling. The printer responded, indifferently: 'O! ma! but we do it every day!'[29] The Tipografia Giuntina was a small printing shop; they had only enough type to set up half the book at a time. The first half was printed, proof-read, and sheets for 1,200 copies printed, 200 more being kept in reserve. The type was then distributed, and the second half printed. Even for a private press book, it turned out large and remarkably heavy.[30] Lawrence chose the paper for the text – there were delays in getting hold of enough of it – and also the mulberry-coloured paper for the binding; he signed and numbered the copies. He even drew the phoenix printed on the cover, and thus liberated a symbol which has been associated with him ever since; in 1929, he would write a poem about it, and about the loss of self involved in radical change.[31]

Orioli was helpful to the book project in innumerable ways; Lawrence and Frieda both spent a lot of time in Florence with him. We can picture them on the Ponte Santa Trinita one warm spring morning, Orioli dandyish in bicoloured shoes, pale trousers and dark jacket, carrying a cane, both the Lawrences dressed up for a day in town: Frieda in open shoes, a smart silk dress and a pearl necklace, Lawrence in stylish suit and hat and breast-pocket handkerchief (no turned suits any more). This, at least, is what Illustration 34 shows.[32]

Advance orders for the book started to arrive and it became clear that Lawrence was at least going to cover his costs. He started to feel proud of what he had accomplished. He had written a book, designed it, had it printed and bound, and was now successfully by-passing all the usual procedures of publication. The content was also something absolutely new: 'the full natural *rapprochement* of a man and a woman; and the re-entry into life of a bit of the old phallic awareness and the old phallic insouciance'. That was what he told Ottoline Morrell, to whom he had written on hearing that she had been ill: a cheering letter, but one also full of regrets.

If only one could have two lives: the first, in which to make one's mistakes, which seem as if they *had* to be made; and the second in which to profit by them. If it could only be so, what a lovely Garsington we could all have, and no bitterness at the end of it! ... I wish, and wish deeply, there could be Ottoline again and Garsington again, and we could start afresh.[33]

From a person who so rarely excused himself, this was the nearest Lawrence was likely to get to making an apology.

Starting afresh was a haunting idea; the book was, after all, a reminiscence of the time when sexual desire had impelled him and had changed his life. He was all the characters. As the person once condemned to repeating the past, and rescued by a liberating relationship with an older, sexually experienced partner who tranformed everything, he knew Constance's situation very well; but he was also Mellors, the working-class man who had moved into the middle class but who felt at home nowhere, now putting behind him a marriage with a sexually rapacious woman. And he was Clifford the writer, the husband now no longer feeling desire, prepared for his wife to have an affair with another man so long as she remained *his* partner. In such ways the final version of the novel got very close to Lawrence; its 'phallic reality' so haunting, its anger and regret so palpable. It was also a book which, he knew, 'will in a way set me apart even more definitely than I am already set apart. It's destiny.' It was not destiny, however: it was his choice. He was enormously pleased with the book; but he could not have produced anything more likely to arouse righteous anger against him, or to fortify his sense of being an outsider. In August 1928, he would comment gleefully: 'Amusing how people disliked *Lady* C. I'm afraid I've lost 9/10 of my few remaining friends.'[34] Another result of his success in getting such a text into print was that he was now prepared to experiment with other private press publications. When the rich American Harry Crosby, living in Paris, asked Lawrence to sell him the original manuscript of the story 'Sun', and it turned out that Curtis Brown could not lay their hands on it, Lawrence wrote out for Crosby a new, longer version, with a sexually explicit ending; and this would be published by Crosby's Black Sun Press in Paris, in October 1928.

Back in April, Frieda had been able to make a trip to see Ravagli, while escorting her sister Else to visit Barby in Alassio. She had again felt rather desperate when Lawrence decided to leave Italy and give up the Mirenda at the end of April 1928: 'we began to pack: but Frieda became so gloomy, that I hung the pictures up again and paid six months' rent.'[35] She was fond of the place, they had domestic help, and she had an appreciative Florence circle; and leaving northern Italy would also have cut her off from Ravagli. The Alassio trip seems, however, to have marked some kind of a turning point in her relationship with him. When she came back, Lawrence commented to Maria Huxley: 'Frieda has changed since she went away with Barby.'[36] A letter from Frieda to her mother dating from the end of April or the start of May 1928 suggests how she had changed. She was now admitting that Lawrence's health was preventing her from living her own life, in which Ravagli had become central. Her letter throws a very different light upon the picture of busy domesticity at the Mirenda portrayed in her biography or in Lawrence's letters. The latter show a man working hard to organize printer, binder and paper-supplier, and trying to interest friends in the book; he seems overflowing with energy and spirits. But, writing in confidence to her mother, Frieda reveals just how trapped by his illness she felt, and what she intended to do about it.

But you know very well, just as I want to travel, L. gets ill . . . I'm well otherwise, but with every bit of inward strength I make myself slowly freer, I can't bear always just living this illness – and always *just* sacrificing myself – that's not what I understand by life . . . we're keeping the Mirenda for another six months, then we'll see – should a letter come to you from Gradisca (I told him to if there were anything special) send it to *Orioli*, then I'll say *you're* writing to me *privately* about L's illness . . .[37]

Her mother was helping Frieda keep in touch with Ravagli, now stationed at a military base at Gradisca, northwest of Trieste. Frieda was apparently held up on her journey to rejoin Lawrence from Baden-Baden in June 1928, when Lawrence met train after train, but she arrived twenty-four hours late;[38] such occurrences suggest that she was continuing to see Ravagli when and where she could. But that was the price Lawrence now had to pay. Her daughter Barby later commented about her mother: 'She was rather infatuated and foolish about Ravagli, but it's important to remember that she'd been under immense strain with Lawrence by then, so long with this virtually dying man who clung to her and was so irritable and difficult.'[39] That was certainly how Frieda saw it.

It has been pointed out how our 'concern with history . . . is a concern with pre-formed images already imprinted on our brains, images at which we keep staring while the truth lies elsewhere, away from it all, somewhere as yet undiscovered'.[40] Because Frieda lived with Lawrence until his death in 1930 and only then had an affair with Murry, only went to America with Angelo Ravagli in 1931, in 1934 published an extremely moving book about her life with Lawrence, and until her death in 1956 continued to write about him and speak up for him, the image imprinted on our collective consciousness is that she was wonderfully faithful to Lawrence to the end. Yet by 1928 she was growing very tired of his illness. She felt trapped; she wanted more freedom; and she seems to have determined on maintaining a relationship with Ravagli while remaining married to Lawrence. She had, after all, tried for a similar kind of marriage in 1912, when she had attempted to be like her sisters, remaining married but enjoying her freedom and her lover. In 1912, she lost her husband and children, while acquiring another husband. In the autumn of 1923, she made her first serious attempt to live her own life while staying married. It looks as if, in 1928, she finally achieved her ambition.

24

Searching: 1928–1929

Robert Hobart Davis[1] photographed Lawrence twice in Orioli's shop in May 1928; his small camera, with a portrait lens, allowed him to take pictures in natural light, though with an exposure of six or seven seconds. In the first picture, Lawrence's smile is frozen by being held: the face appears fine, narrowed, pale, ascetic, the beard silky. Davis arranged Lawrence for a second portrait, telling him, 'You looked bored.' Lawrence 'smiled and wet his lips' and asked how he could avoid that. 'By fixing your gaze on some object outside. Select a spot on the opposite bank of the river and show some concern in it. Project your mind and the eye will record interest. Anyhow, that's my theory about portrait photography.'[2] A few seconds later, another photograph was taken, and it shows a very different Lawrence: a Socratic nose, a pugnacity of outlook and intent, a rough beard. Lawrence thought the pictures 'not bad'. But Frieda exclaimed: 'These are you. They are wonderful. Nothing could be more natural. Just as you are, without artifice.'[3] The photographer's art ensured that the photographs (Illustrations 35 and 36) show opposing, equally characteristic things.

The writing and then the publishing of *Lady Chatterley's Lover* had been a great adventure: Lawrence's practical side working in tandem with his idealism. However, although he had not wanted to leave Florence until the book was out, it was delayed; the specially ordered hand-made paper had been late arriving. The book was still at the printers on the advertised publication date of 15 May. Lawrence stayed on until early June, but then felt he had to escape the summer heat of Florence for his health's sake. It was not until 28 June that he had a copy in his hands: Orioli was left to deal with receiving the subscriptions and posting the copies.

For the summer, Lawrence's only plan was to go somewhere reasonably cheap, cool and at altitude. He chose Switzerland: 'I don't particularly *want* to be in Switzerland. But the doctors say this is where I ought to be – so we'll try it. – I really want to try to get rid of this beastly cough – it's no worse – and no danger in it – but it is such a nuisance.' That, at least, was what he wrote to his sister Emily, as reassuringly as possible. There were problems, none the less. One hotel turned him out 'because I coughed. They said they didn't have anybody who coughed. I felt very mad.'[4] However, he felt rather better after three weeks with the Brewsters in the Grand Hotel in Chexbres-sur-Vevey, on the north side of Lake Geneva.

While in Switzerland waiting for *Lady Chatterley's Lover* to arrive, Lawrence, in a most unusual way for him, wrote a second part to his previously finished and published story 'The Escaped Cock', to make it a fitting partner to the enterprise of the novel. The man who had died is now not only a man who has abandoned his old mission – *Salvator Mundi*, attracting disciples and changing people – but one who finds a relationship with a woman too. Christ is the Egyptian god Osiris, restored, made whole, revivified, resurrected to life and sexual desire. 'I think it's lovely,' Lawrence remarked. 'I don't want to let it go out of my hands.' It was, he said, one of his 'thin-skinned' stories,[5] meaning that it said more about *him* and his feelings than some of his other work. The writer of fiction could still fully imagine and create a situation that the man could no longer inhabit; the Christ figure, coming back to full bodily life with a woman, realizes and experiences what Lawrence had once experienced. The story in effect reversed his own narrative, as it moved from the state of a man nearly dead and desire-less to one rediscovering vitality and desire. Thin-skinned indeed.

Real life was more mundane. In June 1928, Lawrence characterized himself to an American acquaintance threatening a visit: 'Here I am, forty-two, with rather bad health: and a wife who is by no means the soul of patience . . . a stray individual with not much health and not much money.' What above all he lacked, he had come to feel, was a life with 'a milieu of its own, and a rhythm and a ritual of its own'.

The word 'stray' articulates that lack. Such needs had lain behind the fiction of Rananim, and had surfaced again when he had asked for the support of his friends at the Café Royal. His continuing lack of such a milieu, back in Europe, was now not likely to change, for all his circles of acquaintance and their pleasure in his company. The only thing that really changed for the better during these years was the money. His formal English and American publication was down to a trickle: his only mainstream publications since *The Plumed Serpent* had been *Mornings in Mexico* in 1927 and *The Woman Who Rode Away* in 1928, not enough to make his living. But it quickly turned out that *Lady Chatterley's Lover* was going to be a success; it would earn him more than he had ever made in his life. In the end, it probably earned more than all his other books combined. He invested the money it earned him in stocks and shares he bought in New York; by October 1929, he held shares to a total value of over $6,000. Not bad for that 'stray individual with . . . not much money'.[6]

It also quickly made him a household name, if a notorious one, and he found that popular newspapers were now keen on commissioning topical articles from him; he contributed to the *Sunday Dispatch*, the *Daily Express* and the *Daily Chronicle*. He enjoyed doing these pieces, finding that he could sometimes write them in a single morning, and earn more from them than a long and serious story would ever have brought in. The *Sunday Dispatch*, for example, paid him '£25. for a 2000 word article, written in an hour and a half': that was the essay 'Sex Locked out'.[7] It was in Chexbres that a piece he wrote for the *Evening News*, 'Over-Earnest Ladies', first printed on 12 July, beautifully created the hot, still afternoon and two men mowing the grass below the hotel: 'the uncanny glassiness of the lake this afternoon, the sulkiness of the mountains, the vividness of near green in thunder-sun, the young man in bright blue trousers lightly tossing the grass from the scythe, the elderly man in a boater stiffly shoving his scythe-strokes, both of them sweating in the silence of the intense light'.

By the time the piece was published, a very natural attempt to recover the happiness of Les Diablerets in February had led him and Frieda to go on by train to the village of Gstaad, only a few miles further up the valley of the Reuschbach, and by road thence to Gsteig; and here they had found and rented the Chalet Kesselmatte for the summer.[8] Frieda found it 'very plain and simple and terribly clean', with 'lovely saucepans in the kitchen'; they had 'a very shy little wild calf of a Lina' as a maid, who brought them wild strawberries and 'Alpenrosen'. The chalet was at over 4,000 ft: 'the upper world – rather lovely – has a bit of the Greater Day atmosphere.'[9] That was what he told the Brewsters, to whom he must by now have read 'The Flying Fish', probably at Chexbres; they would follow the Lawrences to Gsteig, and stay in a nearby hotel. Lawrence, however, found himself marooned: confined to the chalet and the area immediately around it. The extreme steepness of the hills made walking imposs- ible: 'its all up and down, and I simply gasp going uphill.' His friends found even 'trudging up' to the chalet the mile from Gsteig an effort. For the first fortnight he was 'weaker and more upset' than at the Mirenda.[10]

He nevertheless spent nine weeks at Kesselmatte, in the belief that it would do him good; in spite of which Achsah Brewster once found him in bed there after a slight haemorrhage. Lawrence was painting quite a lot; Brewster would often join him, they would work together, and he was now thinking of exhibiting his paintings. But he was also writing essays, reviews, a short story ('The Blue Moccasins'), and doing his best via Orioli and various friends in London and America to ensure that copies of Lady Chatterley's Lover were safely distrib- uted, in spite of action against the book by bookshops, the police and the customs on both sides of the Atlantic. No official ban could be imposed, for the book had not been published in England (nor would it be until 1960); and very few reviews appeared. But word of mouth advertised it. One bookshop (William Jackson Ltd) in London decided, when they saw the copies they had ordered, that they wanted them off the premises. Lawrence was enraged but had to act fast; he needed friends in London who could collect the seventy copies and hide them. This turned out to be a blessing in disguise, in fact; for on both sides of the Atlantic the book was quickly added to the list of pornographic publications that would naturally be seized by customs authorities, the postal services and the police, if they came across it. As orders were subsequently received in Florence, copies of the book could be posted in England to those who had placed the orders, without arousing suspicion. Other bookshops took the same decision; Koteliansky, Richard Aldington and Enid Hilton all helped in collecting, secreting and redistributing the copies. All this needed an extensive correspondence, and although Orioli was posting copies from Florence, dealing with many of the letters, and earning himself 10 per cent of the profits for so doing, Lawrence wrote numerous business letters over the months the distribution lasted. He tried, for example, to make the William Jackson bookshop compensate him for postage from Florence to London, but only provoked a letter from their solicitor: 'dirty dirty swine!'[11] Although the novel was, hugely to his annoyance, widely pirated from the start (it could only have been copyrighted if published in England or America, with copies deposited at the copyright libraries), Lawrence proved able to sell every copy he had; and he was immeasurably helped by the book's success, as his health grew worse. He was enabled to publish other material fairly easily, as well as to work as much or as little as he chose; he could live in hotels as often as he liked, travel where he liked, and afford medical treatment.

At the end of August, following his offer to send them the money for the journey (something else he could now afford to do), his sister Emily and his nineteen-year-old niece Peggy came to stay at Gsteig; the first time they had ever left England, and the first time Lawrence had seen any of his family for a couple of years. The visit seems not to have created any tension between him and Frieda, though he did grumble at feeling 'stuck among several women, alone'.[12] But Emily was not as possessive of her brother as Ada had been; and if ever she tried to be, it was in a way that Lawrence was able to resist. She would call him 'our Bert' but he was confident that 'I am not really "our Bert". Come to that, I never was.' He had once been, for sure; but was so no longer. On the other hand, Lawrence was sadly struck by the gulf, 'always yawning, horribly obvious to me', between him and his sister: 'somehow it depresses me terribly'. A sense of being cut off from the past, from his family, from his old self, haunted him in these years. He became aware how far even Emily and Peggy were 'from my active life . . . I have to hide *Lady C.* like a skeleton in my cupboard.'[13] He would in the end give Emily a copy of the book, but very sensibly counselled her to keep her copy 'uncut', as it would then be more valuable. It would have made it uniquely valuable; but Peggy subsequently cut the pages of her mother's copy and read it one wet Good Friday, which would have pleased Lawrence more.[14]

But the revelation of quite how far he had travelled since his childhood in the Midlands made him angry, too. 'How I *hate* the attitude of ordinary people to life. How I loathe ordinariness! How from my soul I abhor nice simple people, with their eternal price-list.' Emily and Peggy got on his nerves with their talk of 'dear England, with its eternal "expensive" and "not at all dear, you know"'. At such moments, he knew very well why he had left, and how far he had distanced himself from the world of his mother. Yet it wasn't as if he were any happier receiving literary plaudits. Achsah Brewster found him one day 'holding in his hands a long and hectic letter from an admirer. He said emphatically how much he hated what he called literary letters.'[15] What would he now have made of his old letters to Blanche Jennings or Rachel Annand Taylor? Like anyone who has remade himself, he was peculiarly sensitive on the subject of his old self. After staying in Switzerland until mid September, with his cough remaining an 'unspeakable nuisance', he and Frieda and the Brewsters went down to Baden-Baden for ten days, to visit Frieda's mother; and while they were there Frieda tried to persuade him to see a 'famous physician', and even spoke of a nun in a nearby convent who had 'the power of healing with the touch of her hands'. 'I shall not be in. He'll not see me!' was Lawrence's response to the first; 'all he needed was the south and the sun' his answer to the second.[16]

It was in Baden-Baden that the Lawrences finally decided to give up the Villa Mirenda. Although they had enjoyed living there, the Mirenda was now irresistibly linked in Lawrence's mind with his haemorrhages of July 1927. Places he associated with illness (like Oaxaca and Mexico City) he never wanted to go back to, and he was now convinced that the Mirenda 'didn't suit my health'.[17] He had never been really happy there the previous winter; and now the peasant families they had got to know so well were being sent away, the Wilkinson family had left in March, and the place was starting to feel distant from the friends on whom they now particularly depended: the Brewsters and the Huxleys. Frieda returned to the Mirenda to see to the packing up of their belongings; Lawrence waited for her in the port of Le Lavandou, near Toulon. They had been invited for the winter to the island of Port Cros, where Richard Aldington, Arabella Yorke and Brigit Patmore (whom they had known for years: she had played her part as 'Clariss Browning' in *Aaron's Rod*) had taken a house. Aldington was both malicious and discreet when he commented that Frieda's task of giving up the Mirenda was 'a complicated process, since it involved a journey to Trieste'.[18] Frieda had seen rather little of Ravagli since April; Lawrence once more had to sit and wait for her.

La Vigie was a borrowed house at the top of the island of Port Cros: another place with the most marvellous view. But Lawrence's health was a real problem. Aldington, who had not seen him since October 1926, was surprised how much frailer he was. Although Lawrence liked the place, and liked the people there, he was far too ill to take part in their expeditions, 'or indeed to rough it in so remote and exposed a place'. The steepness of the road from the harbour up to La Vigie meant that he was 'perched, as at Kesselmatte', and could not go with the others when they went swimming each afternoon. Aldington remembered how he would listen to Lawrence's 'dreadful hollow cough at night, and wonder what on earth I should do if he got worse'; they agreed that one of them would always stay with him when the rest of the party went off for the day or the afternoon. Frieda had come back from Italy with a cold, which of course Lawrence instantly caught. He also had 'two days hemorrhage' and felt 'rather rotten': 'this is worse than the Mirenda'.[19] When Brigit took his breakfast to him in bed in the mornings, and put a coat round his shoulders, 'I could feel his pyjamas soaked with perspiration.' He would give her one of his newly arrived, very splendidly produced copies of *Sun*, inscribing it 'to Brigit / the angel in the Vigie'.[20]

But things went wrong at La Vigie. Aldington was starting an affair with Brigit Patmore, and the Lawrences sided with Arabella, of whom they were very fond. Lawrence ended up violently angry with Aldington. His poem 'I know a noble Englishman', written immediately afterwards, would insist that 'Ronald . . . never wants a woman, he doesn't like women', because 'he's an instinctive homosexual'.[21] One afternoon when the others were off swimming – they all bathed, Aldington recalled with relish more than thirty years later, '*naked* daily together on one of the plages of Port-Cros, and then lay in the sun' – Lawrence told Brigit a little about his desolation and lack of desire ('you have something in your life which makes up for everything, and then find you haven't got it'). Whether they meant to or not, Frieda, Brigit and Aldington (and in her own way poor Arabella) were making horribly clear to him the continuing importance of sexual desire in their lives. Brigit felt that Lawrence 'was far away in a loneliness where nothing but what he desired could be of use to him'. She tried to tell him that his writing had mattered immensely to her in re-establishing her sense of herself after she had been ill; but found she was only making matters worse. He replied: 'Yes. Once I could do that. But I can't any more.'[22] In the past, he could convey his experience of the body and its desires directly in his writing. He felt that that no longer happened; such writing was now inevitably either nostalgic or reminiscent. A letter from Jessie Chambers's younger brother David came while he was at La Vigie, and received a response, quoted in Chapter 3, of loving, nostalgic reminiscence of the old days: 'whatever else I am, I am somewhere still the same Bert who rushed with such joy to the Haggs.'[23] The farm had been one of the very few places in Lawrence's life where he had felt absolutely at home; and he never forgot it. His response, nevertheless, contained not a mention of Jessie.

He spent a good deal of time in bed, writing; he was doing a new translation from the Italian, of the Renaissance writer Lasca's *The Story of Dr Manente*, for a series of books which he had encouraged Orioli to start. But he was also beginning to write clusters of new little poems which he called 'Pensées', which would become the collection *Pansies*: 'he was intensely happy and proud of the *Pansies*; he would read out the newest ones with delight.'[24] They were an interesting experiment: short-winded, often satirical stabs at things that irritated him; sometimes just thoughts. Written fast, not much revised, they were a resolution of the conflict between a need to conserve his diminishing energy, and a desire to comment on the world and its affairs. They could hardly have been more different from the laboriously crafted early poetry that he had so comprehensively revised for his *Collected Poems* earlier in the year. One he probably wrote around this time suggests one of his moods at La Vigie:

I have no desire any more
towards woman or man, bird, beast or creature or thing.

All day long I feel the tide rocking, rocking
though it strikes no shore
in me.

Only mid-ocean – [25]

That mid-ocean feeling of the undesiring, detached self seems to have been something Lawrence experienced not just in 1928, but more than once with his sexual partners: perhaps with Dorothy Brett a couple of years earlier, probably with Jessie Chambers before that. Now it could be a sharp, sad little poem.

Not surprisingly, the person who suffered most because of Lawrence's unhappiness at La Vigie was Frieda. Brigit remembered 'burning words of accusation flung at Frieda, who had always to bear the worst. We occasionally received a cool flick, but she got it straight from the electric current.' All idea of spending the whole autumn and winter there vanished. The place was too lonely – 'storms, torrents, no boat, no bread' – the situation too dangerous for Lawrence, the disharmony too troubling.[26]

So where should the Lawrences go? At La Vigie, they had talked about Taos, and Lawrence was still fantasizing about going back: 'You think this place is beautiful . . . it's nothing to those [New] Mexican mountains. The light and clarity kill you, but it's worth it. Other things seem so small after you've lived on that plateau. Yes, we'll all go back there.' A month later, at Christmas 1928, he wrote his last essay about it: 'Never shall I forget the Christmas dances at Taos, twilight, snow, the darkness coming over the great wintry mountains and the lonely pueblo, then suddenly, again, like dark calling to dark, the deep Indian cluster-singing around the drum, wild and awful, suddenly rousing on the last dusk as the procession starts.' But he could not go there any more, except in his writing. All the same, 'it seems like losing one's youth and glamour of freedom, to part with Lobo';[27] he could neither bear to give it up, nor to give up the thought of it. The Lawrences simply went from La Vigie by boat to Toulon and from there along the coast for just a couple of weeks, before moving on, perhaps to

Spain. The only question was: where in the south, probably along the Mediterranean coast, should they live?

They ended up at the Hotel Beau-Rivage in Bandol, where Katherine Mansfield had stayed in 1915 before she moved into the Villa Pauline, also in Bandol. It turned out that Bandol was small, warm and attractive, the Beau-Rivage was nice, and its food 'quite good and imaginative . . . especially nice fishes which I like so much'. Lawrence felt more at home there than anywhere for a long time, and wrote to Maria Huxley about it: one of the creations of everyday life that he did incomparably well.

It is incredibly lovely weather, and the place very lovely, swimming with milky gold light at sunset, and white boats half melted on the white twilight sea, and palm trees frizzing their tops in the rosy west, and their thick dark columns down in the dark where we are, with shadowy boys running and calling, and tiny orange lamps under foliage, in the under dusk. Then we come in and have tea in my room looking south where the moon is, and get sticky with the jammy cake.[28]

He was happy to go on working at his *Pansies* and at the newspaper articles that were currently providing him with a decent small income. The Florentine edition of *Lady Chatterley* was now almost disposed of; he was happy to double the price of the remaining copies to £4, though sufficiently embarrassed at doing so to pretend that the decision had been Orioli's. All he had left to sell was the edition of 200 unsigned copies on cheaper paper; he would go on wishing that he had more of them.

And because his health was not any worse in Bandol, they stayed; having expected to spend a fortnight there, they stayed for five months. Lawrence had no major writing project on his hands except for *Pansies* and the still-unfinished Etruscan book, which Secker wanted as his next 'Lawrence book' for the autumn of 1929. One obvious possibility was to go back to Italy to finish it. Yet friends came to Bandol to stay: Rhys Davies, a young Welsh writer whose work Lawrence liked, came twice; P. R. Stephensen, who ran a private press in London and had had the idea of bringing out an edition of Lawrence's paintings (published in June 1929), also came for a couple of days. 'I was glad to see somebody young with a bit of energy and fearlessness,' Lawrence told him. Lawrence's visitors were in turn exhilarated by him as a companion – Davies recalled his 'magical talent for burlesque' – though they were distressed by his frailty and his cough. A 1929 visitor observed how he dealt with his illness: 'he gave the slightest coughs, an apologetic throat sound, and took out an envelope. These he had about everywhere from his ample correspondence, and they were kept to expectorate into. In his jacket pocket he kept them, and they were folded up when used and neatly returned into his pocket again.'[29] Barby Weekley came at New Year, and Aldous and Maria also stayed for a week; Julian and Juliette Huxley passed through early in January and stayed later in the month; while an admirer of Lawrence's from California, Brewster Ghiselin, also came to visit.

Throughout his life, person after person recorded their amazement at Lawrence's talk; his letters are now perhaps the only way of experiencing it. 'I think I have never heard better,' said Richard Aldington. 'It was a great spectacle to see Lawrence building up a "situation," starting from the merest silly gossip and rising, like a sharp-tongued hawk, in sweep after sweep of words to a literary display of the first order.' Aldous Huxley remembered hearing Lawrence 'talking wonderfully': 'Of most other eminent people I have met I feel that at any rate I belong to the same species as they do. But this man has something different and superior in kind, not degree.'[30] The visits from young people in Bandol were particularly pleasing, and were one of the things that made the place so bearable: Lawrence told Davies, 'All you young writers have me to thank for what freedom you enjoy, even as things are.'[31] Even Ada came for ten days in February, without any kind of row or bitterness with Frieda.

However, like Emily, she brought Lawrence 'tortures of angry depression'. Once again, his past came back to haunt him: 'I feel all those Midlands behind her, with their sort of despair.' She made him want to 'put my pansies in the fire, and myself with them'. Back in December, she had asked for a copy of *Lady Chatterley's Lover* and Lawrence had sent her one, with many misgivings; as he feared, she reacted badly, accusing him of having always hidden a side of himself from her.[32] Lawrence felt that she was 'too "pure" and unphysical, unsensual'. On her visit to Bandol, however, Lawrence discovered that she was miserable too, 'and I don't know what to say or do'. She was agonized about the way she had spent her life dedicated to her husband's business; she wanted 'to abandon all the life she's so deliberately built up there in the Midlands, and have a new one – "away from it all" '. Lawrence could only sympathize: 'I hope one day we may all live in touch with one another, away from business and all that sort of world, and really have a *new* sort of happiness together.' In practical terms, such a new life was unimaginable; Lawrence told Maria Huxley that Ada 'wanted – secretly – the moon'.[33] But his feelings for his sister as someone like him, in so many ways, who had *not* managed to break away from the old life, led him now to a tender sympathy with her: a response which showed his frustrated need for 'touch with one another'. One of the *Pansies* written in Bandol had located precisely his kind of loneliness, and again linked it with a lack of sexual desire:

> I cannot help but be alone
> for desire has died in me, silence has grown,
> And nothing now reaches out to draw
> Another's flesh to my own.[34]

But the months went past in Bandol: 'it's sunny here all the time, and quiet and very pleasant: the people are all very nice: why should one hurry away to something worse!' The only real problem was that Frieda wanted a place of her own. Unlike Lawrence, happy either to write or to do nothing, Frieda in a hotel really had nothing to do. Her remark 'we live quietly enough, day by day' attempts to conceal the fact that she got 'most awfully fidgetty'.[35] Her restlessness had acquired a new edge: that of a homeless woman, stranded with a sick husband, and with the man she wanted far away.

So, even in pleasant Bandol, life was not always easy. For Lawrence by far the most annoying thing was the fact that, early in January 1929, a registered package containing his two typed copies of the almost completed *Pansies* collection, sent to his agent in London, was opened by the English postal authorities, officially in consequence of a random search of the mail to check 'whether letters or other matter not conveyed at that rate' were in the packet. The truth was that ever since most of the copies of *Lady Chatterley's Lover* sent to England the previous summer had entered the country before the authorities were alerted, packages from Lawrence had been suspect. The authorities were now rewarded with a sight of the word 'shits' in the quotation from Jonathan Swift in the Introduction. The typescripts were seized and sent to the Home Office, and the Home Secretary, Sir William Joynson Hicks, was advised that 'there is no possible doubt whatever that these contain indecent matter and, as such, are liable to seizure'.[36] Lawrence was enraged by the absurdity of such action, and went on the attack. Although, on the one hand, the money he was earning from *Lady Chatterley's Lover* (he would die worth £2,438 16s 5d)[37] meant that he did not have to bother about bringing out a new book, even if Secker wanted one, the *Pansies* seizure inspired him to keep up his campaign against hypocrisy and censorship: and he was also very fond of these 'real doggerel' poems. The Home Secretary stated in the House of Commons in February that the package containing the *Pansies* materials had been 'sent through the open book post from abroad',[38] which was untrue: it had been registered. Lawrence was given two months to establish that the material in the package was not indecent, but either failed or refused to do so. The typescripts were destroyed.

Another way of keeping up the campaign against censorship would have very practical advantages. Lawrence was already very annoyed that piracy of *Lady Chatterley's Lover* was flourishing: an expert on the subject has concluded that the 'variety and number of unauthorised printings suggests that *Lady Chatterley* may be the most-pirated twentieth-century novel in English'.[39] One American bookseller sent Lawrence a cheque for $180 representing a 10 per cent royalty on the pirated copies he had been selling, apologizing that it was no more than 'a drop in the bucket'. 'He meant, of course,' Lawrence commented, 'a drop out of the bucket. And since, for a drop, it was quite a nice little sum, what a beautiful bucketful there must have been for the pirates!'[40] Letters exchanged with the Huxleys, now living in Suresnes near Paris, convinced Lawrence that Paris would be the place to bring out a cheap edition of the novel, to undercut the pirates. He and Frieda had been thinking of trying Spain as a place to live, and had agreed to go to Mallorca in the spring; but Lawrence decided first to go to Paris, to bring out *Lady Chatterley's Lover* in a paperback edition: 'a little fat book that will go in your pocket'.[41] As well as earning a tidy sum of money, he would thus carry the fight to those who disapproved of him and his book.

25

Somewhere not Ill: 1929

To go to Paris, in the spring of 1929, was for Lawrence an act of righteous anger as well as commercial self-interest: he wanted to get the pirated book back under his control. French laws on censorship, coupled with the city's central location for Britons and Americans, meant that books could be published there in English-language versions which could attract surprisingly large sales. Joyce had published *Ulysses* in Paris in 1922; Radclyffe Hall's banned *The Well of Loneliness* had just been issued there. Publishing an edition of *Lady Chatterley's Lover* in Paris meant that Lawrence was choosing the best outlet in the world for material which would be banned elsewhere; though he was also positioning it squarely in the pornographic book market.

However, what made the whole enterprise not only more attractive but far easier was being able to stay some of the time with the Huxleys; and he travelled there with Rhys Davies, meaning that changing trains and carrying bags was easier, too. Frieda had taken the chance of going to her mother in Baden-Baden while he was away, though it would have been unlike her not to try to fit in a visit to Ravagli too, at some point. Such a visit might help to explain why Lawrence complained about her so 'bitterly'[1] to the Huxleys while he was with them; but he may, too, have been complaining about her usual impatience with illness. Frieda was starting to adopt the role of seeing Lawrence through to what she called 'the bitter end':[2] it would be bitter in more than one way.

Finding a publisher took Lawrence a month. Sylvia Beach (who had published *Ulysses*) turned *Lady Chatterley's Lover* down, and in the end it was an almost unknown publisher, Edward Titus, who accepted it; Lawrence wrote him a 'little peppery foreword' for his edition.[3] Lawrence also saw Harry Crosby, who had brought out the Black Sun

Press edition of *Sun* the previous year, and arranged for him to do the book publication of the full-length *Escaped Cock* too. Now they met, Crosby's admiration for Lawrence diminished: 'He is indirect. I am direct. He admits of defeat. I do not. He is commonplace. I am not. He is unthoroughbred. I am thoroughbred.' Crosby saw, however, 'no excuse for writing *Lady Chatterley's Lover*'; the rich man's opinions were oddly conventional.[4] Davies's memories of Lawrence in Paris were dominated by illness and anger: Lawrence tempted by but eventually furious with a 'pirate' who made him an offer to publish the novel; Lawrence enraged with a cab driver who lost his way; Lawrence agonized by his cough at night and asking Davies to sit beside his bed for a while; Davies's own shock at Lawrence's 'frail, wasted body, so vulnerable looking'.[5]

Away from Frieda, the Huxleys made efforts to get Lawrence X-rayed by 'a first-class specialist in bronchial diseases'; Huxley still believed that the seriousness of his illness would bring him to behave sensibly.[6] They had got him to the doctor, who told Maria afterwards that 'one lung was practically gone and the other affected'. Lawrence knew that he 'must be x-rayed again', but, Davies remembered, 'Half an hour before the time fixed, and ready dressed to go to the specialist, he suddenly refused to leave the hotel. It seemed to me that he believed a submission to medical art was an act of treachery to the power within him, his gods.'[7] The truth, however, seems to have been rather different. Frieda had arrived in Paris. The Huxleys were outraged at the consequences of her return; Huxley wrote to his brother Julian:

L. felt himself reinforced. He refused to go back to the Dr., refused to think of the treatment and set off with Frieda (of whom he had bitterly complained when he was alone with us) to Majorca. So that's that. It's no good. He doesn't *want* to know how ill he is: that, I believe, is the fundamental reason why he won't go to Doctors and homes. He only went in Paris because he was feeling iller than usual and was even more frightened of dying at once than of hearing how ill he was.

The Huxleys told Mark Gertler, who had submitted to sanatorium treatment for tuberculosis, that 'it is mostly Frieda's fault and . . . it really seems almost as if it is she who is slowly killing him'.[8]

*

Blaming Frieda for Lawrence's state of health is unfair. People often observed what a bad nurse she was: her 'bust-up' with Ada in 1926 had been about it, and the Huxleys would be shocked in 1930 by her behaviour when Lawrence was dying.[9] What was actually wrong was far more complex. Lawrence's illness dominated him during the last eighteen months of his life; yet he endeavoured to live as if it didn't. He claimed in 1928 that in spite of 'delicate health' he had a 'strong constitution', which was absolutely true; an X-ray of his lungs in 1930 showed only one 'cavity' (that is, seat of infection) in spite of 'very extensive scarring' (evidence of previous attacks which his body had successfully combated, at the cost of damage to the lung). Lawrence preferred to believe that a combination of the right location and the right attitude to life would lead to his recovery; Brewster noted, 'Never did he give me the impression that he thought his recovery doubtful.'[10] He had always treated illness as a relatively unimportant fact; as early as 1910 he had told Louie Burrows: 'always abuse me if I say I'm sick: I'm never ill unless I want to luxuriate in a little bath of sympathy.' The Huxleys were enraged by his attitude in 1929, and concluded: 'He rationalizes the fear in all kinds of ways which are, of course, quite irrelevant.' They believed his 'gradually approaching dissolution' was unnecessary, 'the result simply of the man's strange obstinacy against professional medicine'.[11]

Lawrence, however, had spent a lot of time over the previous two and a half years counselling and advising Gertie Cooper. In the summer of 1926, he had wanted her X-rayed, and an analysis of her sputum carried out. After she was admitted to a sanatorium in the autumn of 1926, he had advised her about the doctors: 'try and do as they tell you.' During the winter of 1926–7, his letters show how well he understood the treatment of tuberculosis, and sympathized with the patient. She was worried at being kept in bed: 'You know, they keep you in bed until the temperature *never* rises above one degree *below* normal.' She wanted to go home: 'in a case like yours it's bound to be difficult to stop the germ working. And while the germ is active, you'll have a temperature. But the fact that you're getting fatter shows that the germ is making no headway at all. That's a great deal.'[12] How could someone ignore his own illness who so perfectly understood the disease and its progress?

For one thing, he hated the subjection and humiliation of illness. 'He did so hate admitting he was ill,' noted a visitor to Florence when Lawrence had to take a rest in the middle of the day. He was determined (as he advised Gertie) to have 'the courage to live, and live well': accepting that he was ill would have changed his life.[13] But he also ignored his illness because being ill had always been a problem with Frieda. After his dreadful influenza attack in the spring of 1919, when he had almost died, Lawrence had written to Kot: 'If this illness hasn't been a lesson to her, it has to me.'[14] It was necessary for their marriage that he should not be ill. Frieda knew how her radiant vitality became a kind of standing reproach to him: 'When Lorenzo feels ill, it infuriates him to have me well.' He made a point, in his letters, of noting when Frieda was ill: 'she never has anything wrong, so when she *does*, she minds.'[15]

She also believed that she could, in the most extraordinary way, revive Lawrence when he was ill and depressed. 'I roused him into the determination to accept the challenge of my virility, he was not going to succumb.' Lawrence participated in her belief that she kept him alive: he told her how he could 'always trust your instinct to know the right thing for me'. When she returned to Paris from Baden-Baden, for example, Davies was embarrassed to come across her in the very act of knowing the right thing for him: 'The couple lay in bed under a tumbled counterpane of crimson velvet, Lawrence's bearded head nestling contentedly on a hearty bosom refreshed by a fortnight's breathing of its native air.'[16] Because it was Frieda's belief that she naturally healed him – 'miracles happen if one lets them!' – real illness always tended to increase the tension between them, and to make her impatient, especially with what she increasingly came to feel was his dependence. Lawrence was aware of this; in the winter of 1929–30, he would tell Barby: 'Your mother is repelled by the death in me.' In the spring of 1929, Mabel Luhan had written to Frieda accusing her of trying to 'hang on to Lawrence like grim death'. Frieda protested loudly that 'it's the other way about . . . Much too much for my taste is he dependent on me.'[17] The longer Lawrence survived, the more his dependence on Frieda was a problem for them both. His illness gave her a kind of effortless upper hand over him, and that he could not bear. Nor could she; in May 1929 she complained, 'He is so frail and anything emotional is more than he can stand. I just leave him alone and give him as much as I can, but make no demands.'[18] Leaving each other alone and making no demands was not, however, what their marriage was about. This was another reason why Lawrence refused to admit to serious illness: why he refused the X-ray in Paris and went to Mallorca with Frieda. Towards the end of her life, she remarked, 'I never heard him complain about his health.' Everyone else did; so she must have meant that he 'never felt like an invalid, I saw to that! Never should he feel a poor sick thing as long as I was there and his spirit!'[19]

This linked up with what Lawrence knew about the tubercular patient in the hands of contemporary doctors. There would be months of absolute rest in a sanatorium, perhaps surgery; life would become narrowed in every way, with perhaps no cure, simply a slower decline. Gertie Cooper survived twelve years longer than Lawrence, but only by living as an invalid. The surgery she underwent in 1927 made Lawrence despair: 'If one let it work on one's imagination, one would get ill out of very horror.'[20] Lawrence, powerfully imaginative, was not going to let anything like that happen to him. It was his conviction that the more he *thought* about his illness, the more he let it work on his imagination, the more ill he would be.

Friends saw it very differently. When Aldous Huxley wrote that agonized letter about Lawrence's irresponsibility in refusing to face up to illness, or to consult a proper doctor, he blamed Frieda. 'We've told her that she's a fool and a criminal; but it has no more effect than telling an elephant.' Yet Huxley also knew that the doctor whom Lawrence had seen in Paris 'doubted whether very much cd be done', while Hans Carossa had realized as early as 1927 that 'no medical treatment can really save him'.[21] Was it so irrational of Lawrence to behave as if he were *not* ill, simply spending more time in bed because of his wretched bronchials and asthma? His friends certainly had to collaborate in the fiction. Brigit Patmore recalled how, at Port Cros, it was 'against the rules to suggest that anything was wrong'. Lawrence showed tremendous courage, and never relapsed into self-pity; and that certainly contributed to the fact that he lived far longer than anyone could have predicted. Even Huxley noticed with awe how for 'the last two years he was like a flame burning on in miraculous disregard of the fact that there was no more fuel to justify its existence'.[22]

Frieda wrote, after his death, about his instinct for health: 'he knew so well what was good for him, what he needed, by an unfailing instinct, or he would have died many years ago.' Lawrence intended to go on working, and to be partnered by Frieda (not by a nurse), and to lead his life, terribly diminished though it eventually came to be. 'Somewhere I am not ill,' he would write wistfully in December 1929. 'I feel so strongly as if my illness weren't really me – I feel perfectly well and all right, *in myself*. Yet there is this beastly torturing chest superimposed on me, and it's as if there was a demon lived there, triumphing, and extraneous to me.'[23] Above all, he remained convinced of the role played in illness by mental attitude. 'What is the matter with us is primarily chagrin. Then the microbes pounce.' A doctor he consulted in Baden-Baden sustained his belief that lungs were not the problem, 'but the asthma very bad. And asthma is basically nerves, chagrin.'[24] This was his way of making illness non-physical; but it also shows that he felt he had been over-anxious, had self-consciously nursed his disappointment, because of being unhappy, disappointed and thwarted in the course of his life. He wrote in *Pansies* about this:

I am ill because of wounds to the soul, to the deep emotional self
and the wounds to the soul take a long, long time, only time can help
and patience, and a certain difficult repentance
long, difficult repentance, realisation of life's mistake, and the freeing
    oneself
from the endless repetition of the mistake[25]

'Life's mistake' for Lawrence in 1929 had been to believe in love, to give himself up to love, and so to be endlessly disappointed. The more completely he could break out of that pattern, he now believed, the better it would be for him. It is natural to link this with his discovery that what in his case had made up for everything, desire, was something he no longer experienced. He wrote about this in *Pansies* too:

When love is gone, and desire is dead, and tragedy has left the heart
then grief and pain go too, withdrawing
from the heart and leaving strange cold stretches of sand . . .
Yet even waste, grey foreshores, sand, and sorry, far-out clay

are sea-bed still, through their hour of bare denuding.
It is the moon that turns the tides.
The beaches can do nothing about it.[26]

He had talked about this with the Brewsters late in 1928, trying to make a virtue, or at least a way of life, out of loss: 'We must let things go, one after another, finally even love – only keeping oneself true to oneself, just that integrity. Nothing else matters in life or death.'[27]

At times he still lived vividly. His writing of three versions of *Lady Chatterley's Lover* between 1926 and 1928 had been miraculous. So would be his creation of his last prose book, *Apocalypse*, in the winter of 1929. Huxley believed Lawrence's health so bad that, by the summer of 1929, he could no longer do anything creative: 'He hasn't written a line or painted a stroke for the last 3 months.'[28] But Lawrence remained creative to the last. A poem like 'Nothing to Save' suggests what it was like for him during the last year of his life, feeling almost overwhelmed by the prospect of death, and yet determinedly and miraculously alive.

> There is nothing to save, now all is lost,
> but a tiny core of stillness in the heart
> like the eye of a violet.[29]

Putting himself into the hands of doctors, or being 'reasonable', as Huxley wanted him to be,[30] was not an option. One highly intelligent person, in an excellent position to understand Frieda, appreciated what she and Lawrence were doing. Else Jaffe believed that they 'had come to a rational way of dealing with his illness – everyone must live and die according to his own precept'. It *was* rational, as a way of coping with the irrational fact of incurable disease.[31] They still lived in some ways as they wanted to, in spite of terrible restrictions and Lawrence's increasing discomfort.

Having arranged for the publication of *Lady Chatterley's Lover* in Paris with Titus, he and Frieda went to Mallorca, where they would spend two generally happy months. The island was 'a bit reminiscent of Sicily, but not nearly so beautiful as Taormina, just much quieter, the quietest place I've ever known, seems rather boring, but I like it and it certainly is good for my health'. That would have been true.

The worst thing was the wine at the hotel, and Lawrence's denunciation offers the rich taste of his conversation: 'cat-piss is champagne compared, this is the sulphureous urination of some aged horse.'[32] He wasn't sure he could work much while there, but the success of *Lady Chatterley's Lover* had probably given him the idea for his next project: an unexpurgated edition of his volume of poems *Pansies*, which Secker would be bringing out in the normal (that is, censored) way that summer. Secker had already omitted a number of poems, though fewer than he would have liked; as Lawrence had insisted: 'make the *Pansies* into a good, "innocuous", bourgeois little book I will not, and you shall not.'[33] The fact that its typescripts had been seized made Lawrence still more determined to put the uncensored version before the public. So Secker produced a trade edition; and a London bookshop owner and friend of Rhys Davies, Charles Lahr, brought out an unexpurgated *Pansies* in August 1929. Lawrence also wrote the second of his articles about censorship, 'Pornography and Obscenity'; he had written a brief introduction to the subject when doing his 'peppery' foreword for the Paris *Lady Chatterley's Lover*. And he continued to write poems along the lines of the *Pansies* collection. His inventiveness and wit, as well as his capacity for mimicry, remained undiminished; a poem from this time may well have been provoked by encountering the English abroad, as well as becoming freshly aware of the 'dirty snivelling cant'[34] of the bourgeois sensibility hiding behind its 'niceness'.

> The English are so nice
> so awfully nice
> they are the nicest people in the world.
>
> And what's more, they're very nice about being nice
> about your being nice as well!
> If you're not nice they soon make you feel it.
>
> Americans and French and Germans and so on
> they're all very well
> but they're not *really* nice, you know.
> They're not nice in *our* sense of the word, are they now?
>
> That's why one doesn't have to take them seriously.
> We must be nice to them, of course,

of course, naturally –

But it doesn't really matter what you say to them,

they don't really understand

The poem ends with the advice to be 'nice enough, just nice enough / to let them feel they're not quite as nice as they might be'.[35] The speaking voice is wonderfully audible in such poetry: sharp, ironic, arch, malicious. It was in Mallorca, too, that he drew one of his best pictures: a self-portrait in red chalk, full of character and malice.[36]

But the main excitement of life in the summer of 1929 was over his paintings; the book of reproductions was to be published around the time of an exhibition being staged in London. Lawrence had been painting with enthusiasm over the past three years: and however imperfect in technical terms his paintings were – 'I know they're rolling with faults, Sladeily considered'[37] – he created a series of images sufficiently impressive to make the owner of a London gallery want to show them. This was Dorothy Warren, whom Lawrence had thought 'beautiful'[38] at Garsington in 1915 (Ottoline Morrell was her aunt) and whom Barby Weekley now knew. The idea of an exhibition had first come up in August 1927, but Lawrence did nothing about it until the late spring of 1928, when he and Frieda were preparing to leave the Villa Mirenda, and his pictures had to be packed up anyway. At this point, the Warren Gallery agreed to show them, and by the summer of 1928 the pictures were arriving in London. A series of delays then postponed the exhibition. By the time the gallery opened its doors to the public in July 1929, following an exhibition of work by another coal-miner's son, the then unknown Henry Moore, the large and handsome book of reproductions of Lawrence's paintings was already in existence. When Stephensen visited Lawrence in Bandol in January 1929, they had agreed to publish the book in the spring; by the end of January, Lawrence had some of the first proofs, as well as having produced a couple more new paintings which he forwarded to London; he had also written a long introductory essay.[39] The Mandrake Press advertised the book at ten guineas and sold out the edition before publication; it was yet another of those private press publications that were making money for Lawrence in these years.

But, exactly as with *Lady Chatterley's Lover* and *Pansies*, Lawrence would again find himself and his work targeted as obscene. His anger, these years, was directed into a running battle with the English authorities: what he was producing was aimed straight at prudishness and bourgeois 'niceness'. And he enjoyed the confrontation. It still threatened his livelihood, as it had back in 1915; but he had acquired ways of outmanoeuvring his opponents. The novel had been published, and was being republished, abroad; Lahr would produce an unexpurgated volume of *Pansies*; and Lawrence and his literary agent were able to get a question asked in Parliament about the Home Office's interference with his private correspondence when they seized the typescripts. When he heard that the printers of the *Paintings* volume were refusing to undertake the reproductions of some of the works, he assumed the reason was his notoriety since the seizure of *Pansies*. In fact, the volume was issued as he wanted it; but each of these ventures offered him a new public role as a polemicist, rather as his newspaper journalism had.

Lawrence and Frieda left Mallorca just as it was getting hot, in mid June. He claimed that Frieda had wanted to go from the end of May, after her bottom had been pinched in a tram; the event had made her despise 'every letter in the word Mallorca', so that she was now 'rampant' to sail to Italy: 'to Marseille anyhow . . . where her squeamish rear has never been nipped'.[40] After weeks during which it seemed as if Lawrence's illness was again in some kind of remission, as that buoyant letter to Rhys Davies suggests, things began to go badly wrong, however. Frieda travelled to England to see the paintings exhibition open on 4 July; Lawrence could not have faced the journey, but his London agent had also advised him that, following the *Pansies* seizure, he was in danger of being arrested if ever he did enter England. Before moving to Orioli's flat in Florence, he first went to stay with the Huxleys at Forte dei Marmi, on the Italian coast. They observed with distress how awful his health was: he 'coughs more, breathes very quickly and shallowly, has no energy'.[41] While Frieda was in London, and following some savage press attacks on the exhibition, the Warren Gallery was raided by the police, and thirteen of Lawrence's pictures (all those showing any trace of pubic hair, plus a couple of others) were taken down and removed, along with four copies of the Mandrake Press *Paintings. Family on a Verandah* (Illustration 37) shows how Lawrence had made pubic hair the very centre and focus of the picture; for this the painting was seized. Until it was pointed out to them that William Blake was a famous artist, the police looked likely to be taking a copy of his *Pencil Drawings* with them as well. The gallery was prosecuted for having obscene oil paintings, watercolours and books on its premises *'for purposes of sale and gain'*.[42] The case to determine whether they were obscene, in which case they would be destroyed, would be heard at Bow Street Magistrates court early in August; Dorothy Warren and her husband, Philip Trotter, mounted a campaign to justify them as works of art.

The episode left Lawrence feeling outraged. He wrote a new series of poems (to be called *Nettles*) about what had happened: 'Virginal, pure policemen came / and hid their faces for very shame.' But he had no desire to risk his pictures. 'I do not want my pictures to be burned, under any circumstance or for any cause . . . If you have to promise never to show them again in England, I do not care. England can change its mind later if it wants to – it can never call back a burnt picture.' The magistrate declared that it was 'utterly immaterial' whether the pictures in questions were works of art; it was enough if they were obscene.[43] By promising that they would not again be exhibited in England, the gallery was, however, able to prevent the pictures' destruction. Only the books of the *Paintings* were destroyed, and the gallery ordered to pay costs.

Lawrence had fallen ill in Florence. As usual, he made light of the matter – 'I got a bad cold on Friday afternoon – like a shot in the back'; but Orioli was sufficiently alarmed by his condition to wire Frieda to come back at once.[44] When she arrived, she produced the usual miraculous change for the better in Lawrence. That is, she believed she would do so, and he wanted to believe that she would: after a few days, they both went to Baden-Baden for the seventy-seventh birthday of Frieda's mother, in spite of Lawrence's previous determination not to go.

This turned out to be a bad move. His improvement was not something either he or Frieda could sustain. His previous visits to Baden-Baden had been happy ones, and he had always liked the Baroness's energy and spirit; in 1923 he had thought her 'a thousand times lovelier and more cheerful' than Mabel Luhan's mother, and as recently as

September 1927 had described her as 'really very nice – and whatever she can do for me, she does it – thinks of everything possible'.[45] This time, however, he found her unbearable, the climate bad, and the place horrible. A visit to the Kurhaus Plättig in the Black Forest, at a higher altitude, made things still worse: 'though it's supposed to be good for me, I really hate it'; 'I am neither writing nor painting, but letting the clock go round.' It was better back at the Hotel Löwen, near Baden-Baden, though he was very aware of the contrast between his thinness and the large German women sitting round him 'like mountains'; but he was still desperate to leave.[46] What had happened?

He had told Emily how 'I get depressed here', quickly following that with the reassuring 'which is not usual for me, I am very rarely depressed'.[47] What affected him most powerfully was the Baroness herself, who, at the age of seventy-seven, expressed a kind of parodic version of Frieda's radiant vitality, which Lawrence found both platitudinous and oppressive. He mocked her ecstasies over 'das Brünnele, das Bächlein' ('the little fountain, the little stream'), while her exclamatory chat to Frieda is ridiculed in another letter: 'The pine-forest is all around – really in the forest, my little Frieda, do you realise? in the great, wonderful pine-forest! ah! and the air! – and the nice people who so kindly chat with me! – ah, aren't *we* lucky, shouldn't *we* be grateful! When I think of men working in coal-mines – in great factories –!!!!'[48] Such an attitude to her health on the one hand depressed Lawrence and on the other enraged him. He portrayed her 'in an awful state, thinking her time to die may be coming on. So she fights in the ugliest fashion, greedy and horrible, to get everything that will keep her alive – food, high air, pine-trees, Frieda or me, *nothing* exists but just for the purpose of giving her a horrible strength to hang on a few more years.'[49] She had insisted on staying on at the Kurhaus Plättig even though it rained a good deal and was bitterly cold for late July. And although Lawrence was in bed most of the time, and badly wanted to go back down to Baden-Baden,

that old woman would see me die by inches and yards rather than relinquish her 'mountain air'. She stands in the road and gulps the air in greedy gulps – and says – 'it does me so much good! it gives me strength, strength!' . . . It's the most ghastly state of almost insane selfishness I ever saw – and all comes of her hideous terror of having to die. At the age of seventy-eight! May god preserve me from ever sinking so low. I never felt so cruelly humiliated.[50]

Humiliation was always a problem for him: he had told Dorothy Brett, in 1925, how 'I hate "situations", and feel humiliated by them'.[51] But why was he humiliated now? The reason would seem to be that he could bear neither the Baroness's lack of inhibition in her greed for life, nor what it told him about himself. His mother-in-law would indeed outlive him, if only by seven months, and her fearful craving made him embarrassed for her. By contrast, his own self-contained, proud and lonely battle in the face of death seemed – if principled – also a little ridiculous. Mollie Skinner's brother Jack (one of the sources of inspiration for *The Boy in the Bush*) had died at the age of forty-four in 1925. On hearing of his death, a few months after learning of his own tuberculosis, Lawrence had written Mollie a note of sympathy: 'And after all, he lived his life and had his mates wherever he went. What more does a man want? So many old bourgeois people live on and on, and *can't* die, because they have never been in life at all. Death's not sad, when one has lived.'[52] Lawrence now cast the Baroness in the role of the sad old person who (like Lydia Lawrence) '*can't* die'.[53] But, then, could *he*? That was perhaps the real problem. Back at the Hotel Löwen he felt better, though he continued to cough 'to the general annoyance or cold commiseration of a nervous universe';[54] but he could not leave Baden-Baden fast enough.

Yet he and Frieda had very much enjoyed being in Bavaria in the autumn of 1927, and Lawrence had felt well there; so this year they accepted an invitation from the German doctor-writer Max Mohr to stay in Rottach-am-Tegernsee, in the Bavarian Alps. But here, unfortunately, just as at the Kurhaus Plättig, Lawrence felt that the altitude was wrong for him, and the medical advice he took did him no good at all. One doctor told him that 'in a few weeks, with diet and a bit of breathing, I ought to be well', and prescribed him a diet of simple food, without salt. 'They say I can get well in quite a short time.' Another doctor prescribed him 'arsenic and phosphorus twice a day', though he quickly stopped that: it 'made me feel I was *really* being poisoned'.[55] All that happened was that he felt worse: Frieda told Ottoline Morrell, 'Lorenzo is often depressed, it's hard to put up with, I suppose for him too.' When Frieda watched him playing with the Mohrs' three-year-old daughter, she saw it with the eyes of a parent, and thought of infection; Mohr recorded how she 'asks me, if I do not think it dangerous. But I deny it as so often before. For nobody can believe that any harm can come from Lorenzo.' Frieda was under no illusions about her husband's illness; Mohr, although a doctor, clearly was. Else came down to see them and found Lawrence 'lying in a bare room in the mean village inn. Beside him stood a great bush of pale blue autumn gentians as the only furnishing.'[56] But the bareness was not a problem for him; and the flowers gave rise to one of his greatest poems, 'Bavarian Gentians'. 'Not every man has gentians in his house / In Soft September, at slow, sad Michaelmas' begins one version; the 'smoking blueness' of the flowers is 'Pluto's dark-blue blaze': the darkness of the underworld.

> Reach me a gentian, give me a torch!
> let me guide myself with the blue, forked torch of this flower
> down the darker and darker stairs, where blue is darkened on blueness

At the end of the journey will be Persephone, the bride kept underground by Pluto,

> enfolded in the deeper dark
> of the arms Plutonic, and pierced with the passion of dense gloom,
>   among the splendour of torches of darkness, shedding darkness on
>   the lost bride
> and her groom.[57]

Lawrence gave the old myth magnificent new energy; his vivid imagination now attuned to the ideas of loss and ending.

Living was harder. He and Frieda had no idea where they wanted to go. The constant travelling and staying with friends and in hotels was a little desperate; even Lawrence felt 'really fed up with moving about, and should be glad to have a place of my own'.[58] They decided to return south, to Italy or the south of France: but where? Lawrence was normally reluctant to revisit places, preferring to travel to somewhere new. He did not go back to Chapala in 1924 but to Oaxaca: he had gone to Spotorno in 1925, rather than return to any of the Italian places he knew. But he could not forget having been 'cheerful and well' at Bandol the previous winter and spring when, although coughing, he had felt surprisingly fit: 'not *ill*'. He had been proud of not having been a day in bed all winter, and of having been able to 'work away'.[59] Accordingly, after the wretched summer and autumn in Italy and Germany, he and Frieda returned to Bandol, in the hope that what had suited him the previous year might suit him again.

And at first it seemed to. As soon as they were there, late in September 1929, Lawrence felt 'already nearly myself again here – the sun and sea, the great light, and the *natural* people. I can breathe. In the north, I can't breathe.' After a few days at the Beau-Rivage, they rented a six-room 'chalet-bungalow' named Villa Beau Soleil on the outskirts of town, right on the sea. With its heliotrope-tinted walls and gold-framed mirrors (the Brewsters thought it 'must have been designed for some lady-love') it was not beautiful, and its walls were so thin that, as Lawrence put it, 'everybody hears everybody brushing their teeth'. But it was 'wonderfully in the air and light': and that now mattered most.[60]

26

Dying Game: 1929–1930

Frieda's own writing never became more lyrical than when she was contemplating, in retrospect, this last winter in Bandol: 'The sun rose magnificently opposite his bed in red and gold across the bay and the fishermen standing up in their boats looked like eternal mythological figures dark and alive against the lit-up splendour of the sea and sky . . .'[1] The Beau Soleil was nevertheless an odd place for them to have ended up. Lawrence would tell Mabel Luhan in January 1930: 'I am too much cut off.'[2] Frieda and he knew few people in Bandol apart from the hotel staff, though the Huxleys regularly travelled along that stretch of coast, and the Brewsters were prepared to move down because the Lawrences were living there. But other friends came to the hotel; and Bandol's position by the Mediterranean was especially important to Lawrence: 'it is lovely here by the sea . . . it still seems young as Odysseus, in the morning.'[3] In Bandol, he regained some peace after the wretchedness of the summer, though by now his ill-health dominated almost everything he did. He wrote to Ottoline Morrell insisting again that unhappiness arose from the disappointed body, and was nurtured by it too: 'the body has a strange will of its own, and nurses its own chagrin.'[4] Frieda, the partner who had always brought life and health, was now incapable of doing that, although she was at this stage as tender and as little impatient as she could be. But she too was waiting for an end: 'Deep down I knew "something is going to happen, we are steering toward some end" but every nerve was strained and every thought and every feeling . . . I had to see him day by day getting nearer to the end, his spirit so alive and powerful that the end and death seemed unthinkable and always will be, for me.'[5]

Lawrence had not written very much in previous months except some more 'Pansies' and poems he would include in the collection of stinging *Nettles*; he would write no more fiction, in spite of hoping to do so. But in Bandol, he began to work concentratedly once again. He was writing some extremely beautiful poems, many about preparing for death, so that most of his *Last Poems* date from this second period in Bandol; and he prepared *Nettles* for publication. He was also doing another couple of magazine articles, and turning his first introduction to the French *Lady Chatterley's Lover* into the essay 'A Propos of *Lady Chatterley's Lover*'. For a desperately sick man, all this writing, lucid and distinctive, was remarkable. Often confined to bed in the mornings, he could still work, 'propped up . . . with many pillows, knees bent up with a writing pad on the uplifted legs, allowing him to write'.[6] Most significantly, he began work on what would be his final book, *Apocalypse*. The artist and astrologer Frederick Carter, whom he had met in Shropshire at the start of 1924, had written a book about primitive religious symbolism; Lawrence, having promised to write an introduction, found it turning into a work in its own right. Accordingly, he wrote Carter a separate introduction, and followed his own work through to its own conclusion. It took him from late October to the end of December 1929, and began with a renewal of his old excitement at the 'Chaldean vision of the living heavens', the old world he had sketched in his Etruscan essays. What he wanted to do was make this old, pagan vision something which modern man would have to concede was lacking in his own experience; Lawrence was writing a book offering his contemporaries a kind of psychic recovery of their connections with the old world. They needed to admit that their individualism

is really an illusion. I am a part of the great whole, and I can never escape. But I *can* deny my connections, break them, and become a fragment. Then I am wretched.

What we want is to destroy our false, inorganic connections . . . and re-establish the living organic connections, with the cosmos, the sun and earth, with mankind and nation and family. Start with the sun, and the rest will slowly, slowly happen.[7]

Too often read as a kind of exhortation from the moral high ground, such writing is attempting to make actual, in Lawrence's own life, what he had been writing and thinking since his experience at Kiowa. It was a kind of cheering up of himself; writing against the grain of actual experience, in the way he had always done. When he wrote, 'What we want . . .', it was a literal truth; he desperately wanted it. Individualism, and its wretchedness, were things he knew terribly well. The renewal of connection – 'with mankind and nation and family' – was the dream of his own life; he wanted a sense of the larger milieu of which he might be a part. He would write on the book's last page how 'I am part of the sun as my eye is part of me' and, more simply: 'That I am part of the earth my feet know perfectly.'[8] These are compelling versions of truths by no means self-evident; but they are what Lawrence very much wanted to feel and to communicate. Thinking back to New Mexico (Ida Rauh had arrived in Bandol at Christmas), he even considered a new kind of communal life at Kiowa: that very special 'part of the earth'. It would be 'a sort of old school, like the Greek philosophers, talks in a garden – that is, under the pine-trees. I feel I might perhaps get going with a few young people, building up a new unit of life out there . . . and not bother much more about my own personal life. Perhaps now I should submit, and be a teacher. I have fought so against it.'[9]

Another part of the earth his feet in particular never forgot were the pavements and the field paths of Eastwood. A friend visiting him in Bandol in November 1929, just three months before his death, recalled his 'gossiping stories about his own family and his youth where he clearly lived again, very often, in memory'. As he had remarked at the end of September: 'Very still and sunny here – olvidar – vergessen – oublier – dimenticare – forget – So difficult to forget –'[10] On the one hand, he would have liked to have put it behind him, yet his writing life had so often depended on recreating the past and understanding it: 'we can only go forward step by step through realisation, full, bitter, conscious realisation . . . And then we can surpass.'[11] Ada and Emily planned to come out to Bandol together around the middle of February 1930 to see him, which would have given Frieda a chance to get away for a few days. But in the event Lawrence postponed their visit. 'I didn't want you both to come there to that little Beausoleil house – it would have upset me too much and been too much for me'; he told Barby that Ada would 'cry all the time and it upsets me'.[12] There was, moreover, a compelling reason to put them off. In April 1929, the Parisian doctor who *had* examined him reckoned that 'he might drag on for quite a little time like this', but that if 'he got a cold which turned into bronchitis or pneumonia . . . he'd simply be asphyxiated'. Over Christmas, he had had what he called 'a bit of extra bronchitis' and then, on New Year's Day, he got cold in a cutting wind; 'the exposed situation of Bandol aggravated his bronchitis,' a doctor noted.[13] From now onwards, he was in a great deal of pain and lost a lot of weight. The early flowers were coming out, a 'beautiful orange striped cat' they called Monsieur Beau Soleil or Mickie Mussolini had happily adopted them, and they had even been given some goldfish (the cat got one and was spanked). 'Everything flourishes,' Frieda told him: 'why can't you?' 'And he said: "I want to, I want to, I wish I could." '[14]

The English tuberculosis specialist Andrew Morland, who by chance was travelling to the south of France, was asked by Gertler and Koteliansky to go and see him. It was a sign of Lawrence's desperation that he let Morland examine him on 17 January. In the doctor's judgement, 'a really long period of strict rest is the only possible treatment now'. His recommendation was that Lawrence give up work of all kinds for two months and see nobody; simply lie and rest. And if that had no effect, then he should go into a sanatorium like the one at Vence; not because his treatment of strict rest and good food would be so very different there, but because he would have 'proper nursing & attention'. Morland was deeply impressed by Lawrence's resistance to the disease, which had enabled him to survive so long 'while doing all the wrong things'.[15]

In Bandol during the second half of January, Lawrence tried just lying still and doing nothing. Frieda wrote to her daughter: 'They say I must have a nurse; he says "Can't I have Barby?"' And by the end of the month, Barby had joined them, which Lawrence very much appreciated; she 'helps to keep things going, and is very nice. Frieda needs someone to keep her balanced.' On fine days, he 'lay still on a couch screened off in a sheltered corner of the garden. He lay there meditating, with a great calm over his face.'[16] That at least was how Achsah Brewster saw him. Earl massaged him with oil, and was terrified on seeing 'how emaciated and martyrized was his body', like 'one of the haggard, mediaeval, carved figures of the crucified Jesus'; Frieda grieved to see his 'strong, straight, quick legs gone so thin, so thin'. Achsah remembered him preparing to read aloud his recent poems – 'some verses about death' – and then not doing so: 'shaking his head wistfully, he closed the book, saying: "I can't read them now." '[17] He wrote very tellingly, out of his own desperate state, to Caresse Crosby late in January 1930, offering her caring and compassionate advice. Her husband Harry had killed himself and his mistress in New York. What could one say after such a horror? Lawrence wrote: 'don't you try to recover yourself too soon – it is much better to be a little blind and stunned for a time longer, and not make efforts to see or to feel. Work is the best, and a certain numbness, a merciful numbness. It was too dreadful a blow – and it was wrong.'[18]

He was past the stage of conserving his energies. He did accept that he should not have many visitors; but being told not to work by Morland hardly affected him. He went on believing, as he told Caresse, in work. One of the last things he wrote was: 'Happy, intense absorption in any work, which is to be brought as near to perfection as possible, this is a state of being with God, and the men who have not known it have missed life itself.'[19] He wrote as usual; Achsah saw him 'propped up in bed, galley sheets piled thick about him, correcting proofs of his *Nettles*'.[20] His poetry writing had alternated between poems about death, and the characteristic flashes of spiky wit and anger which make his various *Pansies* and *Nettles* so attractive when you like them, and so irritating when you don't. What was new in them was a raw temper coming from the frustrations of being so ill. He suffered from the anger, the sheer blackness of mood, which so often infiltrated his language, but the anger could now sound almost comical, coming from the emaciated body. Frieda once heard him saying, 'I can't die, I can't die, I hate them too much!' But several people beside her saw how capable he now was, through the autumn of 1929 and into 1930, of a new kind of stillness and contemplation, whether sitting on his rock by the sea and looking out, or lying in the garden of the Beau Soleil. Something of this appears in his *Last Poems*. And when Frieda said to him, 'No, Lawrence, you don't hate them as much as all that', it 'seemed to comfort him'.[21]

But what other writer imagined the process of dying, the actual process of the self voyaging out, losing the body, losing memory and desire, losing self, as Lawrence did? He had always wanted to write directly from the experience of being in the body, and was set on completing what he had done, by describing the experience of bodily dying. He had written to Gertie Cooper in 1927, at the start of her treatment, 'While we live, we must be game. And when we come to die, we'll die game too.' This was what 'game' meant: being unflinching, clear-sighted. He had insisted, eight years earlier still, that 'This struggle for verbal consciousness should not be left out in art. It is a very great part of life. It is not superimposition of a theory. *It is the passionate struggle into conscious being.*'[22] As an experimental writer, he was committed to struggling through into conscious understanding of his own experiences. He had written in February 1929: 'My field is to know the feelings inside a man, and to make new feelings conscious. What really torments civilized people is that they are full of feelings they know nothing about; they can't realize them, they can't fulfil them, they can't *live* them.'[23] He would now live his feelings about his own coming death, and write them too, just as he had lived and written his feelings about sex, and loss, and isolation. He could write compellingly of how for 'man, the vast marvel is to be alive'; and while terribly aware how reduced and narrowed his life was – at times indeed, in the autumn of 1929, 'only the leavings of a life' – he could still experience

> snatches of lovely oblivion, and snatches of renewal
> odd, wintry flowers upon the withered stem, yet new, strange flowers
> such as my life has not brought forth before, new blossoms of me – [24]

Such new blossoms could, for example, be poems drawing on the central idea of the ship of death: constructing the ship, readying it and stocking it, setting out in it towards the experience of dying, imaginatively:

> Drift on, drift on, my soul, towards the most pure
> most dark oblivion.
>
> And at the penultimate porches, the dark-red mantle
> of the body's memories slips and is absorbed
> into the shell-like, womb-like convoluted shadow.

And round the great final bend of unbroken dark
the skirt of the spirit's experience has melted away,
the oars have gone from the boat, and the little dishes
gone, gone, and the boat dissolves like pearl
as the soul at last slips perfect into the goal, the core
of sheer oblivion and of utter peace,
the womb of silence in the living night.

These were the feelings of the end of the body which he made it his business to live and write, just as he had written the feelings of life. We might award him the same praise he had found for Maurice Magnus: 'In the great spirit of human consciousness he was a hero . . .'[25]

Just lying down, seeing few people, and only working a little during January 1930, as Morland had suggested, did not help, however. He felt no better; and he did not put on weight. In despair – 'Of course I hate the thought of going' – he agreed to try the sanatorium; and as he was supposed to have visitors there only a couple of times a week, he finally told Ada and Emily not to visit: 'wait a bit, till I'm walking about'. Ada was upset, naturally, and blamed Frieda and Barby for refusing to let her see her brother. Lawrence also told Emily: 'I'm not in any sudden danger – but in slow danger.'[26]

The fact that Frieda took the idea of his going to the sanatorium so badly confirms what, after his death, she called 'my conceit' that 'I thought I could give Lawrence *complete* health, I fought so hard'. But if *she* felt that, she also knew that 'It's so bitter for him'. He certainly behaved as if it were a final sentence. 'With a set face Lawrence made me bring all his papers on to his bed and he tore most of them up and made everything tidy and neat and helped to pack his own trunks, and I never cried . . . His self-discipline kept me up, and my admiration for his unfailing courage.' On the other hand, Frieda reported and denied the truth of a remark he made to Barby: 'Your mother does not care for me anymore, the death in me is repellent to her.'[27] It sounds terribly likely to have been something Lawrence would have felt, and said. He also asked Frieda whether he ought to make a new will: Frieda thought the answer 'yes' would tell him he was going to die. 'Don't you bother about wills,' she answered.[28]

On 6 February 1930, he was admitted into the sanatorium Morland

411

knew about, with the ominous name Ad Astra ('To the Stars'), five hours' travel to the east of Bandol, up in the mountains in Vence. When Lawrence got there, he reported that the 'weather is sunny, the almond trees are all in blossom, beautiful, but I am not allowed any more to go out and see them'.[29] All he had was a view of the distant Mediterranean from his balcony. Not being allowed to work or to go out would have been the most difficult part of the treatment, although he did continue to work at some things, like a review of Eric Gill's *Art-Nonsense*. By committing himself to the Ad Astra, however, Lawrence had taken another step on the 'longest journey' he had written about in the 'Ship of Death': increasingly and inevitably, he was now also on his own. Frieda reported how his 'eyes were so grateful and bright' when she volunteered to spend a night in his room. She was glad he was slightly deaf and so could not hear the girl in the next room calling out to her mother, during the night, 'Mama, Mama, je souffre tant!'[30]

Frieda felt a little reassured that he was in safe hands and thought of visiting her mother. She also thought of seeing Ravagli, now in Savona, quite close. She would shamefacedly tell a friend later in the year that it had only been 'by chance' that she had been with Lawrence when he died: 'the Capitano himself had written and forbidden her to come knowing how desperately ill Lawrence was.'[31] For the sanatorium was having no effect. Lawrence started to suffer from pleurisy, and lost his appetite. By the end of February, he was in an appalling state of pain and dissolution, and Frieda told herself: 'It is enough, it is enough; nobody should have to stand this.' She slept in his room again, but this time he told her: 'Your sleeping here does me no good.' She ran away and cried; such a remark undermined one of the central tenets of their life. When she came back, 'he said so tenderly: "Don't mind, you know I want nothing but you."' It was as true as it had been in Oaxaca in 1925, when he had said to her: 'But if I die, nothing has mattered but you, nothing at all.'[32] Who or what else could he have wanted, at this point in his life?

On Wednesday 26 February 1930, a beautiful sunny day, the American sculptor Jo Davidson visited the sanatorium to do a clay head of Lawrence; H. G. Wells, who had visited Lawrence a couple of days earlier, had suggested the idea. Wells had been more than a little unpleasant, telling Lawrence that 'his illness was mainly hysteria',[33] but Lawrence was up and dressed to receive his visitor. Davidson started to work while they talked of mutual friends:

I knew Lawrence had painted, and I asked him if he had ever done any modeling. He had – once, in plasteline [i.e. plasticine].[34] But he hated the material, its feel and odor, and never touched it again. I gave him a piece of my clay. He liked the feel of it – because it was clean and cool. I promised to send him the very clay I was using as soon as the bust was completed. He thought he would like to do some little animals in clay.[35]

Davidson went on for 'an hour or so', then took a break while Lawrence had a sleep. Before they started again, Lawrence asked if Davidson would mind if this time he sat up in bed while Davidson worked; and Davidson went on for another hour. 'When I told Lawrence I had been experimenting in polychrome sculpture, he asked me to do him in color, and not to forget the blue of his dressing gown, of which he was very fond.'[36] Davidson made their time together sound entirely amicable, but Lawrence offered his own weary judgement the next day: 'Joe Davidson (?) came and made a clay head of me – made me tired – result in clay mediocre.' Those were the last words he ever wrote: the final postscript to his last letter. Davidson's piece (see Illustration 38), though conventional, is striking for work initiated in two or three hours; he probably continued after the sessions were over.[37] The head Lawrence saw late on that Wednesday afternoon may have been rather different, though he would have objected on principle to its ethereal quality. The hair on the finished piece is lank on the forehead, the cheeks sunken, the attitude one of slightly forced concentration, which may well reflect the conditions of the sitting: but the face is also beautiful. What Davidson gives us is an image of how Lawrence appeared to a sympathetic onlooker just four days before he died. He is almost unbearably emaciated and fragile: yet concentrated and unflinching.

Being in the Ad Astra was hastening his death. Morland had not expected it to do much – 'I do not think much of French sanatoria' – but came to wish that he had never urged Lawrence to go: 'I am afraid my efforts only made his last weeks more unhappy.'[38] Lawrence had expected, if not improvement, at least some stabilization of his terrible weight loss; early in 1929, reckoning in stone, he had been 'over seven, nearly eight', but at the start of February 1930 had been under six-and-a-half.[39] And he hated to be given up to the hands of doctors and nurses: he hated the institution. It was what he had been struggling against all his adult life. For the first time since Mexico in 1925, he found himself giving up: 'such bad nights, and cough, and heart, and pain decidedly worse'.[40]

His response was characteristic: he challenged it 'as he challenged everything'. Huxley reported that Lawrence told Frieda 'you have killed me' on the Thursday or Friday after Davidson's visit.[41] She had helped him discount doctors and treatment because, with her, he was not ill. Feeling 'the death in me', he hit back. But what they did next, together, is utterly characteristic. He decided to break out, as he always had. After three useless weeks in a sanatorium, he would move into another of his own homes, with Frieda beside him. It was his last, absurd, agonized, wonderful gesture of refusal and self-determination. *Game.*

With some difficulty, Frieda and Barby rented a house in Vence, the Villa Robermond, and arranged for an English nurse to attend. When Lawrence left the Ad Astra on Saturday 1 March, Frieda had to tie his shoes for him: 'It was the only time . . . everything else he always did for himself.' He was taken by shaking taxi to the new house, helped up the steps and indoors by Frieda and the taxi-driver, and put to bed. And 'that night, as every night at the Sanatorium, he refused to let anybody help him with his toilet'. Frieda slept on the couch in his room, where he could see her. Morland would wonder whether 'the effort of leaving may have produced a further setback': the expenditure of energy cannot have helped. But by now, it was necessary that Lawrence do what he most wanted. If he could rest 'and regain a little strength', he had even been dreaming of returning to Kiowa: 'I believe I should get better there' (he was probably thinking of the spring of 1925). Barby had actually been down to Nice to enquire about passports.[42] The dream was stronger than any reality, and could not be given up.

On Sunday morning, 2 March, he told Frieda, 'Don't leave me', 'don't go away'. He 'got up, washed and brushed his teeth'; he was preparing for another day. Frieda sat by his bed, reading. Barby cooked lunch, which Lawrence ate sitting up in bed; he was reading, of all things, Irving's *Life and Voyages of Columbus*.[43] Another voyage, another shore and landfall. In the afternoon, the Huxleys came for a while.

But towards the end of the afternoon, Lawrence began to suffer dreadfully. As usual, he diagnosed himself and decided what was happening: 'I must have a temperature, I am delirious. Give me the thermometer.' And now he desperately needed morphia. Frieda recalled that this was 'the only time, seeing his tortured face, that I cried, and he said: "Don't cry," in a quick, compelling voice'. The doctor was sent for but did not come; Barby held Lawrence in her arms. Eventually she went out to get the doctor, and Lawrence asked Frieda: 'Put your arm round me like Barby did; it made me feel better.' By now, the Huxleys had returned, but Lawrence could no longer hide his pain from them: 'for the first time he cried out to them in his agony.'[44] It was perhaps the first time he had cried out to anyone; he remained utterly self-contained, heroically or crazily proud according to one's perspective, to the end. His head was 'giving him acute agony': Maria took her turn in holding him. He told her that 'she had his mother's hands'. He suffered the dislocation of self so common *in extremis*: 'Hold me, hold me, I don't know where I am, I don't know where my hands are . . . where am I?' Maria told a friend that he kept saying, 'Look at *him* there in the bed!'[45]

Barby had finally discovered that the Corsican doctor whom they had been trying to find was away for the day. With some difficulty, she managed to persuade the superintendent of the Ad Astra to come and give his ex-patient a morphia injection. Lawrence became quieter; but it was dark by now, and Huxley and Barby went out again, to try to secure some kind of treatment that would see him through till morning. Frieda remembered: 'The minutes went by, Maria Huxley was in the room with me. I held his left ankle from time to time, it felt so full of life, all my days I shall hold his ankle in my hand.'[46] Before Aldous and Barby returned, he died, at about 10.15 at night. One account has those commonest of last words: 'I am better now.' The other version has Lawrence saying to Frieda, 'Wind my watch.' He intended going on: he would want to know the time during the night, when his coughing woke him.[47]

Barby saw the body next morning and was shocked by Lawrence's face: 'a mask of something like mockery – a grimace'. The end of his life had been agonizing. Lawrence had once described how his own mother's face, 'with more smile wrinkles than anything', had as she lay dying 'fallen like a mask of bitter cruel suffering'. Frieda's account of Lawrence offers a very different way of seeing him. 'So proud, manly and splendid he looked, a new face there was. All suffering had been wiped from it, it was as if I had never seen him or known him in all the completeness of his being.'[48]

They buried him in Vence on the Tuesday afternoon, with Frieda refusing melancholy, in a 'gay dress'. Old and new friends (including Edward Titus from Paris) came for the funeral, and one of them, Robert Nichols, wrote a long account. The Huxleys were both there:

Maria . . . looked terribly forlorn and greyer in the face than ever. Aldous came back and took charge of her and I took charge of Frieda. She was quite wonderful. 'It's how he would like it,' she said, 'just friends. And see, the sun's come out!' And so it had and the landscape was beautiful – it's lovely up at Vence and the birds were singing and the huge mass of rocks above the villa towered in a perfect sky . . .

The sky became more and more beautiful for it was just after four and the drama of nature was just beginning to move again after the stillness . . . I led the way with Frieda. She said: 'It's like being all old soldiers together.' And so it was.

We came out on the lowest terrace of the cemetery: a beautiful position. Below the rampart of the cemetery the ground falls away through an orange orchard. A wonderful valley opens out and far away the sea glitters among haze. We all paused. 'How beautiful it is,' said Frieda . . . advanced and dropped some flowers on the coffin. Two or three of us did that and I said 'Goodbye, dear Lawrence,' because I couldn't bear to let him go absolutely without a word. At that I heard Maria begin to cry softly behind me . . . She stood like one about whom the heavens had fallen.[49]

Frieda's own commentary on these last weeks and days was the most moving thing she ever wrote, though its lyricism at times suppresses more disturbing things: such as the fact that (as her Vence friend pointed out) 'had it not been for the Capitano's foresight, her story of Lawrence's deathbed would have had to be second hand'. But this is the end of her account:

Then we buried him, very simply, like a bird we put him away, a few of us who loved him. We put flowers into his grave and all I said was: 'Good-bye Lorenzo' as his friends and I put lots and lots of mimosa on his coffin. Then he was covered over with earth while the sun came out on to his small grave in the little cemetery of Vence which looks over the Mediterranean that he cared for so much.[50]

At the start of 1931, Frieda went back to the Kiowa ranch; it was what she had always planned. But Angelo Ravagli travelled with her – 'o scandal!' – and would stay at her side until her death in 1956. In Lawrence, she had had bad health to combat: and lost. Her desire for Ravagli brought her another problem. 'This time I am beaten trying to give a *mind* to a man who hasn't got one – But he is honest & charming & gentle –'[51] Money was another problem, to start with. Lawrence's will (made in Greatham in 1914) had been mislaid; and because he had died intestate, his estate had to be administered jointly by Frieda and Lawrence's brother George. Two and a half years of quarrels and recriminations led (in the end) to a lawsuit. George and his sister Emily were happy for Frieda to have the income of the estate during her lifetime, so long as the copyrights reverted to the Lawrence family after her death. Frieda, supported by Lawrence's sister Ada, wanted income and copyrights, on the grounds that Lawrence would have wanted her to have them. The dispute culminated in a hearing in London in November 1932, which awarded Frieda the estate: capital, income, copyrights, everything. Frieda gave the Lawrence family members a sum of money and a number of manuscripts and paintings, in compensation. But from that day to this, not a single relative of Lawrence's has earned a penny from the sale of his books.

When Frieda died in 1956, her estate was one of the most valuable literary properties in the Western world; it was divided equally between her three children and her third husband, Angelo Ravagli (they had married in 1950), so that the continuing income of the estate – payment for copyright quotations in this biography, for example – goes to the relatives of Frieda's children by her marriage to Ernest Weekley, whom she left for Lawrence, and to the relatives of Angelo Ravagli, with whom she frequently betrayed Lawrence before his death. But what Lawrence earned, especially between 1928 and 1930, had brought

Frieda both security and freedom, so that she could continue to live where she wanted and as she wanted. As so often before and after, it was Frieda and others who profited, after his death, from the extraordinary legacy of writing Lawrence had left behind him.

It was Ravagli's task in 1935 to return to Vence to have Lawrence exhumed, cremated and then brought back to America, as Frieda wanted; Ravagli would also build a suitable shrine for the ashes on the hill just above the ranch. There are many stories about the fate of the ashes, but it seems likely that Ravagli failed to carry out his commission. He confessed, after Frieda's death, 'I threw away the D. H. cinders', probably in Marseille, and perhaps into the harbour. He dispatched empty to New York the 'beautiful vase' that Frieda had specified, and filled it with ashes when he arrived. These were eventually sealed into a block of concrete that he made to prevent anyone from stealing them.[52] But so far as Frieda was concerned, she had brought Lawrence back; she died in 1956 ignorant of what had happened, and was buried just outside the shrine, under a stone with the von Richthofen crest proudly cut on it. She had once told Mabel Luhan how Lawrence had 'evaded' her with another woman, and how she had seen her opponent off.[53] Lawrence may finally have managed to evade her again, and to finish his career solitary, free, unhoused, with no lid sealing him down or block containing him: scattered, perhaps into the estranging sea he had so often contemplated.

But Frieda's instinct had been to bring him back to the ranch. It was where between 1932 and 1934 she wrote her biography of him, "*Not I, But the Wind . . .*"; she then spent the rest of her life trying to write her own autobiography. Lawrence continued to dominate her life: 'that small, intense space of life is over and yet I feel he loves me still and forever and whatever I do.'[54] In February 1935, she wrote to a friend how Kiowa in winter reminded her of Vence, five years earlier: 'I must remember him lying dead in that cold, bare room and I singing as if I could make him listen to me.' He had always listened to her, even when he was angry. She had sung to him again the night he died: this lonely, 'uncompromising fearless' man, who had travelled so far, and lived so hard, and died still so young.[55]

Acknowledgements

I want to thank my friends Mark Kinkead-Weekes and David Ellis for allowing me unrestricted access to the working materials for their Cambridge Lawrence biographies, in every possible way advising me and saving me from errors of interpretation as well as of fact. This is not a book which either of them would have chosen to have written in quite this way; their generosity is therefore a particular gift of friendship. All three of us acknowledge the helpfulness of Andrew Brown, of Cambridge University Press, not only in encouraging this particular publication, but in giving me permission to draw upon the three volumes of the Cambridge Biography of D. H. Lawrence. This book has been made possible by the whole Cambridge Lawrence project, the helpfulness of the individual editors, and in particular the volumes of *Letters* compiled by James T. Boulton.

Gerald Pollinger, of the D. H. Lawrence Estate, granted me permission to quote from such work of D. H. Lawrence as remains within copyright, and I am very grateful to him.

At Penguin Books, Hilary Laurie oversaw the project and was supportive and helpful at every stage; Laura Barber made many extremely useful suggestions and wonderfully eased my progress through the business of publication; Lin Vasey read the penultimate draft of the book with the extraordinary care characteristic of her, and saved me from vagueness, repetition, inconsistency and error. Kate Parker asked a host of necessary questions about the final draft and played a crucial role in making the book ready for publication.

Dorothy Johnson and the staff of the MSS Department at the University of Nottingham (in particular Julie Allinson, Jayne Amat,

Barbara Andrews, Caroline Kelly and Linda Shaw) have been enormously kind and helpful over many years, and I would like to thank them here.

One of my epigraphs is identical with an epigraph used by Edward Nehls at the start of his three volumes of *Composite Biography*; I have been an admirer of this biography ever since my parents presented me with it in September 1965, at the very start of my work on Lawrence.

For their particular help, I would like to thank Gary Akers, Helen Baron, Dorottya Bíró, Michael Black, Margaret Boulton, Linda Bree, Nick Ceramella, Bert Clarke†, John Coffey, Adriana Craciun, Geneviève Ellis, Roger Epperstone, Ron Faulks, Andrew Harrison, George Haynes, Paul Heapy, Ann Howard, Rosemary Howard, Bethan Jones, Joan King, Joan Kinkead-Weekes, Carl Kröckel, Clive Leivers, Jack and Pam Leivers, Jonathan Long, Molly Mahood, Joan McCluskey, Sandro Mirenda, Peggy Needham†, Ruth Neller and an observant reader at Mablethorpe Library, Leslie Parkes, Terence Pepper and the staff of the National Portrait Gallery, Christopher Pollnitz, Peter and Barbara Preston, Neil Reeve, Keith Sagar, Fred Skillington, Michael Squires, Lynn Talbot, John Turner, P. M. Wilson†, Dorothy Worthen, Peter Worthen† and Joanne Wright. Molly Chan-Williams influenced this book in ways she will understand. Simon Collins was his usual speedy, efficient and helpful self in doing all kinds of photographic work for me. Chloë Green advised me on the relations between Lawrence and her mother, Rosalind Baynes. Stefania Michelucci helped with many matters Italian. Sue Wilson read the Preface more ferociously and helpfully than I had imagined possible.

I also wish to acknowledge Harry Acton, Bingbin Bi, Richard Burdon, Valeria Faravelli, Jane Gibson, Susan Gilchrist, Laura Greenwood, Kevin Harvey, Sélène Hinton, Peggy Hung, Junko Iwasaki, Anna Johncock, Clare McCauley, Xu Ming, Malathy Nair, Masami Nakabayashi, James Oldring, Stephen Parr, Renate Pechova, Ben Shelton, Roger Simmonds, Phil Skelton, Robert Skilling, Meg Stokes, Brenda Summer, Magda Vaughan, Julie Williams, Ben Woolhead and Jie Zhou – together with many other students who came to study Lawrence at Swansea and Nottingham and, whether they knew it or not, helped me.

ACKNOWLEDGEMENTS

Cornelia Rumpf-Worthen has lived with me and thus with Lawrence for a quarter of a century. I owe her far more than I can write here in this, my valedictory book on Lawrence.

Sources, Cue-titles and Abbreviations

Some of the materials in this biography will be found in the three volumes of the Cambridge University Press biography of Lawrence (*The Early Years, Triumph to Exile, Dying Game*). References have usually been made to the sources upon which those volumes drew; references to the Cambridge biographies have been given when the material there is more accessible than the sources on which they drew, or at times because the further discussion of the material in the Cambridge volume is helpful. At one or two points (such as the events of May 1912, and the relationship with the Wilkinsons 1926–8)new arguments have been developed or new material has become available, so that this volume is able to supplement the Cambridge biography. An endnote in Chapter 1 (note 24) describes how *Sons and Lovers* has been used as a source; note 54 in Chapter 7 describes how *Mr Noon* has been used in Chapters 7, 8 and 9. The occasional phrase taken directly from the Cambridge biographies records the author's admiration for language on which he cannot improve; the rare head-on disagreement has been recorded in the endnotes.

Place of publication is London unless otherwise specified.

WORKS BY LAWRENCE

A   *Apocalypse*, ed. Mara Kalnins (Cambridge: Cambridge University Press, 1980)

AR   *Aaron's Rod*, ed. Mara Kalnins (Cambridge: Cambridge University Press, 1988)

BinB	*The Boy in the Bush*, ed. Paul Eggert (Cambridge: Cambridge University Press, 1990)
EmyE	*England, My England and Other Stories*, ed. Bruce Steele (Cambridge: Cambridge University Press, 1990)
Fox	*The Fox · The Captain's Doll · The Ladybird*, ed. Dieter Mehl (Cambridge: Cambridge University Press, 1992)
FSCL	*The First and Second Lady Chatterley Novels*, ed. Dieter Mehl and Christa Jansohn (Cambridge: Cambridge University Press, 1999)
FWL	*The First 'Women in Love'*, ed. John Worthen and Lindeth Vasey (Cambridge: Cambridge University Press, 1998)
Hardy	*Study of Thomas Hardy and Other Essays*, ed. Bruce Steele (Cambridge: Cambridge University Press, 1985)
K	*Kangaroo*, ed. Bruce Steele (Cambridge: Cambridge University Press, 1994)
L, i	*The Letters of D. H. Lawrence*, vol. i, ed. James T. Boulton (Cambridge: Cambridge University Press, 1979)
L, ii	*The Letters of D. H. Lawrence*, vol. ii, ed. George J. Zytaruk and James T. Boulton (Cambridge: Cambridge University Press, 1981)
L, iii	*The Letters of D. H. Lawrence*, vol. iii, ed. James T. Boulton and Andrew Robertson (Cambridge: Cambridge University Press, 1984)
L, iv	*The Letters of D. H. Lawrence*, vol. iv, ed. Warren Roberts, James T. Boulton and Elizabeth Mansfield (Cambridge: Cambridge University Press, 1987)
L, v	*The Letters of D. H. Lawrence*, vol. v, ed. James T. Boulton and Lindeth Vasey (Cambridge: Cambridge University Press, 1989)
L, vi	*The Letters of D. H. Lawrence*, vol. vi, ed. James T. Boulton and Margaret H. Boulton with Gerald M. Lacy (Cambridge: Cambridge University Press, 1991)
L, vii	*The Letters of D. H. Lawrence*, vol. vii, ed. Keith

	Sagar and James T. Boulton (Cambridge: Cambridge University Press, 1993)
L, viii	*The Letters of D. H. Lawrence*, vol. viii, ed. James T. Boulton (Cambridge: Cambridge University Press, 2001)
LAH	*Love Among the Haystacks and Other Stories*, ed. John Worthen (Cambridge: Cambridge University Press, 1987)
LCL	*Lady Chatterley's Lover*, ed. Michael Squires (Cambridge: Cambridge University Press, 1993)
LEA	*Late Essays and Articles*, ed. James T. Boulton (Cambridge: Cambridge University Press, 2004)
LG	*The Lost Girl*, ed. John Worthen (Cambridge: Cambridge University Press, 1981)
MinM	*Mornings in Mexico* (Secker, 1927)
MM	*Memoir of Maurice Magnus*, ed. Keith Cushman (Santa Rosa: Black Sparrow Press, 1987)
MN	*Mr Noon*, ed. Lindeth Vasey (Cambridge: Cambridge University Press, 1984)
Movements	*Movements in European History*, ed. Philip Crumpton (Cambridge: Cambridge University Press, 1988)
P	*Phoenix: The Posthumous Papers of D. H. Lawrence*, ed. Edward D. McDonald (New York: Viking, 1936)
PII	*Phoenix II: Uncollected, Unpublished and Other Prose Works by D. H. Lawrence*, ed. Warren Roberts and Harry T. Moore (Heinemann, 1968)
PFU	*Psychoanalysis and the Unconscious* and *Fantasia of the Unconscious*, ed. Bruce Steele (Cambridge: Cambridge University Press, 2004)
Plays	*The Plays*, ed. Hans Schwarze and John Worthen (Cambridge: Cambridge University Press, 1999)
PM	*Paul Morel*, ed. Helen Baron (Cambridge: Cambridge University Press, 2003)
PO	*The Prussian Officer and Other Stories*, ed. John Worthen (Cambridge: Cambridge University Press, 1983)

Poems	*The Complete Poems of D. H. Lawrence*, ed. Vivian de Sola Pinto and Warren Roberts, revised edn. (Harmondsworth: Penguin Books, 1977)
PS	*The Plumed Serpent*, ed. L. D. Clark (Cambridge: Cambridge University Press, 1987)
R	*The Rainbow*, ed. Mark Kinkead-Weekes (Cambridge: Cambridge University Press, 1989)
Reflections	*Reflections on the Death of a Porcupine and Other Essays*, ed. Michael Herbert (Cambridge: Cambridge University Press, 1988)
S&S	*Sea and Sardinia*, ed. Mara Kalnins (Cambridge: Cambridge University Press, 1997)
SEP	*Sketches of Etruscan Places and Other Italian Essays*, ed. Simonetta de Filippis (Cambridge: Cambridge University Press, 1999)
SL	*Sons and Lovers*, ed. Helen Baron and Carl Baron (Cambridge: Cambridge University Press, 1991)
St.M	*St. Mawr and Other Stories*, ed. Brian Finney (Cambridge: Cambridge University Press, 1983)
Studies	*Studies in Classic American Literature*, ed. Ezra Greenspan, Lindeth Vasey and John Worthen (Cambridge: Cambridge University Press, 2003)
T	*The Trespasser*, ed. Elizabeth Mansfield, with an Introduction and Notes by John F. Turner (Harmondsworth: Penguin Books, 1994)
TI	*Twilight in Italy and Other Essays*, ed. Paul Eggert (Cambridge: Cambridge University Press, 1994)
WL	*Women in Love*, ed. David Farmer, Lindeth Vasey and John Worthen (Cambridge: Cambridge University Press, 1987)
WP	*The White Peacock*, ed. Andrew Robertson (Cambridge: Cambridge University Press, 1983)
WWRA	*The Woman Who Rode Away and Other Stories*, ed. Dieter Mehl and Christa Jansohn (Cambridge: Cambridge University Press, 1995)

OTHER PRINTED AND
ELECTRONIC WORKS

Ada	Ada Lawrence and G. Stuart Gelder, *The Early Life of D. H. Lawrence* (Secker, 1932)
Bedford	Sybille Bedford, *Aldous Huxley: A Biography*, 2 vols. (Chatto & Windus, 1973–4)
Brett	Dorothy Brett, *Lawrence and Brett: A Friendship* (Philadelphia: J. B. Lippincott, 1933)
Brett (1974)	Dorothy Brett, *Lawrence and Brett: A Friendship*, ed. John Manchester (Santa Fe: Sunstone, 1974)
Bynner	Witter Bynner, *Journey with Genius: Recollections and Reflections Concerning the D. H. Lawrences* (Peter Nevill, 1953)
Crotch	Martha Gordon Crotch, *Memories of Frieda Lawrence* (Edinburgh: Tragara Press, n.d.)
Delavenay	Émile Delavenay, *D. H. Lawrence: L'Homme et la genèse de son oeuvre. Les années de formation: 1885–1919*, 2 vols. (Paris: Libraire C. Klincksieck, 1969)
DG	David Ellis, *D. H. Lawrence: Dying Game 1922–1930* (Cambridge: Cambridge University Press, 1998)
E	Section E of Warren Roberts and Paul Poplawski, *A Bibliography of D. H. Lawrence*, 3rd edn. (Cambridge: Cambridge University Press, 2001)
E. T.	E. T. [Jessie Chambers Wood], *D. H. Lawrence: A Personal Record* (Jonathan Cape, 1935)
EY	John Worthen, *D. H. Lawrence: The Early Years 1885–1912* (Cambridge: Cambridge University Press, 1991)
Frieda	Frieda Lawrence, *"Not I, But the Wind . . ."* (Santa Fe: Rydal Press, 1934)
Hignett	Sean Hignett, *Brett: From Bloomsbury to New Mexico: A Biography* (Hodder and Stoughton, 1984)
KJB	*The Holy Bible Containing the Old and New Testaments (Authorised King James Version)*

Luhan   Mabel Luhan, *Lorenzo in Taos* (New York: Knopf, 1932)

Memoirs   *Frieda Lawrence: The Memoirs and Correspondence*, ed. E. W. Tedlock (Heinemann, 1961)

Merrild   Knud Merrild, *A Poet and Two Painters: A Memoir of D. H. Lawrence* (New York: Viking Press, 1939)

Nehls   *D. H. Lawrence: A Composite Biography*, ed. Edward Nehls, 3 vols. (Madison: University of Wisconsin Press, 1957–9)

OED2   *The Oxford English Dictionary (Second Edition)* on CD-ROM, Version 2.0 (Oxford: Oxford University Press, 1994)

Patmore   Brigit Patmore, *My Friends When Young: The Memoirs of Brigit Patmore*, ed. Derek Patmore (Heinemann, 1968)

SP   Catherine Carswell, *The Savage Pilgrimage* [1932] (Cambridge: Cambridge University Press, 1981)

TE   Mark Kinkead-Weekes, *D. H. Lawrence: Triumph to Exile 1912–1922* (Cambridge: Cambridge University Press, 1996)

Tedlock   E. W. Tedlock, *The Frieda Lawrence Collection of D. H. Lawrence Manuscripts: A Descriptive Bibliography* (Albuquerque: University of New Mexico Press, 1948)

Wilkinson   John Turner, 'D. H. Lawrence in the Wilkinson Diaries', *D. H. Lawrence Review*, xxx (2002), 5–63

MANUSCRIPT LOCATIONS

BL   British Library
BucU   Bucknell University
NCL   Nottingham County Libraries
NRO   Nottingham Record Office
NWU   North Western University
NYPL   New York Public Library
SIU   University of Southern Illinois

UCB	University of California at Berkeley
UCin	University of Cincinnati
UCLA	University of California at Los Angeles
UIll	University of Illinois
UN	University of Nottingham
UNM	University of New Mexico
UT	University of Texas at Austin
UTul	University of Tulsa
YU	Yale University

PEOPLE

DHL	David Herbert Lawrence
Frieda	Frieda Weekley Lawrence Ravagli (*née* von Richthofen)
CR-W	Cornelia Rumpf-Worthen
JW	John Worthen

Endnotes

Preface

1. 'Which Class I Belong To', *LEA* 38.
2. 'Autobiographical Sketch', *PII* 302. See John Worthen, *D. H. Lawrence: A Literary Life* (1989), pp. xxiv–xxv, for a comparison of what DHL sold and earned in contrast with two of his successful contemporaries, Compton Mackenzie (1883–1972) and Arnold Bennett (1867–1931): e.g. in 1914, when his pre-war reputation was at its height, DHL received only 2 guineas for a newspaper piece of 1,400 words for the *Manchester Guardian*: Bennett thought 2½ guineas per 1,000 words for his writing an insult, expecting 6 guineas or more (p. xxv).
3. *L*, vi. 513.
4. *L*, vii. 294.
5. *L*, iv. 243, ii. 95; 'A Propos of *Lady Chatterley's Lover*', *LCL* 308.
6. To Edward Garnett, 13 April 1914 (*Letters from John Galsworthy 1900–1932*, ed. Edward Garnett, 1934, p. 218); *After Strange Gods* (1934), p. 61; *Observer*, 9 March 1930, p. 6.
7. *Daily Telegraph*, 'A Mind Diseased', 4 March 1930, p. 12; HO 45 / 13944.
8. Cf. *L*, vi. 491. The friend was Harry Crosby: see *DG* 472; Nehls, iii. 260. The phrase to which DHL was responding was probably the comment in *John Bull*: 'There is no law to prevent a man shutting himself up in an English study and creating a literary cesspool' (Nehls, iii. 262). In which case, he may well have been informed that 'this review calls your book a cesspool!' to which he had perhaps responded: 'Nobody *likes* their book being called a cesspool.'
9. See Jay A. Gertzman, *A Descriptive Bibliography of* Lady Chatterley's Lover (1989), Section 2 ('Piracies, 1928–50') and Section 4 ('Continental Editions in English', 1933–60').
10. Penguin Books had published much of Lawrence's writing in paperback between 1949 and 1960 (*The White Peacock*; *The Trespasser*; *Sons and*

Lovers; The Rainbow; Women in Love; The Lost Girl; England, My England; The Ladybird; Kangaroo; The Plumed Serpent; The Woman Who Rode Away and Other Stories; Love Among the Haystacks and Other Stories; Twilight in Italy; Mornings in Mexico and *Etruscan Places; Selected Essays; Selected Letters; Selected Poems*).

11. Philip Larkin, 'Annus Mirabilis', *High Windows* (1974), p. 34: 'Sexual intercourse began / In nineteen sixty-three / (Which was rather late for me) – / Between the end of the *Chatterley* ban / And the Beatles' first LP.'

12. The attacks on DHL by Simone de Beauvoir in *Le Deuxième Sexe* (Paris, 1949, tr. 1953 as *The Second Sex*) had, in contrast, been careful, measured and scholarly: e.g. DHL's 'statement that women *should* not experience the orgasm is arbitrary. It is a mistake to try to induce it at any cost; it is also wrong to withhold it at all times, as does Don Cipriano in *The Plumed Serpent*' (1953), p. 135.

13. *Poems* 205.

14. *L*, i. 503, 71, ii. 95, 102.

15. *A* 149.

16. *New Statesman*, 16–30 December 2002, p. 110; Ursula K. Le Guin, quoted in Gary Adelman, *Reclaiming D. H. Lawrence: Contemporary Writers Speak Out* (2002); Sandra Gilbert, 'Lawrence in Question', Foreword to Adelman, *Reclaiming Lawrence*, p. 9.

17. *L*, i. 23; *SP* 71; *PFU* 158; Frieda 52.

18. *Movements* 263, 262.

19. See *L*, i. 81.

20. *LCL* 204. Cf. Ursula K. Le Guin, quoted in Adelman, *Reclaiming Lawrence*, p. 26: 'He was a . . . man who wrote (I may not have the exact words of the quote), "fucking a black woman would be like fucking mud".'

21. DHL used the words 'Jew' and 'Jewess' perfectly unselfconsciously, according to the conventions of the time, and without bigotry or contempt: e.g. 'Jew's villas' (*L*, ii. 39), 'a tiny Jew' (*L*, iv. 366). Cf. M. Jane Taylor's comment that Virginia Woolf's 1909 phrase 'fat Jewess' is 'no more racist or bigoted than it would be to call someone a "pompous Frenchman" or a "pushy American" today' (*Guardian*, Review section, 21 June 2003, p. 8).

22. I draw upon the three-volume Cambridge biography of Lawrence, though I obviously cannot match the 'reasonably complete story' which was that project's aim. This book also attempts the 'definition of D. H. Lawrence's "me", his essential self' which is deliberately avoided in the Cambridge biography (*DG* 536), and which he also refused: 'I hate "understanding" people, and I hate more still to be understood. Damn understanding more than anything' (*L*, iv. 108).

1 Birthplace: 1885–1895

1. Cf. the half-timbered, ten-roomed, bourgeois house in Stratford-upon-Avon; the elegant stone-built town-house in Cockermouth (its seventeen large windows overlooking the street); the rambling, seven-roomed thatched cottage with three chimneys at Higher Bockhampton: the birthplaces of William Shakespeare (b. 1564), William and Dorothy Wordsworth (b. 1770, 1771) and Thomas Hardy (b. 1840) respectively.

2. *Studies* 83.

3. 'The Bad Side of Books', *P* 232, corrected from E36a (UT).

4. The weekly wage for a 'butty' (in charge of a team of miners) would vary – according to the demand for coal, and the shifts he was allowed to work – between 50 or 55 shillings in winter and 20 or 25 shillings in summer; see *EY* 36–8.

5. Noel M. Kader, *William Edward Hopkin* (1976), p. 11.

6. Nehls, i. 21; Kader, *Hopkin*, p. 11; 'Mushrooms', *LEA* 335.

7. *Eastwood & Kimberley Advertiser*, 8 October 1897, p. 2.

8. Ada 37; Arthur was probably born on 26 February 1848 (see *Notes and Queries*, 1, no. 4, September 2003, pp. 327–8).

9. *L*, iii. 282.

10. Roy Spencer, *D. H. Lawrence Country* (1979), pp. 67–8.

11. Nehls, iii. 564.

12. The Lawrence family sustained a story that Lydia had run a school bought for her by her father before he lost his job (Edward Gilbert, 'An Account of My Eastwood Visits of 1948–9', p. 15, JW's collection). Spencer found that, having been dismissed as a pupil-teacher, Lydia apparently took in girls for coaching in a room in Marine Town in Sheerness (Spencer, *D. H. Lawrence Country*, pp. 74, 79).

13. *SL* 301.

14. *EY* 5.

15. Ada 22–3; Frieda to Louis Gibbons, 27 September 1954 (quoted Michael Squires and Lynn K. Talbot, *Living at the Edge*, 2002, p. 8).

16. E. T. 20.

17. 'Getting On', *LEA* 29.

18. Ada 9.

19. Ada 21; 'Nottingham and the Mining Countryside', *P* 134 (the Squares were the Eastwood mining company houses built in blocks around a common unpaved 'square' for washing-lines, etc.).

20. Kelly's *Directory of Nottinghamshire*, 1888.

21. *Studies* 83; *L*, i. 192.

22. 'Autobiographical Sketch', *PII* 300; the 1895 catalogue of *The Library of the Eastwood and Greasley Mechanics' and Artizans' Institute* survives (NCL), the institute resulting from a movement begun in Edinburgh in 1821 by George Birkbeck (1776–1841) to provide free education for working men: there were 100 institutes by 1826 and 300 by 1841; Ada 21.

23. See *EY* 128–9.

24. DHL's 1913 novel is autobiographical, but this biography will use it sparingly for illustrations of events in the Lawrence household, and only where other evidence confirms its versions of family life. Many things in the novel are not true of real life; many things from real life do not appear in the novel.

25. John Shuttleworth to JW, Ilkeston, 3 July 1983.

26. *L*, iii. 303.

27. *L*, i. 190; see *Eastwood & Kimberley Advertiser*, 18 June 1897, p. 2, for a case in which the husband was taken to court and fined. *SL* 33–6 shows Mrs Morel waking her husband and getting back into the house; Lydia implied she had spent the night in an outhouse (Nehls, iii. 584).

28. At his christening in St Mary's Parish Church, Eastwood, 'Richards' was added after 'Herbert'; Lydia's sister Lettie wished to commemorate a clergyman who had died (see *EY* 135). DHL never acknowledged or used the name. Beauvale School records give him as 'Lawrence, B.' in 1897 (School Log-book, p. 133). When young, he attempted to drop his first name 'David' ('Enslaved by Civilisation', *PII* 581); some friends nevertheless used it (see *EY* 532). By the age of eighteen, he was styling himself 'DHL' or using his surname and initials (see e.g. *L*, i. 23, 28); from 1913, and probably earlier, Frieda called him 'Lorenzo' (people in Italy could not pronounce 'Lawrence' and had called him 'Signor Lorenze': *L*, i. 538). This biography will call him 'Lawrence' and will use the surname form for its male characters (normal period usage in these circles): e.g. Garnett, Murry. Female characters will normally be called by their first names (e.g. Frieda, Katherine); a notable exception is Dorothy Brett, who was universally called 'Brett'.

29. Nehls, iii. 553.

30. *L*, i. 190.

31. Nehls, i. 200, iii. 566.

32. *L*, i. 190; E. T. 149.

33. Ada 24; Nehls, ii. 126.

34. Interview with W. E. Lawrence (NCL).

35. *L*, i. 190, 471.

36. *L*, vi. 114–15; *OED*2. DHL linked chagrin with his mother specifically when, in December 1922, he referred to those who 'are pushed out of life in

chagrin' and who as a result die 'vengeful' (*Studies* 42); in *Sons and Lovers*, the dying Mrs Morel, like the Beardsalls, has to be 'pushed from behind, inch by inch' (*SL* 431), not hauled out of life by the neck like the Morels. In so far as Lydia Lawrence was in some ways Gertrude Morel, DHL linked Lydia with chagrin. See Chapter 25, n. 53.

37. *L*, v. 406.

38. George Neville, *A Memoir of D. H. Lawrence*, ed. Carl Baron (1981), pp. 57–8.

39. *MN* 225.

40. *MN* 224.

41. *SL* 58–60.

42. E. T. xvi.

43. J. D. Chambers, 'Memories of D. H. Lawrence', *Renaissance and Modern Studies*, xvi (1972), pp. 6–7.

44. *Eastwood & Kimberley Advertiser*, 18 October 1901, p. 2; '[Return to Bestwood]', *PII* 260.

45. *SL* 85; 'Getting On', p. 3; Nehls, iii. 570.

2 Rising in the World: 1895–1902

1. A school under the management of a School Board, as established by the Elementary Education Act of 1870.

2. DHL's letter of 15 September 1913 records: 'I was pretty ill two years ago ... with pneumonia [November 1911] – which was the third time I'd had it' (*L*, ii. 72). The second time was in December 1901, when he was sixteen; the first time must have been earlier in his childhood. See *EY* 523, n. 2, for a further discussion.

3. *PM* 33; *SL* 113; 'Enslaved by Civilisation', *PII* 580; but see too *EY* 75. DHL began his autobiographical novel in the autumn of 1910, wrote a lengthy but incomplete version of it in 1911 (published as *Paul Morel*), revised it extensively between November 1911 and May 1912, then rewrote it as *Sons and Lovers* between July and November 1912: it was published in May 1913.

4. Mabel Thurlby Collishaw interview (NCL).

5. Nehls, i. 25; David Lindley, 'Eastwood Revisited', *Human World* (May 1973), p. 51.

6. Nehls, i. 23; Noel M. Kader, *William Edward Hopkin*, (Eastwood, 1976), p. 11; Nehls, i. 72.

7. *SL* 97.

8. '[Return to Bestwood]', *PII* 261; George Neville, *A Memoir of D. H. Lawrence*, ed. Carl Baron (1981), p. 38; Kader, *Hopkin*, p. 11.

9. 'Autobiographical Sketch', *PII* 300.

10. By Morgan's Studio, 7 Cavendish Street, Chesterfield (La Phot 1/78/1, UN).

11. It can be seen in John Middleton Murry, *Son of Woman* (1931), opposite p. 40.

12. Nehls, iii. 610.

13. Nehls, i. 72; George Lawrence interview (NCL); Nehls, i. 29.

14. '*Stoppages*, deductions from miners' wages, such as rent, candles, blacksmith's work . . . etc.' (*OED*2); *SL* 96. Algebra and French are, however, the very subjects that, as an adolescent, Paul teaches Miriam Leivers (*SL* 186); they are an indication of the advanced education that he has (somehow) acquired.

15. Ada 34 (corrected from Ada Lawrence and G. Stuart Gelder, *Young Lorenzo*, 1931, p. 40).

16. Ada 36.

17. The school took £9 in fees; the balance was sent to the scholar only after his term reports had been examined.

18. Letter from E. J. Woodford to Michael Sharpe, 4 November 1957, p. 2 (UN); 'Autobiographical Sketch', *PII* 300.

19. 'A rod of steel, fluted or plain, fitted with a handle, used for sharpening table . . . knives' (*OED*2 8b).

20. See *EY* 45–7, 87–8.

21. The prize book – W. H. Fitchett, *Fights for the Flag* (1898) – is now in the High School, signed by the headmaster James Gow.

22. E. J. Woodford notes (UN).

23. A contemporary at Beauvale School in the late 1890s told his granddaughter that he remembered DHL as a 'snotty-nosed kid', meaning not only 'always with a cold' but 'small and contemptible' (see *OED*2; reminiscence reported to JW 13 March 2002).

24. Letter from H. Goddard to Émile Delavenay, 8 October 1933 (La T 65, UN).

25. *R* 18.

26. *L*, i. 39, 119.

27. *R* 389; *L*, i. 208.

28. Nehls, iii. 393.

29. *SL* 128.

30. *EY* 100.

31. F. Lyons, *The Hills of Annesley* (1973), p. 236; Neville, *A Memoir of D. H. Lawrence*, p. 90.

32. E. T. 19.

33. Nehls, iii. 561.

34. *Eastwood & Kimberley Advertiser*, 18 October 1901, p. 2; Nehls, iii. 561; see *EY* 520, 526.

35. *Eastwood & Kimberley Advertiser*, 18 October 1901, p. 2.

36. Recreated as Louisa Lily Denys Western, also known as 'Gipsy' or 'Gyp', in *SL* 126.

37. See *EY* Illustrations 5 and 6.

38. E. T. 19; Ernest Lawrence to DHL, 7 October 1897 (MS Clarke).

39. E. T. 26.

40. *Eastwood & Kimberley Advertiser*, 18 October 1901, p. 2; *SL* 77.

41. *L*, i. 477.

42. *SL* 106, 147.

43. E. T. 31.

44. *SL* 171.

45. Nehls, iii. 44; *SL* 171.

46. *SL* 70.

47. *L*, i. 190.

48. *SL* 91.

49. Nehls, iii. 575: an unreliably reported anecdote of Edmund Chambers from the spring of 1902 shows him calling on the Lawrences, to find the lanky sixteen-year-old sitting on his mother's lap (UT); *L*, i. 45.

50. *PFU* 65, 150.

51. 'Autobiographical Sketch', *PII* 301; Nehls, iii. 565.

52. *R* 349–76; e.g. Jessie Chambers in Underwood (Nehls, iii. 537) and Louie Burrows in Leicester (*L*, i. 93, 94).

53. Nehls, iii. 583; Charles Leeming, recorded interview (NCL).

54. Log-book 303, 28 October 1902 (NRO).

3 A Collier's Son a Poet: 1902–1905

1. J. D. Chambers, 'Memories of D. H. Lawrence', *Renaissance and Modern Studies*, xvi (1972), pp. 6–7; E. T. 15–16; Nehls, iii. 555.

2. E. T. 22, 24; Nehls, iii. 561.

3. Nehls, iii. 536. Miriam's comment – 'Mother said to me – "there is one thing in marriage that is always dreadful, but you have to bear it"' (*SL* 334) – suggests that Ann Chambers may have said something similar.

4. *SL* 158.

5. The present tower at Crich was built in 1923, replacing a monument, 'sturdy and squat', erected in 1821, which Paul can see from Bestwood (*SL* 206).

6. Emily King during *Son and Lover*, BBC Third Programme, 8 May 1955 (La Av 3/2, UN); *EmyE* 201.

7. His second mathematics prize at the High School, signed and dated 28 July 1900 (Jean Temple).

8. Chambers, 'Memories', p. 10; Nehls, iii. 578.

9. Compton Mackenzie, *My Life and Times: Octave Five 1915–1923* (1966), p. 168. Mackenzie, however (knowing DHL's background), recalled that he had loved a 'young coal-miner'.

10. Nehls, iii. 537.

11. See *EY* Illustration 21; Nehls, iii. 537.

12. *SL* 96.

13. E. T. 30; 'The Collected Letters of Jessie Chambers', ed. George J. Zytaruk, *D. H. Lawrence Review*, xii (Spring–Summer 1979), p. 58.

14. 'Collected Letters', ed. Zytaruk, p. 49. The Ellis family at the farm at Wandoo in *The Boy in the Bush* (1924) was a later recreation of the Chambers family, in particular their singing and laughter: 'the family! the family! Jack still loved it. It seemed to fill the whole of life for him' (*BinB* 71).

15. *L*, vi. 618. See too 'The Shades of Spring' (1914): 'To his last day, he would dream of this place' (*PO* 102). The writing of the letter is discussed in Chapter 24.

16. Chambers, 'Memories', p. 11.

17. May Holbrook to David Chambers, 25 March 1949 (Ann Howard).

18. *L*, i. 103; Nehls, iii. 611.

19. E. T. 30.

20. E. T. 32.

21. Chambers, 'Memories', p. 12; E. T. 134.

22. Nehls, iii. 565; E. T. 28.

23. Nehls, iii. 591.

24. Nehls, iii. 588.

25. Cf. the picture-postcard which DHL sent to Mabel Limb from London on 28 November 1908 ('Picturesque Devon'): 'Doesn't this picture remind you of our old days?' (*L*, i. 95).

26. E. T. 96.

27. Nehls, iii. 590; *EY* 119.

28. *SL* 161.

29. E. T. 95.

30. E. T. 18; Nehls, iii. 593.

31. 'Collected Letters', ed. Zytaruk, p. 58.

32. E. T. 96.

33. Nehls, iii. 596.

34. Testimonial, written 18 July 1908 (UN).

35. Albert Street School (Boys) Log-book, pp. 318–19 (NRO).

36. Gilbert Noon, of Cotmanhay, may at this stage have been no more than an acquaintance, but would eventually give his name and some of his experience to *Mr Noon*.

37. Nehls, i. 43–4.

38. *Plays* 536.

39. The original of the photograph (see *EY* Illustration 12) reveals that it was taken indoors by Holderness, but its owner will not sanction its reproduction.

40. Nehls, iii. 584.

41. *L*, i. 27.

42. 'Foreword to *Collected Poems*', *Poems* 849.

43. Ron Faulks and Clive Leivers have generously shared with me their researches showing that there is, in fact, no link between the family of the divine and hymn-writer John Newton (1725–1807) and DHL's maternal grandfather, the lace-worker and composer John Newton (1802–86); Lettie Berry's acrostic on DHL's death survives in private hands.

44. Nehls, iii. 560.

45. *L*, i. 23, 27, viii. 1.

46. *L*, vi. 535.

47. 'Autobiographical Sketch', *PII* 301; see e.g. *SL* 88–9; *L*, i. 513.

48. E. T. 57.

49. E. T. 57.

50. George Neville, *A Memoir of D. H. Lawrence*, ed. Carl Baron (1981), p. 188.

51. 'Getting On', *LEA* 30.

52. E317 (UN). The pink campions which Connie threads into Mellors's pubic hair in *Lady Chatterley's Lover* (*LCL* 227) may be a sly reference to the poem for 'young ladies'.

53. See e.g. Richard Ellman, *James Joyce* (1982), pp. 50–51, 78–80.

54. Ada 55–8: see too *EY* 136. DHL's letter writing had certainly developed since the 'long descriptive letters' he had sent in the spring of 1901 from Skegness to the Chambers family, 'in one of which he said that he could stand in his aunt's drawing room and watch the tide rolling in through the window'. The sharp-tongued May Chambers commented: 'what an uncomfortable drawing-room his aunt's must be, with the tide rolling in through the window!' (E. T. 28).

55. Albert Street School (Boys) Log-book, 27–9 March 1906, p. 335 (NRO); *L*, i. 39; 'Autobiographical Sketch', *PII* 593.

4 Getting Weaned: 1905–1908

1. *LAH* 33.
2. *Plays* 29.
3. Sarah Elizabeth Walker (b. 1896); *EY* 159, 535.
4. *L*, i. 62, 29; *PM* 298 (note on 240: 4): the comments refer to the characters Paul and Miriam, but as Jessie is treating them as direct biographical counterparts of DHL and herself, they are evidence of what Jessie thought had happened to her and DHL between 1902 and 1906.
5. *PM* 85.
6. *PM* 243; E. T. 133.
7. 'The State of Funk', *PII* 568; 'Nathaniel Hawthorne and *The Scarlet Letter*', *Studies* 92.
8. Nehls, i. 54–5.
9. E. T. 66.
10. *EY* 162.
11. E. T. 67.
12. E. T. 68.
13. The family traditionally went on holiday with others: with Jessie in 1906, Jessie and Mabel and Frances Cooper in 1907, Alan and Jessie Chambers and Alvina Reeve in 1908 (when they also met up with the Burrows family), and yet another group (but not Jessie) in 1909.
14. In May 1908, DHL referred to working on the book at the start of his college career, having begun it 'some months before – two years last Easter' (*L*, i. 49).
15. E. T. 117; *L*, i. 49.
16. *PM* 94. DHL commented in 1913: 'I love *Tristram Shandy*' (*L*, ii. 90).
17. E. T. 103.
18. Jessie's novel was called *The Rathe Primrose*: see Chapter 9; *L*, i. 551; *SL* 190.
19. *SL* 232.
20. *SL* 232.
21. *L*, i. 141.
22. *L*, i. 89.
23. 'Getting On', E144, p. 4; *LAH* 33. For another photograph taken that day, see *EY* Illustration 14.
24. *LAH* 35.
25. University College Students' Register (UN).
26. *EY* 288; *L*, i. 193.
27. *L*, i. 41.

28. Minute book (La Z 7/1, UN).

29. *Plays* 6; see *MN* 3. Ethical socialism – sometimes called 'utopian social-ism' by Marxists – argued that a socialist society could rely on the ethical obligations of people to help each other.

30. Alice Hall Holditch, interview (NCL).

31. *SL* 267.

32. *L*, i. 99, 101, 36–7, 39–41.

33. See *EY* 175; *L*, i. 99, 40–41, 256.

34. *L*, i. 256.

35. Emily King during *Son and Lover*, BBC Third Programme, 8 May 1955 (La Av 3/2, UN).

36. *L*, i. 98, 101.

37. J. D. Chambers, 'Memories of D. H. Lawrence', *Renaissance and Modern Studies*, xvi (1972), p. 15.

38. *L*, i. 527.

39. Chambers, 'Memories', p. 15.

40. E. T. 127–8.

41. Nehls, i. 49.

42. *L*, ii. 73.

43. *L*, i. 39.

44. *L*, i. 58.

45. E. T. 76.

46. *L*, i. 72.

47. *R* 403.

48. University College Students' Register.

49. See *WP* xvii–xviii; 'Getting On', p. 5.

50. *LAH* 5.

51. *L*, v. 86.

52. E317, E320.1 (UN).

53. See *EY* Illustration 15.

54. *L*, i. 49.

55. *SL* 25.

56. E. T. 89.

57. *L*, i. 73.

58. *L*, i. 80.

59. Alice Hall Holditch recording (NCL); George Neville, *A Memoir of D. H. Lawrence*, ed. Carl Baron (1981), pp. 72–4. See Fiona MacCarthy, *Eric Gill* (1989), p. 46, for an account of the nineteen-year-old Gill's similar ignorance in 1901.

60. Nehls, iii. 618.

61. *L*, i. 117; Nehls, iii. 611.
62. E. T. 149; Nehls, iii. 611.
63. E. T. 150.
64. *L*, i. 154.

5 Croydon: 1908–1910

1. *L*, i. 83–4; Helen Corke, *In Our Infancy* (1975), p. 133; *L*, i. 121.
2. E. T. 152.
3. *L*, i. 82, 106.
4. University College Students' Register (UN); *L*, i. 85.
5. *L*, i. 93.
6. *L*, i. 89, 124. DHL wrote an account of those free breakfasts in 'Lessford's Rabbits' (*LAH* 21–7).
7. *L*, i. 84.
8. *L*, i. 93, 164, 85.
9. *L*, i. 39; *L*, i. 93–4; University College Students' Register.
10. *L*, i. 93, 94, 117. The improvement was permanent; on 20 December 1910, a reference created for the Education Committee in Croydon (presumably using information supplied by Philip Smith) would describe DHL as 'a sympathetic and capable disciplinarian' (MS Clarke).
11. Nehls, i. 98; Corke, *In Our Infancy*, p. 160; *T* 218–19; *L*, i. 465 and n. 1.
12. Nehls, i. 90; *T* 218.
13. *L*, i. 118. Björnsterne Björnson (1832–1910) was a Norwegian poet, novelist and dramatist.
14. See *EY* 210–12.
15. 'Education of the People', *Reflections* 89; Nehls, i. 86.
16. Nehls, i. 87; *L*, i. 89; *The Letters of D. H. Lawrence and Amy Lowell 1914–1925*, ed. E. Claire Healey and Keith Cushman (1985), p. 132.
17. Nehls, i. 90, 86.
18. *L*, v. 479; 'Education of the People', *Reflections* 89.
19. *L*, i. 208.
20. 'The Fly in the Ointment', *LAH* 25, 51.
21. Corke, *In Our Infancy*, p. 135.
22. *L*, i. 106.
23. *L*, i. 84, 85.
24. *WP* 264.
25. *L*, i. 103, 91, 128.
26. *L*, i. 450.
27. *L*, i. 115. DHL wrote poems about Hilda Mary that (as opposed to

poems like 'Campions') still find readers: 'Baby Songs: Ten Months Old', 'Baby Movements: Running Barefoot' and 'Trailing Clouds' (*Poems* 863, 918–19).

28. See e.g. 'I've got six kiddies to buy for' (*L*, i. 208): in addition to Peggy, his brother George's children, Ernest (b. 1897), Edward Arthur (b. 1900) and Flossie (b. 1905), and the two Jones children.

29. *L*, i. 92, 85.

30. *L*, i. 69; E. T. 117.

31. *WP* 222–3.

32. *L*, i. 118; Nehls, i. 91.

33. She was certainly reading his work in 1910; see *EY* 142–4.

34. *L*, i. 99.

35. E. T. 168.

36. E. T. 155–6.

37. *L*, i. 89, 139, 181.

38. *L*, i. 165, ii. 90.

39. *L*, i. 85.

40. *L*, i. 146. Grace Crawford (1889–1977) was a young American woman brought to Europe by her parents for her education.

41. E. T. 157.

42. Nehls, i. 109; E. T. 158.

43. Ford Madox Ford, *Return to Yesterday* (1931), p. 399; E. T. 159; *L*, i. 138. Years later, DHL would actually invent the working-class Midlands poet in his story 'Jimmy and the Desperate Woman': he created appropriately stark industrial verse for Mrs Pinnegar, disappointed wife of a miner, to catch the eye of a London literary editor. See *WWRA* 101–3.

44. Nehls, i. 111–12; 'Dreams Old and Nascent – I: Old. II: Nascent', 'Baby Movements – I: Running Barefoot. II: Trailing Clouds', 'Discipline' (*Poems* 908–9, 909–11, 916, 916, 929).

45. Nehls, i. 109.

46. 'Autobiographical Sketch', *PII* 593–4.

47. Nehls, i. 126; *L*, i. 171; 'Autobiographical Sketch', *PII* 594.

48. *L*, i. 144–5, viii. 3, i. 152, viii. 3.

49. E. T. 179; *L*, i. 130, 286.

50. *L*, i. 319, 137; Mollie Skinner, *The Fifth Sparrow: An Autobiography* (1973), pp. 115–16.

51. *L*, i. 164; Nehls, i. 129–31.

52. Nehls, ii. 268; Wilkinson 43 (though see Nehls, iii. 138–9).

53. 'Autobiographical Sketch', *PII* 593.

54. *L*, i. 141.

55. *WP* 226; E. T. 168; *L*, i. 153.

56. E. T. 180–81. Writing *c*. 1935, Jessie remembered DHL using the word 'engaged' to describe his period of sexual relationship with her in 1910 (Delavenay, ii. 703); to her at least, the commitment *was* an engagement. It seems likely that she meant the same when she used the language of engagement (E. T. 165) for DHL's relationship with Agnes Holt.

57. *L*, i. 153.

58. See *MN* 51–6.

59. 'Restlessness', E317 no. 55, ll. 30–31, revised in *Poems* 178; *L*, i. 188.

60. *WP* 230.

61. *L*, i. 153.

62. Nehls, i. 293.

6 Love and Death: 1910

1. E. T. 164–5.

2. E. T. 167–8; Delavenay, ii. 702.

3. Delavenay, ii. 702.

4. E. T. 167.

5. Nehls, iii. 537.

6. E. T. 167.

7. 'The Collected Letters of Jessie Chambers', ed. George J. Zytaruk, *D. H. Lawrence Review*, xii (Spring–Summer 1979), p. 117; E. T. 182.

8. E. T. 133.

9. 'The State of Funk', *PII* 568; 'Pornography and Obscenity', *LEA* 245; *PFU* 139. Such references to masturbation are unusual in the period from a non-medical or non-moralistic writer: it was characteristic of DHL to write up to the limit (and beyond) of the acceptable, and because he did so, we can extrapolate from his writing some of the likelihoods of his life. James C. Cowan has said rather similar things on the subject in his book *D. H. Lawrence: Self and Sexuality* (2002).

10. In March 1912, DHL came across it and called it 'a story I wrote three years back, and had forgotten' (*L*, i. 372).

11. E. T. 133; *LAH* 47.

12. George Neville, *A Memoir of D. H. Lawrence*, ed. Carl Baron (1981), p. 86.

13. When DHL rewrote his early life from the perspective of Oliver Mellors in the third version of *Lady Chatterley's Lover*, late in 1927, he would put an even cruder gloss on his desires, and on how Jessie had responded: 'I got thinner and crazier. Then I said we'd got to be lovers. I talked her into it, as

usual. So she let me. I was excited, and she never wanted it. She just didn't want it. She adored me, she loved me to talk to her and kiss her: in that way, she had a passion for me. But the other, she just didn't want ... And it was just the other that I *did* want' (*LCL* 200). However much of a self-parody that is, its account of a relationship in which the man talks his way into what he wants has an honesty that, in 1909–10, DHL could not manage.

14. 'Pornography and Obscenity', *LEA* 246.

15. *L*, i. 154.

16. *L*, i. 191.

17. *L*, i. 154.

18. Helen Corke, *Neutral Ground* (1933) p. 194.

19. *T* 241, 267. (References to the Cambridge edition, 1981, of the novel subsequent to p. 230 are located exactly fifty pages later.)

20. *T* 249.

21. *T* 274, 214, 265.

22. Delavenay, ii. 702; *L*, i. 157. DHL had been struck by the way Rochester, in *Jane Eyre*, calls Jane a 'thing' (E. T. 98): 'you strange – you almost unearthly thing!' (vol. ii, ch. viii).

23. *L*, i. 157.

24. Delavenay, ii. 703; *L*, i. 158.

25. *WP* 389 (note on 255: 16).

26. *T* 268.

27. Helen Corke, *In Our Infancy* (1975), p. 162.

28. *L*, i. 160; Delavenay, ii. 704.

29. 'Lilies in the Fire', E213a (UT), ll. 33, 42; E. T. 181; *L*, i. 166.

30. *T* 74.

31. *L*, i. 162, 160, 155. Cf. his comment to Helen Corke on 1 June 1910: 'C'est moi qui perdrai le jeu' ('It is I who will be the loser') (*L*, i. 162).

32. E. T. 182.

33. *L*, i. 173.

34. *L*, i. 173, 190, 191.

35. Corke, *In Our Infancy*, p. 168.

36. Corke, *In Our Infancy*, p. 191; *L*, i. 175.

37. Helen Corke, *D. H. Lawrence: The Croydon Years* (1965), p. 21.

38. Jessie Chambers wrote a novel, *The Rathe Primrose* (see Chapter 9), now lost, and a memoir, *D. H. Lawrence: A Personal Record* (1935), by 'E. T.'. Helen Corke published her novel *Neutral Ground* and her book *Lawrence and Apocalypse* in 1933; later came her *D. H. Lawrence: The Croydon Years* (1965) and *In Our Infancy* (1975).

39. Corke, *In Our Infancy*, p. 181.

40. Cf. 'She belonged to that class of "Dreaming Women", with whom passion exhausts itself at the mouth' (*T*64); 'Passing Visit to Helen', *Poems* 150.

41. 'Lilies in the Fire', E213a, ll. 30–33.

42. *L*, i. 359.

43. *SL* 340–41.

44. 'Collected Letters', ed. Zytaruk, p. 11.

45. *L*, i. 477: 'the split begins to tell again. But, almost unconsciously, the mother realises what is the matter, and begins to die.'

46. *L*, i. 175, 373; Neville, *A Memoir of D. H. Lawrence*, p. 152.

47. *L*, i. 190.

48. *L*, i. 193, 190; Gilbert papers, p. 6 (UN).

49. *L*, i. 179; Corke, *The Croydon Years*, p. 51; *L*, i. 180.

50. *L*, i. 488, 330.

51. See *EY* 276–80.

52. *L*, viii. 4.

53. *L*, i. 190.

54. *L*, i. 195.

55. *L*, i. 185, 181 n. 5 (a note she wrote much later in life); *EY* 340.

56. *L*, i. 189.

57. *SL* 437; *L*, i. 189.

58. *L*, i. 194 and n. 2; Nehls, iii. 618.

59. *L*, i. 193, 192.

60. *L*, i. 198, 343.

61. *L*, i. 197; Nehls, iii. 618.

62. *L*, i. 189.

63. *L*, i. 192, 195; *SL* 435.

64. *L*, i. 195.

65. Lina D. Waterfield, *Castle in Italy* (1961), p. 139: see too *SL* 437–8.

66. *L*, i. 199.

67. *L*, i. 199, 202.

68. In the Walker Street Gallery, Liverpool. DHL's copy for Ada is reproduced in colour on the dust jacket of the hardback edition of *EY*. The copies he gave to Ada and to Louie Burrows are in private hands; the copy for Agnes Holt is at UN; the fourth copy (for Arthur McLeod) is unlocated.

69. *L*, i. 103.

70. *L*, i. 181, 190.

71. *SL* 355.

7 The Sick Year: 1911–1912

1. *L*, i. 220.
2. *L*, i. 222, 223, 191.
3. *L*, i. 293.
4. *L*, i. 266.
5. *L*, i. 225–6.
6. *L*, i. 272.
7. *L*, i. 339.
8. *L*, i. 285.
9. *WP* 132.
10. *EY* 314.
11. *L*, i. 237.
12. *L*, i. 239. In *Lady Chatterley's Lover*, Mellors is a thoroughly jaundiced commentator on a Helen figure: 'She was a soft, white-skinned, soft sort of woman, older than me, and played the fiddle . . . She loved everything about love, except the sex. Clinging, caressing, creeping into you in every way: but if you forced her to the sex itself, she just ground her teeth and sent out hate' (*LCL* 200–201).
13. *L*, ii. 91.
14. *L*, i. 298; see Chapter 7 and *L*, i. 364.
15. *L*, i. 286; Delavenay, ii. 706.
16. *Daily News* (14 February 1911), p. 3; see too *WP* xliv–xlvi.
17. *L*, i. 339.
18. *L*, i. 289, 218. Cf. too his remark to Rachel Annand Taylor, probably in the winter of 1910: 'Oh, I'll probably die of drink like my father' (Nehls, i. 137).
19. *L*, i. 285, 286.
20. *AR* 22.
21. *L*, i. 298–9.
22. *L*, i. 289.
23. *L*, i. 315.
24. *L*, i. 315.
25. *L*, i. 315.
26. *L*, i. 317.
27. *R* 21.
28. *L*, i. 321.
29. *EY* 320, 316.
30. *Memoirs* 247; *L*, i. 48.
31. Enid Hilton Memoir, p. 2 (UN); Alice Hall Holditch recording (NCL).

32. Émile Delavenay, 'Sandals and Scholarship', *D. H. Lawrence Review*, ix (Fall 1976), p. 411.

33. *R* 21; *L*, i. 101, iii. 209.

34. *WL* 500; *Memoirs* 245–8.

35. *L*, i. 322.

36. 'Paul Morel', E373e (UCB), p. 25 (original reading).

37. E. T. 188; *L*, i. 323, 328, 326. Complaint: not just an 'utterance of grief' but a 'bodily ailment, indisposition, disorder (*esp.* of chronic nature)' (*OED2*).

38. *EY* 322.

39. *L*, i. 337. DHL did not, however, resign from the Davidson Road School until the end of February 1912.

40. *L*, i. 358. In 1915 he would comment: 'I would like to see all adjectives banned from the English language for twenty years, and writers compelled to describe things without their help' (Nehls, i. 294).

41. *L*, i. 215; Cyril Beardsall in *The White Peacock*, Bernard Coutts in the 1911 version ('Intimacy') of 'The Witch à la Mode', Edward Severn in 'The Old Adam': while Paul Morel has a French grandfather (also claimed by the Lawrence family): see *EY* 7–8, 24, 62, 308.

42. *L*, i. 358–9.

43. *L*, i. 362.

44. *L*, i. 361.

45. *L*, i. 363.

46. *L*, i. 364.

47. See *EY* 320, 555.

48. I explored in the Cambridge biography another rather similar case – 'Pauline B.' in Lawrence's address book (*EY* 320, 355–6).

49. 'Bromley House' has never been accepted into the 'canon' of Lawrence family houses in Eastwood, but was a striking final location for them: two large rooms downstairs as well as the kitchen, and four bedrooms (presumably one for Arthur Lawrence, one for Emily, Sam and the three-year-old Peggy, one for Ada and one for DHL). They may have used the middle room downstairs as a sitting room, but family life (especially in winter) would have centred on the kitchen; during the day, only Emily, Peggy and DHL would have been at home.

50. *L*, i. 363.

51. *L*, i. 365–6.

52. *EY* 338. It is tempting to link this occasion with the episode in *Sons and Lovers* when Paul goes to the theatre in evening dress with the married woman Clara, and that night makes love to her (*SL* 375–84).

53. *L*, i. 322.

54. *MN* 291. *Mr Noon* offers a fictionalized and reworked account of some of the crucial events in DHL's life between May and September 1912. Details unsupported by other material cannot be relied on, but the novel is nevertheless indispensable for our understanding. When I draw on the novel in Chapters 7, 8 and 9, I either name it in the text or use the word 'apparently'; in these chapters the word always indicates that *Mr Noon* is the source.

55. *L*, iii. 353. Louie acquired a copy of the letter, now at UN: DHL's aunt Ada Krenkow probably sent it to her.

56. See 'The Miner at Home' (*LAH* 123–7), 'Her Turn' (*LAH* 128–33), 'Strike-Pay' (*LAH* 134–42) and 'A Sick Collier' (*PO* 165–71).

57. Delavenay, ii. 706.

58. Ibid.

59. *SL* 345.

60. *L*, i. 51 n. 1. The poem 'The Blessed Damozel' is by D. G. Rossetti (1828–82).

8 Frieda Weekley: 1912

1. John Worthen, *Cold Hearts and Coronets: Lawrence, the Weekleys and the von Richthofens* (1995), p. 10: see too *Memoirs* 420.

2. *Memoirs* 390.

3. *L*, iii. 571; Frieda 55. DHL regularly quoted such soldier songs: e.g. 'Ach, schön Zwanzig' (*LG* 84–5), 'Mach mir auf, mach mir auf, du Stolze' (*WL* 419), 'Dans les Gardes Françaises' (see *PS* 549, textual apparatus entry for 444: 28: this is the 'old song').

4. *L*, i. 502. The frontispiece of Frieda's biography of DHL consists of the von Richthofen coat of arms, which was also carved on her tombstone at the Kiowa ranch.

5. The photograph was cut down to fit inside a watch or locket and was found in Ernest Weekley's desk after his death (information from Ian Weekley). The original (showing a cherry tree, the garden, the house and a view over the landscape) is Illustration 6 in Kirsten Jüngling and Brigitte Roßbeck, *Frieda von Richthofen: Biographie* (1998).

6. *Memoirs* 79–80.

7. William Enfield Dowson (1864–1934), godfather to Barby; when the Weekleys were living at 10 Vickers Street, he lived at 10 Mapperley Road, just eight minutes' walk away.

8. *Memoirs* 89.

9. Frieda 22; 'Introduction', *Look! We Have Come Through!* (1991), p. 10.

10. *SL* 252–4; *Hamlet* III. iv. 161–72; *Memoirs* 351. I am grateful to John Turner for drawing my attention to the coincidence of DHL's writing this scene and his meeting with Frieda on 3 March.

11. Barbara Barr to JW, 26 March 1994. Brenda Maddox, *The Married Man: A Life of D. H. Lawrence* (1994), p. 114, tells the story, and cites William Hopkin as its source: Hopkin's story (itself at second hand) is retold by a third person, Lewis Richmond (UT). The version in *Mr Noon*, cited by Maddox as evidence of how the sexual encounter came about, is quite different: it does not draw on the first meeting between Gilbert and Johanna (see *MN* 136–7). Maddox also ignores the fact of children and servants being in the Weekley house when DHL arrived. The myth is, however, regularly repeated: e.g. 'Frieda seduced Lawrence between soup and the main course within 20 minutes of first setting eyes on him. By the time Weekley arrived home, his marriage was over' (Sebastian O'Kelly, 'Was this peasant the real Lady Chatterley's Lover?', *Mail on Sunday*, 2 December 2001, p. 65).

12. *Evening Standard*, 18 October 1913, p. 4.

13. *TE* 321.

14. *L*, i. 397. Cf. DHL to May Holbrook: 'We . . . often wish we had your cottage' (*L*, i. 500) and *L*, i. 387.

15. *L*, i. 384, 376.

16. 'Lotus hurt by the Cold' (later 'Lotus and Frost'), E320.2; Nehls, ii. 78.

17. Nehls, i. 71.

18. When in 1920–21 he wrote *Mr Noon* (a fictional version of this part of his life), for a while he called it 'Lucky Noon': see *L*, iii. 645–6, 722, iv. 35.

19. E. T. 213.

20. Barbara Barr, 'Step-daughter to Lawrence', *London Magazine*, xxxiii (August/September 1993), p. 26; *Memoirs* 92.

21. Frieda 23.

22. *L*, i. 362, 400, 386.

23. Barr, 'Step-daughter to Lawrence', p. 26.

24. Frieda Gross to Else Jaffe, 'Ascona, 6 Mai' [1912], tr. CR-W and JW. The correspondence is at Tufts University.

25. John Turner with Cornelia Rumpf-Worthen and Ruth Jenkins, 'The Otto Gross–Frieda Weekley Correspondence', *D. H. Lawrence Review*, xxii (Summer 1990), p. 165.

26. *Memoirs* 178.

27. Frieda 25; *FWL* 355; *WL* 387.

28. *L*, i. 392.

29. *MN* 150–54.

30. *L*, i. 391.

31. *L*, i. 392–3.

32. *L*, i. 409, 388.

33. *Memoirs* 92–3; *L*, i. 392–3, 400.

34. 'A Foreword by Frieda Lawrence', D. H. Lawrence, *The First Lady Chatterley* (1972), p. 14.

35. *MN* 216.

36. *L*, i. 394, 392.

37. *Memoirs* 178 (letter misdated 11 April); *L*, i. 409.

38. *MN* 181.

39. *L*, i. 398.

40. 'Bei Hennef', *Poems* 203; *L*, i. 421; Frieda to A. S. Frere-Reeves, n.d. ('Thursday, Kingsley Hotel'); cf. DHL's letters of 21 May, 2 June and 3 July 1912 (*L* i. 408–10, 414–15, 420–22).

41. *L*, viii. 113; Frieda 53.

42. Frieda 25; *Memoirs* 178–81.

43. *L*, i. 401.

44. *L*, i. 410.

45. *L*, i. 406. 'In Fortified Germany, I', about Metz and its soldiers, got as far as galley proof but was pulled (the paper was careful not to print material politically offensive to Germany); 'French Sons of Germany', drafted in Metz, was published on 3 August 1912; 'Hail in the Rhineland', set in Waldbröl, on 10 August. 'How a Spy is Arrested' – the most offensive – only reached print in 1994 (*TI* 11–15).

46. *L*, i. 403.

47. 'First Morning', *Poems* 204; Frieda 56.

48. *L*, i. 418.

49. *L*, i. 420, 419, 421, 440.

50. Conclusion reached by combining *L*, i. 467 ('Ernst offered me a flat in London with the children') with the play *The Fight for Barbara* ('much of it is word for word true . . . Ernst's very words' – *L*, i. 466–7): 'you're to go and live with your mother . . . Then he's going to have a separation and will allow you an income, so long as you'll see no more of me' (*Plays* 254).

51. 'A Foreword by Frieda Lawrence', *The First Lady Chatterley*, p. 14; see *L*, ii. 244: according to *Mr Noon* he told her that when she accosted him 'in Piccadilly' – i.e. when she was reduced to being a prostitute – he would hand her over to the police (*MN* 196).

52. *L*, i. 415.

53. *L*, i. 421 n. 4. Heinemann may also have resented Lawrence's starting to publish with Duckworth.

54. *L*, i. 422.

55. Barr, 'Step-daughter to Lawrence', p. 27; *L*, i. 421.

56. *L*, i. 420.

57. Frieda 24, 53. There can be no certainty about why Frieda and DHL did not have children themselves. At one stage, very early on, Frieda apparently thought she was pregnant and then found that she wasn't. DHL comforted her – 'Never mind about the infant' – and went on: 'If it should come, we will be glad, and stir ourselves to provide for it – and if it should not come, ever – I shall be sorry. I do not believe, when people love each other, in interfering there' (*L*, i. 402). Frieda seems to have been a little surprised to believe herself pregnant, while DHL seems prepared for her *not* to have been. They were clearly not using contraceptives (Barbara Barr confirmed to me on 26 March 1994 that according to her mother they never did), so it would seem that either or both were now infertile. It has been asserted, without evidence, that DHL's childhood illnesses had left him sterile (see *EY* 527 n. 82). It is perhaps significant that although Frieda had a number of lovers between 1904 and 1912 (Dowson, Gross, Frick, von Henning, Hobson), she did not get pregnant. After May 1912, she appears to have had no more false alarms. Frieda herself (Barbara Barr told me on 26 March 1994) believed that Lawrence's creativity went into his writing, which is why they had no children.

58. *L*, i. 430.

59. *L*, i. 430; six 'Schoolmaster' poems in the *Saturday Westminster Gazette* and 'Snapdragon' in the *English Review*.

60. See 'A Chapel Among the Mountains' and 'A Hay-Hut Among the Mountains', *TI* 27–35, 36–42.

61. *L*, i. 433, 441.

62. *L*, i. 442; David Garnett, *Great Friends* (1979), p. 80.

63. *MN* 276.

64. *L*, i. 392.

65. Garnett, *Great Friends*, p. 81.

66. *MN* 279.

67. *MN* 285.

68. *New York Times Book Review*, 17 November 1912, p. 667.

69. *L*, ii. 99, i. 456; Frieda to Anna von Richthofen *c.* 15 September 1912 (UT). 'Inrooted' means 'Deeply rooted, fixed, or established' (*OED*2).

9 *Sons and Lovers* and Marriage: 1912–1914

1. *L*, i. 449, 467.

2. *EY* 411 and Illustration 42.

3. *L*, i. 460.

4. *L*, i. 477.

5. Frieda to Anna von Richthofen, *c.* 15 September 1912 (UT), tr. CR-W and JW.

6. Frieda 58; *L*, i. 485.

7. Rosie Jackson, *Frieda Lawrence* (1994), p. 23: see too p. 58.

8. *Memoirs* 410 (Frieda to Mabel Luhan, 28 April 1930, YU).

9. Frieda to Richard Aldington, 2 January 1949, *Frieda Lawrence and Her Circle*, ed. Harry T. Moore and Dale B. Montague (1981), p. 91; Barbara Barr, 'Step-daughter to Lawrence', *London Magazine*, xxxiii (August/September 1993), p. 26; *Memoirs* 95.

10. Barr, 'Step-daughter to Lawrence', p. 31.

11. *L*, i. 486.

12. E320.1; *EY* 412.

13. *L*, i. 509.

14. *L*, i. 455, ii. 73.

15. *L*, i. 521, 551.

16. *L*, i. 489, 497.

17. See *Memoirs* 98–9; *L*, i. 489.

18. *L*, i. 462, 545.

19. *L*, i. 481.

20. See 'Foreword', *SL* 467–73; *L*, i. 503.

21. *L*, i. 503–4.

22. *L*, i. 503.

23. Nehls, i. 173.

24. *L*, ii. 470.

25. *L*, i. 518. The other abandoned novels were the 'Burns Novel' (*LAH* 200–211) and 'Elsa Culverwell' (*LG* 342–58), while 'The Insurrection of Miss Houghton' was later totally rewritten as *The Lost Girl* (*LG* xxii–xxv); *L*, i. 536.

26. Edward Thomas (1878–1917): see *Bookman*, xliv (April 1913), p. 47; *L*, i. 500–501, 462.

27. *L*, i. 549; 'New Eve and Old Adam', *LAH* 170. It is an odd phrase to describe Paula's non-writing businessman/husband, Richard, in 'New Eve and Old Adam', and is probably autobiographical.

28. *Memoirs* 97; at the hearing in October 1913, a 'sister of the petitioner said she saw the respondent and co-respondent together in Italy in January this year' (*Nottingham Guardian*, 20 October 1913, p. 11).

29. *L*, i. 546.

30. 'New Eve and Old Adam', *LAH* 167, 181–2.

31. *L*, i. 542, ii. 20–21, 23.

32. In DHL's January 1926 story, 'The Virgin and the Gipsy', which drew on reminiscences of their Chiswick home provided by Barby and Elsa Weekley, 'She-who-was-Cynthia' is how the adults think of the wife who has abandoned her husband, marriage and daughters (*The Virgin and the Gipsy*, 1930, pp. 11–12).

33. *L*, i. 440.

34. *L*, i. 545, 551; John Milton, *Lycidas* (1637), l. 142. Jessie would also have known Scott's *Rokeby* (1813): 'Where the rathe primrose decks the mead' (IV, ii).

35. 'Review of *The Peep Show*', *P* 373; *L*, ii. 595.

36. *L*, ii. 21, 23.

37. *L*, ii. 25; Richard Garnett, *Constance Garnett: A Heroic Life* (1991), p. 281.

38. Garnett, *Constance Garnett*, p. 281; *L*, ii. 54, 27.

39. 'Introduction', *Look! We Have Come Through!* (1991), p. 12; Nehls, i. 197.

40. *L*, ii. 23; Garnett, *Constance Garnett*, p. 281.

41. Nehls, i. 197.

42. Records of the High Court, Divorce and Admiralty Division.

43. All that survives is Frieda's quotation of the phrase to Else (*L*, ii. 48–9). The CUP translator misunderstands it: '*Ernst's "verfaulte Leiche" liegt mir noch in den Knochen!*' should be translated 'Ernest's "decomposed corpse" still troubles me deeply!'

44. *L*, ii. 30.

45. David Garnett, *Great Friends* (1979), p. 81.

46. One of the photographs taken that day appeared e.g. in 'Books of the Day' in *The Ladies' Field*, 26 July 1913, p. 424.

47. Nehls, i. 173, 207.

48. Nehls, i. 198.

49. Nehls, i. 200.

50. Frieda to Frieda Gross, September 1913, from Baden-Baden (UT), tr. CR-W and JW.

51. *L*, ii. 6.

52. *L*, ii. 33; see too ii. 49 ('L, after being *thoroughly* miserable the days here, is recovering').

53. 'The Shadow in the Rose Garden', *Smart Set*, xlii (March 1914), p. 77.

54. '*Es ist so schön hier, so wunderschön, die Tage am Meer, im Meer, auf dem Meer, um's Meer herum*': John Turner with Cornelia Rumpf-Worthen and Ruth Jenkins, 'The Otto Gross–Frieda Weekley Correspondence', *D. H. Lawrence Review*, xxii (Summer 1990), pp. 195, 216.

55. *L*, ii. 42.

56. *L*, ii. 39.

57. *L*, ii. 49, 172; Nehls, i. 199.

58. *L*, ii. 46.

59. Nehls, i. 200, 255; *L*, ii. 37.

60. *L*, ii. 50.

61. *SL* lxix; *Westminster Gazette*, xli (14 June 1913), p. 17; *L*, ii. 47. The novel made relatively little money, selling only 1,500 copies in England during its first twelve months; for the moment it made DHL no more than his original advance (in England) of £100, and £35 in America. He was informed by knowledgeable people in the literary world that 'that fine novel hasn't had the success it deserved' (*L*, ii. 135). The book would, of course, go on selling; but another 1,000 copies supplied all English demand for the next three years, leaving DHL still positioned firmly at the non-popular, highbrow end of the publishing market. A successful commercial writer like Arnold Bennett would make some £11,000 in 1912, with sales of his novels reaching 30,000 copies, of which library sales were a significant percentage. DHL earned something like £200 in 1913, with sales of less than 2,000 copies. That enabled him to survive, but no more – 'I can't live under £200 a year' (*L*, i. 506). Even a young writer like Compton Mackenzie (only two years older than DHL) would sell 35,000 copies of his 1913 novel *Sinister Street* in six months and would soon be offered advances of between £750 and £1,000 (Compton Mackenzie, *My Life and Times: Octave Four*, 1965, p. 190). DHL made his living by publishing a good deal; but he needed to publish, in effect, a novel every year, as well as four or five stories or articles, and some poems, to maintain the income of around £200 he was making.

62. *L*, ii. 51, 50 (Frieda to Else Jaffe ?22 July 1913, UT, tr. CR-W and JW).

63. Beatrice Lady Glenavy, *'Today we will only gossip'* (1964), p. 95.

64. *L*, ii. 57.

65. Frieda to Else Jaffe, ?30 September 1913 (UT), tr. CR-W and JW; *L*, i. 530–31, 532. The painting *Hope* (1885–6) is by G. F. Watts (1817–1904).

66. *L*, ii. 29, 49.

67. Frieda to Else Jaffe, ?30 September 1913 (UT), tr. CR-W and JW.

68. *TI* 210.

69. *L*, viii. 9.

70. Nehls, i. 210.

71. *EY* 412.

72. *MN* 228.

73. *L*, viii. 7.

74. *L*, ii. 94.

75. *L*, i. 490.

76. *L*, ii. 88, 82, 88; Frieda to Edward Garnett, 7 November 1913 (NYPL).

77. Frieda to Else Jaffe, 2 November 1912 (UT), tr. CR-W and JW; *LAH* 165.

78. *News of the World*, 19 October 1913, p. 1. See too reports in the *Evening Standard*, 18 October 1913, p. 4, and *Nottingham Guardian*, 20 October 1913, p. 11. DHL was, oddly, referred to as 'B. H. Lawrence' in two of the reports, and 'W. H. Lawrence' in the third.

79. Atti di Matrimonio, 29 November 1913, Parish of Tellaro, no. 9. I am grateful to Adriana Craciun for providing me with a photocopy of this entry.

80. *L*, ii. 116.

81. *L*, ii. 164.

82. Garnett, *Constance Garnett*, p. 281; see *R* 473–9.

83. Joseph Conrad (1857–1924): see Cedric Watts, 'Marketing Modernism: How Conrad Prospered', *Modernist Writers and the Marketplace*, ed. Ian Willison, Warwick Gould and Warren Cherniak (1996), p. 82.

84. *L*, ii. 182–3.

85. Frieda 85. We know very little about Lewis, but the British Consul in La Spezia, Thomas Dunlop – who had become a friend, and whose wife, Madge, had been typing Lawrence's novel for him (*TE* 785) – may have been the contact.

86. *L*, ii. 189, 211, 165.

87. *L*, ii. 196.

88. *L*, ii. 199.

89. Barr, 'Step-daughter to Lawrence', p. 31.

90. *Memoirs* 432.

91. *L*, ii. 268.

92. *L*, ii. 268.

93. 'Put paid': first recorded in 1919 with reference to hunting German U-boats; from 'pay' in the sense of 'to inflict bodily chastisement upon, beat, flog' (*OED*2).

10 In England at War: 1914–1915

1. i.e. £150 (paid on submission of the MS) minus Pinker's 10 per cent.

2. *L*, ii. 206.

3. Evelyn Blücher, *An English Wife in Berlin* (1920), p. 137.

4. In 1909, Mary (1867–1950) had left her husband, the *Peter Pan* author J. M. Barrie (1860–1937); she married Gilbert (1884–1955) in 1910.

5. *L*, ii. 208; Nehls, i. 247.

6. *L*, ii. 210, 214, 216–17: J. W. von Goethe, *Wilhelm Meister* (1795–6), book iii, ch. 1 ('Do you know the land where the lemon trees flower?': i.e. Italy).

7. Frieda 109.

8. *L*, iii. 251; Nehls, i. 264–5.

9. *TI* 81, 84.

10. *L*, ii. 218.

11. David Garnett, *Great Friends* (1974) p. 134; Claire Tomalin, *Katherine Mansfield: A Secret Life* (1988), p. 129.

12. *The Times*, 9 August 1914, p. 9; Lyn Macdonald, *1914: The Days of Hope* (1987), p. 48; *L*, ii. 268, 211.

13. *L*, ii. 268.

14. The German armies pushed deep into Belgium during the first fortnight, but it was not yet clear whether they would make much headway in France. Stories of brutality began appearing in *The Times*, 18–20 August; a report ('The Invaders in Belgium') on 23 August cited several incidents of brutality out of the 'hundreds which have been substantiated beyond all doubt' (p. 2); the first official report of atrocities in Belgium was printed on 26 August 1914 (p. 7); the first apparent use of the word 'atrocity' had occurred the previous day (p. 5).

15. Nehls, i. 263.

16. *L*, i. 57. Cf. Walt Whitman, 'I Sing the Body Electric', *The Complete Poems*, ed. Francis Murphy (1977), p. 132: 'Each has his or her place in the procession. / (All is a procession, / The universe is a procession with measured and perfect motion.)'

17. *L*, i. 511, 424, 544; *L*, iii. 84.

18. *Studies* 42.

19. *PFU* 67; *TI* 81.

20. *L* ii. 302.

21. Cf. the patriotic poem 'England' (1900) by William Ernest Henley (1849–1903): 'What have I done for you, / England, my England?'; *LCL* 156.

22. Five books in the series (all either 127 or 128 pages long) came out in 1914–15: Rebecca West, *Henry James* (1914); F. J. Harvey Darton, *Arnold Bennett* (1915); W. L. George, *Anatole France* (1915); John Palmer, *Rudyard Kipling* (1915); J. D. Beresford, *H. G. Wells* (1915). A volume on *Thomas Hardy*, by Harold Child, replacing the one that DHL did not write, was published in 1916. Victoria Reid enlightened me about the series.

23. See e.g. *L*, ii. 81 n. 1; *L*, ii. 193.

24. *L*, ii. 235, 220.

25. *L*, ii. 219.

26. *L*, ii. 255.

27. In the Botany laboratory, she observes a unicellular 'plant-animal' (*R* 408) and has a sudden revelation: 'To be oneself was a supreme, gleaming triumph of infinity' (409). I am grateful to Molly Mahood for pointing out to me the link with Bunny Garnett; see his *The Flowers of the Forest* (1955), p. 13.

28. *Memoirs* 323.

29. *L*, ii. 224.

30. Nehls i. 256.

31. *SP* 26–7; *L*, ii. 219.

32. Beatrice Lady Glenavy, *'Today we will only gossip'* (1964), p. 78.

33. *L*, ii. 244. 'Quondam' means 'former'.

34. *Memoirs* 432; *L*, ii. 377, iii. 232; see *TE* 436, 465.

35. *Memoirs* 97.

36. Merrild 139.

37. 'Introduction', *Look! We Have Come Through!* (1991), p. 12.

38. *Plays* 296.

39. Nehls, i. 257.

40. *TE* 156.

41. Nehls, i. 263. The man was Francis Carco (1886–1958): see Tomalin, *Katherine Mansfield*, p. 134.

42. *L*, ii. 191.

43. Frieda to Ottoline Morrell, 'Littlehampton' (UT); see *TE* 240, 808; Frieda 51.

44. *L*, iii. 239, ii. 343.

45. Nehls, i. 252; Frieda 52.

46. *SP* 26.

47. See *L*, ii. 252 n. 3.

48. *L*, v. 3; see e.g. *L*, iv. 20 ('recruits for Lawrence's New World Rananim'); Frieda 100.

49. Nehls, i. 263; *L*, iii. 673, ii. 259.

50. *Ottoline: The Early Memoirs of Lady Ottoline Morrell*, ed. R. Gathorne-Hardy (1963), p. 273.

51. *L*, ii. 359, 634. See e.g. 'the way to immortality is in the fulfilment of desire ... what intimation of immortality have we, save our spontaneous wishes? God works in me (if I use the term God) as my desire' (*L*, ii. 634).

52. See Ray Monk, *Bertrand Russell: The Spirit of Solitude* (1996), pp. 410–12.

53. *L*, ii. 302.

54. *L*, ii. 299.

55. *EmyE* 225.

56. *L*, ii. 392; 'The Crown', *Reflections* 472.

57. Bertrand Russell to Ottoline Morrell, 11 and 8 July 1915 (UT).

58. 'The Crown', *Reflections* 472–3.

59. Ibid. 475, 474. Cf. DHL's comment to Ottoline Morrell, 18 April 1916: 'the spring might be perfect but for the gas-fumes that blow in' (*L*, ii. 598).

60. See Mellors's account of his early relationship with the woman who 'egged me on to poetry and reading': 'We were the most literary-cultured couple in ten counties. I held forth with rapture to her, positively with rapture. I simply went up in smoke' (*LCL* 200).

61. *L*, ii. 320–21.

62. *L*, ii. 320. For a full discussion, see Chapter 11.

63. *L*, ii. 319.

64. *L*, ii. 344; see *TE* 257, 809.

65. See e.g. his praise of Blake's 'substantial quality, his solidity' (*L*, vii. 508); *L*, iii. 56.

66. *L*, ii. 302.

67. 'Note to The Crown', *Reflections* 249.

68. See *SP* 34, 41–2; Mark Kinkead-Weekes and John Worthen, 'More about *The Rainbow*', *D. H. Lawrence Review*, xxix (2000), 7–10.

69. James Douglas, *Star*, 22 October 1915, p. 4.

70. *R* l.

71. Nehls, ii. 415.

72. *L*, ii. 548; Nehls, ii. 415; *L*, ii. 429.

73. *L*, ii. 462.

74. *L*, ii. 459–60. DHL wrote of the 'bursten flood of life' in 'Virgin Youth' (*Poems* 899); see e.g. Algernon Charles Swinburne, 'the whelming wave of time', 'On the South Coast' (1894), l. 19; 'Drop tears for dew upon me who am dead', *Atalanta in Calydon* (1865), l. 2,293; 'But the fair gold sides upon the ship, / They were bursten with the sea', 'But when she saw the sides bursten, / I wot her very heart brak', 'Lady Maisie's Bairn' (1889), ll. 9–10, 21–22. See too *Ottoline at Garsington: Memoirs of Lady Ottoline Morrell 1915–1918*, ed. R. Gathorne-Hardy (1974), p. 69.

75. *L*, ii. 302.

76. 'The Crown', *Reflections* 472.

77. *MM* 55. See the discussion of DHL's experience at Monte Cassino in Chapter 13.

78. The scheme devised by Edward George Stanley, Earl of Derby (1865–1948), in which men voluntarily attested their willingness to serve and then awaited call-up: see *Encyclopaedia Britannica* (1922), xxx. 212–13.

79. *L*, ii. 474–5.

80. *L*, ii. 489.

81. *L*, ii. 491, 487 (German).

82. *K* 259.

11 Zennor: 1916–1917

1. *L*, ii. 569.

2. In an unpublished photograph taken during the same session (National Portrait Gallery x36136), DHL – in the same pose and with the same expression – has acquired the prop of a jaunty trilby hat.

3. *L*, i. 85; see e.g. *L*, i. 467, iii. 45, 337, etc. A photograph of DHL at Garsington (see e.g. Miranda Seymour, *Ottoline Morrell*, 1992, first photographic insert) apparently shows them in his hand. A charcoal drawing (15 × 9¾ in.) made around 1923–5 by Xavier Martinez (1869–1943), supposedly of DHL, shows a bearded man wearing glasses; I am grateful to Roger Epperstone for letting me see it.

4. *L*, ii. 521: i.e. before he met Frieda.

5. *L*, ii. 493, 501. *TE* 297 and 818 n. 30 suggest that the January 1916 story was 'The Prodigal Husband', the early version of 'Samson and Delilah', but that story depends so completely upon the setting of the Tinners Arms in Zennor (which DHL did not see until 29 February) that it is hard to imagine what it could have been like without the setting. Bruce Steele suggests November 1916 as the composition date for 'The Prodigal Husband' and says that 'The Miracle' was written in November (*EmyE* xliii, xlv); he does not identify the January story. Keith Sagar in *D. H. Lawrence: A Calendar of his Works* (1979) argues for 'The Miracle' as the January story (p. 68).

6. See *L*, ii. 500.

7. *L*, ii. 491, 498.

8. *L*, ii. 498, 499.

9. S. Dik-Cunningham, 'PREFACE AND SYNOPSIS', *New Age*, 2 March 1916, pp. 428–9. I am very grateful to John Turner for telling me of his discovery of this item.

10. Eleanor Farjeon (1881–1965): Nehls, i. 293.

11. See e.g. *Memoirs* 312.

12. *L*, ii. 666.

13. *L*, ii. 549.

14. *WL* 481.

15. *TI* 173, 178.

16. Barbara Schapiro, *D. H. Lawrence and the Paradoxes of Psychic Life* (1999), p. 51.

17. *L*, i. 418.

18. Nehls, i. 177; *L*, i. 442.

19. *L*, ii. 501.

20. *L*, iii. 245.

21. *L*, i. 509.

22. *L*, ii. 512, 549; *TE* 321.

23. He was getting 'long, wonderful letters' from Juliette Baillot (1896–1995), who was acting as governess to Ottoline's daughter Julian.

24. *L*, ii. 571, iii. 468.

25. *Memoirs* 142.

26. *L*, ii. 563.

27. *L*, ii. 571, 591. Cf. DHL insisting to Frieda in 1912: 'Don't they just work hard, those lilies ... They have to bring up their sap, produce their leaves, flowers and seeds!' (Nehls, i. 168).

28. *L*, ii. 601; *WL*, 97, *L*, ii. 460.

29. *L*, ii. 610, 602.

30. The statuette of the horse in the novel (*WL* 429: 2–39) is a brilliant recreation, in every detail, of the 1906 statuette *Godiva* made by the German sculptor Josef Moest (1873–1914), who visited the Lago di Garda in March 1913: DHL must have met him and seen a photograph. See J. B. Bullen, 'D. H. Lawrence and Sculpture in "Women in Love"', *Burlington Magazine*, cxlv (December 2003), pp. 841–6.

31. *Memoirs* 343; *The Collected Letters of Katherine Mansfield*, ed. V. O'Sullivan and M. Scott (1984), i. 262; *TE* 325, *L*, iii. 127; Nehls, i. 276.

32. *L*, ii. 512; Frieda to Ottoline Morrell, n.d. [?22/23 January 1916] (UT); Nehls, i. 306.

33. Her two accounts – written three days apart – differ in many details, and in the actual words recorded: see *Letters of Katherine Mansfield*, ed. O'Sullivan and Scott, i. 262–4, 267–8. Both accounts were 'written up' for the pleasure of their readers (Koteliansky the first, Ottoline Morrell the second), not for accuracy.

34. In her second account, Katherine made DHL the one who came in, and Frieda the one who walked up and down outside.

35. *Letters of Katherine Mansfield*, ed. O'Sullivan and Scott, i. 262–4.

36. *L*, iii. 656; *SP* 71.

37. *L*, iii. 595; *TE* 308; Brett 272.

38. *Letters of Katherine Mansfield*, ed. O'Sullivan and Scott, i. 264.

39. *Journal of Katherine Mansfield*, Definitive Edition, ed. J. M. Murry (1954), p. 146; *L*, ii. 623. In 1955, Frieda commented about Katherine: 'She is so right when she says that she was like Lawrence' (*Memoirs* 350).

40. *L*, ii. 617.

41. *Letters of Katherine Mansfield*, ed. O'Sullivan and Scott, i. 267.

42. Letter from Ernst Frick to Frieda, 12 June 1912 (Martin Green).

43. See *TE* 321; '*monstrum, horrende, informe, ingens*' is Virgil's description of the Cyclops Polyphemus (*Aeneid*, iii. 658); see *DG* 145, 640–41, 534.

44. *TE* 519. See e.g. Bertrand Russell in malicious old age: 'Lawrence, though most people did not realize it, was his wife's mouthpiece. He had the eloquence, but she had the ideas' (*The Autobiography of Bertrand Russell*, 1968, ii. 23).

45. Nehls, i. 209.

46. Nehls, i. 240–41, 441, 289. Forty years later, Frieda was indignant: 'I never said: those "dirty Belgians", I never felt like that!' (*Memoirs* 352).

47. *L*, ii. 667.

48. *L*, ii. 618; *Letters of Katherine Mansfield*, ed. O'Sullivan and Scott, i. 272.

49. *L*, ii. 635.

50. *L*, ii. 656.

51. *L*, iii. 19.

52. *L*, ii. 659; *WL* 485.

53. *WL* 315, 438; *Studies* 125; *L*, ii. 649; *Studies* 132.

54. *L*, ii. 648, 650; *FWL* 96.

55. *L*, ii. 650, 659, 669.

56. See *WL* 488–518.

57. *L*, ii. 619.

58. *L*, iii. 89.

59. *L*, ii. 661.

60. *L*, ii. 659.

61. *WL* 451, 318.

62. *L*, iii. 75.

63. Nehls, i. 409; *L*, iii. 673 ('Shall I bring you some junk? Do you love it? What sort do you like? I hate it myself'). The fact that DHL asked these questions in February 1921, when planning to come to the USA and see Mountsier for the first time since January 1917, suggests that Mountsier may well have been taking drugs the last time they were together.

64. *L*, iii. 65–6, 75, 64. He gave Mountsier the copy of Anton Chekhov, *The Bet and Other Stories*, tr. S. Koteliansky and J. M. Murry (1915), which Koteliansky had presented to him (*L*, ii. 447 and n. 2) in November 1915 ('A Lorenzo Vivo / da Koteliansky morto'), re-inscribing it: 'New Years Eve / 1916 / da Lorenzo doloroso' (NWU).

65. *L*, i. 337: see e.g. David Garnett in 1913 (Nehls, i. 197). Frieda, however, insisted in 1918: 'it isn't tuberculosis, it *isn't*' (Nehls, i. 461).

66. To Claire Tomalin in *Katherine Mansfield: A Secret Life* (1988) DHL was

the 'glaringly obvious candidate' to have infected Katherine Mansfield with the disease (p. 163); there is no evidence for that, and a great deal against. As a New Zealander, she would have been particularly vulnerable to infection in Europe.

67. Frieda 306.

68. *L*, iii. 76, 78, 92.

69. *L*, iii. 215, 81, 47, 56.

70. *L*, ii. 529.

71. *L*, iii. 150.

72. *L*, iii. 125, 143, 239.

73. Her source was Frieda, but Mabel confused one woman with another; what she recounted about Esther (Luhan 51) applied to Rosalind Baynes in 1920. See Chapter 14.

74. Nehls, i. 416–18.

75. Nehls, i. 417.

76. Luhan 51; *L*, viii. 27.

77. Letter from Austin Harrison to J. B. Pinker, April 1917 (UN). The guinea was £1 1s (one pound, one shilling) and was a professional man's unit for fees. Doctors would often charge in guineas (see e.g. *SL* 417: 35) and a magazine might pay in them. Twenty guineas were £20 20s, i.e. £21.

78. *L*, iii. 125.

79. *WL* 481. Cf. the similar ending to DHL's *The Lost Girl* (*LG* 339).

80. *L*, iii. 94, 84, 87.

81. *L*, ii. 662.

82. *WL* 201, 148. The poem 'One Woman to All Women' actually contains the line 'the way of the stars' (*Poems* 251–2).

83. I am grateful for information about submarine activity from Tom Richards, 9 June 1997; *L*, viii. 20.

84. Frieda 106.

85. Nehls, i. 430. Marjorie Kennedy-Fraser had been publishing volumes of *Songs of the Hebrides* (with piano accompaniment) since 1908.

86. *L*, iii. 436; Nehls, i. 365–6; Frieda 105.

87. *L*, ii. 664; *K* 175.

88. Perhaps because DHL was spending time with Hocking, Frieda saw a good deal of Gray during the summer and early autumn (she was over at Bosigran with him the afternoon their cottage was raided in October), and a brief affair with him is a possibility; see *TE* 405. Frieda's friendships with men very often had an overtly sexual component, especially when she had something to prove, as she would have felt she had in Cornwall this summer: see H. D., *Bid Me To Live* (1960), p. 139.

89. *L*, ii. 664. DHL gave the gesture to Gerald in *Women in Love* (see *FWL* 252 and *WL* 275).
90. Nehls, i. 366.
91. *TE* 855.
92. Nehls, i. 275.
93. *AR* 96–8; *WL* 504.
94. *St Ives Times*, 5 October 1917.
95. Interview with Stanley Hocking © Roger Slack, St Ives (recorded July 1964, Tregerthen Farm House); *TE* 347–8.
96. *L*, iii. 168, 175; *K* 241, 245.
97. E320.1; Nehls, i. 426.
98. Lady Cynthia Asquith, *Diaries 1915–1918* [ed. E. M. Horsley] (1968), pp. 356–7.
99. *L*, iii. 305; see *L*, iii. 237: DHL had commented on his book of poems *Bay* that 'Even the *Daily News* could swallow it and not know but what it was drinking water'; Frieda 108.

12 Isolated and Independent: 1917–1919

1. *L*, iii. 176, 221.
2. Nehls, i. 429, 449–50; Frieda 109–10.
3. Nehls, i. 454; *L*, iii. 364 n. 4, 190.
4. *L*, iii. 215.
5. *L*, iii. 125, 161.
6. *L*, iii. 173, 175, 319–20.
7. *L*, iii. 183, 190.
8. H. D., *Bid Me To Live* (1960).
9. *L*, iii. 179–80.
10. *L*, iii. 190.
11. *L*, viii. 112; *Bid Me To Live*, pp. 111–14, 120–22; *K* 248, 249.
12. *L*, iii. 190.
13. *L*, iii. 173–4, 175.
14. *L*, iii. 179.
15. *L*, iii. 302.
16. *L*, iii. 216.
17. *L*, iii. 226.
18. *L*, iii. 195, 211, 206, 217.
19. *L*, iii. 224, 239.
20. *L*, iii. 209, 270, 276.
21. *L*, iii. 224.

22. *L*, iii. 226, 240, 233.

23. *L*, iii. 232, 242, 240, 254, 242.

24. *L*, iii. 240, 256, 245.

25. *L*, iii. 251, 245, 247.

26. *L*, iii. 259, 245.

27. 'Education of the People', *Reflections* 121.

28. Nehls, i. 303–6, 455; Rosalind Thornycroft, *Time Which Spaces Us Apart*, completed by Chloë Baynes (1991), p. 58; *TE* 510.

29. *L*, iii. 251; *Memoirs* 225.

30. *L*, iii. 283, 248, 315.

31. *L*, iii. 274, 211, 278.

32. *L*, iii. 282; *K* 215.

33. *K* 214; *L*, iii. 190; Nehls, i. 508. DHL told his old Croydon friend Arthur McLeod, before a planned meeting in October 1918, '*Don't* be scared of me because I have a beard' (*L*, iii. 291).

34. *K* 256.

35. *K* 261, 255.

36. *L*, iii. 287, 288.

37. *L*, iii. 288.

38. They were away from 30 September to 28 November; *L*, iii. 285; Nehls, i. 434; *L*, iii. 295.

39. *L*, ii. 597.

40. *L*, iii. 293.

41. *L*, iii. 239, 322, 309.

42. 'Curried' combines the sense of 'brushed up, combed' with 'employing flattery and blandishment, to win favour' (*OED*2 1 and 4b); *L*, iii. 311; 'Education of the People', *Reflections* 100, 97.

43. *L*, iii. 306, 297–8, 323.

44. *L*, iii. 299, 522.

45. *L*, iii. 294, 303.

46. *L*, iii. 328.

47. *L*, iii. 338, 337.

48. *L*, iii. 330, 335, 340.

49. *L*, iii. 337.

50. *L*, iii. 335; *The Collected Letters of Katherine Mansfield*, ed. V. O'Sullivan and M. Scott (1987) ii. 303.

51. Luhan 60.

52. *L*, iii. 302.

53. *L*, iii. 344, 335.

54. *L*, iii. 352.

55. *L*, iii. 355.

56. *L*, iii. 332, 346. In September 1916, Murry had acquired a job in the War Office as translator.

57. *L*, iii. 296, 466.

58. *L*, iii. 391.

59. *L*, iii. 381, 383, 186, 351, 389; Nehls, i. 503.

60. *L*, iii. 412; *Mark Gertler: Selected Letters*, ed. Noel Carrington (1965), p. 175.

61. Nehls, i. 507.

62. *LG* 294.

63. *L*, iii. 391; *K* 247.

64. *L*, ii. 58; *K* 259; *L*, iii. 318.

65. *AR* 22; *K* 250. David Garnett, who had seen DHL on 11 November 1918 after a gap of more than three years, was struck by the fact that he had 'no trace of that sparkling love of life in his eyes which had been his most attractive feature six years before' (Nehls, i. 478).

66. *L*, iii. 194; *AR* 22.

67. *K* 258; *L*, ii. 414, iii. 730.

68. *LG* 294.

13 Italy and Sicily: 1919–1920

1. *L*, iii. 415. DHL has been criticized for exaggerating his poverty (the £9 being compared with the 'more than £40' he recorded changing into lire by the end of November – *L*, iii. 425); e.g. Brenda Maddox, *The Married Man* (1994), p. 299, and Louise E. Wright, 'Disputed Dregs: D. H. Lawrence and the Publication of Maurice Magnus' *Memoirs of the Foreign Legion*', *Journal of the D. H. Lawrence Society* (1996), pp. 57–73. Both accuse him of lying, without considering that a writer's income arrives irregularly; it only needed a cheque to arrive from (say) Huebsch for DHL to have, quite suddenly, cash in hand (£50 would arrive unexpectedly from America on 6 December – *L*, iii. 428).

2. Cf. *TE* Illustration 6.

3. Nehls, ii. 12; *L*, iii. 421, 417.

4. Nehls, ii. 12–13.

5. Douglas had fled from England before he could be put on trial, after being arrested for making advances to a schoolboy in the Natural History Museum.

6. *MM* 31.

7. *MM* 107–32; *L*, viii. 49 n. 3; *MM* 29; *L*, iv. 129.

8. Norman Douglas to Reggie Turner, November 1919 (UCLA); Nehls, iii. 35.

9. *SP* 207; *AR* 194.

10. *L*, vii. 475–6 n. 6.

11. *L*, i. 232 n. 1; *WL* xlix–l; *L*, iv. 93–4; Mollie Skinner, *The Fifth Sparrow: An Autobiography* (1973), pp. 115–16; *L*, i. 232, iii. 36.

12. See *AR* 313–17, 319, 322–5, 328.

13. 'The Blind Man' might be cited for Catherine Carswell, but the house (at Upper Lydbrook in the Forest of Dean, Monmouthshire) is more closely reproduced than the person: see *EmyE* 238.

14. Derek Britton, *Lady Chatterley: The Making of the Novel* (1988), p. 40.

15. *MM* 124; *AR* 217–18.

16. *L*, iv. 131; Nehls, ii. 14.

17. *OED2* senses 15 h, 34, 55 b, c and i.

18. *L*, iv. 318.

19. See William Wordsworth, 'Preface' (1800) to *Lyrical Ballads*, ed. R. L. Brett and A. R. Jones (1991), p. 266.

20. *L*, iii. 416.

21. Frieda 116; *MM* 30.

22. *L*, iii. 422, 450, 435; Frieda 116.

23. *L*, iii. 429.

24. *L*, iii. 432.

25. *L*, iii. 431–2, 434, 442.

26. *L*, iii. 450, 442, 432.

27. *L*, iii. 437.

28. *L*, iii. 439, 454.

29. *L*, iii. 444, 442, 443, 469.

30. *PFU* 39, 43; *L*, iii. 493.

31. *L*, iii. 307, 309.

32. *L*, iii. 439, 453.

33. *L*, iii. 499.

34. Compton Mackenzie, *My Life and Times: Octave Five 1915–1923* (1966), p. 169; *L*, iii. 460 n. 1, 458.

35. *L*, iii. 467.

36. *The Collected Letters of Katherine Mansfield*, ed. V. O'Sullivan and M. Scott (1993), iii. 183. These are extracts from a letter she wrote to Ottoline Morrell on 20 January 1920; her letter to DHL was probably very similar.

37. *L*. iii. 470; *L*, iii. 307, and see n. 5. The translator of *L*, although technically correct in translating the reflexive 'one is not dying', ignores the fact that the reflexive form in French is archaic and 'literary' (the last thing DHL is being).

38. See Aldous Huxley's comments (Haruhide Mori, *A Conversation on D. H. Lawrence*, 1974, p. 39). Eighteen months later, DHL sent her a single-word

postcard – 'Ricordi' (remembrances) – from Wellington when he and Frieda landed there in August 1922 (*L*, iv. 283), which she was pleased to get, and she left him a book in her will (which Murry never passed on): see *TE* 559–64; *L*, iv. 114.

39. *Katherine Mansfield: The Memories of LM* ['Leslie Moore', i.e. Ida Constance Baker] (1971), pp. 145–6; *Journal of Katherine Mansfield*, ed. John Middleton Murry (1954), p. 198.

40. John Middleton Murry to Katherine Mansfield, 'Friday' [6 February 1920] (Turnbull Library); *Letters of Katherine Mansfield*, ed. O'Sullivan and Scott, iii. 214.

41. F. A. Lea, *The Life of John Middleton Murry* (1959), p. 83.

42. See e.g. *Letters between Katherine Mansfield and John Middleton Murry*, ed. Cherry A. Hankin (1988), pp. 276, 281, 282.

43. *Katherine Mansfield: Selected Letters*, ed. Vincent O'Sullivan (1989), pp. 234, 266.

44. *L*, v. 408; Adam Phillips, *Promises Promises* (2000), p. 59.

45. For the source of the unexpected windfall see *L*, iii. 445 and n. 1. Magnus apparently didn't tell DHL that charges had been laid by Leone Colleoni of the Excelsior Hotel in Rome as well as by Amadeo Brocco of the Hotel Vittoria in Anzio (information from Louise Wright).

46. *MM* 56–7.

47. *MM* 38.

48. Rosalind Thornycroft, *Time Which Spaces Us Apart*, completed by Chloë Baynes (1991), p. 78; *MM* 57.

49. *L*, iv. 327, 102.

50. *MM* 56; *L*, iv. 327, 154.

51. I owe the word to Michael Squires and Lynn K. Talbot; it appears in their *Living at the Edge: A Biography of D. H. Lawrence and Frieda von Richthofen* (2002), p. 223.

52. *L*, iii. 471.

53. The Brett Youngs would pass on an anecdote of DHL sharing a room with them: 'In less than five minutes he was talking, groaning and quarrelling with someone (one might guess whom) in his sleep' (*TE* 570). They assumed it must have been a dream of Frieda, but DHL habitually talked in his sleep. Cf. George Lawrence's memory of him in 1911 (E. T. 188) quoted in Chapter 7, and Mabel Luhan's recollection of him 'mumbling and groaning in his uneasy sleep' in June 1924 (Luhan 233).

54. *L*, iii. 491, 498, 497, 491.

55. *L*, iii. 498.

56. *L*, iii. 481.

57. *L*, iii. 650, 655, 729–30, 701.

58. *L*, iii. 486, iv. 111.

14 Ending with Love: 1920–1921

1. *LG* 1; *L*, iii. 503.

2. Maurice Magnus to Norman Douglas, 9 May 1920 (YU); *MM* 67.

3. See e.g. *MM* 40, 66, 76, 80, etc.

4. *MM* 83.

5. *L*, iii. 552; *MM* 84; see Chapter 11; *MM* 57.

6. *L*, iii. 574.

7. *L*, iii. 533, 570, 573, 590.

8. *L*, iii. 463.

9. *L*, iii. 603, 592.

10. David Garnett, *Great Friends* (1979), p. 36.

11. Rosalind Thornycroft, *Time Which Spaces Us Apart*, completed by Chloë Baynes (1991), pp. 78–9; 'Education of the People', *Reflections* 122.

12. Thornycroft, *Time Which Spaces Us Apart*, p. 79; there is a longer quotation of the memoir in *TE* 602–3.

13. He posted three of his 'Fruit Studies' to Mountsier 15–16 September (*L*, iii. 596 and n. 1, 597 and n. 2): by 30 September he had finished his 'Tortoise' poems, which cannot have been started earlier than 3 September (*L*, iii. 605 and n. 2).

14. Rosalind Baynes noted 'Pomegranate', 'Peach', 'Medlars and Sorb-Apples', 'Grapes' and 'Figs' as '*Villa La Canovaia*' in her copy of *Birds, Beasts and Flowers*, 'Cypresses' and 'Turkey-Cock' as '*Villa Belvedere*' (*TE* 858–9).

15. 'Medlars and Sorb-Apples', *New Republic*, xxv (5 January 1921), p. 169.

16. 'Lui et Elle', *Poems* 361.

17. 'Tortoise Gallantry', *Poems* 362. Rosalind noted only 'Tortoise Shell' as '*Villa La Canovaia*' (*TE* 858–9), suggesting that it may have been the only one of the 'Tortoise' poems she saw at the time.

18. *L*, iii. 629.

19. Luhan 40, 51. Catherine Carswell noted that Mabel's account of Esther Andrews was 'both misleading and incorrect . . . I heard the particulars from both Lawrence and Frieda' (*SP* 87n.).

20. *L*, iii. 599.

21. Luhan 51. Mabel also reported Frieda saying – 'with a kind of bitter triumph' – 'But it was unsuccessful' (p. 40).

22. So far as we can tell, Rosalind kept all his letters, so the lack of any tenderer ones is perhaps significant.

23. *L*, iii. 615.

24. DHL sent Rosalind *Sea and Sardinia* in February 1922 (*L*, iv. 193 n. 1); but the fact that she wrote to him in Sicily sometime in the second half of 1923 (*L*, iv. 532) suggests how out of touch she too had become.

25. *AR* 124–5.

26. *L*, iii. 608–9, 616. The poem was 'Sicilian Cyclamens' (*Poems* 310–12).

27. See *LG* xxxix–xl.

28. See *WL* xlv–xlviii; *L*, iii. 625, 665.

29. *The Times Literary Supplement*, 2 December 1920, p. 795; *L*, iii. 638; *MN* 142, 292.

30. *MM* 100; 'Education of the People', *Reflections* 134.

31. The ideal is visible in a letter from Frieda to her sister Else of 2 November 1912: 'However, we are so "intimate", Lawrence and I, and love is simply an identification with the other' (UT), tr. CR-W and JW.

32. *MN* 227–8.

33. *MN* 228. This point of view cannot be reconciled with *TE* 620–21, which argues that Gilbert's feelings at this point refer entirely to the 1920 DHL.

34. See *MN* 292, 290–91; 'New Heaven and Earth', Section VII, *Poems* 260: 'at whose side I have lain for over a thousand nights' asserts the poem (located as '*Greatham*', where DHL and Frieda lived 23 January – 30 July 1915).

35. *MN* 291; *L*, iii. 660.

36. *L*, iii. 635, 655, iv. 299.

37. *L*, iii. 645, 647, 660; *Letters from a Publisher: Martin Secker to D H Lawrence & Others* (1970), p. 10; *L*, iii. 674–5, 732, 728.

38. *L*, iii. 632, 659. For 'far country' see Luke, xx. 9.

39. *L*, iii. 668–9.

40. *L*, iii. 629; *MM* 69.

41. *L*, iv. 240, iii. 435.

42. See e.g. *L*, iii. 383 ('the thought of U.S.A. . . . sickens me') and *L*, iv. 273 ('As for America, I go to it rather with dread').

43. *L*, iii. 521, 689; *K* 240.

44. *L*, iii. 732–3.

45. *Studies* 17.

46. *L*, iii. 649.

47. *L*, iii. 693, 645.

48. *S&S* 9.

49. *S&S* 95–6.

50. He left its first part as a self-standing short text (see *L*, iii. 667), which was published in *A Modern Lover* (1934). The full text was not published until 1984.

51. *L*, iii. 699.

52. *L*, iii. 682, 683.

53. *L*, iii. 698, 712, 710.

54. *L*, iii. 712.

55. *L*, iii. 712, iv. 25, iii. 725, 626.

56. *AR* 264.

57. *AR* 158.

58. *AR* 159–60.

59. See *EY* 412; *LAH* 167; *L*, i. 39, ii. 130.

60. *AR* 194.

61. *AR* 298.

62. *AR* 289.

63. *PFU* 197; *L*, iii. 655; *L*, i. 533.

64. *AR* 257.

65. *AR* 257–8, 260; Thornycroft, *Time Which Spaces Us Apart*, p. 78; *AR* 261, 262–3; *WL* 439–40.

66. *AR* 265–6, 267.

67. *AR* 271–5; Nehls, ii. 59.

68. The Marchesa's first name in *Aaron's Rod* is 'Nan' (*AR* 250: 10) – the name of Rosalind's youngest child: also suggestive is the fact that when Aaron is with her on the terrace of her house (in theory on the south side of the Arno) they are close enough to see an open window in a pension on the Lungarno, and yet the dome of the cathedral is 'in the distance' (*AR* 253: 5). The dome is huge from where they are, but it was indeed 'in the distance' from either the Canovaia or the Villino Belvedere.

69. For Frieda and Hobson, see Chapter 8.

70. *LCL* 176, 208. Constance's appearance, however – 'a soft, ruddy, country-looking girl inclined to freckle, with big blue eyes and curling brown hair' (*LCL* 19) – does not match Rosalind, who 'had hazel eyes, not blue; nor was she freckled' (Chloë Green to JW, 9 July 2003).

71. *MN* 145–6. Cf. Alice Dax's comment that DHL as a lover could 'come back to a woman time after time' (Émile Delavenay, *D. H. Lawrence: The Man and his Work*, 1972, p. 155). See too James C. Cowan, *D. H. Lawrence: Sex and Sexuality* (2002), pp. 73–4.

72. *L*, iii. 718, 694.

73. *AR* 266.

74. *L*, iii. 685; 'Education of the People', *Reflections* 134–5.

75. *WL* 439–40.

76. Compton Mackenzie, *My Life and Times: Octave Five 1915–1923* (1966), pp. 167–8. It is possible, however, that Mackenzie was importing into his

recollection of his discussions with DHL in Capri what he later read of Mellors and Constance in *LCL* 134–5.

77. Nehls, i. 503; *L*, iii. 223; *L*, iv. 269. In Taos, their house had 'four rooms and a kitchen' (*L*, iv. 305), and they had a bedroom each.

78. The only marital sexual encounter in *Kangaroo* (*K* 146–7) occurs after Somers has been sexually aroused by another woman the previous evening (*K* 142–3); Somers's statement about sex appears in the cancelled first conclusion (*K* 474).

79. *L*, iv. 57.

80. *L*, iii. 720; see *BinB* 149.

81. *L*, iv. 92–3.

82. *L*, iv. 57, 116, 124, 125.

83. *PFU* 197.

84. *PFU* 94: the passage is written into E125b (UT).

85. *L*, i. 493, 492; *PFU* 158.

15 Forwards, not Back: 1921–1922

1. *L*, iii. 708, iv. 46.

2. *L*, iii. 678, iv. 113.

3. *L*, iv. 57, 130, 113.

4. *L*, iv. 63–4.

5. *L*, iv. 90.

6. *L*, iii. 435, 312.

7. *L*, iv. 139: so that the less worn inner side becomes the new outside (*OED2* 11 c). An Italian tailor in the early 1920s would charge 120 francs (about £1 10s) to 'turn' a suit of 'beautiful English cloth' from 'before the war' (*AR* 234): see Illustration 27 for the result.

8. *L*, iii. 486, iv. 90, 125, iii. 486.

9. *L*, iv. 93, 111.

10. E47a, p. 3 (UCB), a diary DHL kept briefly about his literary affairs while without an English agent: see E. W. Tedlock, *The Frieda Lawrence Collection of the Manuscripts of D. H. Lawrence: A Descriptive Bibliography* (1948), pp. 87–99.

11. *Nation & Athenaeum*, xxix (13 August 1921), p. 713; xxx (1 October 1921), p. 122.

12. *L*, iv. 93; E47a, p. 3 (UCB). He also changed details of Halliday's flat and manservant.

13. *L*, iv. 129; Nehls, ii. 93–4, 91; *L*, iv. 104.

14. *L*, iv. 114, 97, 141.

15. *Fox* 153.

16. *L*, viii. 48–50; *SP* 117.

17. *K*, 107; *MM* 92, 99.

18. *MM* 99, 101. DHL's introduction has been reprinted a number of times, but Magnus's text was only printed in the 1924 (London) and 1925 (New York) first editions of *Memoirs of the Foreign Legion*; two excerpts of unprinted material appear in *MM* 141–7. Although the full manuscript of Magnus's book is now unlocated, there is a xerox at UN.

19. Nehls, ii. 64.

20. *L*, iv. 103.

21. *L*, iv. 110–11.

22. *L*, iv. 115. Verga (b. 1840) would die in Catania (just 25 miles south of Taormina) on 27 January 1922.

23. *L*, iv. 225, 151.

24. *AR* xxxiii; *L*, iv. 132, 167.

25. E126b (UT).

26. *L*, iv. 105.

27. *L*, iv. 163, 165; *MM* 60.

28. *L*, iv. 165.

29. *L*, iv. 174, 190.

30. I am deliberately not going down the road invitingly prepared in *TE* 697–8 that DHL's insistence on masculine superiority in the autumn of 1921, in work like 'The Fox', 'The Ladybird' and (in some ways) 'The Captain's Doll', might conceivably be 'explained' by Frieda's unfaithfulness that autumn: *TE* 696 is convincing about the unreliability of the (solitary) account of her unfaithfulness.

31. Nehls, ii. 32; 'Snake', *Poems* 349. DHL sent the poem to Mountsier on 28 January 1921 (*L*, iii. 657); the volume it was destined for was growing almost daily, and the poem probably written in the previous few days.

32. *Memoirs* 142; Luhan 7.

33. *L*, iv. 171, 182, 202, 191, iii. 693; 'The Evening Land', *Poems* 291.

34. *L*, iv. 90, 180, 95, 123.

35. *L*, iv. 175, 213, iii. 337, 656. See too *L*, iii. 425 for 'that pressure' of England.

36. *L*, iv. 191, iv. 31, iii. 249 n. 2, iv. 146.

37. *L*, iv. 157, iii. 348, iv. 157.

38. *L*, iv. 198, 206; *L*, iv. 204–5 translates DHL's 'Trennungschmerz' as 'pain of parting', but it was the *separation*, the cutting off, not just the (de)parting which mattered; *L*, iii. 693, viii. 53.

16 On and On: 1922

1. *L*, iv. 213.

2. *L*, iii. 656. The jacket is a lot baggier and more crumpled than in his 1919 passport photograph (see *TE* Illustration 6). Frieda's passport photographs for the equivalent dates are Illustration 19 here and *TE* Illustration 11.

3. Magnus 30.

4. *L*, iv. 208.

5. *L*, iv. 208, 234.

6. *L*, iv. 212.

7. *L*, iv. 213.

8. 'Elephant', *Poems* 387–8.

9. *L*, iv. 213, 214, 215.

10. *L*, iv. 216, 214, 227.

11. *L*, iv. 225, 216; Nehls, ii. 129; *L*, iv. 218.

12. Nehls, iii. 83; Richard Aldington, *Portrait of a Genius, But . . .* (1950), p. 248; Nehls, ii. 124.

13. *L*, iv. 193, 217, 224.

14. Nehls, ii. 120; *L*, iv. 225.

15. *L*, iv. 225, 226, 227.

16. Nehls, ii. 119; *L*, iv. 227, 228, 181, 192.

17. *L*, iv. 216, 234; Frieda 135; *L*, iv. 234, 226, 219.

18. *L*, iv. 219, 227; *K* 21; *L*, iv. 219.

19. *L*, iv. 226; Nehls, ii. 127.

20. *L*, iv. 220, 241, 245, 228, 239.

21. *L*, iii. 522.

22. *L*, iv. 233, 238.

23. Mollie Skinner, *The Fifth Sparrow: An Autobiography* (1973), p. 110.

24. *K* 20.

25. *L*, iv. 253, 249, 265, 263.

26. *L*, iv. 267. DHL also described to Seltzer, in October 1921, 'a proper *story* novel – in the Venetian lagoons: not pretty pretty – but no sex and no problems: no love particularly' which came to nothing (*L*, iv. 93); he had apparently started it in September 1921 as 'a story about Venice' (*L*, iv. 81).

27. *L*, iv. 247.

28. *K* 333.

29. *K* 175.

30. *K* 332; *L*, iv. 267.

31. *L*, iv. 275. Cf. Birkin in *WL*: 'still, he was damned and doomed to the old effort at serious living' (*WL* 302).

32. *L*, iv. 282.

33. *L*, iv. 275, 268.

34. *L*, iv. 268.

35. *K* xxxix, 358, 476–8, 259.

36. *L*, iv. 286, 285, 284; *Studies* 126.

37. Frieda to Anna von Richthofen, 25 August – 1 September 1922 (UT), tr. CR-W and JW; Luhan 47.

38. *L*, iv. 289.

39. *L*, iv. 292, 290, 289.

17 New Mexico: 1922–1923

1. Witter Bynner, 'Foreword', Nehls, ii. x.

2. 'New Mexico', *P* 142–3.

3. 'Indians and an Englishman', *P* 92; *L*, iv. 300.

4. *L*, iv. 304, 312, 313, 362.

5. *L*, iv. 313, 305.

6. *L*, iv. 305.

7. *L*, iv. 311; Luhan 70.

8. *L*, iv. 315, 330, 304, 314.

9. *L*, iv. 326; Ben Hecht, *Fantazius Mallare: A Mysterious Oath* (1922), p. 55; MS [no E no.] (Yale), p. 1.

10. *L*, iv. 319; *St.M* 199. A parallel would be with *The Trespasser*, a work of fiction based entirely on a friend's experience but written without consulting them, rather than with DHL's collaborative work with (e.g.) Mollie Skinner on *The Boy in the Bush* in 1924 and potentially with Catherine Carswell in 1914 and 1923 (see *SP* 18, 201–4).

11. Frieda 152; *L*, iv. 319, 344, 310, 324.

12. Susan Sontag, 'The Fragile Alliance', *Guardian*, Review section, 18 October 2003, p. 4.

13. *Studies* 41. 'Stunt' in this sense is a specifically US word suggesting something done primarily for the sake of attracting attention.

14. *L*, iv. 375.

15. *L*, iv. 327, viii. 127.

16. 'Spirits Summoned West', *Poems* 411–12.

17. 'The Virgin Mother', *Poems* 101.

18. 'Spirits Summoned West', *Poems* 412, 411.

19. See p. 125 above and *EY* 411–12.

20. Luhan 64; *Memoirs* 410.

21. 'The Future of the Novel [Surgery for the Novel – Or a Bomb]', *Hardy* 154.

22. Luhan 88.

23. *L*, iv. 337.

24. *L*, iv. 576, 330.

25. *L*, iv. 314, 311.

26. *L*, iv. 333; Frieda to Anna von Richthofen, '*Donnerstag*' (UT).

27. *L*, iv. 386.

28. *L*, iv. 336, 352, 360, 514; cf. Luhan 112–13.

29. Merrild 73, 208. If Merrild had heard the 'gossip' in 1922, he cannot yet have been influenced by the attack on DHL as a pervert in Joseph Collins's book *The Doctor Looks at Literature* (1923).

30. *Studies* 571.

31. Merrild 135, 232.

32. See e.g. 'Reflections on the Death of a Porcupine', *Reflections* 355–6.

33. 'Bibbles', *Poems* 395; *L*, iv. 434, viii. 76, iv. 470. Frieda also believed she owned the dog, referring to 'my darling Pips' and regretting that the journey to Mexico would be 'too painful' for her (Frieda to Anna von Richthofen, 23 February 1922, UT, tr. CR-W and JW).

34. *L*, iv. 367.

35. Merrild 175.

36. Bynner 62.

37. *L*, v. 423; Adam Phillips, *Promises Promises* (2000), p. 270.

38. *EmyE* 215–16.

39. *L*, iv. 366, 375.

40. Merrild 174; *MN* 225.

41. Luhan 88, 87.

42. *L*, iv. 406–7, 344.

18 Loyalty and Betrayal: 1923

1. *L*, iv. 412; 'Au Revoir, U.S.A.', *P* 105; *L*, iv. 419.

2. Carleton Beals, Frederick W. Leighton and Witter Bynner: see Nehls, ii. 227–8, 230–31, Bynner 26–7.

3. Bynner 31.

4. Letter to John Middleton Murry, 10 December 1955 (*Memoirs* 368); Bynner 32; Gui de Angulo, *Jaime in Taos: The Taos Papers of Jaime de Angulo* (1985), pp. 49–52; Frieda to John Middleton Murry, 10 December 1955; Luhan 72.

5. Bynner 43; 'Au Revoir, U.S.A.', *P* 104–6.

6. Bynner 79–80.

7. The first version has been published as *Quetzalcoatl: The Early Version of*

'*The Plumed Serpent*', ed. Louis I. Martz (1995); *L*, iv. 457; 'Au Revoir, U.S.A.', *P* 105.

8. Hilary Mantel, 'No passport required', *Guardian*, Review section, 12 October 2002, p. 5.

9. *DG* 126.

10. Nehls, ii. 236.

11. Bynner 84. Nickolas Muray, in the summer of 1923, remembered Lawrence as the shyest person he had ever photographed, and regretted that he had not managed to produce 'a single smiling picture' but explained that Lawrence 'wasn't the smiling type' (*The Revealing Eye*, 1967, p. 170): see e.g. *DG* Illustration 15. At Cuernavaca, Bynner had taken a photograph that DHL especially liked (see *DG* Illustration 9). DHL sent copies to four people, remarking to one of them, 'Isn't this a nice photograph' (*L*, iv. 435). The photograph reveals a bright-eyed face, the mouth opening in a smile. He may have preferred to see himself lively; he was more likely to have been relieved that his self-consciousness had not rendered him stiff or grim-faced. Catherine Carswell had been especially proud of a photograph she took of him in Florence in 1921 because it had showed him smiling (see *SP* 148 and frontispiece); like Idella Purnell, she used the word 'sparkling'.

12. *L*, iv. 139; Barbara Barr, 'Step-daughter to Lawrence – II', *London Magazine*, xxxiii (October–November 1993), p. 15; 'New Mexico', *P* 143.

13. *L*, viii. 81.

14. J. Middleton Murry, *Reminiscences of D. H. Lawrence* (1933), p. 240; *L*, iv. 437.

15. *Adelphi*, i (June 1923), pp. 9, 6; *L*, iv. 458.

16. *L*, iv. 483, 327.

17. *L*, iv. 479, 483, 484.

18. *SP* 190: 'one of the worst quarrels – perhaps the very worst – of their life together'; *D. H. Lawrence: Letters to Thomas and Adele Seltzer*, ed. Gerald M. Lacy (1976), p. 106.

19. *Memoirs* 92–3.

20. *L*, iv. 480, i. 551.

21. See Merrild 139–40; Luhan 105.

22. *DG* 126; F. A. Lea, *The Life of John Middleton Murry* (1959), pp. 117–18.

23. Frieda to Anna von Richthofen, ?17 or 22 September 1923 and 5 November 1923 (UT), tr. CR-W and JW.

24. Address Book (?second used: 3 × 4⅞ in.), entry under 'London County Westminster & Parrs Bank' (UT); *L*, iv. 529.

25. Nehls, iii. 289; *L*, iv. 501, 507.

26. *L*, viii. 86, 85.

27. *BinB* 334.

28. Ibid.

29. *L*, iv. 506; 'A Second Contemporary Verse Anthology', *P* 324; *BinB* 338.

30. Merrild 343.

31. *L*, iv. 532, 529.

32. *Memoirs* 231; *L*, iv. 505–6, 541.

33. *St.M* 221–2.

34. *Memoirs* 231.

35. 'On Coming Home', *Reflections* 179.

36. *L*, iv. 542, 545, 543, 550, 544–5; 'On Coming Home', *Reflections* 183; *L*, v. 94, iv. 545.

37. *L*, iv. 480, 483; Hignett 139; Murry, journal entry of 18 December 1955, quoted in Lea, *Life of John Middleton Murry*, p. 118.

38. *Memoirs* 282, 330; Frieda to Anna von Richthofen, 5 November 1923 (UT), tr. CR-W and JW. Michael Squires and Lynn K. Talbot, *Living at the Edge: A Biography of D. H. Lawrence and Frieda von Richthofen* (2002), p. 462, note on 282, unwisely suggest that Murry and Frieda after all became lovers in 1923, in spite of Murry's memory of holding back and his statement that in 1923 'I couldn't have you' (*Memoirs* 331). For her part, Frieda recalled how – on the 1923 journey to Germany – 'I had a hunch you were fond of me too' (*Memoirs* 312): hardly the language of consummated passion.

39. Hignett 135, 143.

40. John Middleton Murry, *Son of Woman* (1931), p. 388; *SP* 205–14; Murry, *Reminiscences of D. H. Lawrence*, pp. 11–12, 190–95. All these accounts were written down within eight years of the event, and – as they corrected each other – we can be reasonably sure that, where they do not do so, they are accurate.

41. *L*, iv. 541.

42. *SP* 212.

43. *L*, iv. 513.

44. See Claire Tomalin, *Katherine Mansfield: A Secret Life* (1988), pp. 194–5.

45. Murry, journal entry of 21 July 1932, quoted in Lea, *Life of John Middleton Murry*, p. 119.

46. Luhan 131. Frieda had told Mabel Luhan about the events at the Café Royal, and the latter's version of what she heard is in general unreliable; but this single haunting detail comes in her version after his loving friends had all 'cheered him and drank his health'.

47. *L*, v. 205; Murry, *Son of Woman*, p. 388.

48. Frieda 132. Willard Johnson remembered an evening in Chapala when

Witter Bynner had 'fed Lorenzo on several drinks in the Plaza' and Lawrence had been 'a perfect scream, burlesquing the Bohemian set of London. He is a born mimic when he lets himself go. And I was fairly rolling on the floor in mirth' (*DG* 117: cf. Nehls, ii. 236).

49. *SP* 200; *L*, v. 46–7.

50. *L*, iv. 572; Murry, *Son of Woman*, p. 13.

51. *L*, iv. 546; *Mark Gertler: Selected Letters*, ed. Noel Carrington (1965), p. 219; *SP* 200.

52. Hignett 146–7; see Brett's letter to S. S. Koteliansky, 25 February 1924, *D. H. Lawrence Review*, vii (Fall 1974), pp. 269–70.

53. *BinB* 344, 346, 347.

54. *L*, iv. 552; Nehls, ii. 318.

55. *WWRA* 133; *L*, iv. 581.

56. See the early version of the story, *WWRA* 285–94.

57. Bedford, ii. 231.

58. *L*, iv. 572, 574.

59. 'Letter from Germany', *P* 109–10.

60. *L*, iv. 597, 581.

19 America Again: 1924

1. E47a, pp. 9–10, demonstrates DHL's careful listing of his accounts with Seltzer and the National Chase Bank: see too John Worthen, *D. H. Lawrence: A Literary Life* (1989), pp. 114–35.

2. *L*, iv. 578, v. 22.

3. Luhan 166, 188.

4. 'Indians and Entertainment', *MinM* 102. Bandelier (1840–1914), pioneer archaeologist of the Southwest, had also written a novel (*The Delight Makers*, 1890) about the betrayal of the prehistoric New Mexican Pueblo tribe to the Navajos, which DHL read in May 1924 (*L*, v. 42) and (along with *The Gilded Man*, 1893) later recommended (Nehls, iii. 290).

5. 'Indians and Entertainment', *MinM* 112–13.

6. *L*, v. 23.

7. Brett 171–2; Frieda 161.

8. *L*, v. 40–41, 45.

9. Luhan 209–10.

10. *L*, v. 43; *DG* 233; *L*, v. 203.

11. *L*, v. 65. When Frieda's next partner, Angelo Ravagli (see Chapter 21), saw the ranch in 1931, he immediately proposed building a 'proper' house there (and did, in the mid 1930s).

12. *L*, v. 75.

13. *L*, v. 47, 44; *St.M* 148, 150.

14. *L*, v. 75; see e.g. *L*, v. 277.

15. *St.M* 146; *L*, v. 63.

16. *L*, v. 47, 75.

17. *St.M* 140.

18. *L*, v. 79, 208, 147–8.

19. Brett 104; 'Medlars and Sorb-Apples', *New Republic*, xxv (5 January 1921), p. 169.

20. Brett 137–8.

21. *WWRA* 69–71.

22. *L*, v. 77.

23. *L*, v. 86, 122, 91.

24. Brett 139–40.

25. *WL* 201.

26. Luhan 268; *The Letters of D. H. Lawrence*, ed. Aldous Huxley (1932), p. 609; *L*, v. 109.

27. 'The Hopi Snake Dance', *MinM* 166–8.

28. See *L*, v. 125, 129–30; Luhan 278–9.

29. *L*, v. 124; *DG* 652 suggests that the fiction fragment 'A Pure Witch' (*WWRA* 377: written by June 1924 and probably started the previous winter) may offer a brief fictional portrait of Arthur Lawrence as DHL saw him for the last time, on his visit to the Midlands at New Year 1924, but it seems at least as much a reminiscence of DHL's grandfather John Lawrence (1815–1901).

30. *L*, v. 143: 'Where is that Jason?' (Latin: DHL recalls the legend of Jason and the golden fleece).

31. See e.g. 'Dolour of Autumn' and 'Brooding Grief' (*Poems* 107–8, 110–11).

32. *Memoirs* 131.

33. Nehls, ii. 126.

34. *St.M* 159–96.

20 The Lost Depths of Mexico: 1924–1925

1. See e.g. the three photographs taken by Edward Weston (1886–1957) in Mexico City on 4 November 1924: (1) *DG* Illustration 17 (reversed) (see *L*, v. 185); (2) *D. H. Lawrence: Letters to Thomas and Adele Seltzer*, ed. Gerald M. Lacy (1976), frontispiece; (3) *L*, iv. Illustrations between pp. 252 and 253 (see *L*, v. 185).

2. Brett 159.

3. *L*, v. 164.

4. Brett 168; *L*, v. 166; Brett 174.

5. *L*, v. 191, 166, 184.

6. 'Corasmin and the Parrots', *MinM* 9.

7. *L*, v. 174, 170, 191, 192.

8. *L*, v. 191, 196; Frieda 165.

9. *PS* 274, 332.

10. *L*, v. 199.

11. *Quetzalcoatl: The Early Version of 'The Plumed Serpent'*, ed. Louis I. Martz (1995), p. 321.

12. Frieda 165.

13. *Memoirs* 121.

14. *L*, v. 192; Brett 206.

15. *L*, v. 202, 204.

16. *L*, vi. 409.

17. *L*, v. 216; Frieda 165; Frieda to Anna von Richthofen, 19 February 1925 (UT), tr. CR-W and JW.

18. *L*, v. 216.

19. Frieda 166–7; Frieda to Dorothy Brett, 12 August 1930, *D. H. Lawrence Review*, ix (Spring 1976), p. 101.

20. See *St.M* xxxiv–xxxvi. The manuscript is lost, so it cannot now be said exactly where Frieda's writing ended, but as she wrote almost a quarter of the whole (nine pages out of a total of forty: Tedlock 55), it is probable that DHL dictated pp. 207–10 of the CUP edition.

21. *St.M* 211.

22. *St.M* 209–10.

23. *L*, v. 229; Brett 216; *L*, vii. 144.

24. *L*, v. 233; Nehls, ii. 416; Frieda to Dorothy Brett [Spring 1925], *D. H. Lawrence Review*, ix (Spring 1976), p. 47.

25. *L*, v. 233, 235–6.

26. *DG* 238; *L*, v. 293.

27. Frieda to Dorothy Brett [Spring 1925], *D. H. Lawrence Review*, ix (Spring 1976), p. 49.

28. Brett 252; Nehls, ii. 411.

29. 'Morality and the Novel', *Hardy* 175.

30. 'Morality and the Novel', *Hardy* 171; 'Aristocracy', *Reflections* 374; 'Him With His Tail in His Mouth', *Reflections* 313.

31. Frieda to Dorothy Brett, [Spring 1925], *D. H. Lawrence Review*, ix (Spring 1976), pp. 47, 49; *L*, v. 254, 260.

32. Cf. 'A Note to the Crown', written ?July 1925, for DHL's attempt to

argue the opposite: 'John Middleton Murry said to me: "Let us *do* something" . . . I can't believe in "doing things" like that . . . There is still nothing to be "done" ' (*Reflections* 249).

33. Nehls, ii. 414.

34. *L*, v. 291.

35. '[Return to Bestwood]', *PII* 260–61 (corrected).

36. E. T. 168.

37. 'Which Class I Belong To', *LEA* 38.

38. *DG* 265; *L*, v. 296.

39. *St.M* 143; *L*, iv. 95.

40. *L*, v. 272.

41. *L*, v. 278; 'New Mexico', *P* 142–3.

21 Return to Europe: 1925–1926

1. *L*, v. 312.

2. *L*, iv. 520, v. 269, 273, 287.

3. The caption read: 'DAVID. H. LAWRENCE AND HIS WIFE SAIL FROM NEW YORK FOR ENGLAND EN ROUTE TO EGYPT, AFTER FIVE YEARS SPENT IN MEXICO AND AUSTRALIA.' (*D. H. Lawrence: Letters to Thomas and Adele Seltzer*, ed. Gerald M. Lacy, 1976, facing p. 148). Cf. *L*, v. 287 for DHL wondering about Egypt in mid August 1925.

4. Luhan 36; '. . . Love Was Once a Little Boy', *Reflections* 336; Crotch 3; Luhan 314. Cf. Richard Aldington, recalling bathing with her in 1928: 'Frieda naked wasn't really *fat* – just opulent like other Rubens ladies!' (*Richard Aldington & H. D.: The Later Years in Letters*, ed. Caroline Zilboorg, 1995, p. 251).

5. *L*, v. 343.

6. *L*, v. 312, 311.

7. *L*, v. 332; *SP* 227.

8. *L*, v. 311, 313.

9. *L*, v. 311; 'Note to the Crown', *Reflections* 249; *L*, v. 311.

10. *L*, v. 316, 318, 319.

11. '[Autobiographical Fragment]', *P* 831, 817; *L*, v. 318, 322.

12. '[Autobiographical Fragment]', *P* 817.

13. DHL was doubtless introduced to Hopkin's new wife, Olive Lizzie Slack (1895–1988), whom Hopkin had married on 17 September.

14. *L*, v. 319; *St.M* 209.

15. *SP* 229; '[Autobiographical Fragment]', *P* 821.

16. Nehls, iii. 9. The friends were Rollo and Luisa Hewitt.

17. '[Autobiographical Fragment]', *P* 817, 819; *L*, v. 332.

18. Nehls, iii. 8; *St.M* 208; '[Autobiographical Fragment]', *P* 819.

19. *L*, v. 332–3.

20. *L*, v. 309, 321, 324.

21. Nehls, iii. 10; *L*, v. 326, 483.

22. *L*, v. 332.

23. *L*, v. 368, 374, 380.

24. *L*, v. 331, 329, 335, 327.

25. *L*, v. 341, 425–6.

26. 'The Last Laugh', 'The Border Line', 'Jimmy and the Desperate Woman'; *WWRA* 200.

27. *WWRA* 281.

28. *L*, v. 352.

29. 'New Mexico', *P* 146–7; 'November by the Sea', 'Mediterranean in January', *Poems* 455, 815.

30. The Bersaglieri were riflemen or sharpshooters in the Italian army: Illustration 30 shows Ravagli wearing their hat with its dark plume of cock's feathers; *L*, v. 350.

31. Nehls, iii. 18; *DG* 348; Crotch 13. I am not persuaded that there is any kind of truth in the account given by Alberto Bevilacqua in his novel *Attraverso il tuo corpo* (2002), p. 225, of DHL writing a letter to Ravagli to encourage the affair. The document survives in Bevilacqua's reconstruction, more than twenty years after the event, in a fiction, of what Ravagli told him in 1974 about a document he himself had seen nearly forty years earlier (Bevilacqua insists, however, that he also saw the document). I provide the reconstruction here for readers unable to access the novel: '*Attraverso il tuo corpo, amico mio, ho ritrovato l'ultima vita del mio corpo, attraverso il tuo corpo, Frieda, ho ritrovato l'ultimo splendore dei sensi che tu hai vissuto attraverso il corpo di Angelo, e attraverso il mio corpo voi avete dato ai vostri corpi il senso di un Dio che, se glielo chiediamo, prende sostanza nel tutto che è desiderio d'amore*' (Through your body, my friend, I have recovered my body's last breath of life. Through your body, Frieda, I have recovered the last splendour of the senses which you have lived through Angelo's body. And through my body you two have given your own bodies the feeling of a God who, if we ask him, takes on substance in the whole which is desire for love). I am grateful to Nick Ceramella for helping me access this material and saving me from various errors.

32. See David Garnett, *Great Friends* (1979), p. 81; Crotch 13; Frieda to Mabel Luhan, 2 July [1931] (Berkeley); Barbara Barr, 'Step-daughter to Lawrence – II', *London Magazine*, xxxiii (October–November 1993), p. 16.

33. *K* 143.

34. Bynner 62.

35. Ibid.

36. Harry T. Moore, *The Intelligent Heart* (rev. edn., 1960), p. 477.

37. See e.g. Richard Aldington, *Portrait of a Genius, But . . .* (1950), p. 335 ('there is every reason to suppose that when he wrote the book [*Lady Chatterley's Lover*] he was already virtually if not completely impotent'); Robert Lucas, *Frieda Lawrence: The Story of Frieda von Richthofen and D. H. Lawrence* (1973), p. 238 ('towards the end of 1926 [Lawrence] had become sexually impotent'); Derek Britton, *Lady Chatterley: The Making of the Novel* (1988), p. 2 ('the loss of sexual potency which afflicted [Lawrence] in his fortieth year'); Rosie Jackson, *Frieda Lawrence* (1994), p. 41 ('by 1926, he was impotent'); James C. Cowan, *D. H. Lawrence: Self and Sexuality* (2002), p. 136 ('Lawrence was, at this time, unable to function sexually'). The accusation may well have been part of the homophobic Aldington's revenge on DHL for calling *him* 'an instinctive homosexual' (see Chapter 24): as late as 1958, Aldington was drawing attention to 'the undoubted homosexual streak' in DHL (Nehls, iii. xv).

38. Frieda to A. S. Frere-Reeves, n.d., but between 1931 and 1936: quoted Sotheby catalogue at sale of letters, item 87, p. 49. A study of 96 male sanatorium patients clinically on the upgrade from tuberculosis found that the sexual urge was or remained diminished in 14 per cent, perturbed in 10 per cent but unchanged in 74 per cent (Cowan, *D. H. Lawrence: Self and Sexuality*, p. 138).

39. Nehls, iii. 21, 26.

40. Nehls, iii. 26; *L*, v. 332–3.

41. See e.g. Barr, 'Step-daughter to Lawrence – II', p. 14: Lucille resembles Elsa, Aunt Cissie resembles Aunt Maude, Granny resembles Agnes Weekley.

42. D. H. Lawrence, *The Virgin and the Gipsy* (1930), p. 21.

43. Nehls, iii. 22; Barbara Weekley to JW, 28 April 1994.

44. *L*, v. 388, 390.

45. *L*, v. 394.

46. *L*, v. 392, 401.

47. Frieda 194.

48. *L*, v. 394–5; Nehls, iii. 44; *L*, v. 392, 403.

49. See Nehls, ii, frontispiece.

50. Nehls, iii. 278; Brett 208.

51. Brett (1974) II–IV; Hignett 191–2.

52. *PS* 257 ('Not you, poor boobs'). Although 'boobs' meaning breasts was first apparently used around 1918, it did not become current until after the

Second World War: cf. David Ellis, 'D. H. Lawrence and the Female Body', *Essays in Criticism*, xlvi (April 1996), pp. 136–52.

53. Brett (1974) V.

54. Frieda to S. S. Koteliansky, 'Sunday' [28 February 1932] (BL, Add. Mss. 48975); Brett 208; *L*, v. 203.

55. Dorothy Brett to Alfred Stieglitz [2 June 1931], YU; *L*, v. 406. See *DG* 292–6 for an extended argument that – however unreliable in detail – Brett's later version of events 'must be true in substance'.

56. *L*, v. 408.

57. Brett left so quickly that DHL had to send her washing after her (*L*, v. 405). Mark Kinkead-Weekes disagrees with the comparison with Rosalind Baynes: see *TE* 603–6.

58. *L*, v. 417; *WWRA* 331.

59. *L*, v. 421.

60. *L*, v. 406, 420.

61. *L*, v. 413–14.

62. *L*, v. 429, 437, 418.

63. *L*, v. 448, 453, 447, 464. *Poderi* are estates, lands.

64. Nehls, iii. 59; *L*, v. 483.

65. *L*, v. 472; Norman Douglas, *D. H. Lawrence and Maurice Magnus: A Plea for Better Manners* (1924), reprinted (slightly revised) as 'Postscript – A Plea for Better Manners' in *Experiments* (1925), pp. 221–67. See Chapter 13.

66. *L*, v. 395–7, 472.

67. *L*, v. 472, 403.

68. *WWRA* 154–5, 164, 170, 173; *L*, vi. 205, 218, v. 473. The book was published in 1932 as *Etruscan Places*.

69. *L*, v. 496, 482, 472.

70. The recording, made by David Gerard of Monty (an accomplished mimic) in old age, is the closest we can now get to the sound of DHL's voice (NCL).

71. *L*, v. 507, 509, 513, 512.

72. Illustration 32 misses out Peggy King but includes Maude Beardsall, the handicapped daughter of DHL's maternal uncle Herbert. Joan King is holding her parasol from the beach photograph, Illustration 31.

73. *L*, v. 514, 522, 518, 534.

74. Lady Cynthia Asquith, *Diaries 1915–1918* [ed. E. M. Horsley] (1968), p. 98; Sarah Walker, 'Memories of Eastwood', *Staple* (Winter 1983), p. 51.

75. *L*, v. 522, 524, 536; '[Return to Bestwood]', *PII* 257.

76. *L*, v. 539–40, 534.

77. *D. H. Lawrence: The Critical Heritage*, ed. R. P. Draper (1969), p. 276; *L*, v. 559.

22 Other Forces: 1926–1927

1. *L*, v. 611; see Jay A. Gertzman, *A Descriptive Bibliography of* Lady Chatterley's Lover (1989), p. 5: by the end of 1930, the novel had sold over 30,000 copies (see John Worthen, 'Lawrence and the "Expensive Edition Business"', *Modernist Writers and the Marketplace*, ed. Ian Willison, Warwick Gould and Warren Cherniak, 1996, p. 121); memorandum by DHL, NWU.

2. *L*, vi. 569; 'A Foreword by Frieda Lawrence', *The First Lady Chatterley* (1973), p. 9; *LCL* xx.

3. *FSLC* 215; Frieda 203. DHL noted after first acquiring it that the house was 'the opposite direction to Fiesole' (*L*, v. 459). For links between Rosalind Baynes and Constance Chatterley, see Derek Britton, *Lady Chatterley: The Making of the Novel* (1988), pp. 83–6.

4. *L*, v. 569; Wilkinson 27–8.

5. *FSLC* 211, 28.

6. Wilkinson 28.

7. *FSLC* 381.

8. *FSLC* 59, 38. The sexual words 'fucker' and 'fucking' are used unexpectedly in the novel's last paragraph by Constance (*FSLC* 220) when she is thinking back to how Parkin used to talk. They look like an aide-mémoire, to record something not to be omitted from a revision; it was 114 pages since such language had previously been used.

9. He may e.g. have been aware of the sexually explicit Frank Harris memoir volumes, *My Life and Loves*, published in Paris from 1922, but there is no direct evidence of it.

10. *L*, v. 605.

11. Enid Hilton Hopkin, *More Than One Life: A Nottinghamshire Childhood with D. H. Lawrence* (1993), p. 53.

12. See *LCL* 200–201: see Chapter 6, n. 13, and Chapter 7, n. 12.

13. *Memoirs* 309.

14. Patmore 138. Cf. DHL's comment to his sister Ada on 22 February 1929: 'The things that seemed to make up one's life die into insignificance, and the whole state is wretched. I've been through it these last three years – and suffered, I tell you' (*L*, vii. 186).

15. *L*, vi. 254–5, 261–2, 264–5, 275.

16. 'Making Pictures', *PII* 604.

17. Merrild 209 and facing 128 (I am indebted to Joanna Wright for the identification): see too Luhan 344; 'Making Pictures', *PII* 604.

18. See e.g. the back of the jacket of *DG*.

19. *L*, v. 637.

20. *L*, vii. 271.

21. *L*, v. 648.

22. *L*, vi. 82, vi. 333.

23. 'A Foreword by Frieda Lawrence', *The First Lady Chatterley*, pp. 9–10.

24. *L*, v. 609–10, 616; 'Autobiographical Sketch', *PII* 595. *Ambiente* means 'ambience'.

25. *L*, v. 655, vi. 90, 220.

26. *SEP* 178, 54.

27. *SEP* 126; Nehls, iii. 226.

28. *L*, vi. 93.

29. *WWRA* 257.

30. *WWRA* 274; 'The Virgin Mother', 'Spirits Summoned West', *Poems* 101, 411; *WWRA* 274.

31. *L*, vi. 37.

32. *L*, vi. 72.

33. *L*, viii. 103, v. 588, vi. 59; Wilkinson 38, 41, 42, 43.

34. *L*, v. 630, vi. 42, 137.

35. *L*, vi. 48, 59.

36. *L*, vi. 72–3, 75; Wilkinson 45.

37. Frieda 208.

38. Wilkinson 49; Frieda 209; Crotch 7.

39. Wilkinson 51; *L*, vi. 119, 120.

40. Wilkinson 48; Bedford, i. 186; Wilkinson 47.

41. *Letters of Aldous Huxley*, ed. Grover Smith (1969), p. 288.

42. 'Introduction', *The Letters of D. H. Lawrence*, ed. Aldous Huxley (1932), pp. xxi–xxii; Wilkinson 50.

43. *L*, vi. 103. Other references to 'chagrin' appear at *L*, vi. 114–15, 409, vii. 440, 623: see too Chapter 1, n. 36.

44. *L*, vi. 136.

45. *L*, vi. 154, 139, 158, 151.

46. *L*, vi. 154, 172; Nehls, iii. 160.

23 *Lady Chatterley's Lover*: 1927–1928

1. *L*, vi. 186, 177, 179.
2. *L*, vi. 200; Wilkinson 52; *L*, vi. 203–4.
3. *L*, vi. 198–9, 207, 195.
4. *L*, vi. 202; '[Autobiographical Fragment]', *P* 830, 833.
5. Nehls, iii. 226; *L*, vi. 180–81, 190–91, 203–4, 225, 233, 247.
6. Richard Aldington, *Life for Life's Sake* (1968), p. 342.
7. 'Memoranda' (NWU); *L*, vi. 225, 222.
8. *L*, vi. 215.
9. *FSLC* 406.
10. *L*, vi. 308; Wilkinson 10.
11. 'A Foreword by Frieda Lawrence', *The First Lady Chatterley* (1973), p. 10.
12. *L*, vi. 414.
13. *FSLC* 100.
14. *L*, vi. 99.
15. *WL* 315, 363.
16. 'Review of *The Social Basis of Consciousness*', *P* 377–82; *L*, vi. 115, v. 648.
17. *L*, v. 521: see too *L*, vi. 419.
18. *L*, vi. 215, 238, 256.
19. Frieda to Anna von Richthofen, 28 December 1927 (UT), tr. CR-W and JW.
20. *The Letters of D. H. Lawrence*, ed. Aldous Huxley (1932), p. xxx.
21. *L*, vi. 247.
22. *L*, vi. 223; 'Foreword to *Collected Poems*', *Poems* 850.
23. 'Whether or Not', *Poems* 84: cf. *Poems* 924–31.
24. 'To Clarinda', *Poems* 550.
25. *L*, vi. 208, 290.
26. Nehls, iii. 182; Bedford, i. 179; *L*, vi. 329.
27. Juliette Huxley, *Leaves of the Tulip Tree: Autobiography* (1986), pp. 122, 118; *L*, vi. 315. The title survived until March 1928 when DHL distributed his subscription forms (see paragraph below in this chapter) but not into the published novel.
28. Bedford, i. 179, 228; Huxley, *Leaves of the Tulip Tree*, p. 125.
29. *LCL* 334.
30. *Lady Chatterley's Lover* measured $8^{15}/_{16} \times 7^{3}/_{8}$ in. and weighed 2 lb; *The Plumed Serpent* $7^{5}/_{16} \times 4^{7}/_{8}$ in., 1 lb 6 oz.

31.

> The phoenix renews her youth
> only when she is burnt, burnt alive, burnt down
> to hot and flocculent ash.
> Then the small stirring of a new small bub in the nest
> with strands of down like floating ash
> shows that she is renewing her youth like the eagle,
> immortal bird. (*Poems* 728)

The phoenix was, however, more commonly seen in the early twentieth than it is in the early twenty-first century. Insurance companies were fond of the name and its associations, the catalogue of Haywoods (the firm DHL had worked for in 1901) had incorporated it (see *Young Bert: An Exhibition of the Early Years of D. H. Lawrence*, Castle Museum, Nottingham, 1972, p. 21), and there had been a Phoenix Coffee Tavern in Eastwood when DHL was a boy, while a row of houses called Phoenix Cottages had been erected in Nottingham Road, Eastwood, in 1875.

32. For another photograph taken at the same time, see *The Letters of D. H. Lawrence*, ed. Huxley, plate facing p. 692.

33. *L*, vi. 410, 409.

34. *L*, vi. 332, 502.

35. *L*, vi. 391.

36. Barbara Barr, 'Step-daughter – II', *London Magazine*, xxxiii (October– November 1993), p. 16.

37. Frieda to Anna von Richthofen, ?April 1928 (UT), tr. CR-W and JW.

38. Nehls, iii. 219.

39. Rosie Jackson, *Frieda Lawrence* (1994), p. 47.

40. W. G. Sebald, *Austerlitz*, tr. Anthea Bell (2001), p. 101.

24 Searching: 1928–1929

1. American writer, editor and photographer (1869–1942); his papers are in NYPL.

2. Nehls, iii. 211–12.

3. *L*, vii. 242; Nehls, iii. 212.

4. *L*, vi. 457, 428.

5. *L*, vi. 469, 526.

6. *L*, vi. 419: the acquaintance was Maria Christina Chambers (d. 1965), born in Mexico, who regularly corresponded with DHL; see John Worthen, *D. H. Lawrence: A Literary Life* (1989), pp. xx, 172.

7. *L*, vii. 26: printed in the *Sunday Dispatch* on 25 November 1928

and republished in *Assorted Articles* as 'Sex versus Loveliness' (*PII* 527–31).

8. Published in *Assorted Articles* as 'Insouciance' (*PII* 534). *Kessel* is a hollow or basin; *Matte* an alpine meadow.

9. *L*, vi. 487, 452.

10. *L*, vi. 456, 459, 476.

11. *L*, vi, 496, 515.

12. *L*, vi. 546.

13. *L*, vi. 535, 533.

14. *L*, vii. 69; personal communication from Margaret Needham. Cf. 'Little prigs like Peg, at her age ought to be made to read *Lady C* aloud and in company' (*L*, vii. 127). Books used to be sold with their leaves still 'uncut' and the pages joined at the top or side; the book's first reader would use a sharp knife to open them.

15. *L*, vi. 542; Nehls, iii. 228.

16. *L*, vi. 522; Nehls, iii. 246.

17. *L*, vi. 573, vii. 37.

18. Nehls, iii. 253.

19. *L*, vi. 593; Nehls, iii. 253; *L*, vi. 598.

20. Nehls, iii. 255; see *D. H. Lawrence*, Catalogue 51 (Simon Finch Rare Books Ltd, 2002), item 75.

21. '[I know a noble Englishman]', *Poems* 953–5 (variant version). The poem was the very first 'Pansy' and its writing seems to have inspired the series.

22. Richard Aldington to H. D., 17 October 1960 (*Richard Aldington & H. D.: The Later Years in Letters*, ed. Caroline Zilboorg, 1995, p. 251); Patmore 138.

23. *L*, vi. 618.

24. Nehls, iii. 274.

25. 'Desire goes down into the Sea', *Poems* 454 (corrected from E302g).

26. Patmore 141; *L*, vi. 609.

27. Patmore 142; 'New Mexico', *P* 145; *L*, vii. 288.

28. *L*, vii. 22, 21.

29. *L*, vii. 78; Nehls, iii. 277, 415. The observer was the English artist, astrologer and writer Frederick Carter (1883–1967).

30. Nehls, iii. 457–8; 'Introduction', *Letters of D. H. Lawrence*, ed. Aldous Huxley (1932), p. xxx.

31. Nehls, iii. 275.

32. *L*, vii. 183, 127.

33. *L*, vii. 214, 186, 190, 186–7. Cf. too Chapter 22, n. 15.

34. 'Man Reaches a Point –', *Poems* 507 (original text: see *DG* 701).

35. *L*, vii. 41; *Memoirs* 239 (dated 10 November 1929 at *Memoirs* 238, the letter belongs to February or early March 1929); *L*, vii. 104.

36. *Poems* 419–20 (I am grateful to Christopher Pollnitz for pointing this out; the poems only contained words like 'turds' and 'turd' in 'The Jeune Fille' and 'Be a Demon', and 'arse' and 'member' in 'Demon Justice', *Poems* 563–5: see too *Letters*, vii. 237 and n. 2); Nehls, iii. 311.

37. Information from researchers of the *Dictionary of National Biography* into the probate grant, 1930.

38. Nehls, iii. 311.

39. Jay A. Gertzman, *A Descriptive Bibliography of* Lady Chatterley's Lover (1989), p. 12. There were at least sixteen pirated and thirty-one continental publications, many of them derivative editions.

40. *LCL* 306. The sum was $180 'for royalties on 30 printed copies' (*LCL* 367).

41. *L*, vii. 208.

25 Somewhere not Ill: 1929

1. *L*, vii. 9.

2. *Memoirs* 312.

3. *L*, vii. 229.

4. *Shadows of the Sun: The Diaries of Harry Crosby*, ed. Edward Germain (1977), p. 241.

5. Nehls, iii. 313–15; Rhys Davies, *Print of a Hare's Foot: An Autobiographical Beginning* (1969), p. 155.

6. Nehls, iii. 315; *Letters of Aldous Huxley*, ed. Grover Smith (1969), p. 288.

7. *L*, vii. 9, 229; Nehls, iii. 315.

8. *L*, vii. 9; *Mark Gertler: Selected Letters*, ed. Noel Carrington (1965), p. 228.

9. Bedford, i. 226.

10. 'Autobiographical Sketch', *PII* 300; Nehls, iii. 425, 406.

11. *L*, i. 206–7, vii. 9; *Letters of Aldous Huxley*, ed. Smith, p. 315.

12. *L*, v. 545, 566, 582, 526.

13. Nehls, iii. 206; *L*, v. 545.

14. *L*, iii. 337.

15. Bynner 61; *L*, vii. 50.

16. Crotch 7 (see too Enid Hilton Hopkin, *More Than One Life: A Nottinghamshire Childhood with D. H. Lawrence*, 1993, pp. 53–4); Frieda to Dorothy Brett, 12 August 1930 (*D. H. Lawrence Review*, ix, Spring 1976, p. 101); Frieda 303; Davies, *Print of a Hare's Foot*, p. 157. Frieda's insistence on her 'virility' was characteristic: she wrote to Koteliansky in

1923 that she was 'six times the "man" than any of you are!' (*Memoirs* 230).

17. Frieda to Ottoline Morrell [25 January 1929] (UT); Nehls, iii. 428; *Memoirs* 408.

18. Luhan 344.

19. 'Introduction', *Look! We Have Come Through!* (1971), p. 11; Nehls, iii. 439.

20. *L*, vi. 48.

21. *L*, vii. 9; Nehls, iii. 160.

22. Patmore 134; 'Introduction', *The Letters of D. H. Lawrence*, ed. Aldous Huxley (1932), p. xxxii.

23. Frieda 305; *L*, vii. 595, 546.

24. *L*, vi. 409, vii. 440.

25. 'Healing', *Poems* 620.

26. 'After all the Tragedies are over', *Poems* 509.

27. Nehls, iii. 245.

28. *L*, vii. 9.

29. 'Nothing to Save', *Poems* 658.

30. *L*, vii. 9.

31. Nehls, iii. 426. Cf. 'You can't be a rationalist in an irrational world. It isn't rational' (Joe Orton, *What the Butler Saw* in *The Complete Plays*, 1976, p. 428).

32. *L*, vii. 253–4, 260.

33. *L*, vii. 249.

34. *L*, vii. 206.

35. 'The English are so nice', *Poems* 659–60.

36. Probably drawn in the same week as he went to the photographer Ernesto Guardia in Las Palmas (see *D G* Illustrations 45 and 46). While the photograph shows him pale, ethereal, gaunt, hardly of this world, the self-portrait reveals what he felt (or at least would have wished) himself to be: untamed and angry, as robust as Frieda, his mouth opened as if about to issue some vituperative comment (though also as it had always needed to open, to catch his breath). But with his eyes looking in quite different directions, he is also a man pulled several ways at once. He thought his drawing '*basically* like me': an odd, sharp-eared malcontent, sketched by Van Gogh. But, he went on: 'my wife thinks it is awful – chiefly because she doesn't understand' (*L*, vii. 333): did not understand, perhaps, his need to be so combative. The picture is determinedly not of someone dying.

37. *L*, vi. 406: i.e. according to the standards of London's Slade School of Art (which e.g. Dorothy Brett and Mark Gertler had attended).

38. *L*, ii. 516.

39. DHL made copious suggestions for corrections in the reproductions (see *L*, vii. 149–50, 270–71, 279–80); a surviving partial set of proofs (UN) shows how successfully these were carried out by the printers. The essay was 'Introduction to These Paintings' (*P* 551–84).

40. *L*, vii. 309.

41. *L*, vii. 222; *Letters of Aldous Huxley*, ed. Smith, p. 313.

42. Nehls, iii. 354.

43. 'Innocent England', *Poems* 579; *L*, vii. 369; Nehls, iii. 383.

44. *L*, vii. 364.

45. *L*, viii. 82, vi. 179–80.

46. *L*, vii. 393, 395, 449.

47. *L*, vii. 436.

48. *L*, vii. 384, 388.

49. *L*, vii. 397–8.

50. *L*, vii. 398.

51. *L*, v. 192. The row over his paintings had led DHL to feel 'humiliated at the very thought of being an Englishman' (*L*, vii. 424), as he both identified himself with and hated the very English folk who attacked him.

52. *L*, v. 292–3.

53. In 1929, DHL may well have been thinking back to his own mother as one who '*can't* die': see Chapter 1, n. 36.

54. *L*, vii. 427.

55. *L*, vii. 466, 470, 477.

56. Frieda to Ottoline Morrell, 29 September 1929 (UT); Nehls, iii. 397, 426.

57. 'Bavarian Gentians', *Poems* 697, 963.

58. *L*, vii. 473–4.

59. *L*, vii. 486, 205.

60. *L*, vii. 494, 492, 509; Nehls, iii. 402; *L*, vii. 591, 494.

26 Dying Game: 1929–1930

1. Frieda 302.

2. *L*, vii. 617.

3. *L*, vii. 495, 509.

4. *L*, vii. 623.

5. Frieda 305.

6. Edith Hilton Hopkin, *More Than One Life: A Nottinghamshire Childhood with D. H. Lawrence* (1993), p. 53.

7. *A* 55, 149.

8. *A* 149.

9. *L*, vii. 616.

10. Nehls, iii. 415; *L*, vii. 505.

11. *MM* 100.

12. *L*, vii. 646; Barbara Barr, 'Step-daughter to Lawrence – II', *London Magazine*, xxxiii (October–November 1993), p. 18.

13. *L*, vii. 9, 611; Nehls, iii. 421, 424.

14. Harwood Brewster Picard, 'Remembering D. H. Lawrence', *D. H. Lawrence Review*, xvii (Fall 1984), p. 197; Frieda 303. Benito Mussolini (1883–1945) had been head of government in Italy since 1923; DHL had joked about him before (see *L*, v. 558, 570), and in 1927 had mocked the slogan chalked on walls in Italy: '*Mussolini is always right!*' (*SEP* 159).

15. *The Quest for Rananim: D. H. Lawrence's Letters to S. S. Koteliansky*, ed. George Zytaruk (1970), p. 402; Nehls, iii. 424–5.

16. Barr, 'Step-daughter to Lawrence – II', p. 18; *L*, vii. 632; Nehls, iii. 421.

17. Nehls, iii. 413; Frieda 303; Nehls, iii. 421.

18. *L*, vii. 634.

19. 'Review of *Art-Nonsense and Other Essays*, by Eric Gill', *P* 396.

20. Nehls, iii. 429.

21. Frieda 305.

22. *L*, v. 632; 'Foreword to *Women in Love*', *WL* 486.

23. 'The State of Funk', *PII* 567.

24. *A* 149; 'Shadows', *Poems* 727.

25. 'Ship of Death', *Poems* 966–7; *MM* 101.

26. *L*, vii. 636, 639, 646.

27. Frieda to A. S. Frere-Reeves, from Chateau Brun, St. Cyr Var., 'Saturday' [1930]; Frieda to Edward Titus, 5 February 1930 (SIU at Carbondale); Frieda 306, 307.

28. *Memoirs* 103.

29. *L*, vii. 633.

30. 'Ship of Death', *Poems* 967; Frieda 307, 308.

31. See Frieda's letter to her mother of 6 February 1930, the day DHL went into the sanatorium: 'I'd like just a fortnight's quietness to myself, but I'm really very relieved about no longer bearing the responsibility all by myself . . . How are you? I have hardly had time to think of you – Now I think I'll just appear –' (UT), tr. CR-W and JW; Crotch 13.

32. Frieda 308, 165.

33. Nehls, iii. 435.

34. 'Plasticine' is the proprietary name for a plastic substance regularly used as a substitute for clay in art teaching from the late 1890s onwards.

35. Nehls, vii. 433.

36. Nehls, iii. 433–4.

37. *L*, vii. 653. Illustration 38 is of the clay head itself: a bronze cast (17 in. high) survives in the Harry Ransom Humanities Research Center (UT).

38. *The Quest for Rananim*, ed. Zytaruk, p. 403–4.

39. *L*, vii, 646, 643. Seven stone is 98 lb, eight stone is 112 lb and six and a half stone is 91 lb.

40. *L*, vii. 651.

41. Nehls, ii. 318; Bedford, i. 228. Cf. the dying Kangaroo, who accuses Somers, 'You've killed me' (*K* 335), and Mrs Holroyd's remorse ('I've killed him'), in *The Widowing of Mrs. Holroyd*, when her husband has been killed in a mining accident (*Plays* 107).

42. Frieda 308; *SP* 291; *The Quest for Rananim*, ed. Zytaruk. p. 405; Nehls, iii. 435; *L*, vii. 633.

43. Frieda 308; *DG* 530; Nehls, iii. 435. The frequently reprinted book (1829) by Washington Irving (1783–1859) acquired a number of variant titles: Frieda's suggests the 1912 edition in the Herbert Strang Library.

44. Frieda 309; Nehls, iii. 435.

45. Barr, 'Step-daughter to Lawrence – II', p. 19; Nehls, iii. 436; Frieda 309; Bedford, i. 224.

46. Frieda 309.

47. Frieda 309; *DG* 531: cf. the nightly habit of the narrator in 'The Fly in the Ointment', *LAH* 53.

48. Barr, 'Step-daughter to Lawrence – II', p. 16; *L*, i. 192; Frieda 309–10. Frieda was probably thinking of the end of 'Odour of Chrysanthemums', *PO* 197–9.

49. Crotch 5; Bedford, i. 227–8.

50. Crotch 13; Frieda 310.

51. Frieda to Martha Gordon Crotch, 22 July 1931, from the Kiowa ranch; Frieda to A. S. Frere-Reeves from Chateau Brun, St. Cyr Var., 'Saturday' [1930].

52. See Émile Delavenay, 'A Shrine without Relics?', *D. H. Lawrence Review*, xvi (Summer 1983), pp. 111–31. In old age, Ravagli claimed that he was scared of the expense of transporting the wooden box containing the ashes to Villefranche, where he was due to sail, but Delavenay has demonstrated the extent to which he was exaggerating the problem. It seems likely that he was spending his time (and Frieda's money) visiting his family in Spotorno, and wished to conceal the purpose of his visit from them.

53. Luhan 53.

54. Her fragmentary writings were published after her death as *Memoirs*; Frieda to Catherine Carswell, n.d. [*c.* 1932], quoted by John Carswell in his 'Introduction' to *SP* (p. xxvi).

55. Frieda to A. S. Frere-Reeves, 2 February 1935; *Memoirs* 116, 304.

Index

'DHL' indicates D. H. Lawrence, 'Frieda' indicates Frieda von Richthofen, Frieda Weekley, Frieda Lawrence and Frieda Ravagli. For individual entries on Lawrence's works *see* Lawrence, David Herbert, WORKS

Luhan, Mabel – *cont.*
Woman who Rode Away' 308, 311; and
Hopi snake dance 313, 314; and 'Things'
359
Luhan, Tony 276, *see* Illustration 24;
relationship with Mabel Sterne 272; drives
DHL to Arizona 273; marries Mabel Sterne
274; house inhabited by DHL and Frieda
274; lends DHL and Frieda horses 280;
accompanies group to Arroyo Seco 307;
drives group to Hotevilla 313
Lynn Croft (Eastwood) 34

Mablethorpe 41, 45, 50, 347
'Mabeltown' *see* Luhan, Mabel
Macartney, Herbert Baldwin 76, 77, 78, 79,
80, 82, 93
Mackenzie, Compton 214, 227, 271; finds
DHL and Frieda Capri flat 220; DHL
describes 220–21; assists DHL 222; success
222, 327, 429n, 453n; DHL discusses sex
with 248; part inspiration for 'The Man
Who Loved Islands' 345–6; *Sinister Street*
453n
Mackenzie, Faith 214
Magnus, Maurice 237, *see* Illustration 21;
homosexuality 190, 225, 254; DHL
interested by 190, 218, 225; on Malta 190,
230, 254; recreated in 'Memoir' 213–14,
218, 254–5, 345, 411; recreated in *The
Lost Girl* 214; 'Dregs' 214, 254, 255; serves
in Foreign Legion 214, 254, 255; DHL
visits at Monte Cassino 225–6;
recommends Sicily to DHL 226–7; begs for
DHL's assistance 229–30; suicide 231, 254
Maistre, Violet le 300, 308
Majorca *see* Mallorca
Mallorca 389, 391, 394, 396, 398, 399
Malta 190, 230, 254
Manby hot springs (New Mexico) 281, 284
Manchester 54; Lydia Lawrence's birthplace 3
Manchester Guardian 149, 429n
Manchester, John: and Dorothy Brett 341, 342
Mandrake Press 398, 399
Mansfield Road 107
Mansfield, Katherine 167, 186, 188, 205,
281, *see* Illustration 16; edits *Rhythm* 130,
135; and Murry 135, 137, 156, 175, 176,
177, 223, 300; meets DHL and Frieda 135;
friendship with DHL and Frieda 136–8,
144–5; with DHL and Frieda in Bucks 149,
154; affair with Francis Carco 156, 456n; at
New Year parties in Bucks 157–8;
antagonism to 'Rananim' 158; and *The*

Signature 163, 480n; and *The Rainbow*
164; and Cornwall 172, 175, 176–7,
179–80; in France 175, 223, 386; rejects
communal life 176; and Ottoline Morrell
176, 179; and Frieda 177–81; corresponds
with DHL 204, 206, 221, 252; quarrel with
DHL 222–4, 225, 322; death 277; and
Brett 297, 298, 308; DHL writes to from
Wellington 466n
Marbahr, Karl von 109
Margate 136, 137
Marseille 399, 418
Marsh, Edward 137, 145, 146, 152
Martinez, Xavier: drawing of DHL by 458n
Marylebone station 102
Mason, Agnes 57, 59, 67, 76, 77, 137
Mayne, Ethel Colburn: reviewer of *Sons and
Lovers* 138
Mayrhofen 122, 173
Mazatlán 294
McLeod, Arthur 87, 137; DHL's liking for 59,
172, 173; and DHL's writing 64; DHL gives
copy of *An Idyll* 88
Mechanics' Institute 8, 34
Mecklenburgh Square 173, 194, 195, 347
Mediterranean Sea 220, 329, 334, 386, 405,
412, 417
Melville, Hermann 182, 184, 271; *Typee* 271
Meran 123
Merrild, Knud 155, 286, 292, 294, 354;
spends winter with DHL and Frieda
280–83; suspicious of DHL's sexuality 281;
opinion of DHL 282; describes DHL and
Bibbles 283–4; sees DHL (1923) 293
Messina 227, 260, 288
Methuen and Co. 143, 144, 146, 148, 152,
163, 182, 238
Metz 108, 109, 112, 114, 115, 116, 118, 138,
142
Mexico 280, 283, 287, 290, 299, 307, 315;
DHL plans to visit 285; DHL and Frieda in
Mexico City and Chapala 286–90, 306,
310; gods and goddesses in Teotihuacán
286; recreated in fiction 288; DHL returns
to with Götzsche 293–6; DHL plans return
to 304, 314; DHL and Frieda in Oaxaca
317–22; DHL 'a bit sick of' 319; DHL ill in
Mexico City 322–3, 414; DHL recalls 'with
nausea' 326; Kiowa ranch 'Mexican really'
328; DHL's created Mexico 331, 365
Mexico City 286, 287, 316, 318, 321, 322,
323, 324, 335, 382
Meynell, Viola 158
Michelangelo ('Michael Angelo') 46